READINGS FOR A HISTORY
OF AN

READINGS FOR A HISTORY OF ANTHROPOLOGICAL THEORY

edited by
Paul A. Erickson
and
Liam D. Murphy

broadview press

National Library of Canada Cataloguing in Publication Data

Main entry under title:

Readings for A history of anthropological theory

Includes bibliographical references.
ISBN 1-55111-411-9

1. Anthropology – Philosophy.   2. Anthropology – History.
I. Erickson, Paul A.   II. Murphy, Liam Donat.   III. Erickson, Paul A.
History of anthropological theory.

GN33.E74 1998 Suppl.   301'.01   C2001-930200-2

Broadview Press, Ltd.
is an independent, international publishing house, incorporated in 1985.

North America
Post Office Box 1243, Peterborough, Ontario, Canada K9J 7H5
3576 California Road, Orchard Park, New York, USA 14127
TEL: (705) 743-8990; FAX (705) 743-8353;
E-MAIL: customerservice@broadviewpress.com

United Kingdom and Europe
Thomas Lyster, Ltd.,
Unit 9, Ormskirk Industrial Park, Old Boundary Way, Burscough Rd, Ormskirk,
Lancashire L39 2YW Tel: (1695) 575112; Fax: (1695) 570120;
E-Mail: books@tlyster.co.uk

Australia
St. Clair Press, Post Office Box 287, Rozelle, NSW 2039
TEL: (612) 818-1942; FAX: (612) 418-1923

www.broadviewpress.com

Broadview Press gratefully acknowledges the support of the Ministry of Canadian Heritage through the Book Publishing Industry Development program.

Printed in Canada

CONTENTS

PREFACE

This book is a joint effort of the editors and reflects our shared views on the history of anthropological theory. While we do not, and in fact could not, necessarily concur with the views of all the anthropologists we have cited or included as authors, we consider them sufficiently important and influential to warrant the characterizations they receive in our text. We have conceived the book as a resource for teaching upper-level undergraduate or graduate university courses in anthropological history, anthropological theory, or the history of anthropological theory. In a way, it is a follow-up to our jointly-authored textbook, *A History of Anthropological Theory*, first published by Broadview Press in 1998. Then, as now, Broadview has been generous, expeditious, and highly professional in its support. *Readings for a History of Anthropological Theory* reflects the contributions of several outstanding members of the Broadview "team." President Don LePan and vice-president Michael Harrison nurtured the project from its beginning; production editor Barbara Conolly shepherded it through several stages to completion; and permissions editor Betsy Struthers conducted the sometimes frustrating "paper chase" to secure permission to reprint 36 selections. We thank these dedicated publishers, as well as the several anonymous reviewers who, on behalf of Broadview, constructively critiqued the book prospectus.

The intellectual framework for *Readings for a History of Anthropological Theory* is anthropology as we know it, have learned it, and, in the case of Erickson, have taught it for more than 20 years. For these reasons, we are indebted to both our anthropological "ancestors" and, in the case of our students who become anthropologists, our anthropological "descendants," who will have engaged us in dialogue during their intellectually formative years. The relationship between Erickson and Murphy is itself generational, with Erickson entering anthropology in the late 1960s and Murphy entering it in the early 1990s. This generational spread is advantageous, because, as anthropology has evolved, the "wisdom of hindsight" is best achieved from more than one temporal vantage point.

The motivation to create a book comes from both "within" and "without," two sources that in reality are intertwined. Each of us has benefitted from the encouragement and indulgence of "significant others," including parents, spouses, children, friends, and professional mentors, whose values and commitments we have internalized as our own. Erickson would like to acknowledge the special support of his wife Dawn, and Murphy would especially like to thank Stephanie Seery, Joanne and Chris Robertson, Jennifer Arzt, Stephen Parks, and Hal Scheffler and Jan Simpson, for all their support. Each of us hopes that this book, already the result of so many positive influences, can have further positive results by exciting interest and appreciation for the rich history of anthropological theory. Professor Julia Harrison of Trent University once lamented that students approached her course in the history of anthropological theory with the preconception that the course would be "one dead guy a week." We hope that, with exciting resources, professors can overcome this preconception and make the course come alive.

Paul A. Erickson
Halifax, Nova Scotia

Liam D. Murphy
Brooklyn, New York

INTRODUCING ANTHROPOLOGICAL HISTORY AND THEORY

Why study the history of anthropological theory? Many students ask this question, and the answer is straightforward: anthropology is a product of its past, so to understand anthropology with sophistication, students need to know how it developed. This need is especially great for "theory," or schools of thought, because theories develop in response to one another, sometimes positively and sometimes negatively, and they develop in the context of particular times, places, and personalities. To foster a sophisticated understanding of anthropology, many academic departments encourage, or require, advanced undergraduate or graduate students to complete a course in the history of anthropological theory. This book of readings is designed for such a course. It can also be used in other anthropology courses where professors adopt a historical or theoretical perspective.

There is, of course, no *one* history of anthropological theory. History depends on the historian, who is selective in presenting theories and who is influenced, consciously or unconsciously, by personal background, education, or "agenda." For this reason, no one textbook in the history of anthropological theory can ever be definitive, including the textbook written by the current editors, *A History of Anthropological Theory* (1998). Helping to counterbalance any unconscious or conscious "slant" of a textbook is a "reader," or collection of original writings. These writings, called primary sources, allow anthropologists to speak for themselves rather than to be spoken for in textbooks, called secondary sources. *Readings for a History of Anthropological Theory* is designed to provide such counterbalance.

There is also no one *reader* in the history of anthropological theory. Therefore, an explanation of the choice of readings and the format of their presentation is warranted. For a reader to be useful, it must contain selections that will be read. The selections in this reader have been read with benefit by the editors in courses they have taught or been taught. Almost all of the readings have also been approved, and in some cases recommended, by anonymous reviewers. The editors believe that anthropology is linked closely to Western history and to interactions among Western and non-Western peoples. In their textbook, they begin their history with Antiquity and continue it through the Medieval, Renaissance, and early modern periods, including the episodes of European geographical expansion, the Scientific Revolution, and the eighteenth-century Enlightenment. While this broad scope has merit, it would be impractical to reproduce in this reader because its numerous and substantial readings would make the reader necessarily lengthier and more expensive. Rather than raise the price or reduce the number or length of selections, the editors have decided to concentrate on the nineteenth and twentieth centuries when anthropology by name achieved recognition. As partial compensation, they have summarized the history of pre-nineteenth-century anthropology later in this introduction.

The 36 readings in *Readings for a History of Anthropological Theory* are grouped into four sections, arranged thematically and chronologically. Four sections are neither too numerous to be connected nor too few to be meaningful. Part One, with 7 readings, focuses on key nineteenth-century foundations and forerunners. Part Two, with 10 readings, looks at the early twentieth century, when the discipline came of age. Part Three, with 7 readings, examines the middle twentieth century, when anthropological concepts of structure, history, and evolution were "revisited." Part Four, with 12 readings, focuses on the late twentieth and emerging twenty-first centuries, when anthropologists became self-critical, analytical, and uncertain of what they could know.

Although it is desirable to let past and present anthropologists speak for themselves, students need some historical background in order to appreciate what the anthropologists are saying. Therefore, each section is preceded by an introduction that summarizes the historical period, introduces the anthropologists, and helps explain the readings. These introductions are aimed at students who are already familiar with anthropology, and preferably also with Western history, but who at the same time will be learning a more detailed history of anthropological theory from their teachers or textbooks. A general conclusion summarizes historical trends and interprets what they might mean for anthropology in the present and into the near future.

Certain unfamiliar words and phrases are **boldfaced** the first time they appear in the text and are defined in a glossary. The editors have also provided lists of study questions and recommended supplementary readings. Despite these learning aids, students should not be lulled into a false sense of complacency that they are being given everything they need. To the contrary, understanding these 36 readings will require *work*, and, when working, students should be prepared to be as resourceful as need be.

Early Anthropological Theory

Despite its technical vocabulary, special concepts, and unique intellectual history, anthropology is a collection of answers to fundamental questions about human existence, questions such as: Where did humanity come from? Why do people differ? What gives life meaning? Because these questions are fundamental, they have been asked by people in every cultural tradition. The tradition that gave rise to academic anthropology is the Western literate tradition, which begins with the period of Antiquity.

Anthropology in Antiquity

Antiquity, the period of classical Greece and Rome, nurtured three systems of thought: theology, humanism, and science. These systems can be defined by being contrasted with one another in terms of gods, people, and nature. In theology, people and nature are known through gods, who are paramount; in humanism, gods and nature are known through people, who are paramount; and in science, gods and people are known through nature, which is paramount. In Antiquity, anthropology, or proto-anthropology, was variously theological, humanistic, and scientific. The epic poems of Homer (*c.* eighth century BC) and other early storytellers were theological because they explained human activity in terms of the motivations and machinations of a pantheon of deities. The travelogues of Herodotus (*c.*484-*c.*425) and other early geographers and historians were humanistic because they explained human variation in human terms. And the materialistic schemes of Anaximander (*c.*622-*c.*547), Democritus (*c.*460-*c.*370), and other early philosophers were scientific because they explained the universe in terms of the transformation of natural elements. These early proto-anthropological examples of theological, humanistic, and scientific systems foreshadow later manifestations in anthropology.

The Golden Age of Greece in the fifth and fourth centuries BC was characterized by the distinguished philosophical lineage of Socrates, Plato, and Aristotle. Socrates (*c.*469-399) pioneered a philosophy of self-education, while Plato (*c.*427-347), his famous student, encouraged reflection on the otherworldly, or transcendental, "essences" of things. In contrast, Aristotle (384-22), the equally famous student of Plato, stressed the importance of detailed natural observation, a position later called "empiricism." The difference between Platonic and Aristotelean philosophies can be illustrated by the difference between the Medieval philosophies of realism and nominalism. Realists maintained that innate universal principles are more real than particular observations, while nominalists maintained that particular observations are more real than innate universal principles. Modern anthropological theory is more Aristotelian than Platonic, but this has not been true until recently.

Aristotle tutored Alexander the Great (356-23), who in the fourth century BC consolidated Greece into an empire that stretched from ancient Persia to Egypt. During the Alexandrian period, Greek philosophy splintered into a variety of sects, each elaborating a Platonic or an Aristotelean theme. Aristotle's more scientific tradition was perpetuated by scholars in Alexandrian Egypt, while Plato's potentially more theological tradition was elaborated in the first century BC by the Greek Stoics. The Stoics believed in *logos*, or cosmic world order, and maintained that humanity should accept worldly occurrences as the outcome of divine will. More than any other philosophy, Stoicism bridged the gap between ancient Greece and Rome, which in its early years stressed secular instead of theological pursuits. In the period of the Roman Empire, however, a growing number of religious sects preached allegiance to deities other than the Roman emperor. The most powerful of these sects was Christianity, which became the official religion of Rome under Emperor Constantine I (*c*.288-337 AD).

The initial period of the Christian Church history in Rome is known as the Patristic Age, during which Church "fathers" codified Church doctrine. According to the most influential Church father, Saint Augustine (354-430), humanity had been created by God, who was perfect, but humanity had become sinful. Therefore, God and humanity were in disharmony. God was omniscient, or all-knowing, and omnipotent, or all-powerful, but also fundamentally inscrutable, or unable to be known, except through revelations in scripture. This combination of tenets thwarted both humanism and science. Science presupposes human curiosity and a sense that nature presents mysteries to be solved. If God knows everything, but people cannot know God, why bother to be curious, and why develop a sense of mystery?

At the end of the fourth century AD, despite adopting Christianity, the Roman Empire declined and then "fell" to barbarians. Europe entered the Dark and Middle Ages, during which time monastic scholars perpetuated the Western literate tradition dominated by the theological tenets of Augustine.

The Middle Ages

The Dark Ages are called dark because they followed the "illumination" of Rome, which, through conquest, had kept Europeans in contact with different kinds of peoples. The Middle Ages are called middle because they intervened between Antiquity and the Renaissance, when Europeans renewed these different contacts. During this era, spanning almost one thousand years, the locus of learning shifted to the Eastern Roman Empire, whose capitol Constantinople became headquarters of the Eastern Orthodox Church. Contrasted with the vestigial Western Church, where Augustinian orthodoxy was infused with the transcendental otherworldliness of Plato, the Eastern Church was more open to the rational and empirical approach of Aristotle. Eastern scholars kept the Aristotelean tradition alive in centres of learning such as Alexandria, founded in 332 BC by Alexander the Great.

Meanwhile in the European West, monastic Christian commentators upheld the scriptural word of God. Although many modern intellectuals, certainly many anthropologists, regard the Middle Ages as regressive, the Medieval Church established at least one lasting intellectual foundation for modern anthropology: the concept of human history. Because scriptures were revealed to a succession of human beings, the record of past human accomplishments became important. Moreover, human history was cumulative and linear, not discontinuous or cyclical, as conceptualized in other religions. This foundation underlines modern anthropological concepts such as prehistory and evolution.

In the sixth century AD, the prophet Mohammed (*c*.570-632) was born in what is now Saudi Arabia. This event had profound implications for the subsequent history of Christianity. Mohammed became the founder of Islam, a religion embracing the outlook of Aristotle. Islam spread rapidly across North Africa to Morocco, from where, in the eighth century AD, Islamic Moors invaded Christian Spain. There, they introduced Aristotle to scholars who had been cloistered with Plato for centuries. The result was a revolutionary epistemological shift.

The blending of Aristotelean and Platonic outlooks revitalized Medieval Christianity and led to a new orthodoxy formulated by Saint Thomas Aquinas (1225-74). Contrasted with Augustinian Christianity, Thomistic Christianity, as the Christianity of Aquinas is called, encouraged human reasoning and observation. If God had created nature, then God could be known *through* nature, and studying nature would glorify God. Moreover, if God had created humanity, then humanity could, and should, use its God-given powers of reason to glorify God by studying nature. While the moral qualities professed in Augustinian Christianity were ignorance, supplication, and faith, the moral qualities professed in Thomistic Christianity were alertness, mental engagement, and reason. Aquinas even provided several rational "proofs" that God exists.

Thomistic Christianity was a Medieval intellectual synthesis of the elements constituting the three major Ancient systems of thought. In Thomism, God, humanity, and nature were harmonious, because humanity studied nature to glorify God. Theology, humanism, and science were also harmonious, because pursuit of one of these systems reinforced pursuit of them all. For the first time in centuries, humanity was curious and nature mysterious. The hidden danger in this self-contained system was that in exercising reason to study nature, humanity would make observations and reach conclusions that *contradict* God. In subsequent Western history, this is precisely what happened in the Renaissance, as a result of voyages of geographical discovery, and in the Scientific Revolution.

The Renaissance
The Renaissance was the early post-Medieval period during which pre-Medieval arts and philosophy were rediscovered and then celebrated. Concentrated in the fourteenth through sixteenth centuries, and first expressed in the

emerging city states of northern Italy, the Renaissance saw a proliferation of the integration of Ancient into Christian world views. As if reawakened from a thousand-year slumber, Renaissance thinkers and practitioners of all kinds began to appreciate the writings and artifacts of classical Greece and Rome as richer and more satisfying than those of dogmatic Medieval Christianity. In Italy, where the new city states sought to break out of the Medieval hierarchy of governance, the past "glories" of Rome were especially attractive, because they demonstrated the viability of a form of governance that was, by contrast, secular. Wealthy leaders of the new city states patronized Renaissance scholars to create the trappings of a secular state culture. The result was a grand secular humanism.

The secular humanism of the Renaissance manifested itself in a wide range of intellectual pursuits in which human accomplishments and modes of conduct were evaluated on a human rather than a theological scale. When the human scale contradicted the theological scale, the authority of Christianity suffered. For example, Leonardo da Vinci (1452-1519), the quintessential "Renaissance man," showed what human genius could achieve in breathtaking feats of art and engineering. Scientist Andreas Vesalius (1514-64) dissected human cadavers to learn human anatomy and in the process exposed errors in the text-based traditional anatomy of Galen (*c*.129-*c*.199). In the field of political philosophy, Nicolò Machiavelli (1469-1527) expounded the human qualities of character that would make a good secular leader in *The Prince* (1513); Saint Thomas More (1478-1535) critiqued the evils of modern society based on an ideal secularized world constructed in *Utopia* (1516); and Desiderius Erasmus (*c*.1466-1536) argued against the Christian concept of original sin in *The Praise of Folly* (1509). In undermining the authority of Medieval Christianity, these and other Renaissance thinkers and practitioners paved the way for the active *opposition* to Medieval Christianity in the sixteenth-century Protestant Reformation.

The implications of the Renaissance for anthropological theory are subtle but important. By nurturing humanism, Renaissance artists, scientists, and intellectuals nurtured the study of humanity in human terms. Moreover, by contrasting Ancient with Medieval world views, they showed that the world was not static but had changed over time. They also practiced an early form of cross-cultural analysis, which anthropologists have used to counteract ethnocentrism, or the sense of the absolute superiority of one culture over others. Until Europe expanded more geographically, however, this analysis was largely restricted to civilizations of the West.

Voyages of Geographical Discovery

Metaphorically, for European intellectuals the Renaissance was a voyage backward in time. Literally, the voyages of geographical discovery were voyages outward in space. In late Roman times, Saint Augustine had pronounced that no "antipodes"—places on the opposite side of the Earth—exist. In making this pronouncement, Augustine believed that Europeans already knew about all living peoples. He was mistaken. Beginning in earnest in the thirteenth century, Europeans journeyed to far-away places and discovered peoples whose appearance and behaviour exceeded some of their wildest expectations.

The European voyages of geographical discovery, preceded by the Christian crusades, were sponsored by new city states and later by nations who competed with one another for access to routes for profitable trade. Beginning with Marco Polo (c.1254-c.1324), who spent many years at the court of Kublai Khan in China, and ending with Ferdinand Magellan (c. 1480-1521), who first circumnavigated the globe, famous early explorers showed Europeans that riches awaited them to the east, which could be accessed more quickly by sailing west. In 1492, the quest for a western route to Asia led Christopher Columbus (1451-1506) to discover the "New" World—new, of course, only to Europeans. The discovery of the New World had profound implications for anthropology. Once Europeans realized that the New World was not Asia, they realized that it was an antipode. They then had to make sense of a place supposedly nonexistent and to incorporate its inhabitants, or "Indians," into Christian theology.

At a time when Europeans understood race, language, and culture to be inextricably linked, the aboriginal inhabitants of the New World appeared innately and profoundly different. Were these inhabitants even human? A difference of such magnitude created a problem for Christian theology. Saint Thomas Aquinas had regarded aboriginals as "natural slaves," but natural slaves lacked the quality of free agency, which was required if they were to convert to Christianity of their own volition. Without free agency, the efforts of Christian missionaries were futile. To solve this problem, after long deliberations by the Church, Spanish theologians Bartolomé de Las Casas (1474-1566) and José de Acosta (1539-1600) recast aboriginals in the image of "natural children" endowed with the potential to become adults and make a valid conversion. This theological change brought aboriginals and Europeans closer together. It led to the anthropological doctrine of monogenesis, the belief that human races share a common origin and constitute a single biological species. Monogenesis remained popular until the nineteenth century, when, as anthropology distanced itself from Christianity, the opposing doctrine of polygenesis became ascendant. Polygenesists believed that human races have separate origins and constitute separate biological species. The theoretical debate between monogenesists and polygenesists was a preoccupation of anthropology for centuries.

The voyages of geographical discovery launched an era of Western colonialism, imperialism, and political and economic global domination. Modern anthropology developed in this context, and anthropologists are currently engaged in a discussion about its theoretical significance.

The Scientific Revolution

Nowhere did the Medieval synthesis unravel as clearly, if not as quickly, as in the sequence of events that constitute the Scientific Revolution. These events, which took place from the thirteenth through the seventeenth centuries, generated revolutionary changes in scientific cosmology, or views of the universe, and epistemology, or ways of knowing.

Thomistic Christianity embraced a cosmology that blended elements of Medieval theology with Ancient Aristotelean science. In this cosmology, which depicted everything as static, the earth was the centre of the universe. Surrounding the earth were concentric layers made up of the natural elements of earth, water, air, and fire and, in the outer layers, rarified elements that bordered the ultimate, empyrean heavens. The earth was stationary, and celestial bodies such as planets and stars rotated around it in fixed spheres, or orbs. The Ancient astronomer Ptolemy (127-51) had calculated the number and velocity of the orbs in such a manner that they accommodated the celestial bodies known at that time. As new astronomical observations accumulated, however, it became difficult to keep the orbs and bodies in synchrony. Even by the time of Aquinas, the old cosmology was showing considerable signs of internal strain.

The now-famous scientists who contributed to the Scientific Revolution were motivated by a fundamental desire to preserve the old cosmology. This, they thought, could be accomplished if some of its features were altered. Nicholaus Copernicus (1473-1543) proposed that the sun, not the earth, is the centre of the universe and that the earth rotates on its own axis and revolves around the sun with other planets. Tycho Brahe (1546-1601), tackling the problem of intersecting orbs, decided simply that orbs do not exist. Johannes Kepler (1571-1630) described the orbits of planets as ellipses, not perfect circles. Galileo Galilei (1564-1642), reflecting on the views of his predecessors, systematically contrasted the Ptolemaic and Copernican views. Finally, Sir Isaac Newton (1642-1727), in his magnum opus *Principles of Mathematics* (1687), solved the problem of what caused planets to move by devising the law of universal gravitation. The end result of this sequence was a revolutionary new cosmology. According to historian of science Thomas Kuhn, author of *The Structure of Scientific Revolutions* (1962), the whole process amounts to a paradigm shift, during which one paradigm, or scientific model, is replaced by another when the former paradigm presents too many problems to solve in old ways.

Although the Scientific Revolution occurred primarily in astronomy and physics, there were equally revolutionary implications for anthropology. If the earth was not the centre of the universe, how could humanity, for whom the earth was created, be special? Might there be other earths? Other humanities? Moreover, in the Medieval cosmology, everything had a fixed place in a universe in which God was actively involved. By contrast, in the Newtonian cosmology, everything in the universe was dynamic and explained by natural laws, of which God was merely the creator. With God and humanity relegated to the sidelines, the Newtonian system of thought was clearly much more scientific than humanistic or theological.

During the period of the Scientific Revolution, as science came to supplant humanism and theology, it became necessary to devise epistemologies to replace faith and intuition. Two scientific epistemologies emerged: deduction and induction. Deduction, or drawing a logical conclusion from axiomatic principles, is a key feature of formal sciences such as mathematics. The most distinguished early philosopher of induction was René Descartes (1596-1650), who reasoned most famously that "I exist, therefore God exists, therefore the real world exists." Descartes also believed in a fundamental dualism of the world divided into categories such as mind and body, subject and object, and culture and nature. Induction, or reaching general conclusions from particular observations, is a key feature of empirical sciences such as the physical, biological, and many social sciences. The most distinguished early philosophers of induction were Francis Bacon (1561-1626) and, especially, John Locke (1632-1704), who argued that every human being is born with a mind like an "empty slate," or *tabula rasa*, written on by life experience. In the subsequent history of anthropological theory, the epistemology of Descartes, sometimes called French rationalism, and the epistemology of Locke, sometimes called British empiricism, both attracted followers. Almost immediately, the great achievements of natural scientists in the seventeenth-century Scientific Revolution inspired social scientists to emulate them in the eighteenth-century Enlightenment.

The Enlightenment

The Enlightenment, sometimes called the Age of Reason, refers to a fluorescence of rational intellectual activity in eighteenth-century Europe and elsewhere. Inspired by Newton and Locke, Enlightenment thinkers sought to make rational sense of human affairs. As a result, they pioneered modern "social science."

Newtonian science was "mechanistic" because it explained the natural world in terms of the motion of inter-related parts, and it was "deistic" because, according to Newton, after creating the world, God exerted no direct control over its operations. Mechanism contrasts with vitalism, the older view that life possesses a unique inner force; deism contrasts with theism, the older view that God is immanent in the world and controls what happens. The mechanistic and deistic character of Newtonian science made social applications of it appear radical and irreligious. In France, Enlightenment thinkers called *philosophes* were especially bold, some of them—for example, François Marie Arouet de Voltaire (1694-1778)—actively attacking the Church and tracing the growth of Christianity in secular terms. Other *philosophes* created analogies between nature and people—for example, Julien Offray de La Mettrie (1709-51) in *Man, A Machine* (1748). This practice became widespread in later anthropology, when theorists portrayed society as a metaphor for biology.

During the eighteenth century, the voyages of geographical discovery made Europeans more aware of the global diversity of plants, animals, and people. This awareness motivated scientists to impose order on such diversity through classification. To classify plants and animals, Swedish biologist Carolus Linnaeus (1707-78) developed the modern system of biological nomenclature, or naming, involving such categories as kingdom, phylum, class, order, and species. In the emerging social science of anthropology, classification was based on early ethnographies, or descriptions of aboriginal peoples, by explorers and missionaries, notably Jesuits. While, judged by modern standards, these early ethnographies were relatively ethnocentric, or culturally biased, they nevertheless made valuable contributions to early ethnology, the comparative study of aboriginal peoples.

The grandest social theoretical frameworks of the Enlightenment incorporated two important eighteenth-century anthropological concepts: progress and culture. Eighteenth-century Europeans recognized great differences between themselves and their relatively "primitive" Medieval ancestors. They recognized even greater differences between themselves and their primitive aboriginal contemporaries, whom they considered "frozen" in earlier time. Reflecting on these differences, Europeans judged themselves superior and therefore the changes leading to themselves progressive. But how had these changes occurred? Extending the reasoning of Locke, who believed that changes occur as a result of experiences accumulated during a single lifetime, Enlightenment thinkers reasoned that changes can also occur as a result of experiences accumulated during multiple lifetimes—essentially the modern concept of culture, or "nurture" contrasted with "nature." By joining the concepts of progress and culture, Enlightenment thinkers came up with theoretical frameworks that foreshadowed later frameworks of cultural evolutionism. These frameworks opposed the traditional framework of Christianity, which interpreted human history critically as a fall from the grace of God.

The grandest social theoreticians of the Enlightenment were called universal historians. They divided human history into stages—usually three—and attempted to explain how one stage led progressively into another. In so doing, they used aboriginal primitives to represent the earliest stages, about which, in the absence of archaeology, little could be known directly. In the nineteenth century, this practice became known as the "comparative method." Universal historian Giambattista Vico (1668-1744) proposed the three stages of Gods, heroes, and men, while Anne Robert Jacques Turgot (1727-81) and William Robertson (1721-93) proposed the more anthropologically familiar three stages of hunting/ pastoralism/ farming and savagery/ barbarism/ civilization. One of the most elaborate frameworks was proposed by Marie Jean de Condorcet (1743-94), who in *Outline of the Intellectual Progress of Mankind* (1795) divided human history into ten stages, the later of which were ushered in by the French Revolution. For all Enlightenment thinkers, human progress was achieved by using human reason to solve human problems. When, with years of warfare and violence, the French Revolution turned out unreasonably, it signalled the end of the Enlightenment era.

Further Readings

Barrett, Stanley R. 1996. *Anthropology: A Student's Guide to Theory and Method.* Toronto: University of Toronto Press.

Erickson, Paul A., & Murphy, Liam D. 1998. *A History of Anthropological Theory.* Peterborough, ON: Broadview Press.

Gacs, U., Khan, A., McIntyre, J., & Weinberg, R. (eds.). 1988. *Women Anthropologists: A Biographical Dictionary.* New York: Greenwood Press.

Garbarino, Merwyn S. 1977. *Sociocultural Theory in Anthropology: A Short History.* Prospect Heights, IL: Waveland Press.

Harris, Marvin. 1968. *The Rise of Anthropological Theory: A History of Theories of Culture.* New York: Thomas Y. Crowell.

Honigmann, John J. 1975. *The Development of Anthropological Ideas.* Ann Arbor, MI: Books on Demand.

Hymes, Dell. 1983. *Essays in the History of Linguistic Anthropology.* Philadelphia: John Benjamins North America.

Kardiner, Abram, & Preble, Edward. 1961. *They Studied Man.* Cleveland, OH: World Publishing Company.

Kroeber, Alfred Louis, & Kluckhohn, Clyde. 1952. *Culture: A Critical Review of Concepts and Definitions.* Cambridge, MA: Peabody Museum of American Archaeology and Ethnology.

Layton, Robert. 1997. *An Introduction to Theory in Anthropology.* Cambridge: Cambridge University Press.

Leaf, Murray J. 1979. *Man, Mind, and Science: A History of Anthropology.* New York: Columbia University Press.

Malefijt, Annemarie de Waal. 1974. *Images of Man: A History of Anthropological Thought*. New York: Alfred A. Knopf.

McGee, R. Jon, & Warms, Richard L. (eds.). 2000. *Anthropological Theory: An Introductory History*. (2nd ed.). Mountain View, CA: Mayfield Publishing Company.

Moore, Jerry D. 1997. *Visions of Culture: An Introduction to Anthropological Theories and Theorists*. Walnut Creek, CA: Altimira Press.

Silverman, Sydel (ed.). 1981. *Totems and Teachers: Perspectives on the History of Anthropology*. New York: Columbia University Press.

Spencer, Frank (ed.). 1997. *History of Physical Anthropology: An Encyclopedia*. New York: Garland.

Thoresen, Timothy H. (ed.). 1975. *Toward a Science of Man: Essays in the History of Anthropology*. Hawthorne, NY: Mouton de Gruyter.

Trigger, Bruce. 1990. *A History of Archaeological Thought*. New York: Cambridge University Press.

Winters, Christopher (ed.). 1991. *International Dictionary of Anthropologists*. New York: Garland.

PART I

NINETEENTH-CENTURY FOUNDATIONS AND FORERUNNERS

INTRODUCTION

During the nineteenth century, anthropology emerged as an intellectual discipline when "founding fathers" pioneered distinctive schools of thought. Meanwhile, intellectuals in other disciplines formulated theories that would influence anthropology in the twentieth century. The nineteenth century began, however, with reactions to the French Revolution.

The French Revolution, which began in 1789 as a fight for human liberty, ended as a series of protracted bloody battles and the rise to power of Emperor Napoleon Bonaparte I (1769-1821), who plunged Europe into warfare lasting until 1815. After Napoleon's defeat at the Battle of Waterloo, Europeans sought peace. Because the Revolution had been fought in the name of the Enlightenment ideals of reason and progress, European intellectuals turned against these ideals. For the next quarter century, various "reactionary" visions promoted the opposite ideals of human *irrationality* and social retrenchment. In Christian theology, for example, there was a surge of Biblical evangelicalism and sects that preached conservative morality as a means of averting apocalyptic doom. In the humanities, artistic movements such as Romanticism celebrated subjective experience and the liberation of sensation from form. In the arena of political philosophy, nationalism superseded universal historicism as the primary interest of ethnographers, who described each European nation and race as possessing its own special spirit, or *volksgeist*. Meanwhile, groups of disenchanted individuals banded together in utopian "socialist" communities, in intent similar to the counter-cultural communes of 1960s' North America. Overarching these trends was a widespread aversion to science, especially social science, as too radical, atheistic, and counterproductive. In this climate of opinion, for a new social scientific theory to succeed, it would need to advocate the investigation of social stability as well as change.

The Rise of Positivism

Positivism was just such a theory. Formulated by French sociologist Auguste Comte (1798-1857), and promulgated in his highly influential work *The Course of Positive Philosophy* (1830-42), Positivism incorporated Enlightenment social thinking into a universal framework for social science. In typical Enlightenment fashion, Comte maintained that human thought progressed through three major stages: theological, metaphysical, and positive. In the theological stage, phenomena were explained in terms of theological principles; in the metaphysical stage, in terms of abstract principles; and in the positive stage, in terms of the

3

phenomena themselves. Throughout the Scientific Revolution, this progression had been completed in the natural sciences, where Newton's law of universal gravitation represented attainment of the positive stage. In the social sciences, or sociology, however, the progression lagged behind. According to Comte, sociology in the Middle Ages had been in the theological stage because social phenomena were explained in terms of the principles of Christianity, and sociology in the Enlightenment had been in the metaphysical phase because social phenomena were explained in terms of the abstract principles of reason and progress. Comte wanted to bring sociology into the positive stage, where social phenomena would be explained in terms of other social phenomena.

According to Comte, in the positive, or truly scientific, stage, sociology would be akin to "social physics" and comprise two complementary sorts of investigations, each modeled on a physical science. "Social dynamics," modeled on the physical science of motion, would investigate how and why societies change, while "social statics," modeled on the physical science of equilibria, would investigate how and why societies remain the same. In modern theoretical terms, social dynamics would be "diachronic," or concerned with the past, present, and future, while social physics would be "synchronic," or concerned only with the present. Like many of his contemporaries, Comte believed that Enlightenment intellectuals had been preoccupied with the investigation of social change at the expense of the investigation of social stability. Positivism would be the balanced investigation of them both.

Because Comte formulated a comprehensive framework for studying social phenomena on their own terms, he is considered a forerunner of modern sociology. In the history of sociological theory, Positivism (with a capital "P") usually refers to his views narrowly construed. On the other hand, positivism (with a small "p") has come to assume broader significance as the position that social phenomena can, and should, be investigated "objectively," without reference to the personal opinions or the cultural context of the investigator. This position, sometimes taken as synonymous with science, has been both praised and criticized in the history of anthropological theory.

Marxism

Classical Marxism, first proposed by Karl Marx (1818-83) and his collaborator Friedrich Engels (1820-95), is known as the theory of dialectical materialism. Marx and Engels, both German socialists, developed the theory in the throes of the Industrial Revolution as means of ameliorating the plight of the industrial working class. Unlike contemporary political reformers, notably "utopian" socialists, they sought to make reform "scientific" in such a way that socialism would become inevitable.

Dialectical materialism has two fundamental components: dialectics and materialism. Dialectics refers to the process, or form, of change that Marx and

Engels believed operates throughout human history. The process was formulated by German philosopher Friedrich Hegel (1770-1831), who believed that a spirit manifests itself in the world through a sequence of transformations called thesis-antithesis-synthesis. The thesis is the initial manifestation; the antithesis, generated by the thesis, is its opposite; and the synthesis is their merger into a new form. Marx and Engels borrowed this concept from Hegel, but because Hegel was an "idealist," or someone who believes that human consciousness determines human existence, they "stood Hegel on his head" and applied the concept to the material world. Diehard materialists, Marx and Engels believed that human existence determines human consciousness.

Critical to classical Marxism was the concept of class struggle. According to Marx and Engels, throughout civilized human history, humanity had been organized into opposing economic classes with unequal access to the "means of production," or material resources for making a living. Ultimately, these resources depended on access to land as a means of producing food, shelter, and clothing. At each stage in history, one class, the superordinate "ruling class," controlled the means of production, while the other class, the "oppressed class," was subordinate. The ruling class was always supported by the institutions of church and state. The operational definition of superordinate and subordinate depended on the economic system in place at the time. In Antiquity, the opposing classes were masters and slaves; in the Middle Ages, feudal lords and serfs; and in industrializing modern Europe, capitalists, or the middle-class bourgeoisie, and industrial workers, or the proletariat. These opposing classes were dialectical opposites, and the struggle of the subordinate class led to the dialectical transformation of one economic system into another.

Marx and Engels expounded on dialectical materialism in several books, especially *The Communist Manifesto* (1848) and *Capital* (1867). They analyzed the economic stage of capitalism and explained why capitalism would be superseded by socialism and then communism. In classical Marxist analysis, the driving force of capitalism, the economic system of industrializing Europe following the French Revolution, was the quest for economic profit, defined as the difference between the value of commodities sold by the bourgeoisie, who owned the factories, and the lower value of wages paid to the proletariat, who worked in them. Marx and Engels subscribed to the labour theory of value, according to which, on a human scale, the value of a commodity should be determined by the labour that produced it. By selling commodities for more than they were "worth," bourgeois capitalists "stole" value and converted it into profit for themselves. Moreover, by forcing workers to work for money, the bourgeois transformed workers into commodities, whose value in wages was determined by supply and demand. These circumstances were the root of working-class oppression.

In order to maximize profit, bourgeois capitalists attempted to minimize costs, including the cost of labour. When they paid workers less, workers had less money to spend on goods produced. Meanwhile, "petty" capitalists succumbed to capitalist competition and joined the ranks of the proletariat, swelling their numbers. Marx and Engels predicted that capitalist overproduction and underconsumption would lead to cycles of recession, depression, and labour unrest that, despite the global expansion of capitalism, would weaken it and prime it for collapse. At a point when the means of production became concentrated in the hands of a few monopolists, it would be easy for workers to rise up and seize the means of production for themselves. This action would initiate the communist revolution, during which, in the initial stage of socialism, a vanguard of the proletariat would eliminate profit by putting it to public use. In the ultimate stage of communism, economic exploitation and classes would disappear, and everybody would work according to their ability and receive compensation according to their needs.

Selection 1, "Bourgeois and Proletarians," is an excerpt from an 1888 edition of *The Communist Manifesto*. In it, Marx and Engels elaborate key themes of dialectical materialism and acknowledge their indebtedness to nineteenth-century anthropologist Lewis Henry Morgan (1818-81). Morgan, as will be seen in Selection 3, portrayed the origin of civilization as a fundamental shift from egalitarian social organization based on communal kinship to nonegalitarian social organization based on territory owned as private property. For Marx and, especially, for Engels, this observation meant that capitalism was not ingrained in human nature and that, in a way, ultimate communism represented a return to "primitive" communism.

The pronouncements of Marx and Engels have had a profound effect on the real world, as, beginning with the Russian Revolution of 1917, political parties, movements, and states have adopted—and abandoned—Marxism as an ideology of government. In intellectual circles, including anthropology, Marxism has also had considerable periodic appeal. Few anthropologists believe in full-blown dialectical materialism, but twentieth-century schools of anthropological thought such as cultural neo-evolutionism, cultural materialism, structuralism, and culture and political economy incorporate elements of materialism and dialectics interpreted in different ways. "Marxist" anthropologists are a diverse group who disagree on many theoretical points. All of them are united, however, in opposition to the positivist claim that science is objective, or "value-free." All Marxists believe that science embodies values derived from the social class and economic interests of scientists.

Classical Cultural Evolutionism

The classical cultural evolutionists are the first major group of theorists whose theories are recognizably anthropological. They are called evolutionists because they were interested in the transformation of cultural forms, and they are called classical to distinguish them from "neo-" cultural evolutionists of the twentieth century. The heyday of classical cultural evolutionism was the 1860s through the 1890s, but it would be historically inaccurate to represent this school as inspired by the theory of biological evolution introduced by Charles Darwin in *Origin of Species* (1859). The classical cultural evolutionists had much more in common with Enlightenment universal historians than they did with Charles Darwin. In no way, then, should they be confused with "Social Darwinists."

Like universal historians, classical cultural evolutionists were interested in describing human progress in stages. Unlike universal historians, they emphasized "pre" history, or the time before writing. Knowledge of prehistory had accumulated as a result of a series of archaeological developments and discoveries during the first half of the nineteenth century. By 1860, most European scientists accepted that human beings or their ancestors had lived on earth a long time before the appearance of Ancient civilizations. Estimates of the length of this time varied, but all of them far exceeded the traditional Christian, Bible-based estimates of a few thousand years. The task of the cultural evolutionists was to describe what happened in prehistory and explain how in some locations prehistoric cultures evolved into historical civilizations with writing.

In the absence of writing, archaeology provided the only real evidence of prehistory, but this evidence was limited. To embellish the archaeological record, cultural evolutionists turned to ethnography. If the ethnographically observed material culture of an extant people resembled the archaeologically recovered material culture of an extinct people, they reasoned, then the *non*-material cultures of the two peoples could be inferred to resemble one another as well. This practice of using ethnography to embellish archaeology was known as the "comparative method." It was a prominent feature of classical cultural evolutionism that early twentieth-century anthropologists criticized as excessively speculative. In the nineteenth century, the comparative method allowed anthropologists to portray some people as "living in the Stone Age" and, contrasted with Europeans, evolutionarily stunted.

The classical cultural evolutionists can be divided into two groups. Those of greater distinction and influence were Herbert Spencer (1820-1903), John Lubbock (1834-1913), Lewis Henry Morgan (1818-81), Edward Burnett Tylor (1832-1917), and James Frazer (1854-1941). Those of lesser distinction and influence included Henry Maine (1822-88), Johann Bachofen (1815-87), and John McLennan (1827-81). Morgan was American, and Bachofen was German, while all the rest were British. As a group, with few exceptions, they did little ethnographic fieldwork, so their evolutionary reconstructions were based mainly on information culled from other sources. For this reason they are sometimes called "armchair" anthropologists. Living in the era of British Queen Victoria (1819-1901), in many ways they shared the prevailing attitude that their own culture was superior.

Classical cultural evolutionists studied a broad array of institutions and beliefs. Some evolutionists, such as Tylor and Frazer, focused on religion, magic, and other forms of spirituality, while others, such as Morgan, Maine, and McLennan, focused on kinship, domestic arrangements, and institutions of governance. Selection 2, "The Science of Culture," is the first chapter of the 1873 edition of Edward Burnett Tylor's landmark two-volume compendium *Primitive Culture*. Tylor held the first academic position in anthropology, at Oxford University, and is widely recognized as the most important father of the discipline. His selection begins with the most frequently quoted definition of culture: "Culture or Civilization, taken in its wide ethnographic sense, is that complex whole which includes knowledge, belief, art, morals, law, custom, and any other capabilities and habits acquired by man as a member of society." The key phrase here is "... acquired by man as a member of *society* [emphasis added] ...," because it shows that Tylor was committed to the view that culture is neither innate nor biologically inherited. Tylor characterizes anthropological culture not as "high" culture but as the culture of the average person. He argues that culture has coherence and is governed by regularities resembling laws. According to him, the anthropological perspective is indispensable because it shows how things are products of the past. To help reconstruct the past, he advocates reference to "survivals," or vestiges of past cultural states. Especially notable is his discussion of why, just because anthropologists "accept" the exotic beliefs of other people, they do not necessarily accept them as "true."

Selection 3, "Ethnical Periods," is the first chapter of Lewis Henry Morgan's magnum opus *Ancient Society* (1877). Morgan was an upstate New York lawyer who developed an ethnographic interest in nearby Iroquois Indians. Expanding his interest to other ethnographic groups, he formulated a taxonomy, or classification, of kinship systems around the world. In this selection, Morgan situates these and other cultural systems in a sweeping evolutionary framework comprising three main periods: savagery, barbarism, and civilization. Savagery, the earliest period, begins with humanity; barbarism, the intermediate period, with the invention of pottery; and civilization, the latest period, with the invention of the phonetic alphabet and writing. Morgan ranks these periods, dividing them into "lower," "middle," and "upper" divisions, and attempts to "represent" as many of them as possible with extant ethnographic groups. Like many of his contemporaries, he is struck by the profound qualitative difference between ancient society, or *societas*, based on personal relations, and modern society, or *civitas*, based on property relations. This was the insight that made his work attractive to Marx and Engels. Ironically, "Ethnical Periods" shows that Morgan was more of an idealist than a materialist, explaining cultural evolution as the unfolding of "germs of thought."

Selection 4, "The Organic Analogy Reconsidered," consists of excerpts from

Herbert Spencer's multivolume work *The Principles of Sociology* (1876). Contrasted with other classical cultural evolutionists, Spencer was more sociological than anthropological. Nevertheless, his theories were true to the evolutionary form. Spencer proposed a grand evolutionary scheme encompassing all realms of human activity, including the social realm. According to him, society has evolved from a relatively homogeneous state, where components cohered because they were the same, into a relatively heterogeneous state, where components cohere because they are different and interdependent. The main point of this selection is to demonstrate that the social realm "exists" by identifying it as analogous to the organic realm, the realm of living things. Using the vocabulary of biology to represent society as a "body politic" that can structurally and functionally "grow," Spencer builds a case for society being something more than the sum of its individual parts. Ever since the Scientific Revolution, sociologists and anthropologists have used the organic analogy to construct images of society and culture. Reading "The Organic Analogy Reconsidered" will make students aware of this practice and should prompt them to wonder whether, if they are so constructed, society and culture are "real."

In the guise of classical cultural evolutionism, anthropology developed its lasting reputation as iconoclastic and critical. It appeared iconoclastic because it showed that cherished modern institutions and beliefs, including Christianity, incorporated primitive elements from which they had evolved. Many smug Victorians were uncomfortable with this revelation because, by and large, classical cultural evolutionists embraced the concept of "psychic unity," meaning the belief that primitive and modern people have the same fundamental mental capability. Psychic unity implied that differences in stages of cultural evolution were due to differences in time and circumstance rather than to differences in capability of evolving. This attitude caused classical cultural evolutionists to criticize contemporary hereditarians, including some Darwinians, whose views dominated scientific circles in Victorian times.

Darwinism

Darwinism narrowly defined refers to the scientific theories of English evolutionary biologist Charles Darwin (1809-82). Broadly defined, it can refer to almost any philosophy that invokes Darwin's theories for support. This account will keep the definition relatively narrow.

Darwin's main goal was to explain the origin of biological species, or reproductively distinct forms of life. The traditional explanation, derived from Christianity, was that each species was separately and divinely created by God. Before Darwin's time, a number of scientists had called this explanation into question and proposed instead that species were naturally created and transformed, or evolved. The most influential pre-Darwinian evolutionist was naturalist Jean Lamarck (1744-1829), who summarized his views in *Zoological Philosophy* (1809). Lamarck maintained that evolution results from the action of a number of mechanisms, including, most potently, the inheritance of acquired characteristics. According to this mechanism, characteristics acquired during the lifetime of an individual are inherited by the individual's offspring. Modern geneticists have shown that the inheritance of acquired characteristics does not work, but, before modern genetics, it seemed plausible. Acting continuously over several generations, it might transform one species into another.

As a young man, Darwin became enamoured of natural history and, through academic connections, secured an appointment as naturalist on the ship *HMS Beagle*, which began a five-year voyage around the world in 1831. During this time Darwin became convinced of the validity of evolution but doubtful about evolutionary mechanisms. After the *Beagle* returned to England, he spent more than 20 years engaged in scientific research while he drafted a new theory, eventually published in *Origin of Species* (1859). The theory, known as evolution by natural selection, was formulated independently by Darwin and fellow naturalist Alfred Russel Wallace (1823-1913), although subsequently it became known as Darwinism.

Darwin derived the mechanism of natural selection from political economist Thomas Malthus (1766-1834), who argued, pessimistically, that the limited natural resources of earth cannot possibly support all people born. Consequently, there is a competitive "struggle for existence," leading to "survival of the fittest" (a phrase actually coined by Herbert Spencer). Darwin extended this Malthusian idea to all living things, arguing that individuals within a species compete in such a way that the individuals with characteristics conferring a competitive advantage survive in greater numbers and have more offspring, leading to an expansion of the characteristics in subsequent generations. Over time, the characteristics of the species change until, at some point, it becomes a new species. Darwin called this whole mechanism "natural selection." In principle, natural selection obviated the need to invoke the mechanism of the inheritance of acquired characteristics, because selected characteristics already existed and were not acquired in the first place. In practice, because he had problems actually *proving* natural selection, Darwin relied on the inheritance of acquired characteristics and other Lamarckian mechanisms throughout his career— ironic for the foremost "Darwinist."

In *Origin of Species*, Darwin made only one scant reference to *human* evolution: the cryptic statement "Much light will be thrown on the origin of man and his history." His reluctance failed to prevent Social Darwinists from rushing to apply natural selection to society, confident that competition among people was both natural and desirable because it eliminated the weak and perpetuated the strong. (Herbert Spencer has been called a Social Darwinist, but he formulated his views before Darwin). Anthropologists took more time to assimilate Darwin's views, because natural selection appeared inadequate to explain key aspects of human nature. Even Darwin, who presented his own theory of human evolution in *The Descent of Man* (1871), faced major challenges in anthropology.

Selection 5 is the "General Summary and Conclusion" of Darwin's *The Descent of Man*, the complete title of which is *The Descent of Man and Selection in Relation to Sex*. In this selection, Darwin invokes numerous evolutionary mechanisms besides natural selection. One is sexual selection, or competition among males and females for reproductive access to the opposite sex. Darwin uses sexual selection to explain the evolution of differences between people and animals, between males and females, and among human races. This same mechanism figures prominently in sociobiology, a late-twentieth century reformulation of Darwinism. For Darwin, the greatest challenge to human evolutionary theory is to account for the evolution of human morality, which he, like most of his nineteenth-century contemporaries, believed to be highly hereditary. Passages in this selection lend clear support to eugenics, the political movement aimed at controlling human reproduction, promoted by Darwin's cousin Francis Galton (1822-1911).

In histories of science, the nineteenth century is sometimes called "Darwin's century," because his hereditarian views were so widespread. In the early twentieth century, prominent anthropologists, especially American anthropologists, opposed those views and argued instead that human behaviour is governed by nurture, not nature.

Émile Durkheim: Forerunner of Structuralism and Functionalism

The schools of classical cultural evolutionism and Darwinism were rooted in the epistemology of British empiricism. Toward the end of the nineteenth century, theoretician Émile Durkheim (1858-1917) moved social science in the direction of the epistemology of French rationalism. In the twentieth century, this led to the anthropological schools of structuralism and functionalism.

Durkheim was an influential French sociologist who worked in the tradition of René Descartes and Auguste Comte. From Descartes he inherited an interest in *a priori* mental logic, or logic independent of experience, and from Comte he inherited an interest in society, which he conceptualized as more than the sum of individuals, or a realm onto itself, *sui generis*. Durkheim combined these inheritances in a special and powerful way.

In Positivist terms, Durkheim was more interested in social statics than social dynamics, or, in modern terms, he was more synchronic than diachronic. He sought to understand how societies were integrated so that they managed to cohere, maintain themselves, and function harmoniously. In this regard, he was the opposite of Karl Marx and Friedrich Engels, who focused on social divisions, change, and conflict. Durkheim identified two fundamentally different but equivalent integrative patterns: "mechanical solidarity" and "organic solidarity." Societies integrated mechanically were more homogeneous, and individuals got along because they were much the same. Societies integrated organically were more heterogeneous, and individuals got along because they were different, each performing tasks that led to interdependence. Unlike Marx and Engels, who predicted that the communist revolution would lead to a class-less egalitarian state, Durkheim predicted that, as organic solidarity superseded mechanical solidarity in the modern world, institutions of social regulation and control would expand.

For Durkheim, social regulation and control were subtle and largely unconscious. They were achieved by getting people to participate in activities and beliefs that affirmed the importance of their membership in society. Durkheim's special insight was that key social institutions are, in his words, "collective representations" of "collective realities" in the "group mind." With symbols and ceremonies, these institutions instill a sense of the "sacred," which allows them to become more powerful social motivators than if they were merely "profane." An anthropological example is the "totem," a venerated ancestor of a kinship group that serves to remind group members that they are part of a reality bigger and ultimately more important than themselves. Durkheim's main point is that the reality of such a representation is "collective," or social. In his classic monograph *Suicide* (1897), he showed that even suicide, a highly individualistic act, had social dimensions.

Durkheim developed his theories in a series of major publications that straddled the threshold of the twentieth century, beginning with *Division of Labour in Society* (1893) and culminating in *The Elementary Forms of the Religious Life* (1912). Selection 6 is the "Introduction" to the 1915 edition of *The Elementary Forms*. Here, Durkheim presents religion as an especially powerful instrument of social conformity, because religion promotes moral codes that implicitly support society and at the same time are explicitly sacred. This function can be seen more clearly in "primitive" religions, those associated with mechanically integrated societies, because in primitive societies the basic elements, or elementary forms, of religion are widely shared. For Darwin and the classical cultural evolutionists, the origin of religion meant where it came from in the past. For Durkheim, the origin means the wellspring of human needs and curiosity that religion satisfies in the present. Later in the twentieth century, building on a Durkheimian theoretical foundation, French anthropologist Claude Lévi-Strauss developed the concept of elementary forms into the concept of elementary structures, and British anthropologists Alfred Reginald Radcliffe-Brown and Bronislaw Malinowski developed the concept of social solidarity into the concept of social function. The astute reader will detect forerunners of these schools in the central themes of selection 6.

Sigmund Freud as an Anthropologist

Sigmund Freud (1856-1939) is world famous as a psychologist. Far less well known, however, are his ventures into anthropology, which he undertook in order to explain the origin of troublesome psychological states. In so doing, he developed anthropological theories that, in retrospect, appear like classical cultural evolutionism in caricature.

As a medical student in Vienna in the 1880s, Freud became interested in debilitating psychological syndromes such as hysteria that resisted then-standard clinical treatments. Instead, he pioneered a radical new treatment called psychotherapy, based on his insight that patients were troubled by psychological traumas they experienced, usually as children, and then "repressed" without resolution. Repressed, the traumas entered the patient's subconsciousness, where they festered and eventually became maladaptive. Freud learned that by using clinical treatments such as hypnosis and dream analysis the psychotherapist could help patients recall their traumas consciously and begin resolving them after the fact.

Soon Freud's clinical successes led him to formulate a general psychological theory that applied to healthy people as well as to patients who were psychologically ill. He divided the human psyche, or centre of feeling and thought, into three components: the id, ego, and superego. The id, or libido, was the unconscious component where basic biological instincts were experienced and sought expression. One of the strongest instincts was sex. The ego was the conscious component where libidinous instincts came in contact with external reality. The superego, or conscience, was the component that incorporated external moral codes that restrained the id, which, if expressed, would be socially disruptive. Freud believed that, libidinously, all people prefer to act on the "pleasure principle," meaning to seek psychosexual gratification and avoid psychosexual pain. But because people live in groups, gratification of one person can lead to conflict and pain for someone else. Therefore, as they psychologically mature, people must adopt the "reality principle," meaning that the pleasure principle must be abandoned or severely curtailed. Psychologically healthy people adopt the reality principle with success. Their superego restrains their id so that their ego develops normally. But psychologically ill people continue to act on the pleasure principle, experience real or psychological conflict, repress or otherwise mismanage the conflict, and become neurotic or, more seriously, psychotic. For Freud, everybody grows up in a kind of psychological minefield, which some people negotiate satisfactorily but which for others explodes.

How does all this lead to anthropology? Freud himself grew up in the nineteenth century, and his intellectual outlook was evolutionary. As a psychic evolutionist, he believed in the "biogenetic law," or the axiom that ontogeny, the growth of the individual, recapitulates phylogeny, the growth of the species. When he began to look for the origin of the psychic problems of humanity, it was natural for him to look in the primeval past. What he found—or created—were certain events that each person relived as "racial memory."

According to Freud, the primeval human family was monogamous and patriarchal, including a mother and a father in charge. Everybody behaved libidinously. The sons of the couple were sexually attracted to their mother and resented their father for denying them sexual access to her. Eventually, their resentment rose to the point where they banded together and killed their father, an act called the primal patricide. Afterwards, because they also loved and respected their father, the sons felt remorse and realized that such acts in the future would be psychologically and socially devastating. To prevent reoccurrences, "they"—representing what Freud called civilization or culture—installed a number of remedial devices, including the reality principle and the superego, which taught that killing is immoral. Other devices were a cultural taboo against incest and the fabrication of religious totems, which Freud interpreted as "father figures," onto which culture projected reverence in order to keep antagonism toward real fathers in check. As a result, all men were now burdened by the "Oedipus complex," or ambivalence toward their fathers. Because he was patriarchal, Freud treated the problems of women differently, but all women were still burdened by an "Electra complex," or jealous attraction to their fathers. In these fantastic evolutionary reconstructions, Freud's main point was that the essence of culture is *opposition* to human nature, and cultural achievements are built on the "sublimation," or rechanneling, of psychosexual instincts in culturally acceptable ways.

Freud published his anthropological speculations in a trilogy of three books: *Totem and Taboo* (1918), *The Future of an Illusion* (1928), and *Civilization and its Discontents* (1930). While published in the early twentieth century, these books perpetuate classic nineteenth-century thinking. Selection 7, a sample of such thinking, is an excerpt from *Civilization and its Discontents*. Here, Freud sets the scene for his subsequent discussion of the primal patricide by elaborating his central theme that culture is the cause, not the solution, of the problem of human unhappiness. He stands in sharp contrast to Durkheim, for whom all forms of culture are functionally useful. With modern anthropological sensibilities, students should be struck by Freud's likening of primitive adults to modern children. Almost certainly they will be given pause by Freud's explanation of the "taming" of fire, which Freud interprets as a symbolic penis, as the surrender of mens' instinctive habit of extinguishing fire by competitive homosexual urination. Such explanations illustrate why twentieth-century anthropologists might have found Freud provocative but badly in need of theoretical reworking. In fact, twentieth-century anthropology developed in reaction to the kind of nineteenth-century evolutionism that Freud so provocatively caricatured.

1

Bourgeois and Proletarians[1]

KARL MARX AND FRIEDRICH ENGELS

The history of all hitherto existing society[2] is the history of class struggles. Freeman and slave, patrician and plebeian, lord and serf, **guildmaster**[3] and **journeyman**, in a word, oppressor and oppressed, stood in constant opposition to one another, carried on an uninterrupted, now hidden, now open fight, a fight that each time ended, either in a revolutionary reconstitution of society at large, or in the common ruin of the contending classes.

In the earlier epochs of history, we find almost everywhere a complicated arrangement of society into various orders, a manifold gradation of social rank. In ancient Rome we have patricians, knights, plebeians, slaves; in the Middle Ages, feudal lords, vassals, guild-masters, journey-men, apprentices, serfs; in almost all of these classes, again, subordinate gradations.

The modern bourgeois society that has sprouted from the ruins of feudal society, has not done away with class antagonisms. It has but established new classes, new conditions of oppression, new forms of struggle in place of the old ones.

Our epoch, the epoch of the **bourgeoisie**, possesses, however, this distinctive feature: It has simplified the class antagonisms. Society as a whole is more and more splitting up into two great hostile camps, into two great classes directly facing each other—bourgeoisie and **proletariat**.

From the serfs of the Middle Ages sprang the chartered **burghers** of the earliest towns. From these **burgesses** the first elements of the bourgeoisie were developed.

The discovery of America, the rounding of the Cape, opened up fresh ground for the rising bourgeoisie. The East-Indian and Chinese markets, the colonization of America, trade with the colonies, the increase in the means of exchange and in commodities generally, gave to commerce, to navigation, to industry, an impulse never before known, and thereby, to the revolutionary element in the tottering feudal society, a rapid development.

The feudal system of industry, in which industrial production was monopolized by closed guilds, now no longer sufficed for the growing wants of the new markets. The manufacturing system took its place. The guild-masters were pushed aside by the manufacturing middle class; division of labor between the different corporate guilds vanished in the face of division of labor in each single workshop.

Meantime the markets kept ever growing, the demand ever rising. Even manufacture no longer sufficed. Thereupon, steam and machinery revolutionized industrial production. The place of manufacture was taken by the giant, modern industry, the place of the industrial middle class, by industrial millionaires—the leaders of whole industrial armies, the modern bourgeois.

Modern industry has established the world market, for which the discovery of America paved the way. This market has given an immense development to commerce, to navigation, to communication by land. This development has, in its turn, reacted on the extension of industry; and in proportion as industry, commerce, navigation, railways extended, in the same proportion the bourgeoisie developed, increased its capital, and pushed into the background every class handed down from the Middle Ages.

We see, therefore, how the modern bourgeoisie is itself the product of a long course of development, of a series of revolutions in the modes of production and exchange.

Each step in the development of the bourgeoisie was accompanied by a corresponding political advance of that class. An oppressed class under the sway of the feudal nobility, it became an armed and self-governing association in the medieval commune;[4] here independent urban republic (as in Italy and Germany), there taxable **"third estate"** of the monarchy (as in France); afterwards, in the period of manufacture proper, serving either the semi-feudal or the absolute monarchy as a counterpoise against the nobility, and, in fact, cornerstone of the great monarchies in general—the bourgeoisie has at last, since the establishment of modern industry and of the world market, conquered for itself, in the modern representative state, exclusive political sway. The executive of the modern state is but a committee for managing the common affairs of the whole bourgeoisie.

The bourgeoisie has played a most revolutionary role in history.

The bourgeoisie, wherever it has got the upper hand, has put an end to all feudal, patriarchal, idyllic relations. It has pitilessly torn asunder the motley feudal ties that bound man to his "natural superiors," and has left no other bond between man and man than naked self-interest, than callous "cash payment." It has drowned the most heavenly ecstasies of religious fervor, of chivalrous enthusiasm, of philistine sentimentalism, in the icy water of egotistical calculation. It has resolved personal worth into exchange value, and in place of the numberless indefeasible chartered freedoms, has set up that single, unconscionable freedom—Free Trade. In one word, for exploitation, veiled by religious and political illusions, it has substituted naked, shameless, direct, brutal exploitation.

The bourgeoisie has stripped of its halo every occupation hitherto honored and looked up to with reverent awe. It has converted the physician, the lawyer, the priest, the poet, the man of science, into its paid wage-laborers.

The bourgeoisie has torn away from the family its sentimental veil, and has reduced the family relation to a mere money relation.

The bourgeoisie has disclosed how it came to pass that the brutal display of vigor in the Middle Ages, which reactionaries so much admire, found its fitting complement in the most slothful indolence. It has been the first to show what man's activity can bring about. It has accomplished wonders far surpassing Egyptian pyramids, Roman aqueducts, and Gothic cathedrals; it has conducted expeditions that put in the shade all former migrations of nations and crusades.

The bourgeoisie cannot exist without constantly revolutionizing the instruments of production, and thereby the relations of production, and with them the whole relations of society. Conservation of the old modes of production in unaltered form, was, on the contrary, the first condition of existence for all earlier industrial classes. Constant revolutionizing of production, uninterrupted disturbance of all social conditions, everlasting uncertainty and agitation distinguish the bourgeois epoch from all earlier ones. All fixed, fast-frozen relations, with their train of ancient and venerable prejudices and opinions, are swept away, all new-formed ones become antiquated before they can ossify. All that is solid melts into air, all that is holy is profaned, and man is at last compelled to face with sober senses his real conditions of life and his relations with his kind.

The need of a constantly expanding market for its products chases the bourgeoisie over the whole surface of the globe. It must nestle everywhere, settle everywhere, establish connections everywhere.

The bourgeoisie has through its exploitation of the world market given a cosmopolitan character to production and consumption in every country. To the great chagrin of reactionaries, it has drawn from under the feet of industry the national ground on which it stood. All old-established national industries have been destroyed or are daily being destroyed. They are dislodged by new industries, whose introduction becomes a life and death question for all civilized nations, by industries that no longer work up indigenous raw material, but raw material drawn from the remotest zones; industries whose products are consumed, not only at home, but in every quarter of the globe. In place of the old wants, satisfied by the production of the country, we find new wants, requiring for their satisfaction the products of distant lands and climes. In place of the old local and national seclusion and self-sufficiency, we have intercourse in every direction, universal interdependence of nations. And as in material, so also in intellectual production. The intellectual creations of individual nations become common property. National one-sidedness and narrow-mindedness become more and more impossible, and from the numerous national and local literatures there arises a world literature.

The bourgeoisie, by the rapid improvement of all instruments of production, by the immensely facilitated means of communication, draws all nations, even the most barbarian, into civilization. The cheap prices of its commodities are the heavy artillery with which it batters down all Chinese walls, with which it forces the barbarians' intensely obstinate hatred of foreigners to capitulate. It compels all nations, on pain of extinction, to adopt the bourgeois mode of production; it compels them to introduce what it calls civilization into their midst, *i.e.*, to become bourgeois themselves. In a word, it creates a world after its own image.

The bourgeoisie has subjected the country to the rule of the towns. It has created enormous cities, has greatly increased the urban population as compared with the rural, and has thus rescued a considerable part of the population from the idiocy of rural life. Just as it has made the country dependent on the towns, so it has made barbarian and semibarbarian countries dependent on the civilized ones, nations of peasant on nations of bourgeois, the East on the West.

More and more the bourgeoisie keeps doing away with the scattered state of the population, of the means of production, and of property. It has agglomerated population, centralized means of production, and has concentrated property in a few hands. The necessary consequence of this was political centralization. Independent, or but loosely connected provinces, with separate interests, laws, governments and systems of taxation, became lumped together into one nation, with one government, one code of laws, one national class interest, one frontier and one customs tariff.

The bourgeoisie, during its rule of scarce one hundred years, has created more massive and more colossal productive forces than have all preceding generations together. Subjection of nature's forces to man, machinery, application of chemistry to industry and agriculture, steam-navigation, railways, electric telegraphs, clearing of whole continents for cultivation, canalization of rivers, whole populations conjured out of the ground—what earlier century had even a presentiment that such productive forces slumbered in the lap of social labor?

We see then that the means of production and exchange, which served as the foundation for the growth of the bourgeoisie, were generated in feudal society. At a certain stage in the development of these means of production and of exchange, the conditions under which feudal society produced and exchanged, the feudal organization of agriculture and manufacturing industry, in a word, the feudal relations of property became no longer compatible with the already developed productive forces; they became so many fetters. They had to be burst asunder; they were burst asunder.

Into their place stepped free competition, accompanied by a social and political constitution adapted to it, and by the economic and political sway of the bourgeois class.

A similar movement is going on before our own eyes. Modern bourgeois society with its **relations of production**, of exchange and of property, a society that has conjured up such gigantic **means of production** and of exchange, is like the sorcerer who is no longer able to control the powers of the nether world whom he has called up by his spells. For many a decade past the history of industry and commerce is but the history of the revolt of modern productive forces against modern conditions of production, against the property relations that are the conditions for the existence of the bourgeoisie and of its rule. It is enough to mention the commercial crises that by their periodical return put the existence of the entire bourgeois society on trial, each time more threateningly. In these crises a great part not only of the existing products, but also of the previously created productive forces, are periodically destroyed. In these crises there breaks out an epidemic that, in all earlier epochs, would have seemed an absurdity—the epidemic of overproduction. Society suddenly finds itself put back into a state of momentary barbarism; it appears as if a famine, a universal war of devastation had cut off the supply of every means of subsistence; industry and commerce seem to be destroyed. And why? Because there is too much civilization, too much means of subsistence, too much industry, too much commerce. The productive forces at the disposal of society no longer tend to further the development of the conditions of bourgeois property; on the contrary, they have become too powerful for these conditions, by which they are fettered, and no sooner do they overcome these fetters than they bring disorder into the whole of bourgeois society, endanger the existence of bourgeois property. The conditions of bourgeois society are too narrow to comprise the wealth created by them. And how does the bourgeoisie get over these crises? On the one hand by enforced destruction of a mass of productive forces; on the other, by the conquest of new markets, and by the more thorough exploitation of the old ones. That is to say, by paving the way for more extensive and more destructive crises, and by diminishing the means whereby crises are prevented.

The weapons with which the bourgeoisie felled feudalism to the ground are now turned against the bourgeoisie itself.

But not only has the bourgeoisie forged the weapons that bring death to itself; it has also called into existence the men who are to wield those weapons—the modern working class—the proletarians.

In proportion as the bourgeoisie, *i.e.*, **capital**, is developed, in the same proportion is the proletariat, the modern working class, developed—a class of
laborers, who live only so long as they find work, and who find work only so
long as their labor increases capital. These laborers, who must sell themselves
piecemeal, are a commodity, like every other article of commerce, and are consequently exposed to the vicissitudes of competition, to all the fluctuations of
the market.

Owing to the extensive use of machinery and to division of labor, the work
of the proletarians has lost all individual character, and, consequently, all charm
for the workman. He becomes an appendage of the machine, and it is only the
most simple, most monotonous, and most easily acquired knack, that is
required of him. Hence, the cost of production of a workman is restricted,
almost entirely, to the means of subsistence that he requires for his maintenance, and for the propagation of his race. But the price of a commodity, and
therefore also of labor, is equal to its cost of production. In proportion, therefore, as the repulsiveness of the work increases, the wage decreases. Nay more,
in proportion as the use of machinery and division of labor increases, in the
same proportion the burden of toil also increases, whether by prolongation of
the working hours, by increase of the work exacted in a given time, or by
increased speed of the machinery, etc.

Modern industry has converted the little workshop of the patriarchal master
into the great factory of the industrial capitalist. Masses of laborers, crowded
into the factory, are organized like soldiers. As privates of the industrial army
they are placed under the command of a perfect hierarchy of officers and
sergeants. Not only are they slaves of the bourgeois class, and of the bourgeois
state; they are daily and hourly enslaved by the machine, by the overlooker,
and, above all, by the individual bourgeois manufacturer himself. The more
openly this despotism proclaims gain to be its end and aim, the more petty, the
more hateful and the more embittering it is.

The less the skill and exertion of strength implied in manual labor, in other
words, the more modern industry develops, the more is the labor of men superseded by that of women. Differences of age and sex have no longer any distinctive social validity for the working class. All are instruments of labor, more
or less expensive to use, according to their age and sex.

No sooner has the laborer received his wages in cash, for the moment escaping exploitation by the manufacturer, than he is set upon by the other portions
of the bourgeoisie, the landlord, the shopkeeper, the pawnbroker, etc.

The lower strata of the middle class—the small tradespeople, shopkeepers,
and retired tradesmen generally, the handicraftsmen and peasants—all these
sink gradually into the proletariat, partly because their diminutive capital does
not suffice for the scale on which modern industry is carried on, and is

swamped in the competition with the large capitalists, partly because their specialized skill is rendered worthless by new methods of production. Thus the proletariat is recruited from all classes of the population.

The proletariat goes through various stages of development. With its birth begins its struggle with the bourgeoisie. At first the contest is carried on by individual laborers, then by the work people of a factory, then by the operatives of one trade, in one locality, against the individual bourgeois who directly exploits them. They direct their attacks not against the bourgeois conditions of production, but against the instruments of production themselves; they destroy imported wares that compete with their labor, they smash machinery to pieces, they set factories ablaze, they seek to restore by force the vanished status of the workman of the Middle Ages.

At this stage the laborers still form an incoherent mass scattered over the whole country, and broken up by their mutual competition. If anywhere they unite to form more compact bodies, this is not yet the consequence of their own active union, but of the union of the bourgeoisie, which class, in order to attain its own political ends, is compelled to set the whole proletariat in motion, and is moreover still able to do so for a time. At this stage, therefore, the proletarians do not fight their enemies, but the enemies of their enemies, the remnants of absolute monarchy, the landowners, the nonindustrial bourgeois, the **petty bourgeoisie**. Thus the whole historical movement is concentrated in the hands of the bourgeoisie; every victory so obtained is a victory for the bourgeoisie.

But with the development of industry the proletariat not only increases in number; it becomes concentrated in greater masses, its strength grows, and it feels that strength more. The various interests and conditions of life within the ranks of the proletariat are more and more equalized, in proportion as machinery obliterates all distinctions of labor and nearly everywhere reduces wages to the same low level. The growing competition among the bourgeois, and the resulting commercial crises, make the wages of the workers ever more fluctuating. The unceasing improvement of machinery, ever more rapidly developing, makes their livelihood more and more precarious; the collisions between individual workmen and individual bourgeois take more and more the character of collisions between two classes. Thereupon the workers begin to form combinations (trade unions) against the bourgeoisie; they club together in order to keep up the rate of wages; they found permanent associations in order to make provision beforehand for these occasional revolts. Here and there the contest breaks out into riots.

Now and then the workers are victorious, but only for a time. The real fruit of their battles lies, not in the immediate results, but in the ever expanding union of the workers. This union is furthered by the improved means of communication which are created by modern industry, and which place the workers of different localities in contact with one another. It was just this contact that was needed to centralize the numerous local struggles, all of the same character, into one national struggle between classes. But every class struggle is a political struggle. And that union, to attain which the burghers of the Middle Ages, with their miserable highways, required centuries, the modern proletarians, thanks to railways, achieve in a few years.

This organization of the proletarians into a class, and consequently into a political party, is continually being upset again by the competition between the workers themselves. But it ever rises up again, stronger, firmer, mightier. It compels legislative recognition of particular interests of the workers, by taking advantage of the divisions among the bourgeoisie itself. Thus the **ten-hour bill** in England was carried.

Altogether, collisions between the classes of the old society further the course of development of the proletariat in many ways. The bourgeoisie finds itself involved in a constant battle. At first with the aristocracy; later on, with those portions of the bourgeoisie itself whose interests have become antagonistic to the progress of industry; at all times with the bourgeoisie of foreign countries. In all these battles it sees itself compelled to appeal to the proletariat, to ask for help, and thus, to drag it into the political arena. The bourgeoisie itself, therefore, supplies the proletariat with its own elements of political and general education, in other words, it furnishes the proletariat with weapons for fighting the bourgeoisie.

Further, as we have already seen, entire sections of the ruling classes are, by the advance of industry, precipitated into the proletariat, or are at least threatened in their conditions of existence. These also supply the proletariat with fresh elements of enlightenment and progress.

Finally, in times when the class struggle nears the decisive hour, the process of dissolution going on within the **ruling class**, in fact within the whole range of old society, assumes such a violent, glaring character, that a small section of the ruling class cuts itself adrift, and joins the revolutionary class, the class that holds the future in its hands. Just as, therefore, at an earlier period, a section of the nobility went over to the bourgeoisie, so now a portion of the bourgeoisie goes over to the proletariat, and in particular, a portion of the bourgeois ideologists, who have raised themselves to the level of comprehending theoretically the historical movement as a whole.

Of all the classes that stand face to face with the bourgeoisie today, the proletariat alone is a really revolutionary class. The other classes decay and finally disappear in the face of modern industry; the proletariat is its special and essential product.

The lower middle class, the small manufacturer, the shopkeeper, the artisan, the peasant, all these fight against the bourgeoisie, to save from extinction their existence as fractions of the middle class. They are therefore not revolutionary, but conservative. Nay more, they are reactionary, for they try to roll back the wheel of history. If by chance they are revolutionary, they are so only in view of their impending transfer into the proletariat; they thus defend not their present, but their future interests; they desert their own standpoint to adopt that of the proletariat.

The "dangerous class," the social scum (***Lumpenproletariat***), that passively rotting mass thrown off by the lowest layers of old society, may, here and there, be swept into the movement by a proletarian revolution; its conditions of life, however, prepare it far more for the part of a bribed tool of reactionary intrigue.

The social conditions of the old society no longer exist for the proletariat. The proletarian is without property; his relation to his wife and children has no longer anything in common with bourgeois family relations; modern industrial labor, modern subjection to capital, the same in England as in France, in America as in Germany, has stripped him of every trace of national character. Law, morality, religion, are to him so many bourgeois prejudices, behind which lurk in ambush just as many bourgeois interests.

All the preceding classes that got the upper hand, sought to fortify their already acquired status by subjecting society at large to their conditions of appropriation. The proletarians cannot become masters of the productive forces of society, except by abolishing their own previous mode of appropriation, and thereby also every other previous mode of appropriation. They have nothing of their own to secure and to fortify; their mission is to destroy all previous securities for, and insurances of, individual property.

All previous historical movements were movements of minorities, or in the interest of minorities. The proletarian movement is the self-conscious, independent movement of the immense majority, in the interest of the immense majority. The proletariat, the lowest stratum of our present society, cannot stir, cannot raise itself up, without the whole superincumbent strata of official society being sprung into the air.

Though not in substance, yet in form, the struggle of the proletariat with the bourgeoisie is at first a national struggle. The proletariat of each country must, of course, first of all settle matters with its own bourgeoisie.

In depicting the most general phases of the development of the proletariat, we traced the more or less veiled civil war, raging within existing society, up to the point where that war breaks out into open revolution, and where the violent overthrow of the bourgeoisie lays the foundation for the sway of the proletariat.

Hitherto, every form of society has been based, as we have already seen, on the antagonism of oppressing and oppressed classes. But in order to oppress a class, certain conditions must be assured to it under which it can, at least, continue its slavish existence. The serf, in the period of serfdom, raised himself to membership in the commune, just as the petty bourgeois, under the yoke of feudal absolutism, managed to develop into a bourgeois. The modern laborer, on the contrary, instead of rising with the progress of industry, sinks deeper and deeper below the conditions of existence of his own class. He becomes a pauper, and pauperism develops more rapidly than population and wealth. And here it becomes evident, that the bourgeoisie is unfit any longer to be the ruling class in society, and to impose its conditions of existence upon society as an overriding law. It is unfit to rule because it is incompetent to assure an existence to its slave within his slavery, because it cannot help letting him sink into such a state, that it has to feed him, instead of being fed by him. Society can no longer live under this bourgeoisie, in other words, its existence is no longer compatible with society.

The essential condition for the existence and sway of the bourgeois class, is the formation and augmentation of capital; the condition for capital is wage-labor. Wage-labor rests exclusively on competition between the laborers. The advance of industry, whose involuntary promoter is the bourgeoisie, replaces the isolation of the laborers, due to competition, by their revolutionary combination, due to association. The development of modern industry, therefore, cuts from under its feet the very foundation on which the bourgeois produces and appropriates products. What the bourgeoisie therefore produces, above all, are its own gravediggers. Its fall and the victory of the proletariat are equally inevitable.

Notes

1   By "bourgeoisie" is meant the class of modern capitalists, owners of the means of social production and employers of wage-labor; by "proletariat," the class of modern wage-laborers who, having no means of production of their own, are reduced to selling their labor power in order to live.

2   That is, all *written* history. In 1837, the prehistory of society, the social organization existing previous to recorded history, was all but unknown. Since then Haxthausen discovered common ownership of land in Russia, Maurer proved it to be the social foundation from which all Teutonic races started in history, and, by and by, village communities were found to be, or to have been, the primitive form of society everywhere from India to Ireland. The inner organization of this primitive communistic society was laid bare, in its typical form, by Morgan's crowning discovery of the true nature of the *gens* and its relation to the *tribe*. With the dissolution of these primeval communities, society begins to be differentiated into separate and finally antagonistic classes. I have attempted to retrace this process of dissolution in *The Origin of the Family, Private Property and the State*.

3   Guild-master, that is a full member of a guild, a master within, not a head of a guild.

4   "Commune" was the name taken in France by the nascent towns even before they had conquered from their feudal lords and masters local self-government and political rights as the "Third Estate." Generally speaking, for the economic development of the bourgeoisie, England is here taken as the typical country, for its political development, France.

Study Questions

1. What do Marx and Engels mean when they assert that history is the history of class struggle?

2. According to Marx and Engels, how is the proletariat oppressed?

3. According to Marx and Engels, why is the downfall of capitalism inevitable?

Further Readings

Berlin, Isaiah. 1996. *Karl Marx: His Life and Environment*. (4th ed.). New York: Oxford University Press.

Bottomore, Tom (ed.). 1991. *A Dictionary of Marxist Thought*. Oxford: Basil Blackwell.

Engels, Friedrich. 1972 [1884]. *Origin of the Family, Private Property, and the State*. (2nd ed.). Ed. Eleanor B. Leacock. New York: International Publishers Company.

Marx, Karl, and Engels, Friedrich. 1902 [1848]. *The Communist Manifesto*. Ed. David McLellan. New York: Oxford University Press.

—. 1930 [1867]. *Capital: A Critique of Political Economy*. (4th ed.). Trans. Paul Eden and Paul Ceder. New York: E.P. Dutton.

Woolfson, Charles. 1982. *The Labour Theory of Culture: A Re-Examination of Engels' Theory of Human Origins*. London: Routledge.

2

The Science of Culture

EDWARD BURNETT TYLOR

Culture or Civilization—Its phenomena related according to definite Laws—Method of classification and discussion of the evidence—Connexion of successive stages of culture by Permanence, Modification, and Survival—Principal topics examined in the present work.

Culture or Civilization, taken in its wide ethnographic sense, is that complex whole which includes knowledge, belief, art, morals, law, custom, and any other capabilities and habits acquired by man as a member of society. The condition of culture among the various societies of mankind, in so far as it is capable of being investigated on general principles, is a subject apt for the study of laws of human thought and action. On the one hand, the uniformity which so largely pervades civilization may be ascribed, in great measure, to the uniform action of uniform causes: while on the other hand its various grades may be regarded as stages of development or evolution, each the outcome of previous history, and about to do its proper part in shaping the history of the future. To the investigation of these two great principles in several departments of ethnography, with especial consideration of the civilization of the lower tribes as related to the civilization of the higher nations, the present volumes are devoted.

Our modern investigators in the sciences of inorganic nature are foremost to recognize, both within and without their special fields of work, the unity of nature, the fixity of its laws, the definite sequence of cause and effect through which every fact depends on what has gone before it, and acts upon what is to come after it. They grasp firmly the **Pythagorean** doctrine of pervading order in the universal Kosmos. They affirm, with Aristotle, that nature is not full of incoherent episodes, like a bad tragedy. They agree with **Leibnitz** in what he calls "my axiom, that nature never acts by leaps (la nature n'agit jamais par saut)," as well as in his "great principle, commonly little employed, that nothing happens without sufficient reason." Nor again, in studying the structure and habits of plants and animals, or in investigating the lower functions even of man, are these leading ideas unacknowledged. But when we come to talk of the higher processes of human feeling and action, of thought and language, knowledge and art, a change appears in the prevalent tone of opinion. The world at large is scarcely prepared to accept the general study of human life as a branch of natural science, and to carry out, in a large sense, the poet's injunction to "Account for moral as for natural things." To many educated minds there seems something presumptuous and repulsive in the view that the history of mankind is part and parcel of the history of nature, that our thoughts, wills, and actions accord with laws as definite as those which govern the motion of waves, the combination of acids and bases, and the growth of plants and animals.

The main reasons of this state of the popular judgment are not far to seek. There are many who would willingly accept a science of history if placed before them with substantial definiteness of principle and evidence, but who not unreasonably reject the systems offered to them, as falling too far short of a scientific standard. Through resistance such as this, real knowledge always sooner or later makes its way, while the habit of opposition to novelty does such excellent service against the invasions of speculative dogmatism, that we may sometimes even wish it were stronger than it is. But other obstacles to the investigation of laws of human nature arise from considerations of **metaphysics** and theology. The popular notion of free human will involves not only freedom to act in accordance with motive, but also a power of breaking loose from continuity and acting without cause,—a combination which may be roughly illustrated by the simile of a balance sometimes acting in the usual way, but also possessed of the faculty of turning by itself without or against its weights. This view of an anomalous action of the will, which it need hardly be said is incompatible with scientific argument, subsists as an opinion patent or latent in men's minds, and strongly affecting their theoretic views of history, though it is not, as a rule, brought prominently forward in systematic reasoning. Indeed the definition of human will, as strictly according with motive, is the only possible scientific basis in such enquiries. Happily, it is not needful to add here yet another to the list of dissertations on supernatural intervention and natural causation, on liberty, predestination, and accountability. We may hasten to escape from the regions of **transcendental** philosophy and theology, to start on a more hopeful journey over more practicable ground. None will deny that, as each man knows by the evidence of his own consciousness, definite and natural cause does, to a great extent, determine human action. Then, keeping aside from considerations of extra-natural interference and causeless spontaneity, let us take this admitted existence of natural cause and effect as our standing-ground, and travel on it so far as it will bear us. It is on this same basis that physical science pursues, with ever-increasing success, its quest of laws of nature. Nor need this restriction hamper the scientific study of human life, in which the real difficulties are the practical ones of enormous complexity of evidence, and imperfection of methods of observation.

Now it appears that this view of human will and conduct as subject to definite law, is indeed recognized and acted upon by the very people who oppose it when stated in the abstract as a general principle, and who then complain that it annihilates man's free will, destroys his sense of personal responsibility, and degrades him to a soulless machine. He who will say these things will nevertheless pass much of his own life in studying the motives which lead to human action, seeking to attain his wishes through them, framing in his mind theories of personal character, reckoning what are likely to be the effects of new combinations, and giving to his reasoning the crowning character of true scientific enquiry, by taking it for granted that in so far as his calculation turns out wrong, either his evidence must have been false or incomplete, or his judgment upon it unsound. Such a man will sum up the experience of years spent in complex relations with society, by declaring his persuasion that there is a reason for everything in life, and that where events look unaccountable, the rule is to wait and watch in hope that the key to the problem may some day be found. This man's observation may have been as narrow as his inferences are crude and prejudiced, but nevertheless he has been an inductive philosopher "more than forty years without knowing it." He has practically acknowledged definite laws of human thought and action, and has simply thrown out of account in his own studies of life the whole fabric of motiveless will and uncaused spontaneity. It is assumed here that they should be just so thrown out of account in wider studies, and that the true philosophy of history lies in extending and improving the methods of the plain people who form their judgments upon facts, and check them upon new facts. Whether the doctrine be wholly or but partly true, it accepts the very condition under which we search for new knowledge in the lessons of experience, and in a word the whole course of our rational life is based upon it.

"One event is always the son of another, and we must never forget the parentage," was a remark made by a **Bechuana** chief to **Casalis** the African missionary. Thus at all times historians, so far as they have aimed at being more than mere chroniclers, have done their best to show not merely succession, but connexion, among the events upon their record. Moreover, they have striven to elicit general principles of human action, and by these to explain particular events, stating expressly or taking tacitly for granted the existence of a philosophy of history. Should any one deny the possibility of thus establishing historical laws, the answer is ready with which **Boswell** in such a case turned on **Johnson**: "Then, sir, you would reduce all history to no better than an almanack." That nevertheless the labours of so many eminent thinkers should have as yet brought history only to the threshold of science, need cause no wonder to those who consider the bewildering complexity of the problems which come before the general historian. The evidence from which he is to draw his conclusions is at once so multifarious and so doubtful, that a full and distinct view of its bearing on a particular question is hardly to be attained, and thus the temptation becomes all but irresistible to garble it in support of some rough and ready theory of the course of events. The philosophy of history at large, explaining the past and predicting the future phenomena of man's life in the world by reference to general laws, is in fact a subject with which, in the present state of knowledge, even genius aided by wide research seems but hardly able to cope. Yet there are departments of it which, though difficult enough, seem comparatively accessible. If the field of enquiry be narrowed from History as a whole to that branch of it which is here called Culture, the history, not of tribes or nations, but of the condition of knowledge, religion, art, custom, and the like among them, the task of investigation proves to lie within far more moderate compass. We suffer still from the same kind of difficulties which beset the wider argument, but they are more diminished. The evidence is no longer so wildly heterogenous, but may be more simply classified and compared, while the power of getting rid of extraneous matter, and treating each issue on its own proper set of facts, makes close reasoning on the whole more available than in general history. This may appear from a brief preliminary examination of the problem, how the phenomena of Culture may be classified and arranged, stage by stage, in a probable order of evolution.

Surveyed in a broad view, the character and habit of mankind at once display that similarity and consistency of phenomena which led the Italian proverb-maker to declare that "all the world is one country," "tutto il mondo è paese." To general likeness in human nature on the one hand, and to general likeness in the circumstances of life on the other, this similarity and consistency may no doubt be traced, and they may be studied with especial fitness in comparing races near the same grade of civilization. Little respect need be had in such comparisons for date in history or for place on the map; the ancient Swiss lake-dweller may be set beside the mediæval Aztec, and the Ojibwa of North America beside the Zulu of South Africa. As Dr. Johnson contemptuously said when he had read about **Patagonians** and South Sea Islanders in Hawkesworth's Voyages, "one set of savages is like another." How true a generalization this really is, any Ethnological Museum may show. Examine for instance the edged and pointed instruments in such a collection; the inventory includes hatchet, adze, chisel, knife, saw, scraper, awl, needle, spear and arrowhead, and of these most or all belong with only differences of detail to races the most various. So it is with savage occupations; the wood-chopping, fishing with net and line, shooting and spearing game, fire-making, cooking, twisting cord and plaiting baskets, repeat themselves with wonderful uniformity in the museum shelves which illustrate the life of the lower races from **Kamchatka** to Tierra del Fuego, and from **Dahome** to Hawaii. Even when it comes to comparing barbarous hordes with civilized nations, the consideration thrusts itself upon our minds, how far item after item of the life of the lower races passes into analogous proceedings of the higher, in forms not too far changed to be recognized, and sometimes hardly changed at all. Look at the modern European peasant using his hatchet and his hoe, see his food boiling or roasting over the log-fire, observe the exact place which beer holds in his calculation of happiness, hear his tale of the ghost in the nearest haunted house, and of the farmer's niece who was bewitched with knots in her inside till she fell into fits and died. If we choose out in this way things which have altered little in a long course of centuries, we may draw a picture where there shall be scarce a hand's breadth difference between an English ploughman and a negro of Central Africa. These pages will be so crowded with evidence of such correspondence among mankind, that there is no need to dwell upon its details here, but it may be used at once to override a problem which would complicate the argument, namely, the question of race. For the present purpose it appears both possible and desirable to eliminate considerations of hereditary varieties or races of man, and to treat mankind as homogenous in nature, though placed in different grades of civilization. The details of the enquiry will, I think, prove that stages of culture may be compared without taking into account how far tribes who use the same implement, follow the same custom, or believe the same myth, may differ in their bodily configuration and the colour of their skin and hair.

A first step in the study of civilization is to dissect it into details, and to classify these in their proper groups. Thus, in examining weapons, they are to be classed under spear, club, sling, bow and arrow, and so forth; among textile arts are to be ranged matting, netting, and several grades of making and weaving threads; myths are divided under such headings as myths of sunrise and sunset, eclipse-myths, earthquake-myths, local myths which account for the names of places by some fanciful tale, **eponymic** myths which account for the parentage of a tribe by turning its name into the name of an imaginary ancestor; under rites and ceremonies occur such practices as the various kinds of sacrifice to the ghosts of the dead and to other spiritual beings, the turning to the east in worship, the purification of ceremonial or moral uncleanness by means of water or fire. Such are a few miscellaneous examples from a list of hundreds, and the ethnographer's business is to classify such details with a view to making out their distribution in geography and history, and the relations which exist among them. What this task is like, may be almost perfectly illustrated by comparing these details of culture with the species of plants and animals as studied by the naturalist. To the ethnographer the bow and arrow is a species, the habit of flattening children's skulls is a species, the practice of reckoning numbers by tens is a species. The geographical distribution of these things, and their transmission from region to region, have to be studied as the naturalist studies the geography of his botanical and zoological species. Just as certain plants and animals are peculiar to certain districts, so it is with such instruments as the Australian boomerang, the Polynesian stick-and-groove for fire-making, the tiny bow and arrow used as a lancet or **phleme** by tribes about the Isthmus of Panama, and in like manner with many an art, myth, or custom, found isolated in a particular field. Just as the catalogue of all the species of plants and animals of a district represents its Flora and Fauna, so the list of all the items of the general life of a people represents that whole which we call its culture. And just as distant regions so often produce vegetables and animals which are analogous, though by no means identical, so it is with the details of the civilization of their inhabitants. How good a working analogy there really is between the diffusion of plants and animals and the diffusion of civilization, comes well into view when we notice how far the same causes have produced both at once. In district after district, the same causes which have introduced the cultivated plants and domesticated animals of civilization, have brought in with them a corresponding art and knowledge. The course of events which carried horses and wheat to America carried with them the use of the gun and the iron hatchet, while in return the whole world received not only maize, potatoes, and turkeys, but the habit of tobacco-smoking and the sailor's hammock.

It is a matter worthy of consideration, that the accounts of similar phenomena of culture, recurring in different parts of the world, actually supply incidental proof of their own authenticity. Some years since, a question which brings out this point was put to me by a great historian—"How can a statement as to customs, myths, beliefs, &c., of a savage tribe be treated as evidence where it depends on the testimony of some traveller or missionary, who may be a superficial observer, more or less ignorant of the native language, a careless retailer of unsifted talk, a man prejudiced or even wilfully deceitful?" This question is, indeed, one which every ethnographer ought to keep clearly and constantly before his mind. Of course he is bound to use his best judgment as to the trustworthiness of all authors he quotes, and if possible to obtain several accounts to certify each point in each locality. But it is over and above these measures of precaution that the test of recurrence comes in. If two independent visitors to different countries, say a mediæval Mohammedan in **Tartary** and a modern Englishman in Dahome, or a Jesuit missionary in Brazil and a **Wesleyan** in the Fiji Islands, agree in describing some analogous art or rite or myth among the people they have visited, it becomes difficult or impossible to set down such correspondence to accident or wilful fraud. A story by a bushranger in Australia may, perhaps, be objected to as a mistake or an invention, but did a Methodist minister in Guinea conspire with him to cheat the public by telling the same story there? The possibility of intentional or unintentional mystification is often barred by such a state of things as that a similar statement is made in two remote lands, by two witnesses, of whom A lived a century before B, and B appears never to have heard of A. How distant are the countries, how wide apart the dates, how different the creeds and characters of the observers, in the catalogue of facts of civilization, needs no farther showing to any one who will even glance at the footnotes of the present work. And the more odd the statement, the less likely that several people in several places should have made it wrongly. This being so, it seems reasonable to judge that the statements are in the main truly given, and that their close and regular coincidence is due to the cropping up of similar facts in various districts of culture. Now the most important facts of ethnography are vouched for in this way. Experience leads the student after a while to expect and find that the phenomena of culture, as resulting from widely-acting similar causes, should recur again and again in the world. He even mistrusts isolated statements to which he knows of no parallel elsewhere, and waits for their genuineness to be shown by corresponding accounts from the other side of the earth, or the other end of history. So strong, indeed, is this means of authentication, that the ethnographer in his library may sometimes presume to decide, not only whether a particular explorer is a shrewd, honest observer, but also whether what he reports is conformable to the general rules of civilization. "Non quis, sed quid."

To turn from the distribution of culture in different countries, to its diffusion within these countries. The quality of mankind which tends most to make the systematic study of civilization possible, is that remarkable tacit consensus or agreement which so far induces whole populations to unite in the use of the same language, to follow the same religion and customary law, to settle down to the same general level of art and knowledge. It is this state of things which makes it so far possible to ignore exceptional facts and to describe nations by a sort of general average. It is this state of things which makes it so far possible to represent immense masses of details by a few typical facts, while, these once settled, new cases recorded by new observers simply fall into their places to prove the soundness of the classification. There is found to be such regularity in the composition of societies of men, that we can drop individual differences out of sight, and thus can generalize on the arts and opinions of whole nations, just as, when looking down upon an army from a hill, we forget the individual soldier, whom, in fact, we can scarce distinguish in the mass, while we see each regiment as an organized body, spreading or concentrating, moving in advance or in retreat. In some branches of the study of social laws it is now possible to call in the aid of statistics, and to set apart special actions of large mixed communities of men by means of taxgatherers' schedules, or the tables of the insurance office. Among modern arguments on the laws of human action, none have had a deeper effect than generalizations such as those of M. **Quetelet**, on the regularity, not only of such matters as average stature and the annual rates of birth and death, but of the recurrence, year after year, of such obscure and seemingly incalculable products of national life as the numbers of murders and suicides, and the proportion of the very weapons of crime. Other striking cases are the annual regularity of persons killed accidentally in the London streets, and of undirected letters dropped into post-office letter-boxes. But in examining the culture of the lower races, far from having at command the measured arithmetical facts of modern statistics, we may have to judge of the condition of tribes from the imperfect accounts supplied by travellers or missionaries, or even to reason upon relics of prehistoric races of whose very names and languages we are hopelessly ignorant. Now these may seem at the first glance sadly indefinite and unpromising materials for scientific enquiry. But in fact they are neither indefinite nor unpromising, but give evidence that is good and definite as far as it goes. They are data which, for the distinct way in which they severally denote the condition of the tribe they belong to, will actually bear comparison with the statistician's returns. The fact is that a stone arrow-head, a carved club, an idol, a grave-mound where slaves and property have been buried for the use of the dead, an account of a sorcerer's rites in making rain, a table of numerals, the conjugation of a verb, are things which each express the state of a people as to one particular point of culture, as truly as the tabulated numbers of deaths by poison, and of chests of tea imported, express in a different way other partial results of the general life of a whole community.

That a whole nation should have a special dress, special tools and weapons, special laws of marriage and property, special moral and religious doctrines, is a remarkable fact, which we notice so little because we have lived all our lives in the midst of it. It is with such general qualities of organized bodies of men that ethnography has especially to deal. Yet, while generalizing on the culture of a tribe or nation, and setting aside the peculiarities of the individuals composing it as unimportant to the main result, we must be careful not to forget what makes up this main result. There are people so intent on the separate life of individuals that they cannot grasp a notion of the action of the community as a whole—such an observer, incapable of a wide view of society, is aptly described in the saying that he "cannot see the forest for the trees." But, on the other hand, the philosopher may be so intent upon his general laws of society as to neglect the individual actors of whom that society is made up, and of him it may be said that he cannot see the trees for the forest. We know how arts, customs, and ideas are shaped among ourselves by the combined actions of many individuals, of which actions both motive and effect often come quite distinctly within our view. The history of an invention, an opinion, a ceremony, is a history of suggestion and modification, encouragement and opposition, personal gain and party prejudice, and the individuals concerned act each according to his own motives, as determined by his character and circumstances. Thus sometimes we watch individuals acting for their own ends with little thought of their effect on society at large, and sometimes we have to study movements of national life as a whole, where the individuals co-operating in them are utterly beyond our observation. But seeing that collective social action is the mere resultant of many individual actions, it is clear that these two methods of enquiry, if rightly followed, must be absolutely consistent.

In studying both the recurrence of special habits or ideas in several districts, and their prevalence within each district, there come before us ever-reiterated proofs of regular causation producing the phenomena of human life, and of laws of maintenance and diffusion according to which these phenomena settle into permanent standard conditions of society, at definite stages of culture. But, while giving full importance to the evidence bearing on these standard conditions of society, let us be careful to avoid a pitfall which may entrap the unwary student. Of course the opinions and habits belonging in common to masses of mankind are to a great extent the results of sound judgment and practical wisdom. But to a great extent it is not so. That many numerous societies of men should have believed in the influence of the evil eye and the existence of a firmament, should have sacrificed slaves and goods to the ghosts of the departed, should have handed down traditions of giants slaying monsters and men turning into beasts—all this is ground for holding that such ideas were indeed produced in men's minds by efficient causes, but it is not ground for holding that the rites in question are profitable, the beliefs sound, and the history authentic. This may seem at the first glance a truism, but, in fact, it is the denial of a fallacy which deeply affects the minds of all but a small critical minority of mankind. Popularly, what everybody says must be true, what everybody does must be right—"Quod ubique, quod semper, quod ab omnibus creditum est, hoc est vere proprieque Catholicum"—and so forth. There are various topics, especially in history, law, philosophy, and theology, where even the educated people we live among can hardly be brought to see that the cause why men do hold an opinion, or practise a custom, is by no means necessarily a reason why they ought to do so. Now collections of ethnographic evidence bringing so prominently into view the agreement of immense multitudes of men as to certain traditions, beliefs, and usages, are peculiarly liable to be thus improperly used in direct defence of these institutions themselves, even old barbaric nations being polled to maintain their opinions against what are called modern ideas. As it has more than once happened to myself to find my collections of traditions and beliefs thus set up to prove their own objective truth, without proper examination of the grounds on which they were actually received, I take this occasion of remarking that the same line of argument will serve equally well to demonstrate, by the strong and wide consent of nations, that the earth is flat, and nightmare the visit of a demon.

It being shown that the details of Culture are capable of being classified in a great number of ethnographic groups of arts, beliefs, customs, and the rest, the consideration comes next how far the facts arranged in these groups are produced by evolution from one another. It need hardly be pointed out that the groups in question, though held together each by a common character, are by no means accurately defined. To take up again the natural history illustration, it may be said that they are species which tend to run widely into varieties. And when it comes to the question what relations some of these groups bear to others, it is plain that the student of the habits of mankind has a great advantage over the student of the species of plants and animals. Among naturalists it is an open question whether a theory of development from species to species is a record of transitions which actually took place, or a mere ideal scheme serviceable in the classification of species whose origin was really independent. But among ethnographers there is no such question as to the possibility of species of implements or habits or beliefs being developed one out of another, for development in Culture is recognized by our most familiar knowledge. Mechanical invention supplies apt examples of the kind of development which affects civilization at large. In the history of fire-arms, the clumsy wheel-lock, in which a notched steel wheel revolved by means of a spring against a piece of pyrites till a spark caught the priming, led to the invention of the more serviceable flint-lock, of which a few still hang in the kitchens of our farm-houses for the boys to shoot small birds with at Christmas; the flint-lock in time passed by modification into the percussion-lock, which is just now changing its old-fashioned arrangement to be adapted from muzzle-loading to breech-loading. The mediæval astrolabe passed into the quadrant, now discarded in its turn by the seaman, who uses the more delicate sextant, and so it is through the history of one art and instrument after another. Such examples of progression are known to us as direct history, but so thoroughly is this notion of development at home in our minds, that by means of it we reconstruct lost history without scruple, trusting to general knowledge of the principles of human thought and action as a guide in putting the facts in their proper order. Whether chronicle speaks or is silent on the point, no one comparing a long-bow and a cross-bow would doubt that the cross-bow was a development arising from the simpler instrument. So among the fire-drills for igniting by friction, it seems clear on the face of the matter that the drill worked by a cord or bow is a later improvement on the clumsier primitive instrument twirled between the hands. That instructive class of specimens which antiquaries sometimes discover, bronze celts modelled on the heavy type of the stone hatchet, are scarcely explicable except as first steps in the transition from the Stone Age to the Bronze Age, to be followed soon by the next stage of progress, in which it is discovered that the new material is suited to a handier and less wasteful pattern. And thus, in the other branches of our history, there will come again and again into view series of facts which may be consistently arranged as having followed one another in a particular order of development, but which will hardly bear being turned round and made to follow in reversed order. Such for instance are the facts I have here brought forward in a chapter on the Art of Counting, which tend to prove that as to this point of culture at least, savage tribes reached their position by learning and not by unlearning, by elevation from a lower rather than by degradation from a higher state.

Among evidence aiding us to trace the course which the civilization of the world has actually followed, is that great class of facts to denote which I have found it convenient to introduce the term "**survivals**." These are processes, customs, opinions, and so forth, which have been carried on by force of habit into a new state of society different from that in which they had their original home, and they thus remain as proofs and examples of an older condition of culture out of which a newer has been evolved. Thus, I know an old Somersetshire woman whose hand-loom dates from the time before the introduction of the "flying shuttle," which new-fangled appliance she has never even learnt to use, and I have seen her throw her shuttle from hand to hand in true classic fashion; this old woman is not a century behind her times, but she is a case of survival. Such examples often lead us back to the habits of hundreds and even thousands of years ago. The ordeal of the Key and Bible, still in use, is a survival; the Midsummer bonfire is a survival; the Breton peasants' All Souls' supper for the spirits of the dead is a survival. The simple keeping up of ancient habits is only one part of the transition from old into new and changing times. The serious business of ancient society may be seen to sink into the sport of later generations, and its serious belief to linger on in nursery folk-lore, while superseded habits of old-world life may be modified into new-world forms still powerful for good and evil. Sometimes old thoughts and practices will burst out afresh, to the amazement of a world that thought them long since dead or dying; here survival passes into revival, as has lately happened in so remarkable a way in the history of modern spiritualism, a subject full of instruction from the ethnographer's point of view. The study of the principles of survival has, indeed, no small practical importance, for most of what we call superstition is included within survival, and in this way lies open to the attack of its deadliest enemy, a reasonable explanation. Insignificant, moreover, as multitudes of the facts of survival are in themselves, their study is so effective for tracing the course of the historical development through which alone it is possible to understand their meaning, that it becomes a vital point of ethnographic research to gain the clearest possible insight into their nature. This importance must justify the detail here devoted to an examination of survival, on the evidence of such games, popular sayings, customs, superstitions, and the like, as may serve well to bring into view the manner of its operation.

Progress, degradation, survival, revival, modification, are all modes of the connexion that binds together the complex network of civilization. It needs but a glance into the trivial details of our own daily life to set us thinking how far we are really its originators, and how far but the transmitters and modifiers of the results of long past ages. Looking around the rooms we live in, we may try here how far he who only knows his own time can be capable of rightly comprehending even that. Here is the "honeysuckle" of Assyria, there the fleur-de-lis of **Anjou**, a cornice with a Greek border runs around the ceiling, the style of Louis XIV and its parent the Renaissance share the looking-glass between them. Transformed, shifted, or mutilated, such elements of art still carry their history plainly stamped upon them; and if the history yet farther behind is less easy to read, we are not to say that because we cannot clearly discern it there is therefore no history there. It is thus even with the fashion of the clothes men wear. The ridiculous little tails of the German **postilion**'s coat show of themselves how they came to dwindle to such absurd rudiments; but the English clergyman's bands no longer so convey their history to the eye, and look unaccountable enough till one has seen the intermediate stages through which they came down from the more serviceable wide collars, such as **Milton** wears in his portrait, and which gave their name to the "band-box" they used to be kept in. In fact, the books of costume, showing how one garment grew or shrank by gradual stages and passed into another, illustrate with much force and clearness the nature of the change and growth, revival and decay, which go on from year to year in more important matters of life. In books, again, we see each writer not for and by himself, but occupying his proper place in history; we look through each philosopher, mathematician, chemist, poet, into the background of his education,—through Leibnitz into Descartes, through **Dalton** into **Priestly**, through Milton into Homer. The study of language has, perhaps, done more than any other in removing from our view of human thought and action the ideas of chance and arbitrary invention, and in substituting for them a theory of development by the co-operation of individual men, through processes ever reasonable and intelligible where the facts are fully known. Rudimentary as the science of culture still is, the symptoms are becoming very strong that even what seem its most spontaneous and motiveless phenomena will, nevertheless, be shown to come within the range of distinct cause and effect as certainly as the facts of mechanics. What would be popularly thought more indefinite and uncontrolled than the products of the imagination in myths and fables? Yet any systematic investigation of mythology, on the basis of a wide collection of evidence, will show plainly enough in such efforts of fancy at once a development from stage to stage, and a production of uniformity of result from uniformity of cause. Here, as elsewhere, causeless spontaneity is seen to recede farther and farther into shelter within the dark precincts of ignorance; like chance, that still holds its place among the vulgar as a real cause of events otherwise unaccountable, while to educated men it has long consciously meant nothing but this ignorance itself. It is only when men fail to see the line of connexion in events, that they are prone to fall upon the notions of arbitrary impulses, causeless freaks, chance and nonsense and indefinite unaccountability. If childish games, purposeless customs, absurd superstitions, are set down as spontaneous because no one can say exactly how they came to be, the assertion may remind us of the like effect that the eccentric habits of the wild rice-plant had on the philosophy of a Red Indian tribe, otherwise disposed to see in the harmony of nature the effects of one controlling personal will. The Great Spirit, said these Sioux theologians, made all things except the wild rice; but the wild rice came by chance.

"Man," said **Wilhelm von Humboldt**, "ever connects on from what lies at hand (der Mensch knüpft immer an Vorhandenes an)." The notion of the continuity of civilization contained in this maxim is no barren philosophic principle, but is at once made practical by the consideration that they who wish to understand their own lives ought to know the stages through which their opinions and habits have become what they are. Auguste Comte scarcely overstated the necessity of this study of development when he declared at the beginning of his "Positive Philosophy" that "no conception can be understood except through its history," and his phrase will bear extension to culture at large. To expect to look modern life in the face and comprehend it by mere inspection, is a philosophy whose weakness can easily be tested. Imagine any one explaining the trivial saying, "a little bird told me," without knowing of the old belief in the language of birds and beasts, to which Dr. **Dasent**, in the introduction to the Norse Tales, so reasonably traces its origin. Attempts to explain by the light of reason things which want the light of history to show their meaning, may be instanced from **Blackstone**'s Commentaries. To Blackstone's mind, the very right of the commoner to turn his beast out to graze on the common, finds its origin and explanation in the feudal system. "For, when lords of manors granted out parcels of land to tenants, for services either done or to be done, these tenants could not plough or manure the land without beasts; these beasts could not be sustained without pasture; and pasture could not be had but in the lord's wastes, and on the uninclosed fallow grounds of themselves and other tenants. The law therefore annexed this right of common, as inseparably incident, to the grant of the lands; and this was the original of common appendant," &c.[1] Now though there is nothing irrational in this explanation, it does not agree at all with the Teutonic land-law which prevailed in England long before the Norman Conquest, and of which the remains have never wholly disappeared. In the old village-community even the arable land, lying in the great common fields which may still be traced in our country, had not yet passed into separate property, while the pasturage in the fallows and stubbles and on the waste belonged to the householders in common. Since those days, the change from communal to individual ownership has mostly transformed this old-world system, but the right which the peasant enjoys of pasturing his cattle on the common still remains, not as a concession to feudal tenants, but as possessed by the commoners before the lord ever claimed the ownership of the waste. It is always unsafe to detach a custom from its hold on past events, treating it as an isolated fact to be simply disposed of by some plausible explanation.

In carrying on the great task of rational ethnography, the investigation of the causes which have produced the phenomena of culture, and of the laws to which they are subordinate, it is desirable to work out as systematically as possible a scheme of evolution of this culture along its many lines. In the following chapter, on the Development of Culture, an attempt is made to sketch a theoretical course of civilization among mankind, such as appears on the whole most accordant with the evidence. By comparing the various stages of civilization among races known to history, with the aid of archaeological inference from the remains of prehistoric tribes, it seems possible to judge in a rough way of an early general condition of man, which from our point of view is to be regarded as a primitive condition, whatever yet earlier state may in reality have lain behind it. This hypothetical primitive condition corresponds in a considerable degree to that of modern savage tribes, who, in spite of their difference and distance, have in common certain elements of civilization, which seem remains of an early state of the human race at large. If this hypothesis be true, then, notwithstanding the continual interference of degeneration, the main tendency of culture from primæval up to modern times has been from savagery towards civilization. On the problem of this relation of savage to civilized life, almost every one of the thousands of facts discussed in the succeeding chapters has its direct bearing. Survival in Culture, placing all along the course of advancing civilization way-marks full of meaning to those who can decipher their signs, even now sets up in our midst primæval monuments of barbaric thought and life. Its investigation tells strongly in favour of the view that the European may find among the Greenlanders or Maoris many a trait for reconstructing the picture of his own primitive ancestors. Next comes the problem of the Origin of Language. Obscure as many parts of this problem still remain, its clearer positions lie open to the investigation whether speech took its origin among mankind in the savage state, and the result of the enquiry is that consistently with all known evidence, this may have been the case. From the examination of the Art of Counting a far more definite consequence is shown. It may be confidently asserted, that not only is this important art found in a rudimentary state among savage tribes, but that satisfactory evidence proves numeration to have been developed by rational invention from this low stage up to that in which we ourselves possess it. The examination of Mythology contained in the first volume, is for the most part made from a special point of view, on evidence collected for a special purpose, that of tracing the relation between the myths of savage tribes and their analogues among more civilized nations. The issue of such enquiry goes far to prove that the earliest myth-maker arose and flourished among savage hordes, setting on foot an art which his more cultured successors would carry on, till its results came to be fossilized in superstition, mistaken for history, shaped and draped in poetry, or cast aside as lying folly.

Nowhere, perhaps, are broad views of historical development more needed than in the study of religion. Notwithstanding all that has been written to make the world acquainted with the lower theologies, the popular ideas of their place in history and their relation to the faiths of higher nations are still of the mediæval type. It is wonderful to contrast some missionary journals with **Max Müller**'s Essays, and to set the unappreciating hatred and ridicule that is lavished by narrow hostile zeal on Brahmanism, Buddhism, Zoroastrism, besides the catholic sympathy with which deep and wide knowledge can survey those ancient and noble phases of man's religious consciousness; nor, because the religions of savage tribes may be rude and primitive compared with the great Asiatic systems, do they lie too low for interest and even for respect. The question really lies between understanding and misunderstanding them. Few who will give their minds to master the general principles of savage religion will ever again think it ridiculous, or the knowledge of it superfluous to the rest of mankind. Far from its beliefs and practices being a rubbish-heap of miscellaneous folly, they are consistent and logical in so high a degree as to begin, as soon as even roughly classified, to display the principles of their formation and development; and these principles prove to be essentially rational, though working in a mental condition of intense and inveterate ignorance. It is with a sense of attempting an investigation which bears very closely on the current theology of our own day, that I have set myself to examine systematically, among the lower races, the development of **Animism**; that is to say, the doctrine of souls and other spiritual beings in general. More than half of the present work is occupied with a mass of evidence from all regions of the world, displaying the nature and meaning of this great element of the Philosophy of Religion, and tracing its transmission, expansion, restriction, modification, along the course of history into the midst of our own modern thought. Nor are the questions of small practical moment which have to be raised in a similar attempt to trace the development of certain prominent Rites and Ceremonies— customs so full of instruction as to the inmost powers of religion, whose outward expression and practical result they are.

In these investigations, however, made rather from an ethnographic than a theological point of view, there has seemed little need of entering into direct controversial argument, which indeed I have taken pains to avoid as far as possible. The connexion which runs through religion, from its rudest forms up to the status of an enlightened Christianity, may be conveniently treated of with little recourse to dogmatic theology. The rites of sacrifice and purification may be studied in their stages of development without entering into questions of their authority and value, nor does an examination of the successive phases of the world's belief in a future life demand a discussion of the arguments adduced for or against the doctrine itself. The ethnographic results may then be left as materials for professed theologians, and it will not perhaps be long before evidence so fraught with meaning shall take its legitimate place. To fall back once again on the analogy of natural history, the time may soon come when it will be thought as unreasonable for a scientific student of theology not to have a competent acquaintance with the principles of the religions of the lower races, as for a physiologist to look with the contempt of past centuries on evidence derived from the lower forms of life, deeming the structure of mere invertebrate creatures matter unworthy of his philosophic study.

Not merely as a matter of curious research, but as an important practical guide to the understanding of the present and the shaping of the future, the investigation into the origin and early development of civilization must be pushed on zealously. Every possible avenue of knowledge must be explored, every door tried to see if it is open. No kind of evidence need be left untouched on the score of remoteness or complexity, of minuteness or triviality. The tendency of modern enquiry is more and more towards the conclusion that if law is anywhere, it is everywhere. To despair of what a conscientious collection and study of facts may lead to, and to declare any problem insoluble because difficult and far off, is distinctly to be on the wrong side in science; and he who will choose a hopeless task may set himself to discover the limits of discovery. One remembers Comte starting in his account of astronomy with a remark on the necessary limitation of our knowledge of the stars; we conceive, he tells us, the possibility of determining their form, distance, size, and movement, whilst we should never by any method be able to study their chemical composition, their mineralogical structure, &c. Had the philosopher lived to see the application of spectrum analysis to this very problem, his proclamation of the dispiriting doctrine of necessary ignorance would perhaps have been recanted in favour of a more hopeful view. And it seems to be with the philosophy of remote human life somewhat as with the study of the nature of the celestial bodies. The process to be made out in the early stages of our mental evolution lie distant from us in time as the stars lie distant from us in space, but the laws of the universe are not limited with the direct observation of our senses. There is vast material to be used in our enquiry; many workers are now busied in bringing this material into shape, though little may have yet been done in proportion to what remains to do; and already it seems not too much to say that the vague outlines of a philosophy of primæval history are beginning to come within our view.

Note

1   Blackstone, "Commentaries on the Laws of England," bk. II., ch.3. The above example replaces that given in former editions. Another example may be found in his explanation of the origin of deodand, bk. I., ch. 8, as designed, in the blind days of popery, as an expiation for the souls of such as were snatched away by sudden death [rest of sentence omitted].

Study Questions

1.   What does Tylor mean when he represents the study of culture as scientific?

2.   What are Tylor's arguments and evidence that culture has evolved?

3.   How does Tylor respond to the charge that cultural laws are a threat to human free will?

Further Readings

Sanderson, Stephen K. 1992. *Social Evolutionism: A Critical History.* Cambridge, MA: Blackwell.

Stocking, George W., Jr. 1987. *Victorian Anthropology.* New York: The Free Press.

—. 1994. *The Collected Works of E.B. Tylor.* New York: Routledge.

Tylor, Edward Burnett. 1873 [1871]. *Primitive Culture.* New York: Gordon Press.

—. 1898 [1881]. *Anthropology: An Introduction to the Study of Man and Civilization.* New York: D. Appleton.

3

Ethnical Periods

LEWIS HENRY MORGAN

The latest investigations respecting the early condition of the human race are tending to the conclusion that mankind commenced their career at the bottom of the scale and worked their way up from savagery to civilization through the slow accumulations of experimental knowledge.

As it is undeniable that portions of the human family have existed in a state of **savagery**, other portions in a state of **barbarism**, and still other portions in a state of **civilization**, it seems equally so that these three distinct conditions are connected with each other in a natural as well as necessary sequence of progress. Moreover, that this sequence has been historically true of the entire human family, up to the status attained by each branch respectively, is rendered probable by the conditions under which all progress occurs, and by the known advancement of several branches of the family through two or more of these conditions.

An attempt will be made in the following pages to bring forward additional evidence of the rudeness of the early condition of mankind, of the gradual evolution of their mental and moral powers through experience, and of their protracted struggle with opposing obstacles while winning their way to civilization. It will be drawn, in part, from the great sequence of inventions and discoveries which stretches along the entire pathway of human progress; but chiefly from domestic institutions, which express the growth of certain ideas and passions.

As we re-ascend along the several lines of progress toward the primitive ages of mankind, and eliminate one after the other, in the order in which they appeared, inventions and discoveries on the one hand, and institutions on the other, we are enabled to perceive that the former stand to each other in progressive, and the latter in unfolding relations. While the former class have had a connection, more or less direct, the latter have been developed from a few primary germs of thought. Modern institutions plant their roots in the period of barbarism, into which their germs were transmitted from the previous period of savagery. They have had a lineal descent through the ages, with the streams of the blood, as well as a logical development.

Two independent lines of investigations thus invite our attention. The one leads through inventions and discoveries, and the other through primary institutions. With the knowledge gained therefrom, we may hope to indicate the principal stages of human development. The proofs to be adduced will be drawn chiefly from domestic institutions; the references to achievements more strictly intellectual being general as well as subordinate.

The facts indicate the gradual formation and subsequent development of certain ideas, passions, and aspirations. Those which hold the most prominent positions may be generalized as growths of the particular ideas with which they severally stand connected. Apart from inventions and discoveries they are the following:

I. *Subsistence,*   V. *Religion,*

II. *Government,*   VI. *House Life and Architecture,*

III. *Language,*   VII. *Property.*

IV. *The Family,*

First. Subsistence has been increased and perfected by a series of successive arts, introduced at long intervals of time, and connected more or less directly with inventions and discoveries.

Second. The germ of government must be sought in the organization into **gentes** in the Status of savagery; and followed down, through the advancing forms of this institution, to the establishment of political society.

Third. Human speech seems to have been developed from the rudest and simplest forms of expression. Gesture or sign language, as intimated by **Lucretius**, must have preceded articulate language, as thought preceded speech. The monosyllabical preceded the syllabical, as the latter did that of concrete words. Human intelligence, unconscious of design, evolved articulate language by utilizing the vocal sounds. This great subject, a department of knowledge by itself, does not fall within the scope of the present investigation.

Fourth. With respect to the family, the stages of its growth are embodied in systems of **consanguinity** and **affinity**, and in usages relating to marriage, by means of which, collectively, the family can be definitely traced through several successive forms.

Fifth. The growth of religious ideas is environed with such intrinsic difficulties that it may never receive a perfectly satisfactory exposition. Religion deals so largely with the imaginative and emotional nature, and consequently with such uncertain elements of knowledge, that all primitive religions are grotesque and to some extent unintelligible. This subject also falls without the plan of this work excepting as it may prompt incidental suggestions.

Sixth. House architecture, which connects itself with the form of the family and the plan of domestic life, affords a tolerably complete illustration of progress from savagery to civilization. Its growth can be traced from the hut of the savage, through the communal houses of the barbarians, to the house of the single family of civilized nations, with all the successive links by which one extreme is connected with the other. This subject will be noticed incidentally.

Lastly. The idea of property was slowly formed in the human mind, remaining nascent and feeble through immense periods of time. Springing into life in savagery, it required all the experience of this period and of the subsequent period of barbarism to develop the germ, and to prepare the human brain for the acceptance of its controlling influence. Its dominance as a passion over all other passions marks the commencement of civilization. It not only led mankind to overcome the obstacles which delayed civilization, but to establish political society on the basis of territory and of property. A critical knowledge of the evolution of the idea of property would embody, in some respects, the most remarkable portion of the mental history of mankind.

It will be my object to present some evidence of human progress along these several lines, and through successive ethnical periods, as it is revealed by inventions and discoveries, and by the growth of the ideas of government, of the family, and of property.

It may be here premised that all forms of government are reducible to two general plans, using the word plan in its scientific sense. In their bases the two are fundamentally distinct. The first, in the order of time, is founded upon persons, and upon relations purely personal, and may be distinguished as a society (*societas*). The gens is the unit of this organization; giving as the successive stages of integration, in the archaic period, the **gens**, the **phratry**, the tribe, and the confederacy of tribes, which constituted a people or nation (*populus*). At a later period a coalescence of tribes in the same area into a nation took the place of a confederacy of tribes occupying independent areas. Such, through prolonged ages, after the gens appeared, was the substantially universal organization of ancient society; and it remained among the Greeks and Romans after civilization supervened. The second is founded upon territory and upon property, and may be distinguished by a state (*civitas*). The township or ward, circumscribed by **metes and bounds**, with the property it contains, is the basis or unit of the latter, and political society is the result. Political society is organized upon territorial areas, and deals with property as well as with persons through territorial relations. The successive stages of integration are the township or ward, which is the unit of organization; the county or province, which is an aggregation of townships or wards; and the national domain or territory, which is an aggregation of counties or provinces; the people of each of which are organized into a body politic. It taxed the Greeks and Romans to the extent of their capacities, after they had gained civilization, to invent the **deme** or township and the city ward; and thus inaugurate the second great plan of government, which remains among civilized nations to the present hour. In ancient society this territorial plan was unknown. When it came in it fixed the boundary line between ancient and modern society, as the distinction will be recognized in these pages.

It may be further observed that the domestic institutions of the barbarous, and even of the savage ancestors of mankind, are still exemplified in portions of the human family with such completeness that, with the exception of the strictly primitive period, the several stages of this progress are tolerably well preserved. They are seen in the organization of society upon the basis of sex, then upon the basis of kin, and finally upon the basis of territory; through the successive forms of marriage and of the family, with the systems of consanguinity thereby created; through house life and architecture; and through progress in usages with respect to the ownership and inheritance of property.

The theory of human degradation to explain the existence of savages and of barbarians is no longer tenable. It came in as a corollary from the Mosaic **cosmogony**, and was acquiesced in from a supposed necessity which no longer exists. As a theory, it is not only incapable of explaining the existence of savages, but it is without support in the facts of human existence.

The remote ancestors of the Aryan nations presumptively passed through an experience similar to that of existing barbarous and savage tribes. Though the experience of these nations embodies all the information necessary to illustrate the periods of civilization, both ancient and modern, together with a part of that in the Later period of barbarism, their anterior experience must be deduced, in the main, from the traceable connection between the elements of their existing institutions and inventions, and similar elements still preserved in those of savage and barbarous tribes.

It may be remarked finally that the experience of mankind has run in nearly uniform channels; that human necessities in similar conditions have been substantially the same; and that the operations of the mental principle have been uniform in virtue of the specific identity of the brain of all the races of mankind. This, however, is but a part of the explanation of uniformity in results. The germs of the principal institutions and arts of life were developed while man was still a savage. To a very great extent the experience of the subsequent periods of barbarism and of civilization have been expended in the further development of these original conceptions. Wherever a connection can be traced on different continents between a present institution and a common germ, the derivation of the people themselves from a common original stock is implied.

The discussion of these several classes of facts will be facilitated by the establishment of a certain number of Ethnical Periods; each representing a distinct condition of society, and distinguishable by a mode of life peculiar to itself. The terms *"Age of Stone,"* "of *Bronze,"* and "of *Iron,"* introduced by Danish archæologists, have been extremely useful for certain purposes, and will remain so for the classification of objects of ancient art; but the progress of knowledge has rendered other and different subdivisions necessary. Stone implements were not entirely laid aside with the introduction of tools of iron, nor of those of bronze. The invention of the process of smelting iron ore created an ethnical epoch, yet we could scarcely date another from the production of bronze. Moreover, since the period of stone implements overlaps those of bronze and of iron, and since that of bronze also overlaps that of iron, they are not capable of a circumscription that would leave each independent and distinct.

It is probable that the successive arts of subsistence which arose at long intervals will ultimately, from the great influence they must have exercised upon the condition of mankind, afford the most satisfactory bases for these divisions. But investigation has not been carried far enough in this directly to yield the necessary information. With our present knowledge the main result can be attained by selecting such other inventions or discoveries as will afford sufficient tests of progress to characterize the commencement of successive ethnical periods. Even though accepted as provisional, these periods will be found convenient and useful. Each of those about to be proposed will be found to cover a distinct culture, and to represent a particular mode of life.

The period of savagery, of the early part of which very little is known, may be divided, provisionally, into three subperiods. These may be named respectively the *Older*, the *Middle*, and the *Later* period of savagery; and the condition of society in each, respectively, may be distinguished as the *Lower*, the *Middle*, and the *Upper Status* of savagery.

In like manner, the period of barbarism divides naturally into three sub-periods, which will be called, respectively, the *Older*, the *Middle*, and the *Later* period of barbarism; and the condition of society in each, respectively, will be distinguished as the *Lower*, the *Middle*, and the *Upper Status* of barbarism.

It is difficult, if not impossible, to find such tests of progress to mark the commencement of these several periods as will be found absolute in their application, and without exceptions upon all the continents. Neither is it necessary, for the purpose in hand, that exceptions should not exist. It will be sufficient if the principal tribes of mankind can be classified, according to the degree of their relative progress, into conditions which can be recognized as distinct.

I. *Lower Status of Savagery*.

This period commenced with the infancy of the human race, and may be said to have ended with the acquisition of a fish subsistence and of a knowledge of the use of fire. Mankind were then living in their original restricted habitat, and subsisting upon fruits and nuts. The commencement of articulate speech belongs to this period. No exemplification of tribes of mankind in this condition remained to the historical period.

II. *Middle Status of Savagery*.

It commenced with the acquisition of a fish subsistence and a knowledge of the use of fire, and ended with the invention of the bow and arrow. Mankind, while in this condition, spread from their original habitat over the greater portion of the earth's surface. Among tribes still existing it will leave in the Middle Status of savagery, for example, the Australians and the greater part of the Polynesians when discovered. It will be sufficient to give one or more exemplifications of each status.

III. *Upper Status of Savagery*.

It commenced with the invention of the bow and arrow, and ended with the invention of the art of pottery. It leaves in the Upper Status of Savagery the Athapascan tribes of the Hudson's Bay Territory, the tribes of the valley of the Columbia, and certain coast tribes of North and South America; but with relation to the time of their discovery. This closes the period of Savagery.

IV. *Lower Status of Barbarism*.

The invention or practice of the art of pottery, all things considered, is probably the most effective and conclusive test that can be selected to fix a boundary line, necessarily arbitrary, between savagery and barbarism. The distinctness of the two conditions has long been recognized, but no criterion of progress out of the former into the latter has hitherto been brought forward. All such tribes, then, as never attained to the art of pottery will be classed as savages, and those possessing this art but who never attained a phonetic alphabet and the use of writing will be classed as barbarians.

The first sub-period of barbarism commenced with the manufacture of pottery, whether by original invention or adoption. In finding its termination, and the commencement of the Middle Status, a difficulty is encountered in the unequal endowments of the two hemispheres, which began to be influential upon human affairs after the period of savagery had passed. It may be met, however, by the adoption of equivalents. In the Eastern hemisphere, the domestication of animals, and the Western, the cultivation of maize and plants by irrigation, together with the use of adobe-brick and stone in house building have been selected as sufficient evidence of progress to work a transition out of the Lower and into the Middle Status of barbarism. It leaves, for example, in the Lower Status, the Indian tribes of the United States east of the Missouri River, and such tribes of Europe and Asia as practiced the art of pottery, but were without domestic animals.

V. *The Middle Status of Barbarism.*

It commenced with the domestication of animals in the Eastern hemisphere, and in the Western with cultivation by irrigation and with the use of adobe-brick and stone in architecture, as shown. Its termination may be fixed with the invention of the process of smelting iron ore. This places in the Middle Status, for example, the Village Indians of New Mexico, Mexico, Central America and Peru, and such tribes in the Eastern hemisphere as possessed domestic animals, but were without a knowledge of iron. The ancient Britons, although familiar with the use of iron, fairly belong in this connection. The vicinity of more advanced continental tribes had advanced the arts of life among them far beyond the state of development of their domestic institutions.

VI. *Upper Status of Barbarism.*

It commenced with the manufacture of iron, and ended with the invention of a phonetic alphabet, and the use of writing in literary composition. Here civilization begins. This leaves in the Upper Status, for example, the Grecian tribes of the Homeric age, the Italian tribes shortly before the founding of Rome, and the Germanic tribes of the time of Cæsar.

VII. *Status of Civilization.*

It commenced, as stated, with the use of a phonetic alphabet and the production of literary records, and divides into *Ancient* and *Modern*. As an equivalent, hieroglyphical writing upon stone may be admitted.

RECAPITULATION

Periods.	Conditions.
I. Older Period of Savagery,	I. Lower Status of Savagery,
II. Middle Period of Savagery,	II. Middle Status of Savagery,
III. Later Period of Savagery,	III. Upper Status of Savagery,
IV. Older Period of Barbarism,	IV. Lower Status of Barbarism,
V. Middle Period of Barbarism,	V. Middle Status of Barbarism,
VI. Later Period of Barbarism,	VI. Upper Status of Barbarism,

VII. Status of Civilization.

I. Lower Status of Savagery,	From the Infancy of the Human Race to the commencement of the next Period.
II. Middle Status of Savagery,	From the acquisition of a fish subsistence and a knowledge of the use of fire, to etc.
III. Upper Status of Savagery,	From the Invention of the Bow and Arrow, to etc.
IV Lower Status of Barbarism,	From the Invention of the Art of Pottery, to etc.
V. Middle Status of Barbarism,	From the Domestication of animals on the Eastern hemisphere, and in the Western from the cultivation of maize and plants by Irrigation, with the use of adobe-brick and stone, to etc.
VI. Upper Status of Barbarism	From the Invention of the process of Smelting Iron Ore, with the use of iron tools, to etc.
VII. Status of Civilization	From the Invention of a Phonetic Alphabet, with the use of writing, to the present time.

Each of these periods has a distinct culture and exhibits a mode of life more or less special and peculiar to itself. This specialization of ethnical periods renders it possible to treat a particular society according to its condition of relative advancement, and to make it a subject of independent study and discussion. It does not affect the main result that different tribes and nations on the same continent, and even of the same linguistic family, are in different conditions at the same time, since for our purpose the *condition* of each is the material fact, the *time* being immaterial.

Since the use of pottery is less significant than that of domestic animals, of iron, or of a phonetic alphabet, employed to mark the commencement of subsequent ethnical periods, the reasons for its adoption should be stated. The manufacture of pottery presupposes village life, and considerable progress in the simple arts.[1] Flint and stone implements are older than pottery, remains of the former having been found in ancient repositories in numerous instances unaccompanied by the latter. A succession of inventions of greater need and adapted to a lower condition must have occurred before the want of pottery would be felt. The commencement of village life, with some degree of control over subsistence, wooden vessels and utensils, finger weaving with filaments of bark, basket making, and the bow and arrow make their appearance before the art of pottery. The Village Indians who were in the Middle Status of barbarism, such as the Zuñians the Aztecs and the **Cholulans**, manufactured pottery in large quantities and in many forms of considerable excellence; the partially Village Indians of the United States, who were in the Lower Status of barbarism, such as the Iroquois, the Choctas, and the Cherokees, made it in smaller quantities and in a limited number of forms; but the Non-horticultural Indians, who were in the Status of savagery, such as the Athapascans, the tribes of California and of the valley of the Columbia, were ignorant of its use.[2] In **Lubbock**'s *Pre-Historic Times*, in **Tylor**'s *Early History of Mankind*, and in **Peschel**'s *Races of Man*, the particulars respecting this art, and the extent of its distribution, have been collected with remarkable breadth of research. It was unknown in Polynesia (with the exception of the Islands of the Tongans and Fijians), in Australia, in California, and in the Hudson's Bay Territory. Mr. Tylor remarks that "the art of weaving was unknown in most of the Islands away from Asia," and that "in most of the South Sea Islands there was no knowledge of pottery."[3] The Rev. Lorimer Fison, an English missionary residing in Australia, informed the author in answer to inquiries, that "the Australians had no woven fabrics, no pottery, and were ignorant of the bow and arrow." This last fact was also true in general of the Polynesians. The introduction of the ceramic art produced a new epoch in human progress in the direction of an improved living and increased domestic conveniences. While flint and stone implements—which came in earlier and required long periods of time to develop all their uses—gave the canoe, wooden vessels and utensils, and ultimately timber and plank in house architecture,[4] pottery gave a durable vessel for boiling food, which before that had been rudely accomplished in baskets coated with clay, and in ground cavities lined with skin, the boiling being effected with heated stones.[5]

Whether the pottery of the aborigines was hardened by fire or cured by the simple process of drying, has been made a question. Prof E.T. Cox, of Indianapolis, has shown by comparing the analyses of ancient pottery and hydraulic cements, "that so far as chemical constituents are concerned it (the pottery) agrees very well with the composition of hydraulic stones." He remarks further, that "all the pottery belonging to the **mound-builders**' age, which I have seen, is composed of alluvial clay and sand, or a mixture of the former with pulverized fresh-water shells. A paste made of such a mixture possesses in a high degree the properties of hydraulic Puzzuolani and Portland cement, so that vessels formed of it hardened without being burned, as is customary with modern pottery. The fragments of shells served the purpose of gravel or fragments of stone as at present used in connection with hydraulic lime for the manufacture of artificial stone."[6] The composition of Indian pottery in analogy with that of hydraulic cement suggests the difficulties in the way of inventing the art, and tends also to explain the lateness of its introduction in the course of human experience. Notwithstanding the ingenious suggestion of Prof. Cox, it is probable that pottery was hardened by artificial heat. In some cases the fact is directly attested. Thus **Adair**, speaking of the Gulf Tribes, remarks that "they make earthen pots of very different sizes, so as to contain from two to ten gallons, large pitchers to carry water, bowls, dishes, platters, basins, and a prodigious number of other vessels of such antiquated forms as would be tedious to describe, and impossible to name. Their method of glazing them is, they place them over a large fire of smoky pitch-pine, which makes them smooth, black and firm."[7]

Another advantage of fixing definite ethnical periods is the direction of special investigation to those tribes and nations which afford the best exemplification of each status, with the view of making each both standard and illustrative. Some tribes and families have been left in geographical isolation to work out the problems of progress by original mental effort; and have, consequently, retained their arts and institutions pure and homogeneous; while those of other tribes and nations have been adulterated through external influence. Thus, while Africa was and is an ethnical chaos of savagery and barbarism, Australia and Polynesia were in savagery, pure and simple, with the arts and institutions belonging to that condition. In like manner, the Indian family of America, unlike any other existing family, exemplified the condition of mankind in three successive ethnical periods. In the undisturbed possession of a great continent, of common descent, and with homogeneous institutions, they illustrated, when discovered, each of these conditions, and especially those of the Lower and of the Middle Status of barbarism, more elaborately and completely than any other portion of mankind. The far northern Indians and some of the coast tribes of North and South America were in the Upper Status of savagery; the partially Village Indians east of the Mississippi were in the Lower Status of barbarism, and the Village Indians of North and South America were in the Middle Status. Such an opportunity to recover full and minute information of the course of human experience and progress in developing their arts and institutions through these successive conditions has not been offered within the historical period. It must be added that it has been indifferently improved. Our greatest deficiencies relate to the last period named.

Differences in the culture of the same period in the Eastern and Western hemispheres undoubtedly existed in consequence of the unequal endowments of the continents; but the condition of society in the corresponding status must have been, in the main, substantially similar.

The ancestors of the Grecian, Roman, and German tribes passed through the stages we have indicated, in the midst of the last of which the light of history fell upon them. Their differentiation from the undistinguishable mass of barbarians did not occur, probably, earlier than the commencement of the Middle Period of barbarism. The experience of these tribes has been lost, with the exception of so much as is represented by the institutions, inventions and discoveries which they had brought with them, and possessed when they first came under historical observation. The Grecian and Latin tribes of the Homeric and **Romulian** periods afford the highest exemplification of the Upper Status of barbarism. Their institutions were likewise pure and homogeneous, and their experience stands directly connected with the final achievement of civilization.

Commencing, then, with the Australians and Polynesians, following with the American Indian tribes, and concluding with the Roman and Grecian, who afford the highest exemplifications respectively of the six great stages of human progress, the sum of their united experiences may be supposed fairly to represent that of the human family from the Middle Status of savagery to the end of ancient civilization. Consequently, the Aryan nations will find the type of the condition of their remote ancestors, when in savagery, in that of the Australians and Polynesians; when in the Lower Status of barbarism in that of the partially Village Indians of America; and when in the Middle Status in that of the Village Indians, with which their own experience in the Upper Status directly connects. So essentially identical are the arts, institutions and mode of life in the same status upon all the continents, that the archaic form of the principal domestic institutions of the Greeks and Romans must even now be sought in the corresponding institutions of the American aborigines, as will be shown in the course of this volume. This fact forms a part of the accumulating evidence tending to show that the principal institutions of mankind have been developed from a few primary germs of thought; and that the course and manner of their development was predetermined, as well as restricted within narrow limits of divergence, by the natural logic of the human mind and the necessary limitations of its powers. Progress has been found to be substantially the same in kind in tribes and nations inhabiting different and even disconnected continents, while in the same status, with deviations from uniformity in particular instances produced by special causes. The argument when extended tends to establish the unity of origin of mankind.

In studying the condition of tribes and nations in these several ethnical periods we are dealing, substantially, with the ancient history and condition of our own remote ancestors.

Notes

1 Mr. Edwin [sic] B. Tylor observes that Goquet "first propounded, in the last century, the notion that the way in which pottery came to be made, was that people

daubed such combustible vessels as these with clay to protect them from fire, till they found that clay alone would answer the purpose, and thus the art of pottery came into the world."—"Early History of Minkind [sic]," p. 273. Goquet relates of Capt. Gonneville who visited the southeast coast of South America in 1503, that he found "their household utensils of wood, even their boiling pots, but plastered with a kind of clay, a good finger thick, which prevented the fire from burning them."—Ib. 273.

2   Pottery has been found in aboriginal mounds in Oregon within a few years past.—Foster's "Pre-Historic Races of the United States," I, 152. The first vessels of pottery among the Aborigines of the United States seem to have been made in baskets of rushes or willows used as moulds which were burned off after the vessel hardened.—Jones's "Antiquities of the Southern Indians," p. 461. Prof. Rau's article on "Pottery," "Smithsonian Report," 1866, p. 352.

3   "Early History of Mankind," p. 181; "Pre-Historic Times," pp. 437, 441, 462, 477, 533, 542.

4   Lewis and Clarke (1805) found plank in use in houses among the tribes of the Columbia River.—"Travels," Longman's Ed., 1814, p. 503. Mr. John Keast Lord found "cedar plank chipped from the solid tree with chisels and hatchets made of stone," in Indian houses on Vancouver's Island.—"Naturalist in British Columbia," I, 169.

5   Tylor's "Early History of Mankind," p. 265, "et. seq."

6   "Geological Survey of Indians," 1873, p. 119. He gives the following analysis: Ancient Pottery, "Bone Bank," Posey Co., Indiana.

Moisture at 212° F.,	1.00
Silica,	36.00
Carbonate of Lime,	25.50
Carbonate of Magnesia,	3.02
Alumina,	5.00
Peroxide of Iron,	5.50
Sulfuric Acid,	.20
Organic Matter (alkalies and loss),	23.60
	100.00

7   "History of the American Indians," Lond. Ed., 1775, p. 424. The Iroquois affirm that in ancient times their forefathers cured their pottery before a fire.

Study Questions

1. According to Morgan, what causes culture to evolve?

2. How consistent are Morgan's criteria for distinguishing among ethnical periods and subperiods?

3. In Morgan's evolutionary schema, what is the relationship between past and present cultures?

———————

Further Readings

Fortes, Meyer. 1970. *Kinship and Social Order: The Legacy of Lewis Henry Morgan.* Chicago: Aldine.

Morgan, Lewis Henry. 1871. Systems of Consanguinity and Affinity of the Human Family. *Smithsonian Contributions to Knowledge* 218,17. Washington, DC: Smithsonian Institution.

——. 1985 [1877]. *Ancient Society.* Tucson: University of Arizona Press.

Resek, Carl. 1960. *Lewis Henry Morgan: American Scholar.* Chicago: University of Chicago Press.

Trautman, Robert R. 1987. *Lewis Henry Morgan and the Invention of Kinship.* Berkeley: University of California Press.

4

The Organic Analogy Reconsidered

HERBERT SPENCER

What is a Society?

This question has to be asked and answered at the outset. Until we have decided whether or not to regard a society as an entity; and until we have decided whether, if regarded as an entity, a society is to be classed as absolutely unlike all other entities or as like some others; our conception of the subject-matter before us remains vague.

It may be said that a society is but a collective name for a number of individuals. Carrying the controversy between **nominalism** and **realism** into another sphere, a nominalist might affirm that just as there exist only the members of a species, while the species considered apart from them has no existence; so the units of a society alone exist, while the existence of the society is but verbal. Instancing a lecturer's audience as an aggregate which by disappearing at the close of the lecture, proves itself to be not a thing but only a certain arrangement of persons, he might argue that the like holds of the citizens forming a nation.

But without disputing the other steps of his argument, the last step may be denied. The arrangement, temporary in the one case, is lasting in the other; and it is the permanence of the relations among component parts which constitutes the individuality of a whole as distinguished from the individualities of its parts. A coherent mass broken into fragments ceases to be a thing; while, conversely, the stones, bricks, and wood, previously separate, become the thing called a house if connected in fixed ways.

Thus we consistently regard a society as an entity, because, though formed of discrete units, a certain concreteness in the aggregate of them is implied by the maintenance, for generations and centuries, of a general likeness of arrangement throughout the area occupied. And it is this trait which yields our idea of a society. For, withholding the name from an ever-changing cluster such as primitive men form, we apply it only where some constancy in the distribution of parts has resulted from settled life.

But now, regarding a society as a thing, what kind of thing must we call it? It seems totally unlike every object with which our senses acquaint us. Any likeness it may possibly have to other objects, cannot be manifest to perception, but can be discerned only by reason. If the constant relations among its parts make it an entity; the question arises whether these constant relations among its parts are akin to the constant relations among the parts of other entities. Between a society and anything else, the only conceivable resemblance must be one due *to parallelism of principle in the arrangement of components.*

There are two great classes of aggregates with which the social aggregate may be compared—the inorganic and the organic. Are the attributes of society, considered apart from its living units, in any way like those of a not-living body? or are they in any way like those of a living body? or are they entirely unlike those of both?

The first of these questions needs only to be asked to be answered in the negative. A whole of which the parts are alive, cannot, in its general characters, be like lifeless wholes. The second question, not to be thus promptly answered, is to be answered in the affirmative. The reasons for asserting that the permanent relations among the parts of a society, are analogous to the permanent relations among the parts of a living body, we have now to consider.

A Society Is an Organism

When we say that growth is common to social aggregates and organic aggregates, we do not thus entirely exclude community with inorganic aggregates: some of these, as crystals, grow in a visible manner; and all of them, on the hypothesis of evolution, are concluded to have arisen by integration at some time or other. Nevertheless, compared with things we call inanimate, living bodies and societies so conspicuously exhibit augmentation of mass, that we may fairly regard this as characteristic of them both. Many organisms grow throughout their lives; and the rest grow throughout considerable parts of their lives. Social growth usually continues either up to times when the societies divide, or up to times when they are overwhelmed.

Here, then, is the first trait by which societies ally themselves with the organic world and substantially distinguish themselves from the inorganic world.

It is also a character of social bodies, as of living bodies, that while they increase in size they increase in structure. A low animal, or the embryo of a high one, has few distinguishable parts; but along with its acquirement of greater mass, its parts multiply and simultaneously differentiate. It is thus with a society. At first the unlikenesses among its groups of units are inconspicuous in number and degree; but as it becomes more populous, divisions and sub-divisions become more numerous and more decided. Further, in the social organism as in the individual organism, differentiations cease only with that completion of the type which marks maturity and precedes decay.

Though in inorganic aggregates also, as in the entire solar system and in each of its members, structural differentiations accompany the integrations; yet these are so relatively slow, and so relatively simple, that they may be disregarded. The multiplication of contrasted parts in bodies politic and in living bodies, is so great that it substantially constitutes another common character which marks them off from inorganic bodies.

This community will be more fully appreciated on observing that progressive differentiation of structures is accompanied by progressive differentiation of functions.

The multiplying divisions, primary, secondary, and tertiary, which arise in a developing animal, do not assume their major and minor unlikenesses to no purpose. Along with diversities in their shapes and compositions there go diversities in the actions they perform: they grow into unlike organs having unlike duties. Assuming the entire function of absorbing nutriment at the same time that it takes on its structural characters, the alimentary system becomes gradually marked off into contrasted portions; each of which has a special function forming part of the general function. A limb, instrumental to locomotion or prehension, acquires divisions and sub-divisions which perform their leading and their subsidiary shares in this office. So is it with the parts into which a society divides. A dominant class arising does not simply become unlike the rest, but assumes control over the rest; and when this class separates into the more and the less dominant, these, again, begin to discharge distinct parts of the entire control. With the classes whose actions are controlled it is the same. The various groups into which they fall have various occupations: each of such groups also, within itself, acquiring minor contrasts of parts along with minor contrasts of duties.

And here we see more clearly how the two classes of things we are comparing distinguish themselves from things of other classes; for such differences of structure as slowly arise in inorganic aggregates, are not accompanied by what we can fairly call differences of function.

Why in a body politic and in a living body, these unlike actions of unlike parts are properly regarded by us as functions, while we cannot so regard the unlike actions of unlike parts in an inorganic body, we shall perceive on turning to the next and the most distinctive common trait.

Evolution establishes in them both, not differences simply, but definitely-connected differences—differences such that each makes the others possible. The parts of an inorganic aggregate are so related that one may change greatly without appreciably affecting the rest. It is otherwise with the parts of an organic aggregate or of a social aggregate. In either of these the changes in the parts are mutually determined, and the changed actions of the parts are mutually dependent. In both, too, this mutuality increases as the evolution advances. The lowest type of animal is all stomach, all respiratory surface, all limb. Development of a type having appendages by which to move about or lay hold of food, can take place only if these appendages, losing power to absorb nutriment directly from surrounding bodies, are supplied with nutriment by parts which retain the power of absorption. A respiratory surface to which the circulating fluids are brought to be aerated, can be formed only on condition that the concomitant loss of ability to supply itself with materials for repair and growth, is made good by the development of a structure bringing these materials. So is it in a society. What we call with perfect propriety its organization, has a necessary implication of the same kind....

Here let it once more be pointed out that there exist no analogies between the body politic and a living body, save those necessitated by that mutual dependence of parts which they display in common. Though, in foregoing chapters, comparisons of social structures and functions to structures and functions in the human body, have in many cases been made, they have been made only because structures and functions in the human body furnish the most familiar illustrations of structures and functions in general. The social organism, discrete instead of concrete, asymmetrical instead of symmetrical, sensitive in all its units instead of having a single sensitive centre, is not comparable to any particular type of individual organism, animal or vegetal. All kinds of creatures are alike in so far as each shows us co-operation among its components for the benefit of the whole; and this trait, common to them, is a trait common also to communities. Further, among the many types of individual organisms, the degree of this co-operation measures the degree of evolution; and this general truth, too, is exhibited among social organisms. Once more, to effect increasing co-operation, creatures of every order show us increasingly-complex appliances for transfer and mutual influence; and to this general characteristic, societies of every order furnish a corresponding characteristic. Community in the fundamental principles of organization is thus the only community asserted.

But now let us drop this alleged parallelism between individual organizations and social organizations. I have used the analogies elaborated, but as a scaffolding to help in building up a coherent body of sociological inductions. Let us take away the scaffolding: the inductions will stand by themselves.

We saw that societies are aggregates which grow; that in various types of them there are great varieties in the degrees of growth reached; that types of successively larger sizes result from the aggregation and re-aggregation of those of smaller sizes; and that this increase by coalescence, joined with **inter-**

stitial increase, is the process through which have been formed the vast civilized nations.

Along with increase of size in societies goes increase of structure. Primitive wandering hordes are without established unlikenesses of parts. With growth of them into tribes habitually come some differences; both in the powers and occupations of their members. Unions of tribes are followed by more differences, governmental and industrial—social grades running through the whole mass, and contrasts between the differently-occupied parts in different localities. Such differentiations multiply as the compounding progresses. They proceed from the general to the special: first the broad division between ruling and ruled; then within the ruling part divisions into political, religious, military, and within the ruled part divisions into food-processing classes and handicraftsmen; then within each of these divisions minor ones, and so on.

Passing from the structural aspect to the functional aspect, we note that while all parts of a society have like natures and activities there is hardly any mutual dependence, and the aggregate scarcely forms a vital whole. As its parts assume different functions they become dependent on one another, so that injury to one hurts others; until in highly-evolved societies, general perturbation is caused by derangement of any portion. This contrast between undeveloped and developed societies, is due to the fact that, with increasing specialization of functions comes increasing inability in each part to perform the functions of other parts.

The organization of every society begins with a contrast between the division which carries on relations, habitually hostile, with environing societies, and the division which is devoted to procuring necessaries of life; and during the earlier stages of development these two divisions constitute the whole. Eventually there arises an intermediate division serving to transfer products and influences from part to part. And in all subsequent stages, evolution to the two earlier systems of structures depends on evolution of this additional system.

While the society as a whole has the character of its sustaining system determined by the general character of its environment, inorganic and organic, the respective parts of this system differentiate in adaptation to the circumstances of the localities; and, after primary industries have been thus localized and specialized, secondary industries dependent upon them arise in conformity with the same principle. Further, as fast as societies become compounded and recompounded and the distributing system develops, the parts devoted to each kind of industry, originally scattered, aggregate in the most favourable localities; and the localized industrial structures, unlike the governmental structures, grow regardless of the original lines of division.

Increase of size, resulting from the massing of groups, necessitates means of communication; both for achieving combined offensive and defensive actions, and for exchange of products. Scarcely traceable tracks, paths, rude roads, finished roads, successively arise; and as fast as intercourse is thus facilitated, there is a transition from direct barter to trading carried on by a separate class; out of which evolves, in course of time, a complex mercantile agency of wholesale and retail distributors. The movement of commodities effected by this agency, beginning as a slow flux to and reflux from certain places at long intervals, passes into rhythmical, regular, rapid currents; and materials for sustentation distributed hither and thither, from being few and crude become numerous and elaborated. Growing efficiency of transfer with greater variety of transferred products, increases the mutual dependence of parts at the same time that it enables each part to fulfill its function better.

Unlike the sustaining system, evolved by converse with the organic and inorganic environments, the regulating system is evolved by converse, offensive and defensive, with environing societies. In primitive headless groups temporary chieftainship results from temporary war; chronic hostilities generate permanent chieftainship; and gradually from the military control results the civil control. Habitual war, requiring prompt combination in the action of parts, necessitates subordination. Societies in which there is little subordination disappear, and leave outstanding those in which subordination is great; and so there are established societies in which the habit fostered by war and surviving in peace, brings about permanent submission to a government. The centralized regulating system thus evolved is in early stages the sole regulating system. But in large societies that become predominantly industrial, there is added a decentralized regulating system for the industrial structures; and this, at first subject in every way to the original system, acquires at length substantial independence. Finally there arises for the distributing structures also, an independent controlling agency.

Study Questions
1. According to Spencer, why is society an entity onto itself rather than a mere collection of individuals?
2. According to Spencer, in what ways is society like an organism?
3. According to Spencer, what are the major trends in social evolution?

Further Readings
Burrow, J.W. 1966. *Evolution and Society: A Study in Victorian Social Theory.* London: Cambridge University Press.

Maasen, Sabine. 1995. *Biology as Society, Society as Biology: Metaphors.* Ed. Everett Mendelsohn, et al. Norwell, MA: Kluwer Academic Publishers.

Rumney, Jay. 1966. *Herbert Spencer's Sociology: A Study in the History of Social Theory.* New York: Atherton Press.

Spencer, Herbert. 1967. *The Evolution of Society: Selections from Herbert Spencer's Principles of Sociology.* Ed. Robert L. Carneiro. Ann Arbor, MI: Books on Demand.

—. 1885. *The Principles of Sociology.* (2 vols.). New York: Appleton-Century-Crofts.

5

General Summary and Conclusion
[*The Descent of Man*]

CHARLES DARWIN

Main conclusion that man is descended from some lower form—Manner of development—Genealogy of man—Intellectual and moral faculties—Sexual Selection—Concluding remarks.

A brief summary will be sufficient to recall to the reader's mind the more salient points in this work. Many of the views which have been advanced are highly speculative, and some no doubt will prove erroneous; but I have in every case given the reasons which have led me to one view rather than to another. It seemed worth while to try how far the principle of evolution would throw light on some of the more complex problems in the natural history of man. False facts are highly injurious to the progress of science, for they often endure long; but false views, if supported by some evidence, do little harm, for every one takes a salutary pleasure in proving their falseness: and when this is done, one path towards error is closed and the road to truth is often at the same time opened.

The main conclusion here arrived at, and now held by many naturalists who are well competent to form a sound judgment is that man is descended from some less highly organised form. The grounds upon which this conclusion rests will never be shaken, for the close similarity between man and the lower animals in embryonic development, as well as innumerable points of structure and constitution, both of high and of the most trifling importance,—the rudiments which he retains, and the abnormal reversions to which he is occasionally liable,—are facts which cannot be disputed. They have long been known, but until recently they told us nothing with respect to the origin of man. Now when viewed by the light of our knowledge of the whole organic world, their meaning is unmistakable. The great principle of evolution stands up clear and firm, when these groups or facts are considered in connection with others, such as the mutual affinities of the members of the same group, their geographical distribution in past and present times, and their geological succession. It is incredible that all these facts should speak falsely. He who is not content to look, like a savage, at the phenomena of nature as disconnected, cannot any longer believe that man is the work of a separate act of creation. He will be forced to admit that the close resemblance of the embryo of man to that, for instance, of a dog—the construction of his skull, limbs and whole frame on the same plan with that of other mammals, independently of the uses to which the parts may be put—the occasional re-appearance of various structures, for instance of several muscles, which man does not normally possess, but which are common to the **Quadrumana**—and a crowd of analogous facts—all point in the plainest manner to the conclusion that man is the co-descendant with other mammals of a common progenitor.

We have seen that man incessantly presents individual differences in all parts of his body and in his mental faculties. These differences or variations seem to be induced by the same general causes, and to obey the same laws as with the lower animals. In both cases similar laws of inheritance prevail. Man tends to increase at a greater rate than his means of subsistence; consequently he is occasionally subjected to a severe **struggle for existence**, and **natural selection** will have effected whatever lies within its scope. A succession of strongly-marked variations of a similar nature is by no means requisite; slight fluctuating differences in the individual suffice for the work of natural selection; not that we have any reason to suppose that in the same species, all parts of the organisation tend to vary to the same degree. We may feel assured that the inherited effects of the long-continued use or disuse of parts will have done much in the same direction with natural selection. Modifications formerly of importance, though no longer of any special use, are long-inherited. When one part is modified, other parts change through the principle of correlation, of which we have instances in many curious cases of correlated monstrosities. Something may be attributed to the direct and definite action of the surrounding conditions of life, such as abundant food, heat or moisture; and lastly, many characters of slight physiological importance, some indeed of considerable importance, have been gained through **sexual selection**.

No doubt man, as well as every other animal, presents structures, which seem to our limited knowledge, not to be now of any service to him, nor to have been so formerly, either for the general conditions of life, or in the relations of one sex to the other. Such structures cannot be accounted for by any form of selection, or by the inherited effects of the use and disuse of parts. We know, however, that many strange and strongly-marked peculiarities of structure occasionally appear in our domesticated productions, and if their unknown causes were to act more uniformly, they would probably become common to all the individuals of the species. We may hope hereafter to understand something about the causes of such occasional modifications, especially through the study of monstrosities: hence the labours of experimentalists such as those of M. Camille Dareste, are full of promise for the future. In general we can only say that the cause of each slight variation and of each monstrosity lies much more in the constitution of the organism, than in the nature of the surrounding conditions; though new and changed conditions certainly play an important part in exciting organic changes of many kinds.

Through the means just specified, aided perhaps by others as yet undiscovered, man has been raised to his present state. But since he attained to the rank of manhood, he has diverged into distinct races, or as they may be more fitly called, sub-species. Some of these, such as the Negro and European, are so distinct that, if specimens had been brought to a naturalist without any further information, they would undoubtedly have been considered by him as good and true species. Nevertheless all the races agree in so many unimportant details of structure and in so many mental peculiarities that these can be accounted for only by inheritance from a common progenitor; and a progenitor thus characterised would probably deserve to rank as man.

It must not be supposed that the divergence of each race from the other races, and of all from a common stock, can be traced back to any one pair of progenitors. On the contrary, at every stage in the process of modification, all the individuals which were in any way better fitted for their conditions of life, though in different degrees, would have survived in greater numbers than the less well-fitted. The process would have been like that followed by man, when he does not intentionally select particular individuals, but breeds from all the superior individuals, and neglects the inferior. He thus slowly but surely modifies his stock, and unconsciously forms a new strain. So with respect to modifications acquired independently of selection, and due to variations arising from the nature of the organism and the action of the surrounding conditions, or from changed habits of life, no single pair will have been modified much more than the other pairs inhabiting the same country, for all will have been continually blended through free intercrossing.

By considering the embryological structure of man,—the **homologies** which he presents with the lower animals,—the rudiments which he retains,— and the reversions to which he is liable, we can partly recall in imagination the former condition of our early progenitors; and can approximately place them in their proper place in the zoological series. We thus learn that man is descended from a hairy, tailed quadruped, probably arboreal in its habits, and an inhabitant of the Old World. This creature, if its whole structure had been examined by a naturalist, would have been classed amongst the Quadrumana, as surely as the still more ancient progenitor of the Old and New World monkeys. The Quadrumana and all the higher mammals are probably derived from an ancient marsupial animal, and this through a long series of diversified forms, from some amphibian-like creature, and this again from some fish-like animal. In the dim obscurity of the past we can see that the early progenitor of all the Vertebrata must have been an aquatic animal provided with **branchiæ**, with the two sexes united in the same individual, and with the most important organs of the body (such as the brain and heart) imperfectly or not at all developed. This animal seems to have been more like the larvae of the existing marine **Ascidians** than any other known form.

The high standard of our intellectual powers and moral disposition is the greatest difficulty which presents itself, after we have been driven to this conclusion on the origin of man. But every one who admits the principle of evolution, must see that the mental powers of the higher animals, which are the same in kind with those of man, though so different in degree, are capable of advancement. Thus the interval between the mental powers of one of the higher apes and of a fish, or between those of an ant and scale-insect, is immense; yet their development does not offer any special difficulty; for with our domesticated animals, the mental faculties are certainly variable, and the variations are inherited. No one doubts that they are of the utmost importance to animals in a state of nature. Therefore the conditions are favourable for their development through natural selection. The same conclusion may be extended to man: the intellect must have been all-important to him, even at a very remote period, as enabling him to invent and use language, to make weapons, tools, traps, &c., whereby with the aid of his social habits, he long ago became the most dominant of all living creatures.

A great stride in the development of the intellect will have followed, as soon as the half-art and half-instinct of language came into use; for the continued use of language will have reacted on the brain and produced an inherited effect; and this again will have reacted on the improvement of language. As Mr. **Chauncey Wright**[1] has well remarked, the largeness of the brain in man relatively to his body, compared with the lower animals, may be attributed in chief part to the early use of some simple form of language,—that wonderful engine which affixes signs to all sorts of objects and qualities, and excites trains of thought which would never arise from the mere impression of the senses, or if they did arise could not be followed out. The higher intellectual powers of man, such as those of **ratiocination**, abstraction, self-consciousness, &c., probably follow from the continued improvement and exercise of the other mental faculties.

The development of the moral qualities is a more interesting problem. The foundation lies in the social instincts, including under this term the family ties.

These instincts are highly complex, and in the case of the lower animals give special tendencies towards certain definite actions; but the more important elements are love, and the distinct emotion of sympathy. Animals endowed with the social instincts take pleasure in one another's company, warn one another of danger, defend and aid one another in many ways. These instincts do not extend to all the individuals of the species, but only to those of the same community. As they are highly beneficial to the species, they have in all probability been acquired through natural selection.

A moral being is one who is capable of reflecting on his past actions and their motives—of approving of some and disapproving of others; and the fact that man is the one being who certainly deserves this designation, is the greatest of all distinctions between him and the lower animals. But in the fourth chapter I have endeavoured to shew that the moral sense follows, firstly, from the enduring and ever-present nature of the social instincts; secondly, from man's appreciation of the approbation and disapprobation of his fellows; and thirdly, from the high activity of his mental faculties, with past impressions extremely vivid; and in these latter respects he differs from the lower animals. Owing to this condition of mind, man cannot avoid looking both backwards and forwards, and comparing past impressions. Hence after some temporary desire or passion has mastered his social instincts, he reflects and compares the now weakened impression of such past impulses with the ever-present social instincts; and he then feels that sense of dissatisfaction which all unsatisfied instincts leave behind them, he therefore resolves to act differently for the future,—and this is conscience. Any instinct, permanently stronger or more enduring than another, gives rise to a feeling which we express by saying that it ought to be obeyed. A pointer dog, if able to reflect on his past conduct, would say to himself, I ought (as indeed we say of him) to have pointed at that hare and not have yielded to the passing temptation of hunting it.

Social animals are impelled partly by a wish to aid the members of their community in a general manner, but more commonly to perform certain definite actions. Man is impelled by the same general wish to aid his fellows; but has few or no special instincts. He differs also from the lower animals in the power of expressing his desires by words, which thus become a guide to the aid required and bestowed. The motive to give aid is likewise much modified in man: it no longer consists solely of a blind instinctive impulse, but is much influenced by the praise or blame of his fellows. The appreciation and the bestowal of praise and blame both rest on sympathy; and this emotion, as we have seen, is one of the most important elements of the social instincts. Sympathy, though gained as an instinct, is also much strengthened by exercise or habit. As all men desire their own happiness, praise or blame is bestowed on actions and motives, according as they lead to this end; and as happiness is an essential part of the general good, the greatest-happiness principle indirectly serves as a nearly safe standard of right and wrong. As the reasoning powers advance and experience is gained, the remoter effects of certain lines of conduct on the character of the individual, and on the general good, are perceived; and then the self-regarding virtues come within the scope of public opinion, and receive praise, and their opposites blame. But with the less civilised nations reason often errs, and many bad customs and base superstitions come within the same scope, and are then esteemed as high virtues, and their breach as heavy crimes.

The moral faculties are generally and justly esteemed as of higher value than the intellectual powers. But we should bear in mind that the activity of the mind in vividly recalling past impressions is one of the fundamental though secondary bases of conscience. This affords the strongest argument for educating and stimulating in all possible ways the intellectual faculties of every human being. No doubt a man with a torpid mind, if his social affections and sympathies are well developed, will be led to good actions, and may have a fairly sensitive conscience. But whatever renders the imagination more vivid and strengthens the habit of recalling and comparing past impressions, will make the conscience more sensitive, and may even somewhat compensate for weak social affections and sympathies.

The moral nature of man has reached its present standard, partly through the advancement of his reasoning powers and consequently of a just public opinion, but especially from his sympathies having been rendered more tender and widely diffused through the effects of habit, example, instruction, and reflection. It is not improbable that after long practice virtuous tendencies may be inherited. With the more civilised races, the conviction of the existence of an all-seeing Deity has had a potent influence on the advance of morality. Ultimately man does not accept the praise or blame of his fellows as his sole guide, though few escape this influence, but his habitual convictions, controlled by reason, afford him the safest rule. His conscience then becomes the supreme judge and monitor. Nevertheless the first foundation or origin of the moral sense lies in the social instincts, including sympathy; and these instincts no doubt were primarily gained, as in the case of the lower animals, through natural selection.

The belief in God has often been advanced as not only the greatest, but the most complete of all the distinctions between man and the lower animals. It is however impossible, as we have seen, to maintain that this belief is innate or instinctive in man. On the other hand a belief in all-pervading spiritual agencies seems to be universal; and apparently follows from a considerable advance in man's reason, and from a still greater advance in his faculties of imagination, curiosity and wonder. I am aware that the assumed instinctive belief in God has been used by many persons as an argument for His existence. But this is a rash argument, as we should thus be compelled to believe in the existence of many cruel and malignant spirits, only a little more powerful than man: for the belief in them is far more general than in a beneficent Deity. The idea of a universal and beneficent Creator does not seem to arise in the mind of man, until he has been elevated by long-continued culture.

He who believes in the advancement of man from some low organised form, will naturally ask how does this bear on the belief in the immortality of the soul. The barbarous races of man, as Sir J. Lubbock has shewn, possess no clear belief of this kind; but arguments derived from the primeval beliefs of savages are, as we have just seen, of little or no avail. Few persons feel any anxiety from the impossibility of determining at what precise period in the development of the individual, from the first race of a minute germinal **vesicle**, man becomes an immortal being; and there is no greater cause for anxiety because the period cannot possibly be determined in the gradually ascending organic scale.[2]

I am aware that the conclusions arrived at in this work will be denounced by some as high irreligious; but he who denounces them is bound to shew why it is more irreligious to explain the origin of man as a distinct species by descent from some lower form, through the laws of variation and natural selection, than to explain the birth of the individual through the laws of ordinary reproduction. The birth both of the species and of the individual are equally parts of that grand sequence of events, which our minds refuse to accept as the result of blind chance. The understanding revolts at such a conclusion, whether or not we are able to believe that every slight variation of structure,—the union of each pair in marriage,—the dissemination of each seed,—and other such events, have all been ordained for some special purpose.

Sexual selection has been treated at great length in this work; for, as I have attempted to shew, it has played an important part in the history of the organic world. I am aware that much remains doubtful, but I have endeavoured to give a fair view of the whole case. In the lower divisions of the animal kingdom, sexual selection seems to have done nothing: such animals are often affixed for life to the same spot, or have the sexes combined in the same individual, or what is still more important, their perceptive and intellectual faculties are not sufficiently advanced to allow of the feelings of love and jealousy, or of the exertion of choice. When, however, we come to the Arthropoda and Vertebrata, even to the lowest classes in these two great Sub-Kingdoms, sexual selection has effected much.

In the several great classes of the animal kingdom,—in mammals, birds, reptiles, fishes, insects, and even crustaceans,—the differences between the sexes follow nearly the same rules. The males are almost always the wooers; and they alone are armed with special weapons for fighting with their rivals. They are generally stronger and larger than the females, and are endowed with the requisite qualities of courage and pugnacity. They are provided, either exclusively or in much higher degree than the females, with organs for vocal or instrumental music, and with odoriferous glands. They are ornamental with infinitely diversified appendages, and with the most brilliant or conspicuous colours, often arranged in elegant patterns, whilst the females are unadorned. When the sexes differ in more important structures, it is the male which is provided with special sense-organs for discovering the female, with locomotive organs for reaching her, and often with prehensile organs for holding her. These various structures for charming or securing the female are often developed in the male during only part of the year, namely the breeding-season. They have in many cases been more or less transferred to the females; and in the latter case they often appear in her as mere rudiments. They are lost or never gained by the males after emasculation. Generally they are not developed in the male during early youth, but appear a short time before the age for reproduction. Hence in most cases the young of both sexes resemble each other; and the female somewhat resembles her young offspring throughout life. In almost every great class a few anomalous cases occur, where there has been an almost complete transposition of the characters proper to the two sexes; the females assuming characters which properly belong to the males. This surprising uniformity in the laws regulating the differences between the sexes in so many and such widely separated classes, is intelligible if we admit the action of one common cause, namely sexual selection.

Sexual selection depends on the success of certain individuals over others of the same sex, in relation to the propagation of the species; whilst natural selection depends on the success of both sexes, at all ages, in relation to the general conditions of life. The sexual struggle is of two kinds; in the one it is between individuals of the same sex, generally the males, in order to drive away or kill their rivals, the females remaining passive; whilst in the other, the struggle is likewise between the individuals of the same sex, in order to excite or charm those of the opposite sex, generally the females, which no longer remain passive, but select the more agreeable partners. This latter kind of selection is closely analogous to that which man unintentionally, yet effectually, brings to bear on his domesticated productions, when he preserves during a long period the most pleasing or useful individuals, without any wish to modify the breed.

The laws of inheritance determine whether characters gained through sexual selection by either sex shall be transmitted to the same sex, or to both; as well as the age at which they shall be developed. It appears that variations arising late in life are commonly transmitted to one and the same sex. Variability is the necessary basis for the action of selection, and is wholly independent of it. It follows from this, that variations of the same general nature have often been taken advantage of and accumulated through sexual selection in relation to the propagation of the species, as well as through natural selection in relation to the general purposes of life. Hence secondary sexual characters, when equally transmitted to both sexes can be distinguished from ordinary specific characters only by the light of analogy. The modifications acquired through sexual selection are often so strongly pronounced that the two sexes have frequently been ranked as distinct species, or even as distinct genera. Such strongly-marked differences must be in some manner highly important; and we know that they have been acquired in some instances at the cost not only of inconvenience, but of exposure to actual danger.

The belief in the power of sexual selection rests chiefly on the following considerations. Certain characters are confined to one sex; and this alone renders it probable that in most cases they are connected with the act of reproduction. In innumerable instances these characters are fully developed only at maturity, and often during only a part of the year, which is always the breeding-season. The males (passing over a few exceptional cases) are the more active in courtship; they are the better armed, and are rendered the more attractive in various ways. It is to be especially observed that the males display their attractions with elaborate care in the presence of the females; and that they rarely or never display them excepting during the season of love. It is incredible that all this should be purposeless. Lastly we have distinct evidence with some quadrupeds and birds, that the individuals of one sex are capable of feeling a strong antipathy or preference for certain individuals of the other sex.

Bearing in mind these facts, and the marked results of man's unconscious selection, when applied to domesticated animals and cultivated plants, it seems to me almost certain that if the individuals of one sex were during a long series of generations to prefer pairing with certain individuals of the other sex, characterised in some peculiar manner, the offspring would slowly but surely become modified in this same manner. I have not attempted to conceal that, excepting when the males are more numerous than the females, or when **polygamy** prevails, it is doubtful how the more attractive males succeed in leaving a large number of offspring to inherit their superiority in ornaments or other charms than the less attractive males; but I have shewn that this would probably follow from the females,—especially the more vigorous ones, which would be the first to breed,—preferring not only the more attractive but at the same time the more vigorous and victorious males.

Although we have some positive evidence that birds appreciate bright and beautiful objects, as with the bower-birds of Australia, and although they certainly appreciate the power of song, yet I fully admit that it is astonishing that the females of many birds and some mammals should be endowed with sufficient taste to appreciate ornaments, which we have reason to attribute to sexual selection; and this is even more astonishing in the case of reptiles, fish, and insects. But we really know little about the minds of the lower animals. It cannot be supposed, for instance, that male birds of paradise or peacocks should take such pains in erecting, spreading, and vibrating their beautiful plumes before the females for no purpose. We should remember the fact given on excellent authority in a former chapter, that several peahens, when debarred from an admired male, remained widows during the whole season rather than pair with another bird.

Nevertheless I know of no fact in natural history more wonderful than that of the female Argus pheasant should appreciate the exquisite shading of the ball-and-socket ornaments and the elegant patterns on the wing-feathers of the male. He who thinks that the male was created as he now exists must admit that the great plumes, which prevent the wings from being used for flight, and which are displayed during courtship and at no other time in a manner quite peculiar to this one species, were given to him as an ornament. If so, he must likewise admit that the female was created and endowed with the capacity of appreciating such ornaments. I differ only in the conviction that the male Argus pheasant acquired his beauty gradually, through the preference of the females during many generations for the more highly ornamental males; the æsthetic capacity of the females having been advanced through exercise or habit, just as our own taste is gradually improved. In the male through the fortunate chance of a few feathers, being left unchanged, we can distinctly trace how simple spots with a little **fulvous** shading on one side may have been developed by small steps into the wonderful ball-and-socket ornaments; and it is probable that they were actually thus developed.

Everyone who admits the principle of evolution, and yet feels great difficulty in admitting that female mammals, birds, reptiles, and fish, could have acquired the high taste implied by the beauty of the males, and which generally coincides with our own standard, should reflect that the nerve-cells of the brain in the highest as well as in the lowest members of the Vertebrate series, are derived from those of the common progenitor of this great Kingdom. For we can thus see how it has come to pass that certain mental faculties, in various and widely distinct groups of animals, have been developed in nearly the same manner and to nearly the same degree.

The reader who has taken the trouble to go through the several chapters devoted to sexual selection, will be able to judge how far the conclusions at which I have arrived are supported by sufficient evidence. If he accepts these conclusions he may, I think, safely extend them to mankind; but it would be superfluous here to repeat what I have so lately said on the manner in which sexual selection apparently has acted on man, both on the male and female side, causing the two sexes to differ in body and mind, and the several races to differ from each other in various characters, as well as from their ancient and lowly-organised progenitors.

He who admits the principle of sexual selection will be led to the remarkable conclusion that the nervous system not only regulates most of the existing functions of the body, but has indirectly influenced the progressive development of various bodily structures and of certain mental qualities. Courage, pugnacity, perseverance, strength and size of body, weapons of all kinds, musical organs, both vocal and instrumental, bright colours and ornamental appendages, have all been indirectly gained by the one sex or the other, through the exertion of choice, the influence of love and jealousy, and the appreciation of the beautiful in sound, colour or form; and these powers of the mind manifestly depend on the development of the brain.

Man scans with scrupulous care the character and pedigree of his horses, cattle, and dogs before he matches them; but when he comes to his own marriage he rarely, or never, takes any such care. He is impelled by nearly the same motives as the lower animals, when they are left to their own free choice, though he is in so far superior to them that he highly values mental charms and virtues. On the other hand he is strongly attracted by mere wealth or rank. Yet he might by selection do something not only for the bodily constitution and frame of his offspring, but for their intellectual and moral qualities. Both sexes ought to refrain from marriage if they are in any marked degree inferior in body or mind; but such hopes are Utopian and will never be even partially realised until the laws of inheritance are thoroughly known. Everyone does good service, who aids toward this end. When the principles of breeding and inheritance are better understood, we shall not hear ignorant members of our legislature rejecting with scorn a plan for ascertaining whether or not consanguineous marriages are injurious to man.

The advancement of the welfare of mankind is a most intricate problem: all ought to refrain from marriage who cannot avoid abject poverty for their children; for poverty is not only a great evil, but tends to its own increase by leading to recklessness in marriage. On the other hand, as Mr. **Galton** has remarked, if the prudent avoid marriage, whilst the reckless marry, the inferior members tend to supplant the better members of society. Man, like every other animal, has no doubt advanced to his present high condition through a struggle for existence consequent on his rapid multiplication; and if he is to advance still higher, it is to be feared that he must remain subject to a severe struggle. Otherwise he would sink into indolence, and the more gifted men would not be more successful in the battle of life than the less gifted. Hence our natural rate of increase, though leading to many and obvious evils, must not be greatly diminished by any means. There should be open competition for all men; and the most able should not be prevented by laws or customs from succeeding best and rearing the largest number of offspring. Important as the struggle for existence has been and even still is, yet as far as the highest part of man's nature is concerned there are other agencies more important. For the moral qualities are advanced, either directly or indirectly, much more through the effects of habit, the reasoning powers, instruction, religion, &c., than through natural selection; though to this latter agency may be safely attributed the social instincts, which afforded the basis for the development of the moral sense.

The main conclusion arrived at in this work, namely, that man is descended from some lowly organised form, will, I regret to think, be highly distasteful to many. But there can hardly be a doubt that we are descended from barbarians. The astonishment which I felt on first seeing a party of **Fuegians** on a wild and broken shore will never be forgotten by me, for the reflection at once rushed into my mind—such were our ancestors. These men were absolutely naked and bedaubed with paint, their long hair was tangled, their mouths frothed with excitement, and their expression was wild, startled, and distrustful. They possessed hardly any arts, and like wild animals lived on what they could catch; they had no government, and were merciless to every one not of their own small tribe. He who has seen a savage in his native land will not feel much shame, if forced to acknowledge that the blood of some more humble creature flows in his veins. For my own part I would as soon be descended from that heoric little monkey, who braved his dreaded enemy in order to save the life of his keeper, or from that old baboon, who descending from the mountains, carried away in triumph his young comrade from a crowd of astonished dogs—as from a savage who delights to torture his enemies, offers up bloody sacrifices, practises infanticide without remorse, treats his wives like slaves, knows no decency, and is haunted by the grossest superstitions.

Man may be excused for feeling some pride in having risen, though not through his own exertions, to the very summit of the organic scale; and the fact of his having thus risen, instead of having been aboriginally placed there, may give him hope for a still higher destiny in the distant future. But we are not here concerned with hopes or fears, only with the truth as far as our reason permits us to discover it; and I have given the evidence to the best of my ability. We must, however, acknowledge, as it seems to me, that man with all his noble qualities, with sympathy which feels for the most debased, with benevolence, which extends not only to other men but to the humblest living creature, with his god-like intellect which has penetrated into the movements and constitution of the solar system—with all these exalted powers—Man still bears in his bodily frame the indelible stamp of his lowly origin.

Notes
1   "On the Limits of Natural Selection," in the "North American Review," Oct. 1870, p. 295.
2   The Rev. J.A. Picton gives a discussion to this effect in his "New Theories and the Old Faith," 1870.

––––––––––

Study Questions
1.   What are Darwin's evidence and arguments that "man" has biologically evolved from other animals?

2.   Why did Darwin consider it especially challenging to explain the evolution of human morality? What was his explanation?

3.   From the perspective of the early twenty-first century, are any of Darwin's views contestable? If so, which views, and why?

––––––––––

Further Readings
Bowler, Peter J. 1989. *Evolution: The History of an Idea.* (Rev. ed.). Berkeley: University of California Press.

—. 1996. *Charles Darwin: The Man and his Influence.* New York: Cambridge University Press.

Darwin, Charles. 1964 [1859]. *On the Origin of Species: A Facsimile of the First Edition.* Cambridge, MA: Harvard University Press.

—. 1981 [1871]. *The Descent of Man and Selection in Relation to Sex.* Princeton, NJ: Princeton University Press.

Eiseley, Loren C. 1958. *Darwin's Century: Evolution and the Men Who Discovered It.* Garden City, NY: Doubleday.

Greene, John C. 1959. *The Death of Adam: Evolution and its Impact on Western Thought.* Ames: Iowa State University Press.

6

Introduction
[*The Elementary Forms of the Religious Life*]

ÉMILE DURKHEIM

Subject of Our Study:
Religious Sociology and the Theory of Knowledge
In this book we propose to study the most primitive and simple religion which is actually known, to make an analysis of it, and to attempt an explanation of it. A religious system may be said to be the most primitive which we can observe when it fulfils the following two conditions: in the first place, when it is found in a society whose organization is surpassed by no others in simplicity;[1] and secondly, when it is possible to explain it without making use of any element borrowed from a previous religion.

We shall set ourselves to describe the organization of this system with all the exactness and fidelity that an ethnographer or an historian could give it. But our task will not be limited to that: sociology raises other problems than history or ethnography. It does not seek to know the passed forms of civilization with the sole end of knowing them and reconstructing them. But rather, like every **positive** science, it has as its object the explanation of some actual reality which is near to us, and which consequently is capable of affecting our ideas and our acts: this reality is man, and more precisely, the man of to-day, for there is nothing which we are more interested in knowing. Then we are not going to study a very archaic religion simply for the pleasure of telling its peculiarities and its singularities. If we have taken it as the subject of our research, it is because it has seemed to us better adapted than any other to lead to an understanding of the religious nature of man, that is to say, to show us an essential and permanent aspect of humanity.

But this proposition is not accepted before the raising of strong objections. It seems very strange that one must turn back, and be transported to the very beginnings of history, in order to arrive at an understanding of humanity as it is at present. This manner of procedure seems particularly paradoxical in the question which concerns us. In fact, the various religions generally pass as being quite unequal in value and dignity; it is said that they do not all contain the same quota of truth. Then it seems as though one could not compare the highest forms of religious thought with the lowest, without reducing the first to the level of the second. If we admit that the crude cults of the Australian tribes can help us to understand Christianity, for example, is that not supposing that the latter religion proceeds from the same mentality as the former, that it is made up of the same superstitions and rests upon the same errors? This is how the theoretical importance which has sometimes been attributed to primitive religions has come to pass as a sign of a systematic hostility to all religion, which, by prejudging the results of the study, vitiates them in advance.

There is no occasion for asking here whether or not there are scholars who have merited this reproach, and who have made religious history and ethnology a weapon against religion. In any case, a sociologist cannot hold such a point of view. In fact, it is an essential postulate of sociology that a human institution cannot rest upon an error and a lie, without which it could not exist. If it were not founded in the nature of things, it would have encountered in the facts a resistance over which it could never have triumphed. So when we commence the study of primitive religions, it is with the assurance that they hold to reality and express it; this principle will be seen to re-enter again and again in the course of the analyses and discussions which follow, and the reproach which we make against the schools from which we have separated ourselves is that they have ignored it. When only the letter of the formulæ is considered, these religious beliefs and practices undoubtedly seem disconcerting at times, and one is tempted to attribute them to some sort of deep-rooted error. But one must know how to go underneath the symbol to the reality which it represents and which gives it its meaning. The most barbarous and the most fantastic rites and the strangest myths translate some human need, some aspect of life, either individual or social. The reasons with which the faithful justify them may be, and generally are, erroneous; but the true reasons do not cease to exist, and it is the duty of science to discover them.

In reality, then, there are no religious which are false. All are true in their own fashion; all answer, though in different ways, to the given conditions of human existence. It is undeniably possible to arrange them in a hierarchy. Some can be called superior to others, in the sense that they call into play higher mental functions, that they are richer in ideas and sentiments, that they contain more concepts with fewer sensations and images, and that their arrangement is wiser. But howsoever real this greater complexity and this higher ideality may be, they are not sufficient to place the corresponding religions in different classes. All are religions equally, just as all living beings are equally alive, from the most humble **plastids** up to man. So when we turn to primitive religions it is not with the idea of depreciating religion in general, for these religions are no less respectable than the others. They respond to the same needs, they play the same rôle, they depend upon the same causes; they can also well serve to show the nature of the religious life, and consequently to resolve the problems which we wish to study.

But why give them a sort of prerogative? Why choose them in preference to all others as the subject of our study?—It is merely for reasons of method.

In the first place, we cannot arrive at an understanding of the most recent religions except by following the manner in which they have been progressively composed in history. In fact, historical analysis is the only means of explanation which it is possible to apply to them. It alone enables us to resolve an institution into its constituent elements, for it shows them to us as they are born in time, one after another. On the other hand, by placing every one of them in the condition where it was born, it puts into our hands the only means we have of determining the causes which gave rise to it. Every time that we undertake to explain something human, taken at a given moment in history—be it a religious belief, a moral precept, a legal principle, an æsthetic style or an economic system—it is necessary to commence by going back to its most primitive and simple form, to try to account for the characteristics by which it was marked at that time, and then to show how it developed and became complicated little by little, and how it became that which it is at the moment in question. One readily understands the importance which the determination of the point of departure has for this series of progressive explanations, for all the others are attached to it. It was one of Descartes's principles that the first ring has a predominating place in the chain of scientific truths. But there is no question of placing at the foundation of the science of religions an idea elaborated after the **cartesian** manner, that is to say, a logical concept, a pure possibility, constructed simply by force of thought. What we must find is a concrete reality, and historical and ethnological observation alone can reveal that to us. But even if this cardinal conception is obtained by a different process than that of Descartes, it remains true that it is destined to have a considerable influence on the whole series of propositions which the science establishes. Biological evolution has been conceived quite differently ever since it has been known that monocellular beings do exist. In the same way, the arrangement of religious facts is explained quite differently, according as we put naturism, animism or some other religious form at the beginning of the evolution. Even the most specialized scholars, if they are unwilling to confine themselves to a task of pure erudition, and if they desire to interpret the facts which they analyse, are obliged to choose one of these hypotheses, and make it their starting point.

Whether they desire it or not, the questions which they raise necessarily take the following form: how has naturism or animism been led to take this particular form, here or there, or to enrich itself or impoverish itself in such and such a fashion? Since it is impossible to avoid taking sides on this initial problem, and since the solution given is destined to affect the whole science, it must be attacked at the outset: that is what we propose to do.

Besides this, outside of these indirect reactions, the study of primitive religions has of itself an immediate interest which is of primary importance.

If it is useful to know what a certain particular religion consists in, it is still more important to know what religion in general is. This is the problem which has aroused the interest of philosophers in all times; and not without reason, for it is of interest to all humanity. Unfortunately, the method which they generally employ is purely **dialectic**: they confine themselves to analysing the idea which they make for themselves of religion, except as they illustrate the results of this mental analysis by examples borrowed from the religions which best realize their ideal. But even if this method ought to be abandoned, the problem remains intact, and the great service of philosophy is to have prevented its being suppressed by the disdain of scholars. Now it is possible to attack it in a different way. Since all religions can be compared to each other, and since all are species of the same class, there are necessarily many elements which are common to all. We do not mean to speak simply of the outward and visible characteristics which they all have equally, and which make it possible to give them a provisional definition from the very outset of our researches; the discovery of these apparent signs is relatively easy, for the observation which it demands does not go beneath the surface of things. But these external resemblances suppose others which are profound. At the foundation of all systems of beliefs and of all cults there ought necessarily to be a certain number of fundamental representations or conceptions and of ritual attitudes which, in spite of the diversity of forms which they have taken, have the same objective significance and fulfil the same functions everywhere. These are the permanent elements which constitute that which is permanent and human in religion; they form all the objective contents of the idea which is expressed when one speaks of *religion* in general. How is it possible to pick them out?

Surely it is not by observing the complex religions which appear in the course of history. Every one of these is made up of such a variety of elements that it is very difficult to distinguish what is secondary from what is principal, the essential from the accessory. Suppose that the religion considered is like that of Egypt, India or the classical antiquity. It is a confused mass of many cults, varying according to the locality, the temples, the generations, the dynasties, the invasions, etc. Popular superstitions are there confused with the purest dogmas. Neither the thought nor the activity of the religion is evenly distributed among the believers; according to the men, the environment and the circumstances, the beliefs as well as the rites are thought of in different ways. Here they are priests, there they are monks, elsewhere they are laymen; there are mystics and rationalists, theologians and prophets, etc. In these conditions it is difficult to see what is common to all. In one or another of these systems it is quite possible to find the means of making a profitable study of some particular fact which is specially developed there, such as sacrifice or prophecy, monasticism or the mysteries; but how is it possible to find the common foundation of the religious life underneath the luxuriant vegetation which covers it? How is it possible to find, underneath the disputes of theology, the variations of ritual, the multiplicity of groups and the diversity of individuals, the fundamental states characteristic of religious mentality in general?

Things are quite different in the lower societies. The slighter development of individuality, the small extension of the group, the homogeneity of external circumstances, all contribute to reducing the differences and variations to a minimum. The group has an intellectual and moral conformity of which we find but rare examples in the more advanced societies. Everything is common to all. Movements are stereotyped; everybody performs the same ones in the same circumstances, and this conformity of conduct only translates the conformity of thought. Every mind being drawn into the same eddy, the individual type nearly confounds itself with that of the race. And while all is uniform, all is simple as well. Nothing is deformed like these myths, all composed of one and the same theme which is endlessly repeated, or like these rites made up of a small number of gestures repeated again and again. Neither the popular imagination nor that of the priests has had either the time or the means of refining and transforming the original substance of the religious ideas and practices; these are shown in all their nudity, and offer themselves to an examination, it requiring only the slightest effort to lay them open. That which is accessory or secondary, the development of luxury, has not yet come to hide the principal elements.[2] All is reduced to that which is indispensable, to that without which there could be no religion. But that which is indispensable is also that which is essential, that is to say, that which we must know before all else.

Primitive civilizations offer privileged cases, then, because they are simple cases. That is why, in all fields of human activity, the observations of ethnologists have frequently been veritable revelations, which have renewed the study of human institutions. For example, before the middle of the nineteenth century, everybody was convinced that the father was the essential element of the family; no one had dreamed that there could be a family organization of which the paternal authority was not the keystone. But the discovery of **Bachofen** came and upset this old conception. Up to very recent times it was regarded as evident that the moral and legal relations of kindred were only another aspect of the psychological relations which result from a common descent; Bachofen and his successors, **MacLennan**, **Morgan** and many others still laboured under this misunderstanding. But since we have become acquainted with the nature of the primitive clan, we know that, on the contrary, relationships cannot be explained by consanguinity. To return to religions, the study of only the most familiar ones had led men to believe for a long time that the idea of god was characteristic of everything that is religious. Now the religion which we are going to study presently is, in a large part, foreign to all idea of divinity; the forces to which the rites are there addressed are very different from those which occupy the leading place in our modern religions, yet they aid us in understanding these latter forces. So nothing is more unjust than the disdain with which too many historians still regard the work of ethnographers. Indeed, it is certain that ethnology has frequently brought about the most fruitful revolutions in the different branches of sociology. It is for this same reason that the discovery of unicellular beings, of which we just spoke, has transformed the current idea of life. Since in these very simple beings, life is reduced to its essential traits, these are less easily misunderstood.

But primitive religions do not merely aid us in disengaging the constituent elements of religion; they also have the great advantage that they facilitate the explanation of it. Since the facts there are simpler, the relations between them are more apparent. The reasons with which men account for their acts have not yet been elaborated and denatured by studied reflection; they are nearer and more closely related to the motives which have really determined these acts. In order to understand an hallucination perfectly, and give it its most appropriate treatment, a physician must know its original point of departure. Now this event is proportionately easier to find if he can observe it near its beginnings. The longer the disease is allowed to develop, the more it evades observation; that is because all sorts of interpretations have intervened as it advanced, which tend to force the original state into the background, and across which it is frequently difficult to find the initial one. Between a systematized hallucination and the first impressions which gave it birth, the distance is often considerable. It is the same thing with religious thought. In proportion as it progresses in history, the causes which called it into existence, though remaining active, are no longer perceived, except across a vast scheme of interpretations which quite transform them. Popular mythologies and subtle theologies have done their work: they have superimposed upon the primitive sentiments others which are quite different, and which, though holding to the first, of which they are an elaborated form, only allow their true nature to appear very imperfectly. The psychological gap between the cause and the effect, between the apparent cause and the effective cause, has become more considerable and more difficult for the mind to leap. The remainder of this book will be an illustration and a verification of this remark on method. It will be seen how, in the primitive religions, the religious fact still visibly carries the mark of its origins: it would have been well-nigh impossible to infer them merely from the study of the more developed religions.

The study which we are undertaking is therefore a way of taking up again, *but under new conditions*, the old problem of the origin of religion. To be sure, if by origin we are to understand the very first beginning, the question has nothing scientific about it, and should be resolutely discarded. There was no given moment when religion began to exist, and there is consequently no need of finding a means of transporting ourselves thither in thought. Like every human institution, religion did not commence anywhere. Therefore, all speculations of this sort are justly discredited; they can only consist in subjective and arbitrary constructions which are subject to no sort of control. But the problem which we raise is quite another one. What we want to do is to find a means of discerning the ever-present causes upon which the most essential forms of religious thought and practice depend. Now for the reasons which were just set forth, these causes are proportionately more easily observable as the societies where they are observed are less complicated. That is why we try to get as near as possible to the origins.[3] It is not that we ascribe particular virtues to the lower religions. On the contrary, they are rudimentary and gross; we cannot make of them a sort of model which later religions only have to reproduce. But even their grossness makes them instructive, for they thus become convenient for experiments, as in them, the facts and their relations are easily seen. In order to discover the laws of the phenomena which he studies, the physicist tries to simplify these latter and rid them of their secondary characteristics. For that which concerns institutions, nature spontaneously makes the same sort of simplifications at the beginning of history. We merely wish to put these to profit. Undoubtedly we can only touch very elementary facts by this method. When we shall have accounted for them as far as possible, the novelties of every sort which have been produced in the course of evolution will not yet be explained. But while we do not dream of denying the importance of the problems thus raised, we think that they will profit by being treated in their turn, and that it is important to take them up only after those of which we are going to undertake the study at present.

II

But our study is not of interest merely for the science of religion. In fact, every religion has one side by which it overlaps the circle of properly religious ideas, and there, the study of religious phenomena gives a means of renewing the problems which, up to the present, have only been discussed among philosophers.

For a long time it has been known that the first systems of representations with which men have pictured to themselves the world and themselves were of religious origin. There is no religion that is not a **cosmology** at the same time that it is a speculation upon divine things. If philosophy and the sciences were born of religion, it is because religion began by taking the place of the sciences and philosophy. But it has been less frequently noticed that religion has not confined itself to enriching the human intellect, formed beforehand, with a certain number of ideas; it has contributed to forming the intellect itself. Men owe to it not only a good part of the substance of their knowledge, but also the form in which this knowledge has been elaborated.

At the roots of all our judgments there are a certain number of essential ideas which dominate all our intellectual life; they are what philosophers since Aristotle have called the categories of the understanding: ideas of time, space,[4] class, number, cause, substance, personality, etc. They correspond to the most universal properties of things. They are like the solid frame which enclosed all thought; this does not seem to be able to liberate itself from them without destroying itself, for it seems that we cannot think of objects that are not in time and space, which have no number, etc. Other ideas are contingent and unsteady; we can conceive of their being unknown to a man, a society or an epoch; but these others appear to be nearly inseparable from the normal working of the intellect. They are like the framework of the intelligence. Now when primitive religious beliefs are systematically analysed, the principal categories are naturally found. They are born in religion and of religion; they are a product of religious thought. This is a statement that we are going to have occasion to make many times in the course of this work.

This remark has some interest of itself already; but here is what gives it its real importance.

The general conclusion of the book which the reader has before him is that religion is something eminently social. Religious representations are **collective representations** which express collective realities; the rites are a manner of acting which takes rise in the midst of the assembled groups and which are destined to excite, maintain or recreate certain mental states in these groups. So if the categories are of religious origin, they ought to participate in this nature common to all religious facts; they too should be social affairs and the product of collective thought. At least—for in the actual condition of our knowledge of these matters, one should be careful to avoid all radical and exclusive statements—it is allowable to suppose that they are rich in social elements.

Even at present, these can be imperfectly seen in some of them. For example, try to represent what the notion of time would be without the process by which we divide it, measure it or express it with objective signs, a time which is not a succession of years, months, weeks, days and hours! This is something nearly unthinkable. We cannot conceive of time, except on condition of distinguishing its different moments. Now what is the origin of this differentiation? Undoubtedly, the states of consciousness which we have already experienced can be reproduced in us in the same order in which they passed in the first place; thus portions of our past become present again, though being clearly distinguished from the present. But howsoever important this distinction may be for our private experience, it is far from being enough to constitute the notion or category of time. This does not consist merely in a commemoration, either partial or integral, of our past life. It is an abstract and impersonal frame which surrounds, not only our individual existence, but that of all humanity. It is like an endless chart, where all duration is spread out before the mind, and upon which all possible events can be located in relation to fixed and determined guide lines. It is not *my time* that is arranged; it is time in general, such as it is objectively thought of by everybody in a single civilization. That alone is enough to give us a hint that such an arrangement ought to be collective. And in reality, observation proves that these indispensable guide lines, in relation to which all things are temporally located, are taken from social life. The divisions into days, weeks, months, years, etc., correspond to the periodical recurrence of rites, feasts, and public ceremonies.[5] A calendar expresses the rhythm of the collective activities, while at the same time its function is to assure their regularity.[6]

It is the same thing with space. As Hamelin has shown,[7] space is not the vague and indetermined medium which **Kant** imagined; if purely and absolutely homogeneous, it would be of no use, and could not be grasped by the mind. Spatial representation consists essentially in a primary co-ordination of the data of sensuous experience. But this co-ordination would be impossible if the parts of space were qualitatively equivalent and if they were really interchangeable. To dispose things spatially there must be a possibility of placing them differently, of putting some at the right, others at the left, these above, those below, at the north of or at the south of, east or west of, etc., etc., just as to dispose states of consciousness temporally there must be a possibility of localizing them at determined dates. That is to say that space could not be what it is if it were not, like time, divided and differentiated. But whence come these divisions which are so essential? By themselves, there are neither right nor left, up nor down, north nor south, etc. All these distinctions evidently come from the fact that different sympathetic values have been attributed to various regions. Since all the men of a single civilization represent space in the same way, it is clearly necessary that these sympathetic values, and the distinctions which depend upon them, should be equally universal, and that almost necessarily implies that they be of social origin.[8]

Besides that, there are cases where this social character is made manifest. There are societies in Australia and North America where space is conceived in the form of an immense circle, because the camp has a circular form;[9] and this spatial circle is divided up exactly like the tribal circle, and is in its image. There are as many regions distinguished as there are clans in the tribe, and it is the place occupied by the clans inside the encampment which has determined the orientation of these regions. Each region is defined by the totem of the clan to which it is assigned. Among the Zuñi, for example, the pueblo contains seven quarters; each of these is a group of clans which has had a unity: in all probability it was originally a single clan which was later subdivided. Now their space also contains seven quarters, and each of these seven quarters of the world is in intimate connection with a quarter of the pueblo, that is to say with a group of clans.[10] "Thus," says **Cushing**, "one division is thought to be in relation with the north, another represents the west, another the south," etc.[11] Each quarter of the pueblo has its characteristic colour, which symbolizes it; each region has its colour, which is exactly the same as that of the corresponding quarter. In the course of history the number of fundamental clans has varied; the number of the fundamental regions of space has varied with them. Thus the social organization has been the model for the spatial organization and a reproduction of it. It is thus even up to the distinction between right and left which, far from being inherent in the nature of man in general, is very probably the product of representations which are religious and therefore collective.[12]

Analogous proofs will be found presently in regard to the ideas of class, force, personality and efficacy. It is even possible to ask if the idea of contradiction does not also depend upon social conditions. What makes one tend to believe this is that the empire which the idea has exercised over human thought has varied with times and societies. To-day the principle of identity dominates scientific thought; but there are vast systems of representations which have played a considerable rôle in the history of ideas where it has frequently been set aside: these are the mythologies, from the grossest up to the most reasonable.[13] There, we are continually coming upon beings which have the most contradictory attributes simultaneously, who are at the same time one and many, material and spiritual, who can divide themselves up indefinitely without losing anything of their constitution; in mythology it is an axiom that the part is worth the whole. These variations through which the rules which seem to govern our present logic have passed prove that, far from being engraven through all eternity upon the mental constitution of men, they depend, at least in part, upon factors that are historical and consequently social. We do not know exactly what they are, but we may presume that they exist.[14]

This hypothesis once admitted, the problem of knowledge is posed in new terms.

Up to the present there have been only two doctrines in the field. For some, the categories cannot be derived from experience: they are logically prior to it and condition it. They are represented as so many simple and irreducible data, imminent in the human mind by virtue of its inborn constitution. For this reason they are said to be *a priori*. Others, however, hold that they are constructed and made up of pieces and bits, and that the individual is the artisan of this construction.[15]

But each solution raises difficulties.

Is the **empirical** thesis the one adopted? Then it is necessary to deprive the categories of all their characteristic properties. As a matter of fact they are distinguished from all other knowledge by their universality and necessity. They are the most general concepts which exist, because they are applicable to all that is real, and since they are not attached to any particular object they are independent of every particular subject; they constitute the common field where all minds meet. Further, they must meet there, for reason, which is nothing more than all the fundamental categories taken together, is invested with an authority which we could not set aside if we would. When we attempt to revolt against it, and to free ourselves from some of these essential ideas, we meet with great resistances. They do not merely depend upon us, but they impose themselves upon us. Now empirical data present characteristics which are diametrically opposed to these. A sensation or an image always relies upon a determined object, or upon a collection of objects of the same sort, and expresses the momentary condition of a particular consciousness; it is essentially individual and subjective. We therefore have considerable liberty in dealing with the representations of such an origin. It is true that when our sensations are actual, they impose themselves upon us *in fact*. But *by right* we are free to conceive them otherwise than they really are, or to represent them to ourselves as occurring in a different order from that where they are really produced. In regard to them nothing is forced upon us except as considerations of another sort intervene. Thus we find that we have here two sorts of knowledge, which are like the two opposite poles of the intelligence. Under these conditions forcing reason back upon experience causes it to disappear, for it is equivalent to reducing the universality and necessity which characterize it to pure appearance, to an illusion which may be useful practically, but which corresponds to nothing in reality; consequently it is denying all objective reality to the logical life, whose regulation and organization is the function of the categories. Classical empiricism results in irrationalism; perhaps it would even be fitting to designate it by this latter name.

In spite of the sense ordinarily attached to the name, the **apriorists** have more respect for the facts. Since they do not admit it as a truth established by evidence that the categories are made up of the same elements as our sensual representations, they are not obliged to impoverish them systematically, to draw from them all their real content, and to reduce them to nothing more than verbal artifices. On the contrary, they leave them all their specific characteristics. The apriorists are the **rationalists**; they believe that the world has a logical aspect which the reason expresses excellently. But for all that, it is necessary for them to give the mind a certain power of transcending experience and of adding to that which is given to it directly; and of this singular power they give neither explanation nor justification. For it is no explanation to say that it is inherent in the nature of the human intellect. It is necessary to show whence we hold this surprising prerogative and how it comes that we can see certain relations in things which the examination of these things cannot reveal to us. Saying that only on this condition is experience itself possible changes the problem perhaps, but does not answer it. For the real question is to know how it comes that experience is not sufficient onto itself, but presupposes certain conditions which are exterior and prior to it, and how it happens that these conditions are realized at the moment and in the manner that is desirable. To answer these questions it has sometimes been assumed that above the reason of individuals there is a superior and perfect reason from which the others emanate and from which they get this marvellous power of theirs, by a sort of mystic participation: this is the divine reason. But this hypothesis has at least the one grave disadvantage of being deprived of all experimental control; thus it does not satisfy the conditions demanded of a scientific hypothesis. More than that, the categories of human thought are never fixed in any one definite form; they are made, unmade and remade incessantly; they change with places and times. On the other hand, the divine reason is immutable. How can this immutability give rise to this incessant variability?

Such are the two conceptions that have been pitted against each other for centuries; and if this debate seems to be eternal, it is because the arguments given are really about equivalent. If reason is only a form of individual experience, it no longer exists. On the other hand, if the powers which it has are recognized but not accounted for, it seems to be set outside the confines of nature and science. In the face of these two opposed objections the mind remains uncertain. But if the social origin of the categories is admitted, a new attitude becomes possible, which we believe will enable us to escape both of the opposed difficulties.

The fundamental proposition of the apriorist theory is that knowledge is made up of two sorts of elements, which cannot be reduced into one another, and which are like two distinct layers superimposed one upon the other.[16] Our hypothesis keeps this principle intact. In fact, that knowledge which is called empirical, the only knowledge of which the theorists of empiricism have made use in constructing the reason, is that which is brought into our minds by the direct action of objects. It is composed of individual states which are completely explained[17] by the psychical nature of the individual. If, on the other hand, the categories are, as we believe they are, essentially collective representations, before all else, they should show the mental states of the group; they should depend upon the way in which this is founded and organized, upon its morphology, upon its religious, moral and economic institutions, etc. So between these two sorts of representations there is all the difference which exists between the individual and the social, and one can no more derive the second from the first than he can deduce society from the individual, the whole from the part, the complex from the simple.[18] Society is a reality *sui generis*; it has its own peculiar characteristics, which are not found elsewhere and which are not met with again in the same form in all the rest of the universe. The representations which express it have wholly different contents from purely individual ones and we may rest assured in advance that the first add something to the second.

Even the manner in which the two are formed results in differentiating them. Collective representations are the result of an immense co-operation, which stretches out not only into space but into time as well; to make them, a multitude of minds have associated, united and combined their ideas and sentiments; for them, long generations have accumulated their experience and their knowledge. A special intellectual activity is therefore concentrated in them which is infinitely richer and complexer than that of the individual. From that one can understand how the reason has been able to go beyond the limits of empirical knowledge. It does not owe this to any vague mysterious virtue but simply to the fact that according to the well-known formula, man is double. There are two beings in him: an individual being which has its foundation in the organism and the circle of whose activities is therefore strictly limited, and a social being which represents the highest reality in the intellectual and moral order that we can know by observation—I mean society. This duality of our nature has as its consequence in the practical order, the irreducibility of a moral idea to a utilitarian motive, and in the order of thought, the irreducibility of reason to individual experience. In so far as he belongs to society, the individual transcends himself, both when he thinks and when he acts.

This same social character leads to an understanding of the origin of the necessity of the categories. It is said that an idea is necessary when it imposes itself upon the mind by some sort of virtue of its own, without being accompanied by any proof. It contains within it something which constrains the intelligence and which leads to its acceptance without preliminary examination. The apriorist postulates this singular quality, but does not account for it; for saying that the categories are necessary because they are indispensable to the functioning of the intellect is simply repeating that they are necessary. But if they really have the origin which we attribute to them, their ascendancy no longer has anything surprising in it. They represent the most general relations which exist between things; surpassing all our other ideas in extension, they dominate all the details of our intellectual life. If men did not agree upon these essential ideas at every moment, if they did not have the same conception of time, space, cause, number, etc., all contact between their minds would be impossible, and with that, all life together. Thus society could not abandon the categories to the free choice of the individual without abandoning itself. If it is to live there is not merely need of a satisfactory moral conformity, but also there is a minimum of logical conformity beyond which it cannot safely go. For this reason it uses all its authority upon its members to forestall such dissidences. Does a mind ostensibly free itself from these forms of thought? It is no longer considered a human mind in the full sense of the word, and is treated accordingly. That is why we feel that we are no longer completely free and that something resists, both within and outside ourselves, when we attempt to rid ourselves of these fundamental notions, even in our own conscience. Outside of us there is public opinion which judges us; but more than that, since society is also represented inside of us, it sets itself against these revolutionary fancies, even inside of ourselves; we have the feeling that we cannot abandon them if our whole thought is not to cease being really human. This seems to be the origin of the exceptional authority which is inherent in the reason and which makes us accept its suggestions with confidence. It is the very authority of society,[19] transferring itself to a certain manner of thought which is the indispensable condition of all common action. The necessity with which the categories are imposed upon us is not the effect of simple habits whose yoke we could easily throw off with a little effort; nor is it a physical or metaphysical necessity, since the categories change in different places and times; it is a special sort of moral necessity which is to the intellectual life what moral obligation is to the will.[20]

But if the categories originally only translate social states, does it not follow that they can be applied to the rest of nature only as metaphors? If they were made merely to express social conditions, it seems as though they could not be extended to other realms except in this sense. Thus in so far as they aid us in thinking of the physical or biological world, they have only the value of artificial symbols, useful practically perhaps, but having no connection with reality. Thus we come back, by a different road, to nominalism and empiricism.

But when we interpret a sociological theory of knowledge in this way, we forget that even if society is a specific reality it is not an empire within an empire; it is a part of nature, and indeed its highest representation. The social realm is a natural realm which differs from the others only by a greater complexity. Now it is impossible that nature should differ radically from itself in the one case and the other in regard to that which is most essential. The fundamental relations that exist between things—just that which it is the function of the categories to express—cannot be essentially dissimilar in the different realms. If, for reasons which we shall discuss later,[21] they are more clearly disengaged in the social world, it is nevertheless impossible that they should not be found elsewhere, though in less pronounced forms. Society makes them more manifest but it does not have a monopoly upon them. That is why ideas which have been elaborated on the model of social things can aid us in thinking of another department of nature. It is at least true that if these ideas play the rôle of symbols when they are thus turned aside from their original signification, they are well-founded symbols. If a sort of artificiality enters into them from the mere fact that they are constructed concepts, it is an artificiality which follows nature very closely and which is constantly approaching it still more closely.[22] From the fact that the ideas of time, space, class, cause or personality are constructed out of social elements, it is not necessary to conclude that they are devoid of all objective value. On the contrary, their social origin rather leads to the belief that they are not without foundation in the nature of things.[23]

Thus renovated, the theory of knowledge seems destined to unite the opposing advantages of the two rival theories, without incurring their inconveniences. It keeps all the essential principles of the apriorists; but at the same time it is inspired by that positive spirit which the empiricists have striven to satisfy. It leaves the reason its specific power, but it accounts for it and does so without leaving the world of observable phenomena. It affirms the duality of our intellectual life, but it explains it, and with natural causes. The categories are no longer considered as primary and unanalysable facts, yet they keep a complexity which falsifies any analysis as ready as that with which the empiricists content themselves. They no longer appear as very simple notions which the first comer can very easily arrange from his own personal observations and which the popular imagination has unluckily complicated, but rather they appear as priceless instruments of thought which the human groups have laboriously forged through the centuries and where they have accumulated the best of their intellectual capital.[24] A complete section of the history of humanity is resumed therein. This is equivalent to saying that to succeed in understanding them and judging them, it is necessary to resort to other means than those which have been in use up to the present. To know what these conceptions which we have not made ourselves are really made of, it does not suffice to interrogate our own consciousnesses; we must look outside of ourselves, it is history that we must observe, there is a whole science which must be formed, a complex science which can advance but slowly and by collective labour, and to which the present work brings some fragmentary contributions in the nature of an attempt. Without making these questions the direct object of our study, we shall profit by all the occasions which present themselves to us of catching at their very birth some at least of these ideas which, while being of religious origin, still remain at the foundation of human intelligence.

Notes

1 In the same way, we shall say of these societies that they are primitive, and we shall call the men of these societies primitives. Undoubtedly the expression lacks precision, but that is hardly evitable, and besides, when we have taken pains to fix the meaning, it is not inconvenient.

2 But that is not equivalent to saying that all luxury is lacking to the primitive cults. On the contrary, we shall see that in every religion there are beliefs and practices which do not aim at strictly utilitarian ends (Bk. III, ch. iv, § 2). This luxury is indispensable to the religious life; it is at its very heart. But it is much more rudimentary in the inferior religions than in the others, so we are better able to determine its reason for existence here.

3 It is seen that we give a wholly relative sense to this word "origins," just as to the word "primitive." By it we do not mean an absolute beginning, but the most simple social condition that is actually known or that beyond which we cannot go at present. When we speak of the origins or of the commencement of religious history or thought, it is in this sense that our statements should be understood.

4 We say that time and space are categories because there is no difference between the rôle played by these ideas in the intellectual life and that which falls to the ideas of class or cause (on this point see, Hamelin, *Essay sur les éléments principaux de la représentation*, pp. 63, 76).

5 See the support given this assertion in Hubert and Mauss, *Mélanges d'Histoire des Religions (Travaux de l'Année Sociologique)*, chapter on *La Représentation du Temps dans la Religion*.

6 Thus we see all the difference which exists between the group of sensations and images which serve to locate us in time, and the category of time. The first are the summary of individual experiences, which are of value only for the person who experienced them. But what the category of time expresses is a time common to the group, a social time, so to speak. In itself it is a veritable social institution. Also, it is peculiar to man; animals have no representations of this sort.

   This distinction between the category of time and the corresponding sensations could be made equally well in regard to space or cause. Perhaps this would aid in clearing up certain confusions which are maintained by the controversies of which these questions are the subject. We shall return to this point in the conclusion of the present work (§ 4).

7 *Op. cit.*, pp. 75ff.

8   Or else it would be necessary to admit that all individuals, in virtue of their organo-physical constitution, are spontaneously affected in the same manner by the different parts of space: which is more improbable, especially as in themselves the different regions are sympathetically indifferent. Also, the divisions of space vary with different societies, which is a proof that they are not founded exclusively upon the congenital nature of man.

9   See Durkheim and Mauss, *De quelques formes primitives de classification*, in *Année Sociologique*. VI, pp. 47ff.

10 See Durkheim and Mauss, *De quelques formes primitives de classification*, in *Année Sociologique*, VI, p. 34.

11 *Zuñi Creation Myths*, in *13th Rep. Of the Bureau of Amer. Ethnol.*, pp. 367ff.

12 See Hertz, *La prééminence de la main droite. Étude de polarité religieuse*, in the *Revue Philosophique*, Dec., 1909. On this same question of the relations between the representation of space and the form of the group, see the chapter in Ratzel, *Politische Geographie*, entitled *Der Raum in Geist der Völker*.

13 We do not mean to say that the mythological thought ignores it, but that it contradicts it more frequently and openly than scientific thought does. Inversely, we shall show that science cannot escape violating it, though it holds to it far more scrupulously than religion does. On this subject, as on many others, there are only differences of degree between science and religion; but if these differences should not be exaggerated, they must be noted, for they are significant.

14 This hypothesis has already been set forth by the founders of the *Völkerpsychologie*. It is especially remarked in a short article by Windelbrand entitled *Die Erkenntnisslehre unter dem Völkerpsychologischen Gesichtspunke*, in the same *Zeitsch. f. Völkerpsychologie*, viii, pp. 166ff. Cf. A note of Steinthal on the same subject, *ibid.*, pp. 178ff.

15 Even in the theory of Spencer, it is by individual experience that the categories are made. The only difference which there is in this regard between ordinary empiricism and evolutionary empiricism is that according to this latter, the results of individual experience are accumulated by heredity. But this accumulation adds nothing essential to them; no element enters into their composition which does not have its origin in the experience of the individual. According to this theory, also, the necessity with which the categories actually impose themselves upon us is the product of an illusion and a superstitious prejudice, strongly rooted in the organism, to be sure, but without foundation in the nature of things.

16 Perhaps some will be surprised that we do not define the apriorist theory by the hypothesis of innateness. But this conception really plays a secondary part in the doctrine. It is a simple way of stating the impossibility of reducing rational knowledge to empirical data. Saying that the former is innate is only a positive way of saying that it is not the product of experience, such as it is ordinarily conceived.

17 At least, in so far as there are any representations which are individual and hence wholly empirical. But there are in fact probably none where the two elements are not found closely united.

18 This irreducibility must not be taken in any absolute sense. We do not wish to say that there is nothing in the empirical representations which shows rational ones, nor that there is nothing in the individual which could be taken as a sign of social life. If experience were completely separated from all that is rational, reason could not operate upon it; in the same way, if the psychic nature of the individual were absolutely opposed to the social life, society would be impossible. A complete analysis of the categories should seek these germs of rationality even in the individual consciousness. We shall have occasion to come back to this point in our conclusion. All that we wish to establish here is that between these indistinct germs of reason and the reason properly so called, there is a difference comparable to that which separates the properties of the mineral elements out of which a living being is composed from the characteristic attributes of life after this one has been constituted.

19 It has frequently been remarked that social disturbances result in multiplying mental disturbances. This is one more proof that logical discipline is a special aspect of social discipline. The first gives way as the second is weakened.

20 There is an analogy between this logical necessity and moral obligation, but there is not an actual identity. To-day society treats criminals in a different fashion than subjects whose intelligence only is abnormal; that is a proof that the authority attached to logical rules and that inherent in moral rules are not of the same nature, in spite of certain similarities. They are two species of the same class. It would be interesting to make a study on the nature and origin of this difference, which is probably not primitive, for during a long time, the public conscience has poorly distinguished between the deranged and the delinquent. We confine ourselves to signalizing this question. By this example, one may see the number of problems which are raised by the analysis of these notions which generally pass as being elementary and simple, but which are really of an extreme complexity.

21 This question will be treated again in the conclusion of this work.

22 The rationalism which is imminent in the sociological theory of knowledge is thus midway between the classical empiricism and apriorism. For the first, the categories are purely artificial constructions; for the second, on the contrary, they are given by nature; for us, they are in a sense a work of art, but of an art which imitates nature with a perfection capable of increasing unlimitedly.

23 For example, that which is at the foundation of the category of time is the rhythm of social life; but if there is a rhythm in collective life, one may rest assured that there is another in the life of the individual, and more generally, others. In the same way, we shall see that the notion of class is founded on that of the human group. But if men form natural groups, it can be assumed that among things there exists groups which are at once analogous and different. Classes and species are natural groups of things.

If it seems to many minds that a social origin cannot be attributed to the categories without depriving them of all speculative value, it is because society is still too frequently regarded as something that is not natural; hence it is concluded that the representations which express it express nothing in nature. But the conclusion is not worth more than the premise.

24 This is how it is legitimate to compare the categories to tools; for on its side, a tool is material accumulated capital. There is a close relationship between the three ideas of tool, category and institution.

Study Questions

1. On what basis does Durkheim assert that no religions are false?

2. What does Durkheim mean by "elementary forms"? Where are they to be found?

3. What does Durkheim mean when he asserts that religious representations are collective representations expressing collective realities? How does this assertion bear on the distinction between rational and empirical knowledge?

Further Readings

Durkheim, Émile. 1982 [1895]. *The Rules of Sociological Method*. New York: The Free Press.

—. 1984 [1893]. *The Division of Labor in Society*. Trans. W. D. Hall. New York: The Free Press.

—. 1995 [1912]. *The Elementary Forms of the Religious Life*. Trans. Karen E. Fields. New York: The Free Press.

Lukes, Steven. 1985. *Émile Durkheim: His Life and Work: A Historical and Critical Study*. Stanford, CA: Stanford University Press.

Parkin, Frank. 1992. *Durkheim*. Oxford: Oxford University Press.

Turner, Stephen P. 1993. *Émile Durkheim: Sociologist and Moralist*. New York: Routledge.

7

[Part] III
[*Civilization and Its Discontents*]

SIGMUND FREUD

Our enquiry concerning happiness has not so far taught us much that is not already common knowledge. And even if we proceed from it to the problem of why it is so hard for men to be happy, there seems no greater prospect of learning anything new. We have given the answer already by pointing to the three sources from which our suffering comes: the superior power of nature, the feebleness of our own bodies and the inadequacy of the regulations which adjust the mutual relationships of human beings in the family, the state and society. In regard to the first two sources, our judgement cannot hesitate long. It forces us to acknowledge those sources of suffering and to submit to the inevitable. We shall never completely master nature; and our bodily organism, itself a part of that nature, will always remain a transient structure with a limited capacity for adaptation and achievement. This recognition does not have a paralysing effect. On the contrary, it points the direction for our activity. If we cannot remove all suffering, we can remove some, and we can mitigate some: the experience of many thousands of years has convinced us of that. As regards the third source, the social source of suffering, our attitude is a different one. We do not admit it at all; we cannot see why the regulations made by ourselves should not, on the contrary, be a protection and a benefit for every one of us. And yet, when we consider how unsuccessful we have been in precisely this field of prevention and suffering, a suspicion dawns on us that here, too, a piece of unconquerable nature may lie behind—this time a piece of our own psychical constitution.

When we start considering this possibility, we come upon a contention which is so astonishing that we must dwell upon it. This contention holds that what we call civilization is largely responsible for our misery, and that we should be much happier if we gave it up and returned to primitive conditions. I call this contention astonishing because, in whatever way we may define the concept of civilization, it is a certain fact that all the things with which we seek to protect ourselves against the threats that emanate from the sources of suffering are part of that very civilization.

How has it happened that so many people have come to take up this strange attitude of hostility to civilization? I believe that the basis of it was a deep and long-standing dissatisfaction with the then existing state of civilization and that on that basis a condemnation of it was built up, occasioned by certain specific historical events. I think I know what the last and the last but one of those occasions were. I am not learned enough to trace the chain of them far back enough in the history of the human species; but a factor of this kind hostile to civilization must already have been at work in the victory of Christendom over the heathen religions. For it was very closely related to the low estimation put upon earthly life by the Christian doctrine. The last but one of these occasions was when the progress of voyages of discovery led to contact with primitive peoples and races. In consequence of insufficient observation and a mistaken view of their manners and customs, they appeared to Europeans to be leading a simple, happy life with few wants, a life such as was unattainable by their visitors with their superior civilization. Later experience has corrected some of those judgements. In many cases the observers had wrongly attributed to the absence of complicated cultural demands what was in fact due to the bounty of nature and the ease with which the major human needs were satisfied. The last occasion is especially familiar to us. It arose when people came to know about the mechanism of the **neuroses**, which threaten to undermine the modicum of happiness enjoyed by civilized men. It was discovered that a person becomes neurotic because he cannot tolerate the amount of frustration which society imposes on him in the service of its cultural ideals, and it was inferred from this that the abolition or reduction of those demands would result in a return to possibilities of happiness.

There is also an added factor of disappointment. During the last few generations mankind has made an extraordinary advance in the natural sciences and in their technical application and has established his control over nature in a way never before imagined. The single steps of this advance are common knowledge and it is unnecessary to enumerate them. Men are proud of those achievements, and have a right to be. But they seem to have observed that this newly-won power over space and time, this subjugation of the forces of nature, which is the fulfilment of a longing that goes back thousands of years, has not increased the amount of pleasurable satisfaction which they may expect from life and has not made them feel happier. From the recognition of this fact we ought to be content to conclude that power over nature is not the *only* precondition of human happiness, just as it is not the *only* goal of cultural endeavour; we ought not to infer from it that technical progress is without value for the economics of our happiness. One would like to ask: is there, then, no positive gain in pleasure, no unequivocal increase in my feeling of happiness, if I can, as often as I please, hear the voice of a child of mine who is living hundreds of miles away or if I can learn in the shortest possible time after a friend has reached his destination that he has come through the long and difficult voyage unharmed? Does it mean nothing that medicine has succeeded in enormously reducing infant mortality and the danger of infection for women in childbirth, and, indeed, in considerably lengthening the average life of a civilized man? And there is a long list that might be added to benefits of this kind which we owe to the much-despised era of scientific and technical advances. But here the voice of pessimistic criticism makes itself heard and warns us that most of these satisfactions follow the model of the "cheap enjoyment" extolled in the anecdote—the enjoyment obtained by putting a bare leg from under the bed-clothes on a cold winter night and drawing it in again. If there had been no rail-way to conquer distances, my child would never have left his native town and I should need no telephone to hear his voice; if travelling across the ocean by ship had not been introduced, my friend would not have embarked on his sea-voyage and I should not need a cable to relieve my anxiety about him. What is the use of reducing infantile mortality when it is precisely that reduction which imposes the greatest restraint on us in the begetting of children, so that, taken all round, we nevertheless rear no more children than in the days before the reign of hygiene, while at the same time we have created difficult conditions for our sexual life in marriage, and have probably worked against the benefi-cial effects of natural selection? And, finally, what good to us is a long life if it is difficult and barren of joys, and if it is so full of misery that we can only wel-come death as a deliverer?

It seems certain that we do not feel comfortable in our present-day civiliza-tion, but it is very difficult to form an opinion whether and in what degree men of an earlier age felt happier and what part their cultural conditions played in the matter. We shall always tend to consider people's distress objectively—that is, to place ourselves, with our own wants and sensibilities, in *their* conditions, and then to examine what occasions we should find in them for experiencing happiness or unhappiness. This method of looking at things, which seems objective because it ignores the variations in subjective sensibility, is, of course, the most subjective possible, since it puts one's own mental states in the place of any others, unknown though they may be. Happiness, however, is something essentially subjective. No matter how much we may shrink with horror from certain situations—of a galley-slave in antiquity, of a peasant dur-ing the **Thirty Years' War**, of a victim of the **Holy Inquisition**, of a Jew await-ing a pogrom—it is nevertheless impossible for us to feel our way into such people—to divine the changes which original obtuseness of mind, a gradual stupefying process, the cessation of expectations, and cruder or more refined methods of narcotization have produced upon their receptivity to sensations of pleasure and unpleasure. Moreover, in the case of the most extreme possibility of suffering, special mental protective devices are brought into operation. It seems to me unprofitable to pursue this aspect of the problem any further.

It is time for us to turn our attention to the nature of this civilization on whose value as a means of happiness doubts have been thrown. We shall not look for a formula in which to express that nature in a few words, until we have learned something by examining it. We shall therefore content ourselves with saying once more that the word "civilization"[1] describes the whole sum of the achievements and the regulations which distinguish our lives from those of our animal ancestors and which serve two purposes—namely to protect men against nature and to adjust their mutual relations.[2] In order to learn more, we will bring together the various features of civilization individually, as they are exhibited in human communities. In doing so, we shall have no hesitation in letting ourselves be guided by linguistic usage or, as it is also called, linguistic feeling, in the conviction that we shall thus be doing justice to inner discernments which still defy expression in abstract terms.

The first stage is easy. We recognize as cultural all activities and resources which are useful to men for making the earth serviceable to them, for protecting them against the violence of the forces of nature, and so on. As regards this side of civilization, there can be scarcely any doubt. If we go back far enough, we find that the first acts of civilization were the use of tools, the gaining of control over fire and the construction of dwellings. Among these, the control over fire stands out as a quite extraordinary and unexampled achievement,[3] while the others opened up paths which man has followed ever since, and the stimulus to which is easily guessed. With every tool man is perfecting his own organs, whether motor or sensory, or is removing the limits to their functioning. Motor power places gigantic forces at his disposal, which, like his muscles, he can employ in any direction; thanks to ships and aircraft neither water nor air can hinder his movements; by means of spectacles he corrects defects in the lens of his own eye; by means of the telescope he sees into the far distance; and by means of the microscope he overcomes the limits of visibility set by the structure of his retina. In the photographic camera he has created an instrument which retains the fleeting visual impression, just as a gramophone disc retains the equally fleeting auditory ones; both are at bottom materializations of the power he possesses of recollection, his memory. With the help of the telephone he can hear at distances which would be respected as unattainable even in a fairy tale. Writing was in its origin the voice of an absent person; and the dwelling-house was a substitute for the mother's womb, the first lodging, for which in all likelihood man still longs, and in which he was safe and felt at ease.

These things that, by his science and technology, man has brought about on this earth, on which he first appeared as a feeble animal organism and on which each individual of his species must once more make its entry ("oh inch of nature!") as a helpless suckling—these things do not only sound like a fairy tale, they are an actual fulfilment of every—or of almost every—fairy-tale wish. All these assets he may lay claim to as his cultural acquisition. Long ago he formed an ideal conception of omnipotence and omniscience which he embodied in his gods. To these gods he attributed everything that seemed unattainable to his wishes, or that was forbidden to him. One may say, therefore, that these gods were cultural ideals. To-day he has come very close to the attainment of this ideal, he has almost become a god himself. Only, it is true, in the fashion in which ideals are usually attained according to the general judgement of humanity. Not completely; in some respects not at all, in others only half way. Man has, as it were, become a kind of prosthetic God. When he puts on all his auxiliary organs he is truly magnificent; but those organs have not grown on to him and they still give him much trouble at times. Nevertheless, he is entitled to console himself with the thought that this development will not come to an end precisely with the year 1930 A.D. Future ages will bring with them new and probably unimaginably great advances in this field of civilization and will increase man's likeness to God still more. But in the interests of our investigations, we will not forget that present-day man does not feel happy in his Godlike character.

We recognize, then, that countries have attained a high level of civilization if we find that in them everything which can assist in the exploitation of the earth by man and in his protection against the forces of nature—everything, in short, which is of use to him—is attended to and effectively carried out. In such countries rivers which threaten to flood the land are regulated in their flow, and their water is directed through canals to places where there is a shortage of it. The soil is carefully cultivated and planted with the vegetation which it is suited to support; and the mineral wealth below ground is assiduously brought to the surface and fashioned into the required implements and utensils. The means of communication are ample, rapid and reliable. Wild and dangerous animals have been exterminated, and the breeding of domesticated animals flourishes. But we demand other things from civilization besides these, and it is a noticeable fact that we hope to find them realized in these same countries. As though we were seeking to repudiate the first demand we made, we welcome it as a sign of civilization as well if we see people directing their care too to what has no practical value whatever, to what is useless—if, for instances, the green spaces necessary in a town as playgrounds and as reservoirs of fresh air are also laid out with flower-beds, or if the windows of the houses are decorated with pots of flowers. We soon observe that this useless thing which we expect civilization to value is beauty. We require civilized man to reverence beauty wherever he sees it in nature and to create it in the objects of his handwork so far as he is able. But this is far from exhausting our demands on civilization. We expect besides to see the signs of cleanliness and order. We do not think highly of the cultural level of an English country town in Shakespeare's time when we read that there was a big dung-heap in front of his father's house in Stratford; we are indignant and call it "barbarous" (which is the opposite of civilized) when we find the paths of the **Wiener Wald** littered with paper. Dirtiness of any kind seems to us incompatible with civilization. We extend our demand for cleanliness to the human body too. We are astonished to learn of the objectionable smell which emanated from the *Roi Soleil*; and we shake our heads on the **Isola Bella** when we are shown the tiny wash-basin in which Napoleon made his morning toilet. Indeed, we are not surprised by the idea of setting up the use of soap as an actual yardstick of civilization. The same is true of order. It, like cleanliness, applies solely to the works of man. But whereas cleanliness is not to be expected in nature, order, on the contrary, has been imitated from her. Man's observation of the great astronomical regularities not only furnished him with a model for introducing order into his life, but gave him the first points of departure for doing so. Order is a kind of compulsion to repeat which, when a regulation has been laid down once and for all, decides when, where and how a thing shall be done, so that in every similar circumstance one is spared hesitation and indecision. The benefits of order are incontestable. It enables men to use space and time to the best advantage, while conserving their psychical forces. We should have a right to expect that order would have taken its place in human activities from the start and without difficulty; and we may well wonder that this has not happened—that, on the contrary, human beings exhibit an inborn tendency to carelessness, irregularity and unreliability in their work, and that a laborious training is needed before they learn to follow the example of their celestial models.

Beauty, cleanliness and order obviously occupy a special position among the requirements of civilization. No one will maintain that they are as important for life as control over the forces of nature or as some other factors with which we shall become acquainted. And yet no one would care to put them in the background as trivialities. That civilization is not exclusively taken up with what is useful is already shown by the example of beauty, which we decline to omit from among the interests of civilization. The usefulness of order is quite evident. With regard to cleanliness, we must bear in mind that it is demanded of us by hygiene as well, and we may suspect that even before the days of scientific prophylaxis the connection between the two was not altogether strange to man. Yet utility does not entirely explain these efforts; something else must be at work besides.

No feature, however, seems better to characterize civilization than its esteem and encouragement of man's higher mental activities—his intellectual, scientific and artistic achievements—and the leading role that it assigns to ideas in human life. Foremost among those ideas are the religious systems, on whose complicated structure I have endeavoured to throw light elsewhere. Next come the speculations of philosophy; and finally what might be called man's "ideals"—his ideas of a possible perfection of individuals, or of peoples or of the whole of humanity, and the demands he sets up on the basis of such ideas. The fact that these creations of his are not independent of one another, but are on the contrary closely interwoven, increases the difficulty not only of describing them but of tracing their psychological derivation. If we assume quite generally that the motive force of all human activities is a striving towards the two confluent goals of utility and a yield of pleasure, we must suppose that this is also true of the manifestations of civilization which we have been discussing here, although this is easily visible only in scientific and aesthetic activities. But it cannot be doubted that the other activities, too, correspond to strong needs in men—perhaps to needs which are only developed in a minority. Nor must we allow ourselves to be misled by judgements of value concerning any particular religion, or philosophic system, or ideal. Whether we think to find in them the highest achievements of the human spirit, or whether we deplore them as aberrations, we cannot but recognize that where they are present, and, in especial, where they are dominant, a high level of civilization is implied.

The last, but certainly not the least important, of the characteristic features of civilization remains to be assessed: the manner in which the relationships of men to one another, their social relationships, are regulated—relationships which affect a person as a neighbour, as a source of help, as another person's sexual object, as a member of a family and of a State. Here it is especially difficult to keep clear of particular ideal demands and to see what is civilized in general. Perhaps we may begin by explaining that the element of civilization enters on the scene with the first attempt to regulate these social relationships. If the attempt were not made, the relationships would be subject to the arbitrary will of the individual: that is to say, the physically stronger man would decide them in the sense of his own interests and instinctual impulses. Nothing would be changed in this if the stronger man should in his turn meet someone even stronger than he. Human life in common is only made possible when a majority comes together which is stronger than any separate individual and which remains united against all separate individuals. The power of this community is then set up as "right" in opposition to the power of the individual, which is condemned as "brute force." This replacement of the power of the individual by the power of a community constitutes the decisive step of civilization. The essence of it lies in the fact that the members of the community restrict themselves in their possibilities of satisfaction, whereas the individual knew no such restriction. The first requisite of civilization, therefore, is that of justice—that is, the assurance that a law once made will not be broken in favour of an individual. This implies nothing as to the ethical value of such a law. The further course of cultural development seems to tend towards making the law no longer an expression of the will of a small community—a caste or a stratum of the population or a racial group—which, in its turn, behaves like a violent individual towards other, and perhaps more numerous, collections of people. The final outcome should be a rule of law to which all—except those who are not capable of entering a community—have contributed by a sacrifice of their instincts, and which leaves no one—again with the same exception—at the mercy of brute force.

The liberty of the individual is no gift of civilization. It was greatest before there was any civilization, though then, it is true, it had for the most part no value, since the individual was scarcely in a position to defend it. The development of civilization imposes restrictions on it, and justice demands that no one shall escape those restrictions. What makes itself felt in a human community as a desire for freedom may be their revolt against some existing injustice, and so may prove favourable to a further development of civilization; it may remain compatible with civilization. But it may also spring from the remains of their original personality, which is still untamed by civilization and may thus become the basis in them of hostility to civilization. The urge for freedom, therefore, is directed against particular forms and demands of civilization or against civilization altogether. It does not seem as though any influence could induce a man to change his nature into a termite's. No doubt he will always defend his claim to individual liberty against the will of the group. A good part of the struggles of mankind centre round the single task of finding an expedient accommodation—one, that is, that will bring happiness—between this claim of the individual and the cultural claims of the group; and one of the problems that touches the fate of humanity is whether such an accommodation can be reached by means of some particular form of civilization or whether this conflict is irreconcilable.

By allowing common feeling to be our guide in deciding what features of human life are to be regarded as civilized, we have obtained a clear impression of the general picture of civilization; but it is true that so far we have discovered nothing that is not universally known. At the same time we have been careful not to fall in with the prejudice that civilization is synonymous with perfecting, that it is the road to perfection pre-ordained for men. But now a point of view presents itself which may lead in a different direction. The development of civilization appears to us as a peculiar process which mankind undergoes, and in which several things strike us as familiar. We may characterize this process with reference to the changes which it brings about in the familiar instinctual dispositions of human beings, to satisfy which is, after all, the economic task of our lives. A few of these instincts are used up in such a manner that something appears in their place which, in an individual, we describe as a character-trait. The most remarkable example of such a process is found in the anal erotism of young human beings. Their original interest in the excretory function, its organs and products, is changed in the course of their growth into a group of traits which are familiar to us as parsimony, a sense of order and cleanliness—qualities which, though valuable and welcome in themselves, may be intensified till they become markedly dominant and produce what is called the anal character. How this happens we do not know, but there is no doubt about the correctness of the finding.[4] Now we have seen that order and cleanliness are important requirements of civilization, although their vital necessity is not very apparent, any more than their suitability as sources of enjoyment. At this point we cannot fail to be struck by the similarity between the process of civilization and the **libidinal** development of the individual. Other instincts are induced to displace the conditions for their satisfaction, to lead them into other paths. In most cases this process coincides with that of the *sublimation* (of instinctual aims) with which we are familiar, but in some it can be differentiated from it. Sublimation of instinct is an especially conspicuous feature of cultural development; it is what makes it possible for higher psychical activities, scientific, artistic or ideological, to play such an important part in civilized life. If one were to yield to a first impression, one would say that sublimation is a vicissitude which has been forced upon the instincts entirely by civilization. But it would be wiser to reflect upon this a little longer. In the third place, finally, and this seems the most important of all, it is impossible to overlook the extent to which civilization is built up upon a renunciation of instinct, how much it presupposes precisely the non-satisfaction (by suppression, repression or some other means?) of powerful instincts. This "cultural frustration" dominates the large field of social relationships between human beings. As we already know, it is the cause of the hostility against which all civilizations have to struggle. It will also make severe demands on our scientific work, and we shall have much to explain here. It is not easy to understand how it can become possible to deprive an instinct of satisfaction. Nor is doing so without danger. If the loss is not compensated for economically, one can be certain that serious disorders will ensue.

But if we want to know what value can be attributed to our view that the development of civilization is a special process, comparable to the normal maturation of the individual, we must clearly attack another problem. We must ask ourselves to what influences the development of civilization owes its origin, how it arose, and by what its course has been determined.

Notes

1   *"Kultur."* For the translation of this word see the Editor's Note to *The Future of an Illusion.*

2   See *The Future of an Illusion.*

3   Psycho-analytic material, incomplete as it is and not susceptible to clear interpretation, nevertheless admits of a conjecture—a fantastic-sounding one—about the origin of this human feat. It is as though primal man had the habit, when he came in contact with fire, of satisfying an infantile desire connected with it, by putting it out with a stream of his urine. The legends that we possess leave no doubt about the originally phallic view taken of tongues of flame as they shoot upwards. Putting out fire by micturating—a theme to which modern giants, Gulliver in Lilliput and Rabelais' Gargantua, still hark back—was therefore a kind of sexual act with a male, an enjoyment of sexual potency in a homosexual competition. The first person to renounce this desire and spare the fire was able to carry it off with him and subdue it to his own use. By damping down the fire of his own sexual excitation, he had tamed the natural force of fire. This great cultural conquest was thus the reward for his renunciation of instinct. Further, it is as though woman had been appointed guardian of the fire which was held captive on the domestic hearth, because her anatomy made it impossible for her to yield to the temptation of this desire. It is remarkable, too, how regularly analytic experience testifies to the connection between ambition, fire and urethral erotism.

4   Cf. my "Character and Anal Erotism" (1908*b*), and numerous further contributions, by Ernest Jones and others.

Study Questions

1.   According to Freud, why have people become unhappy with civilization?

2.   According to Freud, what do people require from civilization?

3.   According to Freud, what is the relationship between civilization and human instinct?

Further Readings

Freud, Sigmund. 1960 [1913]. *Totem and Taboo.* Trans. Abraham A. Brill. New York: Random House.

—. 1961 [1930]. *Civilization and its Discontents.* Trans. James Strachey. New York: W.W. Norton.

—. 1973 [1928]. *The Future of an Illusion.* (Rev.) Ed. James Strachey. London: Hogarth Press and the Institute of Psycho-Analysis.

Manson, William C. 1988. *The Psychodynamics of Culture: Abram Kardiner and Neo-Freudian Anthropology*. Westport, CT: Greenwood.

Ritvo, Lucile B. 1990. *Darwin's Influence on Freud: A Tale of Two Sciences*. New Haven, CT: Yale University Press.

Spindler, George Dearborn (ed.). 1978. *The Making of Psychological Anthropology*. Berkeley: University of California Press.

Wallace, Edwin R., IV. 1983. *Freud and Anthropology: A History and Reappraisal*. Madison, CT: International Universities Press.

PART II

THE EARLY TWENTIETH CENTURY: ANTHROPOLOGY COMES OF AGE

INTRODUCTION

In the early twentieth century, anthropology in the United States and Great Britain moved in new directions as it sought to distance itself from nineteenth-century cultural evolutionism and hereditarianism, now construed as "racism." Meanwhile, German sociologist Max Weber formulated theories that late-twentieth century anthropologists would find appealing. In each case, as before, the history of anthropological theory was affected by powerful and persuasive personalities.

American Cultural Historicism

In the United States, early twentieth-century anthropology was largely the vision of Franz Boas (1858-1942) and his students, beginning with Robert Lowie (1883-1957) and Alfred Louis Kroeber (1876-1960). These individuals were the great "generalists" who set American anthropology on its modern course.

Franz Boas was a German scientist raised in an intellectual environment that demanded dedication and empirical rigor. He was trained as a physicist but, following a research expedition to Baffin Island in Canada, switched to geography and then to anthropology. Although Boas was scientific, he did not try to model anthropology on the natural sciences. Following the Southwest School of German philosophy, he maintained that the natural and human sciences were different. The natural sciences, or *naturwissenshaften*, could achieve explanatory generalizations, a characteristic that, in modern terms, makes them "nomothetic." In contrast, the human sciences, or *geisteswis-senshaften*, were sciences of the human mind and could only achieve particular descriptions, a characteristic that makes them "idiographic." Partly for this reason, historian of anthropology Marvin Harris has labelled the Boasian school "American historical particularism."

A large part of Boas's career was devoted to a critique of classical cultural evolutionism and its associated comparative method. For Boas, classical cultural evolutionists such as Lewis Henry Morgan had been too doctrinaire, insisting that there was only *one* evolutionary trajectory. This "unilineal" position, he argued, was not supported by the facts. What facts? Chiefly the facts of history, which gave evidence of considerable cultural "diffusion," or spreading by human migration, borrowing, and assimilation. During the first quarter of the twentieth century, diffusionist ideas became popular in some anthropology circles. Boas thought that, while sometimes extreme, these ideas had merit and ought to be incorporated into comprehensive histories of particular peoples. Each of these histories would be unique, showing that two or more peoples at the same "stage" of cultural development need not have arrived there independently in parallel fashion. Despite varying rates of change, cultures are not static, so no extant culture could be perpetuated from prehistory intact. Furthermore, why "rank" stages and judge the later ones superior? This practice smacked of "ethnocentrism," or cultural bias, an attitude that Boas worked long and hard to counteract. Altogether, Boas's preferences amounted to what can be called "cultural historicism," a label that captures his commitment to comprehend history without theoretical preconceptions.

"Cultural historicism" also captures Boas's commitment to demonstrate the power of culture over biology to explain past and present variation in human behaviour. Himself a target of anti-Semitic racism, Boas designed anthropology to be a discipline that would show that culture is separate from biology in the sense that culture change does not depend on a change in genes. His action was a clear reaction to the thrust of nineteenth-century anthropology, which, as exemplified by Darwinism and a widespread racial polygenism, was strongly hereditarian. In a landmark scientific demonstration, Boas showed that the human head form, supposedly highly heritable, could vary in a single generation under the influence of culture. His scientific mission to combat racism and ethnocentrism made anthropology appeal to a core of highly gifted students with a heightened social conscience. These students responded to Boas's urgent call to "salvage" ethnographic information before aboriginal cultures disappeared upon the death of peoples or their assimilation to Western ways.

Before 1900, following appointments elsewhere, Boas became a professor of anthropology at Columbia University in New York City, a position he held until his death in 1942. During his near half-century at Columbia, he "mentored" almost all early American anthropologists of distinction, including Lowie and Kroeber. Of these two, Lowie remained truer to the Boasian vision, devoting much of his career to a refutation of cultural evolutionism in favour of the facts of culture history. In his influential book *Primitive Society* (1920), Lowie theoretically reworked anthropology to update it from the days of Morgan's *Ancient Society* (1877). Kroeber, while essentially Boasian, sometimes veered in a more nomothetic direction, searching for cultural configurations and laws that dominated individuals and denied them freedom of cultural choice. While Boas was still at Columbia, Lowie and Kroeber assumed positions at the University of California at Berkeley. Thereafter, Boasian anthropology flourished on both the American west and east coasts.

Selections 8 to 10 represent American cultural historicism in excerpts from key works by Boas, Lowie, and Kroeber. Selection 8, "The Methods of Ethnology" by Boas, was originally published as an article in a 1920 issue of *American Anthropologist*, a journal that Boas nurtured with editorial support. The "methods" are those of cultural historicism. After reviewing the histories of cultural evolutionism and diffusionism in some detail, Boas makes his case for American anthropology as a compromise between these two theoretical extremes. His central theme is the process of cultural change, which he portrays as a dynamic series of causes and effects involving individuals. Because culture change involves individuals, psychology is relevant, but Boas finds Freudian psychology one-sided, and he questions Freud's preoccupation with culture as merely symbolic of disturbed psychological states. Besides psychology, Boas promotes anthropological linguistics, because he understands that languages filter the expression and reception of culture. The relationship between language and culture was explored more fully by his student Edward Sapir.

Selection 9 is the "Conclusion" to Robert Lowie's *Primitive Society*. Here, he systematically critiques cultural evolutionism by assessing the pros and cons—mainly cons—of unilinear, parallel, and convergent evolutionary schemas. Under his scrutiny, none holds up. Therefore, he concludes that there are no historical "laws." The final paragraph of *Primitive Society* is frequently quoted:

> Nor are the facts of culture history without bearing on the adjustment of our own future. To that planless hodgepodge, that thing of shreds and patches called civilization, its historian can no longer yield superstitious reverence. He will realize better than others the obstacles to infusing design into the amorphous product; but in thought at least he will not grovel before it in fatalistic acquiescence but dream of a rational scheme to supplant the chaotic jumble.

To some anthropologists, particularly those unsympathetic with Lowie's theoretical position, this passage implies that Lowie was a near-fanatical particularist who disavowed the search for any sort of historical generalization. An alternative interpretation, and one that is based on the broader Boasian context, is that Lowie, following Boas, wanted to postpone generalizations for the future and concentrate instead on the pressing need to salvage pertinent ethnographic facts in the present.

Selection 10, "What Anthropology is About" by Alfred Louis Kroeber, is essentially the first chapter of his classic textbook *Anthropology* (1923). In this selection, students should be able to recognize anthropology much as they know it, purged of nineteenth-century hereditarianism. Kroeber surveys the anthropological landscape, making room for both biology and culture, but he keeps these two realms separate and gives examples of how cultural and biological evolution differ. In the tradition of predecessors like Auguste Comte and successors like the middle-twentieth century anthropologist Leslie White, he demarcates culture as a realm unto itself, *sui generis*, which he describes elsewhere as "above" biology, or "superorganic." While other academics might be interested in particular aspects of cultures, Kroeber stipulates that anthropologists are interested in "culture as such." In other publications, he develops the theme of superorganic cultural configurations and trends that predetermine human behaviour and refute the "Great Man Theory of History."

Together, Boas, Lowie, and Kroeber formed a powerful triumvirate of early American anthropologists. Building on their foundation, some of their students next moved American anthropology clearly in a psychological direction.

Psychological Anthropology

Boas and his students gave anthropology a human touch. They were curious about the relationship between culture and the individual, and they explored this relationship through fieldwork, during which they became acquainted with native informants "one on one." Because Boas was the first person to teach general anthropology at an American university, his students did not have academic backgrounds in the subject. Many of them, including Kroeber, came from classics, literature, and the "arts," where the intellectual outlook was humanistic. All this made Boasian anthropology ripe for psychology, but the psychology of Freud, being formulated at the time, was anathema to the Boasian program. Freud's views were evolutionary and excessively speculative; his theories of instinct and racial memory were hereditarian; his scenario for the primal family was ethnocentric; and, judged by modern standards, his views on the differences between men and women were sexist. If Freudian psychology were to prove useful, it would have to be purged of these elements.

Toward the middle of the twentieth century, psychoanalyst Abram Kardiner (1891-1981) blended a purged version of Freudian psychology into anthropology to create what is known as the American "psychodynamic" school. Before that, Boasian anthropologists used psychology idiosyncratically. The two early Boasians to use psychology to greatest effect were Margaret Mead and her colleague and teacher Ruth Benedict.

Margaret Mead (1901-78) became the most famous anthropologist of the middle twentieth century. She came to anthropology from psychology and literature and, inspired by Boas at Columbia, abandoned aspirations to write poetry in favour of a career that she felt "mattered." Boas was impressed with Mead and took charge of her career, encouraging her to do fieldwork in Samoa, where she spent nine months in the early 1920s. Mead was then in her early 20s, an age that critics such as Derek Freeman (see Selection 26) have subsequently observed to be extremely young. Boas wanted Mead to find ethnographic evidence that would disprove psychological assertions that certain human behaviours are universal and biologically fixed. Mead chose to study the behaviour of adolescent Samoan girls, whom she found to be calmer and less troublesome than adolescents in the United States. She attributed this difference to the relative sexual permissiveness of Samoan culture, so she, and Boas, concluded that his mission had been accomplished. Mead published her findings in her first book, *Coming of Age in Samoa* (1928), which she wrote for a general audience and which became an American bestseller, launching her career as an outspoken social critic.

Selection 11 is the "Introduction" to *Coming of Age in Samoa*. In it, Mead unequivocally sets forth her agenda, pronouncing that culture, not race, shapes personality, so that children grow up exhibiting whatever personality traits their culture rewards. Personality is "plastic," not fixed, a point that can be made clear by studying cultures simpler and more homogenous than the United States. Mead's statement that "...a trained student can master the fundamental structure of a primitive society in a few months.... " has been criticized as naive. Her justification of anthropologists studying exotic peoples, however, is still recognized as wise: the exotic are a mirror that reflects what the familiar really means. Throughout her career, Mead developed these and related themes in a series of ethnographically based books, including *Growing Up in New Guinea* (1930) and *Sex and Temperament in Three Primitive Societies* (1935). These books advanced the principle of cultural relativism, or the principle that ethnocentrism is wrong. Cultural relativism is an enduring legacy of Boasian anthropology.

Ruth Benedict (1887-1948) also wrote poetry and had professional literary aspirations that she set aside to become an anthropologist under the tutelage of Boas. Benedict was a faculty member at Columbia by the time Mead arrived there, so she was also Mead's teacher. Benedict's paramount publication was *Patterns of Culture* (1934), an ethnographic contrast of three cultures: the Kwakiutl of the Pacific Northwest, the Zuñi of the American Southwest, and the Dobuans of the South Pacific. Drawing somewhat on her own fieldwork, but mainly on the fieldwork of others, she characterized each culture by a dominant personality pattern or configuration—a gestalt. A major source of this idea was the configurationalism of fellow Boasian Alfred Louis Kroeber, which Benedict elaborated literarily. Borrowing labels from the German philosopher Friedrich Nietzsche (1844-1900), she characterized the Kwakiutl as Dionysian, or megalomaniacal and prone to excess in excruciating vision quests and extravagant ceremonies such as the potlatch. She characterized the Zuñi as Apollonian, or pacific, and engaging in ceremonies with moderation of sexual expression. The Dobuans were "paranoid," or preoccupied with theft and the fear that they might be accused of stealing sweet potatoes through witchcraft. For Benedict, these characterizations demonstrated the cultural relativity of personality traits. For decades, owing to its persuasiveness, *Patterns of Culture* remained an anthropology "classic."

Selection 12, "The Individual and the Pattern of Culture," is the final chapter of *Patterns of Culture*. In it, Benedict argues that the individual and culture are not antagonistic, as Freud maintained, because the personality of the individual is drawn *from* culture. This relationship is difficult to discern in complex cultures because they appear to regulate personality and deny it freedom of expression. On the other hand, ethnographic analysis of simpler cultures shows how cultures select from an array of potential personalities those that are culturally appropriate and then nurture and define them as normal. Most people grow up conforming their personalities to these cultural forces, but a minority do not, and their personalities are disapproved and defined as abnormal. Benedict's main point is that what is abnormal in one culture can be normal in another culture; for example, homosexuals and seizure-prone individuals are looked down upon in the United States but acclaimed elsewhere as berdaches and shamen. The unflattering and self-deprecating features of "abnormal" personalities are part of an inferiority complex instilled by cultures. If cultures would be more tolerant, fewer people would feel like misfits, and the world would be a better place.

During World War II, Mead, Benedict, and other Boasian anthropologists worked for the American government to help defeat the enemy Axis and the racist ideology of Nazism. One of their contributions was to study enemy cultures "at a distance" to determine how they worked. This approach produced "national character" studies such as Benedict's ethnography of Japan, *The Chrysanthemum and the Sword* (1946). Meanwhile, other anthropologists employed extreme Freudian frameworks that attributed the personality of entire nations to a single child-rearing practice such as premature toilet training or the restrictive swaddling of infants. For a while, these studies gave more sophisticated examinations of culture and personality a bad reputation, until Kardiner's psychodynamic model took hold. In the rich history of psychological anthropology, Mead and Benedict remain distinguished pre-psychodynamic pioneers.

Language and Culture

One of Boas's specializations was anthropological linguistics. Language was important for fieldwork, and it was inextricably bound up with culture, so Boas encouraged his students to study as many languages as possible in order to become better ethnographers and theorists. The student who pursued the study of language with the greatest diligence and sophistication was Edward Sapir.

Edward Sapir (1884-1939) was a close friend of Margaret Mead and Ruth Benedict, with whom he exchanged poetry and other literary efforts. Like Mead and Benedict, he was interested in the relationship between culture and personality. More than them, however, he saw culture as conditioned by language, a theme he developed in numerous publications, including "The Unconscious Patterning of Behavior in Society," first published in 1927 and reproduced in this reader as Selection 13. Unlike Durkheim, for whom society was a realm onto itself, Sapir sees society as an extension of individuals and therefore considers it appropriate to study society using psychological concepts. These concepts lead to linguistics, because language is a set of formal rules carried around in peoples's heads. These rules, or—again in the spirit of Kroeber—patterns, are unconscious, meaning that people act on them but are not always aware of them and cannot always identify them even when asked. Nevertheless, they are powerful conditioners of culture. For example, the linguistic expression of plurality, or number, has a bewildering variety of patterns in different languages, no one of which is absolutely better than another. For Sapir, anthropological linguistics illustrates the principle of cultural relativism.

In Selection 13, Sapir makes a case for culture being *like* language, more intuited than consciously perceived. This insight has major implications for anthropological theory, which can be discerned in the following passage:

> Let anyone who doubts this try the experiment of making a painstaking report of the actions of a group of natives engaged in some form of activity, say religious, to which he has not the cultural key. If he is a skillful writer, he may succeed in giving a picturesque account of what he sees and hears, or thinks he sees and hears, but the chances of his being able to give a relation of what happens in terms that would be intelligible and acceptable to the natives themselves are practically nil. He will be guilty of all manner of distortion. His emphasis will be constantly askew. He will find interesting what the natives take for granted as a casual kind of behavior worthy of no particular comment, and he will utterly fail to observe the crucial turning points in the course of action that give formal significance to the whole in the minds of those who do possess the key to its understanding.

Astute students will discern in this passage germs of "emics," a term coined in the 1950s by linguist Kenneth Pike. Emics is the suffix of the word "phonemics" and means the insider's, or native's, interpretation of culture. Pike contrasted emics with "etics," the suffix of the word "phonetics" and meaning the outsider's, or anthropologist's, interpretation of culture. In the middle twentieth century, emics versus etics became a topic of anthropological debate, prompted mainly by theorist Marvin Harris. If not always by name, emics also became incorporated into the middle-twentieth century school of cognitive anthropology, which portrayed cultures as "codes" that could be cracked with so-called ethnosemantic techniques. Furthermore, emics became implicit in late twentieth-century theories of some symbolic anthropologists, interpretive anthropologists, and postmodernists, who, like Sapir in 1927, argued that it is impossible to really "know" another culture because cultures are indistinct, incommensurable, or untranslatable.

In the late 1930s, as the Boasian era of American anthropology was drawing to a close, Sapir collaborated with Benjamin Lee Whorf (1897-1941) to formulate what is called the Sapir-Whorf hypothesis. This hypothesis, for which Sapir is best remembered in anthropological theory, states that patterns, or categories, of language and culture are isomorphic, or exhibit corresponding forms. These forms are mutually reinforcing, so that language and culture contribute to one another—but language predominates. The Sapir-Whorf hypothesis is a bridge to middle twentieth-century anthropological theories. The core of the hypothesis appears in Sapir's 1927 essay. Its seeds were planted by Boas and nurtured by the anthropological theories he inspired.

British Social Anthropology

While Franz Boas and his students were establishing the school of cultural historicism in the United States, Alfred Reginald Radcliffe-Brown (1881-1955) and Bronislaw Malinowski (1884-1942) were establishing the school of social anthropology in Great Britain. Like Boasians, British social anthropologists wanted to distance themselves from the evolutionism and hereditarianism of nineteenth-century anthropology—but in a different way. The key influences on British social anthropology were Émile Durkheim and a group of anthropologists known as the Cambridge School.

From Durkheim, British social anthropologists, especially Radcliffe-Brown, borrowed the idea of the organic analogy, the idea that society is like an organism. Accordingly, analogous to what biologists would study in anatomy and physiology, society had social structures and functions. The structures were the social components that functioned together to maintain social equilibrium, or what Durkheim had called social solidarity. Whereas Marxists saw society riven with conflict and potential dysfunction, British social anthropologists saw it, despite internal differences, as essentially harmonious and intact. Whereas Freud saw society as opposed to human nature, British social anthropologists, especially Malinowski, saw it as an instrument to satisfy human needs. And whereas Boas saw society, or culture, as a diachronic product of the past, British social anthropologists saw it as a synchronic composition of structures functioning together in the present. These theoretical outlooks made British social anthropology different from contemporary American anthropology and from nineteenth-century anthropology in both the United States and Europe.

The focus of British anthropologists on society rather than culture derives in large part from the Cambridge School, a group of anthropologists active at Cambridge University at the turn of the twentieth century. Its most influential members were Alfred Cort Haddon (1855-1940), Charles Seligman (1873-1940), and William H.R. Rivers (1864-1922), who undertook an expedition to the Torres Strait region of New Guinea to pioneer the "genealogical method" of ethnographic research. This method was based on the insight that the nub of primitive social organization is kinship, a complex web of social relationships governing individuals. Although kinship has many cultural dimensions, including ideological and economic dimensions, British anthropologists focused on its social dimension. As a result, contrasted with contemporary American cultural anthropology, their focus appears narrow.

The prototypical British social anthropologist was Alfred Reginald Radcliffe-Brown, who was trained at Cambridge University and held academic appointments at several other Commonwealth universities, including Oxford. Radcliffe-Brown's best-known fieldwork was done in the Andaman Islands near India in the Bay of Bengal. Selection 14, "Social Structure," is an excerpt from his unfinished introductory textbook, published posthumously in *Method in Social Anthropology* (1958). In this selection, he asks, "Just what is it that social anthropologists study?" His answer, of course, is "society," but not society as a discrete entity in the vision of Herbert Spencer. Rather, society comprises the *processes* of the social life of individuals. Although Radcliffe-Brown acknowledges that societies have histories, his preference is to study them for limited periods of time, as he does in examining the structures and functions of Australian aboriginal society, with its kin-based tribes, hordes, and sections. In "Social Structure" students will find a succinct statement of classic British social anthropological theory.

Bronislaw Malinowski differed from Radcliffe-Brown in both theory and intellectual style. Polish by birth, Malinowski studied anthropology at the London School of Economics. He was visiting the South Pacific when World War I broke out but was allowed to remain on the Trobriand Islands, where he spent years engaged in ethnographic research. In the early twentieth century, ethnographic fieldwork became broader and more intense than it had been in the nineteenth century. Malinowski was the early twentieth-century fieldworker *par excellence*. Although his classic Trobriand Islands fieldwork was multidimensional—including an ethnographic evaluation of the theories of Sigmund Freud—its central theme was the *kula* ring of inter-island trade. This theme is invoked in the title of his classic ethnography *Argonauts of the Western Pacific* (1922).

Selection 15 is the "Introduction" to Malinowski's *Argonauts*. It serves as an instructive contrast with the introduction to Margaret Mead's *Coming of Age in Samoa*, published just six years later. While Mead makes her fieldwork sound relatively easy, Malinowski makes his sound like extremely demanding and difficult work. He describes what has been called the "participant-observation" method of fieldwork, meaning the artful balance of the "insider" perspective of the native and the "outsider" perspective of the anthropologist—or, a balance between emics and etics. As a primer in how to do ethnography, *Argonauts of the Western Pacific* has been read by generations of anthropologists in preparation for their own first fieldwork experiences. Malinowski warns about the personal stresses of fieldwork, which he detailed in diaries published posthumously as *A Diary in the Strict Sense of the Term* (1967).

Although Malinowski was a functionalist, his version of functionalism differed from that of Radcliffe-Brown. For Malinowski, culture functioned simply to satisfy human needs, which began as basic biological needs and, through culture, were transformed into instrumental and integrative needs. A lot of those needs were sexual, which Malinowski described in books with provocative titles such as *Sex and Repression in Savage Society* (1927) and *The Sexual Life of Savages* (1929). In so doing, he joined Mead and other Boasians in earning a reputation for anthropology as iconoclastic and bold.

British social anthropologists conducted much of their fieldwork in British colonies, notably in Africa. In 1940, social anthropologists Meyer Fortes (1902-73) and E.E. Evans-Pritchard (1906-83) edited a major volume of essays on African ethnology titled *African Political Systems*. In this volume, prefaced by Radcliffe-Brown, they presented descriptions of eight African political systems divided into two groups, those with centralized authority, or states, and those without centralized authority, or non-states. *African Political Systems* has been the subject of controversy in anthropology, with some anthropologists citing its deficiencies in diachronic and cultural perspectives and criticizing its implied acceptance of the British colonial policy of indirect rule. Selection 16 is the editors' "Introduction" to *African Political Systems*. In it, Fortes and Evans-Pritchard make the point that political systems are embedded in social systems. Declaring the origins of political systems undeterminable, and the connection between society and culture problematic, they seek to expose the structural similarities among societies by stripping them of their cultural "idiom." This selection is a classic expression of British social anthropology in its later phase. By reading the selection carefully, students will be in a better position to decide for themselves whether British social anthropology deserves all the criticism it has received.

Beginning in the late 1930s, a number of second-generation British social anthropologists sought to revitalize the school by incorporating diverse theoretical perspectives. Along with C. Daryll Forde, both Fortes and Evans-Pritchard, author of the classic African ethnography *The Nuer* (1940), attempted to show how social structures have cultural dimensions. Meanwhile, in *We, the Tikopia* (1936), Raymond Firth (b.1901) added ingredients of history and economics, and in *Political Systems of Highland Burma* (1954), Edmund Leach (1910-89) undertook a structural-functional analysis of conflict. These efforts were symptomatic of the beginning of major changes in anthropological theory, marked by the deaths of Malinowski (1942), Radcliffe-Brown (1955), and Boas (1942). With the passing of these early twentieth-century "giants," British and American anthropology entered a new, middle-twentieth-century phase.

Max Weber: Forerunner of Culture and Political Economy and Postmodernism

Anthropology is the study of people, but until the early twentieth century, anthropologists did not very often portray people in the flesh and blood. Instead, they concentrated on human institutions, beliefs, traits, races, languages, and artifacts in the abstract, devoid of individuals. This situation began to change with the introduction of long-term ethnographic fieldwork, as the pioneering ethnographies of Bronislaw Malinowski and Margaret Mead can attest. Still, at the level of *theory*, there was a lack of vision of people as creative agents of their own destiny and cultural change. Not until the late twentieth century did anthropologists began to construct theories based on human "agency," or action, operation, and power. When they did so, they referred to early twentieth-century German sociologist Max Weber (1864-1920).

Contrasted with other early intellectual "giants" such as Darwin, Marx, Durkheim, and Freud, Weber saw people as more than shaped by external forces, whether these forces be hereditary, material, social, or psychic. Instead, situated in these forces was the "ideational," or imaginative, potentiality of individuals who could transform the circumstances of their own lives and the lives of others. For Weber, this potentiality was best expressed in religion, which in turn was rooted in the material conditions of life.

Weber's theory of religion is explicated in two of his best-known works, *The Protestant Ethic and the Spirit of Capitalism* (1920) and *The Sociology of Religion* (1922). In these works, he describes how, in the evolution of complex societies, human labour intensifies and differentiates, leading to stratified socioeconomic classes. The lower classes, which he refers to as "relatively non-privileged," feel marginalized and alienated. The discrepancy between their world as it *is* and—if God is fair-minded—their world as it *should be* causes existential stress, which is expressed in religion, which in turn drives social transformation. Because the world seems unfair, religion promises salvation from the world, which is accomplished through a radical restructuring of beliefs about the world and associated ethical standards. This whole process entails what Weber calls "inner-worldly asceticism," or a retreat from worldly corruption. A crucial feature of his theory of religion is his belief that material prosperity is not inherently corrupting and, in fact, is evidence of good standing before God. The prime example of his theory was the Calvinist Protestant reform movement of sixteenth-century Europe. According to Weber, the founder of Calvinism, John Calvin (1509-64), was a charismatic religious prophet who alleviated the stress of middle-class artisans and merchants by elevating hard work and material acquisitiveness to a standard of ethical superiority that, if followed, would be rewarded in the here-and-now and hereafter. The Protestant ethic, then, nurtured capitalism with spiritual support.

Selection 17, "The Sociology of Charismatic Authority," is excerpted from Weber's *Wirtschaft und Gesellschaft* [*Domestic Economy and Society*], a work written mainly before 1914 but published posthumously in 1922. In this work, Weber contrasts major forms of political authority, including "patriarchialism," "patrimonialism," "feudalism," and "charismatic authority." With the authority of charisma, prophets such as Calvin are able to instigate religious renewal on the basis of their claim to having received a revelation of divine Truth, which re-integrates beliefs and conduct and achieves spiritual harmony. The opposite of bureaucrats, charismatic figures draw their authority not from office but from outstanding personal qualifications and "gifts," including seizure and trance. Transporting themselves and others beyond everyday experience, as, for example, do sorcerers and shamans, they suspend the old spiritual order and make it possible to synthesize a new order that is more satisfying in a new material world. In this way, charismatics are model agents of cultural reconstruction and change.

In anthropology, Weber's ideas lay dormant for several decades until, beginning in the 1960s, they were "discovered" by anthropologists seeking to humanize anthropological theory. In particular, "culture and political economists" and, later, "postmodernists" were attracted to Weber because he provided a powerful theoretical framework for analyzing the impact of global capitalism and Western hegemony, or predominance. A classic ethnographic adaptation of Weber's ideas was Peter Worsley's *The Trumpet Shall Sound* (1968), which featured an analysis of Melanesian "cargo cults" as revitalizing responses to culture stress. Anthony F.C. Wallace used a similar mode of analysis in *The Death and Rebirth of the Seneca* (1972). Wallace also incorporated Weberian themes into his general theory of psychology and religion, which identified the need for periodic "mazeway" resyntheses, or reorientations of world view. A more recent use of Weber's ideas can be found in Jean and John Comaroff's *Of Revelation and Revolution* (1991), which analyzes the impact of colonialism in South Africa. These and like-minded anthropologists are indebted to Weber for bringing to their theoretical attention the culturally transforming power of people.

8

The Methods of Ethnology[1]

FRANZ BOAS

During the last ten years the methods of inquiry into the historical development of civilization have undergone remarkable changes. During the second
half of the last century evolutionary thought held almost complete sway and
investigators like **Spencer**, Morgan, Tylor, Lubbock, to mention only a few,
were under the spell of the idea of a general, uniform evolution of culture in
which all parts of mankind participated. The newer development goes back in
part to the influence of **Ratzel** whose geographical training impressed him
with the importance of **diffusion** and migration. The problem of diffusion was
taken up in detail particularly in America, but was applied in a much wider
sense by **Foy** and **Graebner**, and finally seized upon in a still wider application by **Elliot Smith** and **Rivers**, so that at the present time, at least among
certain groups of investigators in England and also in Germany, ethnological
research is based on the concept of migration and dissemination rather than
upon that of evolution.

A critical study of these two directions of inquiry shows that each is founded on the application of one fundamental hypothesis. The evolutionary point of
view presupposes that the course of historical changes in the cultural life of
mankind follows definite laws which are applicable everywhere, and which
bring it about that cultural development is, in its main lines, the same among
all races and all peoples. This idea is clearly expressed by Tylor in the introductory pages of his classic work "Primitive Culture." As soon as we admit that
the hypothesis of a uniform evolution has to be proved before it can be accepted, the whole structure loses its foundation. It is true that there are indications
of parallelism of development in different parts of the world, and that similar
customs are found in the most diverse and widely separated parts of the globe.
The occurrence of these similarities which are distributed so irregularly that
they cannot readily be explained on the basis of diffusion, is one of the foundations of the evolutionary hypothesis, as it was the foundation of **Bastian**'s

psychologizing treatment of cultural phenomena. On the other hand, it may be recognized that the hypothesis implies the thought that our modern Western European civilization represents the highest cultural development toward which all other more primitive cultural types tend, and that, therefore, retrospectively, we construct an **orthogenetic** development towards our own modern civilization. It is clear that if we admit that there may be different ultimate and co-existing types of civilization, the hypothesis of one single general line of development cannot be maintained.

Opposed to these assumptions is the modern tendency to deny the existence of a general evolutionary scheme which would represent the history of the cultural development the world over. The hypothesis that there are inner causes which bring about similarities of development in remote parts of the globe is rejected and in its place it is assumed that identity of development in two different parts of the globe must always be due to migration and diffusion. On this basis historical contact is demanded for enormously large areas. The theory demands a high degree of stability of cultural traits such as is apparently observed in many primitive tribes, and it is furthermore based on the supposed coexistence of a number of diverse and mutually independent cultural traits which reappear in the same combinations in distant parts of the world. In this sense, modern investigation takes up anew **Gerland**'s theory of the persistence of a number of cultural traits which were developed in one center and carried by man in his migrations from continent to continent.

It seems to me that if the hypothetical foundations of these two extreme forms of ethnological research are broadly stated as I have tried to do here, it is at once clear that the correctness of the assumptions has not been demonstrated, but that arbitrarily the one or the other has been selected for the purpose of obtaining a consistent picture of cultural development. These methods are essentially forms of classification of the static phenomena of culture according to two distinct principles, and interpretations of these classifications as of historical significance, without, however, any attempt to prove that this interpretation is justifiable. To give an example: It is observed that in most parts of the world there are resemblances between decorative forms that are representative and others that are more or less geometrical. According to the evolutionary point of view, their development is explained by arranging the decorative forms in such order that the most representative forms are placed at the beginning, the others being so placed that they show a gradual transition from representative to purely conventional geometric forms. This order is then interpreted as meaning that geometric designs originated from representative designs which gradually degenerated. This method has been pursued, for instance, by **Putnam, Stolpe, Balfour**, and **Haddon**, and by Verworn and, in his earlier writings, by **von den Steinen**. While I do not mean to deny that this development may have occurred, it would be rash to generalize and to claim that in every case the classification which has been made according to a definite principle represents an historical development. The order might as well be reversed and we might begin with a simple geometric element which, by the addition of new traits, might be developed into a representative design, and we might claim that this order represents an historical sequence. Both of these possibilities were considered by **Holmes** as early as 1885. Neither the one nor the other theory can be established without actual historical proof.

The opposite attitude, namely, origin through diffusion, is exhibited in **Heinrich Schurtz**'s attempt to connect the decorative art of Northwest America with that of Melanesia. The simple fact that in these areas elements occur that may be interpreted as eyes, induced him to assume that both have a common origin, without allowing for the possibility that the pattern in the two areas—each of which shows highly distinctive characteristics—may have developed from independent sources. In this attempt Schurtz followed Ratzel who had already tried to establish connections between Melanesia and Northwest America on the basis of other cultural features.

While ethnographical research based on these two fundamental hypotheses seems to characterize the general tendency of European thought, a different method is at present pursued by the majority of American anthropologists. The difference between the two directions of study may perhaps best be summarized by the statement that American scholars are primarily interested in the dynamic phenomena of cultural change, and try to elucidate cultural history by the application of the results of their studies; and that they relegate the solution of the ultimate question of the relative importance of parallelism of cultural development in distant areas, as against worldwide diffusion, and stability of cultural traits over long periods to a future time when the actual conditions of cultural change are better known. The American ethnological methods are analogous to those of European, particularly of Scandinavian, archaeology, and of the researches into the prehistoric period of the eastern Mediterranean area.

It may seem to the distant observer that American students are engaged in a mass of detailed investigations without much bearing upon the solution of the ultimate problems of a philosophic history of human civilization. I think this interpretation of the American attitude would be unjust because the ultimate questions are as near to our hearts as they are to those of other scholars, only we do not hope to be able to solve an intricate historical problem by a formula.

First of all, the whole problem of cultural history appears to us as an historical problem. In order to understand history it is necessary to know not only how things are, but how they have come to be. In the domain of ethnology, where, for most parts of the world, no historical facts are available except those that may be revealed by archaeological study, all evidence of change can be inferred only by indirect methods. Their character is represented in the researches of students of comparative philology. The method is based on the comparison of static phenomena combined with the study of their distribution. What can be done by this method is well illustrated by **Lowie**'s investigations of the military societies of the plains Indians, or by the modern investigation of American mythology. It is, of course, true that we can never hope to obtain incontrovertible data relating to the chronological sequence of events, but certain general broad outlines can be ascertained with a high degree of probability, even of certainty.

As soon as these methods are applied, primitive society loses the appearance of absolute stability which is conveyed to the student who sees a certain people only at a certain given time. All cultural forms rather appear in a constant state of flux and subject to fundamental modifications.

It is intelligible why in our studies the problem of dissemination should take a prominent position. It is much easier to prove dissemination than to follow up developments due to inner forces, and the data for such a study are obtained with much greater difficulty. They may, however, be observed in every phenomenon of **acculturation** in which foreign elements are remodeled according to the patterns prevalent in their new environment, and they may be found in the peculiar local developments of widely spread ideas and activities. The reason why the study of inner development has not been taken up energetically, is not due to the fact that from a theoretical point of view it is unimportant, it is rather due to the inherent methodological difficulties. It may perhaps be recognized that in recent years attention has been drawn to this problem, as is manifested by the investigations on the processes of acculturation and of the interdependence of cultural activities which are attracting the attention of many investigators.

The further pursuit of these inquiries emphasizes the importance of a feature which is common to all historic phenomena. While in natural sciences we are accustomed to consider a given number of causes and to study their effects, in historical happenings we are compelled to consider every phenomenon not only as effect but also as cause. This is true even in the particular application of the laws of physical nature, as, for instance, in the study of astronomy in which the position of certainly heavenly bodies at a given moment may be considered as the effect of gravitation, while, at the same time, their particular arrangement in space determines future changes. This relation appears much more clearly in the history of human civilization. To give an example: a surplus of food supply is liable to bring about an increase of population and an increase of leisure, which gives opportunity for occupations that are not absolutely necessary for the needs of every day life. In turn the increase of population and of leisure, which may be applied to new inventions, give rise to a greater food supply and to a further increase in the amount of leisure, so that a cumulative effect results.

Similar considerations may be made in regard to the important problem of the relation of the individual to society, a problem that has to be considered whenever we study the dynamic conditions of change. The activities of the individual are determined to a great extent by his social environment, but in turn his own activities influence the society in which he lives, and may bring about modifications in its form. Obviously, this problem is one of the most important ones to be taken up in a study of cultural changes. It is also beginning to attract the attention of students who are no longer satisfied with the systematic enumeration of standardized beliefs and customs of a tribe, but who begin to be interested in the question of the way in which the individual reacts to his whole social environment, and to the differences of opinion and of mode of action that occur in primitive society and which are the causes of far-reaching changes.

In short then, the method which we try to develop is based on a study of the dynamic changes in society that may be observed at the present time. We refrain from the attempt to solve the fundamental problem of the general development of civilization until we have been able to unravel the processes that are going on under our eyes.

Certain general conclusions may be drawn from this study even now. First of all, the history of human civilization does not appear to us as determined entirely by psychological necessity that leads to a uniform evolution the world over. We rather see that each cultural group has its own unique history, dependent partly upon the peculiar inner development of the social group, and partly upon the foreign influences to which it has been subjected. There have been processes of gradual differentiation as well as processes of leveling down differences between neighboring cultural centers, but it would be quite impossible to understand, on the basis of a single evolutionary scheme, what happened to any particular people. An example of the contrast between the two points of view is clearly indicated by a comparison of the treatment of the Zuñi civilization by Frank Hamilton Cushing on the one hand, on the other by modern students, particularly by **Elsie Clews Parsons**, **Leslie Spier**, **Ruth Benedict** and **Ruth Bunzel**. Cushing believed that it was possible to explain Zuñi culture entirely on the basis of the reaction of the Zuñi mind to its geographical environment, and that the whole of Zuñi culture could be explained as the development which followed necessarily from the position in which the people were placed. Cushing's keen insight into the Indian mind and his thorough knowledge of the most intimate life of the people gave great plausibility to his interpretations. On the other hand, Dr. Parsons' studies prove conclusively the deep influence which Spanish ideas have had upon Zuñi culture, and, together with

Professor **Kroeber**'s investigations, give us one of the best examples of acculturation that have come to our notice. The psychological explanation is entirely misleading, notwithstanding its plausibility, and the historical study shows us an entirely different picture, in which the unique combination of ancient traits (which in themselves are undoubtedly complex) and of European influences, have brought about the present condition.

Studies of the dynamics of primitive life also show that an assumption of long-continued stability such as is demanded by Elliot Smith is without any foundation in fact. Wherever primitive conditions have been studied in detail, they can be proved to be in a state of flux, and it would seem that there is a close parallelism between the history of language and the history of general cultural development. Periods of stability are followed by periods of rapid change. It is exceedingly improbable that any customs of primitive people should be preserved unchanged for thousands of years. Furthermore, the phenomena of acculturation prove that a transfer of customs from one region into another without concomitant changes due to acculturation, are very rare. It is, therefore, very unlikely that ancient Mediterranean customs could be found at the present time practically unchanged in different parts of the globe, as Elliot Smith's theory demands.

While on the whole the unique historical character of cultural growth in each area stands out as a salient element in the history of cultural development, we may recognize at the same time that certain typical parallelisms do occur. We are, however, not so much inclined to look for these similarities in detailed customs as rather in certain dynamic conditions which are due to social or psychological causes that are liable to lead to similar results. The example of the relation between food supply and population to which I referred before may serve as an example. Another type of example is presented in those cases in which a certain problem confronting man may be solved by a limited number of methods only. When we find, for instance, marriage as a universal institution, it may be recognized that marriage is possible only between a number of men and a number of women; a number of men and one woman; a number of women and one man; or one man and one woman. As a matter of fact, all these forms are found the world over and it is, therefore, not surprising that analogous forms should have been adopted quite independently in different parts of the world, and, considering both the general economic conditions of mankind and the character of sexual instinct in the higher animals, it also does not seem surprising that group marriage and **polyandrous** marriages should be comparatively speaking rare. Similar considerations may also be made in regard to the philosophical views held by mankind. In short, if we look for laws, the laws relate to the effects of physiological, psychological, and social conditions, not to sequences of cultural achievement.

In some cases a regular sequence of these may accompany the development of the psychological or social status. This is illustrated by the sequence of industrial inventions in the Old World and in America, which I consider as independent. A period of food gathering and of the use of stone was followed by the invention of agriculture, of pottery and finally of the use of metals. Obviously, this order is based on the increased amount of time given by mankind to the use of natural products, of tools and utensils, and to the variations that developed with it. Although in this case parallelism seems to exist on the two continents, it would be futile to try to follow out the order in detail. As a matter of fact, it does not apply to other inventions. The domestication of animals, which, in the Old World must have been an early achievement, was very late in the New World, where domesticated animals, except the dog, hardly existed at all at the time of discovery. A slight beginning had been made in Peru with the taming of the llama, and birds were kept in various parts of the continent.

A similar consideration may be made in regard to the development of rationalism. It seems to be one of the fundamental characteristics of the development of mankind that activities which have developed unconsciously are gradually made the subject of reasoning. We may observe this process everywhere. It appears, perhaps, most clearly in the history of science which has gradually extended the scope of its inquiry over an ever-widening field and which has raised into consciousness human activities that are automatically performed in the life of the individual and of society.

I have not heretofore referred to another aspect of modern ethnology which is connected with the growth of psycho-analysis. Sigmund Freud has attempted to show that primitive thought is in many respects analogous to those forms of individual psychic activity which he has explored by his psycho-analytic methods. In many respects his attempts are similar to the interpretation of mythology by symbolists like Stucken. Rivers has taken hold of Freud's suggestion as well as of the interpretations of Graebner and Elliot Smith, and we find, therefore, in his new writings a peculiar disconnected application of psychologizing attitude and the application of the theory of **ancient transmission**.

While I believe some of the ideas underlying Freud's psycho-analytic studies may be fruitfully applied to ethnological problems, it does not seem to me that the one-sided exploitation of this method will advance our understanding of the development of human society. It is certainly true that the influence of impressions received during the first few years of life have been entirely underestimated and that the social behavior of man depends to a great extent upon the earliest habits which are established before the time when connected memory begins, and that many so-called racial or hereditary traits are to be considered rather as a result of early exposure to certain forms of social conditions.

Most of these habits do not rise into consciousness and are, therefore, broken with difficulty only. Much of the difference in the behavior of adult male and female may go back to this cause. If, however, we try to apply the whole theory of the influence of suppressed desire to the activities of man living under different social forms, I think we extend beyond their legitimate limits the inferences that may be drawn from the observation of normal and abnormal individual psychology. Many other factors are of greater importance. To give an example: The phenomena of language show clearly that conditions quite different from those to which psycho-analysts direct their attention determine the mental behavior of man. The general concepts underlying language are entirely unknown to most people. They do not rise into consciousness until the scientific study of grammar begins. Nevertheless, the categories of language compel us to see the world arranged in certain definite conceptual groups which, on account of our lack of knowledge of linguistic processes, are taken as objective categories and which, therefore, impose themselves upon the form of our thoughts. It is not known what the origin of these categories may be, but it seems quite certain that they have nothing to do with the phenomena which are the subject of psycho-analytic study.

The applicability of the psycho-analytic theory of symbolism is also open to the greatest doubt. We should remember that symbolic interpretation has occupied a prominent position in the philosophy of all times. It is present not only in primitive life, but the history of philosophy and of theology abounds in examples of a high development of symbolism, the type of which depends upon the general mental attitude of the philosopher who develops it. The theologians who interpreted the Bible on the basis of religious symbolism were no less certain of the correctness of their views, than the psycho-analysts are of their interpretations of thought and conduct based on sexual symbolism. The results of a symbolic interpretation depend primarily upon the subjective attitude of the investigator who arranges phenomena according to his leading concept. In order to prove the applicability of the symbolism of psycho-analysis, it would be necessary to show that a symbolic interpretation from other entirely different points of view would not be equally plausible, and that explanations that leave out symbolic significance or reduce it to a minimum, would not be adequate.

While, therefore, we may welcome the application of every advance in the method of psychological investigation, we cannot accept as an advance in ethnological method the crude transfer of a novel, one-sided method of psychological investigation of the individual to social phenomena the origin of which can be shown to be historically determined and to be subject to influences that are not at all comparable to those that control the psychology of the individual.

Note
1   *American Anthropologist*, N.S., vol. 22 (1920), pp. 311-322.

Study Questions
1.   What are Boas's criticisms of cultural evolutionist and diffusionist methods of ethnology?

2.   What method of ethnology does Boas propose as an alternative to cultural evolutionist and diffusionist methods?

3.   What does Boas think about psychological methods of ethnology?

Further Readings
Boas, Franz. 1989. *A Franz Boas Reader: The Shaping of American Anthropology, 1883-1911*. Ed. George W. Stocking, Jr. Chicago: University of Chicago Press.

Herskovits, Melville J. 1953. *Franz Boas*. New York: Scribner.

Hyatt, Marshall. 1990. *Franz Boas, Social Activist: The Dynamics of Ethnicity*. New York: Greenwood Press.

Stocking, George W., Jr. (ed.). 1996. *Volksgeist as Method and Ethic: Essays on Boasian Ethnography and the German Anthropological Tradition*. Madison: University of Wisconsin Press.

Williams, Vernon J., Jr. 1996. *Rethinking Race: Franz Boas and His Contemporaries*. Lexington: University Press of Kentucky.

9

Conclusion
[*Primitive Society*]

ROBERT LOWIE

Primitive society wears a character rather different from that popularized by Morgan's school. Instead of dull uniformity, there is mottled diversity; instead of the single **sib** pattern multiplied in fulsome profusion we detect a variety of social units, now associated with the sib, now taking its place. Let us visualize the actual aspect of primitive conditions by a concrete example from a by no means unusually complicated social environment.

In the Mountain Crow band, some eighty years ago, a woman of the Thick-lodge sib gives birth to a boy. Her husband summons a renowned warrior of his sib, the Bad-leggings, who dubs the child Strikes-three-men in memory of one of his own exploits. As Strikes-three-men grows up, he learns how to act towards the relatives on either side of his family and what conduct to expect in return. The female Thick-lodges make for him beaded shirts and moccasins, on the male members he can rely for aid in any difficulty. His father he comes to regard as the natural provider and protector of the immediate family circle; to all the other men of the Bad-leggings sib he gives presents when he can and treats them with respect. On their part they become his official eulogists as soon as he distinguishes himself by skill as a hunter or by bravery in battle; and the bond between him and them is so close that when one of them commits an offense against tribal etiquette an appropriate nickname is attached to his own person. With the children of his "fathers" a curious reciprocal relationship unites him. They are his mentors and he is theirs. They throw in his teeth his foibles and misdemeanors, and he retaliates in kind. To these various relations based on family and sib ties associational ones are soon added. He enters a league of playmates mimicking the warrior societies and tries to gain glory by striking deer and buffalo as the older braves count coup on Dakota or Cheyenne foe-men. As he grows older, Albino-bull, one of his companions, becomes a bosom friend. Together they go courting and share each other's mistresses; together they set out on war parties, each shielding the other at the risk of his own life; together they join the Fox society to which Albino-bull has been invited; and together they leave it when the rival Lumpwoods, impressed by the young men's war record, bribe them into their fold. Now a novel set of relations ensues. Strikes-three-men aids his fellow-Lumpwoods as he aids his sibmates; he and his comrade participate in all of the society's feasts and dances; and they while away leisure hours lounging and smoking in the tents of their new associates and singing Lumpwood songs. When Strikes-three-men buys a wife, still another unit is added to his social groups; added rather than substituted for the old family group because the tie that links him with his brothers and sisters remains not only unsnapped but in full force. About this time a fancy may seize our hero to cast in his lot with the band hunting about the Yellowstone confluence. Henceforth its political relations become his. With his new fellows he pays visits to the friendly Village tribes of the upper Missouri, with them he pursues a gang of Dakota raiders, and when the Mountain Crow decline to join a punitive war party against the hereditary enemy he is as vociferous as any River Crow in denouncing the pusillanimity of the band of his nativity. From the start he has been no stranger in the strange land: there are Thick-lodges on the Yellowstone who greet him as a brother, and he mingles without formality with the Lumpwoods there resident. The illness of one of his children may evoke a vow: on its recovery he pledges himself to seek admission into the Tobacco order. Four-bears, of the Weasel chapter, is willing to initiate him, and so Strikes-three-men and his wife become members, privileged to join in the annual planting of the sacred week and in all other ceremonial activities of their branch. A special bond of intimacy unites them henceforth with their sponsor Four-bears, from whom an occasional horse may be expected as a token of paternal affection.

Thus our Crow comes to be a member of some half-a-dozen well-defined groups. By birth he belongs to a sib, a family and a band. Later a life-long friendship couples him with Albino-bull; he joins the Fox and subsequently the Lumpwood organization; and is finally admitted to the religious Tobacco order. As a mature man he is simultaneously a Thick-lodge, Albino-bull's partner, a Lumpwood, a River Crow, a Weasel, besides forming the center of an individual household. Manifold as are his affiliations, they are hardly above the average in number and complexity. Under special circumstances a variety of others could be added. Through distinguished valor he may become a chief; the purchase of one medicine would establish a ceremonial tie between him and the seller; by buying another he would come to join still another definite organization, the Horse Dancers. On the whole, there is remarkably little collision of interests through this varied allegiance; and an extension of sentimental attachment takes place rather than a clash of emotions associated with diverse groups. Doubtless some obligations sit more lightly than others. If one of two comrades were affronted by their military society, both would leave it and seek entrance into another. It is also safe to infer that regard for one's wife would be readily sacrificed either to one's blood kin or to one's club. Not in the real life of the Crow bourgeois, but by the swashbuckling standard of honor to which he is content to make public obeisance, a woman is only a woman and to show overmuch solicitude on her account would mean a loss of face. But the occasions for such demonstrations are not over-numerous and the average tribesman does not suffer much distress from the variety of his memberships.

The multiplicity of social relations could be as strikingly illustrated by other examples. In the sibless **Andamans** we should have to reckon with status as determined by dietary restrictions, conjugal and parental position. A **Banks Islander** would be found to belong at once to a sib, a grade in the club, and half a dozen Ghost societies. Among the **Vedda** territorial grouping would figure prominently, and in Polynesia distinctions of caste would come to the foreground. In each and every case, however, diverse coëxisting units would have to be considered.

Multiplicity by itself would not be fatal to a generalized scheme of social evolution, for abstractly it is conceivable that at a certain definite stage in the history of the sib organization status groups would supervene, at another age-classes, and so forth. But empirically it turns out that the several types of social unit are combined in a purely capricious fashion. In one region we find secret societies with sibs; in another, sibs but no secret societies; in a third, a secret society without sibs; a fourth tribe has either or both features in combination with all sorts of associations; a fifth lacks both. Upon what principles can be fixed the chronological order of the observed combinations? Shall we say that Andamanese siblessness plus status grouping is anterior to **Maidu** siblessness and lack of status grouping plus a secret organization? And is the Melanesian union of mother-sibs, sex dichotomy with graded clubs, and Ghost societies, earlier or later than the **Hidatsa** complex of mother-sibs, military age organizations and **bundle societies**? An attempt to embody the exuberant variety of phenomena in a single chronological sequence seems hopeless. Probably even adherents of **unilinear evolution** would admit that the totality of social manifestations cannot be dealt with in this fashion and would be content with maintaining that only each distinct type of social unit or phenomenon taken by itself tends to develop through a fixed series of stages.

But this contention has been proved erroneous for practically every department of social organization. Its fallacy becomes patent as soon as we place side by side the institutions of tribes in distinct areas but on the same general level of cultural advancement. The aboriginal Australians were economically hunters and seed-gatherers, and that was the condition of the **Paviotso** of Nevada, both representing technologically the **Neolithic** stage of European archaeologists. Yet, whatever branch of their social life we compare, there is complete dissimilarity. The Australians have sibs, **moieties**, totemism, classes; among the Paviotso not even the faintest germ of these institutions is to be detected so that there is no reason to assume that they ever would have risen or fallen to a similar form of organization. Politically, too, there is no suggestion of resemblance: there is no Paviotso body with powers comparable to those of the Australian **gerontocracy**; on the other hand, there is nothing in Australia comparable to a director of the rabbit-hunt, in whom is vested what meager central authority exists in Nevada. Australians and Plateau **Shoshoneans** prove not only different but incommensurable; they represent not one line of development but two separate lines. If it be suggested that these are arbitrarily selected cases, let others be substituted. The Andamanese represent the same stage of general advancement and they are sibless like the Paviotso. But to their division into married couples, bachelors and spinsters there is no parallel among the Nevada people; and though the segregation of bachelors occurs in Australia, this partial resemblance was found to be probably the result of historical connection with the same peoples rather than of independent, spontaneous evolution.

There is no loop-hole for the specious plea that general cultural advancement and social advancement may proceed in mutual independence of each other. That argument has already been examined in another context and its worthlessness appears when peoples are grouped precisely according to the complexity of their *social* institutions. From that angle, the Negroes and the Polynesians, who would occupy quite different rungs technologically, may be regarded as roughly equivalent. Yet to compare Uganda and Hawaii is to pass from one cultural universe to another: the Africans are devoid of the Polynesian caste system founded on divine lineage; and throughout Polynesia not a trace appears of that complicated jurisprudence that is so marked a trait of Negro Africa. If the assumed laws of social evolution operate neither among peoples of like general condition nor among peoples of generally like complexity of social organization, where can they possibly be conceived to operate?

But what of the resemblances that undoubtedly do occur in widely separated areas? Is it not an inherent law that produces polyandry in Eskimo and **Toda** communities or sibs among the Pueblo and **Gros Ventre** Indians? At this point it is desirable to discriminate more sharply than has hitherto been done between the theory of independent development, which I have again and again advocated, and a belief in laws regulating the independent reproduction of the same *series* of stages which I now at the close of my investigation formally abjure. Undoubtedly there are certain conditions that may recur in different areas and produce similar results. Scarcity of women and polyandry were seen to be thus causally linked, but as I have already shown in the appropriate place the parallelism is of strictly limited scope. The common cause of polyandry is female infanticide, but the cause of infanticide was seen to vary, while the implications of polyandry again show divergence in the two regions after the brief span of likeness. Generally speaking, the duplication of conditions may indeed produce the duplication of one sequence but there the matter ends. For the course of cultural evolution depends not on that single element of similarity but on the whole complex of associated features as well, and since *these* are not alike nor indeed well can be alike in peoples with a distinct body of cultural traditions, the effect is almost inevitably divergence so far as any advancement occurs at all. But it should be noted that often enough such advancement is not observed; development terminates in a blind alley with no possibility of further parallelism. When we have recognized how a like social point of view can produce a similar term of opprobrium among Australian blacks and Crow Indians, that is as far as we can go. There is no further social result flowing from the use of similar vituperative epithets, nor can any further consequence therefrom be readily imagined. At this juncture it is well to revert to the linguistic analogy of the introductory chapter. When the Shoshoni and the Greeks independently evoke a dual number, this is the result of similar classificatory processes, but what is the general import of the isolated resemblance? Precisely nil. It has not inaugurated a series of morphological changes making both languages conform to a common linguistic pattern. To be sure, it is conceivable that a classification of the type mentioned might be correlated with certain other features that are descriptively distinct though psychologically linked. The total resemblance in structure would nevertheless remain remarkably slight. Now this example illustrates my conception of the independent development of sociological or cultural traits. Independent development occurs; but its products have a negligible influence on the total course of events in their respective series, which remain essentially distinct.

The occurrence of convergent evolution—of like results achieved through different channels—might be cited as evidence of laws consummating predestined ends. But in by far the greater number of instances the likeness dissolves on closer scrutiny into a superficial or only partial resemblance. Thus **teknonymy** appeared as a possible result of a system of status designations, of feminine inferiority, or of a paucity of kinship terms. Evidently the import of the custom is quite different in these cases; or rather there are three customs which it is sometimes convenient to call by a common name. In the same way we find it convenient to group together as democracies the polities of ancient Athens and of the United States. This sets them apart for certain purposes from certain other constitutions but implies no recognition of either genetic or psychological affinity. But even where genuine likeness has been achieved we find divergence setting in after convergence, as in the case of polyandry.

Thus neither the examples of independent evolution from like causes nor those of convergent evolution from unlike causes establish an innate law of social progress. One fact, however, encountered at every stage and in every phase of society, by itself lays the axe to the root of any theory of historical laws—the extensive occurrence of diffusion. Creating nothing, this factor nevertheless makes all other agencies taper almost into nothingness beside it in its effect on the total growth of human civilization. An explanation of the ultimate origin of the Omaha sib would account for *one* sib organization; transmission accounts for that organization among a dozen tribes or more. Diffusion not merely extends the range of a feature, but in so doing it is able to level the differences of race, geographical environment, and economic status that are popularly assumed as potent instrumentalities in cultural evolution. Through diffusion the Chinese come to share Western notions of government; through diffusion the Southern Plains Indians come to share with the Iroquois of the Woodlands a type of sib that distinguishes them from their fellow-Siouans living under the same geographical conditions; through diffusion fishermen, reindeer nomads, and tillers of the soil come to entertain the identical conception of feminine disabilities. Any conceivable tendency of human society to pursue a fixed sequence of stages must be completely veiled by the incessant tendency to borrowing and thus becomes an unknowable **noumenon** that is scientifically worthless. Strangely enough, it was a jurist who clearly recognized this fact at a time when anthropologists were still chasing the will-o'-the-wisp of historical laws; and Maitland's memorable words in *Domesday Book and Beyond* may well be quoted in full: "Even had our anthropologists at their command material that would justify them in prescribing that every independent portion of mankind must, if it is to move at all, move through one fated series of stages which may be designated as Stage A, Stage B, Stage C, and so forth, we still should have to face the fact that the rapidly progressive groups have been just those which have not been independent, which have not worked out their own salvation, but have appropriated alien ideas and have thus been enabled, for anything that we can tell, to leap from Stage A to Stage X without passing through any intermediate stages. Our Anglo-Saxon ancestors did not arrive at the alphabet or at the **Nicene Creed**, by traversing a long series of 'stages'; they leapt to the one and to the other." Present ethnographical knowledge warrants us in extending Maitland's argument; we know that the relatively stationary no less than the relatively progressive peoples have evolved their culture through contact with alien ideas, and that accordingly the conditions for the operation of social laws among independent peoples nowhere exist. By all means let us register such sequences as may be found to recur in separated regions, but let us not dignify these strictly limited and sometimes trivial relations, such as that between polyandry and a paucity of women, by the pretentious title of historical laws.

To recognize the complexity and singularity of cultural phenomena, mainly as a consequence of diffusion, is then to abandon that quest of short-hand formulas prescribed by **Professor Pearson**, and it will be abandoned not from any foolish disdain for a simplification of facts but because we prefer to have the facts unsimplified than a simple statement that fails to correspond with them. The evolutionary views until recently current among anthropologists are of the category of those "laws" denounced by **Sir Henry Maine** when in 1861 he wrote as follows: "Theories, plausible and comprehensive, but absolutely unverified, ... enjoy a universal preference over sober research into the primitive history of society and law." The period has come for eschewing the all-embracing and baseless theories of yore and to settle down to that sober historical research involved in the intensive study of specific regions.

Must we, then, resign all hope of rising from a contemplation of unique series of events to an interpretation? By no means. First of all the renunciation of historical laws does not imply the renunciation of uniformities *independent of the time factor* and veritably inherent in the essence of social existence. The universality of borrowing is itself a generalization of this type, as is the implied aversion from or inability for creative effort, which in turn is correlated with the persistence of cultural features once established. Secondly, it is precisely the singular combination of traits forming the context or past history of a given feature that, in conjunction with such general sociological principles as these, furnishes an interpretation of its meaning, *as nothing else whatsoever can.* An example from Maine, that champion of sane historical methods, will elucidate the point. Maine was confronted with the fact that the later Roman republic dispensed with the death penalty, a fact which had led to explanations based on the supposed psychology of the Romans. But Maine discovered that at the time in question permanent judicial bodies were commissions holding a delegated authority from the legislative assembly, which itself lacked power of inflicting capital punishment, hence could not delegate such authority to one of its creatures. The interpretation completely clarifies the problem, carries immediate conviction, and at once exposes the speciousness of any type of explanation not founded on similar principles. When we desire to understand **Masai** age-classes or Hidatsa age-societies, we shall do well to follow not Morgan or Schurtz, but Maine; to saturate ourselves with the spirit and history of Masai and Hidatsa culture, respectively, and with that of their neighbors, rather than to fly for aid to a chimerical law of social evolution.

The principles that underlie the growth of social organization do not differ from the principles operative in culture generally. It was once believed that the stages which archaeological research reveals in western Europe must be stages mankind have everywhere been obliged to traverse. But the case of African technology suffices to disprove the assumption: the Africans did not pass from a Stone Age to an Age of Copper and Bronze and then to an Iron Age; whether through **autochthonous** advancement or through borrowing from Asiatic sources, they passed directly from the manufacture of stone tools to the manufacture of iron tools. In another phase of material civilization the American natives, except in Peru, completely failed to domesticate animals for economic use, clearly proving that, as in Yucatan and Mexico, a fairly complex cultural structure can be reared without resting on domestication as one of its supports. In the absence of an inherent law of evolution, then, social history merely conforms to the facts of culture history generally.

There is nevertheless an important difference not so much objectively as from the point of view of the appraising observer between the history of material culture and that of social organization. In the former there are periods of retrogression or stagnation alternating with eras of advancement, and the very use of these words implies criteria for judging progress. Nor is it difficult to fathom their foundation. Tools are contrivances for definite practical purposes; if these are accomplished more expeditiously and efficiently by one set of tools, then that set is better. Hence it is a purely objective judgment that metal axes are superior to those of stone. So economic activity has for its object the sustenance of human existence, and when the possibilities for supporting life are enlarged, as by the domestication of an eatable and milkable species, we are justified in speaking of a *progressive* change. But in the sphere of social life there is no objective criterion for grading cultural phenomena. The foremost philosophers are not agreed as to the ultimate ideals to be sought through social existence. Within a century Western thought and action have swung from one pole to the other, from the extremes of **Manchesterian** individualism to the extremes of state socialism; and the student's evaluation of, say, the communistic bias of Eskimo society will not be the same if he is a disciple of Herbert Spencer as it would be if he were a disciple of **Prince Kropotkin**. Democracy has become a slogan of modern times, but it has also roused the impassioned protests of men of genius and of reactionary biologists, some of whom doubtless cast wistful glances in the direction of Micronesia, lamenting the decay of that spirit of loyalty to superior rank so nobly preserved in the Marshall Islands. Again, the unqualified emancipation of woman may be the only goal consistent with strict individualism, but what if individualistic aspirations are subordinated to others, say, to the perpetuation of traditional family ideals or to **eugenic** aims? Here, too, judgment of primitive conceptions must depend on one's subjective reaction to moot-problems of modern speculation. Even where the verdict of modern society tends to unanimity, the critical investigator cannot accept it as absolutely valid. It is not obvious that obligatory monogamy is in an absolute sense the most preferable form of marriage, least of all when it is tempered with a system of **libertinage** producing something not wholly different from the system of the Masai.

In short, the appraisal of sociological features is wholly different from that of technological features of culture. The latter may be rated according to the closeness with which they accomplish known ends; the former have unknown ends or ends whose value is a matter of philosophic doubt, hence they can be graded only on subjective grounds and must scientifically be treated as incommensurable.

Of course it is true that social organizations differ in complexity, but that difference fails to provide a criterion of progress. When the Andamanese evolved or borrowed the notion of segregating bachelors from spinsters, and both from married couples, their social culture gained in complexity, but it is not easy to prove that it experienced either improvement or deterioration. If our enlightened communities coped as successfully with, say, the problem of maintaining order as ruder peoples in a simpler environment, then it might be conceded that our complex administrative machinery represents an intellectual advance. But the condition is contrary to fact, and our cumbersome method of preserving the peace and the more elegant solution of the same problem in simpler circumstances remain incommensurable.

When from definite customs and institutions we turn to the dynamics of social history, the result is again the impossibility of grading cultures, but for a different reason. Institutions are generally different and not comparable; processes are not only comparable but identical in the simpler and the higher civilizations. Thus we find the cooperative motive and the need for congenial companionship incarnated in a variety of forms among primitive peoples and at times even simulating the semblance of quite modern institutions, as in the case of the Samoan trade unions. As an invariable component of primitive life we further encounter the eternal striving for prestige, which is thus clearly a characteristic of all social aggregates. The peacock theory of primitive man does away with that shopworn commonplace that primitive society wholly merges the individual in his group. It is true that at bottom it despises individuality, for it prizes variation only in a direction it has predetermined and conformity to its standards is the price exacted for recognition. But in this respect primitive and civilized society coincide in principle, however they may differ in detail. History records a transfer of power from one mystically sanctified source of authority to another, from a church to a book, from a book to a state, or to an intangible public opinion. But with unfailing tenacity every society from the simplest to the most complex has adhered to the principle that the one unpardonable sin consists in setting up one's private judgment against the recognized social authority, in perpetrating an infraction of tribal taboos. When, therefore, Sir Henry Maine points out the growing importance of contractual instead of status relations in modern society, his argument is of formal rather than substantial significance for the history of individual freedom. In the disposal of his property an **Ewe** is not so free as an American, in other regards he is freer; and both are hedged about by a set of conventions whose breach may subject them to indignity, ostracism, and death. Neither morphologically nor dynamically can social life be said to have progressed from a stage of savagery to a stage of enlightenment.

The belief in social progress was a natural accompaniment of the belief in historical laws, especially when tinged with the evolutionary optimism of the 'seventies of the nineteenth century. If inherent necessity urges all societies along a fixed path, metaphysicians may still dispute whether the underlying force be divine or diabolic, but there can at least be no doubt as to which community is retarded and which accelerated in its movement toward the appointed goal. But no such necessity or design appears from the study of culture history. Cultures develop mainly through the borrowings due to chance contact. Our own civilization is even more largely than the rest a complex of borrowed traits. The singular order of events by which it has come into being provides no schedule for the itinerary of alien cultures. Hence the specious pleas that a given people must pass through such or such a stage in *our* history before attaining this or that destination can no longer be sustained. The student who has mastered Maitland's argument will recognize the historical and ethnologic absurdity of this solemn nonsense. In prescribing for other peoples a social programme we must always act on subjective grounds; but at least we can act unfettered by the pusillanimous fear of transgressing a mock-law of social evolution.

Nor are the facts of culture history without bearing on the adjustment of our own future. To that planless hodgepodge, that thing of shreds and patches called civilization, its historian can no longer yield superstitious reverence. He will realize better than others the obstacles to infusing design into the amorphous product; but in thought at least he will not grovel before it in fatalistic acquiescence but dream of a rational scheme to supplant the chaotic jumble.

Study Questions

1. Why does Lowie begin his selection with a lengthy description of the multiplicity of social relations among Crow Indians?

2. According to Lowie, what is the significance of diffusionism contrasted with independent and convergent evolutionism?

3. What are Lowie's views on cultural progress and historical laws?

Further Readings

Lowie, Robert H. 1937. *History of Ethnological Theory*. New York: Rinehart and Company.

—. [1959]. *Robert H. Lowie, Ethnologist: A Personal Record*. Ann Arbor, MI: Books on Demand.

—. 1960 [1920]. *Primitive Society*. London: Routledge and Kegan Paul.

Murphy, Robert Francis. 1972. *Robert H. Lowie*. New York: Columbia University Press.

Murra, John V. (ed.). 1976. *American Anthropology: The Early Years*. St. Paul, MN: West.

10

What Anthropology Is About

ALFRED LOUIS KROEBER

1. Anthropology, Biology, History 2. Organic and Sociocultural Elements 3. Organic or "Physical" Anthropology 4. Sociocultural Anthropology 5. Evolutionary Processes and Evolutionistic Fancies 6. Society and Culture 7. Anthropology and the Social Sciences

1. Anthropology, Biology, History

Anthropology is the science of man. Of course, this literal, **etymological** meaning is too broad and general. More precise would be: "the science of man and his works and behavior." But even this needs an addition to make it sufficiently specific, since no one means to claim sciences like physiology and psychology as parts of anthropology. Now physiology and psychology focus their attention on particular men, whom they examine as individuals. This gives a clue to the additional limitation we are seeking. Anthropology obviously is concerned not with particular men as such, but with men in groups, with races and peoples and their happenings and doings. So let us take as our provisional basic definition the following: "Anthropology is the science of groups of men and their behavior and productions." This will include any findings on the total human species, since this constitutes an aggregate of races or peoples, a sort of supergroup or total society.

However, man is an animal or organism and he is also a civilized being having a history and social qualities. Thus he is investigated—different aspects of him are investigated—both by the organic or biological or life sciences and by what are sometimes called the historical and more generally the social sciences. True, this latter term, "the social sciences," though commonly used, is not easy to define satisfactorily. But we can leave this difficulty for the philosopher of science. In practice, anthropology is mostly classified as being both a biological science and a social science. Some universities recognize this fact by having certain courses of anthropological study count as the one and certain as the other, or perhaps even the same course counting either way. Such a situation of double participation is unusual among the sciences. If anthropology is not concerned so predominantly with man as an animal, or with man as a social human having a history, that it can be set outright in either the life or the social-historical science category, both aspects are evidently represented significantly in its subject matter. Could it be that the specific subject of anthropology is the interrelation of what is biological in man and what is social and historical in him? The answer is Yes. Or, more broadly, anthropology does at least concern itself with both organic and social factors in man, whereas nearly all other sciences and studies deal with one or the other. Anthropology concerns itself with both sets of factors because these come associated in human beings in nature. Often they are even intertwined in one and the same phenomenon, as when a person is born with hereditary musical capacity and develops this further by studying and training. They are not always easy to disentangle; but they must be separated if the processes at work are to be understood. That job is peculiarly the anthropologist's.

2. Organic and Sociocultural Elements

To the question why a Louisiana Negro is black and longheaded, the answer is ready. He was born so. As cows produce calves, and lions, cubs, so Negro springs from Negro and Caucasian from Caucasian. We call the force at work heredity. Our same Negro is reputed amiable and easy-going. Is this too an innate quality? Offhand most of us might reply Yes. He sings at his corn-hoeing more frequently than the white man across the fence. Is this also because of his heredity? "Of course—he is made so," might be a common answer, "Probably—why not?" a more cautious one. But now our Negro is singing the "Memphis Blues," which his great-grandfather in Africa assuredly did not sing. As for the specific song, heredity can obviously no longer be the cause. Our Negro may have learned it from an uncle, or perhaps from his schoolmates; quite likely he acquired it from human beings who were not his ancestors, or over the radio, acquired it as part of his customs, like being a member of the Baptist Church and wearing overalls, and the thousand other things that come to him from without instead of from within. At these points heredity is displaced by tradition, nature by nurture, to use a familiar jingle. The efficient forces are now quite different from those which made his skin black and his head long. They are causes of another order.

The particular song of the Negro and his complexion represent the clear-cut extremes of the matter. Between them lie the good nature and the inclination to melody. Obviously these traits may also be the result of human example, of "social environment," of contemporary tradition. There are those who so believe, as well as those who see in them chiefly the effects of inborn biological impulse. Perhaps these intermediate dubious traits are the results of a blending of nature and nurture, the strength of each varying according to the trait or the individual examined. Clearly, at any rate, there is room here for investigation and weighing of evidence. A genuine problem exists. This problem cannot be solved by the historical or social sciences alone, because they do not concern themselves with heredity. Nor can it be solved by biology, which deals with heredity and allied factors but does not go on to operate with the nonbiological principle of tradition or with what is acquired by men when they live in societies.

Here, then, is one distinctive task for anthropology: the interpretation of those phenomena into which both innate organic factors and "social" or acquired factors enter or may enter.

The word "social" is the customary untechnical one for the nonorganic or more-than-organic phenomena referred to. It is, however, an ambiguous word and therefore sometimes a confusing one. As will shortly be pointed out, "social" refers to both social and cultural phenomena. Until the distinction between them has been made, we shall either put "social" into quotation marks or use "sociocultural" instead.

3. Organic or "Physical" Anthropology

The organic sciences underlie the sociocultural ones. They are more immediately "natural," less "humanized" in their concern. Anthropology therefore accepts and uses the general principles of biology: the laws of heredity and the doctrines of cell development and evolution, for instance, and all the findings of anatomy, physiology, embryology, zoology, palaeontology, and the rest. Its business has been to ascertain how far these principles apply to man, what forms they take in his particular case. This has meant a concentration of attention, the devising of special methods of inquiry. Many biological problems, including most physiological and hereditary ones, can be most profitably attacked in the laboratory, or at least under experimental conditions. The experimental method, however, is but rarely available for human beings living in groups. Sociocultural phenomena have to be taken as they come and laboriously sifted and resifted afterward, instead of being artificially simplified in advance, as is done in laboratory experimentation.

Then, too, since anthropology is operating biologically within the narrow limits of one species, it has sometimes been driven to concern itself with minute traits, such as the zoologist is rarely troubled with: the proportions of the length and the breadth of the skull—the famous **cephalic index**—for instance; the number of degrees the arm bones are twisted, and the like. Also, as these data had to be used in the gross, unmodifiable by artificially varied conditions, it has been necessary to secure them from all possible varieties of men, different races, sexes, ages, and their nearest brute analogues. The result is that biological or physical anthropology—"**somatology**" it is sometimes called in Anglo-Saxon countries, and sometimes simply "anthropology" in continental Europe—has in part constituted a sort of specialization or sharpening of certain aspects of general biology. It has become absorbed to a considerable degree in certain particular phenomena, such as human species or sub-races and methods of studying them, about which general biologists, physiologists, and students of medicine are usually but vaguely informed.

4. Sociocultural Anthropology

The sociocultural sciences, usually, but somewhat loosely, called the social sciences, overlie the organic sciences. Men's bodies and inborn equipment are back of their deeds and accomplishments as shaped by tradition, and are primary to their culture or civilization as well as to their aggregations in societies. The relation of anthropology to sociocultural science has therefore been in a sense the opposite of its relation to biological science. Instead of specializing, anthropology has been occupied with trying to generalize the findings of history. Historians can never experiment; sociologists, economists, and other social scientists only rarely. Historians deal with the unique; for to a degree every historical or social or cultural event has something unparalleled about it. They do not lay down laws, nor do they verify them by the artificial trials of experiment. But anthropology looks for such general and recurrent processes as may occur in the multifarious events of history and in the diverse societies, institutions, customs, and beliefs of mankind. So far as such processes can be extricated or formulated, they are generalizations.

It has sometimes been said that social and cultural anthropology—that part of the subject which is concerned with the more-than-merely-organic aspects of human behavior—seems preoccupied with ancient and savage and exotic and extinct peoples. The cause is a desire to understand better all civilizations, irrespective of time and place, in the abstract, or as generalized principles if possible. It is not that cave men are more illuminating than Romans, or flint knives more interesting than fine porcelains or the art of printing, which has led anthropology to bear heavily on the former, but the fact that it wanted to know about cave men and flint knives, which no one else was studying, as well as about the Romans and printing presses that history tells us about so fully. It would be arbitrary to prefer the exotic and remote to the familiar, and in principle anthropology has never accepted the adjudication sometimes tacitly rendered that its proper field should be restricted to the primitive as such. As well might zoology confine its interest to eggs or to protozoans. It is probably true that some researches into early and savage history, especially in the initial stages of anthropology, have sprung from an emotional predilection for the forgotten or the neglected, the obscure and the strange, the unwonted and the mysterious. But such occasional personal aesthetic trends cannot delimit the range of a science or determine its aims and methods. Innumerable historians have been inveterate gossips, but one does not therefore insist that the only proper subject of history is backstairs intimacies.

This, then, is the reason for the special development of those subdivisions of anthropology known as archaeology, "the science of what is old" in the career of humanity, especially as revealed by excavations of the sites of prehistoric occupation, and ethnology, "the science of peoples" and their cultures and life histories as groups, irrespective of their degree of advancement.[1]

5. Evolutionary Processes and Evolutionistic Fancies

In their more elementary aspects the two strands of the organic or hereditary and the sociocultural or "environmental" run through all human life. They are distinct as mechanisms, and their products are distinct. Thus a comparison of the acquisition of the power of flight respectively by birds in their organic development out of the ancestral reptile stem millions of years ago, and by men as a result of cultural progress in the field of invention during the past generation, reveals at once the profound differences of process that inhere in the ambiguous concept of "evolution." The bird gave up a pair of walking limbs to acquire wings. It added a new faculty by transforming part of an old one. The sum total of its parts or organs was not greater than before. The change was transmitted only to the blood descendants of the altered individuals. The reptile line went on as it had been before, or if it altered, did so for causes unconnected with the evolution of the birds. The airplane, on the contrary, gave men a new faculty without diminishing or even impairing any of those they had previously possessed. It led to no visible bodily changes, no alterations of mental capacity. The invention has been transmitted to individuals and groups not derived by descent from the inventors; in fact, it has already influenced the fortunes of all of us. Theoretically, the invention is transmissible to ancestors if they happen to be still living. In sum, it represents an accretion to the stock of existing civilization rather than a transformation.

Once the broad implications of the distinction which this example illustrates have been grasped, many common errors are guarded against. The program of eugenics, for instance, loses much of its force. There is certainly much to be said in favor of intelligence and discrimination in mating, as in everything else. There is need for the acquisition of more exact knowledge on human heredity. But, in the main, the claims sometimes made that eugenics is necessary to preserve civilization from dissolution, or to maintain the flourishing of this or that nationality, rest on the fallacy of recognizing only organic causes as operative, when sociocultural as well as organic ones are active — when indeed the super-hereditary factors may be much the more powerful ones. So, in what are mis-called race problems, the average thought of the day still reasons confusedly between sociocultural and organic causes and effects.[2] Anthropology is not yet in a position always to state just where the boundary lies between the con-tributing organic causes and the **superorganic** or "sociocultural" causes of such phenomena. But it does hold to their fundamental distinctness and to the importance of their distinction, if true understanding is the aim. Without sure grasp of this principle, many of the arguments and conclusions in the present volume will lose their significance.

Accordingly, a designation of anthropology as "the child of Darwin" is mis-leading. Darwin's essential achievement was that he imagined, and substanti-ated by much indirect evidence, a mechanism through which organic evolution appeared to be taking place. The whole history of man, however, being much more than an organic matter, a merely or strictly Darwinian anthropology would be largely misapplied biology. One might almost as justly speak of a **Copernican** or a **Newtonian** anthropology.

What has greatly influenced some of the earlier anthropology, mainly to its damage, has been not Darwinism, but the vague idea of progress, to the organ-ic aspect of which Darwin happened incidentally to give such support and apparent substance that the whole group of evolutionistic ideas, sound and unsound, has luxuriated rankly ever since. It became common practice in the older anthropology to "explain" any part of human civilization by arranging its several forms in an evolutionary sequence from lowest to highest and allowing each successive stage to flow spontaneously, without specific cause, from the preceding one. At bottom this logical procedure was astonishingly naïve. In these schemes we of our land and day stood at the summit of the ascent. What-ever seemed most different from our customs was therefore reckoned as earli-est, and other phenomena were disposed wherever they would best contribute to the straight evenness of the climb upward. The relative occurrence of phe-nomena in time and space was disregarded in favor of their logical fitting into a plan. It was argued that since we hold to definitely monogamous marriage, the beginnings of human sexual union probably lay in the opposite condition of indiscriminate promiscuity. Since we accord precedence to descent from the father, and generally know him, early society must have reckoned descent from the mother and no one knew his own father. We abhor incest; therefore the most primitive men normally married their sisters. These are fair samples of the con-clusions or assumptions of the classic evolutionistic school of anthropology of, say, 1860 to 1890, which still believed that primal origins or ultimate causes could be determined, and that they could be discovered by speculative reason-ing. The roster of this evolutionistic-speculative school was graced by some illustrious names. Needless to say, these men tempered the basic crudity of their opinions by wide knowledge, acuity or charm of presentation, and frequent insight and sound sense in concrete particulars. In their day, two generations or three ago, under the spell of the concept of evolution in its first flush, and of the postulate of progress at its strongest, such methods of reasoning were almost inevitable. Today they are long since threadbare; they have descended to the level of newspaper science or have become matter for idle amateur guessing. They are evidence of a tendency toward the easy smugness of feeling oneself superior to all the past. These ways of thought are mentioned here only as an example of the beclouding that results from bad transference of biologically legitimate concepts into the realm of the history of human society and culture, or viewing these as unfolding according to a simple scheme of progress.

6. Society and Culture

The relation between what is biological and what is sociocultural has just been said to be a sort of central pivot of anthropology, from which the range of the subject then extends outward on both sides, into the organic and into the more-than-organic. It is now necessary to consider the more precise relation of society and culture within the "organic-plus." In man, social and cultural phenomena normally occur associated much as the joint sociocultural phenomena co-occur with the organic ones. Nevertheless, the social and the cultural aspects within the larger sociocultural field can nearly always be distinguished.

The Latin word *socius* denotes a companion or ally, and in their specific sense the words "society" and "social" refer to associations of individuals, to group relations. When we speak of social structure, or the organization of society, it is clear what is meant: the way a mass of people is constituted into families, clans, tribes, states, classes, sets, clubs, communities, and the like. A society is a group of interrelated individuals.

But in a much wider sense the word "social" is also used, loosely, for whatever transcends the biological individual: for what we have so far designated as more-than-organic or sociocultural. Thus popular usage and university curricula recognize the physical, the biological, and the social sciences. The last-named usually comprise history, government, economics, sociology, anthropology, human geography.[3] All these branches of study deal not only with man but with men. In fact they deal primarily with the interrelations of men, or groups of men.

It so happens that man is an essentially unique animal in that he possesses speech faculty and the faculty of symbolizing, abstracting, or generalizing. Through these two associated faculties he is able to communicate his acquired learning, his knowledge and accomplishments, to his fellows and his descendants—in fact, even to his ancestors, if they happen to be still alive and are willing to listen to him. So he transmits much of his ideas, habits, and achievements to succeeding generations of men. This is something that no other animal can do, at least not to any significant degree. This special faculty is what was meant when someone called man the "time-binding" animal. He "binds" time by transcending it, through influencing other generations by his actions.

Now the mass of learned and transmitted motor reactions, habits, techniques, ideas, and values—and the behavior they induce—is what constitutes culture. Culture is the special and exclusive product of men, and is their distinctive quality in the cosmos.

Not only is culture a unique phenomenon, but it can be said to have a large degree of influence. Of course culture can appear and go on only in and through men, men in some kind of societies; without these it could not come into being nor maintain itself. But, given a culture, the human beings that come under its influence behave and operate quite differently from the way they would behave under another culture, and still more differently from the way they would act under no culture. In the latter case they would be merely animals in their behavior. They are human beings precisely because they are animals plus a culture. Somehow human beings began long ago to produce culture and have continued ever since to produce it. In that sense culture derives wholly from men. But the other side of the picture is that every human being is influenced by other men who in turn have been influenced by still others in the direction of maintaining and developing certain ideas, institutions, and standards. And a shorthand way of expressing this is to say that they are all influenced by the culture they grow up in; in fact, in a broad way, they are dependent on it for most of the specific things they do in their lives. Culture is therefore a powerful force in human behavior—in both individual and social behavior. Any given form of culture, whether of the Eskimo or of our contemporary Western civilization, has behind it a long history of other forms of culture by which it was conditioned and from which it derives. And in turn each culture is changing and shaping the forms of culture that will succeed it and which therefore more or less depend on it. Culture thus is a factor that produces enormous effects, and as such we study it.

To be concrete, the reason our Louisiana Negro of a few pages back sings the blues, goes to a Baptist church, and cultivates corn is that these things are parts of American culture. If he had been reared in the Africa of some of his forefathers, his dress, labor, food, religion, government, and amusements would have been quite different, as well as his language. Such is what culture does to men. And, as has been pointed out, the process of transmission, a process of acquisition by learning by which culture is perpetuated and operates on new generations, is quite different from the process by which heredity—

another indubitable force—operates on them. Equally distinct are the results. No religion, no tool, no idea was ever produced by heredity.

Culture, then, is all those things about man that are more than just biological or organic, and are also more than merely psychological. It presupposes bodies and personalities, as it presupposes men associated in groups, and it rests upon them; but culture is something more than a sum of psychosomatic qualities and actions. It is more than these in that its phenomena cannot be wholly understood in terms of biology and psychology. Neither of these sciences claims to be able to explain why there are axes and property laws and etiquettes and prayers in the world, why they function and perpetuate as they do, and least of all why these cultural things take the particular and highly variable forms or expressions under which they appear. Culture thus is at one and the same time the totality of products of social men, and a tremendous force affecting all human beings, socially and individually. And in this special but broad sense, culture is universal for man.[4]

This brings us back to the relation of society and culture. Logically, the two are separate, though they also coexist. Many animals are social. Ants and bees and termites are very highly socialized, so much so that they can survive only in societies. But they have no culture. There is no culture on the subhuman level. Ants get along without culture because they are born with many highly specific instincts; but men have only few and general instincts. Society without culture exists on the subhuman level. But culture, which exists only through man, who is also a social animal, presupposes society. The speech faculty makes possible the transmission and perpetuation of culture; and speech could evidently arise only in a somewhat socially inclined species, though the most socialized animals, the social insects, are held together by instinctive drives and do not need speech. In man, however, language helps bind his societies successfully together. And then culture, with its institutions and morals and values, binds each of them together more and helps them to achieve more successful functioning.

Human society and culture are thus perhaps best viewed as two intimately intertwined aspects of a complex of phenomena that regularly occur only in association; whereas on the subhuman level, societies occur but there is no significant culture.

The occurrence of cultureless true societies among the insects makes it clear that, much as living bodies and "minds" underlie societies and cultures, and precede them in evolution, so also, in turn, society precedes and underlies culture, though in man the two always happen to come associated. At any rate, society is a simpler and more obvious concept to grasp than is culture. That is apparently why sociocultural phenomena—the phenomena of man's total history in the broadest sense, which necessarily contain both social facts and cultural facts—usually have their social aspects recognized first. The result has been that the social-plus-cultural combination came at first to be called merely "social," and in popular and general use still carries that ambiguous name.

For those who like their thinking concrete, it may help if they conceive the sociocultural total in man as similar to a sheet of carbon paper, of which the fabric side represents society and the coated side culture. It is obvious that to use carbon paper effectively, we must distinguish the sides. And yet the sheet is also a unit. Moreover, in certain respects, as when we are not concerned with manifolding but only with some operation like sorting, counting, or packing, a sheet of carbon paper is comparable to and is handled like a sheet of uncoated paper—which in turn would correspond to the cultureless animal societies. But if what we are interested in is the use of carbon paper, the impressions made by it, or if we wish to understand how it makes them, then it is the specific carbon coating that we must examine, even though this comes only as a sort of dry-ink film carried by paper of more or less ordinary cellulose fabric and texture. Like all similes, this one has its limitations. But it may be of help in extricating one-self from the confusing difficulty that the word "social" has acquired a precise and limited meaning—society as distinguishable from culture—in anthropology and sociology, while still having a shifting double meaning—society including or excluding culture—in popular usage and in many general contexts.

There is a real difficulty in the confusion that results from the varying usage of the word "society." The difficulty is unfortunate; but it can be met by keeping it constantly in mind. In the present book, the effort is made to be consistent in saying "culture" or "cultural" whenever anything cultural is referred to. "Social" or "society" are used only with specific reference to the organization of individuals into a group and their resulting relations. Culture, on the contrary, whatever else it may also be—such as a tremendous influence on human behavior—is always first of all the product of men in groups: a set of ideas, attitudes, and habits—"rules" if one will—evolved by men to help them in their conduct of life.[5]

7. Anthropology and the Social Sciences

All the so-called social sciences deal with cultural as well as social data. Caesar's reform of the calendar was a cultural innovation. His defeat of the senatorial party was a social event, but it led to institutional and therefore cultural changes, just as it affected thousands of individual lives for better or worse. When a historian analyzes Caesar's character and motivation, he has in fact gone beyond both society and culture and is operating in the field of informal, biographical, individual psychology. In economics, a banking system, the gold standard, commerce by credit or barter, are institutions, and hence cultural phenomena.

Of all the social sciences, anthropology is perhaps the most distinctively culture-conscious. It aims to investigate human culture as such: at all times, everywhere, in all its parts and aspects and workings. It looks for generalized findings as to how culture operates—literally, how human beings behave under given cultural conditions—and for the major developments of the history of culture.

To this breadth of aim, one thing contributed. This was the early anthropological preoccupation with the very ancient and primitive and remote, which we have already mentioned as a possible foible or drawback. Unlettered peoples leave no biographies of their great men to distract one with personalities, no written histories of rulers and battles. The one thing we know about them is their customs; and customs are culture. The earliest men in fact have left us evidence of just two things: parts of their organic bodies, as represented by their bones; and, more abundantly, their culture, as represented by those of their tools and implements which happened to be of stone and imperishable, plus such of their customs as may be inferable from these tools.

Now while some of the interest of anthropology in its earlier stages was in the exotic and the out-of-the-way, yet even this antiquarian motivation ultimately contributed to a broader result. Anthropologists became aware of the diversity of culture. They began to see the tremendous range of its variations. From that, they commenced to envisage it as a totality, as no historian of one period or of a single people was ever likely to do, nor any analyst of his own type of civilization alone. They became aware of culture as a "universe," or vast field, in which we of today and our own civilization occupy only one place of many. The result was a widening of a fundamental point of view, a departure from unconscious **ethnocentricity** toward relativity. This shift from naïve self-centeredness in one's own time and spot to a broader view based on objective comparison is somewhat like the change from the original **geocentric** assumption of astronomy to the Copernican interpretation of the solar system and the subsequent still greater widening to a universe of galaxies.

A considerable differentiation of anthropology occurred on this point. The other social sciences recognized culture in its specific manifestations as they became aware of this or that fragment or aspect of it—economic or juridical or political or social. Anthropologists became aware of culture as such. From that they went on to try to understand its generic features and processes and their results.

This is one of the few points that sets off from anthropology a science which in the main is almost a twin sister: sociology. Sociologists began mainly with the analysis of our own civilization; they kept the exotic in its place. Therefore as regards culture they tended to remain autocentric somewhat longer. Also, in dealing with ourselves, they dealt mainly with the present, and from that they went on to deal with the future, immediate and ultimate. This inevitably gave to much of early sociology some reformist or ameliorative coloring, and often a program for action. On the contrary, the reproach used to be directed at anthropology that it did not concern itself with practical solutions, or aim at betterment. So far as this was true, it had at least the virtue of helping anthropology to remain a general or fundamental science, undistracted by questions of application from its search for basic findings and meanings. One other distinction is that sociology has been more concerned with strictly social problems: the relations of classes, the organization of family and society, the competitions of individuals within a group. The names are indeed significant here: sociology tends to be concerned with society, anthropology with anthropos, man, and his specifically human product, culture.

All in all, however, these are only differences of emphasis. In principle, sociology and anthropology are hard to keep apart. Anthropologists rate **Sumner** as one of the great names in the history of the study of man; and they feel they stand on common ground with American sociologists like Thomas, Ogburn, Chapin, **Sorokin**, Wirth, **MacIver**, **Parsons**, and **Lynd**, to name only a few, and with Britons and Frenchmen like **Hobhouse**, Ginsberg, **Durkheim**, and **Mauss**. Sociologists on their side have been if anything even more hospitable. Almost to a man they are culture-conscious, know anthropological literature well, and use it constantly.

The relations of anthropology to psychology are obviously important. The nature of human personality—or let us say simply human nature—must enter vitally into all of man's social and cultural activity. However, the relations of anthropology and psychology are not easy to deal with. Psychologists began by taking their own culture for granted, as if it were uniform and universal, and then studying psychic behavior within it. Reciprocally, anthropologists tend to take human nature for granted, as if it were uniform, and to study the diverse cultures which rest upon it. In technical language, we have two variables, "mind" and culture, and each science assumes that it can go ahead by treating the other variable as if it were constant. All psychologists and anthropologists now know that such constancy is not actual. But to deal with two variables, each highly complex, is difficult; and as for specific findings, only beginnings have as yet been made. This whole set of problems of cultural psychology is taken up in one of the later chapters of this book.

The foregoing will make clear why anthropology is sometimes still regarded as one of the newer subjects of study. As a distinct science, with a program of its own, it is relatively recent, because it could hardly become well organized until the biological and the social sciences had both attained enough development to specialize and become aware of the gap between themselves, and until culture was recognized as a specific and distinctive field of inquiry.

But as an unmethodical body of knowledge, as an interest, anthropology is plainly one of the oldest of the sisterhood of sciences. It could not well be otherwise than that men were at least as much interested in each other as in stars and mountains and plants and animals. Every savage is a bit of an ethnologist about neighboring tribes and knows a legend of the origin of mankind. **Herodotus**, the "father of history," devoted half of his nine books to pure ethnology. Lucretius, a few centuries later, tried to solve by philosophical deduction and poetical imagination many of the same problems that modern anthropology is more cautiously attacking with concrete methods. Until nearly two thousand years after these ancients, in neither chemistry nor geology nor biology was so serious an interest developed as in anthropology.

Notes

1   Ethnography is sometimes separated, as more descriptive, from ethnology, as more theoretically or more historically inclined.

2   An example is the still lingering fallacy that individual development of organs by use somehow gets incorporated into the heredity of descendants. This fallacy rests on the misapplication to organic situations of a valid sociocultural mechanism. An example in reverse is the ascription of environmentally or historically produced cultural backwardness to organic and hereditary inferiority.

3   Psychology is sometimes also partly included, sometimes reckoned rather with the biological sciences.

4   Culture as dealt with by the anthropologist is obviously different from what is signified by speaking of "a man of culture," or "a cultured person," in the popular sense, when high culture, or special refinement of it, is meant. Similarly with the word "civilization." When we ordinarily, as laymen, speak of "civilized" and "uncivilized" peoples, we mean, more precisely, peoples of advanced and backward culture, respectively. By many anthropologists, ever since Tylor, the words "civilization" and "culture" are often used to denote the same thing; and always they denote only degrees of the same thing.

5   A further complication arises from the fact that human societies are more than merely innate or instinctual associations like beehives or anthills, but are also culturally shaped and modeled. That is, the forms which human association takes— into nations, tribes, sects, cult groups, classes, castes, clans, and the like—all these forms of social structure are as much the result of varying cultural influences as are the particular forms of economies, technologies, ideologies, arts, manners, and morals at different times and places. In short, specific human societies are more determined by culture than the reverse, even though some kind of social life is a precondition of culture. And therewith social forms become part of culture! This seemingly contradictory situation is intellectually difficult. It touches the heart of the most fundamental social theorizing. A good many anthropologists and sociologists still shrink from facing the problem or admitting the situation to be signifi-

cant. The beginner is therefore advised not to try to master the difficulty at this stage, but to wait till he has finished the book. He will then presumably understand what the problem is and be in a position either to accept the solution suggested here, or to give his own answer. And if not, he will still be in the company of a lot of professional social scientists of good standing.

―――――――

Study Questions

1. According to Kroeber, what makes anthropology different from both biological and social sciences?

2. According to Kroeber, what is the difference between organic and superorganic change?

3. According to Kroeber, what are the differences between society and culture and between sociology and anthropology?

―――――――

Further Readings

Driver, Harold Edson. 1962. *The Contributions of A.L. Kroeber to Culture Area Theory and Practice.* Baltimore: Waverly Press.

Kroeber, Alfred Louis. 1917. The Superorganic. *American Anthropologist* 19: 163-213.

―. 1944. *Configurations of Cultural Growth.* Berkeley: University of California Press.

Kroeber, Theodora. 1970. *Alfred Kroeber: A Personal Configuration.* Berkeley: University of California Press.

Steward, Julian Haines. 1973. *Alfred Kroeber.* New York: Columbia University Press.

11

Introduction
[*Coming of Age in Samoa*]

MARGARET MEAD

During the last hundred years parents and teachers have ceased to take child-hood and adolescence for granted. They have attempted to fit education to the needs of the child, rather than to press the child into an inflexible education-al mould. To this new task they have been spurred by two forces, the growth of the science of psychology, and the difficulties and maladjustments of youth. Psychology suggested that much might be gained by a knowledge of the way in which children developed, of the stages through which they passed, of what the adult world might reasonably expect of the baby of two months or the child of two years. And the fulminations of the pulpit, the loudly voiced laments of the conservative social philosopher, the records of juvenile courts and social agencies all suggested that something must be done with the peri-od which science had named adolescence. The spectacle of a younger gener-ation diverging ever more widely from the standards and ideals of the past, cut adrift without the anchorage of respected home standards or group religious values, terrified the cautious reactionary, tempted the radical propagandist to missionary crusades among the defenceless youth, and worried the least thoughtful among us.

In American civilisation, with its many immigrant strains, its dozens of conflicting standards of conduct, its hundreds of religious sects, its shifting economic conditions, this unsettled, disturbed status of youth was more apparent than in the older, more settled civilisation of Europe. American con-ditions challenged the psychologist, the educator, the social philosopher, to offer acceptable explanations of the growing children's plight. As to-day in post-war Germany, where the younger generation has even more difficult adjustments to make than have our own children, a great mass of theorising about adolescence is flooding the book shops; so the psychologist in America tried to account for the restlessness of youth. The result was works like that of **Stanley Hall** on "Adolescence," which ascribed to the period through which the children were passing, the causes of their conflict and distress. Adolescence was characterised as the period in which idealism flowered and rebellion against authority waxed strong, a period during which difficulties and conflicts were absolutely inevitable.

The careful child psychologist who relied upon experiment for his conclusions did not subscribe to these theories. He said, "We have no data. We know only a little about the first few months of a child's life. We are only just learning when a baby's eyes will first follow a light. How can we give definite answers to questions of how a developed personality, about which we know nothing, will respond to religion?" But the negative cautions of science are never popular. If the experimentalist would not commit himself, the social philosopher, the preacher and the pedagogue tried the harder to give a short-cut answer. They observed the behaviour of adolescents in our society, noted down the omnipresent and obvious symptoms of unrest, and announced these as characteristics of the period. Mothers were warned that "daughters in their teens" present special problems. This, said the theorists, is a difficult period. The physical changes which are going on in the bodies of your boys and girls have their definite psychological accompaniments. You can no more evade one than you can the other; as your daughter's body changes from the body of a child to the body of a woman, so inevitably will her spirit change, and that stormily. The theorists looked about them again at the adolescents in our civilisation and repeated with great conviction, "Yes, stormily."

Such a view, though unsanctioned by the cautious experimentalist, gained wide currency, influenced our educational policy, paralysed our parental efforts. Just as the mother must brace herself against the baby's crying when it cuts its first tooth, so she must fortify herself and bear with what equanimity she might the unlovely, turbulent manifestations of the "awkward age." If there was nothing to blame the child for, neither was there any programme except endurance which might be urged upon the teacher. The theorist continued to observe the behaviour of American adolescents and each year lent new justification to his hypothesis, as the difficulties of youth were illustrated and documented in the records of schools and juvenile courts.

But meanwhile another way of studying human development had been gaining ground, the approach of the anthropologist, the student of man in all of his most diverse social settings. The anthropologist, as he pondered his growing body of material upon the customs of primitive people, grew to realise the tremendous rôle played in an individual's life by the social environment in which each is born and reared. One by one, aspects of behavior which we had been accustomed to consider invariable complements of our humanity were found to be merely a result of civilisation, present in the inhabitants of one country, absent in another country, and this without a change of race. He learned that neither race nor common humanity can be held responsible for many of the forms which even such basic human emotions as love and fear and anger take under different social conditions.

So the anthropologist, arguing from his observations of the behaviour of adult human beings in other civilisations, reaches many of the same conclusions which the behaviourist reaches in his work upon human babies who have as yet no civilisation to shape their malleable humanity.

With such an attitude towards human nature the anthropologist listened to the current comment upon adolescence. He heard attitudes which seemed to him dependent upon social environment—such as rebellion against authority, philosophical perplexities, the flowering of idealism, conflict and struggle—ascribed to a period of physical development. And on the basis of his knowledge of the determinism of culture, of the plasticity of human beings, he doubted. Were these difficulties due to being adolescent or to being adolescent in America?

For the biologist who doubts an old hypothesis or wishes to test out a new one, there is the biological laboratory. There, under conditions over which he can exercise the most rigid control, he can vary the light, the air, the food, which his plants or his animals receive, from the moment of birth throughout their lifetime. Keeping all the conditions but one constant, he can make accurate measurement of the effect of the one. This is the ideal method of science, the method of the controlled experiment, through which all hypotheses may be submitted to a strict objective test.

Even the student of infant psychology can only partially reproduce these ideal laboratory conditions. He cannot control the pre-natal environment of the child whom he will later subject to objective measurement. He can, however, control the early environment of the child, the first few days of its existence, and decide what sounds and sights and smells and tastes are to impinge upon it. But for the student of the adolescent there is no such simplicity of working conditions. What we wish to test is no less than the effect of civilisation upon a developing human being at the age of puberty. To test it most rigorously we would have to construct various sorts of different civilisations and subject large numbers of adolescent children to these different environments. We would list the influences the effects of which we wished to study. If we wished to study the influence of the size of the family, we would construct a series of civlisations alike in every respect except in family organisation. Then if we found differences in the behaviour of our adolescents we could say with assurance that size of family had caused the difference, that, for instance, the only child had a more troubled adolescence than the child who was a member of a large family. And so we might proceed through a dozen possible situations—early or late sex knowledge, early or late sex-experience, pressure towards precocious development, discouragement of precocious development, segregation of the sexes or coeducation from infancy, division of labour between the sexes or common tasks for both, pressure to make religious choices young or the lack of such pressure. We would vary one factor, while the others remained quite constant, and analyse which, if any, of the aspects of our civilisation were responsible for the difficulties of our children at adolescence.

Unfortunately, such ideal methods of experiment are denied to us when our materials are humanity and the whole fabric of a social order. The test colony of Herodotus, in which babies were to be isolated and the results recorded, is not a possible approach. Neither is the method of selecting from our own civilisation groups of children who meet one requirement or another. Such a method would be to select five hundred adolescents from small families and five hundred from large families, and try to discover which had experienced the greatest difficulties of adjustment at adolescence. But we could not know what were the other influences brought to bear upon these children, what effect their knowledge of sex or their neighbourhood environment may have had upon their adolescent development.

What method then is open to us who wish to conduct a human experiment but who lack the power either to construct the experimental conditions or to find controlled examples of those conditions here and there throughout our own civilisation? The only method is that of the anthropologist, to go to a different civilisation and make a study of human beings under different cultural conditions in some other part of the world. For such studies the anthropologist chooses quite simple peoples, primitive peoples, whose society has never attained the complexity of our own. In this choice of primitive peoples like the Eskimo, the Australian, the South Sea islander, or the Pueblo Indian, the anthropologist is guided by the knowledge that the analysis of a simpler civilisation is more possible of attainment.

In complicated civilisations like those of Europe, or the higher civilisations of the East, years of study are necessary before the student can begin to understand the forces at work within them. A study of the French family alone would involve a preliminary study of French history, of French law, of the Catholic and Protestant attitudes toward sex and personal relations. A primitive people without a written language present a much less elaborate problem and a trained student can master the fundamental structure of a primitive society in a few months.

Furthermore, we do not choose a simple peasant community in Europe or an isolated group of mountain whites in the American South, for these people's ways of life, though simple, belong essentially to the historical tradition to which the complex parts of European or American civilisation belong.

Instead, we choose primitive groups who have had thousands of years of historical development along completely different lines from our own, whose language does not possess our Indo-European categories, whose religious ideas are of a different nature, whose social organisation is not only simpler but very different from our own. From these contrasts, which are vivid enough to startle and enlighten those accustomed to our own way of life and simple enough to be grasped quickly, it is possible to learn many things about the effect of a civlisation upon the individuals within it.

So, in order to investigate the particular problem, I chose to go not to Germany or to Russia, but to Samoa, a South Sea island about thirteen degrees from the Equator, inhabited by a brown Polynesian people. Because I was a woman and could hope for greater intimacy in working with girls rather than with boys, and because owing to a paucity of women ethnologists our knowledge of primitive girls is far slighter than our knowledge of boys, I chose to concentrate upon the adolescent girl in Samoa.

But in concentrating, I did something very different from what I would do if I concentrated upon a study of the adolescent girl in Kokomo, Indiana. In such a study, I would go right to the crux of the problem; I would not have to linger long over the Indiana language, the table manners or sleeping habits of my subjects, or make an exhaustive study of how they learned to dress themselves, to use the telephone, or what the concept of conscience meant in Kokomo. All these things are the general fabric of American life, known to me as investigator, known to you as readers.

But with this new experiment on the primitive adolescent girl the matter was quite otherwise. She spoke a language the very sounds of which were strange, a language in which nouns became verbs and verbs nouns in the most sleight-of-hand fashion. All of her habits of life were different. She sat cross-legged on the ground, and to sit upon a chair made her stiff and miserable. She ate with her fingers from a woven plate; she slept upon the floor. Her house was a mere circle of pillars, roofed by a cone of thatch, carpeted with water-worn coral fragments. Her whole material environment was different. Cocoanut palm, breadfruit, and mango trees swayed above her village. She had never seen a horse, knew no animals except the pig, dog and rat. Her food was taro, breadfruit and bananas, fish and wild pigeon and half-roasted pork, and land crabs. And just as it was necessary to understand this physical environment, this routine of life which was so different from ours, so her social environment in its attitudes toward children, towards sex, towards personality, presented as strong a contrast to the social environment of the American girl.

I concentrated upon the girls of the community. I spent the greater part of my time with them. I studied most closely the households in which adolescent girls lived. I spent more time in the games of children than in the councils of their elders. Speaking their language, eating their food, sitting barefoot and cross-legged upon the pebbly floor, I did my best to minimise the differences between us and to learn to know and understand all the girls of three little villages on the coast of the little island of Taū, in the Manu'a Archipelago.

Through the nine months which I spent in Samoa, I gathered many detailed facts about these girls, the size of their families, the position and wealth of their parents, the number of their brothers and sisters, the amount of sex experience which they had had. All of these routine facts are summarised in a table in the appendix. They are only the barest skeleton, hardly the raw materials for a study of family situations and sex relations, standards of friendship, of loyalty, of personal responsibility, all those impalpable storm centres of disturbances in the lives of our adolescent girls. And because these less measurable parts of their lives were so similar, because one girl's life was so much like another's, in an uncomplex, uniform culture like Samoa, I feel justified in generalising although I studied only fifty girls in three small neighbouring villages.

In the following chapters I have described the lives of these girls, the lives of their younger sisters who will soon be adolescent, of their brothers with whom a strict taboo forbids them to speak, of their older sisters who have left puberty behind them, of their elders, the mothers and fathers whose attitudes towards life determine the attitudes of their children. And through this description I have tried to answer the question which sent me to Samoa: Are the disturbances which vex our adolescents due to the nature of adolescence itself or to the civilisation? Under different conditions does adolescence present a different picture?

Also, by the nature of the problem, because of the unfamiliarity of this simple life on a small Pacific island, I have had to give a picture of the whole social life of Samoa, the details being selected always with a view to illuminating the problem of adolescence. Matters of political organisation which neither interest nor influence the young girl are not included. Minutiæ of relationship systems or ancestor cults, genealogies and mythology, which are of interest only to the specialist, will be published in another place. But I have tried to present to the reader the Samoan girl in her social setting, to describe the course of her life from birth until death, the problems she will have to solve, the values which will guide her in her solutions, the pains and pleasures of her human lot cast on a South Sea island.

Such a description seeks to do more than illuminate this particular problem. It should also give the reader some conception of a different and contrasting civilisation, another way of life, which other members of the human race have found satisfactory and gracious. We know that our subtlest perceptions, our highest values, are all based upon contrast; that light without darkness or beauty without ugliness would lose the qualities which they now appear to us to have. And similarly, if we would appreciate our own civilisation, this elaborate pattern of life which we have made for ourselves as a people and which we are at such pains to pass on to our children, we must set our civilisation over against other very different ones. The traveller in Europe returns to America, sensitive to nuances in his own manners and philosophies which have hitherto gone unremarked, yet Europe and America are parts of one civilisation. It is with variations within one great pattern that the student of Europe to-day or the student of our own history sharpens his sense of appreciation. But if we step outside the stream of Indo-European culture, the appreciation which we can accord our civilisation is even more enhanced. Here in remote parts of the world, under historical conditions very different from those which made Greece and Rome flourish and fall, groups of human beings have worked out patterns of life so different from our own that we cannot venture any guess that they would ever have arrived at our solutions. Each primitive people has selected one set of human gifts, one set of human values, and fashioned for themselves an art, a social organisation, a religion, which is their unique contribution to the history of the human spirit.

Samoa is only one of these diverse and gracious patterns, but as the traveller who has been once from home is wiser than he who has never left his own door step, so a knowledge of one other culture should sharpen our ability to scrutinize more steadily, to appreciate more lovingly, our own.

And, because of the particular problem which we set out to answer, this tale of another way of life is mainly concerned with education, with the process by which the baby, arrived cultureless upon the human scene, becomes a full-fledged adult member of his or her society. The strongest light will fall upon the ways in which Samoan education, in its broadest sense, differs from our own. And from this contrast we may be able to turn, made newly and vividly self-conscious and self-critical, to judge anew and perhaps fashion differently the education we give our children.

Study Questions

1. According to Mead, what accounts for the popularity of the view that American adolescence is a period of inevitable conflict and stress?

2. According to Mead, what can anthropology contribute to the study of adolescence?

3. Why did Mead focus her fieldwork on young women in Samoa?

Further Readings

Bateson, Mary C. 1994 [1984]. *With a Daughter's Eye: A Memoir of Gregory Bateson and Margaret Mead*. New York: Harper Collins.

Cassidy, Robert. 1982. *Margaret Mead: A Voice for the Century*. New York: Universe Books.

Grosskurth, Phillis. 1988. *Margaret Mead: A Life*. London: Penguin Books.

Mead, Margaret. 1928. *Coming of Age in Samoa: A Psychological Study of Primitive Youth for Western Civilization*. New York: William Morrow.

—. 1930. *Growing Up in New Guinea: A Comparative Study of Primitive Education*. New York: William Morrow.

—. 1935. *Sex and Temperament in Three Primitive Societies*. New York: William Morrow.

—. 1990 [1972]. *Blackberry Winter*. Magnolia, MA: Peter Smith.

Rice, Edward. 1979. *Margaret Mead: A Portrait*. New York: Harper and Row.

12

The Individual and the Pattern of Culture

RUTH BENEDICT

The large corporate behaviour we have discussed is nevertheless the behaviour of individuals. It is the world with which each person is severally presented, the world from which he must make his individual life. Accounts of any civilization condensed into a few dozen pages must necessarily throw into relief the group standards and describe individual behaviour as it exemplifies the motivations of that culture. The exigencies of the situation are misleading only when this necessity is read off as implying that he is submerged in an overpowering ocean.

There is no proper antagonism between the rôle of society and that of the individual. One of the most misleading misconceptions due to this nineteenth-century dualism was the idea that what was subtracted from society was added to the individual and what was subtracted from the individual was added to society. Philosophies of freedom, political creeds of *laissez faire*, revolutions that have unseated dynasties, have been built on this dualism. The quarrel in anthropological theory between the importance of the culture pattern and of the individual is only a small ripple from this fundamental conception of the nature of society.

In reality, society and the individual are not antagonists. His culture provides the raw material of which the individual makes his life. If it is meagre, the individual suffers; if it is rich, the individual has the chance to rise to his opportunity. Every private interest of every man and woman is served by the enrichment of the traditional stores of his civilization. The richest musical sensitivity can operate only within the equipment and standards of its tradition. It will add, perhaps importantly, to that tradition, but its achievement remains in proportion to the instruments and musical theory which the culture has provided. In the same fashion a talent for observation expends itself in some Melanesian tribe upon the negligible borders of the magico-religious field. For a realization of its potentialities it is dependent upon the development of scientific methodology, and it has no fruition unless the culture has elaborated the necessary concepts and tools.

The man in the street still thinks in terms of a necessary antagonism between society and the individual. In large measure this is because in our civilization the regulative activities of society are singled out, and we tend to identify society with the restrictions the law imposes upon us. The law lays down the number of miles per hour that I may drive an automobile. If it takes this restriction away, I am by that much the freer. This basis for a fundamental antagonism between society and the individual is naïve indeed when it is extended as a basic philosophical and political notion. Society is only incidentally and in certain situations regulative, and law is not equivalent to the social order. In the simpler homogeneous cultures collective habit or custom may quite supersede the necessity for any development of formal legal authority. American Indians sometimes say: "In the old days, there were no fights about hunting grounds or fishing territories. There was no law then, so everybody did what was right." The phrasing makes it clear that in their old life they did not think of themselves as submitting to a social control imposed upon them from without. Even in our civilization the law is never more than a crude implement of society, and one it is often enough necessary to check in its arrogant career. It is never to be read off as if it were the equivalent of the social order.

Society in its full sense as we have discussed it in this volume is never an entity separable from the individuals who compose it. No individual can arrive even at the threshold of his potentialities without a culture in which he participates. Conversely, no civilization has in it any element which in the last analysis is not the contribution of an individual. Where else could any trait come from except from the behaviour of a man or a woman or a child?

It is largely because of the traditional acceptance of a conflict between society and the individual, that emphasis upon cultural behaviour is so often interpreted as a denial of the autonomy of the individual. The reading of Sumner's *Folkways* usually rouses a protest at the limitations such an interpretation places upon the scope and initiative of the individual. Anthropology is often believed to be a counsel of despair which makes untenable a beneficent human illusion. But no anthropologist with a background of experience of other cultures has ever believed that individuals were automatons, mechanically carrying out the decrees of their civilization. No culture yet observed has been able to eradicate the differences in the temperaments of the persons who compose it. It is always a give-and-take. The problem of the individual is not clarified by stressing the antagonism between culture and the individual, but by stressing their mutual reinforcement. This rapport is so close that it is not possible to discuss patterns of culture without considering specifically their relation to individual psychology.

We have seen that any society selects some segment of the arc of possible human behaviour, and in so far as it achieves integration its institutions tend to further the expression of its selected segment and to inhibit opposite expressions. But these opposite expressions are the congenial responses, nevertheless, of a certain proportion of the carriers of the culture. We have already discussed the reasons for believing that this selection is primarily cultural and not biological. We cannot, therefore, even on theoretical grounds imagine that all the congenial responses of all its people will be equally served by the institutions of any culture. To understand the behaviour of the individual, it is not merely necessary to relate his personal life-history to his endowments, and to measure these against an arbitrarily selected normality. It is necessary also to relate his congenial responses to the behaviour that is singled out in the institutions of his culture.

The vast proportion of all individuals who are born into any society always and whatever the idiosyncrasies of its institutions, assume, as we have seen, the behaviour dictated by that society. This fact is always interpreted by the carriers of that culture as being due to the fact that their particular institutions reflect an ultimate and universal sanity. The actual reason is quite different. Most people are shaped to the form of their culture because of the enormous malleability of their original endowment. They are plastic to the moulding force of the society into which they are born. It does not matter whether, with the Northwest Coast, it requires delusions of self-reference, or with our own civilization the amassing of possessions. In any case the great mass of individuals take quite readily the form that is presented to them.

They do not all, however, find it equally congenial, and those are favoured and fortunate whose potentialities most nearly coincide with the type of behaviour selected by their society. Those who, in a situation in which they are frustrated, naturally seek ways of putting the occasion out of sight as expeditiously as possible are well served in Pueblo culture. Southwest institutions, as we have seen, minimize the situations in which serious frustration can arise, and when it cannot be avoided, as in death, they provide means to put it behind them with all speed.

On the other hand, those who react to frustration as to an insult and whose first thought is to get even are amply provided for on the Northwest Coast. They may extend their native reaction to situations in which their paddle breaks or their canoe overturns or to the loss of relatives by death. They rise from their first reaction of sulking to thrust back in return, to "fight" with property or with weapons. Those who can assuage despair by the act of bringing shame to others can register freely and without conflict in this society, because their proclivities are deeply channelled in their culture. In **Dobu** those whose first impulse is to select a victim and project their misery upon him in procedures of punishment are equally fortunate.

It happens that none of the three cultures we have described meets frustration in a realistic manner by stressing the resumption of the original and interrupted experience. It might even seem that in the case of death this is impossible. But the institutions of many cultures nevertheless attempt nothing less. Some of the forms the restitution takes are repugnant to us, but that only makes it clearer that in cultures where frustration is handled by giving rein to this potential behaviour, the institutions of that society carry this course to extraordinary lengths. Among the Eskimo, when one man has killed another, the family of the man who has been murdered may take the murderer to replace the loss within its own group. The murderer then becomes the husband of the woman who has been widowed by his act. This is an emphasis upon restitution that ignores all other aspects of the situation—those which seem to us the only important ones; but when tradition selects some such objective it is quite in character that it should disregard all else.

Restitution may be carried out in mourning situations in ways that are less uncongenial to the standards of Western civilization. Among certain of the Central Algonkian Indians south of the Great Lakes the usual procedure was adoption. Upon the death of a child a similar child was put into his place. The similarity was determined in all sorts of ways: often a captive brought in from a raid was taken into the family in the full sense and given all the privileges and the tenderness that had originally been given to the dead child. Or quite as often it was the child's closest playmate, or a child from another related settlement who resembled the dead child in height and features. In such cases the family from which the child was chosen was supposed to be pleased, and indeed in most cases it was by no means the great step that it would be under our institutions. The child had always recognized many "mothers" and many homes where he was on familiar footing. The new allegiance made him thoroughly at home in still another household. From the point of view of the bereaved parents, the situation had been met by a restitution of the *status quo* that existed before the death of their child.

Persons who primarily mourn the situation rather than the lost individual are provided for in these cultures to a degree which is unimaginable under our institutions. We recognize the possibility of such solace, but we are careful to minimize its connection with the original loss. We do not use it as a mourning technique, and individuals who would be well satisfied with such a solution are left unsupported until the difficult crisis is past.

There is another possible attitude toward frustration. It is the precise opposite of the Pueblo attitude, and we have described it among other **Dionysian** reactions of the Plains Indians. Instead of trying to get past the experience with the least possible discomfiture, it finds relief in the most extravagant expression of grief. The Indians of the plains capitalized the utmost indulgences and exacted violent demonstrations of emotion as a matter of course.

In any group of individuals we can recognize those to whom these different reactions to frustration and brief are congenial: ignoring it, indulging it by uninhibited expression, getting even, punishing a victim, and seeking restitution of the original situation. In the psychiatric records of our own society, some of these impulses are recognized as bad ways of dealing with the situation, some as good. The bad ones are said to lead to maladjustments and insanities, the good ones to adequate social functioning. It is clear, however, that the correlation does not lie between any one "bad" tendency and abnormality in any absolute sense. The desire to run away from grief, to leave it behind at all costs, does not foster psychotic behaviour where, as among the Pueblos, it is mapped out by institutions and supported by every attitude of the group. The Pueblos are not a neurotic people. Their culture gives the impression of fostering mental health. Similarly, the paranoid attitudes so violently expressed among the **Kwakiutl** are known in psychiatric theory derived from our own civilization as thoroughly "bad"; that is, they lead in various ways to the breakdown of personality. But it is just those individuals among the Kwakiutl who find it congenial to give the freest expression to these attitudes who nevertheless are the leaders of Kwakiutl society and find greatest personal fulfilment in its culture.

Obviously, adequate personal adjustment does not depend upon following certain motivations and eschewing others. The correlation is in a different direction. Just as those are favoured whose congenial responses are closest to that behaviour which characterizes their society, so those are disoriented whose congenial responses fall in that arc of behaviour which is not capitalized by their culture. These abnormals are those who are not supported by the institutions of their civilization. They are the exceptions who have not easily taken the traditional forms of their culture.

For a valid comparative psychiatry, these disoriented persons who have failed to adapt themselves adequately to their cultures are of a first importance. The issue in psychiatry has been too often confused by starting from a fixed list of symptoms instead of from the study of those whose characteristic reactions are denied validity in their society.

The tribes we have described have all of them their non-participating "abnormal" individuals. The individual in Dobu who was thoroughly disoriented was the man who was naturally friendly and found activity an end in itself. He was a pleasant fellow who did not seek to overthrow his fellows or to punish them. He worked for anyone who asked him, and he was tireless in carrying out their commands. He was not filled by a terror of the dark like his fellows, and he did not, as they did, utterly inhibit simple public responses of friendliness toward women closely related, like a wife or sister. He often patted them playfully in public. In any other Dobuan this was scandalous behaviour, but in him it was regarded as merely silly. The village treated him in a kindly enough fashion, not taking advantage of him or making a sport of ridiculing him, but he was definitely regarded as one who was outside the game.

The behaviour congenial to the Dobuan simpleton has been made the ideal in certain periods of our own civilization, and there are still vocations in which his responses are accepted in most Western communities. Especially if a woman is in question, she is well provided for even today in our *mores*, and functions honourably in her family and community. The fact that the Dobuan could not function in his culture was not a consequence of the particular responses that were congenial to him, but of the chasm between them and the cultural pattern.

Most ethnologists have had similar experiences in recognizing that the persons who are put outside the pale of society with contempt are not those who would be placed there by another culture. Lowie found among the Crow Indians of the plains a man of exceptional knowledge of his cultural forms. He was interested in considering these objectively and in correlating different facets. He had an interest in genealogical facts and was invaluable on points of history. Altogether he was an ideal interpreter of Crow life. These traits, however, were not those which were the password to honour among the Crow. He had a definite shrinking from physical danger, and bravado was the tribal virtue. To make matters worse he had attempted to gain recognition by claiming a war honour which was fraudulent. He was proved not to have brought in, as he claimed, a picketed horse from the enemy's camp. To lay false claim to war honours was a paramount sin among the Crow, and by the general opinion, constantly reiterated, he was regarded as irresponsible and incompetent.

Such situations can be paralleled with the attitude in our civilization toward a man who does not succeed in regarding personal possessions as supremely important. Our hobo population is constantly fed by those to whom the accumulation of property is not a sufficient motivation. In case these individuals ally themselves with the hoboes, public opinion regards them as potentially vicious, as indeed because of the asocial situation into which they are thrust they readily become. In case, however, these men compensate by emphasizing their artistic temperament and become members of expatriated groups of petty artists, opinion regards them not as vicious but as silly. In any case they are unsupported by the forms of their society, and the effort to express themselves satisfactorily is ordinarily a greater task than they can achieve.

The dilemma of such an individual is often most successfully solved by doing violence to his strongest natural impulses and accepting the rôle the culture honours. In case he is a person to whom social recognition is necessary, it is ordinarily his only possible course. One of the most striking individuals in Zuñi had accepted this necessity. In a society that thoroughly distrusts authority of any sort, he had a native personal magnetism that singled him out in any group. In a society that exalts moderation and the easiest way, he was turbulent and could act violently upon occasion. In a society that praises a pliant personality that "talks lots"—that is, that chatters in a friendly fashion—he was scornful and aloof. Zuñi's only reaction to such personalities is to brand them as witches. He was said to have been seen peering through a window from outside, and this is a sure mark of a witch. At any rate, he got drunk one day and boasted that they could not kill him. He was taken before the war priests who hung him by his thumbs from the rafters til he should confess to his witchcraft. This is the usual procedure in a charge of witchcraft. However, he dispatched a messenger to the government troops. When they came, his shoulders were already crippled for life, and the officer of the law was left with no recourse but to imprison the war priests who had been responsible for the enormity. One of these war priests was probably the most respected and important person in recent Zuñi history, and when he returned after imprisonment in the state penitentiary he never resumed his priestly offices. He regarded his power as broken. It was a revenge that is probably unique in Zuñi history. It involved, of course, a challenge to the priesthoods, against whom the witch by his act openly aligned himself.

The course of his life in the forty years that followed this defiance was not, however, what we might easily predict. A witch is not barred from his membership in cult groups because he has been condemned, and the way to recognition lay through such activity. He possessed a remarkable verbal memory and a sweet singing voice. He learned unbelievable stores of mythology, of esoteric ritual, of cult songs. Many hundreds of pages of stories and ritual poetry were taken down from his dictation before he died, and he regarded his songs as much more extensive. He became indispensable in ceremonial life and before he died was the governor of Zuñi. The congenial bent of his personality threw him into irreconcilable conflict with his society, and he solved his dilemma by turning an incidental talent to account. As we might well expect, he was not a happy man. As governor of Zuñi, and high in his cult groups, a marked man in his community, he was obsessed by death. He was a cheated man in the midst of a mildly happy populace.

It is easy to imagine the life he might have lived among the Plains Indians, where every institution favoured the traits that were native to him. The personal authority, the turbulence, the scorn, would all have been honoured in the career he could have made his own. The unhappiness that was inseparable from his temperament as a successful priest and governor of Zuñi would have had no place as a war chief of the Cheyenne; it was not a function of the traits of his native endowment but of the standards of the culture in which he found no outlet for his native responses.

The individuals we have so far discussed are not in any sense psychopathic. They illustrate the dilemma of the individual whose congenial drives are not provided for in the institutions of his culture. This dilemma becomes of psychiatric importance when the behaviour in question is regarded as categorically abnormal in a society. Western civilization tends to regard even a mild homosexual as an abnormal. The clinical picture of homosexuality stresses the neuroses and psychoses to which it gives rise, and emphasizes almost equally the inadequate functioning of the invert and his behaviour. We have only to turn to other cultures, however, to realize that homosexuals have by no means been uniformly inadequate to the social situation. They have not always failed to function. In some societies they have even been especially acclaimed. **Plato**'s *Republic* is, of course, the most convincing statement of the honourable estate of homosexuality. It is presented as a major means to the good life, and Plato's high ethical evaluation of this response was upheld in the customary behaviour of Greece at that period.

The American Indians do not make Plato's high moral claims for homosexuality, but homosexuals are often regarded as exceptionally able. In most of North America there exists the institution of the ***berdache***, as the French called them. These men-women were men who at puberty or thereafter took the dress and the occupations of women. Sometimes they married other men and lived with them. Sometimes they were men with no inversion, persons of weak sexual endowment who chose this rôle to avoid the jeers of the women. The berdaches were never regarded as of first-rate supernatural power, as similar men-women were in Siberia, but rather as leaders in women's occupations, good healers in certain diseases, or, among certain tribes, as the genial organizers of social affairs. They were usually, in spite of the manner in which they were accepted, regarded with a certain embarrassment. It was thought slightly ridiculous to address as "she" a person who was known to be a man and who, as in Zuñi, would be buried on the men's side of the cemetery. But they were socially placed. The emphasis in most tribes was upon the fact that men who took over women's occupations excelled by reason of their strength and initiative and were therefore leaders in women's techniques and in the accumulation of those forms of property made by women. One of the best known of all the Zuñis of a generation ago was the man-woman We-wha, who was, in the words of his friend, Mrs. Stevenson, "certainly the strongest person in Zuñi, both mentally and physically." His remarkable memory for ritual made him a chief personage on ceremonial occasions, and his strength and intelligence made him a leader in all kinds of crafts.

The men-women of Zuñi are not all strong, self-reliant personages. Some of them take this refuge to protect themselves against their inability to take part in men's activities. One is almost a simpleton, and one, hardly more than a little boy, has delicate features like a girl's. There are obviously several reasons why a person becomes a berdache in Zuñi, but whatever the reason, men who have chosen openly to assume women's dress have the same chance as any other persons to establish themselves a functioning members of the society. Their response is socially recognized. If they have native ability, they can give it scope; if they are weak creatures, they fail in terms of their weakness of character, not in terms of their inversion.

The Indian institution of the berdache was most strongly developed on the plains. The Dakota had a saying "fine possessions like a berdache's," and it was the epitome of praise for any woman's household possessions. A berdache had two strings to his bow, he was supreme in women's techniques, and he could also support his *menage* by the man's activity of hunting. Therefore no one was richer. When especially fine beadwork or dressed skins were desired for ceremonial occasions, the berdache's work was sought in preference to any other's. It was his social adequacy that was stressed above all else. As in Zuñi, the attitude toward him is ambivalent and touched with malaise in the face of a recognized incongruity. Social scorn, however, was visited not upon the berdache but upon the man who lived with him. The latter was regarded as a weak man who had chosen an easy berth instead of the recognized goals of their culture; he did not contribute to the household, which was already a model for all households through the sole efforts of the berdache. His sexual adjustment was not singled out in the judgment that was passed upon him, but in terms of his economic adjustment he was an outcast.

When the homosexual response is regarded as a perversion, however, the invert is immediately exposed to all the conflicts to which aberrants are always exposed. His guilt, his sense of inadequacy, his failures, are consequences of the disrepute which social tradition visits upon him; and few people can achieve a satisfactory life unsupported by the standards of the society. The adjustments that society demands of them would strain any man's vitality, and the consequences of this conflict we identify with their homosexuality.

Trance is a similar abnormality in our society. Even a very mild mystic is aberrant in Western civilization. In order to study trance or **catalepsy** within our own social groups, we have to go to the case histories of the abnormal. Therefore the correlation between trance experience and the neurotic and psychotic seems perfect. As in the case of the homosexual, however, it is a local correlation characteristic of our century. Even in our own cultural background other eras give different results. In the Middle Ages when Catholicism made the ecstatic experience the mark of sainthood, the trance experience was greatly valued, and those to whom the response was congenial, instead of being overwhelmed by a catastrophe as in our century, were given confidence in the pursuit of their careers. It was a validation of ambitions, not a stigma of insanity. Individuals who were susceptible to trance, therefore, succeeded or failed in terms of their native capacities, but since trance experience was highly valued, a great leader was very likely to be capable of it.

Among primitive peoples, trance and catalepsy have been honoured in the extreme. Some of the Indian tribes of California accorded prestige principally to those who passed through certain trance experiences. Not all of these tribes believed that it was exclusively women who were so blessed, but among the **Shasta** this was the convention. Their **shamans** were women, and they were accorded the greatest prestige in the community. They were chosen because of their constitutional liability to trance and allied manifestations. One day the woman who was so destined, while she was about her usual work, fell suddenly to the ground. She had heard a voice speaking to her in tones of the greatest intensity. Turning, she had seen a man with drawn bow and arrow. He commanded her to sing on pain of being shot through the heart by his arrow, but under the stress of the experience she fell senseless. Her family gathered. She was lying rigidly, hardly breathing. They knew that for some time she had had dreams of a special character which indicated a shamanistic calling, dreams of escaping grizzly bears, falling off cliffs or trees, or of being surrounded by swarms of yellow-jackets. The community knew therefore what to expect. After a few hours the woman began to moan gently and to roll about upon the ground, trembling violently. She was supposed to be repeating the song which she had been told to sing and which during the trance had been taught her by the spirit. As she revived, her moaning became more and more clearly the spirit's song until at last she called out the name of the spirit itself, and immediately blood oozed from her mouth.

When the woman had come to herself after the first encounter with her spirit, she danced that night her first initiatory shaman's dance. For three nights she danced, holding herself by a rope that was swung from the ceiling. On the third night she had to receive in her body her power from the spirit. She was dancing, and as she felt the approach of the moment she called out, "He will shoot me, he will shoot me." Her friends stood close, for when she reeled in a kind of cataleptic seizure, they had to seize her before she fell or she would die. From this time on she had in her body a visible materialization of her spirit's power, an icicle-like object which in her dances thereafter she would exhibit, producing it from one part of her body and returning it to another part. From this time on she continued demonstrations, and she was called upon in great emergencies of life and death, for curing and for divination and for counsel. She became, in other words, by this procedure a woman of great power and importance.

It is clear that, far from regarding cataleptic seizures as blots upon the family **escutcheon** and as evidences of dreaded disease, cultural approval had seized upon them and made of them the pathway to authority over one's fellows. They were the outstanding characteristic of the most respected social type, the type which functioned with most honour and reward in the community. It was precisely the cataleptic individuals who in this culture were singled out for authority and leadership.

The possible usefulness of "abnormal" types in a social structure, provided they are types that are culturally selected by that group, is illustrated from every part of the world. The shamans of Siberia dominate their communities. According to the ideas of these peoples, they are individuals who by submission to the will of the spirits have been cured of a grievous illness—the onset of the seizures—and have acquired by this means great supernatural power and incomparable vigour and health. Some, during the period of the call, are violently insane for several years; others irresponsible to the point where they have to be constantly watched lest they wander off in the snow and freeze to death; others ill and emaciated to the point of death, sometimes with bloody sweat. It is the shamanistic practice which constitutes their cure, and the extreme exertion of a Siberian séance leaves them, they claim, rested and able to enter immediately upon a similar performance. Cataleptic seizures are regarded as an essential part of any shamanistic performance.

A good description of the neurotic condition of the shaman and the attention given him by his society is an old one by **Canon Callaway**, recorded in the words of an old Zulu of South Africa:

> The condition of a man who is about to become a diviner is this: at first he is apparently robust, but in the process of time he begins to be delicate, not having any real disease, but being delicate. He habitually avoids certain kinds of food, choosing what he likes, and he does not eat much of that; he is continually complaining of pains in different parts of his body. And he tells them that he has dreamt that he was carried away by a river. He dreams of many things, and his body is muddied [as a river] and he becomes a house of dreams. He dreams constantly of many things, and on awakening tells his friends, "My body is muddied today; I dream many men were killing me, and I escaped I know not how. On waking one part of my body felt different from other parts; it was no longer alike all over." At last that man is very ill, and they go to the diviners to enquire.

The diviners do not at once see that he is about to have a soft head [that is, the sensitivity associated with shamanism]. It is difficult for them to see the truth; they continually talk nonsense and make false statements, until all the man's cattle are devoured at their command, they saying that the spirit of his people demands cattle, that it may eat food. At length all the man's property is expended, he still being ill; and they no longer know what to do, for he has no more cattle, and his friends help him in such things as he needs.

At length a diviner comes and says that all the others are wrong. He says, "He is possessed by the spirits. There is nothing else. They move in him, being divided into two parties; some say, 'No, we do not wish our child injured. We do not wish it.' It is for that reason he does not get well. If you bar the way against the spirits, you will be killing him. For he will not be a diviner; neither will he ever be a man again."

So the man may be ill two years without getting better; perhaps even longer than that. He is confined to his house. This continues till his hair falls off. And his body is dry and scurfy; he does not like to anoint himself. He shows that he is about to be a diviner by yawning again and again, and by sneezing continually. It is apparent also from his being very fond of snuff; not allowing any long time to pass without taking some. And people begin to see that he has had what is good given to him.

After that he is ill; he has convulsions, and when water has been poured on him they then cease for a time. He habitually sheds tears, at first slight, then at last he weeps aloud and when the people are asleep he is heard making a noise and wakes the people by his singing; he has composed a song, and the men and women awake and go to sing in concert with him. All the people of the village are troubled by want of sleep; for a man who is becoming a diviner causes great trouble, for he does not sleep, but works constantly with his brain; his sleep is merely by snatches, and he wakes up singing many songs; and people who are near quit their villages by night when they hear him singing aloud and go to sing in concert. Perhaps he sings till morning, no one having slept. And then he leaps about the house like a frog; and the house becomes too small for him, and he goes out leaping and singing, and shaking like a reed in the water, and dripping with perspiration.

In this state of things they daily expect his death; he is now but skin and bones, and they think that tomorrow's sun will not leave him alive. At this time many cattle are eaten, for the people encourage his becoming a diviner. At length [in a dream] an ancient ancestral spirit is pointed out to him. This spirit says to him, "Go to So-and-so and he will churn for you an emetic [the medicine the drinking of which is a part of shamanistic initiation] that you may be a diviner altogether." Then he is quiet a few days, having gone to the diviner to have the medicine churned for him; and he comes back quite another man, being now cleansed and a diviner indeed.

Thereafter for life, when he is possessed by his spirits, he foretells events and finds lost articles.

It is clear that culture may value and make socially available even highly unstable human types. If it chooses to treat their peculiarities as the most valued variants of human behaviour, the individuals in question will rise to the occasion and perform their social rôles without reference to our usual ideas of the types who can make social adjustments and those who cannot. Those who function inadequately in any society are not those with certain fixed "abnormal" traits, but may well be those whose responses have received no support in the institutions of their culture. The weakness of these aberrants is in great measure illusory. It springs, not from the fact that they are lacking in necessary vigour, but that they are individuals whose native responses are not reaffirmed by society. They are, as **Sapir** phrases it, "alienated from an impossible world."

The person unsupported by the standards of his time and place and left naked to the winds of ridicule has been unforgettably drawn in European literature in the figure of **Don Quixote**. **Cervantes** turned upon a tradition still honoured in the abstract the limelight of a changed set of practical standards, and his poor old man, the orthodox upholder of the romantic chivalry of another generation, became a simpleton. The windmills with which he tilted were the serious antagonists of a hardly vanished world, but to tilt with them when the world no longer called them serious was to rave. He loved his **Dulcinea** in the best traditional manner of chivalry, but another version of love was fashionable for the moment, and his fervour was counted to him for madness.

These contrasting worlds which, in the primitive cultures we have considered, are separated from one another in space, in modern **Occidental** history more often succeed one another in time. The major issue is the same in either case, but the importance of understanding the phenomenon is far greater in the modern world where we cannot escape if we would from the succession of configurations in time. When each culture is a world in itself, relatively stable like the Eskimo culture, for example, and geographically isolated from all others, the issue is academic. But our civilization must deal with cultural standards that go down under our eyes and new ones that arise from a shadow upon the horizon. We must be willing to take account of changing normalities even when the question is of the morality in which we were bred. Just as we are handicapped in dealing with ethical problems so long as we hold to an absolute definition of morality, so we are handicapped in dealing with human society so long as we identify our local normalities with the inevitable necessities of existence.

No society has yet attempted a self-conscious direction of the process by which its new normalities are created in the next generation. **Dewey** has pointed out how possible and yet how drastic such social engineering would be. For some traditional arrangements it is obvious that very high prices are paid, reckoned in terms of human suffering and frustration. If these arrangements presented themselves to us merely as arrangements and not as categorical imperatives, our reasonable course would be to adapt them by whatever means to rationally selected goals. What we do instead is to ridicule our Don Quixotes, the ludicrous embodiments of an outmoded tradition, and continue to regard our own as final and prescribed in the nature of things.

In the meantime the therapeutic problem of dealing with our psychopaths of this type is often misunderstood. Their alienation from the actual world can often be more intelligently handled than by insisting that they adopt the modes that are alien to them. Two other courses are always possible. In the first place, the misfit individual may cultivate a greater objective interest in his own preferences and learn how to manage with greater equanimity his deviation from the type. If he learns to recognize the extent to which his suffering has been due to his lack of support in a traditional **ethos**, he may gradually educate himself to accept his degree of difference with less suffering. Both the exaggerated emotional disturbances of the manic-depressive and the seclusion of the schizophrenic add certain values to existence which are not open to those differently constituted. The unsupported individual who valiantly accepts his favourite and native virtues may attain a feasible course of behaviour that makes it unnecessary for him to take refuge in a private world he has fashioned for himself. He may gradually achieve a more independent and less tortured attitude toward his deviations and upon this attitude he may be able to build an adequately functioning existence.

In the second place, an increased tolerance in society toward its less usual types must keep pace with the self-education of the patient. The possibilities in this direction are endless. Tradition is as neurotic as any patient; its overgrown fear of deviation from its fortuitous standards conforms to all the usual definitions of the psychopathic. This fear does not depend upon observation of the limits within which conformity is necessary to the social good. Much more deviation is allowed to the individual in some cultures than in others, and those in which much is allowed cannot be shown to suffer from their peculiarity. It is probable that social orders of the future will carry this tolerance and encouragement of individual difference much further than any cultures of which we have experience.

The American tendency at the present time leans so far to the opposite extreme that it is not easy for us to picture the changes that such an attitude would bring about. **Middletown** is a typical example of our usual urban fear of seeming in however slight an act different from our neighbours. Eccentricity is more feared than parasitism. Every sacrifice of time and tranquility is made in order that no one in the family may have any taint of nonconformity attached to him. Children in school make their great tragedies out of not wearing a certain kind of stockings, not joining a certain dancing-class, not driving a certain car. The fear of being different is the dominating motivation recorded in Middletown.

The psychopathic toll that such a motivation exacts is evident in every institution for mental diseases in our country. In a society in which it existed only as a minor motive among many others, the psychiatric picture would be a very different one. At all events, there can be no reasonable doubt that one of the most effective ways in which to deal with the staggering burden of psychopathic tragedies in America at the present time is by means of an educational program which fosters tolerance in society and a kind of self-respect and independence that is foreign to Middletown and our urban traditions.

Not all psychopaths, of course, are individuals whose native responses are at variance with those of their civilization. Another large group are those who are merely inadequate and who are strongly enough motivated so that their failure is more than they can bear. In a society in which the will-to-power is most highly rewarded, those who fail may not be those who are differently constituted, but simply those who are insufficiently endowed. The inferiority complex takes a great toll of suffering in our society. It is not necessary that sufferers of this type have a history of frustration in the sense that strong native bents have been inhibited; their frustration is often enough only the reflection of their inability to reach a certain goal. There is a cultural implication here, too, in that the traditional goal may be accessible to large numbers or to very few, and in proportion as success is obsessive and is limited to the few, a greater and greater number will be liable to the extreme penalties of maladjustment.

To a certain extent, therefore, civilization in setting higher and possibly more worthwhile goals may increase the number of its abnormals. But the point may very easily be overemphasized, for very small changes in social attitudes may far outweigh this correlation. On the whole, since the social possibilities of tolerance and recognition of individual difference are so little explored in practice, pessimism seems premature. Certainly other quite different social factors which we have just discussed are more directly responsible for the great proportion of our neurotics and psychotics, and with these other factors civilizations could, if they would, deal without necessary intrinsic loss.

We have been considering individuals from the point of view of their ability to function adequately in their society. This adequate functioning is one of the ways in which normality is clinically defined. It is also defined in terms of fixed symptoms, and the tendency is to identify normality with the statistically average. In practice this average is one arrived at in the laboratory, and deviations from it are defined as abnormal.

From the point of view of a single culture this procedure is very useful. It shows the clinical picture of the civilization and gives considerable information about its socially approved behaviour. To generalize this as an absolute normal, however, is a different matter. As we have seen, the range of normality in different cultures does not coincide. Some, like Zuñi and the Kwakiutl, are so far removed from each other that they overlap only slightly. The statistically determined normal on the Northwest Coast would be far outside the extreme boundaries of abnormality in the Pueblos. The normal Kwakiutl rivalry contest would only be understood as madness in Zuñi, and the traditional Zuñi indifference to dominance and the humiliation of others would be the fatuousness of a simpleton in a man of noble family on the Northwest Coast. Aberrant behaviour in either culture could never be determined in relation to any least common denominator of behaviour. Any society, according to its major preoccupations, may increase and intensify even hysterical, epileptic, or paranoid symptoms, at the same time relying socially in a greater and greater degree upon the very individuals who display them.

This fact is important in psychiatry because it makes clear another group of abnormals which probably exists in every culture: the abnormals who represent the extreme development of the local cultural type. This group is socially in the opposite situation from the group we have discussed, those whose responses are at variance with their cultural standards. Society, instead of exposing the former group at every point, supports them in their furthest aberrations. They have a licence which they may almost endlessly exploit. For this reason these persons almost never fall within the scope of any contemporary psychiatry. They are unlikely to be described even in the most careful manuals of the generation that fosters them. Yet from the point of view of another generation or culture they are ordinarily the most bizarre of the psychopathic types of the period.

The **Puritan** divines of New England in the eighteenth century were the last persons whom contemporary opinion in the colonies regarded as psychopathic. Few prestige groups in any culture have been allowed such complete intellectual and emotional dictatorship as they were. They were the voice of God. Yet to a modern observer it is they, not the confused and tormented women they put to death as witches, who were the psychoneurotics of Puritan New England. A sense of guilt as extreme as they portrayed and demanded both in their own conversion experiences and in those of their converts is found in a slightly saner civilization only in institutions for mental diseases. They admitted no salvation without a conviction of sin that prostrated the victim, sometimes for years, with remorse and terrible anguish. It was the duty of the minister to put the fear of hell into the heart of even the youngest child, and to exact of every convert emotional acceptance of his damnation if God saw fit to damn him. It does not matter where we turn among the records of New England Puritan churches of this period, whether to those dealing with witches or with unsaved children not yet in their teens or with such themes as damnation and predestination, we are faced with the fact that the group of people who carried out to the greatest extreme and in the fullest honour the cultural doctrine of the moment are by the slightly altered standards of our generation the victims of intolerable aberrations. From the point of view of a comparative psychiatry they fall in the category of the abnormal.

In our own generation extreme forms of ego-gratification are culturally supported in a similar fashion. Arrogant and unbridled egoists as family men, as officers of the law and in business, have been again and again portrayed by novelists and dramatists, and they are familiar in every community. Like the behaviour of Puritan divines, their courses of action are often more asocial than those of the inmates of penitentiaries. In terms of the suffering and frustration that they spread about them there is probably no comparison. There is very possibly at least as great a degree of mental warping. Yet they are entrusted with positions of great influence and importance and are as a rule fathers of families. Their impress both upon their own children and upon the structure of our society is indelible. They are not described in our manuals of psychiatry because they are supported by every tenet of our civilization. They are sure of themselves in real life in a way that is possible only to those who are oriented to the points of the compass laid down in their own culture. Nevertheless a future psychiatry may well ransack our novels and letters and public records for illumination upon a type of abnormality to which it would not otherwise give credence. In every society it is among this very group of the culturally encouraged and fortified that some of the most extreme types of human behaviour are fostered.

Social thinking at the present time has no more important task before it than that of taking adequate account of cultural relativity. In the fields of both sociology and psychology the implications are fundamental, and modern thought about contacts of people and about our changing standards is greatly in need of sane and scientific direction. The sophisticated modern temper has made of social relativity, even in the small area which it has recognized, a doctrine of despair. It has pointed out its incongruity with the orthodox dreams of permanence and ideality and with the individual's illusions of autonomy. It has argued that if human experience must give up these, the nutshell of existence is empty. But to interpret our dilemma in these terms is to be guilty of an anachronism. It is only the inevitable cultural lag that makes us insist that the old must be discovered again in the new, that there is no solution but to find the old certainty and stability in the new plasticity. The recognition of cultural relativity carries with it its own values, which need not be those of the absolutist philosophies. It challenges customary opinions and causes those who have been bred to them acute discomfort. It rouses pessimism because it throws old formulae into confusion, not because it contains anything intrinsically difficult. As soon as the new opinion is embraced as customary belief, it will be another trusted bulwark of the good life. We shall arrive then at a more realistic social faith, accepting as grounds of hope and as new bases of tolerance the coexisting and equally valid patterns of life which mankind has created for itself from the raw materials of existence.

Study Questions

1. Why does Benedict oppose the view that culture and the individual are antagonistic?

2. On what basis does Benedict criticize traditional definitions of abnormal behavior?

3. What is Benedict's remedy for the problem of social misfits?

Further Readings

Benedict, Ruth. 1946. *The Chrysanthemum and the Sword: Patterns of Japanese Culture*. Boston: Houghton Mifflin.

—. 1977. *An Anthropologist at Work: The Writings of Ruth Benedict*. Ed. Margaret Mead. Westport, CT: Greenwood.

—. 1989 [1934]. *Patterns of Culture*. Boston, MA: Houghton Mifflin.

Caffrey, Margaret M. 1989. *Ruth Benedict: Stranger in this Land*. Austin: University of Texas Press.

Mead, Margaret. 1974. *Ruth Benedict*. New York: Columbia University Press.

Modell, Judith Schachter. 1983. *Ruth Benedict: Patterns of a Life*. Philadelphia: University of Pennsylvania Press.

13

The Unconscious Patterning of Behavior in Society[1]

EDWARD SAPIR

We may seem to be guilty of a paradox when we speak of the unconscious in reference to social activity. Doubtful as is the usefulness of this concept when we confine ourselves to the behavior of the individual, it may seem to be worse than doubtful when we leave the kinds of behavior that are strictly individual and deal with those more complex kinds of activity which, rightly or wrongly, are supposed to be carried on, not by individuals as such, but by the associations of human beings that constitute society. It may be argued that society has no more of an unconscious than it has hands or legs.

I propose to show, however, that the paradox is a real one only if the term "social behavior" is understood in the very literal sense of behavior referred to groups of human beings which act as such, regardless of the mentalities of the individuals which compose the groups. To such a mystical group alone can a mysterious "social unconsciousness" be ascribed. But as we are very far from believing that such groups really exist, we may be able to persuade ourselves that no more especial kind of unconsciousness need be imputed to social behavior than is needed to understand the behavior of the individual himself. We shall be on much safer ground if we take it for granted that all human behavior involves essentially the same types of mental functioning, as well conscious as unconscious, and that the term "social" is no more exclusive of the concept "unconscious" than is the term "individual," for the very simple reason that the terms "social" and "individual" are contrastive in only a limited sense. We will assume that any kind of psychology that explains the behavior of the individual also explains the behavior of society in so far as the psychological point of view is applicable to and sufficient for the study of social behavior. It is true that for certain purposes it is very useful to look away entirely from the individual and to think of socialized behavior as though it were carried on by certain larger entities which transcend the psycho-physical organism. But this viewpoint implicitly demands the abandonment of the psychological approach to the explanation of human conduct in society.

It will be clear from what we have said that we do not find the essential difference between individual and social behavior to lie in the psychology of the behavior itself. Strictly speaking, each kind of behavior is individual, the difference in terminology being entirely due to a difference in the point of view. If our attention is focused on the actual, theoretically measurable behavior of a given individual at a given time and place, we call it "individual behavior," no matter what the physiological or psychological nature of that behavior may be. If, on the other hand, we prefer to eliminate certain aspects of such individual behavior from our consideration and to hold on only to those respects in which it corresponds to certain norms of conduct which have been developed by human beings in association with one another and which tend to perpetuate themselves by tradition, we speak of "social behavior." In other words, social behavior is merely the sum or, better, arrangement of such aspects of individual behavior as are referred to culture patterns that have their proper context, not in the spatial and temporal continuities of biological behavior, but in historical sequences that are imputed to actual behavior by a principle of selection.

We have thus defined the difference between individual and social behavior, not in terms of kind or essence, but in terms of organization. To say that the human being behaves individually at one moment and socially at another is as absurd as to declare that matter follows the laws of chemistry at a certain time and succumbs to the supposedly different laws of atomic physics at another, for matter is always obeying certain mechanical laws which are at one and the same time both physical and chemical according to the manner in which we choose to define its organization. In dealing with human beings, we simply find it more convenient for certain purposes to refer a given act to the psychophysical organism itself. In other cases the interest happens to lie in continuities that go beyond the individual organism and its functioning, so that a bit of conduct that is objectively no more and no less individual than the first is interpreted in terms of the non-individual patterns that constitute social behavior or cultural behavior.

It would be a useful exercise to force ourselves to see any given human act from both of these points of view and to try to convince ourselves in this way that it is futile to classify human acts as such as having an inherently individual or social significance. It is true that there are a great many organismal functions that it is difficult to think of in social terms, but I think that even here the social point of view may often be applied with success. Few social students are interested, for instance, in the exact manner in which a given individual breathes. Yet it is not to be doubted that our breathing habits are largely conditioned by factors conventionally classified as social. There are polite and impolite ways of breathing. There are special attitudes which seem to characterize whole societies that undoubtedly condition the breathing habits of the individuals who make up these societies. Ordinarily the characteristic rhythm of breathing of a given individual is looked upon as a matter for strictly individual definition. But if, for one reason or another, the emphasis shifts to the consideration of a certain manner of breathing as due to good form or social tradition or some other principle that is usually given a social context, then the whole subject of breathing at once ceases to be a merely individual concern and takes on the appearance of a social pattern. Thus, the regularized breathing of the Hindu Yogi, the subdued breathing of those who are in the presence of a recently deceased companion laid away in a coffin and surrounded by all the ritual of funeral observances, the style of breathing which one learns from an operatic singer who gives lessons on the proper control of the voice, are, each and every one of them, capable of isolation as socialized modes of conduct that have a definite place in the history of human culture, though they are obviously not a whit less facts of individual behavior than the most casual and normal style of breathing, such as one rarely imagines to have other than purely individual implications. Strange as it may seem at first blush, there is no hard and fast line of division as to class of behavior between a given style of breathing, *provided that it be socially interpreted*, and a religious doctrine or a form of political administration. This is not to say that it may not be infinitely more useful to apply the social mode of analysis of human conduct to certain cases and the individual mode of analysis to others. But we do maintain that such differences of analysis are merely imposed by the nature of the interest of the observer and are not inherent in the phenomena themselves.

All cultural behavior is patterned. This is merely a way of saying that many things that an individual does and thinks and feels may be looked upon not merely from the standpoint of the forms of behavior that are proper to himself as a biological organism but from the standpoint of a generalized mode of conduct that is imputed to society rather than to the individual, though the personal genesis of conduct is of precisely the same nature, whether we choose to call the conduct individual or social. It is impossible to say what an individual is doing unless we have tacitly accepted the essentially arbitrary modes of interpretation that social tradition is constantly suggesting to us from the very moment of our birth. Let anyone who doubts this try the experiment of making a painstaking report of the actions of a group of natives engaged in some form of activity, say religious, to which he has not the cultural key. If he is a skillful writer, he may succeed in giving a picturesque account of what he sees and hears, or thinks he sees and hears, but the chances of his being able to give a relation of what happens in terms that would be intelligible and acceptable to the natives themselves are practically nil. He will be guilty of all manner of distortion. His emphasis will be constantly askew. He will find interesting what the natives take for granted as a casual kind of behavior worthy of no particular comment, and he will utterly fail to observe the crucial turning points in the course of action that give formal significance to the whole in the minds of those who do possess the key to its understanding. This patterning or formal analysis of behavior is to a surprising degree dependent on the mode of apprehension which has been established by the tradition of the group. Forms and significances which seem obvious to an outsider will be denied outright by those who carry out the patterns; outlines and implications that are perfectly clear to these may be absent to the eye of the onlooker. It is the failure to understand the necessity of grasping the native patterning which is responsible for so much unimaginative and misconceiving description of procedures that we have not been brought up with. It becomes actually possible to interpret as base what is inspired by the noblest and even holiest of motives, and to see altruism or beauty where nothing of the kind is either felt or intended.

Ordinarily a cultural pattern is to be defined both in terms of function and of form, the two concepts being inseparably intertwined in practice, however convenient it may be to dissociate them in theory. Many functions of behavior are primary in the sense that an individual organic need, such as the satisfaction of hunger, is being fulfilled, but often the functional side of behavior is either entirely transformed or, at the least, takes on a new increment of significance. In this way new functional interpretations are constantly being developed for forms set by tradition. Often the true functions of behavior are unknown and a merely rationalized function may be imputed to it. Because of the readiness with which forms of human conduct lose or modify their original functions or take on entirely new ones, it becomes necessary to see social behavior from a formal as well as from a functional point of view, and we shall not consider any kind of human behavior as understood if we can merely give or think we can give, an answer to the question "For what purpose is this being done?" We shall have also to know what is the precise manner and articulation of the doing.

Now it is a commonplace of observation that the reasoning intelligence seeks to attach itself rather to the functions than to the forms of conduct. For every thousand individuals who can tell with some show of reason why they sing or use words in connected speech or handle money, there is barely one who can adequately define the essential outlines of these modes of behavior. No doubt certain forms will be imputed to such behavior if attention is drawn to it, but experience shows that the forms discovered may be very seriously at variance with those actually followed and discoverable on closer study. In other words, the patterns of social behavior are not necessarily discovered by simple observation, though they may be adhered to with tyrannical consistency in the actual conduct of life. If we can show that normal human beings, both in confessedly social behavior and often in supposedly individual behavior, are reacting in accordance with deep-seated cultural patterns, and if, further, we can show that these patterns are not so much known as felt, not so much capable of conscious description as of naïve practice, then we have the right to speak of the "unconscious patterning of behavior in society." The unconscious nature of this patterning consists not in some mysterious function of a racial or social mind reflected in the minds of the individual members of society, but merely in a typical unawareness on the part of the individual of outlines and demarcations and significances of conduct which he is all the time implicitly following. **Jung**'s "racial unconscious" is neither an intelligible nor a necessary concept. It introduces more difficulties than it solves, while we have all we need for the psychological understanding of social behavior in the facts of individual psychology.

Why are the forms of social behavior not adequately known by the normal individual? How is it that we can speak, if only metaphorically, of a social unconscious? I believe that the answer to this question rests in the fact that the relations between the elements of experience which serve to give them their form and significance are more powerfully "felt" or "intuited" than consciously perceived. It is a matter of common knowledge that it is relatively easy to fix the attention on some arbitrarily selected element of experience, such as a sensation or an emotion, but that it is far from easy to become conscious of the exact place which such an element holds in the total constellations of behavior. It is easy for an Australian native, for instance, to say by what kinship terms he calls so and so or whether or not he may undertake such and such relations with a given individual. It is exceedingly difficult for him to give a general rule of which these specific examples of behavior are but illustrations, though all the while he acts as though the rule were perfectly well known to him. *In a sense it is well known to him.* But this knowledge is not capable of conscious manipulation in terms of word symbols. It is, rather, a very delicately nuanced feeling of subtle relations, both experienced and possible. To this kind of knowledge may be applied the term "intuition," which, when so defined, need have no mystic connotations whatever. It is strange how frequently one has the illusion of free knowledge, in the light of which one may manipulate conduct at will, only to discover in the test that one is being impelled by strict loyalty to forms of behavior that one can feel with the utmost nicety but can state only in the vaguest and most approximate fashion. It would seem that we act all the more securely for our unawareness of the patterns that control us. It may well be that, owing to the limitations of the conscious life, any attempt to subject even the higher forms of social behavior to purely conscious control must result in disaster. Perhaps there is a far-reaching moral in the fact that even a child may speak the most difficult language with idiomatic ease but that it takes an unusually analytical type of mind to define the mere elements of that incredibly subtle linguistic mechanism which is but a plaything of the child's unconscious. Is it not possible that the contemporary mind, in its restless attempt to drag all the forms of behavior into consciousness and to apply the results of its fragmentary or experimental analysis to the guidance of conduct, is really throwing away a greater wealth for the sake of a lesser and more dazzling one? It is almost as though a misguided enthusiast exchanged his thousands of dollars of accumulated credit at the bank for a few glittering coins of manifest, though little, worth.

We shall now give a number of examples of patterns of social behavior and show that they are very incompletely, if at all, known by the normal, naïve individual. We shall see that the **penumbra** of unconscious patterning of social behavior is an extraordinarily complex realm, in which one and the same type of overt behavior may have altogether distinct significances in accordance with its relation to other types of behavior. Owing to the compelling, but mainly unconscious, nature of the forms of social behavior, it becomes almost impossible for the normal individual to observe or to conceive of functionally similar types of behavior in other societies than his own, or in other cultural contexts than those he has experienced, without projecting into them the forms that he is familiar with. In other words, one is always unconsciously finding what one is in unconscious subjection to.

Our first example will be taken from the field of language. Language has the somewhat exceptional property that its forms are, for the most part, indirect rather than direct in their functional significance. The sounds, words, grammatical forms, syntactic constructions, and other linguistic forms that we assimilate in childhood have only value in so far as society has tacitly agreed to see them as symbols of reference. For this reason language is an unusually favorable domain for the study of the general tendency of cultural behavior to work out all sorts of formal elaborations that have only a secondary, and, as it were, "after the event" relevance to functional needs. Purely functional explanations of language, if valid, would lead us to expect either a far greater uniformity in linguistic expression than we actually find, or should lead us to discover strict relations of a functional nature between a particular form of language and the culture of the people using it. Neither of these expectations is fulfilled by the facts. Whatever may be true of other types of cultural behavior, we can safely say that the forms of speech developed in the different parts of the world are at once free and necessary, in the sense in which all artistic productions are free and necessary. Linguistic forms as we find them bear only the loosest relation to the cultural needs of a given society, but they have the very tightest consistency as aesthetic products.

A very simple example of the justice of these remarks is afforded by the English plural. To most of us who speak English the tangible expression of the plural idea in the noun seems to be a self-evident necessity. Careful observation of English usage, however, leads to the conviction that this self-evident necessity of expression is more of an illusion than a reality. If the plural were to be understood functionally alone, we should find it difficult to explain why we use plural forms with numerals and other words that in themselves imply plurality. "Five man" or "several house" would be just as adequate as "five men" or "several houses." Clearly, what has happened is that English, like all of the other Indo-European languages, has developed a feeling for the classification of all expressions which have a **nominal** form into singulars and plurals. So much is this the case that in the early period of the history of our linguistic family even the adjective, which is nominal in form, is unusable except in conjunction with the category of number. In many of the languages of the group this habit still persists. Such notions as "white" or "long" are incapable of expression in French or Russian without formal commitments on the score of whether the quality is predicated of one or several persons or objects. Now it is not denied that the expression of the concept of plurality is useful. Indeed, a language that is forever incapable of making the difference between the one and the many is obviously to that extent hampered in its technique of expression. But we must emphatically deny that this particular kind of expression need ever develop into the complex formal system of number definition that we are familiar with. In many other linguistic groups the concept of number belongs to the group of optionally expressible notions. In Chinese, for instance, the word "man" may be interpreted as the English equivalent of either "man" or "men," according to the particular context in which the word is used. It is to be carefully noted, however, that this formal ambiguity is never a functional one. Terms of inherent plurality, such as "five," "all," or "several," or of inherent singularity, such as "one" or "my" in the phrase "my wife," can always be counted upon to render factually clear what is formally left to the imagination. If the ambiguity persists, it is a useful one or one that does not matter. How little the expression of our concept of number is left to the practical exigencies of a particular case, how much it is a matter of consistency of aesthetic treatment, will be obvious from such examples as the editorial "we are in favor of prohibition," when what is really meant is, "I, John Smith, am in favor of prohibition."

A complete survey of the methods of handling the category of number in the languages of the world would reveal an astonishing variety of treatment. In some languages number is a necessary and well developed category. In others it is an accessory or optional one. In still others, it can hardly be considered as a grammatical category at all but is left entirely to the implications of vocabulary and syntax. Now the interesting thing psychologically about this variety of forms is this, that while everyone may learn to see the need of distinguishing the one from the many and has some sort of notion that his language more or less adequately provides for this necessity, only a very competent **philologist** has any notion of the true formal outlines of the expression of plurality, of whether, for instance, it constitutes a category comparable to that of gender or case, whether or not it is separable from the expression of gender, whether it is a strictly nominal category or a verbal one or both, whether it is used as a lever for syntactic expression, and so on. Here are found determinations of a bewildering variety, concerning which few even among the sophisticated have any clarity, though the lowliest peasant or savage head-hunter may have control of them in his intuitive repertoire.

So great are the possibilities of linguistic patterning that the languages actually known seem to present the whole gamut of possible forms. We have extremely analytic types of speech, such as Chinese, in which the formal unit of discourse, the word, expresses nothing in itself but a single notion of thing or quality or activity or else some relational nuance. At the other extreme are the incredibly complex languages of many American Indian tribes, languages of so-called **polysynthetic** type, in which the same formal unit, the word, is a sentence microcosm full of delicate formal elaborations of the most specialized type. Let one example do for many. Anyone who is brought up in English, even if he has had the benefit of some familiarity with the classical languages, will take it for granted that in such a sentence as "Shall I have the people move across the river to the east?" there is rather little elbow room for varieties of formal expression. It would not easily occur to us, for instance, that the notion of "to the east" might be conveyed not by an independent word or phrase but by a mere suffix in complex verb.

There is a rather obscure Indian language in northern California, Yana, which not only can express this thought in a single word, but would find it difficult to express it in any other way. The form of expression which is peculiar to Yana may be roughly analyzed as follows. The first element in the verb complex indicates the notion of several people living together or moving as a group from place to place. This element, which we may call the "verb stem," can only occur at the beginning of the verb, never in any other position. The second element in the complete word indicates the notion of crossing a stream or of moving from one side of an area to the other. It is in no sense an independent word, but can only be used as an element attached to a verb stem or to other elements which have themselves been attached to the verb stem. The third element in the word is similarly suffixed and conveys the notion of movement toward the east.

It is one of a set of eight elements which convey the respective notions of movement toward the east, south, west, and north, and of movement from the east, south, west, and north. None of these elements is an intelligible word in itself but receives meaning only in so far as it falls into its proper place in the complexly organized verb. The fourth element is a suffix that indicates the relation of causality, that is, of causing one to do or be something, bringing it about that one does or is in a certain way, treating one in such and such an indicated manner. At this point the language indulges in a rather pretty piece of formal play. The vowel of the verb stem which we spoke of as occupying the first position in the verb symbolized the intransitive or static mode of apprehension of the act. As soon as the causative notion is introduced, however, the verb stem is compelled to pass to the category of transitivized or active notions, which means that the causative suffix, in spite of the parenthetical inclusion of certain notions of direction of movement, has the retroactive effect of changing the vowel of the stem. Up to this point, therefore, we get a perfectly unified complex of notions which may be rendered "to cause a group to move across a stream in an easterly direction."

But this is not yet a word, at least not a word in the finished sense of the term, for the elements that are still to follow have just as little independent existence as those we have already referred to. Of the more formal elements that are needed to complete the word, the first is a tense suffix referring to the future. This is followed by a pronominal element which refers to the first person singular, is different in form from the suffixed pronoun used in other tenses and modalities. Finally, there is an element consisting of a single consonant which indicates that the whole word, which is a complete proposition in itself, is to be understood in an interrogative sense. Here again the language illustrates an interesting kind of specialization of form. Nearly all words of the language differ slightly in form according to whether the speaker is a man speaking to a man or, on the other hand, is a woman or a man speaking to a woman. The interrogative form that we have just discussed can only be used by a man speaking to a man. In the other three cases the suffix in question is not used, but the last vowel of the word, which in this particular case happens to be the final vowel of the pronominal suffix, is lengthened in order to express the interrogative modality.

We are not in the least interested in the details of this analysis, but some of its implications should interest us. In the first place, it is necessary to bear in mind that there is nothing arbitrary or accidental or even curious about the structure of this word. Every element falls into its proper place in accordance with definitely formulable rules which can be discovered by the investigator but of which the speakers themselves have no more conscious knowledge than of the inhabitants of the moon. It is possible to say, for instance, that the verb stem is a particular example of a large number of elements which belong to the same general class, such as "to sit," "to walk," "to run," "to jump," and so on; or that the element which expresses the idea crossing from one side to another is a particular example of a large class of local elements of parallel function, such as "to the next house," "up the hill," "into a hollow," "over the crest," "down hill," "under," "over," "in the middle of," "off," "hither," and so on. We may quite safely assume that no Yana Indian ever had the slightest knowledge of classifications such as these or ever possessed even an inkling of the fact that his language neatly symbolized classifications of this sort by means of its **phonetic** apparatus and by rigid rules of sequence and cohesion of formal elements. Yet all the while we may be perfectly certain that the relations which give the elements of the language their significance were somehow felt and adhered to. A mistake in the vowel of the first syllable, for instance, would undoubtedly feel to a native speaker like a self-contradictory form in English, for instance "five house" instead of "five houses" or "they runs" instead of "they run." Mistakes of this sort are resisted as any aesthetic transgression might be resisted—as being somehow incongruous, out of the picture, or, if one chooses to rationalize the resistance, as inherently illogical.

The unconscious patterning of linguistic conduct is discoverable not only in the significant forms of language but, just as surely, in the several materials out of which language is built, namely the vowels and consonants, the changes of stress and quantity, and the fleeting intonations of speech. It is quite an illusion to believe that the sounds and the sound dynamics of language can be sufficiently defined by more or less detailed statements of how the speech articulations are managed in a neurological or muscular sense. Every language has a phonetic scheme in which a given sound or a given dynamic treatment of a sound has a definite configurated place in reference to all the other sounds recognized by the language. The single sound, in other words, is in no sense identical with an articulation or with the perception of an articulation. It is, rather, a point in a pattern, precisely as a tone in a given musical tradition is a point in a pattern which includes the whole range of aesthetically possible tones. Two given tones may be physically distinguished but aesthetically identical because each is heard or understood as occupying the same formal position in the total set of recognized tones. In a musical tradition which does not recognize **chromatic** intervals "C sharp" would have to be identified with "C" and would be considered as a mere deviation, pleasant or unpleasant, from "C." In our own musical tradition the difference between "C" and "C sharp" is crucial to an understanding of all our music, and, by unconscious projection, to a certain way of misunderstanding all other music built on different principles. In still other musical traditions there are still finer intervalic differences recognized, none of which quite corresponds to our semitone interval. In these three cases it is obvious that nothing can be said as to the cultural and aesthetic status of a given tone in a song unless we know or feel against what sort of general tonal background it is to be interpreted.

It is precisely so with the sounds of speech. From a purely objective standpoint the difference between the k of "kill" and the k of "skill" is as easily definable as the, to us, major difference between the k of "kill" and the g of "gill" (of a fish). In some languages the g sound of "gill" would be looked upon, or rather would be intuitively interpreted, as a comparatively unimportant or individual divergence from a sound typically represented by the k of "skill," while the k of "kill," with its greater strength of articulation and its audible breath release, would constitute an utterly distinct phonetic entity. Obviously the two distinct k sounds of such a language and the two ways of pronouncing the k in English, while objectively comparable and even identical phenomena, are from the point of view of patterning utterly different. Hundreds of interesting and, at first blush, strangely paradoxical examples of this sort could be given, but the subject is perhaps too technical for treatment in this paper.

It is needless to say that no normal speaker has an adequate knowledge of these submerged sound configurations. He is the unconscious and magnificently loyal adherent of thoroughly socialized phonetic patterns, which are simple and self-evident in daily practice, but subtly involved and historically determined in actual fact. Owing to the necessity of thinking of speech habits not merely in overt terms but as involving the setting up of intuitively mastered relations in suitable contexts, we need not be surprised that an articulatory habit which is perfectly feasible in one set of relations becomes subjectively impossible when the pattern in which it is to be fitted is changed. Thus, an English-speaking person who is utterly unable to pronounce a French nasalized vowel may nevertheless be quite able to execute the necessary articulation in another context, such as the imitation of snoring or of the sound of some wild animal. Again, the Frenchman or German who cannot pronounce the "wh" of our American-English "why" can easily produce the same sound when he gently blows out a candle. It is obviously correct to say that the acts illustrated in these cases can only be understood as they are fitted into definite cultural patterns concerning the form and mechanics of which the normal individual has no adequate knowledge.

We may now summarize our interpretation of these, and thousands of other, examples of language behavior by saying that in each case an unconscious control of very complicated configurations or formal sets is individually acquired by processes which it is the business of the psychologist to try to understand but that, in spite of the enormously varied psychological predispositions and types of conditioning which characterize different personalities, these patterns in their completed form differ only infinitesimally from individual to individual, in many cases from generation to generation. And yet these forms lie entirely outside the inherited biological tendencies of the race and can be explained only in strictly social terms. In the simple facts of language we have an excellent example of an important network of patterns of behavior, each of them with exceedingly complex and, to a large extent, only vaguely definable functions, which is preserved and transmitted with a minimum of consciousness. The forms of speech so transmitted seem as necessary as the simplest reflexes of the organism. So powerfully, indeed, are we in the grip of our phonetic habits that it becomes one of the most delicate and difficult tasks of the linguistic student to discover what is the true configuration of sounds in languages alien to his own. This means that the average person unconsciously interprets the phonetic material of other languages in terms imposed upon him by the habits of his own language. Thus, the naïve Frenchman confounds the two sounds "s" of "sick" and "th" of "think" in a single pattern point—not because he is really unable to hear the difference, but because the setting up of such a difference disturbs his feeling for the necessary configuration of linguistic sounds. It is as though an observer from Mars, knowing nothing of the custom we call war, were intuitively led to confound a punishable murder with a thoroughly legal and noble act of killing in the course of battle. The mechanism of projection of patterns is as evident in the one case as in the other.

Not all forms of cultural behavior so well illustrate the mechanics of unconscious patterning as does linguistic behavior, but there are few, if any, types of cultural behavior which do not illustrate it. Functional considerations of all kinds, leading to a greater degree of conscious control, or apparent control, of the patterns of behavior, tend to obscure the unconscious nature of the patterns themselves, but the more carefully we study cultural behavior, the more thoroughly we become convinced that the differences are but differences of degree. A very good example of another field for the development of unconscious cultural patterns is that of gesture. Gestures are hard to classify and it is difficult to make a conscious separation between that in gesture which is of merely individual origin and that which is referable to the habits of the group as a whole. In spite of these difficulties of conscious analysis, we respond to gestures with an extreme alertness and, one might almost say, in accordance with an elaborate and secret code that is written nowhere, known by none, and understood by all. But this code is by no means referable to simple organic responses. On the contrary, it is as finely certain and artificial, as definitely a creation of social tradition, as language or religion or industrial technology. Like everything else in human conduct, gesture roots in the reactive necessities of the organism, but the laws of gesture, the unwritten code of gestured messages and responses, is the anonymous work of an elaborate social tradition. Whoever doubts this may soon become convinced when he penetrates into the significance of gesture patterns of other societies than his own. A Jewish or Italian shrug of the shoulders is no more the same pattern of behavior as the shrug of a typical American than the forms and significant evocations of the Yiddish or Italian sentence are identical with those of any thinkable English sentence. The differences are not to be referred to supposedly deep-seated racial differences of a biological sort. They lie in the unconsciously apprehended builds of the respective social patterns which include them and out of which they have been abstracted for an essentially artificial comparison. A certain immobility of countenance in New York or Chicago may be interpreted as a masterly example of the art of wearing a poker face, but when worn by a perfectly average inhabitant of Tokio, it may be explainable as nothing more interesting or important than the simplest and most obvious of good manners. It is the failure to understand the relativity of gesture and posture, the degree to which these classes of behavior are referable to social patterns which transcend merely individual psychological significances, which makes it so easy for us to find individual indices of personality where it is only the alien culture that speaks.

In the economic life of a people, too, we are constantly forced to recognize the pervasive influence of patterns which stand in no immediate relation to the needs of the organism and which are by no means to be taken for granted in a general philosophy of economic conduct but which must be fitted into the framework of social forms characteristic of a given society. There is not only an unconscious patterning of the types of endeavor that are classed as economic, there is even such a thing as a characteristic patterning of economic motive. Thus, the acquirement of wealth is not to be lightly taken for granted as one of the basic drives of human beings. One accumulates property, one defers the immediate enjoyment of wealth, only in so far as society sets the pace for these activities and inhibitions. Many primitive societies are quite innocent of an understanding of the accumulation of wealth in our sense of the phrase. Even where there is a definite feeling that wealth should be accumulated, the motives which are responsible for the practice and which give definite form to the methods of acquiring wealth are often signally different from such as we can readily understand.

The West Coast Indians of British Columbia have often been quoted as a primitive society that has developed a philosophy of wealth which is somewhat comparable to our own, with its emphasis on "conspicuous waste" and on the sacrosanct character of property. The comparison is not essentially sound. The West Coast Indian does not handle wealth in a manner which we can recognize as our own. We can find plenty of analogies, to be sure, but they are more likely to be misleading than helpful. No West Coast Indian, so far as we know, ever amassed wealth as an individual pure and simple, with the expectation of disposing of it in the fulness of time at his own sweet will. This is a dream of the modern European and American individualist, and it is a dream which not only brings no thrill to the heart of the West Coast Indian but is probably almost meaningless to him. The concepts of wealth and the display of honorific privileges, such as crests and dances and songs and names, which have been inherited from legendary ancestors are inseparable among these Indians. One cannot publicly exhibit such a privilege without expending wealth in connection with it. Nor is there much object in accumulating wealth except to reaffirm privileges already possessed, or, in the spirit of a **parvenu**, to imply the possession of privileges none too clearly recognized as legitimate by one's fellow tribesmen. In other words, wealth, beyond a certain point, is with these people much more a token of status than it is a tool for the fulfillment of personal desires. We may go so far as to say that among the West Coast Indians it is not the individual at all who possesses wealth. It is primarily the ceremonial **patrimony** of which he is the temporary custodian that demands the symbolism of wealth. Arrived at a certain age, the West Coast Indian turns his privileges over to those who are by kin or marriage connection entitled to manipulate them. Henceforth he may be as poor as a church mouse, without loss of prestige. I should not like to go so far as to say that the concepts of wealth among ourselves and among the West Coast Indians are utterly different things. Obviously they are nothing of the kind, but they are measurably distinct and the nature of the difference must be sought in the total patterning of life in the two communities from which the particular pattern of wealth and its acquirement has been extracted. It should be fairly clear that where the patterns of manipulation of wealth are as different as they are in these two cases, it would be a mere exercise of the academic imagination to interpret the economic activities of one society in terms of the general economy which has been abstracted from the mode of life of the other.

No matter where we turn in the field of social behavior, men and women do what they do, and cannot help but do, not merely because they are built thus and so, or possess such and such differences of personality, or must needs adapt to their immediate environment in such and such a way in order to survive at all, but very largely because they have found it easiest and aesthetically most satisfactory to pattern their conduct in accordance with more or less clearly organized forms of behavior which no one is individually responsible for, which are not clearly grasped in their true nature, and which one might almost say are as self-evidently imputed to the nature of things as the three dimensions are imputed to space. It is sometimes necessary to become conscious of the forms of social behavior in order to bring about a more serviceable adaptation to changed conditions, but I believe it can be laid down as a principle of far-reaching application that in the normal business of life it is useless and even mischievous for the individual to carry the conscious analysis of his cultural patterns around with him. That should be left to the student whose business it is to understand these patterns. A healthy unconsciousness of the forms of socialized behavior to which we are subject is as necessary to society as is the mind's ignorance, or better unawareness, of the workings of the viscera to the health of the body. In great works of the imagination form is significant only in so far as we feel ourselves to be in its grip. It is unimpressive when divulged in the explicit terms of this or that simple or complex arrangement of known elements. So, too, in social behavior, it is not the overt forms that rise readily to the surface of attention that are most worth our while. We must learn to take joy in the larger freedom of loyalty to thousands of subtle patterns of behavior that we can never hope to understand in explicit terms. Complete analysis and the conscious control that comes with a complete analysis are at best but the medicine of society, not its food. We must never allow ourselves to substitute the starveling calories of knowledge for the meat and bread of historical experience. This historic experience may be theoretically knowable, but it dare never be fully known in the conduct of daily life.

Note
1   E.S. Dummer, ed., *The Unconscious: A Symposium* (New York, Knopf, 1927), pp. 114-142.

Study Questions
1. According to Sapir, what is the difference between individual and social behaviour?

2. What does Sapir mean by the unconscious patterning of behaviour in society? How can such patterning be elicited?

3. In his selection, why does Sapir devote so much attention to language behaviour?

Further Readings

Caroll, J.B. (ed.). 1956. *Language, Thought and Reality: Selected Writings of Benjamin Lee Whorf.* New York: John Wiley and Sons.

Darnell, Regna. 1990. *Edward Sapir: Linguist, Anthropologist, Humanist.* Berkeley: University of California Press.

Hymes, Dell (ed.). 1974. *Studies in the History of Linguistics: Traditions and Paradigms.* Ann Arbor, MI: Books on Demand.

Sapir, Edward. 1958. *Culture, Language and Personality: Selected Essays*. Ed. David Mandelbaum. Berkeley: University of California Press.

Sebeok, Thomas Albert (ed.). 1966. *Portraits of Linguistics: A Biographical Source Book for the History of Western Linguistics, 1746-1963*. Bloomington: Indiana University Press.

14

Social Structure

ALFRED REGINALD RADCLIFFE-BROWN

Whewell, in his *Novum organon renovatum*,[1] describes inductive science as "the application of clear and appropriate ideas to a body of facts," and as requiring a double process of "explication of concepts" and **"colligation** of facts." Each science must advance by means of its *appropriate* concepts, and this requires the creation of a coherent system of technical terms. "In an advanced science, the history of the language of the science is the history of the science itself.... The fundamental principle and supreme rule of all scientific terminology is that terms must be constructed and appropriated so as to be fitted to enunciate simply and clearly true general proposition." Social anthropology is not yet an advanced science; it does not yet have a coherent system of concepts denoted by technical terms accepted and used in the same sense by all the students of the subject. This is the result, and at the same time the sign, of the immaturity of the science. One of the difficulties that the reader of the literature of anthropology has to face is the fact that the same word is used in different meanings by different writers, and many anthropological terms are sometimes used ambiguously or without precise definition.

In order to avoid confused and unscientific thinking it is necessary to obtain and keep constantly in mind a clear idea of the nature of the empirical reality with which we have to deal in social anthropology, and to which all our concepts and theories must be referred. Only in this way can we hope to avoid the fallacy of "misplaced concreteness" which results from treating abstractions as though they were concrete realities, a fallacy which it is difficult to avoid. There is a tendency to think of "societies" as if they were separate discrete entities. This is derived from Aristotle, for whom a society was a *koinonia politike*, a political association such as the Greek city state. The collection of persons living in a defined area under a single political authority is only one kind of association. We might ask "Is the British Empire a 'society,' or, if not, how many distinct societies does it contain?" The Roman Church as a religious or ecclesiastical association is as much a society as a political association such as the United States. It is necessary to avoid the tendency to think of societies as discrete entities in the way in which Herbert Spencer did.

The empirical reality with which social anthropology has to deal, by description, by analysis and in comparative studies, is the process of social life of a certain limited region during a certain period of time. The social life as a phenomenal reality is a process consisting of a multitude of actions of human beings, more particularly their interactions and joint actions. The particular events of the social life are the facts to which all our concepts and theories must be applied. To provide a description of social life we have to describe certain *general* features which seem significant or relevant to our enquiries, and it is these generalised descriptions that provide the *data* of the science. It is obvious that importance attaches to the way in which these data are extracted, from direct observation or particular facts, from statements by informants, or from historical records.

Over a limited period the general features of the social life of a particular region may remain unchanged, or may change in only minor respects. In other instances, particularly if a sufficient period be taken, there will be significant changes in some features. We can distinguish between a **synchronic** description in which the social life is taken as it is at a certain time without reference to changes in its general features, and a **diachronic** description which gives an account of such changes.

Two very important concepts are *social structure* and *social organisation*. The concept of structure refers to an arrangement of parts or components related to one another in some sort of larger unity. We can talk of the structure of a house, meaning the arrangement of walls, roof, rooms, stairs, passages, etc., and ultimately as an arrangement of bricks, stone, timber, etc. We can speak of the structure of a piece of music as an arrangement of successive sounds, and we can say that the structure of one fugue or sonata is similar in *form* to that of another. The structure of a molecule is the arrangement of its component atoms in relation to one another. The structure of a human body is in the first instance an arrangement of tissues and organs, but ultimately an arrangement of living and dead cells and interstitial fluids.

In social structure the ultimate components are individual human beings thought of as actors in the social life, that is, as *persons*, and structure consists of the arrangement of persons in relation to each other. The inhabitants of Europe are arranged into nations, and this is therefore a structural feature of the social life of Europe. In a village we may find an arrangement of persons into families or households, which is again a structural feature. In a family the structure consists of the relations of father, mother and children to each other.

Thus in looking for the structural features of social life we look first for the existence of social groups of all kinds, and examine also the internal structure of those groups that we find. But besides the arrangement of persons into groups and within those groups we find also an arrangement into social classes and categories. Social distinctions between men and women, between chiefs or nobles and commoners, between patricians and plebians, between Brahmins, Sundras and untouchables, are important structural features, though we cannot properly speak of these as forming social groups. Further, a most important structural feature is the arrangement of persons in dyadic, person to person, relationships, such as that between master and servant, or, in primitive societies between mother's brother and sister's son. Ultimately, a social structure is exhibited either in interactions between groups, as when one nation goes to war with another, or in interactions between persons.

While structure refers to arrangements of persons, organisation refers to the arrangement of activities. A gardener or peasant may be said to organise his own work when he allots different tasks to different seasons of the year. Social organisation is the arrangement of activities of two or more persons which are adjusted to give a united combined activity. An example is the organisation of work in a factory, whereby the manager, the foremen, the workmen, each have certain tasks to perform as part of the total activity. An organised group, which may consist of only two persons, is one in which the members combine in a joint activity in which each has an allotted part. We cannot, however, regard such groups as features of the social structure unless they have some degree of permanence. A football team is an organised group, but not the assembly of people who help to pull an overturned motor car out of a ditch.

These concepts of structure and organisation can be illustrated by reference to a modern army. The structure consists in the first place of the arrangement into groups—divisions, army corps, regiments, companies, and so on; and secondly of the arrangement of the personnel into ranks—generals, colonels, majors, corporals, "other ranks," etc. A rank is not a group; the majors, for example, do not constitute a social group but form a social category, like plumbers, bookmakers or University Professors. But the arrangement into ranks is an essential feature of the structure of an army. The organisation of the army is the allotment of activities of various kinds to the groups and individuals, whether in time of peace, or in actual military operations. A modern army is the best example of a highly organised structure; a Socialist State would have to be something similar.

The best way to make clear the concept of social structure is by an example, and we may take for this purpose the structural system of the tribes of a part of Western Australia as it was in former times. The essential basis of the structure was provided by the division of the country into a number of recognised distinct territories. Every male was attached by birth and throughout his life to one of these, that of his father and his father's father. The men thus connected with a particular territory formed a distinct social group which we speak of as a "clan," and this was a unit of fundamental importance in the social structure. A woman also belonged to the clan of her father, but since marriage between persons of one clan was forbidden, the women married men from other clans and became attached to the territory of the husband.

The men of a clan, together with their wives, coming from other clans, and their children, formed a group that it is convenient to call a ***horde***, which may be described as occupying the territory of the clan. The horde camped together as a unit whether in their own country or when they were visiting friendly territories. A horde may be described as being politically autonomous, under the authority of the old men, and as being very largely self-sufficient economically. It probably numbered, on the average, not more than fifty persons.

The internal structure of the horde was a division into families, each composed of a man with his wife or wives and their young children. It was a domestic group under the man's authority, having its own family hearth and shelter and its own food-supply. The family as a group was formed by marriage and the birth of children and came to an end as a separate group on the death of the husband, thus having continuous existence for only a limited number of years. The clan was a continuing group which the natives themselves thought of as having come into existence at the beginning of the world, and as being eternal; as members were lost by death they were replaced by the birth of new members. The continuity of the horde as a group of persons living regularly together was somewhat different. The male members of the clan constituted the continuing nucleus of the horde, but the female members moved out when they married, and other women moved in as wives of the men.

There were wider systems of structure. A number of clans had the same language, and had similar customs; they therefore formed a linguistic community, which is referred to as a *tribe*. Unlike what are called tribes in some other regions, this was not a politically united group; the members of a tribe did not unite in any combined action. Hordes of the same tribe or of different tribes might live at peace with one another, or might on occasion engage in fighting.

Persons of different hordes and of different tribes were linked together by means of the kinship system. A man was connected by some relation of kinship, near or distant, with every person with whom he had any social contact, no matter to what horde or tribe they belonged. The basis of the reckoning consisted of actual genealogical relationships, including therein the relations between fellow-members of one clan. The kin of any given person were classified into a limited number of categories, each denoted by one kinship term, but distinguished within the category as being nearer or more distant. The behaviour of any two persons towards one another was dependent on the relationship in which they stood in the kinship structure. The structure was a complex arrangement of dyadic, person to person, relationships. A particular man was closely connected through his mother with her clan and its members. He could always visit their territory and live with the horde though he was not and could not become a member of the clan. Different members of a single clan were connected in this way with different other clans. The same thing results from the fact that a man was connected with the clan of his mother's mother, and with the clan from which he obtained a wife. Each person had his own particular position in the total kinship structure. Even two full brothers might marry into different clans, although they had the same connection with their mother's clan.

There is a division of the society into two moieties, and this division extends through a number of tribes. Each clan belongs to one of the moieties. We may denote the moieties as I and II. Essentially the system is a classification or grouping of clans, which cuts across the classification into tribes or linguistic communities. A man distinguishes the clans with which he is acquainted as belonging to the same moiety as his own or to the other moiety. There is a further dichotomy of society into two alternating generation divisions, which can be denoted as x and y. If a man belongs to the x division his children will be y, and so will his father, while his father's father and his son's son will be x like himself. Each clan therefore contains at all times persons of both divisions. There is therefore a four-fold division of society, into what it is convenient to call "sections," the four being Ix, Iy, IIx and IIy. These sections have names— such as Banaka, Burong, Karimera and Paldjeri. By the laws of these tribes a man may only marry a woman who belongs to one of the categories into which his kin are arranged, that which includes the daughter of his mother's brother. The result is that he must find a wife in his own generation division and in the opposite moiety from his own; a man of Ix has to find a wife in IIx; in the Kariera tribe a man of Banaka section had to find a wife in the Burung section. If by "social group" we mean a body of persons having a certain cohesion, the clans and hordes are groups in this sense, but the sections are not. They provide a kind of classification of persons within the intertribal kinship structure, and are part of that structure.

There are other aspects of social structure that should be mentioned. Each clan is a distinct totemic group, having its own sacred totem-centres within its territory, its own myths of the origin of the topographical features of the territory and of these sacred spots, and its own rites which are carried out with the ostensible purpose of maintaining the continuity of nature and of society. Each clan has its own totemic solidarity and continuity, which differentiates it from other clans. But, in addition, there are totemic ceremonies and religious rites for the initiation of boys in which a number of clans unite and co-operate. Meetings of clans in the territory of one of them are held at intervals; on different occasions it is a different collection of clans that assembles, since a meeting held in the territory of a particular clan will only be attended by neighbouring friendly clans. It is the clans and their meetings that provide the religious structure of society.

Each of these meetings can be regarded as creating a temporary political group, for at them conflicts between clans or between individual members of different clans are settled under the authority of the assembled public opinion. This is the nearest approach that these tribes have to a political organisation wider than the horde.

In these tribes, as elsewhere in Australia, there was a continuous circulation of certain kinds of articles by exchanges of gifts, whereby they passed from one horde to another. These exchanges were less important economically than as maintaining relations of friendship.

In many societies an important element of the structural system is the division into social classes, such as the division between chiefs and commoners in Polynesia. In Australian tribes there are no distinctions of this kind except on the basis of sex and age, but this is of very great importance. Men and women have different occupations. Authority is exercised in all social affairs by the older men, who are also the ritual leaders.

This description of a structural system in a primitive people may help to make clear certain matters. To arrive at a description of a structural system we have not only to consider social groups, such as the family, the clan and the horde, in Western Australia, with the internal structure of the group and the relations between the groups, and also social classes, but we have to examine the whole set of socially fixed relationships of person to person, as in the Australian kinship system. The social reality of groups and classes consists in the way in which they affect the interactions of persons, as belonging to the same or different groups or classes. From this point of view the structure of a region at a particular time consists of the whole set of social relationships in which the persons of that region are involved.

In any of the relationships of which the social structure consists there is an expectation that a person will conform to certain rules or patterns of behaviour. The term *institution* is used to refer to this, an institution being an established or socially recognised system of norms or patterns of conduct referring to some aspect of social life. The family institutions of a society are the patterns of behaviour to which the members of the family are expected to conform in their conduct in relation to one another. There are patterns or norms of conduct for a father towards his children, for a wife to a husband and vice versa, for child to parent, for brother to brother or sister. These institutions are accepted in a particular society, of which they are the institutions, as fixing, with a certain measure of flexibility, the *proper* conduct of a person in a certain relationship. They define for a person how he is expected to behave, and also how he may expect others to behave. Not every one always behaves as he ought, as he is expected to; minor or major deviations are frequent in any society; to deal with these there are *sanctions* of various kinds. Social structure therefore has to be described by the institutions which define the proper or expected conduct of persons in their various relationships. The structural features of social life of a particular region consist of all those continuing arrangements of persons in institutional relationships which are exhibited in the actions and interactions that in their totality make up the social life.

A question that needs to be mentioned, though it can only be dealt with very briefly, is that of structural continuity. We may first consider the continuity of social groups. A group such as a nation, a tribe, or a clan may have a continuous existence although its membership is continually changing, since it loses members by death and gains new members by birth. A learned society loses members by death or resignation but replaces them by electing new members. The French Academy continues to keep its identity although the members are now an entirely different set of persons from the members in the eighteenth century.

The same sort of continuity can be observed in social classes. In a Polynesian society the class of chiefs is continuous since when a chief dies he is replaced, in some instances by his eldest son. An occupational or professional class may have the same kind of continuity; as doctors or lawyers die or retire their places are taken by new recruits to the profession. A regiment in the army may have a continuous existence though there is a more or less continuous change of the persons who form it, and though lieutenants may become captains and then majors, and colonels, the arrangement of ranks remains the same. The United States always has a President, and England has a King, though the person who occupies this position in the social structure changes from time to time. The English House of Commons or the United States House of Representatives maintains its continuity in spite of changes in membership at each election.

Thus, as social structure is an arrangement of persons in institutionalised roles and relationships, structural continuity is the continuity of such arrangements. This may be conveniently expressed by means of the ideas of matter and form. In the static continuity of a building both the matter, the bricks, timber, tiles, etc., and the form remain the same. In a human body the matter consists of molecules, and this is constantly changing; my body does not consist of the same molecules as it did yesterday, and there is a popular idea that at the end of seven years every molecule of a human body has been replaced. But a human organism retains its form, excluding such changes as the amputation of a leg. The structural continuity of an organism is thus a dynamic, not a static, continuity, a process in which the matter of which the organisms is composed is continually changing while the form remains the same. Structural continuity in human societies is dynamic in this sense, the matter being individual human beings, the form being the way in which they are connected by institutional relationships.

An aspect that has to be considered is the fact that individuals change their position in social structure during the course of life. A man may change his nationality, or leave one church to join another. What is everywhere present is the process by which a human being begins life as an infant and grows into an adult; the social position of a person changes, either gradually, or by institutionally defined stages, as from a boy he becomes a young man and finally an elder. In some African societies a very important structural feature is a system of age-grades, an individual passing from one grade to the next in accordance with the institutional pattern.

Social structure, therefore, is to be defined as the continuing arrangement of persons in relationships defined or controlled by institutions, i.e., socially established norms or patterns of behaviour.

Note
1   3rd ed., 1858.

Study Questions
1. According to Radcliffe-Brown, what is the difference between social structure and social organization?

2. According to Radcliffe-Brown, what is the function of social institutions?

3. What does Radcliffe-Brown mean when he characterizes the structural continuity of societies as dynamic?

Further Readings
Goody, Jack. 1995. *The Expansive Moment: The Rise of Social Anthropology in Britain and Africa, 1918-1970*. New York: Cambridge University Press.

Kuper, Adam. 1983. *Anthropology and Anthropologists: The Modern British School*. (Rev. ed.). New York: Routledge.

Langham, Ian G. 1981. *The Building of British Social Anthropology*. Norwell, MA: Kluwer Academic Publishers.

Radcliffe-Brown, Alfred Reginald. 1964 [1922]. *The Andaman Islanders*. New York: Free Press of Glencoe.

—. 1965 [1952]. *Structure and Function in Primitive Society*. New York: The Free Press.

Slobodin, Richard. 1978. *W.H.R. Rivers*. New York: Columbia University Press.

Stocking, George W., Jr. 1995. *After Tylor: British Social Anthropology, 1888-1951*. Madison: University of Wisconsin Press.

Urry, James (ed.). 1993. *Before Social Anthropology: Essays on the History of British Anthropology*. Newark, NJ: Gordon Breach.

15

The Subject, Method and Scope of This Inquiry
[*Argonauts of the Western Pacific*]

BRONISLAW MALINOWSKI

I

The coastal populations of the South Sea Islands, with very few exceptions, are, or were before their extinction, expert navigators and traders. Several of them had evolved excellent types of large sea-going canoes, and used to embark in them on distant trade expeditions or raids of war and conquest. The Papuo-Melanesians, who inhabit the coast and the outlying islands of New Guinea, are no exception to this rule. In general they are daring sailors, industrious manufacturers, and keen traders. The manufacturing centres of important articles, such as pottery, stone implements, canoes, fine baskets, valued ornaments, are localised in several places, according to the skill of the inhabitants, their inherited tribal tradition, and special facilities offered by the district; thence they are traded over wide areas, sometimes travelling more than hundreds of miles.

Definite forms of exchange along definite trade routes are to be found established between the various tribes. A most remarkable form of intertribal trade is that obtaining between the Motu of **Port Moresby** and the tribes of the Papuan Gulf. The Motu sail for hundreds of miles in heavy, unwieldy canoes, called *lakotoi*, which are provided with the characteristic crab-claw sails. They bring pottery and shell ornaments, in olden days, stone blades, to Gulf Papuans, from whom they obtain in exchange **sago** and the heavy dug-outs, which are used afterwards by the Motu for the construction of their *lakatoi* canoes.[1]

Further East, on the South coast, there lives the industrious, sea-faring population of the Mailu, who link the East End of New Guinea with the central coast tribes by means of annual trading expeditions.[2] Finally, the natives of the islands and archipelagoes, scattered around the East End, are in constant trading relations with one another. We possess in Professor **Seligman**'s book an excellent description of the subject, especially of the nearer trades routes between the various islands inhabited by the Southern **Massim**.[3] There exists, however, another, a very extensive and highly complex trading system, embracing with its ramifications, not only the islands near the East End, but also the **Louisiades**, **Woodlark Island**, the **Trobriand Archipelago**, and the **d'Entrecasteaux** group; it penetrates into the mainland of New Guinea, and exerts an indirect influence over several outlying districts, such as **Rossel Island**, and some parts of the Northern and Southern coast of New Guinea. This trading system, the **Kula**, is the subject I am setting out to describe in this volume, and it will be seen that it is an economic phenomenon of considerable theoretical importance. It looms paramount in the tribal life of those natives who live within its circuit, and its importance is fully realised by the tribesmen themselves, whose ideas, ambitions, desires and vanities are very much bound up with the Kula.

II

Before proceeding to the account of the Kula, it will be well to give a description of the methods used in the collecting of the ethnographic material. The results of scientific research in any branch of learning ought to be presented in a manner absolutely candid and above board. No one would dream of making an experimental contribution to physical or chemical science, without giving a detailed account of all the arrangements of the experiments; an exact description of the apparatus used; of the manner in which the observations were conducted; of their number; of the length of time devoted to them, and of the degree of approximation with which each measurement was made. In less exact sciences, as in biology or geology, this cannot be done as rigorously, but every student will do his best to bring home to the reader all the conditions in which the experiment or the observations were made. In Ethnography, where a candid account of such data is perhaps even more necessary, it has unfortunately in the past not always been supplied with sufficient generosity, and many writers do not ply the full searchlight of methodic sincerity, as they move among their facts but produce them before us out of complete obscurity.

It would be easy to quote works of high repute, and with a scientific hallmark on them, in which wholesale generalisations are laid down before us, and we are not informed at all by what actual experiences the writers have reached their conclusion. No special chapter or paragraph is devoted to describing to us the conditions under which observations were made and information collected. I consider that only such ethnographic sources are of unquestionable scientific value, in which we can clearly draw the line between, on the one hand, the results of direct observation and of native statements and interpretations, and on the other, the inferences of the author, based on his common sense and psychological insight.[4] Indeed, some such survey, as that contained in the table, given below (Div. VI of this chapter) ought to be forthcoming, so that at a glance the reader could estimate with precision the degree of the writer's personal acquaintance with the facts which he describes, and form an idea under what conditions information had been obtained from the natives.

Again, in historical science, no one could expect to be seriously treated if he made any mystery of his sources and spoke of the past as if he knew it by divination. In Ethnography, the writer is his own chronicler and the historian at the same time, while his sources are no doubt easily accessible, but also supremely elusive and complex; they are not embodied in fixed, material documents, but in the behaviour and in the memory of living men. In Ethnography, the distance is often enormous between the brute material of information—as it is presented to the student in his own observations, in native statement, in the kaleidoscope of tribal life—and the final authoritative presentation of the results. The Ethnographer has to traverse this distance in the laborious years between the moment when he sets foot upon a native beach, and makes his first attempts to get into touch with the natives, and the time when he writes down the final version of his results. A brief outline of an Ethnographer's tribulations, as lived through by myself, may throw more light on the question, than any long abstract discussion could do.

III

Imagine yourself suddenly set down surrounded by all your gear, alone on a tropical beach close to a native village, while the launch or dinghy which has brought you sails away out of sight. Since you take up your abode in the compound of some neighbouring white man, trader or missionary, you have nothing to do, but to start at once on your ethnographic work. Imagine further that you are a beginner, without previous experience, with nothing to guide you and no one to help you. For the white man is temporarily absent, or else unable or unwilling to waste any of his time on you. This exactly describes my first initiation into field work on the south coast of New Guinea. I well remember the long visits I paid to the villages during the first weeks; the feeling of hopelessness and despair after many obstinate but futile attempts had entirely failed to bring me into real touch with the natives, or supply me with any material. I had periods of despondency, when I buried myself in the reading of novels, as a man might take to drink in a fit of tropical depression and boredom.

Imagine yourself then, making your first entry into the village, alone or in company with your white **cicerone**. Some natives flock round you, especially if they smell tobacco. Others, the more dignified and elderly, remain seated where they are. Your white companion has his routine way of treating the natives, and he neither understands, nor is very much concerned with the manner in which you, as an ethnographer, will have to approach them. The first visit leaves you with a hopeful feeling that when you return alone, things will be easier. Such was my hope at least.

I came back duly, and soon gathered an audience around me. A few compliments in **pidgin**-English on both sides, some tobacco changing hands, induced an atmosphere of mutual amiability. I tried then to proceed to business. First, to begin with subjects which might arouse no suspicion, I started to "do" technology. A few natives were engaged in manufacturing some object or other. It was easy to look at it and obtain the names of the tools, and even some technical expressions about the proceedings, but there the matter ended. It must be borne in mind that pidgin-English is a very imperfect instrument for expressing one's ideas, and that before one gets a good training in framing questions and understanding answers one has the uncomfortable feeling that free communication in it with the natives will never be attained; and I was quite unable to enter into any more detailed or explicit conversation with them at first. I knew well that the best remedy for this was to collect concrete data, and accordingly I took a village census, wrote down genealogies, drew up plans and collected the terms of kinship. But all this remained dead material, which led no further into the understanding of real native mentality or behaviour, since I could neither procure a good native interpretation of any of these items, nor get what could be called the hang of tribal life. As to obtaining their ideas about religion, and magic, their beliefs in sorcery and spirits, nothing was forthcoming except a few superficial items of folk-lore, mangled by being forced into pidgin English.

Information which I received from some white residents in the district, valuable as it was in itself, was more discouraging than anything else with regard to my own work. Here were men who had lived for years in the place with constant opportunities of observing the natives and communicating with them, and who yet hardly knew one thing about them really well. How could I therefore in a few months or a year, hope to overtake and go beyond them? Moreover, the manner in which my white informants spoke about the natives and put their views was, naturally, that of untrained minds, unaccustomed to formulate their thoughts with any degree of consistency and precision. And they were for the most part, naturally enough, full of the biassed and pre-judged opinions inevitable in the average practical man, whether administrator, missionary, or trader, yet so strongly repulsive to a mind striving after the objective, scientific view of things. The habit of treating with a self-satisfied frivolity what is really serious to the ethnographer; the cheap rating of what to him is a scientific treasure, that is to say, the native's cultural and mental peculiarities and independence—these features, so well known in the inferior amateur's writing, I found in the tone of the majority of white residents.[5]

Indeed, in my first piece of Ethnographic research on the South coast, it was not until I was alone in the district that I began to make some headway; and, at any rate, I found out where lay the secret of effective field-work. What is then this ethnographer's magic, by which he is able to evoke the real spirit of the natives, the true picture of tribal life? As usual, success can only be obtained by a patient and systematic application of a number of rules of common sense and well-known scientific principles, and not by the discovery of any marvellous short-cut leading to the desired results without effort or trouble. The principles of method can be grouped under three main headings; first of all, naturally, the student must possess real scientific aims, and know the values and criteria of modern ethnography. Secondly, he ought to put himself in good conditions of work, that is, in the main, to live without other white men, right among the natives. Finally, he has to apply a number of special methods of collecting, manipulating and fixing his evidence. A few words must be said about these three foundation stones of field work, beginning with the second as the most elementary.

IV

Proper conditions for ethnographic work. These, as said, consist mainly in cutting oneself off from the company of other white men, and remaining in as close contact with the natives as possible, which really can only be achieved by camping right in their villages. It is very nice to have a base in a white man's compound for the stores, and to know there is a refuge there in times of sickness and surfeit of native. But it must be far enough away not to become a permanent milieu in which you live and from which you emerge at fixed hours only to "do the village." It should not even be near enough to fly to at any moment for recreation. For the native is not the natural companion for a white man, and after you have been working with him for several hours, seeing how he does his gardens, or letting him tell you items of folk-lore, or discussing his customs, you will naturally hanker after the company of your own kind. But if you are alone in a village beyond reach of this, you go for a solitary walk for an hour or so, return again and then quite naturally seek out the natives' society, this time as a relief from loneliness, just as you would any other companionship. And by means of this natural intercourse, you learn to know him, and you become familiar with his customs and beliefs far better than when he is a paid, and often bored, **informant**.

There is all the difference between a sporadic plunging into the company of natives, and being really in contact with them. What does this latter mean? On the Ethnographer's side, it means that his life in the village, which at first is a strange, sometimes unpleasant, sometimes intensely interesting adventure, soon adopts quite a natural course very much in harmony with his surroundings.

Soon after I had established myself in Omarakana (Trobriand Islands), I began to take part, in a way, in the village life, to look forward to the important or festive events, to take personal interest in the gossip and the developments of the small village occurrences; to wake up every morning to a day, presenting itself to me more or less as it does to the native. I would get out from under my mosquito net, to find around me the village life beginning to stir, or the people well advanced in their working day according to the hour and also to the season, for they get up and begin their labours early or late, as work presses. As I went on my morning walk through the village, I could see intimate details of family life, of toilet, cooking, taking of meals; I could see the arrangements for the day's work, people starting on their errands, or groups of men and women busy at some manufacturing tasks. Quarrels, jokes, family scenes, events usually trivial, sometimes dramatic but always significant, formed the atmosphere of my daily life, as well as of theirs. It must be remembered that as the natives saw me constantly every day, they ceased to be interested or alarmed, or made self-conscious by my presence, and I ceased to be a disturbing element in the tribal life which I was to study, altering it by my very approach, as always happens with a new-comer to every savage community. In fact, as they knew that I would thrust my nose into everything, even where a well-mannered native would not dream of intruding, they finished by regarding me as part and parcel of their life, a necessary evil or nuisance, mitigated by donations of tobacco.

Later on in the day, whatever happened was within easy reach, and there was no possibility of its escaping my notice. Alarms about the sorcerer's approach in the evening, one or two big, really important quarrels and rifts within the community, cases of illness, attempted cures and deaths, magical rites which had to be performed, all these I had not to pursue, fearful of missing them, but they took place under my very eyes, at my own doorstep, so to speak. And it must be emphasised whenever anything dramatic or important occurs it is essential to investigate it at the very moment of happening, because the natives cannot but talk about it, are too excited to be reticent, and too interested to be mentally lazy in supplying details. Also, over and over again, I committed breaches of etiquette, which the natives, familiar enough with me, were not slow in pointing out. I had to learn how to behave, and to a certain extent, I acquired "the feeling" for native good and bad manners. With this, and with the capacity of enjoying their company and sharing some of their games and amusements, I began to feel that I was indeed in touch with the natives, and this is certainly the preliminary condition of being able to carry on successful field work.

V

But the Ethnographer has not only to spread his nets in the right place, and wait for what will fall into them. He must be an active huntsman, and drive his quarry into them, and follow it up to its most inaccessible lairs. And that leads us to the more active methods of pursuing ethnographic evidence. It has been mentioned at the end of Division III that the Ethnographer has to be inspired by the knowledge of the most modern results of scientific study, by its principles and aims. I shall not enlarge upon this subject, except by way of one remark, to avoid the possibility of misunderstanding. Good training in theory, and acquaintance with its latest results, is not identical with being burdened with "preconceived ideas." If a man sets out on an expedition, determined to prove certain hypotheses, if he is incapable of changing his views constantly and casting them off ungrudgingly under the pressure of evidence, needless to say his work will be worthless. But the more problems he brings with him into the field, the more he is in the habit of moulding his theories according to facts, and of seeing facts in their bearing upon theory, the better he is equipped for the work. Preconceived ideas are pernicious in any scientific work, but foreshadowed problems are the main endowment of a scientific thinker, and these problems are first revealed to the observer by his theoretical studies.

In Ethnology, the early efforts of Bastian, Tylor, Morgan, the German Völkerpsychologen have remoulded the older crude information of travellers, missionaries, etc., and have shown us the importance of applying deeper conceptions and discarding crude and misleading ones.[6]

The concept of animism superseded that of **"fetichism"** or "devil-worship," both meaningless terms. The understanding of the classificatory systems of relationship paved the way for the brilliant, modern researches on native sociology in the field-work of the **Cambridge school**. The psychological analysis of the German thinkers has brought forth an abundant crop of most valuable information in the results obtained by the recent German expeditions to Africa, South America and the Pacific, while the theoretical works of **Frazer**, Durkheim and others have already, and will no doubt still for a long time inspire field workers and lead them to new results. The field worker relies entirely upon inspiration from theory. Of course he may be also a theoretical thinker and worker, and there he can draw on himself for stimulus. But the two functions are separate, and in actual research they have to be separated both in time and conditions of work.

As always happens when scientific interest turns towards and begins to labour on a field so far only prospected by the curiosity of amateurs, Ethnology has introduced law and order into what seemed chaotic and freakish. It has transformed for us the sensational, wild and unaccountable world of "savages" into a number of well ordered communities, governed by law, behaving and thinking according to consistent principles. The word "savage," whatever association it might have had originally, connotes ideas of boundless liberty, of irregularity, of something extremely and extraordinarily quaint. In popular thinking, we imagine that the natives live on the bosom of Nature, more or less as they can and like, the prey of irregular, phantasmagoric beliefs and apprehensions. Modern science, on the contrary, shows that their social institutions have a very definite organisation, that they are governed by authority, law and order in their public and personal relations, while the latter are, besides, under the control of extremely complex ties of kinship and clanship. Indeed, we see them entangled in a mesh of duties, functions and privileges which correspond to an elaborate tribal, communal and kinship organisation. Their beliefs and practices do not by any means lack consistency of a certain type, and their knowledge of the outer world is sufficient to guide them in many of their strenuous enterprises and activities. Their artistic productions again lack neither meaning nor beauty.

It is a very far cry from the famous answer given long ago by a representative authority who, asked, what are the manners and customs of the natives, answered, "Customs none, manners beastly," to the position of the modern Ethnographer! This latter, with his tables of kinship terms, genealogies, maps, plans and diagrams, proves the existence of an extensive and big organisation, shows the constitution of the tribe, of the clan, of the family; and he gives us a picture of the natives subjected to a strict code of behaviour and good manners, to which in comparison the life at the **Court of Versailles** or **Escurial** was free and easy.[7]

Thus the first and basic ideal of ethnographic field-work is to give a clear and firm outline of the social constitution, and disentangle the laws and regularities of all cultural phenomena from the irrelevances. The firm skeleton of the tribal life has to be first ascertained. This ideal imposes in the first place the fundamental obligation of giving a complete survey of the phenomena, and not of picking out the sensational, the singular, still less the funny and quaint. The time when we could tolerate accounts presenting us the native as a distorted, childish caricature of a human being are gone. This picture is false, and like many other falsehoods, it has been killed by Science. The field Ethnographer has seriously and soberly to cover the full extent of the phenomena in each aspect of tribal culture studied, making no difference between what is commonplace, or drab, or ordinary, and what strikes him as astonishing and out-of-the-way. At the same time, the whole area of tribal culture *in all its aspects* has to be gone over in research. The consistency, the law and order which obtain within each aspect make also for joining them into one coherent whole.

An Ethnographer who sets out to study only religion, or only technology, or only social organisation cuts out an artificial field for inquiry, and he will be seriously handicapped in his work.

VI

Having settled this very general rule, let us descend to more detailed considerations of method. The Ethnographer has in the field, according to what has just been said, the duty before him of drawing up all the rules and regularities of tribal life; all that is permanent and fixed; of giving an anatomy of their culture, of depicting the constitution of their society. But these things, though crystallised and set, are nowhere *formulated*. There is no written or explicitly expressed code of laws, and their whole tribal tradition, the whole structure of their society, are embodied in the most elusive of all materials; the human being. But not even in human mind or memory are these laws to be found definitely formulated. The natives obey the forces and commands of the tribal code, but they do not comprehend them; exactly as they obey their instincts and their impulses, but could not lay down a single law of psychology. The regularities in native institutions are an automatic result of the interaction of the mental forces of tradition, and of the material conditions of environment. Exactly as a humble member of any modern institution, whether it be the state, or the church, or the army, is *of* it and *in* it, but has no vision of the resulting integral action of the whole, still less could furnish any account of its organisation, so it would be futile to attempt questioning a native in abstract, sociological terms. The difference is that, in our society, every institution has its intelligent members, its historians, and its archives and documents, whereas in a native society there are none of these. After this is realised an expedient has to be found to overcome this difficulty. This expedient for an Ethnographer consists in collecting concrete data of evidence, and drawing the general inferences for himself. This seems obvious on the face of it, but was not found out or at least practised in Ethnography till field work was taken up by men of science. Moreover, in giving it practical effect, it is neither easy to devise the concrete applications of this method, nor to carry them out systematically and consistently.

Though we cannot ask a native about abstract, general rules, we can always enquire how a given case would be treated. Thus for instance, in asking how they would treat crime, or punish it, it would be vain to put to a native a sweeping question such as, "How do you treat and punish a criminal?" for even words could not be found to express it in native, or in pidgin. But an imaginary case, or still better, a real occurrence, will stimulate a native to express his opinion and to supply plentiful information. A real case indeed will start the natives on a wave of discussion, evoke expressions of indignation, show them taking sides—all of which talk will probably contain a wealth of definite views, or moral censures, as well as reveal the social mechanism set in motion by the crime committed. From there, it will be easy to lead them on to speak of other similar cases, to remember other actual occurrences or to discuss them in all their implications and aspects. From this material, which ought to cover the widest possible range of facts, the inference is obtained by simple induction. The *scientific* treatment differs from that of good common sense, first in that a student will extend the completeness and minuteness of survey much further and in a pedantically systematic and methodological manner; and secondly, in that the scientifically trained mind, will push the inquiry along really relevant lines, and towards aims possessing real importance. Indeed, the object of scientific training is to provide the empirical investigator with a *mental chart*, in accordance with which he can take his bearings and lay his course.

To return to our example, a number of definite cases discussed will reveal to the Ethnographer the social machinery for punishment. This is one part, one aspect of tribal authority. Imagine further that by a similar method of inference from definite data, he arrives at understanding leadership in war, in economic enterprise, in tribal festivities—there he has at once all the data necessary to answer the questions about tribal government and social authority. In actual field work, the comparison of such data, the attempt to piece them together, will often reveal rifts and gaps in the information which lead on to further investigations.

From my own experience, I can say that, very often, a problem seemed settled, everything fixed and clear, till I began to write down a short preliminary sketch of my results. And only then, did I see the enormous deficiencies, which would show me where lay new problems, and lead me on to new work. In fact, I spent a few months between my first and second expeditions, and over a year between that and the subsequent one, in going over all my material, and making parts of it almost ready for publication each time, though each time I knew I would have to re-write it. Such cross-fertilisation of constructive work and observation, I found most valuable, and I do not think I could have made real headway without it. I give this bit of my own history merely to show that what has been said so far is not only an empty programme, but the result of personal experience. In this volume, the description is given of a big institution connected with ever so many associated activities, and presenting many aspects. To anyone who reflects on the subject, it will be clear that the information about a phenomenon of such high complexity and of so many ramifications, could not be obtained with any degree of exactitude and completeness, without a constant interplay of constructive attempts and empirical checking. In fact, I have written up an outline of the Kula institution at least half a dozen times while in the field and in the intervals between my expeditions. Each time, new problems and difficulties presented themselves.

The collecting of concrete data over a wide range of facts is thus one of the main points of field method. The obligation is not to enumerate a few examples only, but to exhaust as far as possible all the cases within reach; and, on this search for cases, the investigator will score most whose mental chart is clearest. But, whenever the material of the search allows it, this mental chart ought to be transformed into a real one; it ought to materialise into a diagram, a plan, an exhaustive, synoptic table of cases. Long since, in all tolerably good modern books on natives, we expect to find a full list or table of kinship terms, which includes all the data relative to it, and does not just pick out a few strange and anomalous relationships or expressions. In the investigation of kinship, the following up of one relation after another in concrete cases leads naturally to the construction of genealogical tables. Practised already by the best early writers, such as Munzinger, and, if I remember rightly, **Kubary**, this method has been developed to its fullest extent in the works of Dr. Rivers. Again, studying the concrete data of economic transactions, in order to trace the history of a valuable object, and to gauge the nature of its circulation, the principle of completeness and thoroughness would lead to construct tables of transactions, such as we find in the work of Professor Seligman.[8] It is in following Professor Seligman's example in this matter that I was able to settle certain of the more difficult and detailed rules of the Kula. The method of reducing information, if possible, into charts or synoptic tables ought to be extended to the study of practically all aspects of native life. All types of economic transactions may be studied by following up connected, actual cases, and putting them into a synoptic chart; again, a table ought to be drawn up of all the gifts and presents customary in a given society, a table including the sociological, ceremonial, and economic definition of every item. Also, systems of magic, connected series of ceremonies, types of legal acts, all could be charted, allowing each entry to be synoptically defined under a number of headings. Besides this, of course, the genealogical census of every community, studied more in detail, extensive maps, plans and diagrams, illustrating ownership in garden land, hunting and fishing privileges, etc., serve as the more fundamental documents of ethnographic research.

A genealogy is nothing else but a synoptic chart of a number of connected relations of kinship. Its value as an instrument of research consist in that it allows the investigator to put questions which he formulates to himself *in abstracto*, but can put concretely to the native informant. As a document, its value consists in that it gives a number of authenticated data, presented in their natural grouping. A synoptic chart of magic fulfils the same function. As an instrument of research, I have used it in order to ascertain, for instance, the ideas about the nature of magical power. With a chart before me, I could easily and conveniently go over one item after the other, and note down the relevant practices and beliefs contained in each of them. The answer to my abstract problem could then be obtained by drawing a general inference from all the cases, and the procedure is illustrated in Chapters XVII and XVIII.[9] I cannot enter further into the discussion of this question, which would need further distinctions, such as between a chart of concrete, actual data, such as is a genealogy, and a chart summarising the outlines of a custom or belief, as a chart of a magical system would be.

Returning once more to the question of methodological candour, discussed previously in Division II, I wish to point out here, that the procedure of concrete and tabularised presentation of data ought to be applied first to the Ethnographer's own credentials. That is, an Ethnographer, who wishes to be trusted, must show clearly and concisely, in a tabularised form, which are his own direct observations, and which the indirect information that form the bases of his account. The Table on the next page [below] will serve as an example of this procedure and help the reader of this book to form an idea of the trustworthiness of any statement he is specially anxious to check. With the help of this Table and the many references scattered throughout the text, as to how, under what circumstances, and with what degree of accuracy I arrived at a given item of knowledge, there will, I hope remain no obscurity whatever as to the sources of the book.

Chronological List of Kula Events Witnessed by the Writer

First Expedition, August, 1914-March 1915

> *March*, 1915. In the village of Dikoyas (Woodlark Island) a few ceremonial offerings seen. Preliminary information obtained.

Second Expedition, May, 1915-May, 1916

> *June*, 1915. A Kabigidoya visit arrives from Vakuta to Kiriwana. Its anchoring at Kavataria witnessed and the men seen at Omarakana, where information collected.

> *July*, 1915. Several parties from Kitava land on the beach of Kaulukuba. The men examined in Omarakana. Much information collected in that period.

> *September*, 1915. Unsuccessful attempt to sail to Kitava with To'uluwa, the chief of Omarakana.

> *October-November*, 1915. Departure noticed of three expeditions from Kiriwana to Kitava. Each time To'uluwa brings home a haul of *mwali* (armshells).

> *November*, 1915-*March*, 1916. Preparations for a big overseas expedition from Kiriwana to the Marshall Bennett Islands. Construction of a canoe; renovating of another; sail making in Omarakana; launching; *tasasoria* on the beach of Kaulukuba. At the same time, information is being obtained about these and the associated subjects. Some magical texts of canoe building and Kula magic obtained.

Third Expedition, October, 1917–October, 1918

November, 1917–*December*, 1917. Inland Kula; some data obtained in Tuk-waukwa.

December–February, 1918. Parties from Kitava arrive in Wawela. Collection of information about the *yoyova*. Magic and spells of Kaygau obtained.

March, 1918. Preparations in Sanaroa; preparations in the Amphletts; the Dobuan fleet arrives in the Amphletts. The *uvalaku* expedition from Dobu followed to Boyowa.

April, 1918. Their arrival; their reception in Sinaketa; the Kula transactions; the big intertribal gathering. Some magical formulæ obtained.

May, 1918. Party from Kitava seen in Vakuta.

June, *July*, 1918. Information about Kula magic and customs checked and amplified in Omarakana, especially with regard to its Eastern branches.

August, *September*, 1918. Magical texts obtained in Sinaketa.

October, 1918. Information obtained from a number of natives in Dobu and Southern Massim district (examined in Samarai).

To summarise the first, cardinal point of method, I may say each phenomenon ought to be studied through the broadest range possible of its concrete manifestations; each studied by an exhaustive survey of detailed examples. If possible, the results ought to be tabulated into some sort of synoptic chart, both to be used as an instrument of study, and to be presented as an ethnological document. With the help of such documents and such study of actualities the clear outline of the framework of the natives' culture in the widest sense of the word, and the constitution of their society, can be presented. This method could be called *the method of statistic documentation by concrete evidence*.

VII

Needless to add, in this respect, the scientific field-work is far above even the best amateur productions. There is, however, one point in which the latter often excel. This is, in the presentation of intimate touches of native life, in bringing home to us these aspects of it with which one is made familiar only through being in close contact with the natives, one way or the other, for a long period of time. In certain results of scientific work—especially that which has been called "survey work"—we are given an excellent skeleton, so to speak of the tribal constitution, but it lacks flesh and blood. We learn much about the framework of their society, but within it, we cannot perceive or imagine the realities of human life, the even flow of everyday events, the occasional ripples of excitement over a feast, or ceremony, or some singular occurrence. In working out the rules and regularities of native custom, and in obtaining a precise formula for them from the collection of data and native statements, we find that this very precision is foreign to real life, which never adheres rigidly to any rules. It must be supplemented by the observation of the manner in which a given custom is carried out, of the behaviour of the natives in obeying the rules so exactly formulated by the ethnographer, of the very exceptions which in sociological phenomena almost always occur.

If all the conclusions are solely based on the statements of informants, or deduced from objective documents, it is of course impossible to supplement them in actual observed data of real behaviour. And that is the reason why certain works of amateur residents of long standing, such as educated traders and planters, medical men and officials, and last, but not least, the few intelligent and unbiassed missionaries to whom Ethnography owes so much, surpass in plasticity and in vividness most of the purely scientific accounts. But if the specialised field-worker can adopt the conditions of living described above, he is in a far better position to be really in touch with the natives than any other white resident. For none of them lives right in a native village, except for very short periods, and everyone has his own business, which takes up a considerable part of his time. Moreover, if, like a trader or a missionary or an official he enters into active relations with the native, if he has to transform or influence or make use of him, this makes a real, unbiassed, impartial observation impossible, and precludes all-round sincerity, at least in the case of the missionaries and officials.

Living in the village with no other business but to follow native life, one sees the customs, ceremonies and transactions over and over again, one has examples of their beliefs as they are actually lived through, and the full body and blood of actual native life fills out soon the skeleton of abstract constructions. That is the reason why, working under such conditions as previously described, the Ethnographer is enabled to add something essential to the bare outlines of tribal constitution, and to supplement it by all the details of behaviour, setting and small incident. He is able in each case to state whether an act is public or private; how a public assembly behaves, and what it looks like; he can judge whether an event is ordinary or an exciting and singular one; whether natives bring to it a great deal of sincere and earnest spirit, or perform it in fun; whether they do it in a perfunctory manner, or with zeal and deliberation.

In other words, there is a series of phenomena of great importance which cannot possibly be recorded by questioning or computing documents, but have to be observed in their full actuality. Let us call them *the imponderabilia of actual life*. Here belong such things as the routine of a man's working day, the details of his care of the body, or the manner of taking food and preparing it; the tone of conversational and social life around the village fires, the existence of strong friendships or hostilities, and of passing sympathies and dislikes between people; the subtle yet unmistakable manner in which personal vanities and ambitions are reflected in the behaviour of the individual and in the emotional reactions of those who surround him. All these facts can and ought to be scientifically formulated and recorded, but it is necessary that this be done, not by a superficial registration of details, as is usually done by untrained observers, but with an effort at penetrating the mental attitude expressed in them. And that is the reason why the work of scientifically trained observers, once seriously applied to the study of this aspect, will, I believe, yield results of surpassing value. So far, it has been done only by amateurs, and therefore done, on the whole, indifferently.

Indeed, if we remember that these imponderable yet all important facts of actual life are part of the real substance of the social fabric, that in them are spun the innumerable threads which keep together the family, the clan, the village community, the tribe—their significance becomes clear. The more crystalised bonds of social grouping, such as the definite ritual, the economic and legal duties, the obligations, the ceremonial gifts and formal marks of regard, though equally important for the student, are certainly felt less strongly by the individual who has to fulfil them. Applying this to ourselves, we all know that "family life" means for us, first and foremost, the atmosphere of home, all the innumerable small acts and attentions in which are expressed the affection, the mutual interest, the little preferences, and the little antipathies which constitute intimacy. That we may inherit from this person, that we shall have to walk after the hearse of the other, though sociologically these facts belong to the definition of "family" and family life," in personal perspective of what family truly is to us, they normally stand very much in the background.

Exactly the same applies to a native community, and if the Ethnographer wants to bring their real life home to his readers, he must on no account neglect this. Neither aspect, the intimate, as little as the legal, ought to be glossed over. Yet as a rule in ethnographic accounts we have not both but either the one or the other—and, so far, the intimate one has hardly ever been properly treated. In all social relations besides the family ties, even those between mere tribesmen and, beyond that, between hostile or friendly members of different tribes, meeting on any sort of social business, there is this intimate side, expressed by the typical details of intercourse, the tone of their behaviour in the presence of one another. This side is different from the definite, crystalised legal frame of the relationship, and it has to be studied and stated in its own right.

In the same way, in studying the conspicuous acts of tribal life, such as ceremonies, rites, festivities, etc., the details and tone of behaviour ought to be given, besides the bare outline of events. The importance of this may be exemplified by one instance. Much has been said and written about survival. Yet the survival character of an act is expressed in nothing so well as in the concomitant behaviour, in the way in which it is carried out. Take any example from our own culture, whether it be the pomp and pageantry of a state ceremony, or a picturesque custom kept up by street urchins, its "outline" will not tell you whether the rite flourishes still with full vigour in the hearts of those who perform it or assist at the performance or whether they regard it as almost a dead thing, kept alive for tradition's sake. But observe and fix the data of their behaviour, and at once the degree of vitality of the act will become clear. There is no doubt, from all points of sociological, or psychological analysis, and in any question of theory, the manner and type of behaviour observed in the performance of an act is of the highest importance. Indeed behaviour is a fact, a relevant fact, and one that can be recorded. And foolish indeed and short-sighted would be the man of science who would pass by a whole class of phenomena, ready to be garnered, and leave them to waste, even though he did not see at the moment to what theoretical use they might be put!

As to the actual method of observing and recording in fieldwork these *imponderabilia of actual life and of typical behaviour*, there is no doubt that the personal equation of the observer comes in here more prominently, than in the collection of crystalised, ethnographic data. But here also the main endeavour must be to let facts speak for themselves. If in making a daily round of the village, certain small incidents, characteristic forms of taking food, of conversing, of doing work are found occurring over and over again, they should be noted down at once. It is also important that this work of collecting and fixing impressions should begin early in the course of working out a district. Because certain subtle peculiarities, which make an impression as long as they are novel, cease to be noticed as soon as they become familiar. Others again can only be perceived with a better knowledge of the local conditions. An ethnographic diary, carried on systematically throughout the course of one's work in a district would be the ideal instrument for this sort of study. And if, side by side with the normal and typical, the ethnographer carefully notes the slight, or the more pronounced deviations from it, he will be able to indicate the two extremes within which the normal moves.

In observing ceremonies or other tribal events, such, for instance, as the scene depicted in Plate IV [omitted], it is necessary, not only to note down those occurrences and details which are prescribed by tradition and custom to be the essential course of the act, but also the Ethnographer ought to record carefully and precisely, one after the other, the actions of the actors and of the spectators. Forgetting for a moment that he knows and understands the structure of this ceremony, the main dogmatic ideas underlying it, he might try to find himself only in the midst of an assembly of human-beings, who behave seriously or jocularly, with earnest concentration or with bored frivolity, who are either in the same mood as he finds them every day, or else are screwed up to a high pitch of excitement, and so on and so on. With his attention constantly directed to this aspect of tribal life, with the constant endeavour to fix it, to express it in terms of actual fact, a good deal of reliable and expressive material finds it sway into his notes. He will be able to "set" the act into its proper place in tribal life, that is to show whether it is exceptional or commonplace, one in which the natives behave ordinarily, or one in which their whole behaviour is transformed. And he will also be able to bring all this home to his readers in a clear, convincing manner.

Again, in this type of work, it is good for the Ethnographer sometimes to put aside camera, note book and pencil, and to join in himself in what is going on. He can take part in the natives' games, he can follow them on their visits and walks, sit down and listen and share in their conversations. I am not certain if this is equally easy for everyone—perhaps the Slavonic nature is more plastic and more naturally savage than that of Western Europeans—but though the degree of success varies, the attempt is possible for everyone. Out of such plunges into the life of the natives—and I made them frequently not only for study's sake but because everyone needs human company—I have carried away a distinct feeling that their behaviour, their manner of being, in all sorts of tribal transactions, became more transparent and easily understandable than it had been before. All these methodological remarks, the reader will find again illustrated in the following chapters.

VIII

Finally, let us pass to the third and last aim of scientific field-work, to the last type of phenomenon which ought to be recorded in order to give a full and adequate picture of native culture. Besides the firm outline of tribal constitution and crystallised cultural items which form the skeleton, besides the data of daily life and ordinary behaviour, which are, so to speak, its flesh and blood, there is still to be recorded the spirit—the natives' views and opinions and utterances. For, in every act of tribal life, there is, first, the routine prescribed by custom and tradition, then there is the manner in which it is carried out, and lastly there is the commentary to it, contained in the natives' mind. A man who submits to various customary obligations, who follows a traditional course of action, does it impelled by certain motives, to the accompaniment of certain feelings, guided by certain ideas. These ideas, feelings, and impulses are moulded and conditioned by the culture in which we find them, and are therefore an ethnic peculiarity of the given society. An attempt must be made therefore, to study and record them.

But is this possible? Are these subjective states not too elusive and shapeless? And, even granted that people usually do feel or think or experience certain psychological states in association with the performance of customary acts, the majority of them surely are not able to formulate these states, to put them into words. This latter point must certainly be granted, and it is perhaps the real **Gordian knot** in the study of the facts of social psychology. Without trying to cut or untie this knot, that is to solve the problem theoretically, or to enter further into the field of general methodology, I shall make directly for the question of practical means to overcome some of the difficulties involved.

First of all, it has to be laid down that we have to study here stereotyped manners of thinking and feeling. As sociologists, we are not interested in what A or B may feel *qua* individuals, in the accidental course of their own personal experiences—we are interested only in what they feel and think *qua* members of a given community. Now in this capacity, their mental states receive a certain stamp, become stereotyped by the institutions in which they live, by the influence of tradition and folk-lore, by the very vehicle of thought, that is by language. The social and cultural environment in which they move forces them to think and feel in a definite manner. Thus, a man who lives in a polyandrous community cannot experience the same feelings of jealousy, as a strict monogynist, though he might have the elements of them. A man who lives within the sphere of the Kula cannot become permanently and sentimentally attached to certain of his possessions, in spite of the fact that he values them most of all. These examples are crude, but better ones will be found in the text of this book.

So, the third commandment of field-work runs: Find out the typical ways of thinking and feeling, corresponding to the institutions and culture of a given community, and formulate the results in the most convincing manner. What will be the method of procedure? The best ethnographical writers—here again the Cambridge school with Haddon, Rivers, and Seligman rank first among English Ethnographers—have always tried to quote *verbatim* statements of crucial importance. They also adduce terms of native classification; sociological, psychological and industrial *termini technici*, and have rendered the verbal contour of native thought as precisely as possible. One step further in this line can be made by the Ethnographer, who acquires a knowledge of the native language and can use it as an instrument of inquiry. In working with the **Kiriwinian** language, I found still some difficulty in writing down the statement directly in translation which at first I used to do in the act of taking notes. The translation often robbed the text of all its significant characteristics—rubbed off all its points—so that gradually I was led to note down certain important phrases just as they were spoken, in the native tongue. As my knowledge of the language progressed, I put down more and more in Kiriwinian, till at last I found myself writing exclusively in that language, rapidly taking notes, word for word, of each statement. No sooner had I arrived at this point, than I recognised that I was thus acquiring at the same time an abundant linguistic material, and a series of ethnographic documents which ought to be reproduced as I had fixed them, besides being utilised in the writing up of my account.[10] This *corpus inscriptionum Kiriwiniensium* can be utilised, not only by myself, but by all those who, through their better penetration and ability of interpreting them, may find points which escape my attention, very much as the other *corpora* form the basis for the various interpretations of ancient and prehistoric cultures; only, these ethnographic inscriptions are all decipherable and clear, have been almost all translated fully and unambiguously, and have been provided with native cross-commentaries or *scholia* obtained from living sources.

No more need be said on this subject here, as later on a whole chapter (Chapter XVIII) is devoted to it, and to its exemplification by several native texts. The *Corpus* will of course be published separately at a later date.

IX

Our considerations thus indicate that the goal of ethnographic field-work must be approached through three avenues:

1. *The organisation of the tribe, and the anatomy of its culture* must be recorded in firm, clear outline. The method of *concrete, statistical documentation* is the means through which such an outline has to be given.
2. Within this frame, the *imponderabilia of actual life*, and the *type of behaviour* have to be filled in. They have to be collected through minute, detailed observations, in the form of some sort of ethnographic diary, made possible by close contact with native life.
3. A collection of ethnographic statements, characteristic narratives, typical utterances, items of folk-lore and magical formulæ has to be given as a *corpus inscriptionum*, as documents of native mentality.

These three lines of approach lead to the final goal, of which an Ethnographer should never lose sight. This goal is, briefly, to grasp the native's point of view, his relation to life, to realise *his* vision of *his* world. We have to study man, and we must study what concerns him most intimately, that is, the hold which life has on him. In each culture, the values are slightly different; people aspire after different aims, follow different impulses, yearn after a different form of happiness. In each culture, we find different institutions in which man pursues his life-interest, different customs by which he satisfies his aspirations, different codes of law and morality which reward his virtues or punish his defections. To study the institutions, customs, and codes or to study the behaviour and mentality without the subjective desire of feeling by what these people live, of realising the substance of their happiness—is, in my opinion, to miss the greatest reward which we can hope to obtain from the study of man.

These generalities the reader will find illustrated in the following chapters. We shall see there the savage striving to satisfy certain aspirations, to attain his type of value, to follow his line of social ambition. We shall see him led on to perilous and difficult enterprises by a tradition of magical and heroical exploits, shall see him following the lure of his own romance. Perhaps as we read the account of these remote customs there may emerge a feeling of solidarity with the endeavours and ambitions of these natives. Perhaps man's mentality will be revealed to us, and brought near, along some lines which we never have followed before. Perhaps through realising human nature in a shape very distant and foreign to us, we shall have some light shed on our own. In this, and in this case only, we shall be justified in feeling that it has been worth our while to understand these natives, their institutions and customs, and that we have gathered some profit from the Kula.

Notes

1 The *hiri*, as these expeditions are called in Motuan, have been described with a great wealth of detail and clearness of outline by Captain F. Barton, in C. G. Seligman's "The Melanesians of British New Guinea," Cambridge, 1910, Chapter viii.

2 Cf. "The Mailu," by B. Malinowski, in Transactions of the R. Society of S. Australia, 1915; Chapter iv. 4, pp. 612-629.

3 Op. cit. Chapter xl.

4 On this point of method again, we are indebted to the Cambridge School of Anthropology for having introduced the really scientific way of dealing with the question. More especially in the writings of Haddon, Rivers and Seligman, the distinction between inference and observation is always clearly drawn, and we can visualize with perfect precision the conditions under which the work was done.

5 I may note at once that there were a few delightful exceptions to that, to mention only my friends Billy Hancock in the Trobriands; M. Raffael Brudo, another pearl trader; and the missionary, Mr. M.K. Gilmour.

6 According to a useful habit of the terminology of science, I use the word Ethnography for the empirical and descriptive results of the science of Man, and the word Ethnology for speculative and comparative theories.

7 The legendary "early authority" who found the natives only beastly and without customs is left behind by a modern writer, who, speaking about the Southern Massim with whom he lived and worked "in close contact" for many years, says:—
" ... We teach lawless men to become obedient, inhuman men to love, and savage men to change." And again:—"Guided in his conduct by nothing but his instincts and propensities, and governed by his unchecked passions...." "Lawless, inhuman and savage!" A grosser misstatement of the real state of things could not be invented by anyone wishing to parody the Missionary point of view. Quoted from the

Rev. C.W. Abel, of the London Missionary Society, "Savage Life in New Guinea," no date.

8   For instance, the tables of circulation of the valuable axe blades, op. cit., pp. 531, 532.

9   In this book, besides the adjoining Table, which does not strictly belong to the class of document of which I speak here, the reader will find only a few samples of synoptic tables, such as the list of Kula partners mentioned and analysed in Chapter XIII, Division II, the list of gifts and presents in Chapter VI, Division VI, not tabularised, only described; the synoptic data of a Kula expedition in Chapter XVI, and the table of Kula magic given in Chapter XVII. Here, I have not wanted to overload the account with charts, etc., preferring to reserve them till the full publication of my material.

10   It was soon after I had adopted this course that I received a letter from Dr. A.H. Gardiner, the well-known Egyptologist, urging me to do this very thing. From his point of view as archæologist, he naturally saw the enormous possibilities for an Ethnographer of obtaining a similar body of written sources as have been preserved to us from ancient cultures, plus the possibility of illuminating them by personal knowledge of the full life of that culture.

Study Questions

1.   According to Malinowski, what are the proper conditions for ethnographic fieldwork?

2.   According to Malinowski, what is the role of ethnological theory in ethnographic fieldwork?

3.   What ethnographic methods does Malinowski recommend to grasp what he calls the native's point of view?

Further Readings

Ellen, Roy *et al.* (eds.). 1989. *Malinowski: Between Two Worlds: The Polish Roots of an Anthropological Tradition*. New York: Cambridge University Press.

Firth, Raymond (ed.). 1964. *Man and Culture: An Evaluation of the Work of Bronislaw Malinowski*. New York: Harper & Row.

Kuklik, Henrika. 1992. *The Savage Within: The Social History of British Anthropology, 1885-1945*. New York: Cambridge University Press.

Malinowski, Bronislaw. 1955 [1927]. *Sex and Repression in Savage Society*. New York: Harcourt, Brace.

—. 1984 [1922]. *Argonauts of the Western Pacific*. Prospect Heights, IL: Waveland Press, Inc.

—. 1989 [1967]. *A Diary in the Strict Sense of the Term*. Stanford, CA: Stanford University Press.

Spiro, Melford E. 1992. *Oedipus in the Trobriands*. New Brunswick, NJ: Transaction.

Strenski, Ivan. 1992. *Malinowski and the Work of Myth*. Princeton, NJ: Princeton University Press.

16
___

Introduction
[African Political Systems]

MEYER FORTES AND EDWARD EVAN EVANS-PRITCHARD

I. Aims of this Book

One object we had in initiating this study was to provide a convenient reference book for anthropologists. We also hope that it will be a contribution to the discipline of comparative politics. We feel sure that the first object has been attained, for the societies described are representative of common types of African political systems and, taken together, they enable a student to appreciate the great variety of such types. As the sketch-map on p. 2 [omitted] shows, the eight systems described are widely distributed in the continent. Most of the forms described are variants of a pattern of political organization found among contiguous or neighbouring societies, so that this book covers, by implication, a very large part of Africa. We are aware that not every type of political system found in Africa is represented, but we believe that all the major principles of African political organization are brought out in these essays.

Several contributors have described the changes in the political systems they investigated which have taken place as a result of European conquest and rule. If we do not emphasize this side of the subject it is because all contributors are more interested in anthropological than in administrative problems. We do not wish to imply, however, that anthropology is indifferent to practical affairs. The policy of **Indirect Rule** is now generally accepted in British Africa. We would suggest that it can only prove advantageous in the long run if the principles of African political systems, such as this book deals with, are understood.

II. A Representative Sample of African Societies

Each essay is a condensation of a detailed study of the political system of a single people undertaken in recent years by the most advanced methods of fieldwork by students trained in anthropological theory. A degree of brevity that hardly does justice to some important topics has been necessary for reasons of space. Each essay furnishes, nevertheless, a useful standard by which the political systems of other peoples in the same area may be classified. No such classification is attempted in this book, but we recognize that a satisfactory comparative study of African political institutions can only be undertaken after a classification of the kind has been made. It would then be possible to study a whole range of adjacent societies in light of the Ngwato system, the Tale system, the **Ankole** system, the **Bemba** system, and so on, and, by analysis, to state the chief characters of series of political systems found in large areas. An analysis of the results obtained by these comparative studies in fields where a whole range of societies display many similar characteristics in their political systems would be more likely to lead to valid scientific generalizations than comparison between particular societies belonging to different areas and political types.

We do not mean to suggest that the political systems of societies which have a high degree of general cultural resemblance are necessarily of the same type, though on the whole they tend to be. However, it is well to bear in mind that within a single linguistic or cultural area we often find political systems which are very unlike one another in many important features. Conversely, the same kind of political structures are found in societies of totally different culture. This can be seen even in the eight societies in this book. Also, there may be a totally different cultural content in social processes with identical functions. The function of ritual ideology in political organization in Africa clearly illustrates this. Mystical values are attached to political office among the Bemba, the **Banyankole**, the **Kede**, and the **Tallensi**, but the symbols and institutions in which these values are expressed are very different in all four societies. A comparative study of political systems has to be on an abstract plane where social processes are stripped of their cultural idiom and are reduced to functional terms. The structural similarities which disparity of culture conceals are then laid bare and structural dissimilarities are revealed behind a screen of cultural uniformity. There is evidently an intrinsic connexion between a people's culture and their social organization, but the nature of this connexion is a major problem in sociology and we cannot emphasize too much that these two components of social life must not be confused.

We believe that the eight societies described will not only give the student a bird's eye view of the basic principles of African political organization, but will also enable him to draw a few, perhaps elementary, conclusions of a general and theoretical kind. It must be emphasized, however, that all the contributors have aimed primarily at giving a concise descriptive account and have subordinated theoretical speculations to this end. In so far as they have allowed themselves to draw theoretical conclusions, these have been largely determined by the view that they have taken of what constitutes political structure. They do not all take the same view on this matter. In stating our own view we have found it best to avoid reference to the writings of political philosophers, and in doing so we feel sure that we have the support of our contributors.

III. Political Philosophy and Comparative Politics

We have not found that the theories of political philosophers have helped us to understand the societies we have studied and we consider them of little scientific value; for their conclusions are seldom formulated in terms of observed behaviour or capable of being tested by this criterion. Political philosophy has chiefly concerned itself with how men *ought* to live and what form of government they *ought* to have, rather than with what *are* their political habits and institutions.

In so far as political philosophers have attempted to understand existing institutions instead of trying to justify or undermine them, they have done so in terms of popular psychology or of history. They have generally had recourse to hypotheses about earlier stages of human society presumed to be devoid of political institutions or to display them in a very rudimentary form and have attempted to reconstruct the process by which the political institutions with which they were familiar in their own societies might have arisen out of these elementary forms of organization. Political philosophers in modern times have often sought to substantiate their theories by appeal to the facts of primitive societies. They cannot be blamed if, in doing so, they have been led astray, for little anthropological research has been conducted into primitive political systems compared with research into other primitive institutions, customs, and beliefs, and still less have comparative studies of them been made.[1] We do not consider that the origins of primitive institutions can be discovered and, therefore, we do not think that it is worth while seeking for them. We speak for all social anthropologists when we say that a scientific study of political institutions must be inductive and comparative and aim solely at establishing and explaining the uniformities found among them and their interdependencies with other features of social organization.

IV. The Two Types of Political System Studied

It will be noted that the political systems described in this book fall into two main categories. One group, which we refer to as Group A, consists of those societies which have centralized authority, administrative machinery, and judicial institutions—in short, a government—and in which cleavages of wealth, privilege, and status correspond to the distribution of power and authority. This group comprises the **Zulu**, the Ngwato, the Bemba, the Banyankole, and the Kede. The other group, which we refer to as Group B, consists of those societies which lack centralized authority, administrative machinery, and constituted judicial institutions—in short which lack government—and in which there are no sharp divisions of rank, status, or wealth. This group comprises the **Logoli**, the Tallensi, and the **Nuer**. Those who consider that a state should be defined by the presence of governmental institutions will regard the first group as primitive states and the second group as stateless societies.

The kind of information related and the kind of problems discussed in a description of each society have largely depended on the category to which it belongs. Those who have studied societies of Group A are mainly concerned to describe governmental organization. They therefore give an account of the status of kings and classes, the roles of administrative officials of one kind or another, the privileges of rank, the differences in wealth and power, the regulation of tax and tribute, the territorial divisions of the state and their relation to its central authority, the rights of subjects and the obligations of rulers, and the checks on authority. Those who studied societies of Group B had no such matters to discuss and were therefore forced to consider what, in the absence of explicit forms of government, could be held to constitute the political structure of a people. This problem was simplest among the Nuer, who have very distinct territorial divisions. The difficulty was greater for the Logoli and Tallensi, who have no clear spatially-defined political units.

V. Kinship in Political Organization

One of the outstanding differences between the two groups is the part played by the lineage system in political structure. We must here distinguish between the set of relationships linking the individual to other persons and to particular social units through the transient, **bilateral** family, which we shall call the kinship system, and the **segmentary system** of permanent, **unilateral** groups, which we call the lineage system. Only the latter establishes corporate units with political functions. In both groups of societies kinship and domestic ties have an important role in the lives of individuals, but their relation to the political system is of a secondary order. In the societies of Group A it is the administrative organization, in societies of Group B the segmentary lineage system, which primarily regulates political relations between territorial segments.

This is clearest among the Ngwato, whose political system resembles the pattern with which we are familiar in the modern nation-state. The political unit is essentially a territorial grouping wherein the plexus of kinship ties serves merely to cement those already established by membership of the ward, district, and nation. In societies of this type the state is never the kinship system writ large, but is organized on totally different principles. In societies of Group B kinship ties appear to play a more prominent role in political organization, owing to the close association of territorial grouping with lineage grouping, but it is still only a secondary role.

It seems probable to us that three types of political system can be distinguished. Firstly, there are those very small societies, none of which are described in this book, in which even the largest political unit embraces a group of people all of whom are united to one another by ties of kinship, so that political relations are coterminous with kinship relations and the political structure and kinship organization are completely fused. Secondly, there are societies in which a lineage structure is the framework of the political system, there being a precise co-ordination between the two, so that they are consistent with each other, though each remains distinct and autonomous in its own sphere. Thirdly, there are societies in which an administrative organization is the framework of the political structure.

The numerical and territorial range of a political system would vary according to the type to which it belongs. A kinship system would seem to be incapable of uniting such large numbers of persons into a single organization for defence and the settlement of disputes by arbitration as a lineage system and a lineage system incapable of uniting such numbers as an administrative system.

VI. The Influence of Demography

It is noteworthy that the political unit in the societies with a state organization is numerically larger than in those without a state organization. The largest political groups among the Tallensi, Logoli, and Nuer cannot compete in numbers with the quarter to half million of the Zulu state (in about 1870), the 101,000 of the Ngwato state, and the 140,000 of the Bemba state. It is true that the Kede and their subject population are not so populous, but it must be remembered that they form part of the vast **Nupe** state. It is not suggested that a stateless political unit need be very small—Nuer political units comprise as many as 45,000 souls—nor that a political unit with state organization need be very large, but it is probably true that there is a limit to the size of a population that can hold together without some kind of centralized government.

Size of population should not be confused with density of population. There may be some relation between the degree of political development and the size of population, but it would be incorrect to suppose that governmental institutions are found in those societies with greatest density. The opposite seems to be equally likely, judging by our material. The density of the Zulu is 3.5, of the Ngwato 2.5, of the Bemba 3.75 per square mile, while that of the Nuer is higher and of the Tallensi and Logoli very much higher. It might be supposed that the dense permanent settlements of the Tallensi would necessarily lead to the development of a centralized form of government, whereas the wide dispersion of shifting villages among the Bemba would be incompatible with centralized rule. The reverse is actually the case. In addition to the material collected in this book, evidence from other African societies could be cited to prove that a large population in a political unit and a high degree of political centralization do not necessarily go together with great density.

VII. The Influence of Mode of Livelihood

The density and distribution of population in an African society are clearly related to ecological conditions which also affect the whole mode of livelihood. It is obvious, however, that mere differences in modes of livelihood do not determine differences in political structure. The Tallensi and the Bemba are both agriculturalists, the Tallensi having fixed and the Bemba shifting cultivation, but they have very different political systems. The Nuer and Logoli of Group B and the Zulu and Ngwato of Group A alike practise mixed agriculture and cattle husbandry. In a general sense, modes of livelihood, together with environmental conditions, which always impose effective limits on modes of livelihood, determine the dominant values of the peoples and strongly influence their social organizations, including their political systems. This is evident in the political divisions of the Nuer, in the distribution of Kede settlements and the administrative organization embracing them, and in the class system of the Banyankole.

Most African societies belong to an economic order very different from ours. Theirs is mainly a subsistence economy with a rudimentary differentiation of productive labour and with no machinery for the accumulation of wealth in the form of commercial or industrial capital. If wealth is accumulated it takes the form of consumption goods and amenities or is used for the support of additional dependants. Hence it tends to be rapidly dissipated again and does not give rise to permanent class divisions. Distinctions of rank, status, or occupation operate independently of differences of wealth.

Economic privileges, such as rights to tax, tribute, and labour, are both the main reward of political power and an essential means of maintaining it in the political systems of Group A. But there are counterbalancing economic obligations no less strongly backed by institutionalized sanctions. It must not be forgotten, also, that those who derive maximum economic benefit from political office also have the maximum administrative, judicial, and religious responsibilities. Compared with the societies of Group A, distinctions of rank and status are of minor significance in societies of Group B. Political office carries no economic privileges, though the possession of greater than average wealth may be a criterion of the qualities or status required for political leadership; for in these economically homogeneous, equalitarian, and segmentary societies the attainment of wealth depends either on exceptional personal qualities or accomplishments, or on superior status in the lineage system.

VIII. Composite Political Systems and the Conquest Theory

It might be held that societies like the Logoli, Tallensi, and Nuer, without central government or administrative machinery, develop into states like the Ngwato, Zulu, and Banyankole as a result of conquest. Such a development is suggested for the Zulu and Banyankole. But the history of all the peoples treated in this book is not well enough known to enable us to declare with any degree of certainty what course their political development has taken. The problem must therefore be stated in a different way. All the societies of Group A appear to be an amalgam of different peoples, each aware of its unique origin and history, and all except the Zulu and Bemba are still to-day culturally heterogeneous. Cultural diversity is most marked among the Banyankole and Kede, but it is also clear among the Ngwato. We may, therefore, ask to what extent cultural heterogeneity in a society is correlated with an administrative system and central authority. The evidence at our disposal in this book suggests that cultural and economic heterogeneity is associated with a state-like political structure. Centralized authority and an administrative organization seem to be necessary to accommodate culturally diverse groups within a single political system, especially if they have different modes of livelihood. A class or caste system may result if there are great cultural and, especially, great economic divergencies. But centralized forms of government are found also with peoples of homogeneous culture and little economic differentiation like the Zulu. It is possible that groups of diverse culture are the more easily welded into a unitary political system without the emergence of classes the closer they are to one another in culture. A centralized form of government is not necessary to enable different groups of closely related culture and pursuing the same mode of livelihood to amalgamate, nor does it necessarily arise out of the amalgamation. The Nuer have absorbed large numbers of conquered **Dinka**, who are a pastoral people like themselves with a very similar culture. They have incorporated them by adoption and other ways into their lineage system; but this has not resulted in a class or caste structure or in a centralized form of government. Marked divergencies in culture and economic pursuits are probably incompatible with a segmentary political system such as that of the Nuer or the Tallensi. We have not the data to check this. It is clear, however, that a conquest theory of the primitive state—assuming that the necessary historical evidence is available—must take into account not only the mode of conquest and the conditions of contact, but also the similarities or divergencies in culture and mode of livelihood of conquerors and conquered and the political institutions they bring with them into the new combination.

IX. The Territorial Aspect

The territorial aspect of early forms of political organization was justly emphasized by **Maine** in *Ancient Law* and other scholars have given much attention to it. In all the societies described in this book the political system has a territorial framework, but it has a different function in the two types of political organization. The difference is due to the dominance of an administrative and judicial apparatus in one type of system and its absence in the other. In the societies of Group A the administrative unit is a territorial unit; political rights and obligations are territorially delimited. A chief is the administrative and judicial head of a given territorial division, vested often with final economic and legal control over all the land within his boundaries. Everybody living within these boundaries is his subject, and the right to live in this area can be acquired only by accepting the obligations of a subject. The head of the state is a territorial ruler.

In the other group of societies there are no territorial units defined by an administrative system, but the territorial units are local communities the extent of which corresponds to the range of a particular set of lineage ties and the bonds of direct co-operation. Political office does not carry with it juridical rights over a particular, defined stretch of territory and its inhabitants. Membership of the local community, and the rights and duties that go with it, are acquired as a rule through genealogical ties, real or fictional. The lineage principle takes the place of political allegiance, and the interrelations of territorial segments are directly co-ordinated with the interrelations of lineage segments.

Political relations are not simply a reflexion of territorial relations. The political system, in its own right, incorporates territorial relations and invests them with the particular kind of political significance they have.

X. The Balance of Forces in the Political System

A relatively stable political system in Africa presents a balance between conflicting tendencies and between divergent interests. In Group A it is a balance between different parts of the administrative organization. The forces that maintain the supremacy of the paramount ruler are opposed by the forces that act as a check on his powers. Institutions such as the regimental organization of the Zulu, the genealogical restriction of succession to kingship or chiefship, the appointment by the king of his kinsmen to regional chiefships, and the mystical sanctions of his office all reinforce the power of the central authority. But they are counterbalanced by other institutions, like the king's council, sacerdotal officials who have a decisive voice in the king's investiture, queen mothers' courts, and so forth, which work for the protection of law and custom and the control of centralized power. The regional devolution of powers and privileges, necessary on account of difficulties of communication and transport and of other cultural deficiencies, imposes severe restrictions on a king's authority. The balance between central authority and regional autonomy is a very important element in the political structure. If a king abuses his power, subordinate chiefs are liable to secede or to lead a revolt against him. If a subordinate chief seems to be getting too powerful and independent, the central authority will be supported by other subordinate chiefs in suppressing him. A king may try to buttress his authority by playing off rival subordinate chiefs against one another.

It would be a mistake to regard the scheme of constitutional checks and balances and the delegation of power and authority to regional chiefs as nothing more than an administrative device. A general principle of great importance is contained in these arrangements, which has the effect of giving every section and every major interest of the society direct or indirect representation in the conduct of government. Local chiefs represent the central authority in relation to their districts, but they also represent the people under them in relation to the central authority. Councillors and ritual functionaries represent the community's interest in the preservation of law and custom and in the observance of the ritual measures deemed necessary for its well-being. The voice of such functionaries and delegates is effective in the conduct of government on account of the general principle that power and authority are distributed. The king's power and authority are composite. Their various components are lodged in different offices. Without the co-operation of those who hold these offices it is extremely difficult, if not impossible, for the king to obtain his revenue, assert his judicial and legislative supremacy, or retain his secular and ritual prestige. Functionaries vested with essential subsidiary powers and privileges can often sabotage a ruler's acts if they disapprove them.

Looked at from another angle, the government of an African state consists in a balance between power and authority on the one side and obligation and responsibility on the other. Every one who holds political office has responsibilities for the public weal corresponding to his rights and privileges. The distribution of political authority provides a machinery by which the various agents of government can be held to their responsibilities. A chief or a king has the right to exact tax, tribute, and labour service from his subjects; he has the corresponding obligation to dispense justice to them, to ensure their protection from enemies and to safeguard their general welfare by ritual acts and observances. The structure of an African state implies that kings and chiefs rule by consent. A ruler's subjects are as fully aware of the duties he owes to them as they are of the duties they owe to him, and are able to exert pressure to make him discharge these duties.

We should emphasize here, that we are talking of constitutional arrangements, not of how they work in practice. Africans recognize as clearly as we do that power corrupts and that men are liable to abuse it. In many ways the kind of constitution we find in societies of Group A is cumbrous and too loosely jointed to prevent abuse entirely. The native theory of government is often contradicted by their practice. Both rulers and subjects, actuated by their private interests, infringe the rules of the constitution. Though it usually has a form calculated to hold in check any tendency towards absolute despotism, no African constitution can prevent a ruler from sometimes becoming a tyrant. The history of **Shaka** is an extreme case, but in this and other instances where the contradiction between theory and practice is too glaring and the infringement of constitutional rules becomes too grave, popular disapproval is sure to follow and may even result in a movement of secession or revolt led by members of the royal family or subordinate chiefs. This is what happened to Shaka.

It should be remembered that in these states there is only one theory of government. In the event of rebellion, the aim, and result, is only to change the personnel of office and never to abolish it or to substitute for it some new form of government. When subordinate chiefs, who are often kinsmen of the king, rebel against him they do so in defence of the values violated by his malpractices. They have an interest greater than any other section of the people in maintaining the kingship. The ideal constitutional pattern remains the valid norm, in spite of breaches of its rules.

A different kind of balance is found in societies of Group B. It is an equilibrium between a number of segments, spatially juxtaposed and structurally equivalent, which are defined in local and lineage, and not in administrative terms. Every segment has the same interests as other segments of a like order. The set of intersegmentary relations that constitutes the political structure is a balance of opposed local loyalties and of divergent lineage and ritual ties. Conflict between the interests of administrative divisions is common in societies like those of Group A. Subordinate chiefs and other political functionaries, whose rivalries are often personal, or due to their relationship to the king or the ruling aristocracy, often exploit these divergent local loyalties for their own ends. But the administrative organization canalizes and provides checks on such inter-regional dissensions. In the societies without an administrative organization, divergence of interests between the component segments is intrinsic to the political structure. Conflicts between local segments necessarily mean conflicts between lineage segments, since the two are closely interlocked; and the stabilizing factor is not a superordinate juridical or military organization, but is simply the sum total of inter-segment relations.

XI. The Incidence and Function of Organized Force

In our judgement, the most significant characteristic distinguishing the centralized, pyramidal, state-like forms of government of the Ngwato, Bemba, &c., from the segmentary political systems of the Logoli, the Tallensi, and the Nuer is the incidence and function of organized force in the system. In the former group of societies, the principal sanction of a ruler's rights and prerogatives, and of the authority exercised by his subordinate chiefs, is the command of organized force. This may enable an African king to rule oppressively for a time, if he is inclined to do so, but a good ruler uses the armed forces under his control in the public interest, as an accepted instrument of government—that is, for the defence of the society as a whole or of any section of it, for offence against a common enemy, and as a coercive sanction to enforce the law or respect for the constitution. The king and his delegates and advisers use organized force with the consent of their subjects to keep going a political system which the later take for granted as the foundation of their social order.

In societies of Group B there is no association, class, or segment which has a dominant place in the political structure through the command of greater organized force than is at the disposal of any of its **congeners**. If force is resorted to in a dispute between segments it will be met with equal force. If one segment defeats another it does not attempt to establish political dominance over it; in the absence of an administrative machinery there is, in fact, no means by which it could do so. In the language of political philosophy, there is no individual or group in which sovereignty can be said to rest. In such a system, stability is maintained by an equilibrium at every line of cleavage and every point of divergent interests in the social structure. This balance is sustained by a distribution of the command of force corresponding to the distribution of like, but competitive, interests amongst the homologous segments of the society. Whereas a constituted judicial machinery is possible and is always found in societies of Group A, since it has the backing of organized force, the jural institutions of the Logoli, the Tallensi and the Nuer rest on the right of self-help.

XII. Differences in Response to European Rule
The distinctions we have noted between the two categories into which these eight societies fall, especially in the kind of balance characteristic of each, are very marked in their adjustment to the rule of colonial governments. Most of these societies have been conquered or have submitted to European rule from fear of invasion. They would not acquiesce in it if the threat of force were withdrawn; and this fact determines the part now played in their political life by European administrations.

In the societies of Group A, the paramount ruler is prohibited, by the constraint of the colonial government, from using the organized force at his command on his own responsibility. This has everywhere resulted in diminishing his authority and generally in increasing the power and independence of his subordinates. He no longer rules in his own right, but as the agent of the colonial government. The pyramidal structure of the state is now maintained by the latter's taking his place as paramount. If he capitulates entirely, he may become a mere puppet of the colonial government. He loses the support of his people because the pattern of reciprocal rights and duties which bound him to them is destroyed. Alternatively, he may be able to safeguard his former status, to some extent, by openly or covertly leading the opposition which his people inevitably feel towards alien rule. Very often he is in the equivocal position of having to reconcile his contradictory roles as representative of his people against the colonial government and of the latter against his people. He becomes the pivot on which the new system swings precariously. Indirect Rule may be regarded as a policy designed to stabilize the new political order, with the native paramount ruler in this dual role, but eliminating the friction it is liable to give rise to.

In the societies of Group B, European rule has had the opposite effect. The colonial government cannot administer through aggregates of individuals composing political segments, but has to employ administrative agents. For this purpose it makes use of any persons who can be assimilated to the stereotyped notion of an African chief. These agents for the first time have the backing of force behind their authority, now, moreover, extending into spheres for which there is no precedent. Direct resort to force in the form of self-help in defence of the rights of individuals or of groups is no longer permitted; for there is now, for the first time, a paramount authority exacting obedience in virtue of superior force which enables it to establish courts of justice to replace self-help. This tends to lead to the whole system of mutually balancing segments collapsing and a bureaucratic European system taking its place. An organization more like that of a centralized state comes into being.

XIII. The Mystical Values Associated with Political Office

The sanction of force is not an innovation in African forms of government. We have stressed the fact that it is one of the main pillars of the indigenous type of state. But the sanction of force on which a European administration depends lies outside the native political system. It is not used to maintain the values inherent in that system. In both societies of Group A and those of Group B European governments can impose their authority; in neither are they able to establish moral ties with the subject people. For, as we have seen, in the original native system force is used by a ruler with the consent of his subjects in the interest of the social order.

An African ruler is not to his people merely a person who can enforce his will on them. He is the axis of their political relations, the symbol of their unity and exclusiveness, and their embodiment of their essential values. He is more than a secular ruler; in *that* capacity the European government can to a great extent replace him. His credentials are mystical and are derived from antiquity. Where there are no chiefs, the balanced segments which compose the political structure are vouched for by tradition and myth and their interrelations are guided by values expressed in mystical symbols. Into these sacred precincts the European rulers can never enter. They have no mythical or ritual warranty for their authority.

What is the meaning of this aspect of African political organization? African societies are not models of continuous internal harmony. Acts of violence, oppression, revolt, civil war, and so forth, chequer the history of every African state. In societies like the Logoli, Tallensi, and Nuer the segmentary nature of the social structure is often most strikingly brought to light by armed conflict between the segments. But if the social system has reached a sufficient degree of stability, these internal convulsions do not necessarily wreck it. In fact, they may be the means of reinforcing it, as we have seen, against the abuses and infringements of rulers actuated by their private interests. In the segmentary societies, war is not a matter of one segment enforcing its will on another, but is the way in which segments protect their particular interests within a field of common interests and values.

There are, in every African society, innumerable ties which counteract the tendencies towards political fission arising out of the tensions and cleavages in the social structure. An administrative organization backed by coercive sanctions, clanship, lineage and age-set ties, the fine-spun web of kinship—all these unite people who have different or even opposed sectional and private interests. Often also there are common material interests such as the need to share pastures or to trade in a common market-place, or complementary economic pursuits binding different sections to one another. Always there are common ritual values, the ideological superstructure of political organization.

Members of an African society feel their unity and perceive their common interests in symbols, and it is their attachment to these symbols which more than anything else gives their society cohesion and persistence. In the form of myths, fictions, dogmas, ritual, sacred places and persons, these symbols represent the unity and exclusiveness of the groups which respect them. They are regarded, however, not as mere symbols, but as final values in themselves.

To explain these symbols sociologically, they have to be translated into terms of social function and of the social structure which they serve to maintain. Africans have no objective knowledge of the forces determining their social organization and actuating their social behaviour. Yet they would be unable to carry on their collective life if they could not think and feel about the interests which actuate them, the institutions by means of which they organize collective action, and the structure of the groups into which they are organized. Myths, dogmas, ritual beliefs and activities make his social system intellectually tangible and coherent to an African and enable him to think and feel about it. Furthermore, these sacred symbols, which reflect the social system, endow it with mystical values which evoke acceptance of the social order that goes far beyond the obedience exacted by the secular sanction of force. The social system is, as it were, removed to a mystical plane, where it figures as a system of sacred values beyond criticism or revision. Hence people will overthrow a bad king, but the kingship is never questioned; hence the wars or feuds between segments of a society like the Nuer or the Tallensi are kept within bounds by mystical sanctions. These values are common to the whole society, to rulers and ruled alike and to all the segments and sections of a society.

The African does not see beyond the symbols; it might well be held that if he understood their objective meaning, they would lose the power they have over him. This power lies in their symbolic content, and in their association with the nodal institutions of the social structure, such as the kingship. Not every kind of ritual or any sort of mystical ideas can express the values that hold a society together and focus the loyalty and devotion of its members on their rulers. If we study the mystical values bound up with the kingship in any of the societies of Group A, we find that they refer to fertility, health, prosperity, peace, justice—to everything, in short, which gives life and happiness to a people. The African sees these ritual observances as the supreme safeguard of the basic needs of his existence and of the basic relations that make up his social order—land, cattle, rain, bodily health, the family, the clan, the state. The mystical values reflect the general import of the basic elements of existence: the land as the source of the whole people's livelihood, physical health as something universally desired, the family as the fundamental procreative unit, and so forth. These are the common interests of the whole society, as the native sees them. These are the themes of taboos, observances and ceremonies in which, in societies of Group A, the whole people has a share through its representatives, and in societies of Group B all the segments participate, since they are matters of equal moment to all.

We have stressed the fact that the universal aspect of things like land or fertility are the subjects of common interest in an African society; for these matters also have another side to them, as the private interests of individuals and segments of a society. The productivity of his own land, the welfare and security of his own family or his own clan, such matters are of daily, practical concern to every member of an African society; and over such matters arise the conflicts between sections and factions of the society. Thus the basic needs of existence and the basic social relations are, in their pragmatic and utilitarian aspects, as sources of immediate satisfactions and strivings, the subjects of private interests; as common interests, they are non-utilitarian and non-pragmatic, matters of moral value and ideological significance. The common interests spring from those very private interests to which they stand in opposition.

To explain the ritual aspect of African political organization in terms of magical mentality is not enough; and it does not take us far to say that land, rain, fertility, &c., are "sacralized" because they are the most vital needs of the community. Such arguments do not explain why the great ceremonies in which ritual for the common good is performed are usually on a public scale. They do not explain why the ritual functions we have been describing should be bound up, always, with pivotal political offices and should be part of the political theory of an organized society.

Again, it is not enough to dismiss these ritual functions of chiefship, kingship, &c., by calling them sanctions of political authority. Why, then, are they regarded as among the most stringent responsibilities of office? Why are they so often distributed amongst a number of independent functionaries who are thus enabled to exercise a balancing constraint on one another? It is clear that they serve, also, as a sanction against the abuse of political power and as a means of constraining political functionaries to perform their administrative obligations as well as their religious duties, lest the common good suffer injury.

When, finally, it is stated as an observable descriptive fact that we are dealing here with institutions that serve to affirm and promote political solidarity we must ask why they do so. Why is an all-embracing administrative machinery or a wide-flung lineage system insufficient by itself to achieve this?

We cannot attempt to deal at length with all these questions. We have already given overmuch space to them because we consider them to be of the utmost importance, both from the theoretical and the practical point of view. The "supernatural" aspects of African government are always puzzling and often exasperating to the European administrator. But a great deal more of research is needed before we shall be able to understand them fully. The hypothesis we are making use of is, we feel, a stimulating starting-point for further research into these matters. The part of it which has already been stated is, perhaps, least controversial. But it is incomplete.

Any item of social behaviour, and therefore any political relation, has a utilitarian or pragmatic content. It means that material goods change hands, are disbursed or acquired, and that the direct purposes of individuals are achieved. Items of social behaviour and therefore political relations have also a moral aspect; that is, they express rights and duties, privileges and obligations, political sentiments, social ties and cleavages. We see these two aspects clearly in such acts as paying tribute to a ruler or handing over blood-cattle in compensation for murder. In political relations, consequently, we find two types of interests working conjointly, material interests and moral interests, though they are not separated in this abstract way in native thought. Natives stress the material components of a political relation and generally state it in terms of its utilitarian and pragmatic functions.

A particular right or duty or political sentiment occurs as an item of behaviour of an individual or a small section of an African society and is enforceable by secular sanctions brought to bear on these individuals or small sections. But in a politically organized community a particular right, duty, or sentiment exists only as an element in a whole body of common, reciprocal, and mutually balancing rights, duties, and sentiments, the body of moral and legal norms. Upon the regularity and order with which this whole body of interwoven norms is maintained depends the stability and continuity of the structure of an African society. On the average, rights must be respected, duties performed, the sentiments binding the members together upheld or else the social order would be so insecure that the material needs of existence could no longer be satisfied. Productive labour would come to a standstill and the society disintegrate. This is the greatest common interest in any African society, and it is this interest which the political system, viewed in its entirety, subserves. This, too, is the ultimate and, we might say, axiomatic set of premisses of the social order. If they were continually and arbitrarily violated, the social system would cease to work.

We can sum up this analysis by saying that the material interests that actuate individuals or groups in an African society operate in the frame of a body of interconnected moral and legal norms the order and stability of which is maintained by the political organization. Africans, as we have pointed out, do not analyse their social system; they live it. They think and feel about it in terms of values which reflect, in doctrine and symbol, but do not explain, the forces that really control their social behaviour. Outstanding among these values are the mystical values dramatized in the great public ceremonies and bound up with their key political institutions. These, we believe, stand for the greatest common interest of the widest political community to which a member of a particular African society belongs—that is, for the whole body of interconnected rights, duties, and sentiments; for this is what makes the society a single political community. That is why these mystical values are always associated with pivotal political offices and are expressed in both the privileges and the obligations of political office.

Their mystical form is due to the ultimate and axiomatic character of the body of moral and legal norms which could not be kept in being, as a body, by secular sanctions. Periodical ceremonies are necessary to affirm and consolidate these values because, in the ordinary course of events, people are preoccupied with sectional and private interests and are apt to lose sight of the common interest and of their political interdependence. Lastly, their symbolic content reflects the basic needs of existence and the basic social relations because these are the most concrete and tangible elements of all social and political relations. The visible test of how well a given body of rights, duties, and sentiments is being maintained and is working is to be found in the level of security and success with which the basic needs of existence are satisfied and the basic social relations sustained.

It is an interesting fact that under European rule African kings retain their "ritual functions" long after most of the secular authority which these are said to sanction is lost. Nor are the mystical values of political office entirely obliterated by a change of religion to Christianity or Islam. As long as the kingship endures as the axis of a body of moral and legal norms holding a people together in a political community, it will, most probably, continue to be the focus of mystical values.

It is easy to see a connexion between kingship and the interests and solidarity of the whole community in a state with highly centralized authority. In societies lacking centralized government, social values cannot be symbolized by a single person, but are distributed at cardinal points of the social structure. Here we find myths, dogmas, ritual ceremonies, mystical powers, &c., associated with segments and defining and serving to maintain the relationship between them. Periodic ceremonies emphasizing the solidarity of segments, and between segments, as against sectional interests within these groups, are the rule among the Tallensi and Logoli no less than among the Bemba and Kede. Among the Nuer, the leopard-skin chief, a sacred personage associated with the fertility of the earth, is the medium through whom feuds are settled and, hence, inter-segment relations regulated. The difference between these societies of Group B and those of Group A lies in the fact that there is no person who represents the political unity of the people, such unity being lacking, and there may be no person who represents the unity of segments of the people. Ritual powers and responsibility are distributed in conformity with the highly segmentary structure of the society.

XIV. The Problem of the Limits of the Political Group

We conclude by emphasizing two points of very great importance which are often overlooked. However one may define political units or groups, they cannot be treated in isolation, for they always form part of a larger social system. Thus, to take an extreme example, the localized lineages of the Tallensi overlap one another like a series of intersecting circles, so that it is impossible to state clearly where the lines of political cleavage run. These overlapping fields of political relations stretch almost indefinitely, so that there is a kind of interlocking even of neighbouring peoples, and while we can see that this people is distinct from that, it is not easy to say at what point, culturally or politically, one is justified in regarding them as distinct units. Among the Nuer, political demarcation is simpler, but even here there is, between segments of a political unit, the same kind of structural relationship as there is between this unit and another unit of the same order. Hence the designation of autonomous political groups is always to some extent an arbitrary matter.

This is more noticeable among the societies of Group B, but among those of Group A also there is an interdependence between the political group described and neighbouring political groups and a certain overlapping between them. The Ngwato have a segmentary relationship to other Tswana tribes which in many respects is of the same order as that between divisions of the Ngwato themselves. The same is true of the other societies with centralized governments.

This overlapping and interlocking of societies is largely due to the fact that the point at which political relations, narrowly defined in terms of military action and legal sanctions, end is not the point at which all social relations cease. The social structure of a people stretches beyond their political system, so defined, for there are always social relations of one kind or another between peoples of different autonomous political groups. Clans, age-sets, ritual associations, relations of affinity and of trade, and social relations of other kinds unite people of different political units. Common language or closely related languages, similar customs and beliefs, and so on, also unite them. Hence a strong feeling of community may exist between groups which do not acknowledge a single ruler or unite for specific political purposes. Community of language and culture, as we have indicated, does not necessarily give rise to political unity, any more than linguistic and cultural dissimilarity prevents political unity.

Herein lies a problem of world importance: what is the relation of political structure to the whole social structure? Everywhere in Africa social ties of one kind or another tend to draw together peoples who are politically separated and political ties appear to be dominant whenever there is conflict between them and other social ties. The solution of this problem would seem to lie in a more detailed investigation of the nature of political values and of the symbols in which they are expressed. Bonds of utilitarian interest between individuals and between groups are not as strong as the bonds implied in common attachment to mystical symbols. It is precisely the greater solidarity, based on these bonds, which generally gives political groups their dominance over social groups of other kinds.

Note

1   We would except from this stricture Professor R.H. Lowie, though we do not altogether accept his methods and conclusions. See his works *Primitive Society* (1920) and *Origin of the State* (1927). We are referring only to anthropologists. The work of the great legal and constitutional historians like Maine, Vinogradoff, and Ed. Meyer falls into another category. All students of political institutions are indebted to their pioneer researches.

Study Questions

1. According to Fortes and Evans-Pritchard, what is the relationship between political systems and other aspects of culture?

2. In what ways do the two types of political systems studied by Fortes and Evans-Pritchard differ?

3. According to Fortes and Evans-Pritchard, how did the impact of European rule on the two types of political systems differ?

Further Readings

Douglas, Mary. 1980. *Edward Evans-Pritchard*. New York: Viking Press.

Evans-Pritchard, E.E. 1940. *The Nuer: A Description of the Modes of Livelihood and Political Institutions of a Nilotic People*. Oxford: Oxford University Press.

—. 1951. *Social Anthropology*. New York: Free Press.

Fortes, Meyer, and Evans-Pritchard, E.E. 1967 [1940]. *African Political Systems*. London: Oxford University Press.

Henson, Hilary. 1974. *British Social Anthropologists and Language: A History of Separate Development*. Oxford: Clarendon Press.

Moore, Sally Falk. 1944. *Anthropology and Africa: Changing Perspectives on a Changing Scene*. Charlottesville: University Press of Virginia.

Stocking, George W., Jr. (ed.). 1984. *Functionalism Historicized: Essays on British Social Anthropology*. Madison: University of Wisconsin Press.

—, (ed.). 1993. *Colonial Situations: Essays on the Contextualization of Ethnographic Knowledge*. Madison: University of Wisconsin Press.

17

The Sociology of Charismatic Authority

MAX WEBER

1. The General Character of Charisma

Bureaucratic and patriarchal structures are antagonistic in many ways, yet they have in common a most important peculiarity: permanence. In this respect they are both institutions of daily routine. Patriarchal power especially is rooted in the provisioning of recurrent and normal needs of the workaday life. Patriarchal authority thus has its original locus in the economy, that is, in those branches of the economy that can be satisfied by means of normal routine. The patriarch is the "natural leader" of the daily routine. And in this respect, the bureaucratic structure is only the counter-image of patriarchalism transposed into rationality. As a permanent structure with a system of rational rules, bureaucracy is fashioned to meet calculable and recurrent needs by means of a normal routine.

The provisioning of all demands that go beyond those of everyday routine has had, in principle, an entirely heterogeneous, namely, a *charismatic*, foundation; the further back we look in history, the more we find this to be the case. This means that the "natural" leaders—in times of psychic, physical, economic, ethical, religious, political distress—have been neither officeholders nor incumbents of an "occupation" in the present sense of the word, that is, men who have acquired expert knowledge and who serve for remuneration. The natural leaders in distress have been holders of specific gifts of the body and spirit; and these gifts have been believed to be supernatural, not accessible to everybody. The concept of "charisma" is here used in a completely "value-neutral" sense.

The capacity of the Irish culture hero, **Cuchulain**, or of the Homeric **Achilles** for heroic frenzy is a manic seizure, just as is that of the Arabian berserk who bites his shield like a mad dog—biting around until he darts off in raving bloodthirstiness. For a long time it has been maintained that the seizure of the berserk is artificially produced through acute poisoning. In **Byzantium**, a number of "blood beasts," disposed to such seizures, were kept about, just as war elephants were formerly kept. Shamanistic ecstasy is linked to constitutional epilepsy, the possession and testing of which represents a charismatic qualification. Hence neither is "edifying" to our minds. They are just as little edifying to us as is the kind of "revelation," for instance, of the **Sacred Book of the Mormons**, which, at least from an evaluative standpoint, perhaps would have to be called a "hoax." But sociology is not concerned with such questions. In the faith of their followers, the chief of the Mormons has proved himself to be charismatically qualified, as have "heroes" and "sorcerers." All of them have practiced their arts and ruled by virtue of this gift (charisma) and, where the idea of God has already been clearly conceived, by virtue of the divine mission lying therein. This holds for doctors and prophets, just as for judges and military leaders, or for leaders of big hunting expeditions.

It is to his credit that Rudolph Sohm brought out the sociological peculiarity of this category of domination-structure for a historically important special case, namely, the historical development of the authority of the early Christian church. Sohm performed this task with logical consistency, and hence, by necessity, he was one-sided from a purely historical point of view. In principle, however, the very same state of affairs recurs universally, although often it is most clearly developed in the field of religion.

In contrast to any kind of bureaucratic organization of offices, the charismatic structure knows nothing of a form or of an ordered procedure of appointment or dismissal. It knows no regulated "career," "advancement," "salary," or regulated and expert training of the holder of charisma or of his aids. It knows no agency of control or appeal, no local bailiwicks or exclusive functional jurisdictions; nor does it embrace permanent institutions like our bureaucratic "departments," which are independent of persons and of purely personal charisma.

Charisma knows only inner determination and inner restraint. The holder of charisma seizes the task that is adequate for him and demands obedience and a following by virtue of his mission. His success determines whether he finds them. His charismatic claim breaks down if his mission is not recognized by those to whom he feels he has been sent. If they recognize him, he is their master—so long as he knows how to maintain recognition through "proving" himself. But he does not derive his "right" from their will, in the manner of an election. Rather, the reverse holds: it is the *duty* of those to whom he addresses his mission to recognize him as their charismatically qualified leader.

In Chinese theory, the emperor's prerogatives are made dependent upon the recognition of the people. But this does not mean recognition of the sovereignty of the people any more than did the prophet's necessity of getting recognition from the believers in the early Christian community. The Chinese theory, rather, characterizes the charismatic nature of the *monarch's position*, which adheres to his *personal* qualification and to his *proved* worth.

Charisma can be, and of course regularly is, qualitatively particularized. This is an internal rather than an external affair, and results in the qualitative barrier of the charisma holder's mission and power. In meaning and in content the mission may be addressed to a group of men who are delimited locally, ethnically, socially, politically, occupationally, or in some other way. If the mission is thus addressed to a limited group of men, as is the rule, it finds its limits within their circle.

In its economic sub-structure, as in everything else, charismatic domination is the very opposite of bureaucratic domination. If bureaucratic domination depends upon regular income, and hence at least *a potiori* on a money economy and money taxes, charisma lives in, though not off, this world. This has to be properly understood. Frequently charisma quite deliberately shuns the possession of money and of pecuniary income *per se*, as did **Saint Francis** and many of his like; but this is of course not the rule. Even a pirate genius may exercise a "charismatic" domination, in the value-neutral sense intended here. Charismatic political heroes seek booty and, above all, gold. But charisma, and this is decisive, always rejects as undignified any pecuniary gain that is methodical and rational. In general, charisma rejects all rational economic conduct.

The sharp contrast between charisma and any "patriarchal" structure that rests upon the ordered base of the "household" lies in this rejection of rational economic conduct. In its "pure" form, charisma is never a source of private gain for its holders in the sense of economic exploitation by the making of a deal. Nor is it a source of income in the form of pecuniary compensation, and just as little does it involve an orderly taxation for the material requirements of its mission. If the mission is one of peace, individual patrons provide the necessary means for charismatic structures; or those to whom the charisma is addressed provide honorific gifts, donations, or other voluntary contributions. In the case of charismatic warrior heroes, booty represents one of the ends as well as the material means of the mission. "Pure" charisma is contrary to all patriarchal domination (in the sense of the term used here). It is the opposite of all ordered economy. It is the very force that disregards economy. This also holds, indeed precisely, where the charismatic leader is after the acquisition of goods, as is the case with the charismatic warrior hero. Charisma can do this because by its very nature it is not an "institutional" and permanent structure, but rather, where its "pure" type is at work, it is the very opposite of the institutionally permanent.

In order to do justice to their mission, the holders of charisma, the master as well as his disciples and followers, must stand outside the ties of this world, outside of routine occupations, as well as outside the routine obligations of family life. The statutes of the Jesuit order preclude the acceptance of church offices; the members of orders are forbidden to own property or, according to the original rule of St. Francis, the order as such is forbidden to do so. The priest and the knight of an order have to live in celibacy, and numerous holders of a prophetic or artistic charisma are actually single. All this is indicative of the unavoidable separation from this world of those who partake ('χλῆροζ') of charisma. In these respects, the economic conditions of participation in charisma may have an (apparently) antagonistic appearance, depending upon the type of charisma—artistic or religious, for instance—and the way of life flowing from its meaning. Modern charismatic movements of artistic origin represent "independents without gainful employment" (in everyday language, **rentiers**). Normally such persons are the best qualified to follow a charismatic leader. This is just as logically consistent as was the medieval friar's vow of poverty, which demanded the very opposite.

2. Foundations and Instability of Charismatic Authority

By its very nature, the existence of charismatic authority is specifically unstable. The holder may forego his charisma; he may feel "forsaken by his God," as Jesus did on the cross; he may prove to his followers that "virtue is gone out of him." It is then that his mission is extinguished, and hope waits and searches for a new holder of charisma. The charismatic holder is deserted by his following, however, (only) because pure charisma does not know any "legitimacy" other than that flowing from personal strength, that is, one which is constantly being proved. The charismatic hero does not deduce his authority from codes and statutes, as is the case with the jurisdiction of office; nor does he deduce his authority from traditional custom or feudal vows of faith, as is the case with patrimonial power.

The charismatic leader gains and maintains authority solely by proving his strength in life. If he wants to be a prophet, he must perform miracles; if he wants to be a war lord, he must perform heroic deeds. Above all, however, his divine mission must "prove" itself in that those who faithfully surrender to him must fare well. If they do not fare well, he is obviously not the master sent by the gods.

This very serious meaning of genuine charisma evidently stands in radical contrast to the convenient pretensions of present rulers to a "divine right of kings," with its reference to the "inscrutable" will of the Lord, "to whom alone the monarch is responsible." The genuinely charismatic ruler is responsible precisely to those whom he rules. He is responsible for but one thing, that he personally and actually be the God-willed master.

During these last decades we have witnessed how the Chinese monarch impeaches himself before all the people because of his sins and insufficiencies if his administration does not succeed in warding off some distress from the governed, whether it is inundations or unsuccessful wars. Thus does a ruler whose power, even in vestiges and theoretically, is genuinely charismatic deport himself. And if even this penitence does not reconcile the deities, the charismatic emperor faces dispossession and death, which often enough is consummated as a propitiatory sacrifice.

Meng-tse's (**Mencius'**) thesis that the people's voice is "God's voice" (according to him the *only* way in which God speaks!) has a very specific meaning: if the people cease to recognize the ruler, it is expressly stated that he simply becomes a private citizen; and if he then wishes to be more, he becomes a usurper deserving of punishment. The state of affairs that corresponds to these phrases, which sound highly revolutionary, recurs under primitive conditions without any such **pathos**. The charismatic character adheres to almost all primitive authorities with the exception of domestic power in the narrowest sense, and the chieftain is often enough simply deserted if success does not remain faithful to him.

The subjects may extend a more active or passive "recognition" to the personal mission of the charismatic master. His power rests upon this purely factual recognition and springs from faithful devotion. It is devotion to the extraordinary and unheard-of, to what is strange to all rule and tradition and which therefore is viewed as divine. It is a devotion born of distress and enthusiasm.

Genuine charismatic domination therefore knows of no abstract legal codes and statutes and of no "formal" way of adjudication. Its "objective" law emanates concretely from the highly personal experience of heavenly grace and from the god-like strength of the hero. Charismatic domination means a rejection of all ties to any external order in favor of the exclusive glorification of the genuine mentality of the prophet and hero. Hence, its attitude is revolutionary and transvalues everything; it makes a sovereign break with all traditional or rational norms: "It is written, but I say unto you."

The specifically charismatic form of settling disputes is by way of the prophet's revelation, by way of the oracle, or by way of "**Solomonic**" arbitration by a charismatically qualified sage. This arbitration is determined by means of strictly concrete and individual evaluations, which, however, claim absolute validity. Here lies the proper locus of "Kadi-justice" in the proverbial—not the historical—sense of the phrase. In its actual historical appearance the jurisdiction of the Islamic Kadi is, of course, bound to sacred tradition and is often a highly formalistic interpretation.

Only where these intellectual tools fail does jurisdiction rise to an unfettered individual act valuing the particular case; but then it does indeed. Genuinely charismatic justice always acts in this manner. In its pure form it is the polar opposite of formal and traditional bonds, and it is just as free in the face of the sanctity of tradition as it is in the face of any rationalist deductions from abstract concepts.

This is not the place to discuss how the reference to the *aegum et bonum* in the Roman administration of justice and the original meaning of English "equity" are related to charismatic justice in general and to the theocratic Kadi-justice of Islamism in particular. Both the *aegum et bonum* and "equity" are partly the products of a strongly rationalized administration of justice and partly the product of abstract conceptions of natural law. In any case the *ex bona fide* contains a reference to the "mores" of business life and thus retains just as little of a genuine irrational justice as does, for instance, the German judge's "free discretion."

Any kind of ordeal as a means of evidence is, of course, a derivative of charismatic justice. But the ordeal displaces the personal authority of the holder of charisma by a mechanism of rules for formally ascertaining the divine will. This falls in the sphere of the "routinization" of charisma, with which we shall deal below.

3. Charismatic Kingship

In the evolution of political charisma, kingship represents a particularly important case in the historical development of the charismatic legitimization of institutions. The king is everywhere primarily a war lord, and kingship evolves from charismatic heroism.

In the form it displays in the history of civilized peoples, kingship is not the oldest evolutionary form of "political" domination. By "political" domination is meant a power that reaches beyond and which is, in principle, distinct from domestic authority. It is distinct because, in the first place, it is not devoted to leading the peaceful struggle of man with nature; it is, rather, devoted to leading in the violent conflict of one human community with another.

The predecessors of kingship were the holders of all those charismatic powers that guaranteed to remedy extraordinary external and internal distress, or guaranteed the success of extraordinary ventures. The chieftain of early history, the predecessor of kingship, is still a dual figure. On the one hand, he is the patriarchal head of the family or sib, and on the other, he is the charismatic leader of the hunt and war, the sorcerer, the rainmaker, the medicine man—and thus the priest and the doctor—and finally, the arbiter. Often, yet not always, such charismatic functions are split into as many special holders of charisma. Rather frequently the chieftain of the hunt and of war stands beside the chieftain of peace, who has essentially economic functions. In contrast to the latter, the chieftain of war acquires his charisma by proving his heroism to a voluntary following in successful raids leading to victory and booty. Even the royal Assyrian inscriptions enumerate booties of the hunt and cedars from

Lebanon—dragged along for building purposes—alongside figures on the slain enemies and the size of the walls of conquered cities, which are covered with skins peeled off the enemies.

The charismatic position (among primitives) is thus acquired without regard to position in the sibs or domestic communities and without any rules whatsoever. This dualism of charisma and everyday routine is very frequently found among the American Indians, for instance, among the Confederacy of the Iroquois, as well as in Africa and elsewhere.

Where war and the big game hunt are absent, the charismatic chieftain—the "war lord" as we wish to call him, in contrast to the chieftain of peace—is absent as well. In peacetime, especially if elemental calamities, particularly drought and diseases, are frequent, a charismatic sorcerer may have an essentially similar power in his hands. He is a priestly lord. The charisma of the war lord may or may not be unstable in nature according to whether or not he proves himself and whether or not there is any need for a war lord. He becomes a permanent figure when warfare becomes a chronic state of affairs. It is a mere terminological question whether one wishes to let kingship, and with it the state, begin only when strangers are affiliated with and integrated into the community as subjects. For our purposes it will be expedient to continue delimiting the term "state" far more narrowly.

The existence of the war lord as a regular figure certainly does not depend upon a tribal rule over subjects of other tribes or upon individual slaves. His existence depends solely upon a chronic state of war and upon a comprehensive organization set for warfare. On the other hand, the development of kingship into a regular royal administration does emerge only at the stage when a following of royal professional warriors rules over the working or paying masses; at least, that is often the case. The forceful subjection of strange tribes, however, is not an absolutely indispensable link in this development. Internal class stratification may bring about the very same social differentiation: the charismatic following of warriors develops into a ruling caste. But in every case, princely power and those groups having interests vested in it—that is, the war lord's following—strive for legitimacy as soon as the rule has become stable. They crave for a characteristic which would define the charismatically qualified ruler.

Study Questions
1. According to Weber, how does charismatic authority contrast with bureaucratic authority?
2. According to Weber, why is charismatic authority unstable?
3. According to Weber, how does charismatic kingship evolve?

Further Readings

Comaroff, Jean, and Comaroff, John L. 1991. *Of Revelation and Revolution, Vol. 1: Christianity, Colonialism, and Consciousness in South Africa*. Chicago: University of Chicago Press.

Wallace, Anthony F. 1966. *Religion: An Anthropological View*. New York: Random House.

—. 1972. *The Death and Rebirth of the Seneca*. New York: Random House.

Weber, Max. 1978. *Economy and Society: An Outline of Interpretive Sociology*. Eds. Guenther Roth and Claus Wittich. Trans. Ephraim Fischoff. Berkeley: University of California Press.

—. 1993 [1922]. *The Sociology of Religion*. Boston: Beacon Press.

—. 1996 [1920]. *The Protestant Ethic and the Spirit of Capitalism*. Ed. Randall Collins. Los Angeles: Roxbury.

Worsley, Peter. 1968. *The Trumpet Shall Sound*. New York: Schocken Books.

PART III

ANTHROPOLOGY AT MIDLIFE

———

INTRODUCTION

Parts One and Two examined the nineteenth-century development and early twentieth-century coming of age of the discipline of anthropology as the pre-eminent science of humanity. In this part and the next, we will show how anthropologists came to question the truth-value of key assumptions on which the discipline had been erected (among them the objective status of culture), which were the intellectual legacy of the eighteenth and nineteenth centuries. The tale of the past half-century of anthropology opens with structural-functionalism still very much the reigning paradigm in British anthropology and variations of Boasian anthropology still prevailing in the United States. But certainly by the 1980s and 1990s much had changed in terms of how anthropologists understood both themselves and the cultures and societies that they studied.

Structuralism in Bloom and Decline

For anthropologists working on both sides of the Atlantic Ocean, the period roughly extending from the end of World War II through the academically unsettled and politically tumultuous 1960s and 1970s and culminating in the "postmodern turn" of the 1980s, was chiefly characterized by the critical appraisal, rejection, and occasional rebirth of prevailing anthropological theories of social structure and culture. As we have seen, American anthropology in the immediate postwar years was dominated by culture and personality studies and historical ethnography in the Boasian tradition, whereas the course of British social anthropology in the same period was still very much under the personal influence of Malinowski and Radcliffe-Brown.

Still, by the mid-1950s, anthropologists in Britain were engaged in a concerted effort to redefine what it was to do structural-functionalist anthropology. While Radcliffe-Brown's most prominent students, E.E. Evans-Pritchard and Meyer Fortes, had infused their teacher's "classical" structural-functionalist theory with a much-needed dose of empirical rigor, more fundamental problems associated with the "classical" Radcliffe-Brownian paradigm were not so readily dispensed with. In particular, structural-functionalism appeared increasingly ill-suited to address the questions of social and historical change and the role of individuals as cultural innovators—questions rendered more pressing than they had ever been with the end of European colonialism in Africa and elsewhere. These difficulties persisted despite important attempts to temper the concept of social structure with an appreciation of cultural meaning and the rationality behind non-Western social forms, such as Evans-Pritchard's study of witchcraft in the southern Sudan, *Witchcraft, Oracles and Magic among the Azande* (1937).

Attempts to reformulate the Durkheimian tradition in Britain were matched in France by the development of a new school of anthropological theory under Claude Lévi-Strauss (b. 1908). "French Structuralism," like its British counterpart, relied on Durkheim's conception of organic solidarity to provide a centre of theoretical gravity. However, while a prevailing assumption among structural-functionalists was that social structures were empirically-observed, sociologically concrete institutions, customs, etc., that intersected one another in tangible fashion, Lévi-Strauss and his students emphasized the primacy in anthropology of *mental* structures of logic which, ultimately, are shared by all human beings.

Selections included in this part (by Max Gluckman, Claude Lévi-Strauss, and Edmund Leach, respectively) exemplify both British and French efforts to redefine the concepts of structure and function during the 1940s and 1950s. Given the genius of its protagonists—among them, Evans-Pritchard, Meyer Fortes, and the three cited above—it comes as no surprise that this was a period of intense productivity during which anthropology effloresced (especially in Britain) as an academic discipline. Nevertheless, these years were also characterized by critical evaluation of foundational tenets of the Durkheimian tradition of ethnographic research and theory; in particular, the organic analogy fell to close scrutiny. In the face of such uncertainty about the anthropological traditions that had come down to them, the future direction of the discipline was also thrown into doubt. Therefore, the 1940s and 1950s may likewise be thought of as a period in which the discipline experienced "growing pains."

As the personal influence of Radcliffe-Brown and Malinowski waned in the aftermath of World War II, Max Gluckman (1911-75) was among a small cadre of anthropologists credited with redefining what it meant to do anthropology. For instance, in Selection 18, "The Utility of the Equilibrium Model in the Study of Social Change," he addresses the question of how to incorporate a concern for diachronic analysis into the study of social institutions (developing the concept of the "structural duration") and, in so doing, how to develop a more fine-grained appreciation for the relations between social structure and history, social equilibrium and change. A South African who eventually settled in Britain, Gluckman himself became the charismatic leader of a movement in British anthropological theory, centred in Manchester University and frequently referred to as the "Manchester School." In particular, his work on ritual and conflict in Southern and Central Africa was deeply influential for a cadre of 1950s and 1960s social anthropologists—a group that included Victor Turner (see below) and whose collective corpus of research was strongly connected to the Rhodes-Livingstone Institute in Zambia (now the Zambian National Research Institute). Gluckman is best known for his painstakingly detailed, "action" oriented ethnographies of Central Africa that remain classic texts in the sub-discipline of Political Anthropology. These include *Custom and Conflict in Africa* (1955), and *Order and Rebellion in Tribal Africa* (1963).

A key insight of Gluckman's work was that structural relations in Central African society were not easily accounted for by the kind of Durkheimian organic analogy promulgated by Radcliffe-Brown. Instead, Gluckman showed how several among these societies (notably that of the Swazi people of Southern Africa) were characterized by tensions that continually threatened the stability of the social order and hierarchy. Establishing and maintaining the integrity of society were thereby problematic aspects of social relations demanding a far deeper level of analysis than suggested by uncritical acceptance of the organic analogy. For Gluckman and his students, ritual played a key role in this new, more complex structural-functionalism. It was through "rituals of rebellion," for instance, that Swazi kings were able to consolidate and legitimize authority over their subjects by deliberately invoking and dramatizing the danger of social conflict and the consequent need for a stable kingship.

Arguably, the French anthropologist Claude Lévi-Strauss has been more influential for his prolific and innovative approach to theorizing culture than any other single theorist of the last half-century. Selection 19 features key excerpts from a published lecture, "The Scope of Anthropology," which he delivered as the new Chair of Social Anthropology at the Collège de France in 1960. Rather than fully explicate his seminal theoretical approach, the lecture elucidates his general thinking about the importance of studying universal "signs at the heart of social life." Within and across local social worlds, he argues, anthropologists may view coherent symbolic systems and structures as languages that may be translated—a perspective rooted in Durkheim, which dramatically shifts the focus away from social institutions and toward human consciousness. While his great corpus of multifaceted work is difficult to consider in brief, it is at least possible to trace some of its broad contours and the enduring influence of the school of thought he founded, generally referred to as French Structuralism. Excepting Lévi-Strauss himself, the most well known practitioners within the school were the French anthropologist Louis Dumont (b. 1911) and, in a celebrated conversion from the tradition in which he had been trained, the British ethnographer Edmund Leach (1910-89).

As the name suggests, French Structuralism shares roots with its British "cousin," structural-functionalism, in the work of Émile Durkheim. Like Radcliffe-Brown and his intellectual heirs, Lévi-Strauss was concerned about understanding the integrity of social life and the "structures" that make it possible. Here, however, the resemblance all but ends. In contrast to the British School, Lévi-Strauss and the French Structuralists were much closer to their American confrères in the emphasis they placed on understanding cultural meaning, rather than what many considered to be the sterile, bloodless social structure as understood by structural-functionalists. Specifically, Lévi-Strauss has looked for social coherence as a function of symbolic structures of the mind, rather than empirically observed, institutionalized structures of social relations. Though his ethnographic work in Brazil during the late 1930s was for this reason broadly similar to Evans-Pritchard's studies of cultural meaning carried out among the Nuer and the Azande, it was a very far cry indeed from Radcliffe-Brown's and Meyer Fortes's formulations of primitive societies as organisms the structures of which functioned like well-oiled machines.

The most immediate influence on the French school was not Durkheim himself, but his nephew, Marcel Mauss (1872-1950), whose widely read essay, *The Gift* (1952 [1925]), examined relations of exchange and reciprocity between social groups. The acts of giving, receiving, and repaying signified more to Mauss than transactions between concrete sets of relations between people. They were structures of logic innate to the minds of individuals. Moreover, these, the most elementary units of culture, were not confined to economic transactions, but were extended to all spheres of social life. It was upon this insight that Lévi-Strauss has built much of his work.

Having conducted field research in Brazil, Lévi-Strauss developed his theory of structuralism in two of his best known works, *The Elementary Structures of Kinship* (1949) and *Structural Anthropology* (1958). He began with the idea that reciprocal exchange was the basis on which alliances were formed among individuals and groups. Ultimately, this universally distributed "elementary structure," was the foundation for the integration for all human societies. Following Mauss, this structure whereby gift-giving and exchange (particularly of women) became the fundamental principles of social cohesion, was innate and located in the minds of individuals. Lévi-Strauss infused the concept of reciprocity and exchange with his own insight, borrowed from the discipline of structural linguistics, which was centred in Prague around the work of Roman Jakobson (1896-1982). The two had met in New York in the early 1940s while both were in exile from the Nazi regime in Europe. Lévi-Strauss admired Jakobson's methods of phonological analysis, at the core of which was the notion of "phonemes." These were defined as the most elementary pairs of phonetic sounds to have meaning for speakers when contrasted. In the hybrid formulation proposed by Lévi-Strauss, the locus of this apparently universal "grammar" governing exchange was a binary pair of oppositions in the mind. Like phonemes, these binaries held meaning for all individuals because they were innate to the human psyche, opposing such concepts as life and death, the raw and the cooked, and nature and culture. Such oppositions did not exist in isolation from one another, but were instead integrated into networks of cultural logic mediated by the diverse cultures in which they were manifested. Anthropologists hoping to grasp the character of any given culture would therefore need to "unpack" the local expressions of these binary pairs, like peeling layers from an onion.

Among the most iconoclastic and respected figures to emerge in British social anthropology in the postwar period was Edmund Leach. In Selection 20, "Structuralism in Social Anthropology," Leach employs Biblical mythology to demonstrate the merits of a French structural analysis. However, many would argue that his most significant work was well within the tradition of the British school, albeit with a deeper concern for social change and the politics of social life. Trained under Malinowski and Raymond Firth, Leach conducted fieldwork in Burma during the 1940s, later documented in his famous monograph, *Political Systems of Highland Burma* (1954). This work was a significant advancement in political anthropology, in that Leach sought to unhinge the concept of social structure from the increasingly unpalatable notion that non-Western societies were the discrete, fully integrated organisms proposed by Malinowski and Radcliffe-Brown. To account for the interaction of two different social systems existing in Burma, Leach devised a model of "oscillating equilibrium." In this way, his early work shared a certain maverick quality with that of Gluckman and his Manchester students: all were concerned to develop a more sophisticated theory of social structure based on detailed fieldwork and in recognition of the unique histories and tensions that characterized particular social worlds.

As noted above, beyond his insightful ethnography (by all accounts, some of the most detailed work to come out of the British school) and his association with Gluckman and the Manchester School, Leach is remembered also for having dabbled in French Structuralism during the 1950s and 1960s. Indeed, Leach (together with Rodney Needham [b. 1923]) is frequently credited with introducing this body of research and theory to British social anthropology. The best known of his work in this area, in contrast to Lévi-Strauss's ethnography, concerned the structures of Biblical *texts*—work that was to be taken up and continued by other British scholars, most notably Mary Douglas (b. 1921).

Revitalizing the Symbol

In the ways outlined above, Gluckman, Lévi-Strauss, Leach, and others worked through the middle decades of the twentieth century to invest the anthropological truism of social structure with new theoretical coherence by addressing the limitations of the Durkheimian paradigm—most prominently, its inability to account for historical change, the porous character of social boundaries, or the creative agency of individuals. However, these failings were not easily overcome and ultimately demanded more creative solutions. The 1960s and 1970s witnessed the rise of several broad schools or traditions that have continued to exert influence on the direction of anthropological research and theory-building into the new millennium. Of these traditions, two will be examined in turn through the remainder of this part: "symbolic" and "interpretive" approaches on the one hand and "materialist" or "neoevolutionist" perspectives on the other.

Our choice to present these in tandem is not arbitrary. Many anthropologists have viewed the opposition of so-called "idealist" and "materialist" approaches as central to the academic debates of the past 30 years. While these relatively recent controversies owe much to the respective intellectual legacies of Weber and Marx and Kant and Descartes, renewed perceptions of difference between the two "camps" have been the grounds upon which much fresh intradisciplinary debate has proceeded. Moreover, as Ortner discusses in her essay on anthropological theory "Since the Sixties" (Selection 36), the distinction between these mutually-exclusive meta-categories, or "poles" of social and cultural theory has been the foil for those theorists who, in their efforts to develop truly *post*structural approaches to anthropological theory, have cried "a pox on both your houses."

The enormously influential American "interpretive" and British "symbolic" schools of anthropology, represented here by Clifford Geertz (Selections 21) and Victor Turner (Selection 22), share epistemological connections to earlier generations of social theorists. Indirectly, the roots of both approaches are in the neo-Kantian thought of the German philosopher Wilhelm Dilthey, who drew a sharp distinction between the natural sciences, or *naturwissenschaften*, and social sciences, or *geisteswissenschaften*. As we have seen in the historical particularism embraced by Franz Boas and disseminated to his famous students, this distinction has been very influential in American cultural anthropology. This American tradition also owes a debt to the philosophy of nineteenth- and early twentieth-century "phenomenologist" Edmund Husserl (1854-1958), who viewed human life as being unamenable to naturalistic observation. Unlike the natural world about us, Husserl concluded, human life—imbued with meaning—can only be understood through study of the lived experience, or subjectivity, of people.

In the United States, the two central figures in the development of symbolic anthropology were David Schneider (1918-95) and the guru of "interpretive anthropology," Clifford Geertz (b. 1926). Geertz's "Thick Description," from *The Interpretation of Cultures* (1973), is perhaps his most widely read exposition of the interpretive method in anthropology. He has viewed the anthropologist as a student of networks of interpenetrating symbols. In contrast to his British counterpart, Turner, for whom (as we discuss below) symbols were the instruments employed by people in the on-going creation of social solidarity out of conflict, Geertz viewed symbols as the central repositories and carriers of cultural meaning. For this reason, his interests have been firmly grounded in the American tradition, which placed a premium on the particularity of cultures and their component institutions. Symbols were especially important for the ethnographer, he believes, because they are the interpersonal cultural objects to be interpreted—what do they mean in the context of their use, and to whom? Symbols are interpersonal, he has argued, because they are not trapped in the discrete psychologies or inner-worlds of individual social "actors" (as he believed some of his peers in American anthropology had argued). To the contrary, they are overtly public texts of social life. The calling of the anthropologist is therefore to investigate, study, and (if possible) "grasp" these symbols, the vehicles for the native's perspective.

Through his extensive fieldwork in Morocco, Java, and elsewhere, and prolific publishing in the 1960s and 1970s, Geertz deserves much of the credit for introducing Max Weber into American anthropology—in particular, the more "ideational" or "mentalist" aspects of Weberian theory, which (put broadly) suppose that cultural systems are uniquely convincing for those who hold to them because they create a hermeneutic, or a correspondence, between the world "as it appears to be" with the world "as it should be." In a famous phrase which gave name to the approach Geertz proposed, anthropology is not "an experimental science in search of law," but instead "an interpretive one in search of meaning." On the one hand, cultures are integrated systems of public symbols that people inhabit, manipulate, and traffic in. Simultaneously, these same systems "inhabit" the individuals as logical templates of thought and action that make the world both intelligible and perfectly natural.

Geertz stipulated that the most effective role of the anthropologist was to learn the art of translating cultural meaning much as one might translate a language. In his most influential collection of essays, *The Interpretation of Cultures*, he proposed the investigative technique that he dubbed "thick description" as the surest way to accomplish this end. The ethnographic project, therefore, must involve the weaving together of disparate details drawn from the different realms of social life as observed by the ethnographer in the field. This is necessary above all, Geertz argues, because "man is an animal suspended in webs of significance that he himself has spun." For Geertz, as for Turner, ritual was the ethnographic setting, *par excellence*, in which symbolic meaning could be observed on the road to interpretation. For instance, on the subject of the "Balinese cockfight," Geertz described how the Balinese social order was symbolically played out through networks of symbols that established hierarchical relations between people in attendance at the ritual.

As we have seen, historical process, cultural meaning, and the inner "mental" lives of individuals have all been important focuses for research in Boas's distinctive "cultural anthropology"—concerns recapitulated by Geertz and other interpretive anthropologists. While Kantian thought and phenomenology *à la* Husserl have been less explicit in the British tradition of social anthropology than in its American counterpart, they have been represented particularly in the work of E.E. Evans-Pritchard during the 1940s and, especially, Max Gluckman's student Victor Turner (1920-83) in the 1960s and 1970s. For Turner, whose work we now briefly examine, the importance of cultural meaning was grafted onto the prevailing British focus on social structure to create a new and influential branch of theory: symbolic anthropology.

Like many British anthropologists of his generation, Turner had been steeped in orthodox structural functionalism and the Durkheimian tradition while a student under Max Gluckman at Manchester University in the 1940s. Perhaps the most important of Turner's studies examined the role of rites of passage as performances of social solidarity and communitas among the Ndembu of Rhodesia (now Zambia). Selection 22, "Symbols in Ndembu Ritual," is taken from the collection of ethnographic essays on Ndembu ritual, *The Forest of Symbols* (1967). In this essay, Turner focuses on the dynamic character of social structure and, in particular, on the role of symbols in the performance of "human interests, purposes, ends, and means...." He distinguishes between "dominant" symbols—or symbols that are the *sui generis* ground of social life—and "instrumental symbols," which are wielded by social actors in pursuing particular social objectives and individual interests.

Though an innovator, it would be misleading to characterize Turner's thinking as revolutionary. Rather, as Gluckman's student, he was at the forefront of efforts to refine, not do away with, Radcliffe-Brown's structural-functionalism. Gluckman and his students set about this by infusing anthropological research with a concern for the very real complexities and conflicts that they, as accomplished fieldworkers in colonial and postcolonial Africa, had observed at length and could hardly ignore. The painstaking attention to ethnographic detail and the complexity of social structure which characterized the work of many Manchester students, and which had been absent from the writing and theory of Radcliffe-Brown, was to become a central concern for Turner as well, particularly in his early work on the politics of ritual, exemplified in the highly influential *Schism and Continuity in an African Society* (1957).

Like Gluckman's writing, this work at its broadest level was not so much an argument as a dialogue with his "ancestor"—Émile Durkheim. If Durkheim had been correct in thinking that societies cohered "organically," Turner wanted to know how, precisely, the social organism managed to persist when it was so plainly riven by conflict and the vagaries of change through time. Also, echoing Gluckman and in the best tradition of British social anthropology stretching back to Durkheim, he was preoccupied with the role of ritual in this process. Throughout his career, Turner probed the connection of ritual to social order, always seeking to answer the question of how these orchestrated and sustained social relations in the face of the profound tendency to fission that he observed in complex African states and elsewhere.

In spite of the many similarities his thought and work bore to Gluckman's, however, Victor Turner nevertheless carved out a distinctive approach of his own to understanding the coherence of African states. In considering his ethnographic subjects, Turner was influenced by the writings of the late nineteenth- and early twentieth-century linguist Arnold van Gennep (1873-1957), who had developed a tripartite classificatory scheme of the "ritual process." In *The Rites of Passage* (1959 [1909]), van Gennep had argued that ritual involves the passage of individuals through three sequential phases of social being: "separation" from society, "transition" to a different state of being, and, finally, "incorporation" (or *re*-incorporation) into society. Seeking to expand understanding of the social function of ritual beyond where Durkheim had left it—that is, with the idea that rituals represent nothing so much as primitive humanity coming together in a common, psychological need for social solidarity—Turner incorporated van Gennep's formulation of the ritual process into his own theory, reworking the categories devised by the linguist into a new ritual sequence: "separation," "liminality," and "reaggregation."

For both theorists, liminality was the real key to ritual power: it was a "time out of time," in which participants to ritual could mark out differences between the ordinary and the extraordinary, or (*à la* Durkheim) the "profane" and the "sacred." Participants to ritual were thus made to become psychosocially ambiguous through physical and symbolic separation from society. In separation, these individuals ceased to have firm status within that social order. They were "declassified," or "in betwixt" and "in between." For Turner this liminal separation actually signaled the outright negation of social order, a state which he termed "anti-structure." During anti-structure, a society essentially did away with its own rules by violating them. In these ritual moments, therefore, participants were placed beyond the bounds of social structure. Frequently, this process would incorporate a manner of Durkheim-like effervescence, dubbed "communitas," in which participants experienced an ill-defined sensation of social unity. The climax of the ritual process would then involve the recognition and affirmation of social structure through the ritual participant's reintegration, or reaggregation, into society.

Paradigmatic instances of the ritual process can easily be found in the many varieties of initiation rite that exist the world over. Those rituals in which boys are socially transformed into men, girls into women, princes into kings, the merely dead into the graced by God are all examples of transitional moments where people cease to be what they have been, but have not yet become what they will soon be. In such liminal moments, Turner observed, people exist beyond society and are therefore uncontrolled by it. Hence, people in liminal states are often conceived of as powerful and may even represent a danger of contamination to the social order. Examples of anti-structural moments exist in Western societies, Turner observed, as well as among non-Western peoples. These include the orchestrated chaos of carnival, during which normalized social roles and hierarchies are inverted—a profound "social drama" in which kings become paupers and paupers, kings; men become women and women, men; and the old become young, while the young become temporarily aged.

In contrast to Turner's and Geertz's emphasis on symbolic action and meaning and to Lévi-Strauss's semiotic structuralism, the middle decades of the twentieth century also witnessed the development of a more self-consciously *scientific,* and unremittingly materialist anthropology, which is the subject of the next section.

Material Cultures

During the 1950s and 1960s, the Boasian influence continued to dominate American anthropology, particularly in the various historicist and culture and personality approaches of Mead, Benedict, Kroeber, and Lowie, and later in the interpretive analysis of Geertz and Schneider. Nevertheless, within some circles of American anthropological research, these decades witnessed the resurgence of evolutionism and materialism, notably in the work of the University of Michigan "triumvirate," Leslie White, Julian Steward, and (prior to a celebrated conversion to historical and structural approaches) Marshall Sahlins. In representing these overtly nomothetic approaches, we include in this volume selections by two of this heterogeneous perspective's most influential voices: Leslie White and Marvin Harris.

Leslie White (1900-75) was perhaps the single most influential exponent of what has been called cultural "neo-"evolutionism. Though trained in the Boasian tradition, he fell away from its central tenets. Rejecting the idea that cultural meaning and historical particularism should be the central focus of anthropological inquiry, White chose instead to revisit the nomothetic, generalizing, and Cartesian approaches that had been the hallmark of nineteenth-century classical evolutionism. In his best known and (at the time of their publication) highly controversial works, *The Science of Culture* (1949) and *The Evolution of Culture* (1959), White promulgated his scientific approach to analyzing Culture and cultures and likewise persuaded a generation of students at the University of Michigan (where he taught for many years) and elsewhere of the power of this perspective. In Selection 23, "Energy and Tools," White outlines his explicitly scientific formulation of culture as a "thermodynamic system," evolving as a function of efficient energy use. Clearly, this research strategy marked a departure from (and reaction to) the prevailing historically-minded approaches that dominated American anthropology throughout these years.

White's refurbished, empirical take on evolutionism, dubbed "culturology," began with the assumption that culture, like any domain of nature, was subject to *sui generis* system of laws that might be objectively determined. Like other natural systems, cultures were best grasped through thermodynamics, or the study of how energy is converted to matter. According to the second law of thermodynamics, which was particularly intriguing to White, the universe is slowing down, resulting in increased structural disorder, or entropy. According to White's culturology, biology has worked against this pattern, utilizing the universe's "negative entropy" to build ever more complex patterns in the natural world. The development and ongoing evolution of culture has not so much been a qualitative departure from this pattern, as its progressive intensification. Having "replaced" Darwinian evolution as the primary means of environmental adaptation, human culture (and that of human ancestors) has also become a superior means of establishing order.

White proposed that this system of energy conversion could be represented by the equation $E \times T = C$, or energy times technology equals culture. This constituted a thermodynamic law under which culture develops or evolves as a function of human efficiency in utilizing energy, or the amount of energy harnessed per capita per annum. For human history and prehistory, White identified four major "revolutions" to date, in which human beings transformed and rendered more efficient their use of energy. In the first and second of these, the invention of tools increased humanity's capacity to acquire energy from food; this was intensified still further through the domestication of plants and animals in archaeologist V. Gordon Childe's "neolithic revolution." The third and fourth, respectively, involved the development in the last two centuries of technology that allowed extraction of energy from fossil fuels and the atom.

As attested by this incorporation of physics into anthropology, White was an unapologetic materialist who prioritized economic and technological factors in his evolutionary scheme. Much of his thought on cultural evolution derived from Marx, whose writings he embraced while travelling in the Soviet Union in the 1920s, and also from Lewis Henry Morgan, whose perspectives on the evolution of private property he championed. For his part, White's cultural evolution envisaged the progressive refinement of human energy use in a three-tiered model of causation, which he termed the "layer-cake model of culture."

According to this model, the material conditions of life (that is, a social group's level of technological sophistication and economic complexity) constituted the bottom layer of the cultural cake. Because these were the cultural domains in which innovations in energy might be expected to take place, White looked to this bottom layer to exert a deterministic influence on the middle layer, made up of social and political organization. He anticipated that this layer would, in turn, determine the character of "ideology"—the most inconsequential layer of culture with respect to evolution.

Marvin Harris (b. 1927) remains one of the most controversial figures in American anthropology of the late twentieth century. His central contribution to anthropological theory has been the development and strident defense of a neo-materialist and nomothetic perspective that he has labelled "cultural materialism." The best known of Harris's works in which he expounds this viewpoint are *The Nature of Cultural Things* (1964), *Cannibals and Kings* (1977), *Cultural Materialism* (1979), and *Rise of Anthropological Theory* (1968), a staple among students of the history of anthropology and a theoretical tour-de-force in its own right. Here we include a selection from perhaps his most important theoretical study, *Cultural Materialism*. "The Epistemology of Cultural Materialism" (Selection 24) is an important exposition of infrastructural determinism, the epistemology that Harris pioneered. Cultural materialism assumes that the material conditions of existence act to shape, and even determine, those aspects of culture not demonstrably linked to the human needs of production and reproduction. Harris has called this propensity "infrastructural determinism," because it is the "infrastructure"—the means of production and reproduction—that govern how a society develops and in which directions.

Asserting the primacy of scientific anthropology, Harris has argued that there is a qualitative distinction to be drawn between two intersecting sets of criteria. The first of these borrows from linguistics and cognitive anthropology the terms "phonetic" and "phonemic." In Harris's usage, the terms specify a distinction between "emic" and "etic" modes of analysis in cultural anthropology. For Harris, emic aspects of culture are the subjective perceptions held by those being studied—the "insider" perspective, as it were. These are contrasted with the etic, or objective, perspectives on a given culture as viewed from the outside. The second set of criteria employed by Harris are the mental and behavioural aspects of human life which, baldly stated, draw a contrast between what people think and say that they do, and how they actually behave.

While Harris has insisted that both emics and etics, both the mental and behavioural, are the proper province of anthropological inquiry, he has also maintained that scientific, objective analysis of behaviour, *per se*, is the more powerful means of understanding cultural life. It is only through rigorous study of human interaction with the environment and the material circumstances of existence that anthropology will ever have an accurate scientific model of human life. As such, consideration of the intersection of the emic and behavioural domains is problematic, because ethnographic subjects cannot, by definition, view themselves from the outside, much less make objective pronouncements about their own behaviour. Neither can anthropologists working to understand the mental domain of human life from the stance of outsiders expect to access the inner reaches of their subjects' thoughts.

It is in large measure because Harris has denied, or appeared to deny, the centrality of the emic and mental (and the inevitable spectre of what Marx called false consciousness which this perspective raises) that his work has incited much debate in anthropological circles. His views rose to prominence in the late 1960s, at a point in the discipline where perspectives that favoured the cultural and symbolic were in ascendancy in anthropology departments at universities on both sides of the Atlantic. More recent critiques hold that because Cartesian science is itself a "culture," it remains as poorly positioned as ever to make judgements regarding the ontological status of non-Western worldviews. Besides, many argue, when has it not made such judgements in the name of colonial expansion and appeals to the ultimate superiority of Western ways of knowing? This is a point to which we will return shortly, in our discussion of culture and political economy and postmodernism.

18

The Utility of the Equilibrium Model in the Study of Social Change[1]

MAX GLUCKMAN

In this address I hope to clarify some of the implications in the use of the so-called equilibrium model in the study of allegedly stationary societies. I believe that clarification is necessary because of present-day criticisms of the model, some of which, I feel, arise from a misunderstanding of what its exponents were doing, although undoubtedly those exponents did not always themselves make their intentions clear. Obscurity and ambiguity have accumulated around the problem. If we can remove these so the problem becomes clear, I believe discussion will then show that the equilibrium model has what Leach has called great power (1954:4), not only for the analysis of seemingly stationary social systems but also as one method for studying changing social systems,[2] though I shall disagree with Leach about the reasons for this power. I also believe that if we can clarify the situation we may be some steps nearer to an attempt at bringing the results of studies of the structure of institutional systems together with those of the structure of fields of interaction between persons; this seems to me to be one crucial problem facing social anthropologists in the coming years.

I have defined the "equilibrium model" as one method for studying changing social systems. I emphasize that it is only *one method*. First, our field of study is so complex that there are necessarily many different approaches to analysis, each fruitful in its own way; if I argue the merits of one method, this is not to deny that others have advantages. Second, it is a *method*, a manner of approaching the study of social systems, because it illuminates understanding of the structure of those systems in reality. It might be described as a heuristic scheme; or we might follow Merton in calling it an orientation, and perhaps even class it as one of those orientations that he said are neglected at the peril of the investigator (1957:87-89). Third, the equilibrium model is a method, and not in itself a theory, for it is not a body of interdependent propositions about the structure of social systems. But it can form a framework for a set of such propositions (see Homans 1950:1-11).

In his study of *Political Systems of Highland Burma* (1954, 1964) Leach worries about the difficulties of the equilibrium model, though (I repeat) he says it has "great power" in sociological analysis. These worries he sees as emerging from the fact already frequently stressed that "real societies exist in time and space ... Every real society is a process in time..." (1954:5). The problem of time is critical for all studies of social and cultural systems.

Out of our common tradition, I believe we derive a common fascination with customs, and I believe that it is through this fascination with customs that we make our distinctive contribution to the social and behavioral sciences (Devons and Gluckman 1964:254f).[3] But it is a long time since anthropologists operated with single, isolated customs. Cultural (sci. culturological) anthropologists seek *patterns* in customs; and psychological anthropologists seek the interdependent, concomitant relations between patterns of customs and personality structures. We sociological anthropologists see customs as linked together into what some call *institutions*, which are in some way external to, independent of, and constraining on, the individuals within them (to use Durkheim's criteria for what he called "social facts"). I do not want to enter into controversies about the different ways in which the term "institution" has been used in anthropology and sociology. Perhaps you will allow me to use it as a shorthand expression to cover the facts that men act in standardized roles, through specific modes of behavior, with reference to other men, as they aim to achieve certain purposes in an ecological, biological, and social environment; and that these purposes and the means of achieving them are defined by a set of controlling rules with guiding beliefs and values. Finally, in their actions men use types of material goods (cf. Malinowski on institutions, 1931, 1944).

When we deal with customs not as isolates, but as constituting patterns, or as influencing the development of types of personality, or as dominating social relationships within institutions, we come up at once against the problem of time—development in time, and change through time. It is about the significance of time and changes in time that much of the obscurity has accumulated; for "time" exists in social life, as many studies have shown, in different modes. First, there is, as far as we can assess, a "real" history of events that have constituted the past of any personality or culture or society, events that a phylogenetic sense account for its present form. Secondly, as many historians and social scientists have pointed out, there is an incapsulation of past events within the present pattern of society; thus Fortes wrote "Among the Tallensi the lineage system enables us to see the operation of the time factor in social structure in a very concrete way. We see how the lineage structure at a given time incapsulates [with acknowledgements to R.G. Collingwood] all that is structurally relevant of its past phases and at the same time continually thrusts its growing-points forward" (1945:224). There is a similar incapsulation of the past within the present structure of a particular personality. Thirdly, this process of incapsulation produces certain standardized ideas about time and history, in varying social contexts, held by members and sections of a society, on which anthropologists and other scholars have written at length, as we shall see later; while similarly individuals have varied conceptions of their own history and of time arising from the accumulation of experience and reaction to experience. Fourthly—and it is with this problem that I am mainly concerned—a cultural pattern, or a personality, or an institution, has its own time-scale "built into" it, if you will permit me a metaphor. The speed at which a personality operates is extremely high, and has no reference to the means by which we normally measure time; all students of personality are aware of this. Similarly, I would argue that each institution has a specific time-scale built into its structure, and we cannot understand an institution unless we do so in that scale. Fortes has put the problem thus: "social life is a pattern of processes, and the time dimension is a significant factor in social structure everywhere" (1945:ix); and "The dynamic equilibrium of a lineage is an equilibrium in time" (1945:224). To avoid confusion, I shall follow a suggestion made to me by John A. Barnes, with whom I have had fruitful discussions of the general problem, and call the time-scale built into an institution, that institution's "structural duration."

The "structural duration" of an institution is that period of time required to work out the implications of its rules and customs within the biological, ecological, and social environment (see Homans 1950:81 f. on external environment). This period of time, the duration, is contained in the structure of the institution, and it is only in terms of expositing the institution through that duration that we can work out the interdependence, the systematic structure, between the elements that comprise the institution—what Fortes has called the contemporaneous interdependence of variables (with no period attached to "contemporaneous"). Since we are here concerned with establishing constancies, it follows that this type of exposition is in terms of an equilibrium model, with the institution working through a cyclical, or oscillatory, or other form of process at the end of which it presents the same form as it started from.

Three caveats are essential in approaching the model. First, an analysis of this kind does not state that the institution has operated in that way in reality in the past, or will continue to operate thus in the future; the analysis is not dealing with the institution in real, historical time, nor affirming that the institution is in a state of actual equilibrium—a state that we can describe as *stasis*. The idea of an equilibrium through time, with the elements of the institution in a "state of balance," and the fiction of stable equilibrium, "tending to recover equilibrium [stable balance] after disturbance" (Oxford English Dictionary), are devices to enable us to handle the time element involved in the assumed systematic interdependence of elements of the institution. We assume that this interdependence exists because that makes possible scientific analysis; and the assumption is in reality warranted insofar as we observe that the events relevant to the institution occur in a regular and not a haphazard manner.

Time here is handled in an *as if* manner, as Vaihinger would have put it; indeed, Leach speaks of "as if systems" (1964: *Introduction* to reprint of 1954) though he sees the balance as being, for purposes of analysis, one of the facts forced "within the constraining mould of an *as if* system of ideas, composed of concepts treated *as if* they were part of an equilibrium system. I shall argue later that Leach underestimates the dependence of the idea of equilibrium on reality (as Vaihinger underestimated the connection of scientific laws with reality). I myself feel that this model has great power because it "maps reality" in the mathematicians' phrasing. But it is useful to speak of an *"as if"* equilibrium in order to emphasize that it is abstracted from reality, since it may not deal with the whole complexity of reality. I see it as a framework, which is based on observations of reality and then tested against other observations. We employ it in order to handle the time element, the duration, involved in the structure of the institution, since only thus can we analyze the real interdependence that exists within the institution as an organized structure. In reality, many external events, and internal "distortions," prevent the institution working thus perfectly, and these have to be fed in to complete the analysis, a most important step for a fuller study. The equilibrium model is used to provide a framework within which we can formulate propositions about the interdependence of elements; it is these propositions which form our desired theory. They too must contain a time element, since all reality is a process in time. To formulate such propositions we need for the time being to exclude interference.

The second caveat is that the very definition of equilibrium contains the idea of disturbance, with return to the previous state after that disturbance. In short, we assume in advance that they working of an institution will contain, in the very structure of the institution, disturbances occurring without any purposed action on the part of its personnel, as well as from strife between its personnel. If the institution is functioning, balancing forces and redressive mechanisms come into play to restrain the effects of the disturbance in order to preserve, or restore as far as possible, the earlier form.

Third, the model of the system in no way states that the same persons will occupy the same positions relative to one another throughout the duration of the institution's working. Insofar as there is continuity, it is in the roles, not in the people.

Finally, I repeat caveats entered earlier. The use of the equilibrium model is to provide the framework to formulate propositions about the interdependencies between the elements of the institution. If, having analyzed these, we wish to understand how that institution operated through a period of actual time, a real history, we have to feed into the analysis many kinds of other data and analyses of other institutions. But if the analysis of the equilibrium model has been fruitful, the propositions we arrive at give us insight into, and understanding of, what happened in historical reality. Hence the analysis in terms of theoretical propositions within an equilibrium framework does not state that the institution is in practice in stable equilibrium, does not deny that change is occurring, and does not of itself assert that the institution has been as it is for any period in the past or will continue as it is into the future. It is a mode of analysis, not a description of reality, though it is derived from reality. Whether the institution is in actual stable equilibrium, in a state of stasis, is a matter of historical record over a denoted period, or of prediction about the future.

The nature of structural duration is well shown in all studies of family organization. The stability of an institution—i.e., its tendency to maintain its form—is only partially determined by its internal structure. Much depends on the constraining effects of the external environment, or of internal material factors. In family organization the biological processes involved in mating, reproduction, maturation, and death constrain developments, and tend to maintain a particular form of structure. Within the biological framework, and at the same time incapsulating it, there are numerous varied forms of family, but analysis of all of these forms is usually done in terms of much longer periods of generations than the actual period during which observations are made. That is, to understand even a day in the life of a family, it has to be analyzed *as if* its systematic interdependencies were worked out through a "cycle" (in this case) of at least three generations; for each family contains within itself, at any one moment, parents, children or the expectation of children, and the anticipation of those children marrying and having children. It may be better to work with a structural duration of four generations, since the parents were themselves derived from an earlier pair of parents who produced siblings for their children, people who may lie relevant for family structure. I shall argue later that in some societies the relevant number of generations, incapsulated so-to-speak in each moment of a family's existence, may be five generations, and occasionally more. This structural duration within which alone we can understand the life of a family is contained in the combination of specific rules and customs set in the general human biological framework, and set also in a wider sociocultural environment. Not every family can pass through the cycle, even excluding the effect of radical changes: a marriage may be broken early by death of a spouse or divorce; other marriages are childless; and so forth. But in analysis we treat these as deviations from the "standard" cycle, and fit in similarly remarriage, relationship with stepchildren, and such forms of marriage as levirate, ghost-marriage, sororate, woman-marriage-to-a-woman, etc., as well as the effects of there being varying numbers of children born to parental pairs in each of the generations within the structural duration. This is a usual form of presentation; and even when radical change in family law and relationships is occurring, most studies discuss these against the standard cyclical analysis (Goody 1958; Fortes 1962).

Analysis of the structural duration is also the core of studies of political institutions. If I want to analyze any period in the life of the British House of Commons, I must see what is happening during that period in relation to a longer period of somewhere around fifteen years, i.e., the period covered by three five-yearly elections. Activity in the House Commons shortly after an election is influenced by at least two preceding elections and the prospects of the election to come in five years; while as that Parliament moves through its incumbency there comes a shift at a certain point, and activity is influenced more by one past election and the two elections to come. Thus three elections (fifteen years) seem to form the basic structural duration of the House of Commons. Within that duration, there are other durations internal to the parliamentary system; these are set by Budget Day debates, since money is the most crucial need of a government, and subsidiarily by the stages through which bills must pass and the debates thereon, and so forth. Analysis of this structural duration therefore tends to have the form of an equilibrium model. Any period of actual Parliamentary history is affected by other systems of events, some intrinsically involved in the legislature itself. Thus problems of selection of party leaders may be influenced by the age distribution of members in the party, since a man voting for a candidate slightly older than himself may be ruling out leadership for himself, and so on. Other events, in the external system of both Britain and the international world, are "haphazard" in respect to the system of the legislature, though systematic in relation to other events. Seen in this way, we can examine the effect of the House of Commons with its own duration on the history of political life in Britain and vice versa; the institution in its general cultural form has persisted for centuries during which radical changes have occurred both in the external environment and in the internal structure (as in the types of persons who sit in the House of Commons). We can then assess the relation between continuity of form of the legislature and actual political relationships, and we might conclude that the relation is relatively tenuous, though I think it is important. Again, as with the family, the structural duration of the house of Commons is contained in the rules and customs which organize it, but there is not a constraining framework akin to the biological framework which constrains the structural duration of the family.

If this is correct, it follows that whenever we attempt to analyze an institution, we have to "throw it" (forgive the metaphor) into its structural duration, since all social life is a "process in time" and rules and customs contain a time-element. This involves analyzing the institution *as if* it were operating through a far longer period than the actual period during which we observe it or its parts. This may be truistic; but it is fundamental. The failure to appreciate this when reading an analysis of institutions may give the reader a false impression that the writer believes that the institutional form he analyzes has endured in exactly the same form from far in the past, and will thus endure into the future. This is not always the reader's fault, since often the analyst has not made clear that the time element in analysis is a structural duration, and not actual historical time. There is a tendency, however, to overlook the difference between these kinds of "time" or "durations," perhaps because in more recent times anthropologists have been faced with more rapidly changing societies. They then insist, against the analysis of structural durations, that all real societies in real time are always changing and have always been changing—without specifying what is changing, what the changes are, and how far the changes go, in affecting structural forms. It seems obvious that there are very different kinds of change, and we shall have to develop a vocabulary to differentiate between them.

II

I have written above in terms of the structure of a single institution. The problem of analyzing a set of institutions, or a whole social field, is obviously much more complicated. Various institutions have different structural durations, and their "intermesh" has to be analyzed. Events emerging from the operation of one institution may intervene in the operation of another institution in a manner that is haphazard as far as the systematic interdependencies of the recipient institution are concerned. External events from quite different areas of the world may intrude into the field under analysis, again in what, from the point of view of an analyst of systems, is a haphazard manner. But for analysis of institutions we have to carry out our process of mental abstraction, and when we do this I consider that we find that institutions and wider social fields have a marked tendency to endure, that they and/or their parts are resistant to both unintended and deliberately attempted changes, though radical changes will, after some period of time, occur. We might say therefore that an institutional system, or a field of institutional systems, will tend to develop, and even hypertrophy, along the main facets of its organization, until conditions make it quite impossible for the system to continue to work (e.g., major demographic shifts, invention of new tools and machines, and so forth). This excludes the effect of attacks on the system from outside, as by invasion from elsewhere. Even after radical change has occurred, moreover, institutions are so tough that they often survive into, or revive in, the new conditions that eventuate, and operate again within a new overall system of institutions.

If this view of the history of institutions is validated by our knowledge of the actual history of events, it would mean that, as the dialecticians argue, periods of revolution and other forms of rapid and radical change subverting the structure of a system completely appear as sudden crises after the steady accumulation of smaller and more limited structural changes, constrained within the major pattern of the institutions concerned (save where there is external invasion). I consider that here the dialecticians are right, and this implies that to understand even revolutionary change we have to work from the structural duration of institutions (or social fields) in an equilibrium model.

I find support for this view in the methods by which the best analyses of major social developments have been written. It is clear in the Marxist treatment of the movement from primitive communism, to classical slave societies, to feudalism, to bourgeois mercantilism, to early capitalism, and on to monopoly capitalism. In this Marxist model, centuries of *relative* stability of institutions are assumed and analyzed in a *relatively* equilibrated framework, before the conflicts and contradictions inherent within each system lead to revolutionary changes, which are handled largely in the quite different form of narrative (as against institutional analysis) when the movement to a new institutional system occurs. Durkheim handles similarly the movement from the stasis of mechanical solidarity to the institutional structures emerging as the division of labor increases, as does Max Weber the developments from traditional society to rational bureaucratic society; the theories of Sir Henry Maine, Tönnies, Von Wiese, and many others are similarly constructed. I see a similar mode of analysis in the work of all the cultural evolutionists, with quite different theories, who have enriched the history of anthropology. I repeat, they are using a *mode* of approaching history when they use this framework of long periods of relative stasis, to be understood in *as if* equilibriums of structural durations that to a large extent neglect actual historical time in a manner infuriating to many historians; therein they formulate theories of interdependence between social elements. The theories of each of these analysts or types of analysts may differ; the model of approach, the method, is very similar.

If so many thinkers, holding different political views and elaborating diverse theories, all work in this framework, it shows that they are constrained in at least two ways. First, there has been the sheer incapacity of the human mind to work with, and write about more than a limited amount of facts. Second, there is in reality itself something that is reflected in this framework. I consider the second the more important; and therefore I feel that the model of an equilibrium, if used in analyzing many parts of the institutional set-up within a complicated social field, does illuminate what has happened in actuality. It also illuminates the structure within institutions and the structure linking these together in more complex arrangements.

Weber's conception of "ideal types" is clearly a model similar to the one that anthropologists have developed and that I am delineating here. But there are differences between them. Weber's "ideal types" are composed of consistent principles of organization, with one dominant. The "ideal types" are drawn from reality, but they go beyond reality in emphasizing the dominant principle, against which real institutions can be assessed. The other theories I have cited also emphasize dominant principles of association, or economic structure, at each stage or relative stasis. Marxist theories bring in the emergence of a contradicting "submerged" principle that will become dominant; here the relative stasis involves that the groups whose interests are dominant suppress the increasing resistance and revolt of those whose interests are founded in the new potentiality. The models with which anthropologists have worked usually have reference to institutions that are much shorter in their structural durations. And most anthropologists (like many sociologists) have stressed that, though there may be dominant ideological principles, and constraining variables, the equilibrium results from the working out of processes arising from principles of social organization that are independent of one another, while many principles are mutually discrepant, discordant, conflicting, and, eventually, when radical structural change is going to develop, contradictory. These principles of organization are partly contained in social relationships operating on the physical environment through material equipment, partly in the interests and demands of the varied social relationships in which individuals severally participate, and partly in the setting of social relationships in a culture (the "shreds and patches" [Lowie] of values, allegiances, goals, and so forth).

III

A certain ambiguity, and lack of clear exposition that we were analyzing in terms of structural durations and not of real historical time, has contributed to misunderstanding of what we attempted to do. This ambiguity rises from the multivocality of words like equilibrium and stability; Leach (1954:7) therefore alleged that there has been "confusion between the concepts of equilibrium and stability ... so deep-rooted in anthropological literature that any use of either of these terms is liable to lead to ambiguity." I consider that the ambiguity arises because not everyone, writing or above all reading, distinguishes continually between the equilibrium of the relative stability of a system of interdependent relations, and the stability of actual social life. Some readers have regarded a statement about equilibrium as implying that no disturbance occurs, or they have, as is much more easily done, failed to see that there can be stasis or stability at one level of organization and not at another. As a chair maintains a constant stable form (stasis) despite the continuous movement of particles within the molecules of the elements that compose it, so a macroscopic structure might remain stable despite disturbances in the structures of families; conversely, structures of family patterns may remain in stasis while the macroscopic political structure is radically altered (Homans 1950). In the analysis of systems we have constantly to be shifting our viewpoint with the problems we pose.

This confusion seems to me to be inherent in Leach's argument *in Political Systems of Highland Burma* when he says that [all? most? many? some? a few?] anthropologists present a *"stable* equilibrium." He adds that Malinowski, Firth, and Evans-Pritchard "write as if the Trobrianders, and Tikopia, the Nuer are as they are, now and for ever" (1954:7). This does not seem to be correct for any of them, once we see that they were analyzing structural durations, but Leach's statement is presumably explicable on the grounds that they did not make this clear. Evans-Pritchard did however put forward a differentiation between various kinds of time in order to indicate that he did not believe that his analysis showed "the Nuer as they are, now and for ever." I therefore review the implications of his analysis, and particularly of his concept of "structural time" (Evans-Pritchard 1940, and articles from 1934 onwards cited therein). So, after a monstrous deal of sack, I come to the loaf of bread.

Evans-Pritchard seems to me to have made clear that his analysis of the Nuer was not set in actual historical time, when he differentiated for the Nuer what he called "structural time" as against ecological time, social time, and historical time. In the Nuer system of segmentary lineages, rights and duties between male agnates (patrilineally related men) and the fluctuations of amity and hostility between groups, theoretically depend on how recently they share a common agnatic ancestor. Where the lineage system provides the framework for territorial groups, the closer men are on the ground, the less the "structural space" (as Evans-Pritchard called it) between them, and the more recent their linking ancestor on the agnatic genealogy which provides the ideology for political combinations and feuds. Thus depth of structural time is a means of coordinating relationships in the present, rather than a means of coordinating events in the past. Therefore Evans-Pritchard proposed the theorem that depth in structural time is directly proportional to spread in structural space. The depth to the original ancestor of a maximal lineage in the Nuer system is about eleven generations, presumably because this covers the widest spread of groups that can be coordinated in this type of system. We can say this because there is something constant about this depth of eleven generations, since we find it amongst other peoples, some with otherwise very different systems, such as the agnatic Bedouin, Nyakyusa, Zulu, Tallensi and Tikopia, and the matrilineal Ashanti, though there are deeper and shallower systems. Evans-Pritchard argued therefore that the lineage system never grows; its largest structural time is fixed in depth. This shows clearly that he did not believe the system had started eleven generations ago, and that he could not decide how it had been as he found it.

That eleven generations is not a report of real descent is clearly demonstrated by genealogies among the Bedouin of Cyrenaica. We know they invaded the region in 1056, i.e., 900 years ago (Peters 1960, 1967). But the genealogies of their nine tribes show eleven generations to the nine sons of their alleged founding ancestress. Some ancestors may be fictitious; but clearly many actual progenitors have been eliminated from memory.

These eleven generations show a definite break at the fifth or sixth generation level going backwards in "structural time." Up to this point, the genealogies serve to coordinate relationships of everyday cooperation, inheritance, and so on, between living people, related through the recently dead. The upper half of the genealogies relates larger groups together—that is, these genealogical links define political or group relations, rather than interpersonal relations. This is demonstrated by the fact that in shorter lineage-type genealogies we still find five-generation bases for groupings of living people; interconnected at higher levels by a band of two (Cunnison 1951, 1956, 1957, 1959) or three (Watson 1958) generations. This band consists of politically significant relationships in "perpetual kinship" (Cunnison 1959) between groups or political positions; and the names in this band do not alter or shift their relative positions save when there are major changes in the relationships between political groups. The key positions are maintained in perpetuity in themselves and in relation to one another by what Richards (1953) called "positional succession"; they stand now for social positions, not for men or women. I have not space to consider the systems where the genealogies are deeper than eleven generations.

Evans-Pritchard's concept of structural time is thus a means of describing people's modes of thinking about their past, and ideas of structural time may cover institutions of very different durations. The theorem that structural time is directly proportional to structural space leads to further analysis. For the lower five-generation base is presumably connected not only with descent as such, but also with external factors controlling reproduction and education of people and with modes of organizing production, distribution, and consumption of goods in domestic organizations at this technological level. The wide occurrence of a top six-generation band presumably is related to external factors that determine the extent to which cooperation of political groups, and the distribution of power, can be organized by a kinship ideology. Sahlins (1961) has suggested that a developed lineage system of this type emerges from predatory expansion at the cost of other peoples, but he does not discuss, as it is not relevant to his argument, the problem of why this depth.

Nuer ideas about time are thus not merely the ideas of an isolated Sudan people. Nor do they provide us with an analysis of social structure, any more than do Kachin ideas about aristocratic authority (*gumsa*) and democratic orga-nization (*gumlao*) (Leach 1954, 1964) provide us with an analysis of political relations (see Cohen 1966: 72). Such ideas are clues to the structure, and the structural durations, of various institutions.

In the institutional analysis that Evans-Pritchard made of the Nuer system, his first step was in effect an analysis of the structural duration of some insti-tutions in *as if* equilibrium. He then showed that there were occurring changes in systematic structure, and he assessed these against the analysis of the other institutions in equilibrium. After showing that the greatest structural depth in the Nuer time-scale is eleven generations, Evans-Pritchard discusses the rise of the "prophets" who led ephemeral unions of Nuer groups both in attacks on the Dinka and in resistance to Arab and European attacks. He shows the difficul-ties these prophets had in uniting Nuer groups because of the instituted hostil-ities and persistent feuds between them, and he is able to assess what they achieved and how they achieved it. That is, the historical rise of the prophets is made analytically significant only because of the equilibrium analysis involved in treating the Nuer lineage system, this equilibrium analysis being based both on historical data and on observations in the present. Evans-Pritchard's later analysis (1949) of the rise of the Sanusi holy order to religious prestige among the Bedouin of Cyrenaica takes this problem a step further. Again, the setting is an equilibrium analysis of the Bedouin lineage system; only by understand-ing that system in this way can we understand how the Sanusi holy men placed their lodges at key points in the interstices of the lineage system, so that they were not aligned with any local section, yet could exert influence. During the Italian invasion of Cyrenaica, and through continued resistance by the Bedouin into the period of World War II, the Sanusi could emerge as the titular, if not the actual fighting, leaders of the Bedouin until their head became king of the new state of Libya.

It seems that his "structural time" is partly a description of Nuer ideas, part-ly a conception to analyze their relationships. Hence, on Barnes's advice, I adopted "structural duration." I am not stating that Evans-Pritchard's analysis was perfect. My contention is that Evans-Pritchard's analysis shows that in contrast with the study of recurrent or repetitive change of personnel and their inter-relationships within a pattern of institutions, we can develop considerable understanding of radical change in some institutions by setting this radical change against an analysis of the structural durations of certain other institu-tions, held constant in *as if* equilibrium analysis. This enables us to formulate laws of structural change. Evans-Pritchard's studies of the rise of the Nuer prophets also emphasized that they were "foreigners" to the Nuer groups they united, as the Sanusi order were foreigners to the Bedouin. This is a phenome-non we know from many other eras and regions: Peter the Hermit and Joan of

Arc were both "outsiders" in some sense to the disunited groups they brought together in their crusades; in South Africa commoner, and female, prophets, united the divided tribes against the encroaching whites. The equilibrium analysis of disunity between groups in a segmentary system enables us to understand why leaders must he in some sense "foreigners" or "outsiders," who are moved by spirits, by God, or other form of extra-societal force. Other circumstances of *as if* equilibrium allow independent groups to form deliberate, if temporary, alliances. Within the model, we can seek for propositions about the variables involved in particular types of change.[4]

IV

This type of analysis raises many problems for the analyst of institutions for which we have no history—and this applies not only to the anthropologist who is trying to study a previously unstudied tribe, or village, on whom historical records are poor, but also to the sociologist or anthropologist who is studying many institutions in our own society on which information is inadequate. Obviously it were best if we had detailed longitudinal reports on, or studies of, whole social fields and of every institution. But we have not. In these circumstances, our standard technique is to make a series of synchronic observations of present distributions, supported by collecting histories of individuals and groups, and by using such written historical material as is available. We then try to throw these synchronic observations into varied kinds of time, in order to work out the structural duration of the institutions involved, before we assess what kinds of change are occurring. We examine how far observed differences between the groups, relationships, and individuals can be explained in terms of situational changes or phases involved in some institutions' structural duration, and how far the differences indicate that there is more radical change occurring in the basic structure of the institutions.

This is the technique which Evans-Pritchard used in his study of the Nuer. It has been frequently applied to the study of domestic groups whose structural duration, as stated, is largely controlled in an almost cyclical pattern by the processes of birth, maturation, and death. If we collect quantitative and other data on, say, different families with parents and children of different ages, and we study family laws and customs, we have to throw what are mainly synchronic data into diachronic duration or durations, for various families may be at different phases of a patterned movement, or a systematic change of family structure may be occurring, or both processes may be present. If structural change is occurring, how can we assess its incidence except against an *as if* equilibrium analysis of what was the family structural duration in the past, possibly shown in some phases in families observed in the present? Otherwise we would be left with random observations only. We use life histories and other similar data to make this assessment.

Since structural duration of family and domestic organization is largely set by biological processes, this technique is under considerable control. Fortes discussed the technique in his essay "Time and Social Structure" (1949b), where he dealt with Ashanti domestic organization, thus: "An important aspect of domestic organization is the normal duration of the unit. It is an index of the process of growth by which the physical and social replacement of one generation by the next is assured and depends on the functions performed by the domestic unit in the rearing and education of children." Fortes is concerned to demonstrate for the Ashanti both the cyclic duration involved in family processes and the changes occurring in Ashanti families in new conditions, and he therefore focuses his analysis on an argument for the use of quantitative and statistical data to elucidate structure, as against bare statements of principles like matriliny and matrilocality. He presents quantitative data, collected from dispersed situations in two areas of Ashanti, on such matters as age distribution of household heads; age, residence, and marital status of women; and so forth. The structure of matrilineal, mixed virilocal and uxorilocal, patrilocal and matrilocal and avunculocal, societies are well known, so I give summarily Fortes's conclusion:

> elementary statistical analysis is indispensable for the elucidation of certain problems of social structure that arise in a society which is in process of becoming socially diversified. The futility of blanket-terms like "patrilocality" and "matrilocality" in this context is obvious. The use of numerical data has enabled us to see that Ashanti domestic organization is the result of the interaction of a number of fairly precisely defined factors operating both at a given time and over a stretch of time. Granted the dominance of the rule of matrilineal descent and the recognition of paternity in Ashanti law and values, the sex of the household head is the factor of first importance. It determines the main possibilities of the arrangement of kinsfolk in the domestic unit in relation to the polar values of "matricentral" and "patricentral" grouping. The other factors are the tendency to seek a compromise between the opposed ties of marriage and parenthood on the one hand and those of matrilineal kinship on the other; and the ideal that every mature person, especially a man, should have his own household. How these factors interact depends, among other things, on local social conditions and historical circumstances. The domestic arrangements I have described are possible only in the long-established stable capital towns of chiefdoms, where both spouses in every marriage are equally at home. In new villages the ordinary patrilocal household is more common [1949b:3f.].

These domestic arrangements include the movement of children as they mature between different homes, the movement of men, and the movement of women—as well as the movement of food between houses. Fortes's quantitative data, backed by biographical data, here summarize a series of synchronic observations, which are thrown into two distinct diachronic models: the one is of varied types of domestic units moving through patterned durations, the other of a process of limited structural change proceeding through these durations, and possibly leading to radical social change.

The same procedure was followed by Esther Goody (1962) in an analysis of the factors influencing the divorce rate of women at different ages among the Gonja. She collected records of divorces affecting women of different ages through their lives up to that point and illuminated the varying pressures that move a woman at different ages to remain with her husband, or leave her husband for another husband, or return to her brother's home. But when it came to assessing what factors influenced the divorce rate in the past of older women, she had to rely on observations on younger women in the present day. The method is full of dangers, and I suppose it is always vulnerable to logical attack, for it has flaws. But if we are to make progress we must face the dangers, and do what we can (see Barnes 1949, 1951, 1967). Always, in my opinion, we can seek support in the extent of our comparative evidence. Thus Goody finds a high divorce rate among the Gonja, and it is striking to me that they are what we call cognatic; that they do not have levirate, sororate, or ghost marriage; that they disapprove of sororal polygyny; and that they let a child go to its genitor and not its mother's husband. Their institutions resemble those of the Lozi (Gluckman 1950) who are also cognatic and whom we know, from historical records, have had a high divorce rate ever since they came to our knowledge. This makes it seem plausible that the Gonja high divorce rate is unlikely, in this institutional concatenation, to be entirely a product of modern times, for in these respects the Gonja, like the Lozi, contrast sharply with the Zulu type of society (Gluckman 1950) with its agnatic emphasis and distribution of property through wives of a husband. Here we find levirate, sororate, ghost-marriage, and sororal polygyny approved; adulterine children going to the mother's husband; and no divorces, or very few, both in the past and in modern times, a pattern distributed throughout South and (far away) Northeast Africa. Hence we have several types of controls on this kind of investigation and analysis so that it is not sheer guesswork when we try to assess what are the situational changes through a traditionally oriented life-cycle and what are radical changes related to new conditions.

I would argue that here too, if we are to assess the extent and nature of institutional changes in marriage patterns, we have to set these against an equilibrium model. In studying the rate of divorce among the tribes of Zambia,

Malawi, and Rhodesia, my colleagues have worked out divorce rates despite awareness of the difficulties involved in throwing synchronic observations into a diachronic model. Their studies show (Mitchell 1963) that among the patrilineal peoples the rates are lower than among the matrilineal and probably cognatic peoples. (There are some, but very few, exceptions.) Central African patrilineal systems have adelphic succession and inheritance along a line of brothers; and this may be why they have a higher divorce rate than the Zulu type of patrilineal society where position and property are divided up among wives in a polygynous household and devolve through those wives on to their own sons. In this region (and most others) the generalization stands that divorce rates are higher in the nonpatrilineal than in the patrilineal systems. However, in the urban areas the rates of divorce of patrilineal and matrilineal peoples move toward a common norm, as does the amount of the marriage payment— in tribal areas marriage payments are low in matrilineal and cognatic tribes, much higher among patrilineal peoples who have property to give. The indications are therefore that the urban situation is beginning to establish a common institutional pattern in marriage, for the changes in the amount of marriage payment accompany changes in the rights transferred, and duties entered upon, in marriage. This most important set of changes in the institutions of marriage can be understood only in the setting of the equilibrium studies of tribal marriage.

V

It is again not too difficult to work out structural durations, and to isolate continuity with repetitive change from radical change, in such singular institutions as kingships. It is most difficult to do so with groups like villages, which are multiple like families but not so tightly controlled by the biological framework; yet similar methods have been applied with similar gains.

When he studied the Yao of Malawi, Mitchell (1951, a, b; 1956) observed that their villages varied in internal composition, Some consisted of small matrilineal lineages, other of a range of several such lineages grouped in complex association both by more distant matrilineal or other matrilateral links and by patrilateral ties. He examined how some of these matrilineage-based sections within the villages left their parent villages and set themselves up as independent villages, either in search for new land or after quarrels. He related processes of growth in numbers through marriages and births to an ever-increasing complexity of all villages, realized in reality in some of the villages, and then the reduction of expanding villages through division. He thus established the structural duration of various types of Yao village, in dendritic[5] processes of growth and proliferation of sections till divisions occurred. He examined the role of variable prestige, of the custom by which in a dominantly uxorilocal society village headmen brought their wives to their own homes, of beliefs in witchcraft and sorcery and ancestral spirits as causing misfortune, of the rules of positional succession and perpetual kinship between positions, and of other customs and beliefs in these dendritic processes built into varied types of villages. If we judge from written and oral tradition, some villages remained large and complex for long periods, despite shedding some sections. Mitchell was able to specify the social factors associated with this durability. Other villages, denoted by different social factors, never became very complex, and sections breaking off from the large villages tended to fall into the second category. Marwick (1965) confirmed this analysis among the nearby Chewa, and was able to pursue more deeply how sorcery beliefs, and so on, operated to control, expedite, and maintain the system and the structural durations of its parts.

The core of Mitchell's analysis of Yao villages was investigation of a limited number of types of structural durations in a complex *as if* equilibrium model. Then from historical records he examined how far war, slavery, and trade to the coast from Malawi and beyond had in the past contributed to the growth of big villages, in order to assess what were the effects of British conquest and rule. British rule abolished war and slavery and made life more secure. It brought in specialized traders in cloth and other goods formerly fetched from the coast by Yao caravans. New economic opportunities (such as cash cropping and migration to labor for Europeans) affected social relationships, as well as the emergence of new types of land shortage in some areas. But through these radical changes there was considerable continuity; people still lived in villages and many men were ambitious to become village headmen. New wealth was partly expended in traditional social relationships. Even when a man, in this normally uxorilocal society, was allowed to take his wife to live with him where he worked on a European plantation, their children did not form a group regarded as dominantly descended from the husband, but rather, in terms of Yao dogma, a group regarded as a matrilineage descended from his wife (Mitchell 1951b).

Mitchell worked out his analysis from two different kinds of data. He used what historical data he could gather, both from published and unpublished written records and from histories of villages and individual Yao. Secondly, in the field he made a series of synchronic observations of series of different villages. The technique of analysis was to throw these synchronic observations, with the help of historical data, into different kinds of diachronic processes. The skill of the analyst is to assess when the differences he finds are repetitive situational changes and when they are changes in the structure of the system of institutions itself.

Mitchell had some historical records, written by Europeans, to facilitate his diachronic study and to enable him to assess different kinds of change. Similar more or less valid historical data have not been available to those anthropologists who have studied tribes in recently opened up areas, as in New Guinea (and indeed this was largely Evans-Pritchard's position among the Nuer). These anthropologists employed the method of collecting synchronic observations on the distribution of categories of groups and persons, as well as oral traditions and life histories, and examined the situation in the light of cultural rules and customs. They have then thrown their observations into diachronic "structural durations" (see e.g., Pospisil, 1958a, 1958b, 1960; Reay, 1959; Salisbury, 1962; Brookfield and Brown, 1963; Meggitt, 1965), before they tried to detect radical changes. To some extent, they have produced analyses of systems subject to repetitive changes (i.e., in stable equilibrium or stasis), but they have used this device to indicate processes of limited structural change (i.e., changes which do not go to the roots of the system, but which alter its form), and processes of radical structural change (which alter the form of the system). For example, Meggitt shows that Mae-Enga agnatic lineages, at various levels, have had to face a series of conflicts of values. It is wrong to disseise an agnatically related "brother lineage" of land, yet when numbers increase, this is the most suitable land to seize (cf. Peters 1967). Again, it is proper to allow kinsfolk related through women to settle on one's land. If an agnatic group is falling in numbers it needs these other kinsfolk to help it defend its land against more numerous and therefore more powerful "brother lineages." Yet if you invite in other kinsfolk they may, like the cuckoo, seize your nest. Through these persisting traditional dilemmas, he argues that there runs a thread of limited structural change, a tendency to emphasize, where land is short, the primary principle of filiation—agnation (or matriliny in other systems). He cites comparative evidence (which has been criticized, Brookfield and Brown 1963[6]) that this tendency to enforce the dominant cultural rule appears in many tribes, and he specifically quotes the "longitudinal" analyses made by Firth in Tikopia twenty-four years apart as showing this shift (Firth 1936, 1959). This change is here hypothesized not only from throwing synchronic observations among the Mae-Enga into a diachronic process, but also by seeing a general process occurring over several societies analyzed similarly in equilibrium models by several anthropologists. In each of these studies, the process of structural change is seen significantly because of the equilibrium model of structural duration at the core of analysis.

The generalization here put forward by Meggitt can be applied more widely. For instance (Gluckman 1943, 1965b) in a somewhat different situation of land shortage in South-Central Africa, where land has become short, for tribesmen acquiring their main cash-income from labor migration, the basic rule emphasized is the right of every subject to some arable land. This leads eventually to the chiefs restricting by legislation the amount of land each subject may cultivate. The system breaks down completely where land shortage is too acute for even this restriction to allow sufficient land to each subject. This demonstration was possible only in an analysis of the relation between land-holding and the structure of the politico-economic system in an equilibrium model. The nature and setting of radical changes and development again could be assessed only in an analysis of institutional duration.

These processes can be seen as part of a more general proposition already stated, viz., that an institutional system will tend to develop and hypertrophy along the main lines of its organization until external conditions make it quite impossible for the system to continue to work.[7] This proposition in itself emphasizes my main contention, that institutional change is best understood in a setting of equilibrium analysis. It is theoretically possible that in the kind of situation in which Meggitt and his colleagues worked, without any vouched-for historical data, they might not have been able to separate from one another what were repetitive (Gluckman 1940b, Vogt 1960) situational (Mitchell 1966) changes, what were limited structural changes, and what were radical structural changes. In these circumstances, the same methods of analysis might have to be adopted; but two or more possible analyses of structural durations and of types of change might have to be advanced. No anthropologist has yet felt this to be necessary.

Without the diachronic analysis of structural duration and continuity in these studies, it is impossible to assess the nature and extent of change in the institutions under investigation. I emphasize that I am here discussing institutional change and not all types of change. That is, I am arguing that even when we are interested in radical changes, institutional change is clearly one core of our subject. To study institutional change, we must therefore adopt a methodology that focuses on institutions, and this leads us back to *as if* structural durations, with their implicit conception of equilibrium. When we feed in actual historical changes as we move nearer to the reality we observe, we assess changes in relation to diversions of the processes of structural duration, either to show repetitive change of personnel only, or to exhibit processes of sudden or gradual elimination and substitution or of addition and multiplication of components in the social field, or of several of these processes.

VI

Each of the above analyses does not depend entirely on itself: they are mutually supporting. Not only do they conform to a general pattern of orientation and theoretical statement, but they also produce substantial evidence of external facts to which the theoretical statement has to fit. It is for this reason that I cannot agree with Leach (1954:4; 1964:*Introduction*) when he defines an anthropological model thus:

> We first devise for ourselves a set of verbal categories which are nicely arranged to form an ordered system, and we then fit the facts into the verbal categories and hey presto the facts are "seen" to be systematically ordered! But in that case the system is a matter of relations between concepts and not of relations "actually existing" within the raw factual data, as Radcliffe-Brown and same of his followers have maintained [1964: xii-iii].

I gladly enroll myself among these followers of Radcliffe-Brown, even without being conscribed by Leach to serve thus, for he sees me as his "most vigorous opponent in matters theoretical" (1964:ix). For here he and I part company, and it is because this parting is of crucial importance for the whole of the approach I am outlining that I comment on Leach's undoubtedly influential book. I do not consider that our analyses are the ordering only of "a set of vernal categories"; instead, I consider that the "ordered system" actually exists within the institutional realities that we study. The ordered systems are the structural durations which are built into social institutions, and they are, in Durkheim's phrasing within an out-of-date epistemology, "things". That is, we cannot learn their characteristic properties except by investigation, and we cannot change them merely by an act of will. Much of recent history also emphasizes that it is not so easy to alter institutions by legislative acts and major social pressures. Institutions are resistant to radical changes, and patterns of customs and customary beliefs persist and continue into new situations, even though in the end they may be altered. This is not the resistance of isolated customs or ideas, but a resistance born out of the hard reality of the interdependence of elements within institutional patterns, an interdependence that we labor to discover. To some extent, it is true, a body of persons working within a discipline are likely at any period to see similar problems, but the constraint of evidence is always upon us, and not all of us are easily deceived against the evidence.

Before I pursue this point, I must separate off the apparent similarity sometimes present in our subjects' ideas and in our own analyses. We do not merely analyze the set of ideas of the people involved in an institution. These indigenous ideas, as formulations about what social reality is believed by its participants to be, are some of the facts we take into account in our analyses. The actors' ideas, like their behavior, are part of, and influenced by, the total reality in which they live. This reality, as I have said, is something external and constraining. It is hard, and cannot be changed merely by changing the set of ideas. It is sufficiently hard to shape the future in unexpected ways. The actors may have certain ideas about the hard reality in which they live, and in flashes these may be accurate perceptions of what exists and of what is happening or emerging. But actors are often self-deceived about events and motives, and their ideas may be rationalizations. Hence social and individual ideas cannot be taken as accurate perceptions of reality; and they are almost always incomplete (Peters 1967). Comparative study by specialists may be necessary to put these ideas in perspective. Analysis after analysis shows that often the actors do not fully understand what they are doing and why they do it. I cite only anthropological analyses of how particular categories of persons are divined, in various tribes, as the witches responsible for misfortune,[8] and of genealogies as ideologies rather than as ancestral pedigrees. Anyone can multiply examples.

The reality we study is equally external to, and constraining on, us, the anthropologists. It is hard, in that we cannot change it to suit ourselves. Hence our technical *as if* models are not only an order between a set of verbal categories. They have to be logically constructed, and this construction may be fruitful or not.[9] In addition, they have to be more than that. We constantly refer them to the evidence of our observations, and these are hard and constraining, not to be changed by an act of will or merely by altering a verbal category. The observations, as well as the analyses, of our colleagues working in quite different social fields are also external, constraining, and hard for us. For we take these into account in developing our own analyses. We cannot make up institutions and get away with it. No one has yet analyzed that Bantu tribe that emerged from the fertile imagination of Schapera—the Baloni. And Miner's (1956) delightful satire on the Nacirema is too near the truth to be altogether fictitious. All of you have struggled to analyze your field data and know how difficult it is for a trained outside observer, working with the support of what his predecessors and colleagues have done, to get at the real interconnections within a social system, by taking account of all the evidence in order to erect a model. Most of you have changed your models in the light of new facts about the real world, whether found by yourselves or appearing in the criticisms and works of your fellows.

VII

I have spoken about *as if* equilibrium models to demonstrate how useful they are in studying social change. But particular sets of institutions may have been or still be in actual equilibrium, persisting in continuity, for long periods. I repeat, this is not a matter of a priori judgment but of historical record, of present assessment, or of future prediction. Or institutional change theoretically could proceed with a constant readjustment of each part to changes in the other parts—in moving, actual equilibrium. This is more likely to occur in parts, rather than in the whole, of a social field. More often there will be a steady change of magnitudes within and between institutions, until there is a sudden and radical transformation of form. All experience indicates this.

I will describe how I applied the methods I have outlined to radical change in the history of Zululand.[10] From the evidence of shipwrecked mariners, and of oral traditions collected from the Zulu and their offshoots, who are now established many thousands and hundreds of miles apart, and from neighboring tribes, the political field from at least 1400 until about 1800 can be analyzed as being in an actual state of stable equilibrium (in stasis). It was composed of many tribes, varying in size but with a maximum so that if a tribe became too big, sections broke away either peacefully or after struggles between rivals for chieftainship. Through four centuries tribes split, new tribes appeared, others disappeared, and there were raids but not conquests. This was replication in time and duplication in space of pattern and structure, despite many disturbances involving wars and divisions. There was no radical change, either in institutions or in structural duration. It was stable equilibrium through a long period.

Evidence indicates that human, and probably more importantly, cattle, populations increased beyond the point of critical density. The increase accumulated gradually, then suddenly led to change of structure. There was apparently a short period of moving actual equilibrium in which some tribes emerged as dominant, conquering their neighbors. Structural durations, short in period, show tribes trying various means of conquest and defense, until the Zulu, through wars that solved the population problem, established hegemony that lasted sixty years, ending with their defeat by the British. During this period, there was a pattern of civil wars based on the same factors that determined the earlier equilibrium of small tribes: relatively poor tools, simple consumption goods, slow communications, wide spread of population, simple weapons held by every warrior giving each leader a private army. The result was autonomy of local sections not linked to the center by utilitarian organic interdependence and civil war around the kingship. That is, here we have, within the equilibrium model, theoretical propositions arising from the relation between technology, dispersal of population, and authority systems continuing despite some increase in the power and spread of authority. One cannot understand changes in each reign unless one sees this equilibrium in struggles for power; and the analysis can be duplicated, and its variations correlated, from other states in the history of Africa, Europe, and Asia. The change from small tribes to kingdom I would call limited structural change, rather than radical structural change, because relations between parts were still determined by similar basic technological and other factors. Meanwhile, outside of the analytically isolated kingdom, relationships with whites developed slowly, until suddenly the pattern changed and Britain invaded Zululand. After defeat, a temporary equilibrium, with short-term durations, was established between the remnants of the kingdom; then the British set up rule and there was a new temporary equilibrium based almost entirely on force. One can disentangle archival records to find how this temporary equilibrium was extended into a complex set of interdependent ties between British and Zulu in which political institutions involving various white and Zulu officials, and people, had their own structural durations. By making analyses of several periods of relative stability, and of processes of change from one to the other, I could handle both the structural durations of institutions and also types of change. Barnes (1954) has handled in similar frameworks the history of a group of Ngoni from the time they were driven out of Natal up to their position in Nyasaland under British rule. In terms of the equilibrium found at different periods, changes showing both in continuity and innovation can be assessed. Without the conception of equilibriums, one is left with narrative. In a period of rapid radical change of structure it may be necessary to resort almost entirely to narrative, so far as this is possible, and to seek here for different kinds of generalization and propositions (see Gluckman 1969a).

I consider that it is profitable to apply a similar method of analysis to, for example, the history of the English kingship. In the Middle Ages there was constant change and development; some magnates accumulated more land and power, cities grew at specific phases and trade increased, and so forth. But through several centuries it is possible to isolate the institutional relationships between king and magnates in order to understand the pattern of civil wars. These relationships can be assessed in relation, first, to constant material elements such as types of weapons, supply of goods and money, and modes of communication, then also to patterns of law, such as rules about treason (Gluckman 1965b, Chap. II). The result is an analysis of a polity that has many systematic regularities similar to those I have described in the middle period of Zulu history. I would argue again that without some equilibrium model we cannot make sense of either oscillations or of real changes in the relationships between king and magnates, or in relationships between them and the bourgeoisie in the cities, the artisans, and the rural laborers. Moreover, without applying this model to examine some institutional complex or the other, the whole becomes again recitation of a narrative.

VIII

I maintain that the above analysis of the use of equilibrium models brings out the extent to which it was a dynamic method, trying to deal with various types of disturbance and different types of change. Moreover, its exponents were very much concerned to analyze social process, and very deeply aware of the problem of time. Why then the tendency in recent years for younger anthropologists to dismiss the theories that emerged as static and not dynamic, concerned more with an idealized structure than with process? There is now almost an element of abuse in the epithet "a structural-functional study." The answer may in the widest terms be that each new generation wishes to outdo its predecessors, and wholesale condemnation is an easy way of beginning. Specifically I suggest that as far as tribal systems were concerned, the preceding generation brought sense into the variety of cultural forms in which these systems are manifested. From my own experience in training a succession of research workers, I can vouch for the fact that analysis of the institutional systems became easier, in the sense that each new worker could more rapidly observe and work out the structure of his system, in the light of preceding analyses. This liberated them from months or even years of work, and they were able to go on to observe in greater detail the interaction between persons involved in the institutional structures. Hence, particularly as improved methods of field research brought in more and more complicated data, they became involved in study of the structure of interaction patterns. As in the other social sciences, there was a development of extended case-studies, trying to handle variations and deviations from institutional norms. This led to greater interest in the complexity of each unique period and parcel of history; in the life-histories and lives of individuals; in the choices that individuals have available to manipulate to their advantage (Leach 1954; Bailey 1957; Van Velsen 1964).

When these complexities are reduced in a structural analysis, much of the uniqueness and richness of the data disappears. So the anthropologist has to wrestle with a dilemma: if he presents all the data, we cannot see the structure within it; if he emphasizes the structure, we lose much of the process of actual social life on which he has gathered voluminous data. The dilemma is aggravated when we come to consider changes of various kinds, for the more we describe change of all kinds in detail, the less we can analyze the structure of what we are seeing; the more accurately and carefully we delineate the structural relations within the data, the more we lose the movement and change.

I believe this dilemma will always be with us, as our subject swings between the pole of structural analysis and the pole of narrative (though as Mandelbaum, 1967, has shown, considering other work, no one can get to bare narrative itself).

I have here spoken of structural analysis of interaction patterns, and this is somewhat out of accord with modern practice. In that practice the term structural-functional analysis, usually applied to allegedly static equilibrium models, is seen as applying to what we call macroscopic, morphological, anatomical studies, name them as you will. Structural components are seen to be groups and other major entities. I believe this is exacerbating our dilemma and our disputation. I urge that we get rid of the false reification that has crept into the conception of a "structure" and a "social structure." Whatever field we study, we assume that it has within it regularities since observably it is not altogether haphazard, and once we assume there are regularities there must be some kind of systematic interdependence which in turn must have a structure as defined in the dictionaries, something like "an arrangement of parts within an organized whole." Hence on a major scale a society has a structure in its institutions; each piece of interaction between persons has a structure, as Goffman has so vividly demonstrated; each individual personality has a structure. A conversation has a structure; an election campaign has a structure; a nation has a structure (though of course not all events are systematically interconnected). Hence we are all of us structuralists, and all of us are to some extent functionalists, in the sense that we try to assess the significance of each element within in the particular structure we are studying.

I caution therefore that he who abuses another as a structuralist must, insofar as he is essaying a scientific study, be flagellating himself. The trouble is that this distracts attention from a whole field of problems. I have been talking above of institutional structures since this is the field in which I work, and I have argued that institutions have a tendency to continuity over time through the systematic interrelation of positions, roles, material apparatus, values, beliefs, etc. My analysis is developed for this field. But I recognize that within the apparent continuity of form of an institution (e.g., House of Commons) there can be a slow accumulation of change: in types of personnel, through drifts of style, through the operation of choices by individuals, and so forth. Lack of continuity seems marked in many patterns of interaction. Nevertheless, many studies have shown that there is a high degree of continuity in interaction patterns, which makes emphasis on structure equally essential (see Goffman, various). But whether interaction patterns are continuous or unstable or changing, it is important that we try to see whether we can bring together these apparently very diverse modes of analysis. I consider this to be one of the challenges before us in the coming years, and hence I am against false disputation between persons dealing with different types of problems in which one person alleges, often enough, that the other's analysis is wrong in principle because it is not the kind of analysis that he (the first) is interested in.

I would rather draw attention to the fact that the separation of institutions from interaction is to a large extent an analytical distinction. For it is partly from action and interaction that we build up our abstract structure of institutions; and conversely, in studies of interaction, we are concerned with incapsulations from institutions. Somehow we must try to bring these different types of analyses together.

I believe firmly that anthropology is a science and therefore progressive and accumulating in that, speaking for myself, I feel we pass the test that the fool of the later generation outdoes the genius of the previous generation. Clearly past theories and methods have to be superseded: I have I hope sufficiently often in print (1965a and elsewhere; also with Eggan, 1965-66) stated my welcoming awareness of the new types of penetrating research done by younger anthropologists. But I have tried here to argue that they face the same problems as the past generation, because these problems persist within the very nature of our attempt to generalize in finding systems with structures in the "passage of events in space time," which is reality in Whitehead's phrase. I have suggested, too, that the interlinking of our varied sets of structures poses new fields of worthwhile problems; these are immensely difficult, as I see it, since I reject any reductionist essay to explain the system in one set of events out of explanations of the system in other sets of events, whether of larger or smaller scale (see Devons and Gluckman 1964; and for a fine exposition, Mandelbaum 1955). I urge that it is wiser to examine the problems and methods and difficulties of all other workers, rather than to dismiss them summarily with intellectual abuse. One may learn something from examination; dismissal teaches one nothing. If we call others "ass-head," we may be in *A Midsummer Night's Dream*. (Act III, Sc.1), looking through bully Bottom's mask.

Notes

1 I am grateful to Professors J.A. Barnes and M. Fortes with whom I had stimulating preliminary discussions on the problems raised in this paper, and to my several colleagues at Manchester (P. Baxter, K. Garbett, B. Kapferer, N. Long, J.C. Mitchell, E.L. Peters, M. Southwold, R. Werbner), who commented in seminar on an early draft and added much that was valuable. Colleagues at the Center for Advanced Study in the Behavioral Sciences at Stanford gave me valuable help and the Center provided many facilities. Professor Sally F. Moore helped me with a final, constructive criticism.

2 For an effective similar argument see Smelser (1959) among many others.

3 An argument elaborated in Gluckman (1964, 1965a) and Eggan and Gluckman (1965-66).

4 I have a summary discussion of this general problem in Gluckman 1965b: 101 f. Frankenberg (1958) applied Evans-Pritchard's general thesis here to illuminate the role of "strangers" and "outsiders" in the communal life of a Welsh village.

5 "Dendritic" means growing like a tree, with some branches continuing large. There are not cycles of development in these processes for large villages, but there is a cycle for some smaller villages.

6 Note that though Meggitt's book was published in 1965, it went to press before Brookfield and Brown's book was published, so he could not consider their criticisms of an early essay's statement of the hypothesis.

7 I have applied this proposition to developments in quite different types of social relations between Whites and Blacks, and within White and Black groups, in my *Analysis of a Social Situation in Modern Zululand* (first published 1940 and 1942; reprinted 1958).

8   Evans-Pritchard (1937); Wilson (1951); Nadel (1947 and 1954); Mitchell (1956); Bohannan (1957); Turner (1957); Marwick (1965); Middleton and Winter (1963); Gluckman (1965b, 1969a, 1969b) analyze some of these findings.
9   See Smelser (1959:Chaps. II and III) for a discussion on this point and the argument below.
10 Three long essays give my main analysis. My draft book and notes from archives on the Zulu were burnt in a fire that destroyed my base camp in Barotseland. I have since then been occupied with the Barotse and general books, but I am sending to press a full-length study of the period of early tribes and relations with whites in it, and of the rise and establishment of the Zulu kingdom.

References

Bailey, F.G. 1957. *Caste and the economic frontier*. Manchester: Manchester University Press.

Barnes, J.A. 1949. Measures of divorce frequency in simple societies. *Journal of the Royal Anthropological Institute* 79:37-62.

—. 1951. *Marriage in a changing society*. Rhodes-Livingstone Paper 20.

—. 1954. *Politics in a changing society: A political history of the Fort Jameson Ngoni*. London, Oxford University Press.

—. 1967. Measures of divorce frequency in simple societies [revised version of Barnes, 1949]. In *The craft of social anthropology*. A.L. Epstein, ed. London: Tavistock.

Bohannan, P.J. 1957. *Justice and judgment among the Tiv*. London, Oxford University Press.

Brookfield, M.C. and P. Brown. 1963. *Struggle for land: agriculture and group territories among the Chimbu of the New Guinea Highlands*. Melbourne: Oxford University Press.

Cohen, P.S. 1966. Models. *British Journal of Sociology* 17:70-78.

Cunnison, I.G. 1951. *History of the Luapula*. Rhodes-Livingstone Paper 21.

—. 1956. Perpetual kinship: a political institution of the Luapula peoples. *Rhodes-Livingstone Journal* 20:28-48.

—. 1957. History and genealogies in a conquest state. *American Anthropologist* 59:20-31.

—. 1959. *The Luapula peoples of Northern Rhodesia: custom and history in tribal politics*. Manchester: Manchester University Press.

Devons, E. and M.Gluckman. 1964. Introduction and Conclusion. In *Closed systems and open minds*. M. Gluckman, ed. Chicago: Aldine.

Eggan, F. and M.Gluckman. 1965, 1966. Introduction. In *New approaches in social anthropology*. M. Banton, ed. London: Tavistock.

Evans-Pritchard, E.E. 1937. *Witchcraft, oracles and magic among the Azande*. Oxford: Clarendon Press.

—.1940. *The Nuer: A description of the modes of livelihood and political institutions of a Nilotic people*. Oxford: Clarendon Press.

—. 1949. *The Sanusi of Cyrenaica*. Oxford: Clarendon Press.

Firth, R. 1936. *We, the Tikopia*. London: Allen and Unwin.

—.1959. *Social change in Tikopia*. London: Allen and Unwin.

Fortes, M. 1945. *The dynamics of clanship among the Tallensi*. London: Oxford University Press.

—. 1949a. *The web of kinship among the Tallensi*. London: Oxford University Press.

—. 1949b. Time and social structure. In *Social structure: Essays presented to A.R. Radcliffe-Brown*. M. Fortes, ed. Oxford: Clarendon Press.

—. 1962 (ed.). Marriage in tribal societies. *Cambridge Papers in Social Anthropology* 3.

Frankenberg, R.J. 1958. *Village on the border*. London: Cohen and West.

Gluckman, M. 1940a. The kingdom of the Zulu of South Africa. In *African political systems*. M. Fortes and E.E. Evans-Pritchard, eds. London: Oxford University Press.

—. 1940b. Analysis of a social situation in modern Zululand. *Bantu Studies* 14:1-30, 147-174. (Republished as *Rhodes-Livingstone Paper* 28, 1958.)

—. 1942. Some processes of social change illustrated from Zululand. *African Studies* 1:243-260. (Republished in *Rhodes-Livingstone Paper* 28, 1958).

—. 1943. Essays on Lozi land and royal property. *Rhodes-Livingstone Paper* 10.

—. 1950. Kinship and marriage among the Lozi of Northern Rhodesia and the Zulu of Natal. In *African systems of kinship and marriage*. A. R. Radcliffe-Brown and C.D. Forde, eds. London: Oxford University Press for the International African Institute.

—. 1963. *Order and rebellion in tribal Africa*. Glencoe, Ill.: Free Press; London: Cohen and West.

—. 1964 (ed.). *Closed systems and open minds*. Chicago: Aldine; Edinburgh: Oliver and Boyd.

—. 1965a. *Politics, law and ritual in tribal society*. Chicago: Aldine; Oxford: Blackwell.

—. 1965b. *The ideas in Barotse jurisprudence*. New Haven: Yale University Press.

—. 1969a. Tribalism, ruralism and urbanism in changing Africa. In *Profiles of Change: the impact of colonialism on African history*. V.W. Turner, ed. Cambridge: Cambridge University Press.

—. 1969b. Social and moral crises: magical and secular solutions. The Marett Lectures, 1964, 1965. In *Allocation of responsibility*. M. Gluckman, ed. Manchester: Manchester University Press.

Goffman, E. 1956. *The presentation of self in everyday life*. University of Edinburgh Social Sciences Research Centre, Monograph No. 2.

—. 1961. *Encounters*. Indianapolis: Bobbs-Merrill.

Goody, E. 1962. Conjugal separation and divorce among the Gonja of Northern Ghana. In *Marriage in tribal societies*. M. Fortes, ed. Cambridge Papers in Social Anthropology 3.

Goody, J., ed. 1958. *The developmental cycle in domestic groups*. Cambridge Papers in Social Anthropology 2.

Homans, G.C. 1950. *The human group*. New York: Harcourt Brace.

Leach, E.R. 1954. *Political Systems of Highland Burma: A study of Kachin social structure*. London: Bell.

—. 1964. (2d ed., with a new "introduction.") London: Bell.

Malinowski, B. 1931. Culture. In *Encyclopedia of the Social Sciences* 5:621-646. New York: Macmillan.

—. 1944. *A scientific theory of culture*. Chapel Hill: University of North Carolina Press.

Mandelbaum, M. 1955. Societal facts. *British Journal of Sociology*, VI, 4, 305-317.

—. 1967. A note on history as normative. *History and Theory* VI, 3: 413-419.

Marwick, M.G. 1965. *Sorcery in its social setting*. Manchester: Manchester University Press.

Meggitt, M.J. 1965. *The lineage system of the Mae Enga of the New Guinea Highlands*. Edinburgh: Oliver and Boyd.

Merton, R. 1957. *Social theory and social structure*. 2nd ed. revised & enlarged. Glencoe, Ill.: Free Press.

Middleton, J. and E. Winter (eds.). 1963. *Witchcraft and sorcery in East Africa*. London: Routledge and Kegan Paul.

Miner, H. 1956. Body ritual among the Nacirema. *American Anthropologist* 56:503-507.

Mitchell, J.C. 1951a. The Yao of Southern Nyasaland. In *Seven tribes of British Central Africa*. E. Colson and M. Gluckman, eds. London: Oxford University Press.

—.1951b. An outline of the social structure of Malemia Ward. *The Nyasaland Journal* 5: 51-58.

—. 1956. *The Yao village*. Manchester: Manchester University Press.

—. 1963. *Marriage stability and social structure in Bantu Africa*. The International Population Conference, New York, 1961, Vol. 2: 255-263. London: International Population Union.

—. 1966. Theoretical orientations in African urban studies. In *The social anthropology of complex societies*. M. Banton, ed. ASA Monographs 4: 37-68.

Nadel, S.F. 1947. *The Nuba*. London: Oxford University Press.

—. 1954. *Nupe Religion*. London: Routledge and Kegan Paul.

Peters, E.L. 1960. The proliferation of segments in the lineage of the Bedouin of Cyrenaica. *Journal of the Royal Anthropological Institute* 90: 29-53.

—. 1967. Some structural aspects of the feud among the camel-herding Bedouin of Cyrenaica. *Africa* 35,2: 261-282.

Pospisil, L.1958a. Kapauka Papuans and their law. *Yale University Publications in Anthropology* 54.

—. 1958b. Social change and primitive law: consequences of a Papuan legal case. *American Anthropologist* 62: 832-837.

—. 1960. Papuan social structure: rejoinder to Leach. *American Anthropologist* 62:690-691.

Reay, M. 1959. *The Kuma*. Melbourne, Melbourne University Press.

Richards, A.I. 1933. Mother-right in Central Africa. In *Essays presented to C.G. Seligman*. E.E. Evans-Pritchard, R. Firth, B. Malinowski, and I. Schapera, eds. London: Kegan Paul, Trench and Trubner.

Sahlins, M.D. 1961. The segmentary lineage: an organization of predatory expansion. *American Anthropologist* 63: 322-345.

Salisbury, R.F. 1962. *From stone to steel: economic consequences of a technological change in New Guinea*. London: Melbourne University Press.

Smelser, N.J. 1959. *Social change in the industrial revolution*. London: Routledge and Kegan Paul.

Turner, V.W. 1957. *Schism and continuity in an African society*. Manchester: Manchester University Press.

Van Velsen, J. 1964. *The politics of kinship: A study in social manipulation among the Lakeside Tonga of Nyasaland*. Manchester: Manchester University Press.

Vogt, E.Z. 1960. On the concept of structure and process in cultural anthropology. *American Anthropologist* 62:18-33.

Watson, W. 1968. *Tribal cohesion in a money economy*. Manchester: Manchester University Press.

Wilson, M. 1911. Witch beliefs and social structure. *American Journal of Sociology* 56: 307-313.

Study Questions

1. What is the "structural duration" of an institution?

2. What is the concept of "equilibrium" and what relationship does this have to social organization?

3. What is the danger, according to Gluckman, of presenting all the complex historical data in, for instance, extended case studies?

Further Readings

Bailey, F. 1980. *Stratagems and Spoils: A Social Anthropology of Politics*. Oxford: Basil Blackwell.

Gluckman, Max. 1955. *Custom and Conflict in Africa*. Glencoe, IL: The Free Press.

—. 1955. *Judicial Process Among the Barotse of Northern Nigeria*. Manchester: Manchester University Press.

—. 1963. *Order and Rebellion in Tribal Africa*. London: Cohen and West.

—, (ed.). 1962. *Essays on the Ritual of Social Relations*. Manchester: Manchester University Press.

—, (ed.). 1972. *The Allocation of Responsibility*. Manchester: Manchester University Press.

19

The Scope of Anthropology

CLAUDE LÉVI-STRAUSS

Trans. Sherry Ortner Paul and Robert A. Paul

What, then, is social anthropology? No one, it seems to me, was closer to defining it—if only by virtually disregarding its existence—than Ferdinand de Saussure, when, introducing linguistics as part of a science yet to be born, he reserved for this science the name *semiology* and attributed to it as its object of study the life of signs at the heart of social life. Did he not, furthermore, anticipate our adherence when he compared language to "writing, to the alphabet of deaf-mutes, to symbolic rites, to forms of politeness, to military signals, etc."?[1] No one would deny that anthropology numbers within its own field at least some of these systems of signs, along with many others: mythical language, the oral and gestural signs of which ritual is composed, marriage rules, kinship systems, customary laws, and certain terms and conditions of economic exchange.

I conceive, then, of anthropology as a bona-fide occupant of that domain of semiology which linguistics has not already claimed for its own, pending the time when for at least certain sections of this domain, special sciences are established within anthropology.

It is necessary, however, to make this definition more precise in two ways.

First of all, I hasten to recognize that certain items which have just been cited are already within the scope of particular sciences: economics, law, political science. However, these disciplines examine the very facts which are closest to us as anthropologists and are thus of particular interest. Let us say that social anthropology apprehends these facts, either in their most distant manifestations, or from the angle of their most general expression. From this latter point of view, anthropology can do nothing useful without collaborating closely with the particular social sciences; but these, for their part, would not know how to aspire to generality were it not for the cooperation of anthropology, which alone is capable of bringing them the accounts and the inventories which it seeks to render complete.

The second difficulty is more serious, because one can ask oneself whether all the phenomena in which social anthropology is interested really do manifest themselves as signs. This is sufficiently clear for the problems we study most frequently. When we consider some system of belief (let us say **totemism**), some form of social organization (unilineal clans, bilateral cross-cousin marriage), the question which we ask ourselves is indeed, "what does all this mean or *signify*?," and to answer it, we force ourselves to *translate* into our language rules originally stated in a different code.

But is this true of other aspects of social reality, such as a stock of tools, various techniques, and modes of production and of consumption? It would seem that we are concerned here with objects, not with signs—the sign being, according to Peirce's celebrated definition, "that which replaces something for someone." What, then, does a stone ax replace and for whom?

The objection is valid up to a certain point, and it explains the repugnance which some people feel towards admitting phenomena which come from other sciences, such as geography and technology, into the field of social anthropology. The term "cultural anthropology" will be appropriate, then, to distinguish and defend the originality of this part of our studies.

It is well known, however—and it is one of Mauss's claims to fame to have established this, along with Malinowski—that in the societies with which we are concerned above all, though not in them alone, these techniques are pregnant with meaning. From this point of view, they still concern us.

Finally, the intention of being exhaustive which inspires our researches very much transforms their object. Techniques taken in isolation may appear as raw fact, historical heritage, or the result of a compromise between human needs and the constraints of environment. They re-emerge in a new light, however, when one puts them back into that general inventory of societies which anthropology is trying to construct, for then we imagine them as the equivalents of choices which each society seems to make (I here use convenient language, which must be stripped of its anthropomorphism) among the possible ones which will constitute the complete list. In this sense, a certain type of stone axe can be a sign: in a given context, for the observer capable of understanding its use, it takes the place of the different implement which another society employs for the same purpose.

Consequently, then, even the simplest techniques of any primitive society have hidden in them the character of a system, analysable in terms of a more general system. The manner in which some elements of this system have been retained and other excluded permits us to conceive of the local system as a totality of significant choices, compatible or incompatible with other choices, which each society, or each period within its development, has been led to make.

In admitting the symbolic nature of its object, social anthropology does not thereby intend to cut itself off from *realia*. How could it do this, when art, in which all is sign, utilizes material media? One cannot study the gods without knowing their icons; rites, without analysing the objects and the substances which the officiant makes or manipulates; social rules independently of the things which correspond to them. Social anthropology does not confine itself to a part of the domain of ethnology; it does not separate material and spiritual culture. In its own perspective, which we shall have to define, it devotes the same interest to each. If men communicate by means of symbols and signs, then, for anthropology, which is a conversation of man with man, everything is symbol and sign, when it acts as intermediary between two subjects.

By this deference towards objects and techniques, as well as by the conviction that we must work on meanings, social anthropology takes an appreciable degree of leave from Radcliffe-Brown who—right up to his untimely death in 1955—did so much to give autonomy to our science.

According to the English master's wonderfully fluent opinions, social anthropology is to be an inductive science which, like other sciences of this type, observes facts, formulates hypotheses, and submits these to experimental control, in order to discover general laws of nature and society. It thus sets itself apart from ethnology, which tries to reconstruct the past of primitive societies, but with means and methods so precarious that it can teach social anthropology nothing.

When it was formulated, around 1940, this conception—inspired by the Durkheimian distinction between *circumfusa* and *praeterita*—heralded a salutary reaction to the abuses of the diffusionist school. Since then, however, "conjectural history," as Radcliffe-Brown called it, not without contempt, has perfected and refined its methods, thanks especially to stratigraphic excavations, the introduction of statistics into archaeology, the analysis of pollens, of the use of carbon-14, and above all, the even closer collaboration between ethnologists and sociologists, on the one hand, and archaeologists and prehistorians, on the other. One may well ask oneself, then, if Radcliffe-Brown's mistrust of historical reconstructions did not correspond to a stage of scientific development which we will have soon outdistanced.

On the other hand, several of us hold more modest views on the future of social anthropology than those which were encouraged by the great ambitions of Radcliffe-Brown. Such views picture social anthropology not on the model of the inductive sciences as they were conceived of in the nineteenth century, but rather as a taxonomy, whose purpose it to identify and to classify types, to analyse their constituent parts, and to establish correlations between them. Without this preliminary work—which, let us make no mistake, has barely begun—the comparative method recommended by Radcliffe-Brown can only mark time: either the facts which one proposes to compare are so close to each other geographically or historically that one is never certain of dealing with distinct phenomena, or they are too heterogeneous, and the comparison must be considered illegitimate because it brings together things which one cannot compare.

Until a few years ago, we assumed that the aristocratic institutions of Polynesia were recent introductions: the result of the arrival of small groups of foreign conquerors only a few centuries ago. Now the measurement of residual radioactivity in organic remains from Melanesia and Polynesia reveals that the difference between the dates of occupations of the two regions is less than was supposed. All at once, conceptions about the nature and homogeneity of the feudal system must be modified; for at least in this part of the world, it can no longer be denied, after Guiart's excellent research, that such a system existed prior to the arrival of the conquerors, and that certain forms of feudalism can arise in humble gardening societies.[2]

The discovery in Africa of the art of Ife, as refined and sophisticated as that of the European Renaissance, but perhaps earlier by three or four centuries, and preceded in Africa itself by the much more ancient art of the so-called Nok civilization, influences our conceptions of the recent arts of Negro Africa and the corresponding cultures. We are now tempted to see them as impoverished, rustic replicas of high art forms and civilizations.

The shortening of the prehistory of the Old World and the lengthening of that of the New, which carbon-14 dating allows us to predict, will perhaps lead us to decide that the civilizations which developed on the two sides of the Pacific were even more akin to each other than they seem and to understand them differently, each on its own terms.

We must busy ourselves with facts of this order before tackling any classification or comparison. For if we hasten overmuch to postulate the homogeneity of the social field, while cherishing the illusion that it is immediately comparable in all its aspects and on all its levels, we will lose sight of essentials. We shall fail to appreciate that the co-ordinates required for defining two apparently very similar phenomena are not always the same in nature or number; and we shall believe we are formulating sociological laws when in fact we are only describing superficial properties or setting forth tautologies.

Scorning the historical dimension on the pretext that we have insufficient means to evaluate it, except approximately, will result in our being satisfied with an impoverished sociology, in which phenomena are set loose, as it were, from their foundations. Rules and institutions, states and processes seem to float in a void in which one strains to spread a tenuous network of functional relations. One becomes wholly absorbed in this task and forgets the men in whose thought these relationships are established, one neglects their material culture, one no longer knows whence they came and what they are.

Anthropology, indeed, should be in no hurry to claim as its own any phenomena liable to be called social. Espinas, another of the masters we allow ourselves the luxury of forgetting, was certainly right from the point of view of social anthropology when he refused to accept the notion that institutions without biological roots have the same coefficient of reality as others: "The management of a great railroad company," he wrote in 1901, "is not a social reality at all ... nor is an army."[3]

The statement is excessive in so far as managements are subjected to thorough studies in sociology, in social psychology, and in other specialized sciences; but it helps us to specify the difference between anthropology and these other disciplines: the social facts which we study are manifested in societies each of which is a *total entity, concrete and cohesive*. We never lose sight of the fact that existing societies are the result of great transformations occurring in mankind at certain moments in prehistory and in certain places on the globe, and that an uninterrupted chain of real events relates these facts to those which we can observe.

The chronological and spatial continuity between the natural order and the cultural order upon which Espinas insisted strongly (in a language which is no longer our own and which, for that reason, we have trouble understanding sometimes) is also the basis of Boas' historicism. It explains why anthropology, even social anthropology, claims to belong to the same area of concern as physical anthropology, whose discoveries it awaits almost eagerly. For, even if social phenomena ought to be provisionally isolated from the rest and treated as if they arose from a specific level, we know well that, both *de facto* and *de jure*, the emergence of culture will remain a mystery to man. Such a mystery will remain until he succeeds in determining, on the biological level, the modifications of the structure and functioning of the brain of which culture was at one and the same time the natural result and the social mode of apprehension, and which at the same time created the intersubjective milieu indispensable to further transformations. These transformations, although certainly anatomical and physiological, can be neither defined nor studied with reference to the individual alone.

This historian's profession of faith may come as a surprise, since I have at times been criticized for being uninterested in history and for paying scant attention to it in my work. I do not practise it much, but I am determined that its rights should be reserved. I merely believe that in this formative period of social anthropology, nothing would be more dangerous than an unmethodical eclecticism seeking to give the illusion of a finished science by confusing its tasks and mixing its programmes.

Now it happens that in anthropology, experimentation precedes both observation and hypothesis. One of the peculiarities of the small societies which we study is that each constitutes, as it were, a ready-made experiment, because of its relative simplicity and the limited number of variables required to explain its functioning. On the other hand, these societies are alive, and we have neither the time nor the means to manipulate them. By comparison with the natural sciences, we benefit from an advantage and suffer an inconvenience; we find our experiments already prepared but they are uncontrollable. It is therefore understandable that we attempt to replace them with models, systems of symbols which preserve the characteristic properties of the experiment, but which we can manipulate.

The boldness of such an approach is, however, compensated for by the humility—one might almost say the servility—of observation as it is practised by the anthropologist. Leaving his country and his home for long periods; exposing himself to hunger, sickness, and occasional danger; allowing his habits, his beliefs, his convictions to be tampered with, conniving at this, indeed, when, without mental reservations or ulterior motives, he assumes the modes of life of a strange society, the anthropologist practises total observation, beyond which there is nothing except—and there *is* a risk—the complete absorption of the observer by the object of his observations.

This alternation between two methods (each involving its rhythm)—the deductive and the empirical—and the strictness with which we practise each in its extreme and most refined form give social anthropology its distinctive character: of all the sciences, it is without a doubt unique in making the most intimate subjectivity into a means of objective demonstration. We really can verify that the same mind which has abandoned itself to the experience and allowed itself to be moulded by it becomes the theatre of mental operations which, without suppressing the experience, nevertheless transform it into a model which releases further mental operations. In the last analysis, the logical coherence of these mental operations is based on the sincerity and honesty of the person who can say, like the explorer bird of the fable, "I was there; such-and-such happened to me; you will believe you were there yourself," and who in fact succeeds in communicating that conviction.

But this constant oscillation between theory and observation requires that the two levels always remain distinct. To return to history, it seems to me that the same holds true, whether one devotes oneself to the static or to the dynamic, to the order of the structure or to the order of the event. The history of the historians requires no defense, but we do not endanger it by saying (as Braudel admits) that next to a short span there exists a long span; that certain facts arise from a statistical and irreversible time, others from a mechanical and reversible time; and that the idea of structural history contains nothing which could shock historians.[4] The two come together, and it is not contradictory that a history of symbols and signs engenders unforeseeable developments, even though it brings into play a limited number of structural combinations. In a kaleidoscope, each recombination of identical elements yields new results; but it is because the history of the historians is present—in the succession of flicks of the finger, as it were, which brings about the reorganization of the structure—and because the chances are practically nil that the same configuration will appear twice.

I do not mean, then, to take up again, in its original form, the distinction introduced in the *Course in General Linguistics* between the synchronic and the diachronic orders. From this aspect of the Saussurian doctrine, modern structuralism, along with Trubetzkoy and Jakobson, has most energetically diverged; and recent documents show the extent to which the editors of the *Course* may at times have forced and schematized the master's thought.[5]

For the editors of the *Course in General Linguistics*, there exists an absolute opposition between two categories of fact: on the one hand, that of grammer, the synchronic, the conscious; on the other hand, that of the phonetic, the diachronic, the unconscious. Only the conscious system is coherent; the unconscious infra-system is dynamic and off-balance, composed at once of elements from the past and as yet unrealized future tendencies.

In fact, de Saussure had not yet discovered the presence of differential elements behind the phoneme. His position indirectly foreshadowed, on another plane, that of Radcliffe-Brown, who was convinced that structure is of the order of empirical observation, when in fact it lies beyond it. This ignorance of hidden realities leads the two men to opposite conclusions. De Saussure appears to deny the existence of a structure where it not immediately given; Radcliffe-Brown confirms such an existence but, locating it in the wrong place, deprives the whole notion of structure of its full force and significance.

In anthropology, as in linguistics, we know today that the synchronic can be as unconscious as the diachronic. In this sense the divergence between the two is already reduced.

On the other hand, the *Course in General Linguistics* sets forth relations of equivalence between the phonetic, the diachronic, and the individual, which pertain to speech (*parole*); and the grammatical, the synchronic, and the collective, which pertain to language (*la langue*). But we have learned from Marx that the diachronic can also exist in the collective, and from Freud that the grammatical can be achieved entirely within the individual.

Neither the editors of the *Course* nor Radcliffe-Brown sufficiently realized that the history of symbolic systems includes logical evolutions which relate to different levels of the structural process and which it is necessary first to isolate. If a conscious system exists, it can only result from a sort of "dialectical average" among a multiplicity of unconscious systems, each of which concerns one aspect or one level of social reality. Now, these systems do not coincide either in their logical structures or in their historical affiliations. They are as if diffracted upon a temporal dimension, whose thickness gives synchronism its consistency, and lacking which synchronism would dissolve into a tenuous and impalpable essence, a phantom of reality.

It would thus not be over-bold to suggest that in its oral expression, the teaching of de Saussure must not have been very far from these profound remarks by Durkheim, which, published in 1900, seem to have been written today:

> Without a doubt, the phenomena which concern structure are somewhat more stable than functional phenomena, but between the two orders of facts there is only a difference of degree. Structure itself occurs in the process of becoming...it takes shape and breaks down ceaselessly, it is life which has reached a certain degree of consolidation; and to distinguish the life whence it derives from the life which it determines would be to dissociate inseparable things.[6]

. . .

So-called primitive societies, of course, exist in history; their past is as old as ours, since it goes back to the origin of the species. Over thousands of years they have undergone all sorts of transformations; they have known wars, migrations, adventure. But they have specialized in ways different from those which we have chosen. Perhaps they have, in certain respects, remained closer to very ancient conditions of life, but this does not preclude the possibility that in other respects they are farther from those conditions than we are.

Although they exist in history, these societies seem to have elaborated or retained a particular wisdom which incites them to resist desperately any structural modification which would afford history a point of entry into their lives. Those which have best protected their distinctive character appear to be societies predominantly concerned with persevering in their existence. The way in which they exploit the environment guarantees both a modest standard of living and the conservation of natural resources. Their marriage rules, though varied, reveal to the eye of the demographer a common function, namely to set the fertility rate very low and to keep it constant. Finally, a political life based on consent, and admitting of no decisions other than those unanimously arrived at, seems conceived to preclude the possibility of calling on that driving force of collective life which takes advantage of the contrast between power and opposition, majority and minority, exploiter and exploited.

In a word, these societies, which we might define as "cold" in that their internal environment neighbours on the zero of historical temperature, are, by their limited total manpower and their mechanical mode of functioning, distinguished from the "hot" societies which appeared in different parts of the world following the Neolithic revolution. In these, differentiations between castes and between classes are urged unceasingly in order to extract social change and energy from them.

The value of this distinction is mainly theoretical: it is unlikely that any society can be found which would correspond exactly to one or the other type. And in another sense also the distinction remains relative, if it is true, as I believe, that social anthropology responds to a double motivation. First: retrospective, since the various types of primitive life are on the point of disappearing and we must hasten to cull our lessons from them. Second: prospective, to the extent that, being conscious of an evolution whose tempo is constantly accelerating, we experience ourselves already as the "primitives" of our great-grandchildren, so that we seek to validate ourselves by drawing closer to those who were—and still are, for a brief moment—like a part of us which persists in its existence.

On the other hand, neither do those societies which I have called "hot" manifest this character to an absolute degree. When, on the morrow of the Neolithic revolution, the great city-states of the Mediterranean Basin and the Far East perpetrated slavery, they constructed a type of society in which the differential statuses of men—some dominant, others dominated—could be used to produce culture at a rate until then inconceivable and unthought of. By the same logic, the industrial revolution of the nineteenth century represents less an evolution oriented in the same direction, than a rough sketch of a different solution: though for a long time it remained based on the same abuses and injustices, yet it made possible the transfer to *culture* of that dynamic function which the protohistoric revolution had assigned to *society*.

If—Heaven forbid!—it were expected of the anthropologist that he predict the future of humanity, he would undoubtedly not conceive of it as a continuation or projection of present types, but rather on the model of an integration, progressively unifying the appropriate characteristics of the "cold" societies and the "hot" ones. His thought would renew connections with the old Cartesian dream of putting machines, like automatons, at the service of man. It would follow this lead through the social philosophy of the eighteenth century and up to Saint-Simon. The latter, in announcing the passage "from government of men to the administration of things," anticipated in the same breath the anthropological distinction between culture and society. He thus looked forward to an event of which advances in information theory and electronics give us at least a glimpse: the conversion of a type of civilization which inaugurated historical development at the price of the transformation of men into machines into an ideal civilization which would succeed in turning machines into men. Then, culture having entirely taken over the burden of manufacturing progress, society would be freed from the millennial curse which has compelled it to enslave men in order that there be progress. Henceforth, history would make itself by itself. Society, placed outside and above history, would be able to exhibit once again that regular and, as it were, crystaline structure which the best-preserved of primitive societies teach us is not antagonistic to the human condition. In this perspective, utopian as it might seem, social anthropology would find its highest justification, since the forms of life and thought which it studies would no longer have a purely historical or comparative interest. They would correspond to a permanent hope for mankind over which social anthropology, particularly in the most troubled times, would have a mission to keep watch.

Our science would not have been able to stand as a sentinel in this way—and would not even have conceived of the importance and the necessity of it—if, on the remote borders of the earth, men had not obstinately resisted history, and if they had not remained as living testimonials of that which we want to preserve....

Notes

1   *Cours de linguistique générale* (Paris, 1960), p.33.
2   *L'organisation sociale et politique du Nord Malekula* (Noumea: Institut français d'Oceanie, 1963), and *Structure de la Chefferie en Melanésie du Sud* (Institut d'Ethnologie, Paris, 1963).
3   "Être ou ne pas être, ou le postulat de la sociologie," in *Revue Philosophique* I (1901), p. 470.
4   "Histoire et sciences sociales: la longue durée," in *Annales, Economies, Sociétés, Civilisations* (1954).
5   R. Godel, *Les sources manuscrites du cours de linguistique générale de Ferdinand de Saussure* (Geneva, 1957).
6   "La sociologie et son domaine scientifique," in *Où va la sociologie française?* (Paris, 1953), p.190.

Study Questions

1. What is the role of translation in the anthropological vision of Lévi-Strauss?

2. Why, according to Lévi-Strauss, is it important not to ignore the "historical dimension" to social life?

3. Why is "everything symbol and sign" when these mediate between two subjects?

Further Readings

Boon, James A. 1972. *From Symbolism to Structuralism: Lévi-Strauss in a Literary Tradition*. New York: Harper and Row.

Leach, Edmund R. 1989 [1970]. *Claude Lévi-Strauss*. Chicago: Chicago University Press.

Lévi-Strauss, Claude. 1969 [1949]. *The Elementary Structures of Kinship*. Boston: Beacon Press.

—. 1974 [1963]. *Structural Anthropology*. New York: Basic Books.

—. 1976 [1955]. *Tristes Tropiques*. Harmondsworth: Penguin.

20

Structuralism in Social Anthropology

EDMUND LEACH

Even the most enthusiastic adherent of **structuralism** in social anthropology will admit that the relationship between Lévi-Strauss's theoretical ideas and the empirical ethnographic facts in which they are said to be exemplified is very complicated. Summary examples can illustrate what is meant when it is argued that structuralism is, essentially, a "way of looking at things", but they are unlikely to convince the sceptic that this is a means for arriving at the truth. At the end of the lecture, which is printed below, I endeavoured to give the listener a taste of the "new" insights which can be derived from an application of structuralist procedures by offering an extremely condensed analysis of certain very familiar materials from the New Testament. I hope that no reader of this printed version of my lecture will imagine that the arguments presented in this truncated form could persuade any serious Biblical scholar. I intend, in due course, to publish elsewhere a much fuller and more scholarly analysis on the same lines which will give the experts a better opportunity to assess both the merits and the limitations of such devices.

Structuralism is a current intellectual fashion and the word itself has come to mean different things to different people, but for present purposes I shall assume that "Structuralism in Social Anthropology" refers to the social anthropology of Lévi-Strauss and work which derives more or less directly from that source. Thus regarded, structuralism is neither a theory nor a method but "a way of looking at things." To see what is peculiar about this way of looking at things we may usefully look at some of the alternatives.

The subject-matter of social anthropology is customary behaviour. In every sequence of such behaviour there is a practical component which "alters the state of the world" and a ritual, or symbolic, component which "says something" about the social situation. For example, when you take breakfast in the morning, the practical aspect relieves your state of hunger but the nature of the food—whether it be "toast and coffee" or "bacon and eggs"—"says" that this is breakfast and not lunch or dinner.

In the history of social anthropology the bias of interest has lain alternately on one side or the other: Frazer, Durkheim, RadcliffeBrown, Mauss, and Lévi-Strauss have been mainly concerned with "things said"; Malinowski and his followers with "things done." The former have neglected economics and the latter have neglected religion.

Another recurrent uncertainty in social anthropology turns on the relationship between sociology and psychology. Are we concerned with social facts which are out there, external to man in the way that physical inorganic nature is external to man, or must we always remind ourselves that cultural products are *phenomena*, in the sense that they are not merely the perceptions of human minds but the products of human minds? And tied up with this is the question of whether we are ultimately concerned with the diversity of human nature or with its universals.

For if there *are* cultural *universals* then these are part of the "nature of man." They are products of "the human mind" in a quite general sense, as distinct from any particular individual mind.

Frazer and Malinowski in their different ways both supposed that the study of social anthropology can lead to general insights about "the human mind," whereas the "collective consciousness" discussed by Durkheim and his associates was presumed to be a characteristic of particular societies. The metaphysics of such arguments are complicated and most British social anthropologists have wisely preferred to concentrate on the sociological part of the Durkheimian tradition—namely the thesis that society is an articulated system which exists in its own right independently of the individuals who make it up. In this respect, as successors to Durkheim, Malinowski and Radcliffe-Brown both emphasized this articulated interdependence of the institutions which make up a social system. But where Radcliffe-Brown thought of the resulting society as a self-sustaining *organism* and proposed a taxonomy of such organisms, classified as species types, Malinowski thought of culture as a kind of ecological interface between the individual and his social and economic environment. For Malinowski, institutions serve to satisfy the *biological* needs of the individual; for Radcliffe-Brown they satisfy the *mechanical* needs of the *social system as such*.

Lévi-Strauss (by developing ideas initiated by Mauss) has attempted a synthesis of these two positions. The Durkheim-Radcliffe-Brown metaphor by which the articulation of *society* is seen as "like that of an organism" is replaced in Lévi-Strauss by the proposition that the articulation of culture is "like that of a language." The superficial details of this language are peculiar to particular social systems; the way it is manipulated is the outcome of individual self-interest; but the ultimate grammar of the language is a human universal. But now to the matter in hand.

At the risk of repeating, or even contradicting, what Professor Lyons said, let me try to give you a rough—and it must be very rough—indication of where the interests of linguistics and social anthropology overlap.

By and large, social anthropologists prefer to leave the facts of human physiology to the physical anthropologists and the zoologists. This permits them to describe a vast area of human behaviour relating to food, sex, reproduction, respiration, body maintenance, and so on as "natural." All human beings are assumed to have roughly the same physiological needs and the same physiological responses. Behaviour which is the immediate undecorated outcome of these physiological drives—e.g. breathing, sleeping, eating, drinking, defecating, and so on—is looked upon as part of human *nature*. The residual category of "non-natural behaviour" (in this blanket sense) is then treated as either *idiosyncratic*—peculiar to a particular individual—or *cultural*—peculiar to a group of human beings who have been brought up in a particular historical tradition.

In this approach, the capability of human children to learn to speak is a part of their *nature*. But particular languages which are mutually unintelligible are *cultural*. Members of a speech community use their spoken language to communicate information to one another. But they also use many other things to achieve the same purpose. The clothes we wear, the food we eat, the houses we live in, and so on, all convey information to those who understand the "codes" in question. Structuralist social anthropologists start off with the hypothesis that these codes are "languages" in the same sense (or very nearly the same sense) as spoken languages, and hence they postulate that the kind of linkage between nature and culture that has lately been emerging from the work of structural linguists is highly relevant for social anthropology.

Linguists have long recognized that although human languages are enormously varied in their superficial aspects, nevertheless there are principles which are valid for all languages. At one time, these universal principles were thought to be grammatical but from the end of the eighteenth century right through to about 1950 professional linguistic attention concentrated heavily on phonology. The experts attempted to formulate rules which would explain how one language could evolve out of another by regular sound shifts and, more generally, they sought to formulate rules about how noise elements (phonemes) can be distinguished from one another so that, when strung together in chains, they form distinctive words.

Since 1953, under the lead of Noam Chomsky, there has been a dramatic shift back to the study of grammar—the attempt to discover universal rules governing the construction of meaningful utterances.

It is important that you should appreciate that, in so far as structuralist social anthropology depends upon a borrowing of ideas from the linguists, these ideas come mainly from the theory of comparative *phonology* rather than from the general theory of *transformational grammar*. This may be a pity, yet it is so.

Anyway, just as structural linguistics endeavours to establish that there are "deep level" universals which lie at the back of the diversity of human languages, so also structuralist social anthropology seeks to discover "deep level" universals which lie at the back of the diversity of human cultures. Anthropologists have been searching for such universals for over 100 years with very little success. The structuralists think that they now have the key to the problem.

At this point I must explain the special sense in which I am using the word structure. By way of illustration I shall borrow an example from Bertrand Russell. If I listen to a broadcast version of a piano sonata the music has gone through a whole series of transformations. It started out as a score written on a piece of paper; it was interpreted in the head of the pianist and then expressed by movements of the pianist's fingers; the piano then produced a patterned noise imposed on the air which was converted by electronic mechanisms into grooves on a gramophone record; subsequently other electronic devices converted the music into radio frequency vibrations and after a further series of transformations it eventually reached my ears as patterned noise. Now it is perfectly clear that *something* must be common to all the forms through which the music has passed. It is that common something, a patterning of internally organized relationships which I refer to by the word *structure*. It is the very essence of structures (in this sense) that they are capable of expression in multiple forms which are transformations of one another, and further—and this point is often overlooked by practitioners of the structuralist art—that there is no one particular form which is a *more* true or *more* correct expression of the underlying structure than any other.

The notion of structure, thus defined, is a mathematical idea and empirical structures can be recognized in every aspect of the universe—in the physics of outer space just as in the genetic chemistry of molecular biology—but in linguistics and in social anthropology we are only concerned with the special class of structures which are generated by human brains. They have the peculiarity that the surface manifestations of these structures tend to be non-repetitive. New forms are being created all the time.

Structural social anthropologists, like structural linguists, are concerned to explore the mechanisms of communication between conscious human beings but they take a wider view of what constitutes communication. To start with they observe that we have receptor senses of taste, smell, touch, rhythm, sensuality, and so on, besides those of hearing and sight.

The social anthropologist therefore assumes that cultural forms which exploit these non-auditory, non-visual senses may function as instruments of communication *in essentially the same way* as the highly specialized cultural forms which we discuss under the heading of spoken and written verbal language.

Social anthropologists agree that it is language rather than any other special capacity which sharply distinguishes human beings from other primates. But in saying this they are using the word *language* in a rather unusual sense. All animals—including man—communicate with each other by means of complex stimulus-response mechanisms. There are some behaviourist psychologists of the school of B.F. Skinner who have managed to convince themselves that ordinary human speech is itself a mechanism of this sort. The linguists, however—and here I am referring especially to Chomsky—have argued with great vigour that human speech interchanges are wholly *unlike* stimulus-response mechanisms.

Although human speech behaviour is governed by discoverable grammatical rules, the way a sequence of verbal utterances will develop is no more predictable than the moves in a multidimensional game of chess.

In this debate, social anthropologists are on Chomsky's side. The interesting parts of cultural intercommunication do not depend upon stimulus-response mechanisms; they are linguistic in nature—generated within a context of grammatical rules—but the language involved is at least partly "non-verbal." When two individuals are in face-to-face communication "the messages which are conveyed by words" and "the messages which are conveyed by other means" are interwoven.

It is possible that the grammatical and phonological structures which can be incorporated in spoken language are more complicated than those which can be built into non-verbal forms of communication—though this is not self-evident—and I should not want to argue that the whole of structural linguistics can be incorporated *en bloc* into social anthropology by an adroit use of algebra and a switch of terminology. But it is suggested, very seriously, that any normal human being, when wide awake in the company of other human beings, is all the time receiving and conveying messages along a variety of different channels—the vocal/auditory channel being just one of many. The receiver of these messages is all the time integrating the information he is receiving through his different senses and attributing a single integrated meaning to his experience. He does not normally attribute one meaning to what he sees and something else to what he hears and something else again to what he touches ... he fits the messages together into a single whole. It seems to follow that this integrating capacity of the brain (or "mind" if you like) must be "structural." If we recog-

nize that we exist in one world rather than many, it must be because we can recognize that messages that reach us through different senses simultaneously
share a common structure.

But that is viewing matters from the receiving end. The individual who
experiences multiple messages from outside as a unity is also a transmitter of
messages through many channels. It is at least a plausible hypothesis that the
messages which are sent out are just as structurally coherent as those which are
taken in.

I have already cited the example of an English breakfast, and food behaviour in general illustrates the structuralist thesis very well. When we sit down
in company for a formal meal we do not just scrabble for the nearest food available; everything is done in accordance with cultural conventions ... Although
the menu may not be known in advance the individual dishes have been prepared in a special and complicated fashion; they follow one another in predictable order and in predictable combinations. Certainly it is not immediately
"obvious" that the patterning of kinds and combinations of food, of modes of
food preparation, of regulated sequences, etc. is "the same as" the harmonic
and melodic structure of a sheet of music, or the phonological and grammatical structure of a speech utterance, but once this analogic possibility is suggested, it is seen to be plausible. Structuralist social anthropologists go much
further and say that it is so.

At this point the interests of the structural linguist and structuralist social
anthropologist begin to diverge rather fast.

Orthodox experts in structural linguistics are not greatly concerned with
meaning as such. Linguistics seeks to discover how it is possible at all for patterned sound to "convey meaning" and, to this end, linguists are extremely
interested in the fact that we are able to distinguish meaningful sentences from
apparently similar meaning*less* sentences ... for example, even a small child
can recognize that "the cat sat on the mat" and "the gnat sat on the cat" are similar forms both of which make sense. Yet a very small phonetic shift which
changes the second of these sentences into "the mat sat on the cat" turns it into
nonsense. How does this come about? Evidently our perception of meaning
here depends on factors other than sound; this particular example seems to
imply a deep-level classification system which distinguishes animate from
inanimate objects and the relation of such classes to types of verbs.

But this kind of problem—the analysis of how sentences come to have
meaning—is different from the problem of worrying about just what sentences
mean. Specialists in linguistics do not ordinarily concern themselves either
with problems of philosophy or with the task of translating foreign languages.

But the structuralist social anthropologist cannot split up theory and practice
in this way. If he claims that the arrangement of cultural objects in space and

of cultural objects in time is "structurally organized" and that these "structures" serve to convey meaning "like" a grammatically organized spoken language, then he must not only show that the patterns in question exist; he must show what they mean. And that is not easy.

I should add here that I myself consider that a good deal of structuralist social anthropology, both in this country and in France, fails at just this point. The authors exhibit the existence of patterns in the material which they are examining, but they fail to demonstrate that the patterns are significant or how they are significant.

However, ignoring that point, how does the structuralist social anthropologist set about his task?

An analogy which has been used very frequently, particularly by Lévi-Strauss, is that of the music produced by an orchestra. The performers in an orchestra play different instruments; the musical score for each instrument is separate from that of any other instrument, so there is a sense in which each performer is providing a separate "message"; but what is being communicated by the orchestra as a whole is a unity. The individual messages of the separate instruments only "make sense" when they are combined as a whole. The individual messages (or, if you like, part-messages) provided by the individual instruments are like incomplete phrases or sentences in a speech utterance.

In conventional Western music (of the kind with which we are familiar in the works of Mozart and Beethoven) most of the phrases are melodic and the meaning of the sound elements is generated by sequence and contiguity. This of course is what happens in speech utterance also; the sound element, as represented by the letters of the alphabet, do not have meanings in themselves, they acquire meaning only when they are ordered in sequences to form words and sentences.

When structuralists refer to this process in which information elements acquire meaning *by contiguous association in sequence*, they are liable to talk about "syntagmatic chains." The jargon is horrible, but there it is. One important aspect of syntagmatic chains is that they are vehicles for the use of **metonymy**. That I am afraid is another jargon word though you will find it in the dictionary. Metonymy is the device whereby a part of a thing is made to stand for a whole. "A" stands for Apple, "C" for Cat, a Crown stands for a King, a Mitre for a Bishop, and so on. Musical melodies have this quality, the first few bars of a piece of music may serve to recall all the rest.

Shifting our frame of reference altogether, metonymy is what happens when "meaning" is evoked as a signal by a stimulus-response mechanism. We can recognize metonymic messages only when they relate to very familiar highly conventional stereotyped patterns.

But to go back to the music of an orchestra. Each player has a score relating to his own particular instrument; the conductor has a score which combines *all* the instruments, and he reads it not merely from left to right, as a melodic or syntagmatic chain, but also up and down as harmony. The conductor generates musical meaning by getting the individual instruments to produce different noises simultaneously. It is the combination of this chorded dimension with the melodic dimension which produces the "music as a whole."

In speech utterances, metaphor plays the part of harmonic (chorded) association in music. Metaphor is the stuff of poetry; its power to stir the imagination and generate "meaning" depends upon its unexpectedness and the chains of implied metonymic associations, which are unstated, and optional to the listener.

Just to be difficult, the structuralists, who refer to melodic sequences as syntagmatic chains, refer to the kind of shift of register which occurs in metaphor and harmony as "paradigmatic."

I think I have said enough now for you to see how the convinced structuralist approaches his data. He assumes that the cultural stuff within his field of observation, which consists of man-made things and customary behaviours, is all conveying information "like an orchestra." That being so, he assumes that it is possible to record the significant patterns in this cultural stuff on some kind of multidimensional orchestral score. As with orchestral music proper, the "meaning" that is conveyed by the totality of cultural stuff results from a combination of two major types of association: (i) association by contiguity and sequence, melody, syntagmatic chains of data, (ii) association by metaphoric analogy, harmony, switches from one line of the score to quite a different line of the score, paradigmatic links of perceived similarity, e.g. "My love is like a rose."

And let me repeat again: there is a *major* difference between these two kinds of association. With syntagmatic chains you can set up rules which will distinguish between meaningful and non-meaningful combinations, for example in normal English, "if a combination of three letters c.a.t. is to make sense, the letter *t* must come at the end." But if I resort to metaphor I am asserting that $x=y$ and the number of entities which can be represented by either x or y is infinite and subject only to the control of my private imagination. I must emphasize that we are always using both modes of communication all the time, but the mix keeps changing.

But it is high time that I tried to show how this abstract theorizing may be applied to the normal subject-matter of social anthropology.

When I myself started out as an anthropologist as a pupil of Malinowski the fashion was to emphasize that cultural materials must satisfy biological needs.

Human beings cannot survive as individuals; they survive as members of communities, knit together by bonds of reciprocal obligation. To be viable, the cultural systems which generate these networks of interdependence must satisfy the biological requirements of the constituent members, notably those of food, sex, and shelter. Malinowski's style of anthropological thinking is now very unfashionable but its links with structuralism are closer than some of my colleagues seem to appreciate.

Ordinary spoken language is superimposed on a physiological essential, namely breath. In a comparable way the other major codes of human communication are superimposed on other physiological essentials, namely Malinowski's "primary needs" of food, sex, and shelter.

I have already twice mentioned the case of food. All of us must eat, but under normal social conditions no human beings just eat indiscriminately. Cultural rules prescribe a classification which distinguishes between food and not-food. Other cultural rules specify how food shall be collected and prepared and how and when it shall be eaten. In every cultural system there is a "grammar" of food behaviour which is as complex and specific as the grammar of speech.

This is equally true of sexual behaviour. Just as there is cultural discrimination between what is food and what is not food, so also there is cultural discrimination between what is sexually permitted and what is sexually forbidden. These are distinctions of culture and not of nature; they result from rules and conventions, not from inborn animal instincts.

In point of fact, the ordering of these two frames of reference—food and sex—is so similar that metaphoric cross-reference from one to another is almost universal. Even the details of the metaphors are repeated over and over again, e.g. sexual intercourse is "like" eating; parturition is "like" vomiting, and so on.

The fact that such symbolization occurs has been long recognized; it was the original basis for most psycho-analytic theorizing concerning dream interpretation and verbal free association. But the structuralist view of the process seems to be a good deal more sophisticated than that propounded by either Freud or Jung, or even Melanie Klein.

The structuralist proposition is that, in any one cultural system the structure of ideas which relate to food is coherent by itself; similarly the structure of ideas relating to sex is coherent; likewise the structure of ideas relating to space and orientation or, for that matter, the structure of ideas relating to interpersonal relationship—submission and dominance, respect and familiarity, and so on.

But the human brain which generates these coherent sub-systems is itself a unity; hence the structural coherence which is generated in the products of human brains, whether it is manifested as, speech behaviour, or food behaviour, or sex behaviour, or whatever, must be general and mathematical. Metaphorical cross-reference becomes possible and appropriate only because the "structure" is common. Each mode of communication is a transformation of each of the others, as in my example of the music on the gramophone record.

I shall try to give you some examples of how this theory can be applied to empirical anthropological data in a few moments but first let me go back to the source of these ideas—structural linguistics.

Structural linguistics started out as an explanation of phonology. Sound elements such as those we represent by the letters of the alphabet have no meaning in themselves; they acquire meaning only when they are strung together in chains. But how does the human brain distinguish between one sound element and another? Structuralist theory maintains that what we discriminate are not the sound elements (phonemes) as such, but the distinctive features which underlie the sound elements, such distinctions as vowel/consonant, compact high-energy sound/diffuse low-energy sound. These distinctions are, in effect, second-order data, "relations between relations." One merit claimed for this theory is that a small number of distinctive features may account for all the observable sound elements used in all natural languages. If this were true then distinctive feature theory ought to make it feasible to explore the possibility of language universals in a systematic way.

It is this "distinctive feature" version of transformational phonology which has been mainly exploited by Lévi-Strauss in his application of structuralist ideas to social anthropology.

Lévi-Strauss's selection of culturally significant binary oppositions, the equivalents of vowel/consonant, compact/diffuse oppositions in phonology, often seems rather arbitrary but they fit with the ethnographic data surprisingly well. Here are some of them:

I. *Left hand* versus *right hand*. Every human individual is aware of the difference between his left hand and his right. He cannot describe with any precision what the difference is; one hand is, in fact, a complex, topological, transformation of the other. My two hands are alike in being hands; opposite in being left and right. This provides us with a useful basis of metaphor, and it was long ago observed that the usage which makes *"left*=sinister, evil, clumsy, mysterious" as opposed to *"right*=correct, good, and so on" is very widespread and not confined to any language area. Structuralism provides us with a clue as to why this should be so.

II. *Raw* versus *cooked*. Human beings characteristically eat part of their food cooked. The use of fire for cooking is what distinguishes men from beasts.

Lévi-Strauss has argued that the worry about what it is that distinguishes true men—"people like us"—from mere beasts is an anxiety shared by all humanity everywhere. If this is true, then concern with the opposition Culture/Nature is basic even when the concepts as such do not exist. Lévi-Strauss postulates that *Raw* versus *Cooked* is a universal metaphor for *Nature* versus *Culture*. The opposition *wild* versus *tame* is very similar.

III. Spatial opposition. Structuralists find significance in such binary pairs as: Earth/Sky // Earth/Underground; This side of the river// The other side; Land // Sea; Dry // Wet; The City // The Desert. The point about such oppositions is that they are aspects of the non-living world external to man which present themselves directly to the senses but which are particularly appropriate for the crucial *social* opposition Us/Other. Of especial significance are those category pairs which can serve as a metaphoric bridge for the distinction between Culture and Nature since these serve as crucial pivots for religious thinking. In particular, "Life/Death" becomes transferred by metaphor to "This World/Other World" and to "Man versus God."

IV. *Sister* versus *Wife* (see Fig. 1). If we accept the proposition that a sister can never be a wife, then x/y forms a binary dyad and the social relationship A/C (+) will always be in some sense opposite to B/C (-). If we then observe how these two relations A/C and B/C are expressed in customary behaviour we shall get a guide as to the coding involved. For example in some cultural systems A/C=blood (common substance) and B/C=metaphysical influence. This allows us to predict that when A/C=metaphysical influence, then B/C=Common substance. On the whole, empirical ethnography confirms this expectation.

But what, you may well ask, is the point of all this? Well first of all it is characteristic of this kind of argument that it is assumed that the elements of symbolism are not things in themselves but "relations" organized in pairs and sets. Let me give an example. Fifty years ago in the first flush of Freudian enthusiasm it was seriously argued that it is universally the case that elongated objects are treated as penis symbols, while oval and circular objects serve as vagina symbols. The structuralist admits that there is substantial ethnographic evidence for this kind of generalization but makes the interpretation more abstract. The category opposition long/round is part of a much more general structure (Fig. 2).

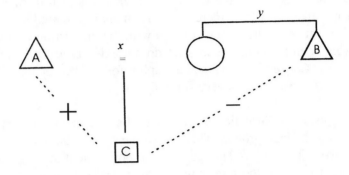

Figure 1

A. For simple-minded Freudians
long object= penis
round object= vagina

B. For structuralists

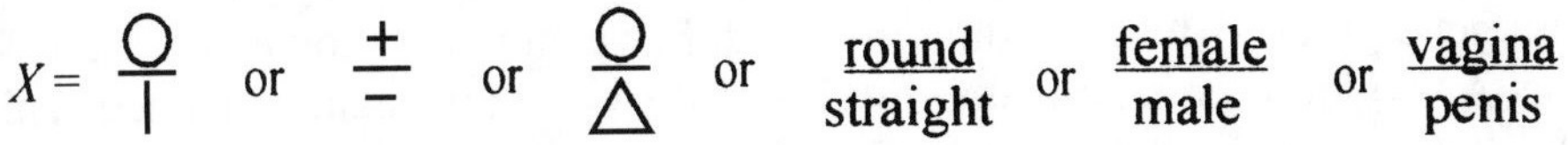

$$X = \frac{\bigcirc}{|} \quad \text{or} \quad \frac{+}{-} \quad \text{or} \quad \frac{\bigcirc}{\triangle} \quad \text{or} \quad \frac{\text{round}}{\text{straight}} \quad \text{or} \quad \frac{\text{female}}{\text{male}} \quad \text{or} \quad \frac{\text{vagina}}{\text{penis}}$$

Figure 2

The crucial point is that the "element of structure" is not a unit *thing* but a relation X.

Applied to ethnographic data this more abstract approach encourages the social anthropologist to perceive that cultural phenomena which he had previously thought of as quite separate are really variations of a common theme.

It is difficult to exemplify this point in detail to a partly nonanthropological audience but here is an example. The fact that some human societies trace descent through the mother and others through the father has been known for centuries. In the mid-nineteenth century this became a central pivot of evolutionary thought. It was argued that since the child's connection with its mother is "more obvious" than its link with its father, therefore **matriliny** is more primitive than **patriliny**. Hence matrilineal societies and patrilineal societies came to be thought of as entities of quite different kinds but no one really bothered to think about just *how* they were different.

According to this traditional classification the Kachins of north Burma are a patrilineal society. The Garo of Assam, who are located about 100 miles further west, are a matrilineal society. Both groups have been known to Western ethnographers for over a century. Both are distinguished by what appear to be rather peculiar marriage rules.

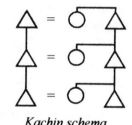

Kachin schema
'marriage with the mothers's
brother's daughter'

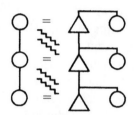

Garo schema
'marriage with the mother-in-law'

Figure 3

Garo men were reputed to marry their mothers-in-law; Kachins allegedly always married their mother's brother's daughter. No one before Lévi-Strauss ever detected any similarity between the two systems.

But a structuralist way of looking at things shows that these two marriage rules are versions of the same principle (Fig. 3), and modern fieldwork has shown that the two cultural systems are in fact remarkably similar right across the board. The contrast patrilineal descent/ matrilineal descent being the only major difference between them. A structuralist therefore regards the two systems as transformations of a single structure.

The "variation on a theme" argument is also the key characteristic of the structuralist analysis of mythology which is the aspect of Lévi-Strauss's work which looms largest in bulk (if not in quality) in the total Lévi-Straussian corpus.

In this field the essential innovation in Levi-Strauss's approach is the recognition that mythological stories always exist as sets rather than isolates. The individual members of the set constitute permutations of the same theme. The moral implication of the mythology, what Malinowski called its force as "a charter for social action," can only be fully apprehended when we take the total set of stories into consideration simultaneously. Once again you need to think of the instruments of an orchestra combining to produce a unitary piece of music.

Lévi-Strauss's theory of myth takes up four very fat volumes of closely argued text. To give a "summary" of that argument seems to me almost impossible. What I propose to do instead is to illustrate the argument by applying it, in very cursory form, to a theme from the New Testament of the Christian Bible. But first some points of general theory about the relationship between mythology and moral precept.

Among human beings, as among other animals, the three primary drives governing the interaction of individuals are hunger, sex, and physical aggression. Among species *other than* man these drives are very largely determined by genetic factors, or by conditioning at a very early stage in the individual's development. As I have already emphasized, in man the rules and conventions which determine with whom we may eat and what we may eat, with whom we may sleep and where we may sleep, whom we may assault with impunity and under what circumstances, are all arbitrary, culturally determined matters. Taken together, these rules and conventions serve to carve up the social environment into a vast array of cross-cutting classes of things and persons in terms of which we organize our daily lives. The tidy ordering of these categories is something to which we all attach great importance. Any infringement of the standard conventions generates a sense of emotional shock which we experience *either* as embarrassment *or* as excitement.

And even in a story, any reference to a transgression of taboo, however oblique, creates vicarious excitement. In this respect the myths of our own society have quite a different quality for *us* from the myths of other people. Myths everywhere make constant reference to moral offences, but unless, as listener or reader, you share the same moral assumptions as the myth narrator, you will not be "shocked" by what he says and you will then have difficulty in picking up the message. For it is the *shock* effect of references to breaches of moral taboo which gives myth its "meaning." That is why the myths which are most widely recognized as powerful and exciting are ones which harp on themes of a very basic moral kind, themes which crop up in all kinds of cultures and not just as local peculiarities.

These *primary* myths are always centrally preoccupied with persons and creatures who are wrongly constructed or wrongly born or in the wrong place, and with such universal moral offences as homicide, sexual misdemeanours, and abnormal food behaviour. Such myths exhibit the limits of normality and the potent dangers of otherness by turning normality back to front.

Men and animals are normally different, so, in myth, the serpent who is abnormally constructed, talks with Eve like a human being; normal boats float on the sea, so Noah's Ark comes to rest on the top of a mountain; parricide and incest are the ultimate sins, so myth tricks Oedipus into killing his own father and marrying his own mother. The moral point is made clear by emphasizing the overwhelming disasters which are directly associated with the mythical breach of normality.

Perhaps *normality* is not quite the right word. The topographical space in which mythical events take place is metaphysical rather than physical. It consists of "the world of common experience," which is *normally* inhabited by normal men and by *tame* animals, plus "the other world" of imagination which is *normally* inhabited by supernatural beings and *wild* animals. But there is also a very important "intermediate world" which is neither here nor there. In myth it is this liminal zone which receives the greatest attention.

Normality and *abnormality* must therefore be viewed in context. Other world beings are "abnormal" when they behave like normal beings of this world; normal men are "abnormal" when they behave like gods; beings of the middle zone, who often appear in myth as deified ancestors (part man, part god), become "abnormal" whenever they lose their ambiguity. The mediating hero is, in all religious systems, a being of the middle zone. One aspect of his essential ambiguity is that he (or she) is always, at one and the same time, impossibly virtuous and impossibly sinful; it is a definitional characteristic of the hero that he is "abnormal when judged by ordinary criteria."

There are dozens of familiar Biblical examples of this principle. The myth makes Abraham marry his half-sister which is incest and it makes Solomon, the Great King, take seven hundred wives and three hundred concubines all from the nations with whom the Israelites were formally forbidden to intermarry. Notice how, on this issue of marriage, the stories of Abraham and Solomon form a contrasted pair. They are concerned with two aspects of the same problem, the *over*emphasis and the *under*emphasis of the same rule of endogamy. This is an example of what I mean when I say that myth stories do not occur as isolates but in sets; the message of the myth is made obliquely by repetitive, yet contrasted, references to the *same* moral injunction which is transgressed in *different* ways.

This sounds all very well in theory, but if I am to show *you* just how myth actually works by storing up emotional feelings of shock and contradiction so as to reveal a religious message, then I have to work through an actual example which you yourselves, or some of you anyway, are liable to find shocking. I must take a myth which is part of *your* own religious background. Hence my choice of Christian New Testament material. The theme which I propose to tackle is that which is implicit in the myth of the birth and death of the paired hero figures, John the Baptist and Jesus Christ.

First you should notice how although the gospels link the careers of these two heroes together in the most emphatic way, the heroes themselves are treated as opposites. In both cases, conception is abnormal, but where John's mother Elizabeth is a woman past the age of childbearing, Jesus' mother Mary is a virgin. Then again the two mothers are cousins, but whereas John belongs to the priestly line of Aaron, Jesus belongs to the royal line of David.

Let me elaborate further some of the structural transformations of this similarity-difference relationship. John is a prophet living in the wilderness, that is to say on the margins of this world and the other; he dresses in animals' skins and feeds off locusts and wild honey; he abstains from alcohol; his companions are wild animals; he is thus a man of *Nature*. Jesus is repeatedly declared to be a king; he lives on normal food in the normal world of the city; he is the son of a carpenter; he fraternizes with publicans and sinners; he is thus a man of *Culture*. Jesus submits to baptism by John yet at this instant John expresses verbally his subordination to Jesus.

Eventually John dies by *decapitation*. Throughout the Old Testament this is a death reserved for kings and princes. In contrast Jesus dies by crucifixion. This is an alien form of execution introduced by the Roman conquerors and reserved for criminals. John's death is brought about by the conspiracy of a wicked Princess Herodias and the sexual guile of her daughter Salome. The women around Jesus play an entirely virtuous sexual role, yet one of them, Mary Magdalene, has been a prostitute.

The context of John's death is a royal feast at which John's severed head is served up on a dish as if it were food. The context of Jesus' death is a Jewish feast of the Passover at which Jesus himself identifies his own body and blood with the food and wine.

I think you must agree that, when the stories are summarized in this selective way, the symmetry of the contrasted patterns is very striking. But what does it mean? We can get an answer to this question by extending the set of stories under examination. For example, we might notice that in the Jewish myth, the *original* Passover commemorated the liberation of *Israelites* from domination by the *Egyptians* and their escape through the *wilderness* to the *Promised Land of Canaan.*

In contrast, the Christian myth of the Last Supper, which is explicitly identified with the Jewish Passover, commemorates the liberation of all *Mankind* from domination by *the cares and suffering of ordinary worldly life,* and *Man's escape,* through the *mysterious wilderness of death* to *the Promised Land of God's Heavenly kingdom and eternal life.* In the *Jewish* myth the final signal of release is the *divine* destruction of all the first born sons of the *Egyptian oppressors.* In the *Christian* myth the final signal of release is the *human* destruction of the first born son of *God.* Thus, the Christian story is, in a quite explicit sense, a new version of the much earlier Jewish story but generalized on to a more metaphysical plane with certain key elements reversed.

If you consider the material in this way you will realize that part at least of the "message" in the New Testament story is that the symbolic heroes John and Jesus exchange their roles. John starts out as a being from the other world; he is "filled with the Holy Ghost even from his mother's womb"; he is a "voice crying in the wilderness"; but he dies in a city in a kingly palace, executed as a king.

Jesus starts out as a being of this world; he belongs initially to the city not the desert; his royal status is emphasized from the start but he becomes filled with the Holy Ghost only when he is baptized by John; he then immediately goes out into the wilderness, but when he does so he is in communication not with God but with Satan; nevertheless Jesus ends up as a being of the Other World. John is a prophet, a spokesman of God, who becomes a murdered king; Jesus is a king who becomes a murdered prophet.

This role reversal is reinforced by many other incidents in the Jesus myth which repeatedly reverses the roles which orthodox Jewish belief seems to offer to the Messiah. For example, where the ancient *Israelites* had escaped from *Pharaoh* by flight *from Egypt into Canaan,* the infant Jesus escapes from Herod by flight from Canaan into Egypt. When Jesus dies he is *not* in a palace but outside the city on a gibbet. He dies *not* as a king, but as a mock king, wearing a crown of thorns. Indeed he dies as a common criminal. Yet, by thus dying, he achieves the status which John had at the beginning; he forms a bridge with the other world and life everlasting.

The drama of the Christian mass, the communion service, recapitulates the myth of the Last Supper. The communicant, by identifying himself with Jesus through the food of the sacred meal, assures himself of life everlasting in the other world, but in doing so, he *also* identifies himself as a criminal and miserable sinner in this world. But the communicant also aspires to improving his personal spiritual status; he seeks to become on some spiritual plane more king-like. But does this mean more like Jesus or more like King Herod? The ambiguity of implication is quite typical of all mythological structures.

Notice that in the process of dramatization the historical context of the story becomes entirely irrelevant. It really does not matter in the least whether *any* of this "actually happened in history." The message of the myth is true in its own terms, not in historical terms.

I realize that such a web of references, cross-references, identifications, inversions, and transformations is difficult to follow. Indeed, if structuralists are right about how myth works, it is an essential feature of the matter that, at a conscious level, the logic of the transformations should be ambiguous. The message of the myth is full of paradox, and it only becomes acceptable as a religious injunction because we do *not* quite understand what is being said.

This is just as well because in this, as in all major myths, the literal sense of what is being said is very terrible. If we leave the metaphysics on one side, we are being told that, in order to achieve the God-like quality of immortality, we must first kill and eat God himself. But we miss the point if we try to constrain our material by imposing any such *literal* interpretation. As a German theologian has put it, "Myth is the expression of unobservable realities in terms of observable phenomena." Myth possesses an *inner* sense which underlies a superficial *non*-sense; we can understand it only as we might understand a kind of universalized poetry.

This I am afraid has been a rather crowded paper. Clearly my Biblical example, if it were to be fully justified, would need much greater elaboration. But I started out by saying that structuralism in social anthropology is a distinctive way of looking at things. I felt that I needed to exemplify this point. Whether, at the end of the day, we have or have not gained any insights which we did not have before will be a matter of opinion.

Study Questions
1. How does Leach employ the metaphor of an orchestra to describe the project of structuralism?

2. What are some of Lévi-Strauss's "binary oppositions" that Leach discusses?

3. How does Leach employ Biblical mythology to illuminate structural analysis?

Further Readings
Leach, Edmund R. 1954. *Political Systems of Highland Burma*. London: G. Bell and Sons.

—. 1961. *Rethinking Anthropology*. London School of Economics Monographs on Social Anthropology 22. New York: Humanities Press.

—. 1969. *Genesis as Myth and Other Essays*. London: Jonathan Cape.

—, (ed.). 1967. *The Structural Study of Myth and Totemism*. London: Tavistock.

21

Thick Description:
Toward an Interpretive Theory of Culture

CLIFFORD GEERTZ

I

In her book, *Philosophy in a New Key*, Suzanne Langer remarks that certain ideas burst upon the intellectual landscape with a tremendous force. They resolve so many fundamental problems at once that they seem also to promise that they will resolve all fundamental problems, clarify all obscure issues. Everyone snaps them up as the open sesame of some new positive science, the conceptual center point around which a comprehensive system of analysis can be built. The sudden vogue of such a *grande idée*, crowding out almost everything else for a while, is due, she says, "to the fact that all sensitive and active minds turn at once to exploiting it. We try it in every connection, for every purpose, experiment with possible stretches of its strict meaning, with generalizations and derivatives."

After we have become familiar with the new idea, however, after it has become part of our general stock of theoretical concepts, our expectations are brought more into balance with its actual uses, and its excessive popularity is ended. A few zealots persist in the old key-to-the-universe view of it; but less driven thinkers settle down after a while to the problems the idea has really generated. They try to apply it and extend it where it applies and where it is capable of extension; and they desist where it does not apply or cannot be extended. It becomes, if it was, in truth, a seminal idea in the first place, a permanent and enduring part of our intellectual armory. But it no longer has the grandiose, all-promising scope, the infinite versatility of apparent application, it once had. The second law of thermodynamics, or the principle of natural selection, or the notion of unconscious motivation, or the organization of the means of production, does not explain everything, not even everything human, but it still explains something; and our attention shifts to isolating just what that something is, to disentangling ourselves from a lot of pseudoscience to which, in the first flush of its celebrity, it has also given rise.

Whether or not this is, in fact, the way all centrally important scientific concepts develop, I don't know. But certainly this pattern fits the concept of culture, around which the whole discipline of anthropology arose, and whose domination that discipline has been increasingly concerned to limit, specify, focus, and contain. It is to this cutting of the culture concept down to size, therefore actually ensuring its continued importance rather than undermining it, that the essays below are all, on their several ways and from their several directions, dedicated. They all argue, sometimes explicitly, more often merely through the particular analysis they develop, for a narrowed, specialized, and, so I imagine, theoretically more powerful concept of culture to replace E.B. Tylor's famous "most complex whole," which, its originative power not denied, seems to me to have reached the point where it obscures a good deal more than it reveals.

The conceptual morass into which the Tylorean kind of *pot-au-feu* theorizing about culture can lead, is evident in what is still one of the better introductions to anthropology, Clyde Kluckhohn's *Mirror for Man*. In some twenty-seven pages of his chapter on the concept, Kluckhohn managed to define culture in turn as: (1) "the total way of life of a people"; (2) "the social legacy the individual acquires from his group"; (3) "a way of thinking, feeling, and believing"; (4) "an abstraction from behavior"; (5) a theory on the part of the anthropologist about the way in which a group of people in fact behave; (6) a "storehouse of pooled learning"; (7) "a set of standardized orientations to recurrent problems"; (8) "learned behavior"; (9) a mechanism for the normative regulation of behavior; (10) "a set of techniques for adjusting both to the external environment and to other men"; (11) "a precipitate of history"; and turning, perhaps in desperation, to similes, as a map, as a sieve, as a matrix. In the face of this sort of theoretical diffusion, even a somewhat constricted and not entirely standard concept of culture, which is at least internally coherent and, more important, which has a definable argument to make is (as, to be fair, Kluckhohn himself keenly realized) an improvement. Eclecticism is self-defeating not because there is only one direction in which it is useful to move, but because there are so many: it is necessary to choose.

The concept of culture I espouse, and whose utility the essays below attempt to demonstrate, is essentially a **semiotic** one. Believing, with Max Weber, that man is an animal suspended in webs of significance he himself has spun, I take culture to be those webs, and the analysis of it to be therefore not an experimental science in search of law but an interpretive one in search of meaning. It is explication I am after, construing social expressions on their surface enigmatical. But this pronouncement, a doctrine in a clause, demands itself some explanation.

II

Operationalism as a methodological dogma never made much sense so far as the social sciences are concerned, and except for a few rather too well-swept corners—Skinnerian behaviorism, intelligence testing, and so on—it is largely dead now. But it had, for all that, an important point to make, which, however we may feel about trying to define charisma or alienation in terms of operations, retains a certain force: if you want to understand what a science is, you should look not in the first instance at its theories or findings, and certainly not at what its apologists say about it: you should look at what the practitioners of it do.

In anthropology, or anyway social anthropology, what the practitioners do is ethnography. And it is in understanding what ethnography is, or more exactly *what doing ethnography is*, that a start can be made toward grasping what anthropological analysis amounts to as a form of knowledge. This, it must immediately be said, is not a matter of methods. From one point of view, that of the textbook, doing ethnography is establishing rapport, selecting informants, transcribing texts, taking genealogies, mapping fields, keeping a diary, and so on. But it is not these things, techniques and received procedures, that define the enterprise. What defines it is the kind of intellectual effort it is: an elaborate venture in, to borrow a notion from Gilbert Ryle, **"thick description."**

Ryle's discussion of "thick description" appears in two recent essays of his (now reprinted in the second volume of his *Collected Papers*) addressed to the general question of what, as he puts it, *"Le Penseur"* is doing: "Thinking and Reflecting" and "The Thinking of Thoughts." Consider, he says, two boys rapidly contracting the eyelids of their right eyes. In one, this is an involuntary twitch; in the other, a conspiratorial signal to a friend. The two movements are, as movements, identical; from an I-am-a-camera, "phenomenalistic" observation of them alone, one could not tell which was twitch and which was wink, or indeed whether both or either was twitch or wink. Yet the difference, however unphotographable, between a twitch and a wink is vast; as anyone unfortunate enough to have had the first taken for the second knows. The winker is communicating, and indeed communicating in a quite precise and special way: (1) deliberately, (2) to someone in particular, (3) to impart a particular message, (4) according to a socially established code, (5) without cognizance of the rest of the company. As Ryle points out, the winker has not done two things, contracted his eyelids and winked, while the twitcher has done only one, contracted his eyelids. Contracting your eyelids on purpose when there exists a public code in which so doing counts as a conspiratorial signal *is* winking. That's all there is to it: a speck of behavior, a fleck of culture, and—voila!—a gesture.

That, however, is just the beginning. Suppose, he continues, there is a third boy, who, "to give malicious amusement to his cronies," parodies the first boy's wink, as amateurish, clumsy, obvious, and so on. He, of course, does this in the same way the second boy winked and the first twitched: by contracting his right eyelids. Only this boy is neither winking nor twitching, he is parodying someone else's, as he takes it, laughable, attempt at winking. Here, too, a socially established code exists (he will "wink" laboriously, over obviously, perhaps adding a grimace—the usual artifices of the clown); and so also does a message. Only now it is not conspiracy but ridicule that is in the air. If the others think he is actually winking, his whole project misfires as completely, though with somewhat different results, as if they think he is twitching. One can go further: uncertain of his mimicking abilities, the would-be satirist may practice at home before the mirror, in which case he is not twitching, winking, or parodying, but rehearsing; though so far as what a camera, a radical behaviorist, or a believer in protocol sentences would record he is just rapidly contracting his right eyelids like all the others. Complexities are possible, if not practically without end, at least logically so. The original winker might, for example, actually have been fake-winking, say, to mislead outsiders into imagining there was a conspiracy afoot when there in fact was not, in which case our descriptions of what the parodist is parodying and the rehearser rehearsing of course shift accordingly. But the point is that between what Ryle calls the "thin description "of what the rehearser (parodist, winker, twitcher…) is doing ("rapidly contracting his right eyelids") and the "thick description" of what he is doing ("practicing a burlesque of a friend faking a wink to deceive an innocent into thinking a conspiracy is in motion") lies the object of ethnography: a stratified hierarchy of meaningful structures in terms of which twitches, winks, fake-winks, parodies, rehearsals of parodies are produced, perceived, and interpreted, and without which they would not (not even the zero-form twitches, which, *as a cultural category*, are as much nonwinks as winks are nontwitches) in fact exist, no matter what anyone did or didn't do with his eyelids.

Like so many of the little stories Oxford philosophers like to make up for themselves, all this winking, fake-winking, burlesque-fake-winking, rehearsed-burlesque-fake-winking, may seem a bit artificial. In way of adding a more empirical note, let me give, deliberately unpreceded by any prior explanatory comment at all, a not untypical excerpt from my own field journal to demonstrate that, however evened off for didactic purposes, Ryles' example presents an image only too exact of the sort of piled-up structures of inference and implication through which an ethnographer is continually trying to pick his way:

The French [the informant said] had only just arrived. They set up twenty or so small forts between here, the town, and the Marmusha area up in the middle of the mountains, placing them on promontories so they could survey the countryside. But for all this they couldn't guarantee safety, especially at night, so although the *mezrag*, trade-pact, system was supposed to be legally abolished it in fact continued as before.

One night, when Cohen (who speaks fluent Berber) was up there, at Marmusha, two other Jews who were traders to a neighboring tribe came by to purchase some goods from him. Some Berbers, from yet another neighboring tribe, tried to break into Cohen's place, but he fired his rifle in the air. (Traditionally, Jews were not allowed to carry weapons; but at this period things were so unsettled many did so anyway.) This attracted the attention of the French and the marauders fled.

The next night, however, they came back, one of them disguised as a woman who knocked on the door with some sort of story. Cohen was suspicious and didn't want to let "her" in, but the other Jews said, "oh, it's all right, it's only a woman." So they opened the door and the whole lot came poring in. They killed the two visiting Jews, but Cohen managed to barricade himself in an adjoining room. He heard the robbers planning to burn him alive in the shop after they removed his goods, and so he opened the door and, laying about him wildly with a club, managed to escape through a window.

He went up to the fort, then, to have his wounds dressed, and complained to the local commandant, one Captain Dumari, saying he wanted his 'ar—i.e., four or five times the value of the merchandise stolen from him. The robbers were from a tribe which had not yet submitted to French authority and were in open rebellion against it, and he wanted authorization to go to his mezrag-holder, the Marmusha tribal sheikh, to collect the indemnity that, under traditional rules, he had coming to him. Captain Dumari couldn't officially give him permission to do this, because of the French prohibition of the mezrag relationship, but he gave him verbal authorization, saying, "if you get killed, it's your problem."

So the *sheikh*, the Jew, and a small company of armed Marmushans went off ten or fifteen kilometers up into the rebellious area, where there were of course no French, and, sneaking up, captured the thief-tribe's shepherd and stole its herds. The other tribe soon came riding out on horses after them, armed with rifles and ready to attack. But when they saw who the "sheep thieves" were, they thought better of it and said, "all right, we'll talk." They couldn't really deny what had happened—that some of their men had robbed Cohen and killed the two visitors—and they weren't prepared to start the serious feud with the Marmusha a scuffle with the invading party would bring on. So the two groups talked, and talked, and talked, there on the plain amid the thousands of sheep, and decided finally on five-hundred sheep damages. The two armed Berber groups then lined up on their horses at opposite ends of the plain, with the sheep herded between them, and Cohen, in his black gown, pillbox hat, and flapping slippers, went out alone among the sheep, picking out, one by one and at his own good speed, the best ones for his payment.

So Cohen got his sheep and drove them back to Marmusha. The French, up in their fort, heard them coming from some a distance ("Ba, ba, ba" said Cohen, happily, recalling the image) and said, "What the hell is that?" And Cohen said, "That is my *'ar*." The French couldn't believe he had actually done what he said he had done, and accused him of being a spy for the rebellious Berbers, put him in prison, and took his sheep. In the town, his family, not having heard from him in so long a time, thought he was dead. But after a while the French released him and he came back home, but without his sheep. He then went to the Colonel in the town, the Frenchman in charge of the whole region, to complain. But the Colonel said, "I can't do anything about the matter. It's not my problem."

Quoted raw, a note in a bottle, this passage conveys, as any similar one similarly presented would do, a fair sense of how much goes into ethnographic description of even the most elemental sort—how extraordinarily "thick" it is. In finished anthropological writings, including those collected here, this fact— that what we call our data are really our own constructions of other people's constructions of what they and their compatriots are up to—is obscured because most of what we need to comprehend a particular event, ritual, custom, idea, or whatever is insinuated as background information before the thing itself is directly examined. (Even to reveal that this little drama took place in the highlands of Morocco in 1912—and was recounted there in 1968—is to determine much of our understanding of it.) There is nothing particularly wrong with this, and it is in any case inevitable. But it does lead to a view of anthropological research as rather more of an observational and rather less of an interpretive activity than it really is. Right down at the factual base, the hard rock, insofar as there is any, of the whole enterprise, we are already explicating: and worse, explicating explanations. Winks upon winks upon winks.

Analysis, then, is sorting out the structure of signification—what Ryle calls established codes, a somewhat misleading expression, for it makes the enterprise sound too much like that of a cipher clerk when it is much more like that of the literary critic—and determining their social ground and import. Here, in our text, such sorting would begin with distinguishing the three unlike frames of interpretation ingredient in the situation, Jewish, Berber, and French, and would then move on to show how (and why) at that time, in that place, their copresence produced a situation in which systematic misunderstanding reduced traditional form to social farce. What tripped Cohen up, and with him the whole, ancient pattern of social and economic relationships within which he functioned, was a confusion of tongues.

I shall come back to this too-compacted aphorism later, as well as to the details of the text itself. The point for now is only that ethnography is thick description. What the ethnographer is in fact faced with—except when (as, of course, he must do) he is pursuing the more automatized routines of data collection—is a multiplicity of complex conceptual structures, many of them superimposed upon or knotted into one another, which are at once strange, irregular, and inexplicit, and which he must contrive somehow first to grasp and then to render. And this is true at the most down-to-earth, jungle field work levels of his activity: interviewing informants, observing rituals, eliciting kin terms, tracing property lines, censusing households ... writing his journal. Doing ethnography is like trying to read (in the sense of "construct a reading of") a manuscript—foreign, faded, full of ellipses, incoherencies, suspicious emendations, and tendentious commentaries, but written not in conventionalized graph of sound but in transient examples of shaped behavior.

III

Culture, this acted document, thus is public, like a burlesqued wink or a mock sheep raid. Though ideational, it does not exist in someone's head; though unphysical, it is not an occult entity. The interminable, because interminable, debate within anthropology as to whether culture is "subjective" or "objective," together with the mutual exchange of intellectual insults ("idealist!"-"materialist!"; "mentalist!"-"behaviorist!"; "impressionist!"-"positivist!") which accompanies it, is wholly misconceived. Once human behavior is seen as (most of the time; there *are* true twitches) symbolic action—action which, like phonation in speech, pigment in painting, line in writing, or sonance in music, signifies—the question as to whether culture is patterned conduct or a frame of mind, or even the two somehow mixed together, loses sense. The thing to ask about a burlesqued wink or a mock sheep raid is not what their ontological status is. It is the same as that of rocks on the one hand and dreams on the other—they are things of this world. The thing to ask is what their import is: what it is, ridicule or challenge, irony or anger, snobbery or pride, that, in their occurrence and through their agency, is getting said.

This may seem like an obvious truth, but there are a number of ways to obscure it. One is to imagine that culture is a self-contained "superorganic" reality with forces and purposes of its own; that is, to reify it. Another is to claim that it consists in the brute pattern of behavioral events we observe in fact to occur in some identifiable community or other; that is, to reduce it. But though both these confusions still exist, and doubtless will be always with us, the main source of theoretical muddlement in contemporary anthropology is a view that developed in reaction to them and is right now very widely held—

namely, that, to quote Ward Goodenough, perhaps its leading proponent, "culture [is located] in the minds and hearts of men."

Variously called **ethnoscience**, **componential analysis**, or cognitive anthropology (a terminological wavering which reflects a deeper uncertainty) this school of thought holds that culture is composed of psychological structures by means of which individuals or groups of individuals guide their behavior. "A society's culture," to quote Goodenough again, this time in a passage which has become the *locus classicus* of the whole movement, "consists of whatever it is one has to know or believe in order to operate in a manner acceptable to its members." And from this view of what culture is follows a view, equally assured, of what describing it is—the writing out of systematic rules, an ethnographic algorithm, which, if followed, would make it possible so to operate, to pass (physical appearance aside) for a native. In such a way, extreme subjectivism is married to extreme formalism, with the expected result: an explosion of debate as to whether particular analyses (which come in the form of taxonomies, paradigms, tables, trees, and other ingenuities) reflect what the natives "really" think or are merely clever simulations, logically equivalent but substantively different, of what they think.

As, on first glance, this approach may look close enough to the one being developed here to be mistaken for it, it is useful to be explicit as to what divides them. If, leaving our winks and sheep behind for the moment, we take, say, a Beethoven quartet as an, admittedly rather special but, for these purposes, nicely illustrative, sample of culture, no one would, I think, identify it with its score, with the skills and knowledge needed to play it, with the understanding of it possessed by its performers or auditors, nor, to take care, *en passant*, of the reductionists and reifiers, with a particular performance of it or with some mysterious entity transcending material existence. The "no one" is perhaps too strong here, for there are always incorrigibles. But that a Beethoven quartet is a temporally developed tonal structure, a coherent sequence of modeled sound—in a word, music—and not anybody's knowledge of or belief about anything, including how to play it, is a proposition to which most people are, upon reflection, likely to assent.

To play the violin it is necessary to possess certain habits, skills, knowledge, and talents, to be in the mood to play, and (as the old joke goes) to have a violin. But violin playing is neither the habits, skills, knowledge, and so on, nor the mood, nor (the notion believers in "material culture" apparently embrace) the violin. To make a trade pact in Morocco, you have to do certain things in certain ways (among others, cut, while chanting Quranic Arabic, the throat of a lamb before the assembled, undeformed, adult male members of your tribe) and to be possessed of certain psychological characteristics (among others, a desire for distant things). But a trade pact is neither the throat cutting nor the desire, though it is real enough, as seven kinsmen of our Marmusha sheikh discovered when, on an earlier occasion, they were executed by him following the theft of one mangy, essentially valueless sheepskin from Cohen.

Culture is public because meaning is. You can't wink (or burlesque one) without knowing what counts as winking or how, physically, to contract your eyelids, and you can't conduct a sheep raid (or mimic one) without knowing what it is to steal a sheep and how practically to go about it. But to draw from such truths the conclusion that knowing how to wink is winking and knowing how to steal a sheep is sheep raiding is to betray as deep a confusion as, taking thin descriptions for thick, to identify winking with eyelid contractions or sheep raiding with chasing woolly animals out of pastures. The cognitivist fallacy—that culture consists (to quote another spokesman for the movement, Stephen Tyler) of "mental phenomena which can [he means "should"] be analyzed by formal methods similar to those of mathematics and logic"—is as destructive of an effective use of the concept as are the behaviorist and idealist fallacies to which it is a misdrawn correction. Perhaps, as its errors are more sophisticated and its distortions subtler, it is even more so.

The generalized attack on privacy theories of meaning is, since early Husserl and late Wittgenstein, so much a part of modern thought that it need not be developed once more here. What is necessary is to see to it that the news of it reaches anthropology; and in particular that it is made clear that to say that culture consists of socially established structures of meaning in terms of which people do such things as signal conspiracies and join them or perceive insults and answer them, is no more to say that it is a psychological phenomenon, a characteristic of someone's mind, personality, cognitive structure, or whatever, than to say that Tantrism, genetics, the progressive form of the verb, the classification of wines, the Common Law, or the notion of a "conditional curse" (as Westermarck defined the concept of 'ar in terms of which Cohen pressed his claim to damages) is. What, in a place like Morocco, most prevents those of us who grew up winking other winks or attending other sheep from grasping what people are up to is not ignorance as to how cognition works (though, especially as, one assumes, it works the same among them as it does among us, it would greatly help to have less of that too) as a lack of familiarity with the imaginative universe within which their acts are signs. As Wittgenstein has been invoked, he may as well be quoted:

We ... say of some people that they are transparent to us. It is, however, important as regards this observation that one human being can be a complete enigma to another. We learn this when we come into a strange country with entirely strange traditions; and, what is more, even given a mastery of the country's language. We do not understand the people. (And not because of not knowing what they are saying to themselves.) We cannot find our feet with them.

IV

Finding our feet, an unnerving business which never more than distantly succeeds, is what ethnographic research consists of as a personal experience; trying to formulate the basis on which one imagines, always excessively, one has found them is what anthropological writing consists of as a scientific endeavor. We are not, or at least I am not, seeking either to become natives (a compromised word in any case) or to mimic them. Only romantics or spies would seem to find point in that. We are seeking, in the widened sense of the term in which it encompasses very much more than talk, to converse with them, a matter a great deal more difficult, and not only with strangers, that is commonly recognized. "If speaking *for* someone else seems to be a mysterious process," Stanley Cavell has remarked, "that may be because speaking *to* someone does not seem mysterious enough."

Looked at in this way, the aim of anthropology is the enlargement of the universe of human discourse. That is not, of course, its only aim—instruction, amusement, practical counsel, moral advance, and the discovery of natural order in human behavior are others; nor is anthropology the only discipline which pursues it. But it is an aim to which a semiotic concept of culture is peculiarly well adapted. As interworked systems of construable **signs** (which, ignoring provisional usages, I would call **symbols**), culture is not a power, something to which social events, behaviors, institutions, or processes can be causally attributed; it is a context, something within which they can be intelligibly—that is, thickly—described.

The famous anthropological absorption with the (to us) exotic—Berber horsemen, Jewish peddlers, French Legionnaires—is, thus, essentially a device for displacing the dulling sense of familiarity with which the mysteriousness of our own ability to relate perceptively to one another is concealed from us. Looking at the ordinary in places where it takes unaccustomed forms brings out not, as has so often been claimed, the arbitrariness of human behavior (there is nothing especially arbitrary about taking sheep theft for insolence in Morocco), but the degree to which its meaning varies according to the pattern of life by which it is informed. Understanding a people's culture exposes their normalness without reducing their particularity. (The more I manage to follow what the Moroccans are up to, the more logical, and the more singular, they seem.) It renders them accessible: setting them in the frame of their own banalities, it dissolves their opacity.

It is this maneuver, usually too casually referred to as "seeing things from the actors point of view," too bookishly as "the *verstehen* approach," or too technically as "emic analysis," that so often leads to the notion that anthropology is a variety of either long-distance mind reading or cannibal-isle fantasizing, and which, for someone anxious to navigate past the wrecks of a dozen sunken philosophies, must therefore be executed with a great deal of care. Nothing is more necessary to comprehending what anthropological interpretation is, and the degree to which it *is* interpretation, than an exact understanding of what it means—and what it does not mean—to say that our formulations of other peoples' symbol systems must be actor-oriented.[1]

What it means is that descriptions of Berber, Jewish, or French culture must be cast in terms of the constructions we imagine Berbers, Jews, or Frenchmen to place upon what they live through, the formulae they use to define what happens to them. What it does not mean is that such descriptions are themselves Berber, Jewish, or French—that is, part of the reality they are ostensibly describing; they are anthropological—that is, part of a developing system of scientific analysis. They must be cast in terms of the interpretations to which persons of a particular denomination subject their experience, because that is what they profess to be descriptions of; they are anthropological because it is, in fact, anthropologists who profess them. Normally, it is not necessary to point out quite so laboriously that the object of study is one thing and the study of it another. It is clear enough that the physical world is not physics, and *A Skeleton Key to Finnegan's Wake* not *Finnegan's Wake*. But, as, in the study of culture, analysis penetrates into the very body of the object—that is, *we begin with our own interpretations of what our informants are up to, or think they are up to, and then systematize those*—the line between (Moroccan) culture as a theoretical entity tends to get blurred. All the more so, as the latter is presented in the form of an actor's-eye description of (Moroccan) conceptions of everything from violence, honor, divinity, and justice, to tribe, property, patronage, and chiefship.

In short, anthropological writings are themselves interpretations, and second and third order ones to boot. (By definition, only a "native" makes first order ones: it's *his* culture.)[2] They are, thus fictions; fictions, in the sense that they are "something made," "something fashioned"—the original meaning of *fictio*—not that they are false, unfactual, or merely "as if" thought experiments. To construct actor-oriented descriptions of the involvements of a Berber chieftain, a Jewish merchant, and a French soldier with one another in 1912 Morocco is clearly and imaginative act, not all that different from constructing similar descriptions of, say, the involvements with one another of a provincial French doctor, his silly, adulterous wife, and her feckless lover in nineteenth century France. In the latter case, the actors are represented as not having existed and the events as not having happened, while in the former they are represented as actual, or as having been so. This is a difference of no mean importance; indeed, precisely the one Madame Bovary had difficulty grasping. But the importance does not lie in the fact that her story was created while Cohen's was only noted. The conditions of their creation, and the point of it (to say nothing of the manner and the quality) differ. But the one is as much a *fictio*—"a making"—as the other.

Anthropologists have not always been as aware as they might be of this fact: that although culture exists in the trading post, the hill fort, or the sheep run, anthropology exists in the book, the article, the lecture, the museum display, or, sometimes nowadays, the film. To become aware of it is to realize that the line between mode of representation and substantive content is as undrawable in cultural analysis as it is in painting; and that fact in turn seems to threaten the objective status of anthropological knowledge by suggesting that its source is not social reality but scholarly artifice.

It does threaten it, but the threat is hollow. The claim to attention of an ethnographic account does not rest on its author's ability to capture primitive facts in faraway places and carry them home like a mask or a carving, but on the degree to which he is able to clarify what goes on in such places, to reduce the puzzlement—what manner of men are these?—to which unfamiliar acts emerging out of unknown backgrounds naturally give rise. This raises some serious problems of verification, all right—or, if "verification" is too strong a word for so soft a science (I, myself, would prefer "appraisal"), of how you can tell a better account from a worse one. But that is precisely the virtue of it. If ethnography is thick description and ethnographers those who are doing the describing, then the determining question for any given example of it, whether a field journal squib or a Malinowski-sized monograph, is whether it sorts winks from twitches and real winks from mimicked ones. It is not against a body of uninterpreted data, radically thinned descriptions, that we must measure the cogency of our explications, but against the power of the scientific imagination to bring us into touch with the lives of strangers. It is not worth it, as Thoreau said, to go round the world to count the cats in Zanzibar.

V

Now, this proposition, that it is not in our interest to bleach human behavior of the very properties that interest us before we begin to examine it, has sometimes been escalated into a larger claim: namely, that as it is only those properties that interest us, we need not attend, save cursorily, to behavior at all. Culture is most effectively treated, the argument goes, purely as a symbolic system (the catch phrase is, "in its own terms"), by isolating its elements, specifying the internal relationships among those elements, and then characterizing the whole system in some general way—according to the core symbols around which it is organized, the underlying structures of which it is a surface expression, or the ideological principles upon which is based. Though a distinct improvement over "learned behavior" and "mental phenomena" notions of what culture is, and the source of some of the most powerful theoretical ideas in contemporary anthropology, this hermetical approach to things seems to me to run the danger (and increasingly to have been overtaken by it) of locking cultural analysis away from its proper object, the informal object of actual life. There is little profit in extricating a concept from the defects of psychologism only to plunge it immediately into those of schematicism.

Behavior must be attended to, and with some exactness, because it is through the flow of behavior—or, more precisely, social action—that cultural forms find articulation. They find it as well, of course, in various sorts of artifacts, and various states of consciousness; but these draw their meaning from the role they play (Wittgenstein would say their "use") in an ongoing pattern of life, not from any intrinsic relationships they bear to one another. It is what Cohen, the sheikh, and "Captain Dumari" were doing when they tripped over one another's purposes—pursuing trade, defending honor, establishing dominance—that created our pastoral drama, and that is what the drama is, therefore, "about." Whatever, or wherever, symbol systems "in their own terms" may be, we gain empirical access to them by inspecting events, not by arranging abstracted entities into unified patterns.

A further implication of this is that coherence cannot be a major test of validity for a cultural description. Cultural systems must have a minimal degree of coherence, else we would not call them systems; and, by observation, they normally have a great deal more. But there is nothing so coherent as a paranoid's delusion or a swindler's story. The force of our interpretations cannot rest, as they are now so often made to do, on the tightness with which they hold together, or the assurance with which they are argued. Nothing has done more, I think, to discredit cultural analysis than the construction of impeccable depictions of formal order in whose actual existence nobody can quite believe.

If anthropological interpretation is constructing a reading of what happens, then to divorce it from what happens—from what, in this time or that place, specific people say, what they do, what is done to them, from the whole vast business of the world—is to divorce it from its applications and render it vacant. A good interpretation of anything—a poem, a person, a history, a ritual, an institution, a society—takes us into the heart of that of which it is an interpretation. When it does not do that, but leads us instead somewhere else—into an admiration of its own elegance, of its author's cleverness, or of the beauties of Euclidean order—it may have its intrinsic charms; but it is something else than what the task at hand—figuring out what all that rigamarole with the sheep is about—calls for.

The rigamarole with the sheep—the sham theft of them, the reparative transfer of them, the political confiscation of them—is (or was) essentially a social discourse, even if, as I suggested earlier, one conducted in multiple tongues and as much in action as in words.

Claiming his *'ar*, Cohen invoked the trade pact; recognizing the claim, the sheikh challenged the offenders' tribe; accepting responsibility, the offenders' tribe paid the indemnity; anxious to make clear to sheikhs and peddlers alike who was now in charge here, the French showed the imperial hand. As in any discourse, code does not determine conduct, and what was actually said need not have been. Cohen might not have, given its illegitimacy in Protectorate eyes, chosen to press his claim. The sheikh might, for similar reasons, have rejected it. The offender's tribe, still resisting French authority, might have decided to regard the raid as "real" and fight rather than negotiate. The French, were they more *habile* and less *dur* (as, under Mareschal Lyautey's seigniorial tutelage, they later in fact became), might have permitted Cohen to keep his sheep, winking—as we say—at the continuance of the trade pattern and its limitation to their authority. And there are other possibilities: the Marshumans might have regarded the French action as too great an insult to bear and gone into dissidence themselves; the French might have attempted not just to clamp down on Cohen but to bring the sheikh himself more closely to heel; and Cohen might have concluded that between renegade Berbers and Beau Geste soldiers, driving trade in the Atlas highlands was no longer worth the candle and retired to the better governed confines of the town. This, indeed, is more or less what happened, somewhat further along, as the Protectorate moved toward genuine sovereignty. But the point here is not to describe what did or did not take place in Morocco. (From this simple incident one can widen out into enormous complexities of social experience.) It is to demonstrate what a piece of anthropological interpretation consists in: tracing the curve of a social discourse; fixing it into an inspectable form.

The ethnographer "inscribes" social discourse; *he writes it down*. In so doing, he turns it from a passing event, which exists only in its own moment of occurrence, into an account, which exists in its transcriptions and can be reconsulted. The sheikh is long dead, killed in the process of being, as the French called it, "pacified"; "Captain Dumari," his pacifier, lives, retired to his souvenirs, in the south of France; and Cohen went last year, part refugee, part pilgrim, part dying patriarch, "home" to Israel. But what they, in my extended sense, "said" to one another on an Atlas plateau sixty years ago is—very far from perfectly—preserved for study. "What," Paul Ricoeur, from whom this whole idea of the inscription of action is borrowed and somewhat twisted, asks, "what does writing fix?"

> Not the event of speaking, but the "said" of speaking, where we understand
> by the "said" of speaking that intentional exteriorization constitutive of the
> aim of discourse thanks to which the *sagen*—the saying—wants to become
> *Aus-sage*—the enunciation, the enunciated. In short, what we write is the
> *noema* ["thought," "content," "gist"] of the speaking. It is the meaning of the
> speech event, not the event as event.

This is not itself so very "said"—if Oxford philosophers run to little stories,
phenomenological ones run to large sentences; but it brings us anyway to a
more precise answer to our generative question, "what does the ethnographer
do?"—he writes.[3] This, too, may seem a less than startling discovery, and to
someone familiar with the current "literature," an implausible one. But as the
standard answer to our question has been, "He observes, he records, he analyses"—a kind of *veni, vidi, vici* conception of the matter—it may have more
deep-going consequences than are at first apparent, not the least of which is
that distinguishing these three phases of knowledge-seeking may not, as a matter of fact, normally be possible; and, indeed, as autonomous "operations" they
may not in fact exist.

The situation is even more delicate, because, as already noted, what we
inscribe (or try to) is not raw social discourse, to which, because, save very
marginally or very specially, we are not actors, we do not have direct access,
but only that small part of it which our informants can lead us into understanding.[4] This is not as fatal as it sounds, for, in fact, not all Cretans are liars,
and it is not necessary to know everything in order to understand something.
But it does make the view of anthropological analysis as the conceptual manipulation of discovered facts, a logical reconstruction of a mere reality, seem
rather lame. To set forth symmetrical crystals of significance, purified of the
material complexity in which they were located, and then attribute their existence to autogenous principles of order, universal properties of the human
mind, or vast, a priori *weltanschauungen*, is to pretend a science that does not
exist and imagine a reality that cannot be found. Cultural analysis is (or should
be) guessing at meanings, assessing the guesses, and drawing explanatory conclusions from the better guesses, not discovering the Continent of Meaning and
mapping out its bodiless landscape.

VI

So, there are three characteristics of ethnographic description: it is interpretive;
what it is interpretive of is the flow of social discourse; and the interpreting
involved consists in trying to rescue the "said" of such discourse from its per-
ishing occasions and fix it in perusable terms. The *kula* is gone or altered; but,
for better or worse, *The Argonauts of the Western Pacific* remains. But there is,

in addition, a fourth characteristic of such description, at least as I practice it: it is microscopic.

This is not to say that there are no large-scale anthropological interpretations of whole societies, civilizations, world events, and so on. Indeed, it is such extension of our analyses to wider contexts that, along with their theoretical implications, recommends them to general attention and justifies our constructing them. No one really cares anymore, not even Cohen (well ... maybe, Cohen), about those sheep as such. History may have its unobtrusive turning points, "great noises in a little room"; but this little go-round was surely not one of them.

It is merely to say that the anthropologist characteristically approaches such broader interpretations and more abstract analyses from the direction of exceedingly extended acquaintances with extremely small matters. He confronts the same grand realities that others—historians, economists, political scientists, sociologists—confront in more fateful settings: Power, Change, Faith, Oppression, Work, Passion, Authority, Beauty, Violence, Love, Prestige; but he confronts them in contexts obscure enough—places like Marmusha and lives like Cohen's—to take the capital letters off them. These all-too-human constancies, "those big words that make us all afraid," take a homely form in such homely contexts. But that is exactly the advantage. There are enough profundities in the world already.

Yet, the problem of how to get a collection of ethnographic miniatures on the order of our sheep story—an assortment of remarks and anecdotes—to wall-sized culturescapes of the nation, the epoch, the continent, or the civilization is not so easily passed over with vague allusions to the virtues of concreteness and the down-to-earth mind. For a science born in Indian tribes, Pacific islands, and African lineages and subsequently seized with grander ambitions, this has come to be a major methodological problem, and for the most part a badly handled one. The models that anthropologists have themselves worked out to justify their moving from local truths to general visions have been, in fact, as responsible for undermining the effort as anything their critics—sociologists obsessed with sample sizes, psychologists with measures, or economists with aggregates—have been able to devise against them.

Of these, the two main ones have been: the Jonesville-is-the-USA "microcosmic" model; and the Easter-Island-is-a-testing-case "natural experiment" model. Either heaven in a grain of sand, or the farther shores of possibility.

The Jonesville-is-America writ small (or America-is-Jonesville writ large) fallacy is so obviously one that the only thing that needs explanation is how people have managed to believe it and expected others to believe it. The notion that one can find the essence of national societies, civilizations, great religions or whatever summed up and simplified in so-called "typical" small towns and villages is palpable nonsense. What one finds in small towns and villages is (alas) small-town or village life. If localized, microscopic studies were really dependant for their greater relevance upon such a premise—that they captured the great world in the little—they wouldn't have any relevance.

But, of course, they are not. The locus of study is not the object of study. Anthropologists don't study villages (tribes, towns, neighborhoods...); they study *in* villages. You can study different things in different places, and some things—for example, what colonial domination does to established frames of moral expectation—you can best study in confined localities. But that doesn't make the place what it is you are studying. In the remoter provinces of Morocco and Indonesia I have wrestled with the same questions other social scientists have wrestled with in more central locations—for example, how comes it that men's most importunate claims to humanity are cast in the accents of group pride?—and with about the same conclusiveness. One can add a dimension—one much needed in the present climate of size-up-and-solve social science; but that is all. There is a certain value, if you are going to run on about the exploitation of the masses in having seen a Javanese sharecropper turning earth in a tropical downpour or a Moroccan tailor embroidering kaftans by the light of a twenty-watt bulb. But the notion that this gives you the thing entire (and elevates you to some moral vantage ground from which you can look down upon the ethically less privileged) is an idea which only someone too long in the bush could possibly entertain.

The "natural laboratory" notion has been equally pernicious, not only because the analogy is false—what kind of laboratory is it where *none* of the parameters are manipulable?—but because it leads to a notion that the data derived from ethnographic studies are purer, or more fundamental, or more solid, or less conditioned (the most favored word is "elementary") than those derived from other sorts of social inquiry. The great natural variation of cultural forms is, of course, not only anthropology's great (and wasting) resource, but the ground of its deepest theoretical dilemma: how is such variation to be squared with the biological unity of the human species? But it is not, even metaphorically, experimental variation, because the context in which it occurs varies along with it, and it is not possible (though there are those who try) to isolate the y's from the x's to write a proper function.

The famous studies purporting to show that the Oedipus complex was backwards in the Trobriands, sex roles were upside down in Tchambuli, and the Pueblo Indians lacked aggression (it is characteristic that they were all negative—"but not in the South"), are, whatever their empirical validity may or may not be, not "scientifically tested and approved" hypotheses. They are interpretations, or misinterpretations, like any others, arrived at in the same way as any others, and as inherently inconclusive as any others, and the attempt to invest them with the authority of physical experimentation is but methodological sleight of hand. Ethnographic findings are not privileged, just particular: another country heard from. To regard them as anything more (*or anything less*) than that distorts both them and their implications, which are far profounder than mere primitivity, for social theory.

Another country heard from: the reason that protracted descriptions of distant sheep raids (and a really good ethnographer would have gone into what kind of sheep they were) have general relevance is that they present the sociological mind with bodied stuff on which to feed. The important thing about the anthropologist's findings is their complex specificness, their circumstantiality. It is with the kind of material produced by long-term, mainly (though not exclusively) qualitative, highly participative, and almost obsessively fine-comb field study in confined contexts that the mega-concepts with which contemporary social science is afflicted—legitimacy, modernization, integration, conflict, charisma, structure, ... meaning—can be given the sort of sensible actuality that makes it possible to think not only realistically and concretely *about* them, but, what is more important, creatively and imaginatively *with* them.

The methodological problem which the microscopic nature of ethnography presents is both real and critical. But it is not to be resolved by regarding a remote locality as the world in a teacup or as the sociological equivalent of a cloud chamber. It is to be resolved—or, anyway, decently kept at bay—by realizing that social actions are comments on more than themselves; that where an interpretation comes from does not determine where it can be impelled to go. Small facts speak to large issues, winks to epistemology, or sheep raids to revolution, because they are made to.

VII

Which brings us, finally, to theory. The besetting sin of interpretive approaches to anything—literature, dreams, symptoms, culture—is that they tend to resist, or to be permitted to resist, conceptual articulation and thus to escape systematic modes of assessment. You either grasp an interpretation or do not, see the point of it or you do not, accept it or you do not. Imprisoned in the immediacy of its own detail, it is presented as self-validating, or, worse, as validated by the supposedly developed sensitivities of the person who presents it; any attempt to cast what it says in terms other than its own is regarded as a travesty—as the anthropologist's severest term of moral abuse, ethnocentric.

For a field of study which, however timidly (although I, myself, am not timid about the matter at all), asserts itself to be a science, this just will not do.

There is no reason why the conceptual structure of a cultural interpretation should be any less formulable, and thus less susceptible to explicit canons of appraisal, than that of, say, a biological observation of a physics experiment— no reason except that the terms in which such formulations can be cast are, if not wholly nonexistent, very nearly so. We are reduced to insinuating theories because we lack the power to state them.

At the same time, it must be admitted that there are a number of characteristics of cultural interpretation which make the theoretical development of it more than usually difficult. The first is the need for theory to stay rather closer to the ground than tends to be the case in sciences more able to give themselves over to imaginative abstraction. Only short flights of ratiocination tend to be effective in anthropology; longer ones tend to drift off into logical dreams, academic bemusements with formal symmetry. The whole point of a semiotic approach to culture is, as I have said, to aid us in gaining access to the conceptual world in which our subjects live so that we can, in some extended sense of the term, converse with them. The tension between the pull of this need to penetrate an unfamiliar universe of symbolic action and the requirements of technical advance in the theory of culture, between the need to grasp and the need to analyze, is, as a result, both necessarily great and essentially irremovable. Indeed, the further theoretical development goes, the deeper the tension gets. This is the first condition for cultural theory: it is not its own master. As it is unseverable from the immediacies thick description presents, its freedom to shape itself in terms of its internal logic is rather limited. What generality it contrives to achieve grows out of the delicacy of its own distinctions, not the sweep of its abstractions.

And from this follows a peculiarity in the way, as a simple matter of empirical fact, our knowledge of culture ... cultures ... a culture ... grows: in spurts. Rather than following a rising curve of cumulative findings, cultural analysis breaks up into a disconnected yet coherent sequence of bolder and bolder sorties. Studies do build on other studies, not in the sense that they take up where the others leave off, but in the sense that, better informed and better conceptualized, they plunge more deeply into the same things. Every serious cultural analysis starts from a sheer beginning and ends where it manages to get before exhausting its intellectual impulse. Previously discovered facts are mobilized, previously developed concepts used, previously formulated hypotheses tried out; but the movement is not from already proven theorems to newly proven ones, it is for an awkward fumbling for the most elementary understanding to a supported claim that one has achieved that and surpassed it. A study is an advance if it is more incisive—whatever that may mean—than those that preceded it; but it less stands on their shoulders than, challenged and challenging, runs by their side.

It is for this reason, among others, that the essay, whether of thirty pages or three hundred, has seemed the natural genre in which to present cultural interpretations and the theories sustaining them, and why, if one looks for systematic treatises in the field, one is so soon disappointed, the more so if one finds any. Even inventory articles are rare here, and anyway of hardly more than bibliographical interest. The major theoretical contributions not only lie in specific studies—that is true in almost any field—but they are very difficult to abstract from such studies and integrate into anything one might call "culture theory" as such. Theoretical formulations hover so low over the interpretations that govern that they don't make much sense or hold much interest apart from them. This is so, not because they are not general (if they are not general, they are not theoretical), but because, stated independently of their applications, they seem either commonplace or vacant. One can, and this in fact is how the field progresses conceptually, take a line of theoretical attack developed in connection with one exercise in ethnographic interpretation and employ it in another, pushing it forward to greater precision and broader relevance; but one cannot write a "General Theory of Cultural Interpretation." Or, rather, one can, but there appears to be little profit in it, because the essential task of theory building here is not to codify abstract regularities but to make thick description possible, not to generalize across cases but to generalize within them.

To generalize within cases is usually called, at least in medicine and depth psychology, clinical inference. Rather than beginning with a set of observations and attempting to subsume them under a governing law, such inference begins with a set of (presumptive) signifiers and attempts to place them within an intelligible frame. Measures are matched to theoretical predictions, but symptoms (even when they are measured) are scanned for theoretical peculiarities—that is, they are diagnosed. In the study of culture the signifiers are not symptoms or clusters of symptoms, but symbolic acts or clusters of symbolic acts, and the aim is not therapy but the analysis of social discourse. But the way in which theory is used—to ferret out the unapparent import of things—is the same.

Thus we are lead to the second condition of cultural theory: it is not, at least in the strict meaning of the term, predictive. The diagnostician doesn't predict measles; he decides that someone has them, or at the very most *anticipates* that someone is rather likely shortly to get them. But this limitation, which is real enough, has commonly been both misunderstood and exaggerated, because it has been taken to mean that cultural interpretation is merely post facto: that, like the peasant in the old story, we first shoot the holes in the fence and then paint the bull's-eyes around them. It is hardly to be denied that there is a good deal of that sort of thing around, some of it in prominent places. It is to be denied, however, that it is the inevitable outcome of a clinical approach to the use of theory.

It is true that in the clinical style of theoretical formulation, conceptualization is directed toward the task of generating interpretations of matters already in hand, not toward projecting outcomes of experimental manipulations or deducing future states of a determined system. But that does not mean that theory has only to fit (or, more carefully, to generate cogent interpretations of) realities past; it has also to survive—intellectually survive—realities to come. Although we formulate our interpretation of an outburst of winking or an instance of sheep-raiding after its occurrence, sometimes long after, the theoretical framework in terms of which such an interpretation is made must be capable of continuing to yield defensible interpretation as new social phenomena swim into view. Although one starts any effort at thick description, beyond the obvious and superficial, from a state of general bewilderment as to what the devil is going on—trying to find one's feet—one does not start (or ought not) intellectually empty-handed. Theoretical ideas are not created wholly anew in each study; as I have said, they are adopted from other, related studies, and, refined in the process, applied to new interpretive problems. If they cease being useful with respect to such problems, they tend to stop being used and are more or less abandoned. If they continue being useful, throwing up new understandings, they are further elaborated and go on being used.[5]

Such a view of how theory functions in an interpretive science suggests that the distinction, relative in any case, that appears in the experimental or observational sciences between "description" and "explanation" appears here as one, even more relative, between "inscription" ("thick description") and "specification" ("diagnosis")—between setting down the meaning particular social actions have for the actors whose actions they are, and stating, as explicitly as we can manage, what the knowledge thus attained demonstrates about the society in which it is found and, beyond that, about social life as such. Our double task is to uncover the conceptual structures that inform our subjects' acts, the "said" of social discourse, and to construct a system of analysis in whose terms what is generic to those structures, what belongs to them because they are what they are, will stand out against the other determinants of human behavior. In ethnography, the office of theory is to provide a vocabulary in which what symbolic action has to say about itself—that is, about the role of culture in human life—can be expressed.

Aside from a couple of orienting pieces concerned with more foundational matters, it is in such a manner that theory operates in the essays collected here. A repertoire of very general, made-in-the-academy concepts and systems of concepts—"integration," "rationalization," "symbol," "ideology," "ethos," "revolution," "identity," "metaphor," "structure," "ritual," "world view," "actor," "function," "sacred," and, of course, "culture" itself—is woven into the body of thick description ethnography in the hope of rendering mere occurrences scientifically eloquent.[6] The aim is to draw large conclusions from small, but very densely textured facts; to support broad assertions about the role of culture in the construction of collective life by engaging them exactly with complex specifics.

Thus it is not only interpretation that goes all the way down to the most immediate observational level: the theory upon which such interpretation conceptually depends does so also. My interest in Cohen's story, like Ryle's in winks, grew out of some very general notions indeed. The "confusion of tongues" model—the view that social conflict is not something that happens when, out of weakness, indefiniteness, obsolescence, or neglect, cultural forms cease to operate, but rather something that happens when, like burlesqued winks, such forms are pressed by unusual situations or unusual intentions to operate in unusual ways—is not an idea I got from Cohen's story. It is one, instructed by colleagues, students, and predecessors, I brought to it.

Our innocent-looking "note in a bottle" is more than a portrayal of the frames of meaning of Jewish peddlers, Berber warriors, and French proconsuls, or even of their mutual interference. It is an argument that to rework the pattern of social relationships is to rearrange the coordinates of the experienced world. Society's forms are culture's substance.

VIII

There is an Indian story—at least I heard it as an Indian story—about an Englishman who, having been told that the world rested on a platform which rested on the back of an elephant which rested in turn on the back of a turtle, asked (perhaps he was an ethnographer; it is the way they behave), what did the turtle rest on? Another turtle? And that turtle? "Ah, Sahib, after that it is turtles all the way down."

Such, indeed, is the condition of things. I do not know how long it would be profitable to meditate on the encounter of Cohen, the sheikh, and "Dumari" (the period has perhaps already been exceeded); but I do know that however long I did so I would not get anywhere near to the bottom of it. Nor have I ever gotten anywhere near to the bottom of anything I have ever written about, either in the essays below or elsewhere. Cultural analysis is intrinsically incomplete. And, worse than that, the more deeply it goes the less complete it is. It is a strange science whose most telling assertions are its most tremulously based, in which to get somewhere with the matter at hand is to intensify the suspicion, both your own and that of others, that you are not quite getting it right. But that, along with plaguing subtle people with obtuse questions, is what being an ethnographer is like.

There are a number of ways to escape this—turning culture into folklore and collecting it, turning it into traits and counting it, turning it into institutions and classifying it, turning it into structures and toying with it. But they *are* escapes.

The fact is that to commit oneself to a semiotic concept of culture and an interpretive approach to the study of it is to commit oneself to a view of ethnographic assertion as, to borrow W.B. Gallie's by now famous phrase, "essentially contestable." Anthropology, or at least interpretive anthropology, is a science whose progress is marked less by a perfection of consensus than by a refinement of debate. What gets better is the precision with which we vex each other.

This is very difficult to see when one's attention is being monopolized by a single party to the argument. Monologues are of little value here, because there are no conclusions to be reported; there is merely a discussion to be sustained. Insofar as the essays here collected have any importance, it is less in what they say than what they are witness to: an enormous increase in interest, not only in anthropology, but in social studies generally, in the role of symbolic forms in human life. Meaning, that elusive and ill-defined pseudoentity we were once more than content to leave philosophers and literary critics to fumble with, has now come back into the heart of our discipline. Even Marxists are quoting Cassirer; even positivists, Kenneth Burke.

My own position in the midst of all this has been to try to resist subjectivism on the one hand and cabbalism on the other, to try to keep the analysis of symbolic forms as closely tied as I could to concrete social events and occasions, the public world of common life, and to organize it in such a way that the connections between theoretical formulations and descriptive interpretations were unobscured by appeals to dark sciences. I have never been impressed by the argument that, as complete objectivity is impossible in these matters (as, of course, it is), one might as well let one's sentiments run loose. As Robert Solow has remarked, that is like saying that as a perfectly aseptic environment is impossible, one might as well conduct surgery in a sewer. Nor, on the other hand, have I been impressed with claims that structural linguistics, computer engineering, or some other advanced form of thought is going to enable us to understand men without knowing them. Nothing will discredit a semiotic approach to culture more quickly than allowing it to drift into a combination of intuitionism and alchemy, no matter how elegantly the intuitions are expressed or how modern the alchemy is made to look.

The danger that cultural analysis, in search of all-too-deep-lying turtles, will lose touch with the hard surfaces of life—with the political, economic, stratificatory realities within which men are everywhere contained—and with the biological and physical necessities on which those surfaces rest, is an ever-present one. The only defense against it, and against, thus, turning cultural analysis into a kind of sociological aestheticism, is to train such analysis on such realities and such necessities in the first place. It is thus that I have written about nationalism, about violence, about identity, about human nature, about legitimacy, about revolution, about ethnicity, about urbanization, about status, about death, about time, and most of all about particular attempts by particular peoples to place these things in some sort of comprehensible, meaningful frame.

To look at the symbolic dimensions of social action—art, religion, ideology, science, law, morality, common sense—is not to turn away from the existential dilemmas of life for some empyrean realm of de-emotionalized forms; it is to plunge into the midst of them. The essential vocation of interpretive anthropology is not to answer our deepest questions, but to make available to us answers that others, guarding other sheep in other valleys, have given, and thus to include them in the consultable record of what man has said.

Notes

1　Not only other peoples': anthropology *can* be trained on the culture of which it is itself a part, and it increasingly is; a fact of profound importance, but which, as it raises a few tricky and rather special second order problems, I shall put to the side for the moment.

2　The order problem is, again, complex. Anthropological works based on other anthropological works (Lévi-Strauss', for example) may, of course, be fourth order or higher, and informants frequently, even habitually, make second order interpretations—what have come to be known as "native models." In literate cultures, where "native" interpretation can proceed to higher levels—in connection with the Maghreb, one has only to think of Ibn Khaldun; with the United States, Margaret Mead—these matters become intricate indeed.

3　Or, again, more exactly, "inscribes." Most ethnography is in fact to be found in books and articles, rather than in films, records, museum displays, or whatever; but even in them there are, of course, photographs, drawings, diagrams, tables, and so on. Self consciousness about modes of representation (not to speak of experiments with them) has been very lacking in anthropology.

4　So far as it has reinforced the anthropologist's impulse to engage himself with his informants as persons rather than as objects, the notion of "participant observation" has been a valuable one. But, to the degree it has lead the anthropologist to block from his view the very special, culturally bracketed nature of his own role and to imagine himself something more than an interested (in both sense of that word) sojourner, it has been our most powerful source of bad faith.

5　Admittedly, this is something of an idealization. Because theories are seldom if ever decisively disproved in clinical use but merely grow increasingly awkward, unproductive, strained, or vacuous, they often persist long after all but a handful of people (though *they* are often most passionate) have lost much interest in them. Indeed, so far as anthropology is concerned, it is almost more of a problem to get exhausted ideas out of the literature than it is to get productive ones in, and so a great deal more of theoretical discussion than one would prefer is critical rather than constructive, and whole careers have been devoted to hastening the demise of moribund notions. As the field advances one would hope that this sort of intellectual weed control would become a less prominent part of our activities. But, for the moment, it remains true that old theories tend less to die than to go into second editions.

6   The overwhelming bulk of the following chapters concern Indonesia rather than Morocco, for have just begun to face up to the demands of my North African material which, for the most part, was gathered more recently. Field work in Indonesia was carried out in 1952-1954, 1957-1958, and 1971; in Morocco in 1964, 1965-1966, 1968-1969, and 1972.

Study Questions

1.   What is meant by the term "thick description?"

2.   What, in Geertz's view, is the role of symbolism in ethnography?

3.   How and why is meaning "public" in Geertz's theory?

Further Readings

Geertz, Clifford. 1963. *Agricultural Involution*. Berkeley: University of California Press.

—. 1968. *Islam Observed*. Chicago: University of Chicago Press.

—. 1973. *The Interpretation of Cultures*. New York: Basic Books.

—. 1983. *Local Knowledge*. New York: Basic Books.

—. 1984. Anti-Anti-Relativism. *American Anthropologist* 86,2: 263-77.

—. 1996. *After the Fact: Two Countries, Four Decades, One Anthropologist*. Cambridge, MA: Harvard University Press.

Schneider, David. 1980 [1968]. *American Kinship: A Cultural Account*. Chicago: University of Chicago Press.

22

Symbols in Ndembu Ritual[1]

VICTOR TURNER

Among the Ndembu of Zambia (formerly Northern Rhodesia), the importance of **ritual** in the lives of the villagers in 1952 was striking. Hardly a week passed in a small neighborhood, without a ritual drum being heard in one or another of its villages.

By "ritual" I mean prescribed formal behavior for occasions not given over to technological routine, having reference to beliefs in mystical beings or powers. The symbol is the smallest unit of ritual which still retains the specific properties of ritual behavior, it is the ultimate unit of specific structure in a ritual context. Since this essay is in the main a description and analysis of the structure and properties of **symbols**, it will be enough to state here, following the *Concise Oxford Dictionary*, that a "symbol" is a thing regarded by general consent as naturally typifying or representing or recalling something by possession of analogous qualities or by association in fact or thought. The symbols I observed in the field were, empirically, objects, activities, relationships, events, gestures, and spatial units in a ritual situation.

Following the advice and example of Professor Monica Wilson, I asked Ndembu specialists as well as laymen to interpret the symbols of their ritual. As a result, I obtained much exegetic material. I felt that it was methodologically important to keep observational and interpretative materials distinct from one another. The reason for this will soon become apparent.

I found that I could not analyze ritual symbols without studying them in a time series in relation to other "events," for symbols are essentially involved in social process. I came to see performances of ritual as distinct phases in the social processes whereby groups became adjusted to internal changes and adapted to their external environment. From this standpoint the ritual symbol becomes a factor in social action, a positive force in an activity field. The symbol becomes associated with human interests, purposes, ends, and means, whether these are explicitly formulated or have to be inferred from the observed behavior. The structure and properties of a symbol become those of a dynamic entity, at least within its appropriate context of action.

Structure and Properties of Ritual Symbols

The structure and properties of ritual symbols may be inferred from three classes of data: (1) external form and observable characteristics; (2) interpretations offered by specialists and by laymen; (3) significant contexts largely worked out by the anthropologist.

Here is an example. At *Nkang'a*, the girl's puberty ritual, a novice is wrapped in a blanket and laid at the foot of a *mudyi* sapling. The *mudyi* tree *Diplorrhyncus condylocarpon* is conspicuous for its white latex, which exudes in milky beads if the thin bark is scratched. For Ndembu this is its most important observable characteristic, and therefore I propose to call it "the milk tree" henceforward. Most Ndembu women can attribute several meanings to this tree. In the first place, they say that the milk tree is the "senior" (*mukulumpi*) tree of the ritual. Each kind of ritual has this "senior" or, as I will call it, "dominant" symbol. Such symbols fall into a special class which I will discuss more fully later. Here it is enough to state that dominant symbols are regarded not merely as means to the fulfillment of the avowed purposes of a given ritual, but also and more importantly refer to values that are regarded as ends in themselves, that is, to axiomatic values. Secondly, the women say with reference to its observable characteristics that the milk tree stands for human breast milk and also for the breasts that supply it. They relate this meaning to the fact that *Nkang'a* is performed when a girl's breasts begin to ripen, not after her first menstruation, which is the subject of another and less elaborate ritual. The main theme of *Nkang'a* is indeed the tie of nurturing between mother and child, not the bond of birth. This theme of nurturing is expressed at *Nkang'a* in a number of supplementary symbols indicative of the act of feeding and of foodstuff. In the third place, the women describe the milk tree as "the tree of a mother and her child." Here the reference has shifted from description of a biological act, breast feeding, to a social tie of profound significance both in domestic relations and in the structure of the widest Ndembu community. This latter meaning is brought out most clearly in a text I recorded from a male ritual specialist. I translate literally.

> The milk tree is the place of all mothers of the lineage (*ivumu*, literally "womb" or "stomach"). It represents the ancestress of women and men. The milk tree is where our ancestress slept when she was initiated. "To initiate" here means the dancing of women round and round the milk tree where the novice sleeps. One ancestress after another slept there down to our grand-

mother and our mother and ourselves the children. That is the place of our tribal custom (*muchidi*),[2] where we began, even men just the same, for men are circumcised under a milk tree.

This text brings out clearly those meanings of the milk tree which refer to principles and values of social organization. At one level of abstraction the milk tree stands for matriliny, the principle on which the continuity of Ndembu society depends. Matriliny governs succession to office and inheritance of property, and it vests dominant rights of residence in local units. More than any other principle of social organization it confers order and structure on Ndembu social life. Beyond this, however, *"mudyi"* means more than matriliny, both according to this text and according to many other statements I have collected. It stands for tribal custom (*muchidi wetu*) itself. The principle of matriliny, the backbone of Ndembu social organization, as an element in the semantic structure of the milk tree, itself symbolizes the total system of interrelations between groups and persons that makes up Ndembu society. Some of the meanings of important symbols may themselves be symbols, each with its own system of meanings. At its highest level of abstraction, therefore, the milk tree stands for the unity and continuity of Ndembu society. Both men and women are components of that spatiotemporal continuum. Perhaps that is why one educated Ndembu, trying to cross the gap between our cultures, explained to me that the milk tree was like the British flag above the administrative headquarters. *"Mudyi* is our flag," he said.

When discussing the milk tree symbolism in the context of the girls' puberty ritual, informants tend to stress the harmonizing, cohesive aspects of the milk tree symbolism. They also stress the aspect of dependence. The child depends on its mother for nutriment; similarly, say the Ndembu, the tribesman drinks from the breasts of tribal custom. Thus nourishment and learning are equated in the meaning content of the milk tree. I have often heard the milk tree compared to "going to school"; the child is said to swallow instruction as a baby swallows milk and *kapudyi*, the thin cassava gruel Ndembu liken to milk. Do we not ourselves speak of "a thirst for knowledge"? Here the milk tree is a shorthand for the process of instruction in tribal matters that follows the critical episode in both boys' and girls' initiation—circumcision in the case of the boys and the long trial of lying motionless in that of the girls. The mother's role is the archetype of protector, nourisher, and teacher. For example, a chief is often referred to as the "mother of his people," while the hunter-doctor who initiates a novice into a hunting cult is called "the mother of huntsmanship (*mama dawuyang'a)*." An apprentice circumciser is referred to as "child of the circumcision medicine." In all the senses hitherto described, the milk tree represents harmonious, benevolent aspects of domestic and tribal life.

However, when the third mode of interpretation, contextual analysis, is applied, the interpretations of informants are contradicted by the way people actually behave with reference to the milk tree. It becomes clear that the milk represents aspects of social differentiation and even opposition between the components of a society which ideally it is supposed to symbolize as a harmonious whole. The first relevant context we shall examine is the role of the milk tree in a series of action situations within the framework of the girls' puberty ritual. Symbols, as I have said, produce action, and dominant symbols tend to become focuses in interaction. Groups mobilize around them, worship before them, perform other symbolic activities near them, and add other symbolic objects to them, often to make composite shrines. Usually these groups of participants themselves stand for important components of the secular social system, whether these components consist of corporate groups, such as families and lineages, or of mere categories of persons possessing similar characteristics, such as old men, women, children, hunters, or widows. In each kind of Ndembu ritual a different group or category becomes the focal social element. In *Nkang'a* this focal element is the unity of Ndembu women. It is the women who dance around the milk tree and initiate the recumbent novice by making her the hub of their whirling circle. Not only is the milk tree the "flag of the Ndembu"; more specifically, in the early phases of *Nkang'a*, it is the "flag" of Ndembu women. In this situation it does more than focus the exclusiveness of women; it mobilizes them in opposition to the men. For the women sing songs taunting the men and for a time will not let men dance in their circle. Therefore, if we are to take account of the operational aspect of the milk tree symbol, including not only what Ndembu say about it but also what they do with it in its "meaning," we must allow that it distinguishes women as a social category and indicates their solidarity.

The milk tree makes further discriminations. For example, in certain action contexts it stands for the novice herself. One such context is the initial sacralization of a specific milk tree sapling. Here the natural property of the tree's immaturity is significant. Informants say that a young tree is chosen because the novice is young. A girl's particular tree symbolizes her new social personality as a mature woman. In the past and occasionally today, the girl's puberty ritual was part of her marriage ritual, and marriage marked her transition from girlhood to womanhood. Much of the training and most of the symbolism of *Nkang'a* are concerned with making the girl a sexually accomplished spouse, a fruitful woman, and a mother able to produce a generous supply of milk. For each girl this is a unique process. She is initiated alone and is the center of public attention and care. From her point of view it is *her Nkang'a*, the most thrilling and self-gratifying phase of her life. Society recognizes and encourages these sentiments, even though it also prescribes certain trials and hardships for the novice, who must suffer before she is glorified on the last day of the ritual. The milk tree, then, celebrates the coming-of-age of a new social personality, and distinguishes her from all other women at this one moment in her life. In terms of its action context, the milk tree here also expresses the conflict between the girl and the moral community of adult women she is entering. Not without reason is the milk tree site known as "the place of death" or "the place of suffering," terms also applied to the site where boys are circumcised, for the girl novice must not move a muscle throughout a whole hot and clamant day.

In other contexts, the milk tree site is the scene of opposition between the novice's own mother and the group of adult women. The mother is debarred from attending the ring of dancers. She is losing her child, although later she recovers her as an adult co-member of her lineage. Here we see the conflict between the matricentric family and the wider society which, as I have said is dominantly articulated by the principle of matriliny. The relationship between mother and daughter persists throughout the ritual, but its context is changed. It is worth pointing out that, at one phase in *Nkang'a*, mother and daughter interchange portions of clothing. This may perhaps be related to the Ndembu custom whereby mourners wear small portions of a dead relative's clothing. Whatever the interchange of clothing may mean to a psychoanalyst—and here we arrive at one of the limits of our present anthropological competence—it seems not unlikely that Ndembu intend to symbolize the termination for both mother and daughter of an important aspect of their relationship. This is one of the symbolic actions—one of very few—about which I found it impossible to elicit any interpretation in the puberty ritual. Hence it is legitimate to infer, in my opinion, that powerful unconscious wishes, of a kind considered illicit by Ndembu, are expressed in it.

Opposition between the tribeswomen and the novice's mother is mimetically represented at the milk tree towards the end of the first day of the puberty ritual. The girl's mother cooks a huge meal of cassava and beans—both kinds of food are symbols in *Nkang'a*, with many meanings—for the women visitors, who eat in village groups and not at random. Before eating, the women return to the milk tree from their eating place a few yards away and circle the tree in procession. The mother brings up the rear holding up a large spoon full of cassava and beans. Suddenly she shouts: "Who wants the cassava of *chipwampwilu*?" All the women rush to be first to seize the spoon and eat from it. "*Chipwampwilu*" appears to be an archaic word and no one knows its meaning. Informants say that the spoon represents the novice herself in her role of married woman, while the food stands both for her reproductive power (*lusemu*) and her role as cultivator and cook. One woman told my wife: "It is lucky if the person snatching the spoon comes from the novice's own village. Otherwise, the mother believes that her child will go far away from her to a distant village and die there. The mother wants her child to stay near her." Implicit in this statement is a deeper conflict than that between the matricentric family and mature female society. It refers to another dominant articulating principle of Ndembu society, namely virilocal marriage according to which women live at their husbands' villages after marriage. Its effect is sometimes to separate mothers from daughters by considerable distances. In the episode described, the women symbolize the matrilineal cores of villages. Each village wishes to gain control through marriage over the novice's capacity to work. Its members also hope that her children will be raised in it, thus adding to its size and prestige. Later in *Nkang'a* there is a symbolic struggle between the novice's matrilineal kin and those of her bridegroom, which makes explicit the conflict between virilocality and matriliny.

Lastly, in the context of action situation, the milk tree is sometimes described by informants as representing the novice's own matrilineage. Indeed, it has this significance in the competition for the spoon just discussed, for women of her own village try to snatch the spoon before members of other villages. Even if such women do not belong to her matrilineage but are married to its male members, they are thought to be acting on its behalf. Thus, the milk tree in one of its action aspects represents the unity and exclusiveness of a single matrilineage with a local focus in a village against other such corporate groups. The conflict between yet another subsystem and the total system is given dramatic and symbolic form.

By this time, it will have become clear that considerable discrepancy exists between the interpretations of the milk tree offered by informants and the behavior exhibited by Ndembu in situations dominated by the milk tree symbolism. Thus, we are told that the milk tree represents the close tie between mother and daughter. Yet the milk tree separates a daughter from her mother. We are also told that the milk tree stands for the unity of Ndembu society. Yet we find that in practice it separates women from men, and some categories and groups of women from others. How are these contradictions between principle and practice to be explained?

Some Problems of Interpretation

I am convinced that my informants genuinely believed that the milk tree represented only the linking and unifying aspects of Ndembu social organization. I am equally convinced that the role of the milk tree in action situations, where it represents a focus of specified groups in opposition to other groups, forms an equally important component of its total meaning. Here the important question must be asked, "meaning for whom?" For if Ndembu do not recognize the discrepancy between their interpretation of the milk tree symbolism and their behavior in connection with it, does this mean that the discrepancy has no relevance for the social anthropologist? Indeed, some anthropologists claim, with Nadel (1954, 108), that "uncomprehended symbols have no part in social enquiry; their social effectiveness lies in their capacity to indicate, and if they indicate nothing to the actors, they are, from our point of view, irrelevant, and indeed no longer symbols (whatever their significance for the psychologist or psychoanalyst)." Professor Monica Wilson (1957, 6) holds a similar point of view. She writes that she stresses "Nyakyusa interpretations of their own rituals, for anthropological literature in bespattered with symbolic guessing, the ethnographer's interpretations of the rituals of other people." Indeed, she goes so far as to base her whole analysis of Nyakyusa ritual on "the Nyakyusa translation or interpretation of the symbolism." In my view, these investigators go beyond the limits of salutary caution and impose serious, and even arbitrary, limitations on themselves. To some extent, their difficulties derive from their failure to distinguish the concept of symbol from that of a mere sign. Although I am in complete disagreement with his fundamental postulate that the collective unconscious is the main formative principle in ritual symbolism, I consider that Carl Jung (1949, 601) has cleared the way for further investigation by making just this distinction. "A sign," he says, "is an analogous or abbreviated expression of a *known* thing. But a symbol is always the best possible expression of a relatively *unknown* fact, a fact, however, which is none the less recognized or postulated as existing." Nadel and Wilson, in treating most ritual symbols as signs, must ignore or regard as irrelevant some of the crucial properties of such symbols.

Field Setting and Structural Perspective

How, then can a social anthropologist justify his claim to be able to interpret a society's ritual symbols more deeply and comprehensively than the actors themselves? In the first place, the anthropologist, by the use of his special techniques and concepts, is able to view the performance of a given kind of ritual as "occurring in, and being interpenetrated by, a totality of coexisting social entities such as various kinds of groups, sub-groups, categories, or personalities, and also barriers between them, and modes of interconnexion" (Lewin 1949, 200). In other words, he can place this ritual in its significant field setting and describe the structure and properties of that field. On the other hand, each participant in the ritual views it from his own particular corner of observation. He has what Lupton has called his own "structural perspective." His vision is circumscribed by his occupancy of a particular position, or even of a set of situationally conflicting positions, both in the persisting structure of his society, and also in the role structure of the given ritual. Moreover, the participant is likely to be governed in his actions by a number of interests, purposes, and sentiments, dependent upon his specific position, which impair his understanding of the total situation. An even more serious obstacle against his achieving objectivity is the fact that he tends to regard as axiomatic and primary the ideals, values, and norms that are overtly expressed or symbolized in the ritual. Thus, in the *Nkang'a* ritual, each person or group in successive contexts of action, sees the milk tree only as representing her or their own specific interests and values at those times. However, the anthropologist who has previously made a structural analysis of Ndembu society, isolating its organizational principles, and distinguishing its groups and relationships, has no particular bias and can observe the real interconnection and conflicts between groups and persons, in so far as these receive ritual representation. What is meaningless for an actor playing a specific role may well be highly significant for an observer and analyst of the total system.

One these grounds, therefore, I consider it legitimate to include within the total meaning of a dominant ritual symbol, aspects of behavior associated with it which the actors themselves are unable to interpret, and indeed of which they may be unaware, if they are asked to interpret the symbol outside its activity context. Nevertheless, there still remains for us the problem of the contradiction between the expressed meanings of the milk tree symbol and the meaning of the stereotyped forms of behavior closely associated with it. Indigenous interpretations of the milk tree symbolism in the abstract appear to indicate that there is no incompatibility or conflict between the persons and groups to which it refers. Yet, as we have seen, it is between just such groups that conflict is mimed at the milk tree site.

Three Properties of Ritual Symbols

Before we can interpret, we must further classify our descriptive data, collected by the methods described above. Such a classification will enable us to state some of the properties of ritual symbols. The simplest property is that of *condensation*. Many things and actions are represented in a single formation. Secondly, a dominant symbol is a *unification of disparate significata*. The disparate *significata* are interconnected by virtue of their common possession of analogous qualities or by association in fact or thought. Such qualities or links of association may in themselves be quite trivial or random or widely distributed over a range of phenomena. Their very generality enables them to bracket together the most diverse ideas and phenomena. Thus, as we have seen, the milk tree stands for, *inter alia*, women's breasts, motherhood, a novice at *Nkang'a*, the principle of matriliny, a specific matrilineage, learning, and the unity and persistence of Ndembu society. The themes of nourishment and dependence run through all these diverse *significata*.

The third important property of dominant ritual symbols is *polarization of meaning*. Not only the milk tree but all other dominant Ndembu symbols possess two clearly distinguishable poles of meaning. At one pole is found a cluster of *significata* that refer to components of the moral and social orders of Ndembu society, to principles of social organization, to kinds of corporate grouping, and to the norms and values inherent in structural relationships. At the other pole, the *significata* are usually natural and physiological phenomena and processes. Let us call the first of these the "ideological pole," and the second the "sensory pole." At the sensory pole, the meaning content is closely related to the outward form of the symbol. Thus one meaning of the milk tree —breast milk—is closely related to the exudation of milky latex from the tree. One sensory meaning of another dominant symbol, the *mukula* tree, is blood; this tree secretes a dusky red gum.

At the sensory pole are concentrated those *significata* that may be expected to arouse desires and feelings; at the ideological pole one finds an arrangement of norms and values that guide and control persons as members of social groups and categories. The sensory, emotional *significata* tend to be "gross" in a double sense. In the first place, they are gross in a general way, taking no account of detail or the precise qualities of emotion. It cannot be sufficiently stressed that such symbols are social facts, "collective representations," even though their appeal is to the lowest common denominator or human feeling. The second sense of "gross" is "frankly, even flagrantly, physiological." Thus, the milk tree has the gross meanings of breast milk, breasts, and the process of breast feeding. These are also gross in the sense that they represent items of universal Ndembu experience. Other Ndembu symbols, at their sensory poles of meaning, represent such themes as blood, male and female genitalia, semen, urine, and feces. The same symbols, at their ideological poles of meaning, represent the unity and continuity of social groups, primary and associational, domestic, and political.

Reference and Condensation

It has long been recognized in anthropological literature that ritual symbols are stimuli of emotion. Perhaps the most striking statement of this position is that made by Edward Sapir in the *Encyclopaedia of the Social Sciences* (XIV, 492-493). Sapir distinguishes, in a way which recalls Jung's distinction, between two principal classes of symbols. The first he calls "referential" symbols. These include such forms as oral speech, writing, national flags, flag signaling, and other organizations of symbols which are agreed upon as economical devices for purposes of reference. Like Jung's "sign," the referential symbol is predominantly cognitive and refers to known facts. The second class, which includes most ritual symbols, consist of "condensation" symbols, which Sapir defines as "highly condensed forms of substitutive behavior for direct expression, allowing for the ready release of emotional tension in conscious or unconscious form." The condensation symbol is "saturated with emotional quality." The chief difference in development between these types of symbolism, in Sapir's view, is that "while referential symbolism grows with formal elaboration in the conscious, condensation symbolism strikes deeper and deeper roots in the unconscious, and diffuses its emotional quality to types of behavior and situations apparently far removed from the original meaning of the symbol."

Sapir's formulation is most illuminating. He lays explicit stress on four main attributes of ritual symbols: (1) the condensation of many meanings in a single form; (2) economy of reference; (3) predominance of emotional or orectic quality; (4) associational linkages with regions of the unconscious. Nevertheless, he tends to underestimate the importance of what I have called the ideological (or, I would add, normative) pole of meaning. Ritual symbols are at one and the same time referential and condensation symbols, though each symbol is multireferential rather than unireferential. Their essential quality consists in their juxtaposition of the grossly physical and the structurally normative, of the organic and the social. Such symbols are coincidences of opposite qualities, unions of "high" and "low." We do not need a detailed acquaintance with any of the current depth psychologies to suspect that this juxtaposition, and even interpenetration, of opposites in the symbol is connected with its social function. Durkheim was fascinated by the problem of why many social norms and imperatives were felt to be at the same time "obligatory" and "desirable." Ritual, scholars are coming to see, is precisely a mechanism that periodically converts the obligatory into the desirable. The basic unit of ritual, the dominant symbol, encapsulates the major properties of the total ritual process which brings about this transmutation. Within its framework of meanings, the dominant symbol brings the ethical and jural norms of society into close contact with strong emotional stimuli. In the action situation of ritual, with its social excitement and directly physiological stimuli, such as music, singing, dancing, alcohol, incense, and bizarre modes of dress, the ritual symbol, we may perhaps say, effects an interchange of qualities between its poles of meaning. Norms and values, on the one hand, become saturated with emotion, while the gross and basic emotions become ennobled through contact with social values. The irksomeness of moral constraint is transformed into the "love of virtue."

Before proceeding any further with our analysis, it might be as well to restate the major empirical properties of dominant symbols derived from our classification of the relevant descriptive data: (1) condensation; (2) unification of disparate meanings in a single symbolic formation; (3) polarization of meaning.

Dominant and Instrumental Symbols

Certain ritual symbols, as I have said, are regarded by Ndembu as dominant. In rituals performed to propitiate ancestor spirits who are believed to have afflicted their living kin with reproductive disorders, illness, or bad luck at hunting, there are two main classes of dominant symbols. The first class is represented by the first tree or plant in a series of trees or plants from which portions of leaves, bark, or roots are collected by practitioners or adepts in the curative cult. The subjects of ritual are marked with these portions mixed with water, or given them, mixed in a potion, to drink. The first tree so treated is called the "place of greeting" (*ishikenu*), or the "elder" (*mukulumpi*). The adepts encircle it several times to sacralize it. Then the senior practitioner prays at its base, which he sprinkles with powdered white clay. Prayer is made either to the named spirit, believed to be afflicting the principal subject of ritual, or to the tree itself, which is in some way identified with the afflicting spirit. Each *ishikenu* can be allotted several meanings by adepts. The second class of dominant symbols in curative rituals consists of shrines where the subjects of such rituals sit while the practitioners wash them with vegetable substances mixed with water and perform actions on their behalf of a symbolic or ritualistic nature. Such shrines are often composite, consisting of several objects in configuration. Both classes of dominant symbols are closely associated with nonempirical beings. Some are regarded as their repositories; others, as being identified with them; others again, as representing them. In life-crisis rituals, on the other hand, dominant symbols seem to represent not beings but nonempirical powers or kinds of efficacy. For example, in the boys' circumcision ritual, the dominant symbol for the whole ritual is a "medicine" (*yitumbu*), called "*nfunda*," which is compounded from many ingredients, e.g., the ash of the burnt lodge which means "death," and the urine of an apprentice circumciser which means "virility." Each of these and other ingredients have many other meanings. The dominant symbol at the camp where the novices' parents assemble and prepare food for the boys is the *chikoli* tree, which represents, among other things, an erect phallus, adult masculinity, strength, hunting prowess, and health continuing into old age. The dominant symbol during the process of circumcision is the milk tree, beneath which novices are circumcised. The dominant symbol in the immediate post-circumcision phase is the red *mukula* tree, on which the novices sit until their wounds stop bleeding. Other symbols are dominant at various phases of seclusion. Each of these symbols is described as "*mukulumpi*" (elder, senior). Dominant symbols appear in many different ritual contexts, sometimes presiding over the whole procedure, sometimes over particular phases. The meaning-context of certain dominant symbols possesses a high degree of constancy and consistency throughout the total symbolic system, exemplifying Radcliffe-Brown's proposition that a symbol recurring in a cycle of rituals is likely to have the same significance in each. Such symbols also possess considerable autonomy with regard to the aims of the rituals in which they appear. Precisely because of these properties, dominant symbols are readily analyzable in a cultural framework of reference. They may be regarded for this purpose as what Whitehead would have called "eternal objects."[3] They are the relatively fixed points in both the social and cultural structures, and indeed constitute points of junction between these two kinds of structure. They may be regarded irrespective of their order of appearance in a given ritual as ends in themselves, as representative of the axiomatic values of the widest Ndembu society. This does not mean that they cannot also be studied, as we have indeed studied them, as factors of social action, in an action frame of reference, but their social properties make them more appropriate objects of morphological study than the class of symbols we will now consider.

These symbols may be termed "instrumental symbols." An instrumental symbol must be seen in terms of its wider context, i.e., in terms of the total system of symbols which makes up a given kind of ritual. Each kind of ritual has its specific mode of interrelating symbols. This mode is often dependent upon the ostensible purposes of that kind of ritual. In other words, each ritual has its own teleology. It has its explicitly expressed goals, and instrumental symbols may be regarded as means of attaining those goals. For example, in rituals performed for the overt purpose of making women fruitful, among the instrumental symbols used are portions of fruit-bearing trees or of trees that possess innumerable rootlets. These fruits and rootlets are said by Ndembu to represent children. They are also thought of as having efficacy to make the woman fruitful. They are means to the main end of the ritual. Perhaps such symbols could be regarded as mere signs or referential symbols, were it not for the fact that the meanings of each are associated with powerful conscious and unconscious emotions and wishes. At the psychological level of analysis, I suspect that these symbols too would approximate to the condition of condensation symbols, but here we touch upon the present limits of competence of anthropological explanation, a problem we will now discuss more fully.

The Limits of Anthropological Interpretation

We now come to the most difficult aspect of the scientific study of ritual symbolism: analysis. How far can we interpret these enigmatic formations by the use of anthropological concepts? At what points to we reach the frontiers of our explanatory competence? Let us first consider the case of dominant symbols. I have suggested that these have two poles of meaning, a sensory and an ideological pole. I have also suggested that dominant symbols have the property of unifying disparate *significata*. I would go so far as to say that at both poles of meaning are clustered disparate and even contradictory *significata*. In the course of its historical development, anthropology has acquired techniques and concepts that enable it to handle fairly adequately the kind of data we have classified as falling around the ideological pole. Such data, as we have seen, include components of social structure and cultural phenomena, both ideological and technological. I believe that study of these data in terms of the concepts and three major subdivisions of anthropology—cultural anthropology, structuralist theory, and social dynamics—would be extremely rewarding. I shall shortly outline how I think such analyses might be done and how the three frameworks might be interrelated, but first we must ask how far and in what respects is it relevant to submit the sensory pole of meaning to intensive analysis, and, more importantly, how far are we, as anthropologists, qualified to do so? It is evident, as Sapir has stated, that ritual symbols, like all condensation symbols, "strike deeper and deeper roots in the unconscious." Even a brief acquaintance with depth psychology is enough to show the investigator that ritual symbols, with regard to their outward form, to their behavioral context, and to several of the indigenous interpretations set upon them, are partially shaped under the influence of unconscious motivations and ideas. The interchange of clothes between mother and daughter at the *Nkang'a* ritual; the belief that a novice would go mad if she saw the milk tree on the day of her separation ritual; the belief that if a novice lifts up the blanket with which she is covered during seclusion and sees her village her mother would die; all these are items of symbolic behavior for which the Ndembu themselves can give no satisfactory interpretation. For these beliefs suggest an element of mutual hostility in the mother-daughter relationship which runs counter to orthodox interpretations of the milk tree symbolism, in so far as it refers to the mother-daughter relationship. One of the main characteristics of ideological interpretations is that they tend to stress the harmonious and cohesive aspect of social relationships. The exegetic idiom feigns that persons and groups always act in accordance with the ideal norms of Ndembu society.

Depth Psychology and Ritual Symbolism
When psychoanalysts like Theodore Reik, Ernest Jones, or Bruno Bettelheim analyze the ritual symbolism of primitive and ancient society, they tend to regard as irrelevant the ideological pole of meaning and to focus their attention on the outward form and sensory meanings of the symbols. They regard most indigenous interpretations of symbols, which form the main component of the ideological pole, almost as though they were identical with the rationalizations by which neurotics explain and justify their aberrant behavior. Furthermore, they tend to look upon ritual symbols as identical with neurotic and psychotic symptoms or as though they had the same properties as the dream symbols of Western European individuals. In effect, their procedure is the exact reverse of that of the social

anthropologists who share the views of Nadel and Wilson. This school of anthropologists, it will be remembered, considers that only conscious, verbalized, indigenous interpretations of symbols are sociologically relevant. The method of the psychoanalysts, on the other hand, is to examine the form, content, and mode of interconnection of the symbolic acts and objects described by ethnographers, and to interpret these by means of concepts formulated in Western European clinical practice. Such psychoanalysts claim to recognize, in the structure and action context of ritual symbols material derived from what they consider to be the universal experiences of human infancy in the family situation. For example, Fenichel (1946, 302) states that two contrary psychic tendencies exist universally in the father-son relationship, namely submission and rebellion, and that both derive from the Oedipus complex. He then goes on to argue that

> since most patriarchal religions also veer between submission to a paternal figure, and rebellion (both submission and rebellion being sexualised), and every god, like a compulsive super-ego, promises protection on condition of submission, there are many similarities in the manifest picture of compulsive ceremonials and religious rituals, due to the similarity of the underlying conflicts.

As against this point of view, we have already shown how the successive symbolic acts of many Ndembu rituals are given order and structure by the explicitly stated purposes of those rituals. We do not need to invoke the nation of underlying conflicts to account for their conspicuous regularity. Psychoanalysts might argue that in patriarchal societies ritual might exhibit a greater rigidity and compulsive quality than among the Ndembu, who are matrilineal. In other words, the formal pattern might be "over-determined" by the unconscious father-son conflict. Ethnographic comparison would seem to refute this view, for the most rigid formalism known to students of comparative religion is found among the Pueblo Indians, who are more strongly matrilineal than the Ndembu, while the Nigerian Nupe, a strongly patrilineal society, possess rituals with a "fluid" and "not over-strict" form (Nadel 1954, 101).[4]

Other psychoanalysts profess to find in symbolic forms traces of orally aggressive, orally dependent, anal-sadistic, and masochistic ideas and drives. Indeed, several anthropologists, after reading psychoanalytical literature, have been tempted to explain ritual phenomena in this way.

Perhaps the most spectacular recent attempt to make a comprehensive interpretation of ritual symbolism by using psychoanalytical concepts is Bruno Bettelheim's book *Symbolic Wounds*. Bettelheim, after observing the behavior of four schizoid adolescent children who formed a secret society, considered that in this behavior lay the clue to an understanding of many features of primitive initiation ritual. From his schizoids, he inferred that one of the (unconscious) purposes of male initiation rites may be to assert that men too can bear children and that "through such operations as subincision men may try to acquire sexual apparatus and functions equal to women's" (1954, 105-123). Womb-envy and an unconscious infantile identification with the mother, in Bettelheim's opinion, were powerful formative factors, both in the *ad hoc* ritual of his four schizoids and in male circumcision rituals all over the world.

Bettelheim's viewpoint is in important respects opposed to that of many orthodox Freudians, who hold that the symbolic events comprising these rituals result principally from the fathers' jealousy of their sons and that their purpose is to create sexual (castration) anxiety and to make the incest taboo secure. Where psychoanalysts disagree, by what criterion can the hapless social anthropologist judge between their interpretations, in a field of inquiry in which he has neither received systematic training nor obtained thorough practical experience?

Provinces of Explanation

I consider that if we conceptualize a dominant symbol as having two poles of meaning, we can more exactly demarcate the limits within which anthropological analysis may be fruitfully applied. Psychoanalysts, in treating most indigenous interpretations of symbols as irrelevant, are guilty of a naïve and one-sided approach. For those interpretations that show how a dominant symbol expresses important components of the social and moral orders are by no means equivalent to the "rationalizations," and the "secondary elaborations" of material deriving from endopsychic conflicts. They refer to social facts that have an empirical reality exterior to the psyches of individuals. On the other hand, those anthropologists who regard only indigenous interpretations as relevant, are being equally one-sided. This is because they tend to examine symbols within two analytical frameworks only, the cultural and the structural. This approach is essentially a static one, and it does not deal with processes involving temporal changes in social relations.

Nevertheless, the crucial properties of a ritual symbol involve these dynamic developments. Symbols instigate social action. In a field context they may even be described as "forces," in that they are determinable influences inclining persons and groups to action. It is in a field context, moreover, that the properties we have described, namely polarization of meanings, transference of affectual quality, discrepancy between meanings, and condensation of meanings, become most significant. The symbol as a unit of action, possessing these properties, becomes an object of study both for anthropology and for psychology. Both disciplines, in so far as they are concerned with human actions must conceptualize the ritual symbol in the same way.

The techniques and concepts of the anthropologist enable him to analyze competently the interrelations between the data associated with the ideological pole of meaning. They also enable him to analyze the social behavior directed upon the total dominant symbol. He cannot, however, with his present skills, discriminate between the precise sources of unconscious feeling and wishing, which shape much of the outward form of the symbol; select some natural objects rather than others to serve as symbols; and account for certain aspects of the behavior associated with symbols. For him, it is enough that the symbol should evoke emotion. He is interested in the fact that emotion is evoked and not in the specific qualities of its constituents. He may indeed find it situationally relevant for his analysis to distinguish whether the emotion evoked by a specific symbol possesses the gross character, say, of aggression, fear, friendliness, anxiety, or sexual pleasure, but he need go no further than this. For him the ritual symbol is primarily a factor in group dynamics, and, as such, its references to the groups, relationships, values, norms, and beliefs of a society are his principal items of study. In other words, the anthropologist treats the sensory pole of meaning as a constant, and the social and ideological aspects as variables whose interdependencies he seeks to explain.

The psychoanalyst, on the other hand, must, I think, attach greater significance than he now does to social factors in the analysis of ritual symbolism. He must cease to regard interpretations, beliefs, and dogmas as mere rationalizations when, often enough, these refer to social and natural realities. For, as Durkheim wrote (1954, 2-3), "primitive religions hold to reality and express it. One must learn to go underneath the symbol to the reality which it represents and which gives it its meaning. No religions are false, all answer, though in different ways, to the given conditions of human existence." Among those giving conditions, the arrangement of society into structured groupings, discrepancies between the principles that organize these groupings, economic collaboration and competition, schism within groups and opposition between groups—in short, all those things with which the social aspect of ritual symbolism is concerned—are surely of at least equal importance with biopsychical drives and early conditioning in the elementary family. After all, the ritual symbol has, in common with the dream symbol, the characteristic, discovered by Freud of being compromise formation between two main opposing tendencies. It is a compromise between the need for social control, and certain innate and universal human drives whose complete gratification would result in a breakdown of that control. Ritual symbols refer to what is normative, general, and characteristic of unique individuals. Thus, Ndembu symbols refer among other things, to the basic needs of social existence (hunting, agriculture, female fertility, favourable climatic conditions, and so forth), and to shared values on which communal life depends (generosity, comradeship, respect for elders, the importance of kinship, hospitality, and the like). In distinguishing between ritual symbols and individual psychic symbols, we may perhaps say that while ritual symbols are gross means of handling social and natural reality, psychic symbols are dominantly fashioned under the influence of inner drives. In analyzing the former, attention must mainly be paid to relations between data external to the psyche; in analyzing the latter, to endopsychic data.

For this reason, the study of ritual symbolism falls more within the province of the social anthropologist than that of the psychologist or psychoanalyst, although the latter can assist the anthropologist by examining the nature and interconnections of the data clustered at the sensory pole of ritual symbolism. He can also, I believe, illuminate certain aspects of the stereotyped behavior associated with symbols in field contexts, which the actors themselves are unable to explain. For, as we have seen, much of this behavior is suggestive of attitudes that differ radically from those deemed appropriate in terms of traditional **exegesis**. Indeed, certain conflicts would appear to be so basic that they totally block exegesis.

The Interpretation of Observed Emotions

Can we really say that behavior portraying conflict between persons and groups, who are represented by the symbols themselves as being in harmony, is in the full Freudian sense unconscious behavior? The Ndembu themselves in many situations outside *Nkang'a*, both secular and ritual, are perfectly aware of and ready to speak about hostility in the relationships between particular mothers and daughters, between particular sublineages, and between particular young girls and the adult women in their villages. It is rather as though there existed in certain precisely defined public situations, usually of a ritual or ceremonial type, a norm obstructing the verbal statement of conflicts in any way connected with the principle and rules celebrated or dramatized in those situations. Evidences of human passion and frailty are just not spoken about when the occasion is given up to the public commemoration and reanimation of norms and values in their abstract purity.

Yet, as we have seen, recurrent kinds of conflict may be acted out in the ritual or ceremonial form. On great ritual occasions, common practice, as well as highest principle, receives its symbolic or stereotyped expression, but practice, which is dominantly under the sway of what all societies consider man's "lower nature," is rife with expressions of conflict. Selfish and factional interests, oath breaking, disloyalty, sins of omission as well as sins of commission, pollute and disfigure those ideal prototypes of behavior which in precept, prayer, formula, and symbol are held up before the ritual assembly for its exclusive attention. In the orthodox interpretation of ritual it is pretended that common practice has no efficacy and that men and women really are as they ideally should be. Yet, as I have argued above, the "energy" required to reanimate the values and norms enshrined in dominant symbols and expressed in various kinds of verbal behavior is "borrowed," to speak metaphorically in lieu at the moment of a more rigorous language, from the miming of well-known and normally mentionable conflicts. The raw energies of conflict are domesticated into the service of social order.

I should say here that I believe it possible, and indeed necessary, to analyze symbols in a context of observed emotions. If the investigator is well acquainted with the common idiom in which a society expresses such emotions as friendship, love, hate, joy, sorrow, contentment, and fear, he cannot fail to observe that these are experienced in ritual situations. Thus, in *Nkang'a* when the women laugh and jeer at the men, tease the novice and her mother, fight one another for the "porridge of *chipwampwilu*," and so on, the observer can hardly doubt that emotions are really aroused in the actors as well as formally represented by ritual custom. ("What's Hecuba to him or he to Hecuba, that he should weep for her?")

These emotions are portrayed and evoked in close relation to the dominant symbols of tribal cohesion and continuity, often by the performance of instrumentally symbolic behavior. However, since they are often associated with the mimesis of interpersonal and intergroup conflict, such emotions and acts of behavior obtain no place among the official, verbal meanings attributed to such dominant symbols.

The Situational Suppression of Conflict from Interpretation

Emotion and praxis, indeed, give life and coloring to the values and norms, but the connection between the behavioral expression of conflict and the normative components of each kind of ritual, and of its dominant symbols, is seldom explicitly formulated by believing actors. Only if one were to personify a society, regarding it as some kind of supra-individual entity, could one speak of "unconsciousness" here. Each individual participant in the *Nkang'a* ritual is well aware that kin quarrel most bitterly over rights and obligations conferred by the principle of matriliny, but that awareness is situationally held back from verbal expression: the participants must behave as if conflicts generated by matriliny were irrelevant.

This does not mean, as Nadel considers, that what is not verbalized is in fact irrelevant either to the participants or to the anthropologist. On the contrary, in so far as the anthropologist considers problems of social action to fall within his purview, the suppression from speech of what might be termed "the behavioral meaning" of certain dominant symbols is highly relevant. The fact is that any kind of coherent, organized social life would be impossible without the assumption that certain values and norms, imperatives and prohibitions, are axiomatic in character, ultimately binding on everyone. However, for many reasons, the axiomatic quality of these norms is difficult to maintain in practice, since in the endless variety of real situations, norms considered equally valid in abstraction are frequently found to be inconsistent with one another, and even mutually to conflict.

Furthermore, social norms, by their very nature, impose unnatural constraints on those whose biopsychical dispositions impel them to supranormal or abnormal behavior, either fitfully or regularly. Social life in all organized groups appears to exhibit a cycle or oscillation between periods when one set of axiomatic norms is observed and periods dominated by another set. Thus, since different norms govern different aspects or sectors of social behavior, and, more importantly, since the sectors overlap and interpenetrate in reality, causing norm-conflict, the validity of several major norms has to be reaffirmed in isolation from others and outside the contexts in which struggles and conflicts arise in connection with them. This is why one so often finds in ritual that dogmatic and symbolic emphasis is laid on a single norm or on a cluster of closely, and on the whole harmoniously, interrelated norms in a single kind of ritual.

Yet, since at major gatherings of this sort, people assemble not as aggregates of individuals but as social personalities arrayed and organized by many principles and norms of grouping, it is by no means a simple matter to assert the clear situational paramountcy of the norms to be commemorated and extolled. Thus, in the Ndembu boys' circumcision ritual, relationships between social categories, such as men and women, old men and young men, circumcised and uncircumcised, and the norms governing such relationships, are given formal representation, but the members of the ritual assembly come as members of corporate groups, such as villages and lineages, which in secular life are in rivalry with one another. That this rivalry is not mysteriously and wonderfully dispelled by the circumcision ritual becomes abundantly clear from the number of quarrels and fights that can be observed during public dances and beer drinks in the intervals between phases of the ritual proper. Here people quarrel as members of groupings that are not recognized in the formal structure of the ritual.

It may be said that any major ritual that stresses the importance of a single principle of social organization only does so by blocking the expression of other important principles. Sometimes the submerged principles, and the norms and customs through which they become effective, are given veiled and disguised representation in the symbolic pattern of the ritual; sometimes, as in the boys' circumcision ritual, they break through to expression in the spatial and temporal interstices of the procedure. In this essay we are concerned principally with the effects of the suppression on the meaning-structure of dominant symbols.

For example, in the frequently performed *Nkula* ritual, the dominant symbols are a cluster of red objects, notably red clay (*mukundu*) and the *mukula* tree mentioned previously. In the context of *Nkula*, both of these are said to represent menstrual blood and the "blood of birth," which is the blood that accompanies the birth of a child. The ostensible goal of the ritual is to coagulate the patient's menstrual blood, which has been flowing away in menorrhagia, around the fetus in order to nourish it. A series of symbolic acts are performed to attain this end. For example, a young *mukula* tree is cut down by male doctors and part of it is carved into the shape of a baby, which is then inserted into a round calabash medicated with the blood of a sacrificed cock, with red clay, and with a number of other red ingredients. The red medicines here, say the Ndembu, represent desired coagulation of the patient's menstrual blood, and the calabash is a symbolic womb. At the ideological pole of meaning, the *mukula* tree and the medicated calabash both represent (as the milk tree does) the patient's matrilineage and, at a higher level of abstraction, the principle of matriliny itself. This is also consistent with the fact that *ivumu*, the term for "womb," also means "matrilineage." In this symbolism the procreative, rather than the nutritive, aspect of motherhood is stressed. However, Ndembu red symbolism, unlike the white symbolism of which the milk tree symbolism is a species, nearly always has explicit reference to violence, to killing, and, at its most general level of meaning, to breach, both in the social and natural orders. Although informants, when discussing this *Nkula* ritual specifically, tend to stress the positive, feminine aspects of parturition and reproduction, other meanings of the red symbols, stated explicitly in other ritual contexts, can be shown to make their influence felt in *Nkula*. For example, both red clay and the *mukula* tree are dominant symbols in the hunter's cult, where they mean the blood of animals, the red meat of game, the inheritance through either parent of hunting prowess, and the unity of all initiated hunters. It also stands for the hunter's power to kill. The same red symbols, in the context of the *Wubanji* ritual performed to purify a man who has killed a kinsman or a lion or leopard (animals believed to be reincarnated hunter kin of the living), represent the blood of homicide. Again, in the boys' circumcision ritual, these symbols stand for the blood of circumcised boys. More seriously still, in divination and in antiwitchcraft rituals, they stand for the blood of witches' victims, which is exposed in necrophagous feasts.

Most of the meanings are implicit in *Nkula*. For example, the female patient, dressed in skins like a male hunter and carrying a bow and arrow, at one phase of the ritual performs a special hunter's dance. Moreover, while she does this, she wears in her hair, just above the brow, the red feather of a lourie bird. Only shedders of blood, such as hunters, man-slayers, and circumcisers are customarily entitled to wear this feather. Again, after the patient has been given the baby figurine in its symbolic womb, she dances with it in a style of dancing peculiar to circumcisers when they brandish aloft the great *nfunda* medicine of the circumcision lodge. Why then is the woman patient identified with male bloodspillers? The field context of these symbolic objects and items of behavior suggests that the Ndembu feel that the woman, in wasting her menstrual blood and in failing to bear children, is actively renouncing her expected role as a mature married female. She is behaving like a male killer, not like a female nourisher. The situation is analogous, though modified by matriliny, to the following pronouncement in the ancient Jewish Code of Qaro: "Every man is bound to marry a wife in order to beget children, and he who fails of this duty is as one who sheds blood."

One does not need to be a psychoanalyst, one only needs sound sociological training, acquaintance with the total Ndembu symbolic system, plus ordinary common sense, to see that one of the aims of the ritual is to make the woman accept her lot in life as a childbearer and rearer of children for her lineage. The symbolism suggests that the patient is unconsciously rejecting her female role, that indeed she is guilty: indeed, *"mbayi,"* one term for menstrual blood, is etymologically connected with *"ku-baya"* (to be guilty). I have not time here to present further evidence of symbols and interpretations, both in *Nkula* and in cognate rituals, which reinforce this explanation. In the situation of *Nkula*, the dominant principles celebrated and reanimated are those of matriliny, the mother-child bond, and tribal continuity through matriliny. The norms in which these are expressed are those governing the behavior of mature women, which ascribe to them the role appropriate to their sex. The suppressed or submerged principles, and norms, in this situation, concern and control the personal and corporate behavior deemed appropriate for man.

The analysis of *Nkula* symbolism throws into relief another major function of ritual. Ritual adapts and periodically readapts the biopsychical individual to the basic conditions and axiomatic values of human social life. In redressive rituals, the category to which *Nkula* belongs, the eternally rebellious individual, is converted for a while into a loyal citizen. In the case of *Nkula*, a female individual whose behavior is felt to demonstrate her rebellion against, or at least her reluctance to comply with, the biological and social life patterns of her sex, is both induced and coerced by means of precept and symbol to accept her culturally prescribed destiny.

Modes of Inference in Interpretation

Each kind of Ndembu ritual, like *Nkula*, has several meanings and goals that are not made explicit by informants, but must be inferred by the investigator from the symbolic pattern and from behavior. He is able to make these inferences only if he has previously examined the symbolic configurations and the meanings attributed to their component symbols by skilled informants, of many other kinds of ritual in the same total system. In other words, he must examine symbols not only in the context of each specific kind of ritual, but in the context of the total system. He may even find it profitable, where the same symbol is found throughout a wide culture area, to study its changes of meaning in different societies in that area.

There are two main types of contexts, irrespective of size. There is the action-field context, which we have discussed at some length. There is also the cultural context in which symbols are regarded as clusters of abstract meanings. By comparing the different kinds and sizes of contexts in which a dominant symbol occurs, we can often see that the meanings "officially" attributed to it in a particular kind of ritual may be mutually consistent. However, there may be much discrepancy and even contradiction between many of the meanings given by informants, when this dominant symbol is regarded as a unit of the total symbolic system. I do not believe that this discrepancy is the result of mere carelessness and ignorance or variously distributed pieces of insight. I believe that discrepancy between *significata* is a quintessential property of the great symbolic dominants in all religions. Such symbols come in the process of time to absorb into their meaning-content most of the major aspects of human social life, so that, in a sense, they come to represent "human society" itself. In each ritual they assert the situational primacy of a single aspect or of a few aspects only, but by their mere presence they suffuse those aspects with the awe that can only be inspired by the human total. All the contradictions of human social life, between norms, and drives, between different drives and between different norms, between society and the individual, and between groups, are condensed and unified in a single representation, the dominant symbols. It is the task of analysis to break down this amalgam into its primary constituents.

The Relativity of "Depth"

Perhaps this breakdown can best be done within different analytical frameworks. I was formerly in favor of talking about "different levels of analysis," but the term "level" contains an implication of depth which I now find misleading, unless we can agree to take "level" to mean any class of abstraction whatsoever. The question of the relative depth of different ways of interpreting symbols is still very much under dispute. For example, psychoanalysts assert that their interpretations of ritual symbols are "deeper" than those of social anthropologists. On the other hand, anthropologists like Monica Wilson hold that at their "deepest level" rituals reveal values, which are sociocultural facts.

I have suggested in this essay different aspects of ritual symbolism can be analyzed within the framework of structuralist theory and of cultural anthropology respectively. As I have said, this would be to treat ritual symbols as timeless entities. Many useful conclusions can be arrived at by these methods, but the essential nature, both of dominant symbols and of constellations of instrumental symbols, is that they are dynamic factors. Static analysis would here presuppose a corpse, and, as Jung says, "a symbol is alive." It is alive only in so far as it is "pregnant with meaning" for men and women, who interact by observing, transgressing, and manipulating for private ends the norms and values that the symbol expresses. If the ritual symbol is conceptualized as a force in a field of social action, its critical properties of condensation, polarization, and unification of disparities become intelligible and explicable. On the other hand, conceptualizing the symbol as if it were an object and neglecting its role in action often lead to a stress on only those aspects of symbolism which can be logically and consistently related to one another to form an abstract unitary system. In a field situation, the unity of a symbol or a symbolic configuration appears as the resultant of many tendencies converging towards one another from different areas of biophysical and social existence. The symbol is an independent force which is itself a product of many opposed forces.

Conclusion: The Analysis of Symbols in Social Processes

Let me outline briefly the way in which I think ritual symbols may fruitfully be analyzed. Performances of ritual are phases in broad social processes, the span and complexity of which are roughly proportional to the size and degree of differentiation of the groups in which they occur. One class of ritual is situated near the apex of a whole hierarchy of redressive and regulative institutions that correct deflections and deviations from customarily prescribed behavior. Another class anticipates deviations and conflicts. This class includes periodic rituals and life-crisis rituals. Each kind of ritual is a patterned process in time, the units of which are symbolic objects and serialized items of symbolic behavior.

The symbolic constituents may themselves be classed into structural elements, or "dominant symbols," which tend to be ends in themselves, and variable elements, or "instrumental symbols," which serve as means to the explicit or implicit goals of the given ritual. In order to give an adequate explanation of the meaning of a particular symbol, it is necessary first to examine the widest action-field context, that, namely, in which the ritual itself is simply a phase. Here one must consider what kinds of circumstances give rise to a performance of ritual, whether these are concerned with natural phenomena, economic and technological processes, human life-crisis, or with the breach of crucial social relationships. The circumstances will probably determine what sort of ritual is performed. The goals of the ritual will have overt and implicit reference to the antecedent circumstances and will in turn help to determine the meaning of the symbols. Symbols must now be examined within the context of the specific ritual. It is here that we enlist the aid of indigenous informants. It is here also that we may be able to speak legitimately of "levels" of interpretation, for laymen will give the investigator simple and exoteric meanings, while specialists will give him esoteric explanations and more elaborate texts. Next, behavior directed towards each symbol should be noted, for such behavior is an important component of its total meaning.

We are now in a position to exhibit the ritual as a system of meanings, but this system acquires additional richness and depth if it is regarded as itself constituting a sector of the Ndembu ritual system, as interpreted by informants and as observed in action. It is in comparison with other sectors of the total system, and by reference to the dominant articulating principles of the total system, that we often become aware that the overt and ostensible aims and purposes of a given ritual conceal unavowed, and even "unconscious," wishes and goals. We also become aware that a complex relationship exists between the overt and the submerged, and the manifest and latent patterns of meaning. As social anthropologists we are potentially capable of analyzing the social aspect of this relationship. We can examine, for example, the relations of dependence and independence between the total society and its parts, and the relations between different kinds of parts, and between different parts of the same kind. We can see how the same dominant symbol, which in one kind of ritual stands for one kind of social group or for one principle of organization, in another kind of ritual stands for another kind of group or principle, and in its aggregate of meanings stands for unity and continuity of the widest Ndembu society, embracing its contradictions.

The Limits of Contemporary Anthropological Competence
Our analysis must needs be incomplete when we consider the relationship between the normative elements in social life and the individual. For this relationship, too, finds its way into the meaning of ritual symbols. Here we come to the confines of our present anthropological competence, for we are now dealing with the structure and properties of psyches, a scientific field traditionally studied by other disciplines than ours. At one end of the symbol's spectrum of meanings we encounter the individual psychologist and the social psychologist, and even beyond them (if one may make a friendly tilt at an envied friend), brandishing his Medusa's head, the psychoanalyst, ready to turn to stone the foolhardy interloper into his caverns of terminology.

We shudder back thankfully into the light of social day. Here the significant elements of a symbol's meaning are related to what it does and what is done to it by and for whom. These aspects can only be understood if one takes into account from the beginning, and represents by appropriate theoretical constructs, the total field situation in which the symbol occurs. This situation would include the structure of the group that performs the ritual we observe, its basic organizing principles and perdurable relationships, and, in addition, its extant division into transient alliances and factions on the basis of immediate interest and ambitions, for both abiding structure and recurrent forms of conflict and selfish interest are stereotyped in ritual symbolism. Once we have collected informants' interpretations of a given symbol, our work of analysis has indeed just begun. We must gradually approximate to the action-meaning of our symbol by way of what Lewin calls (1949, 149) "a stepwise increasing specificity" from widest to narrowest significant action context. Informants' "meanings" only become meaningful as objects of scientific study in the course of this analytical process.

Notes

1   Read at a meeting of the Association of Social Anthropologists of the Commonwealth in London, March 1958. First published in *Closed Systems and Open Minds: The Limits of Naivety, in Social Science,* M. Gluckman, ed. (Edinburgh: Oliver and Boyd, 1964).

2   *Muchidi* also means "category," "kind," "species," and "tribe"itself.

3   I.e., objects not of indefinite duration but to which the category of time is not applicable.

4   Nadel writes: "We might call the very fluidity of the formalism part of the typical form of Nupe ritual."

References

Bettelheim, Bruno. 1954. *Symbolic Wounds: Puberty Rites and the Envious Male.* Glencoe, Ill.: Free Press.

Durkheim, E. 1954. *Elementary Forms of the Religious Life.* London: Allen & Unwin.

Fenichel, Otto. 1946. *The Psychoanalytic Theory of Neuroses.* London: Routledge & Kegan Paul.

Jung, Carl G. 1949. *Psychological Types.* London: Routledge & Kegan Paul.

Lewin, K. 1949. *Field Theory in Social Science.* London: Tavistock Publications.

Nadel, S.F. 1954. *Nupe Religion.* London: Routledge & Kegan Paul.

Sapir, E. n.d. "Symbols." *Encyclopedia of the Social Sciences*, XIV. New York: Macmillan.

Wilson, M. 1957. *Rituals of Kinship among the Nyakyusa*. London: Oxford University Press, for the International African Institute.

Study Questions

1. Why is the milk tree a "dominant" symbol among the Ndembu?

2. How does Turner characterize the difference between "dominant" and "instrumental" symbols?

3. How does ritual affect social stability and/or conflict?

Further Readings

Turner, Victor. 1957. *Schism and Continuity in an African Society: A Study of Ndembu Village Life*. Manchester: Manchester University Press.

—. 1967. *The Forest of Symbols: Aspects of Ndembu Ritual*. Ithaca, NY: Cornell University Press.

—. 1968. *The Drums of Affliction*. Oxford: Clarendon Press.

—. 1969. *The Ritual Process: Structure and Anti-Structure*. Hawthorne, NY: Aldine de Gruyter.

Turner, Victor, and Turner, Edith. 1978. *Image and Pilgrimage in Christian Culture*. New York: Columbia University Press.

Van Gennep, Arnold. 1960. *The Rites of Passage*. Trans. Monika B. Vizedom and Gabrielle L. Caffee. Chicago: University of Chicago Press.

23

Energy and Tools

LESLIE A. WHITE

Everything in the universe may be described in terms of matter and energy, or, more precisely, in terms of energy. Whether we are dealing with galaxies with their millions of blazing suns, a tiny atom with its tightly packed nucleus and darting electrons, a single living cell or a complex multicellular organism, or with a society of ants, apes, or men, we are confronted with a dynamic material system, one that can be described and made intelligible in terms of energy magnitudes and transformations. Energy is the basic and universal concept of science. "Through the various ideas of phlogiston, imponderable fluids, attractions, repulsions, affinities, and forces, science has ended with the simple universal conception of energy," as the eminent British physicist Frederick Soddy observed many years ago.[1]

According to the second law of thermodynamics,[2] the universe is breaking down structurally and running down dynamically; i.e., it is moving in the direction of lesser degrees of order and toward a more uniform distribution of energy. The logical conclusion of this trend is a uniform, random state, or chaos.

In a tiny sector of the cosmos, however, we find a movement in the opposite direction. In the evolution of living material systems, matter becomes more highly organized and energy is raised from lower to higher levels of concentration. This does not mean that living beings constitute an exception to the second law. Animate organisms are able to move in a direction opposite to that specified by the law of entropy only because they are able to draw upon free energy outside themselves and incorporate it within their own systems. All life, as the Austrian physicist Ludwig Boltzmann (1844-1906) pointed out long ago, is a struggle for free energy.[3] All living beings—on our planet at least—are dependent upon energy derived from the sun. Plants obtain energy directly from the sun through radiation and transform it into organic compounds by the process of photosynthesis. All animals live directly or indirectly upon solar energy stored up by plants. Thus, all living organisms are thermodynamic systems which are both expressions and results of a movement toward higher concentrations of energy and greater organization of matter. The process that is life is sustained, perpetuated, and in some instances developed, by energy from the sun.[4]

But, to be precise, the life process, in its maintenance in the individual organism and in its development in orders, phyla, genera, and species, is not merely a matter of capturing quantities of energy and of incorporating them within living systems to take the place of like quantities that have been expended in the process of living. In an adult organism the energy content is a constant, and since one calorie is worth as much as another, a mere exchange would bring no advantage.[5] What is it, then, that sustains the life process and makes possible its evolutionary development?

Schrödinger gives us the answer: by drawing negative entropy from its environment. "A living organism continually increases its entropy," he says, "and thus tends to approach the dangerous state of maximum entropy, which is death. It can only keep aloof from it, i.e., alive, by continually drawing from its environment negative entropy.... What an organism feeds upon is negative entropy"; it continually "sucks orderliness from its environment ... in the case of higher animals we know the kind of orderliness they feed upon well enough, viz., the extremely well-ordered state of matter in more or less complicated organic compounds, which serve them as foodstuffs. After utilizing it they return it in a very much degraded form—not entirely degraded, however, for plants can still make use of it. (These, of course, have their most powerful supply of 'negative entropy' in the sunlight.)"[6]

Schrödinger's emphasis is upon order, upon greater or lesser degrees of orderliness. But the process of life can be described in terms of energy, also. A living organism is a structure through which energy flows, entering the system at higher potentials and leaving it at lower potentials.[7] A living organism is thus a mechanism that is operated by a downward flow of energy, much as a water wheel is turned by a stream flowing downhill.

Living systems are means of arresting, and even of reversing, the cosmic drift toward maximum entropy. Maintenance of life is achieved by offsetting the entropy produced by the very process of living with negative entropy obtained from the environment—by "sucking orderliness from the environment." By obtaining more negative entropy from the environment than the positive entropy produced by the process of living, i.e., by utilizing increasing amounts of energy as it flows through living systems to build more complicated structures, rather than merely to maintain the vital process, living species may evolve.

Thus life and death alike receive their most profound and illuminating definitions in terms of thermodynamics. The maintenance of life is a continuous balancing of positive entropy with negative entropy. The evolution of life is the ascendance of negative entropy. Dying is the losing battle to overcome positive entropy. Death is the state of maximum entropy, of thermodynamical equilibrium.

Living material bodies, like inanimate ones, tend to persevere in the motions proper to them indefinitely; their motions will be terminated only by opposition of one kind or another. Opposition to vital processes may come from the external world, from the habitat of the organism; or it may originate within the organism itself. The articulation of living organism with natural habitat involves a certain amount of wear and tear upon the organism as well as some transformation of habitat. The life process thus encounters opposition or resistance at every point of contact with the external world. And, of course, some outside force may lull an organism instantly, as well as overcome it gradually. In certain habitats, however, some species will continue their vital processes indefinitely. Some organisms perpetuate themselves endlessly by fission. Trees, and even fish, we are told, tend to live forever; they are overcome only by outside forces. Some animal tissues will live indefinitely in certain kinds of solution. But in other sectors of the animate world, the vital motions are gradually overcome by resistances arising within the organisms themselves. In some species, the moving parts of the organism become materially transformed with age; especially, it would appear, do they become less elastic, thus overcoming, eventually, the momentum of the vital process. Thus, the life process is marked by "immortality"—i.e., indefinite continuation—in some areas, and by the death of individuals and the extinction of species, in other sectors.

It is interesting to note that living organisms are organized and structured as energy-capturing systems. The "correlating apparatus [of an organism]," says Lotka, "is primarily an energy-capturing device—its other functions are undoubtedly secondary. Evidence of this is manifold. The close association of the principal sense organs, eyes, ears, nose, taste buds, tactile papillae of the finger tips, with the anterior (head) end of the body, the *mouth* end, all point the same lesson, which is further confirmed by the absence of any well developed sense organs in plants.[8] The second law of thermodynamics thus throws light upon the *structure* of living systems as well as upon the nature of the process called life.

The life process tends to augment itself. The ability to take the first step—the transformation of matter and energy from inanimate to living systems—is also the ability to take the next step, and the next. Once the mechanism of transforming energy from the sun into living material systems was effected, the way was opened for an almost unlimited expansion of the life process; the only limit is that of the earth's capacity to accommodate living beings, for the amount of available solar energy is virtually boundless.

The life process extends itself in two ways: (1) by the mere multiplication of numbers through reproduction; and, (2) by the development of higher forms of life. In some species the rate of reproduction is enormous, thousands of offspring per pair. Here we have an example of the extension of the life process in its merely quantitative aspect: the tendency to transform as much of the external world as possible into organisms of the species in question. "Every living being," observes Bertrand Russell, "is a sort of imperialist, seeking to transform as much as possible of the environment into itself and its seed."[9] In other sectors of the biological world, however, we find a development of higher forms of life, i.e., greater structural organization and higher concentrations of energy. Biological evolution might be defined as the progress of energy organization moving in a direction opposite to that specified for the cosmos by the second law of thermodynamics. Animals are more highly developed thermodynamic systems than plants; mammals, more highly developed than reptiles. "A change that seems often to be involved in progress [in biological evolution]," says Simpson, "is increase in the general energy or maintained level of vital processes.... The metabolic system of reptiles has a low vital minimum.... The mammalian system (typically) has a higher vital minimum.... With regard to energy level, mammals as a whole stand near but not quite at the top among animals; among vertebrates, the birds exceed them...."[10]

Thus we see that the self-augmentation of the process that is life finds expression in two ways: (1) in the multiplication of organisms, a merely quantitative change; and (2) in the development of higher forms, a qualitative change. Considering the animate world as a whole, there appears to be an inverse functional relationship between these two ways in which the life process extends itself: the lower the form of life, the greater the tendency toward self-extension in a quantitative manner, by mere reproduction of numbers. Conversely, the more highly developed the form of life, the less is the tendency toward numerous offspring.

The struggle for existence and survival has two aspects: (1) the adjustment of the organism to its habitat in terms of temperature, humidity, radiation, subsistence, etc.; and (2) the struggle with other living beings for subsistence and favorable habitats. In this struggle, in both its aspects, "the advantage must go to those organisms whose energy-capturing devices are most efficient."[11] Any gains won are kept. The tendency of the life process is always to achieve a maximum of matter-and-energy transformation.[12] This is true regardless of whether the energy is expended quantitatively in mere reproduction of numbers of organisms or in the development of higher forms of living systems.

To understand man in particular we must understand living material systems in general. As we have just seen, the second law of thermodynamics contributes greatly to the understanding of the process that we call life: it illuminates its structure, its functions, and its development. And this law will help us to understand culture also; the fundamental significance of culture cannot be grasped or appreciated without recourse to this great generalization of physics.

Man, like all other living beings, is confronted with the problem of adjustment to habitat in terms of subsistence, protection from the elements, and defense from enemies. In order to effect these adjustments and to perpetuate his kind, man, like all other creatures, must capture and utilize energy. Self-extension, self-augmentation of the life process, finds expression in the human species as well as in others. In short, man is occupied with adjustment to and control over his environment, and with competition with other species for the means of existence, survival, and expansion. This means is energy.

Man employs the organs of his body in the process of adjustment to and control over his environment, as do other animals. But in addition to these somatological mechanisms, man, and man alone, possesses an elaborate extrasomatic mechanism which he employs in the process of living. This extrasomatic mechanism, this traditional organization of tools, customs, language, beliefs, etc., we have called *culture*.

A culture, or sociocultural system,[13] is a material, and therefore a thermodynamic, system. Culture is an organization of things in motion, a process of energy transformations. Whether it be chipping an arrowhead, catching a fish, hoeing a hill of beans, avoiding your mother-in-law, calling your father's sister's son "father," performing a ritual, playing a game, regarding a churinga with awe, or breathing a silent prayer, the event is an expression of energy expended.[14] "Culture" is but the name of the form in which the life forces of man as a human being find expression. It is an organization of energy transformations that is dependent upon symboling.

The principles and laws of thermodynamics are applicable to cultural systems as they are to other material systems. The "laws expressing the relations between energy and matter are not solely of importance in pure science [i.e., physics]," says Soddy, "they necessarily come *first in order ... in the whole record of human experience,* and *they control,* in the last resort, *the rise and fall of political systems, the freedom or bondage of nations, the movements of commerce and industry, the origin of wealth and poverty, and the general physical welfare of the race* [italics supplied]."[15] Schrödinger, like Soddy a Nobel-Prize-winning physicist, is "convinced that this Law [i.e., the second law of thermodynamics] governs all physical and chemical processes, even if they result in the most intricate and tangled phenomena, such as organic life, the genesis of a complicated world of organisms from primitive beginnings, [and] the rise and growth of human cultures."[16] Other physicists and chemists, like Joseph Henry in the United States and Wilhelm Ostwald in

Germany, have contributed to the development of the energy theory of cultural development.[17]

As we noted in the preceding chapter, culture is produced by man and therefore derives its generic nature from its source. Since the fundamental process of man as an organism is the capture and utilization of free energy, it follows that this must be the basic function of culture also: the harnessing of energy and putting it to work in the service of man. And since culture, as an extrasomatic[18] tradition, may be treated logically as a distinct and autonomous kind of system, we may interpret the evolution of culture in terms of the same principles of thermodynamics that are applicable to biological systems.

Cultural systems, like biological organisms, expend the energy that is captured and harnessed in self-extension as well as self-maintenance. Like biological organisms, cultural systems extend themselves both quantitatively and qualitatively. Cultural systems extend themselves quantitatively by multiplication or reduplication; i.e., peoples multiply, tribes divide, forming new tribes and therefore new sociocultural systems. Cultural systems expand qualitatively by developing higher forms of organization and greater concentrations of energy.[19] Degree of organization in any material system is proportional to the amount of energy incorporated in it. As the amount of energy harnessed by sociocultural systems increases per capita per year, the systems not only increase in size, but become more highly evolved; i.e., they become more differentiated structurally and more specialized functionally. We shall see this principle abundantly illustrated as we survey the evolution of culture in general.

Culture, as a thermodynamic system, may be analyzed into the following factors: energy, tools, and product. As we have seen, culture is a mechanism for serving the needs of man. And to do this it must harness energy and put it to work. The use of energy requires technological apparatus, and we may extend the use of the term *tools* to cover all the material means with which energy is harnessed, transformed, and expended. We shall designate all goods and services capable of serving the needs of man that have been produced or formed by the cultural use of energy, the *product*. Thus, catching fish, shooting game, making pottery, cutting hair, piercing ears for pendants, filing teeth for beauty's sake, weaving cloth, and a thousand and one other cultural processes are examples of the control and expenditure of energy by instrumental means in order to serve some need of man. We may, then, think of the culture process in terms of motive power, means of expression, and satisfaction of need. This conception can be expressed by a simple formula, $E \times T > P$, in which E represents the energy involved, T the technological means of utilizing it, and P, the product or result which serves a need of man.

By *energy* we mean "the ability to do work." "... Energy and work are interchangeable terms," says Soddy;[20] one is defined in terms of the other. Thus, a stone is moved from here to there, or its shape is changed by chipping or grinding. Energy is expended; work is done. Energy has both quantitative and qualitative, or formal, aspects. Quantitatively, energy is measurable in terms of definite and standard units, such as ergs, calories, British thermal units, etc. One magnitude of energy may therefore be compared with another. Qualitatively, energy is manifested in a great variety of forms: atomic, molecular, stellar, galactic, cellular, and metazoan, as well as cultural. From the standpoint of cultural systems, solar radiation, plants, animals, wind, water in motion, fuels of various kinds, molecules, and atoms are significant forms of energy, significant because it is in these forms that they are, or may be, incorporated into cultural systems. It is understood, of course, that energy is neither created nor destroyed; it is merely transformed. Cultural systems operate, therefore, only by harnessing energy in one form or another, and by transforming it in the production of human need-serving goods and services.

Cultural systems vary as means of harnessing energy; some are more effective than others. They may be compared in terms of coefficients derived by relating amount of energy harnessed and expended in a given period of time to the number of human beings embraced by the system. Thus one cultural system may harness and use x units of energy per capita per year,[21] another, *3x*, or *10x*. The significance of this coefficient lies, of course, in the relationship between amount of energy harnessed, on the one hand, and the number of human beings whose needs are to be served, on the other. The individual human being thus constitutes the unit in terms of which human need is measured and serves, therefore, as the constant against which varying quantities of energy are measured. Thus, we can compare cultures in terms of amount of energy harnessed and expended per capita per year. Or we can make our comparisons in terms of *power*, the rate of doing work, and classify cultures in terms of horsepower per capita.

The source of energy with which cultural systems were activated at the very beginning of man-and-culture history was, of course, the human organism. The energy with which tools, beliefs, customs, rituals, and sentiments were first organized into a functioning system was derived from man himself; he was, so to speak, the power plant that supplied the first cultural systems with their motive power. The amount of energy derivable by a cultural system from this source is of course small. An average adult man is capable of generating about one-tenth of one horsepower, or 75 watts. But the power coefficient of a cultural system deriving all its energy from human organisms would not be 0.1 horsepower per capita, by any means. When everyone is considered, males and females of all ages from helpless infants to the old and feeble, the sick and crippled, the average would be much less, possibly no more than 0.05 horsepower per capita.[22] Since the amount of human need-serving goods and services produced is proportional to the amount of energy harnessed, or horsepower generated, per capita, other factors remaining constant, a cultural system activated by energy derived from the human organism alone would represent the minimum in the range of capacities of cultural systems. From the standpoint, then, both of energy, or power, per capita and amount of human need-serving goods and services produced per capita, cultures that have the energy of human organisms only, under their control and at their disposal for use in the service of human needs, are at the bottom of the scale.

There is room for variation among cultural systems activated by human energy alone. In our formula $E \times T > P$, E, the energy factor, may vary with daily calorie consumption. T, the tool factor, varies with degrees of efficiency. Quite apart from natural habitat, therefore, which varies from tribe to tribe and from place to place, we are confronted with variation of cultural systems. Amount of energy harnessed per capita per year is the basic factor in this situation; the other two are meaningless or nonexistent without it. Without energy, tools would be meaningless, no work would be done, no product brought forth. The energy factor provides us, therefore, with an objective and meaningful yardstick with which to measure these, and all other, cultures. A culture is high or low depending upon the amount of energy harnessed per capita per year. At bottom, then, cultural development is the process of increasing the amount of energy harnessed and put to work per capita per year, together, with all the consequences attendant upon this increase.

In order to form a conception of primordial cultural systems based upon and activated by energy drawn from the human organism alone, one could examine some of the cultures of modern times having generically similar technological foundations, such as those of the Tasmanians, the Ona, various pygmy groups, and so on.[23] To be sure, technological and environmental factors both operate to produce cultural differences quite apart from source and magnitude of energy harnessed, but we shall deal with these factors later. But however much modern cultures, based upon human energy alone, may vary in specific detail, all are alike in one respect and that a fundamental one: all are extremely limited in their ability to exercise control over the external world, in their ability to produce human need-serving goods per unit of human labor. Sociologically they are all simple, i.e., relatively undifferentiated structurally. And their philosophies—their systems of knowledge and belief—are likewise simple and undeveloped. We have every reason to believe that the earliest cultures of mankind were of the same general type as the cultures of modern times that have had only the energy of human bodies at their disposal, although the latter might be more highly developed technologically. And we may be equally sure that cultural development would never have gone beyond a certain level, and that a low one, had not some way been found to harness additional amounts of energy per capita per year. Mankind would have remained in a condition of savagery indefinitely had not an increase of his available energy resources been made possible. Cultural systems are not developed by intelligence, high ideals, and earnest endeavor alone, as faith is supposed to move mountains; they must have energy—as, we suspect, mountain moving must have also.

Some qualification of our statements regarding the source of energy for the earliest of cultures should be made. The human organism was the principal source for all the earliest systems and the only source for many. There was, however, another source open to some, namely, flowing water. Even the most primitive peoples could float materials downstream instead of carrying them. But water power is insignificant in the course of cultural development until the Iron Age or even later. It is relatively insignificant even today.

Winds were available also to the most primitive peoples, but they had no means to harness them and use their energies. On higher cultural levels winds become significant as a source of energy in watercraft equipped with sails. Mechanical power derived by means of windmills comes very late in culture history, and it has never, in any culture, been of much importance.

Many discussions of harnessing energy begin with a discussion—or rhapsody—of fire. They often degenerate quickly, however, into musings about fire as a symbol of the home, the family fireside, vestal virgins, and what not. Man unquestionably learned to use, and even to make, fire very early in his career. But he did not use it extensively as a form of energy—or more precisely, as a means of doing work—until the recent invention of the steam engine. Fire may be useful in keeping ferocious beasts away from human habitations at night (although it would be easy to exaggerate its value in this respect), and it may constitute a precious symbol in family life and religious ritual. But these uses of fire do not fall within the thermodynamic context *energy*. Even the use of fire in cooking can hardly be put into an energy context because the cooking is not a substitute for something that can be done by an expenditure of muscular energy; fire in this instance cannot be equated with muscular energy or energy in general.

On moderately advanced cultural levels fire assumes considerable importance in the ceramic art, in the firing of pottery. And on still higher levels, fire acquires great importance in the metallurgical arts, in the smelting of ores and in the processing of metals. But in neither of these contexts does fire function as *energy* in the sense in which we are using the term. In pottery making and in metallurgy fire has an *instrumental* significance, as it does in cooking. It is a means of transforming materials. But it cannot be replaced by an expenditure of muscular energy. Since, therefore, we cannot equate fire in the ceramic and metallurgical arts with muscle power, we do not consider it significant as a form of mechanical energy.

There is, however, a very practical use to which fire may be put as a form of energy by very primitive peoples. They may use it to hollow out tree trunks in the manufacture of canoes. Here fire is substituted for, and hence equated with, muscular energy. There is no known cultural system, however, in which energy so derived and used constitutes more than a tiny fraction of the total amount employed. Fire is used also as a form of energy by some peoples to clear land for planting. But when the agricultural level has been reached we are already far advanced culturally and have in agriculture itself a method of harnessing energy compared with which this accessory use of fire is utterly insignificant.

We may distinguish, then, as the first stage of cultural development an era in which the human organism itself was the principal source of energy used by cultural systems, an era in which wind, water, and fire, as sources of energy, were very insignificant indeed. This stage began with the origin of man himself; it ends with the domestication of animals (ruminants), or the cultivation of plants, or both. In duration of time absolutely, and relatively in proportion to the lengths of other periods in culture history, this "human-energy" era is very impressive. If we assume, as many authorities do, that culture began one million years ago, and if we date the beginning of agriculture at about 10,000 years ago,[24] then the human-energy stage of cultural development comprises some 99 per cent of culture history thus far. This fact is as significant as it is remarkable.

The era in which cultural systems derive all but a very little of their energy from the human organism is characterized by another feature, namely, subsistence wholly upon wild food. This gives us another convenient and significant index of cultural development, and a category for the classification of cultures.

When man subsisted wholly upon wild foods he differed but little from the lower animals, who of course did likewise. True enough, he could cook his food, and this was unquestionably an important consideration in his survival. It would be possible to exaggerate the importance of cooking, however, as has been done in the case of fire. While man subsisted wholly upon wild foods he might be considered a wild animal, at least in a sense. He is now a domesticated animal, and it was the agricultural arts primarily that brought about the transition; domesticated man is a by-product of agriculture. Here again we are impressed with the tremendous duration of the wild-food stage as compared with subsequent eras.

The amount of energy per capita per year obtainable by cultural systems from human organisms is of course both small and limited. Unless cultural systems could add to this amount by tapping other sources, they could never have developed beyond a certain level, and that a very low one. And as we have just seen, water, wind, and fire have proved insignificant as sources of usable energy on the lower levels of technological development. Culture could not, and for ages on end did not, develop beyond the limit thus set by the 1/20 horsepower, more or less, per capita. Eventually, however, an effective way of augmenting energy resources for culture building was found, namely, in the domestication of animals and the cultivation of plants; in short, by harnessing solar energy in nonhuman biological forms.

Plants and animals are, of course, forms and magnitudes of energy. Plants receive, transform, and store up energy received directly from the sun. Animals subsist, directly or indirectly, on plants; all life depends, in the last analysis, on the process of photosynthesis performed by plants. But are not wild plants and animals forms and magnitudes of energy just as cultivated and domestic ones are? Yes, they are indeed. But here we must recall the fact that energy is not created or produced; it is merely transformed or controlled. Man is exploiting the energy resources of nature when he appropriates and eats a wild plant or animal, and we may properly say that he is exercising control over these natural forces. But hunting, fishing, and gathering are not forms of *harnessing* plant and animal energies; they are merely acts of appropriation and consumption. To *harness* a force is to lay hold of it, to direct and control it, so that it is not merely introduced into the cultural system but made an integral part of it. A flowing stream is a form and magnitude of energy. But apart from floating materials downstream, this energy does not become significant culturally until it has been harnessed by means of water mills and incorporated into a cultural system. So it is with plants and animals. The domestication of plants and animals was a way of laying hold of them as forces of nature, of directing and controlling them, of incorporating them into cultural systems. This innovation was of tremendous significance, for it tapped new sources of energy and thus freed culture from the limitations imposed by dependence upon man's body for motive power.

The advantages of animal husbandry over hunting wild game are of course numerous. Herds and flocks are within man's grasp and of easy access as contrasted with the difficulty of finding game. Domestication gives man more assurance that he will have food and hides; hunters often return empty-handed. Food supply may be increased as a consequence of domestication. Hunting carried on beyond a certain point will actually decrease man's food supply; game can be killed off faster than it can reproduce. But protection of herds and flocks against attack by wild beasts fosters an increase of numbers under domestication, and hence an increase in food supply. New and valuable materials are made available as a result of domestication. The use of milk, a food whose importance in some cultures it would be hard to exaggerate, is made possible by domestication. Furs and hair were, of course, available to hunters, but the extensive use of wool for textiles was made possible by the domestication and breeding of sheep;[25] the wild varieties did not have wool suitable for such use, apparently.[26]

A tremendous advantage of domestication over hunting lies in the continuous use of animals in the living form instead of the consumption of dead ones. Milk, eggs, and wool can be obtained again and again from animals without killing them. At certain levels of cultural development domestic animals may be used as forms of mechanical power, to pull sledges or travois, to carry burdens including human beings, to draw plows and carts. And through selective breeding, domesticated animals may be greatly improved as food- or wool-producing machines and as forms of mechanical power.

Thus, the domestication of animals is a way of harnessing, controlling, and using solar energy in a variety of forms to produce food, clothing, and mechanical power. All the advantages that we have cited for domestication as compared with hunting can, however, be reduced to a single and simple statement: it is a means of producing more human need-serving goods and services per unit of human labor, and hence, per capita. Culture has advanced as a consequence of increase in the amount of energy harnessed per capita per year.

Much the same observations may be made concerning the advantages of agriculture as compared with gathering wild plants for food and other uses. Horticulture renders the food supply more certain and more abundant. Reducing the competition with weeds gives cultivated plants more chance to grow and yield abundantly. Hoeing, plowing, fertilizing, irrigating, rotation of crops, and selective breeding are also means of increasing yields. Here, as in animal husbandry, agriculture produces more human need-serving goods per unit of human labor than the gathering of wild plants. And this is a consequence of the greater control exercised over the forces of nature by the agricultural arts.

We may express the significance of both animal husbandry and agriculture from the standpoint of cultural development with a simple formula. Instead of $E \times T > P$, energy times technology producing a quantity of human need-serving goods and services, let us write $E (H \times N) \times T > P$, in which H and N are the human and nonhuman components of the energy factor, respectively. If we hold the tool factor constant, we can rewrite our formula simply thus: $H \times N > P$. This expresses the relationship between the amount of energy derived from the human organism and that from other sources. This ratio is an important one in all cultures above the level of 100 per cent subsistence upon wild food and becomes more important as culture advances. As a matter of fact, cultural advance is well expressed in terms of this ratio: *culture advances as the proportion of nonhuman energy to human energy increases*. Or we may define cultural advance in terms of the ratio between the *product* and human labor: *cul-

*ture advances as the amount of human need-serving goods and services pro-
duced per unit of human labor increases.*

Animal husbandry and agriculture are alike, therefore, in being means of
extending control over the forces of nature and of advancing culture as a consequence. But these arts are not equal in their potential capacities for culture
building; agriculture has a much greater capacity for culture building than has
animal husbandry. The difference in their respective capacities rests upon a
simple zoological fact: herds and flocks must feed upon plants; cultivated
plants harness solar energy directly. A pastoral system, for all its control over
animals, still rests upon a wild-food basis in the last analysis: the plants upon
which the herds or flocks feed. The growth and abundance of these plants lie
outside cultural control. If pasturage fails, the herds diminish or die. Control
over forces of nature is greater and more immediate in agriculture. Plants harness solar energy directly. Fields may be fertilized, excess water drawn off,
crops irrigated, advantages derived from use of hotbeds, and so on. It goes
without saying that the control exercised through agriculture, though greater
than that in animal husbandry, is never complete and perfect; the farmer is of
course never wholly immune from natural disaster. But the extent to which culture can develop on a pastoral basis is limited, theoretically and practically. It
cannot develop beyond the limit set by the natural production of pasturage.
Attempts to increase herds beyond this point merely produce the opposite
effect: a diminution of herds as a result of deterioration of pasture caused by
overgrazing. In the agricultural arts, on the other hand, there may be a limit to
the extent to which human need-serving goods can be produced per unit of
human labor, but this limit has not been reached even to this day. Indeed, we
seem not to be close enough to it yet even to foresee it and to distinguish its
characteristics.

If an agricultural system is superior to a pastoral system in its capacity to
harness energy for culture building, a system combining agriculture and animal husbandry is superior to agriculture by itself. In such a system, the production of crops is facilitated by the use of animals as beasts of burden and
motive power—to draw plows and other agricultural implements, to transport
crops, to "tread out grain," to operate machines for grinding grain, irrigating
fields, etc.—and as producers of manure for fertilizer. Agriculture aids animal
husbandry, not only in making the food supply of herds and flocks more
secure and abundant, but in making it easier and more advantageous to keep
certain types of animals such as pigs and fowls. In no culture without agriculture are these kinds of animals domesticated and kept in large numbers. In systems with agriculture, however, they may become of considerable importance.
Agriculture and animal husbandry have combined and cooperated to produce
the greatest cultures of history prior to the Age of Fuels, except in those

regions like Mexico and Middle America where domesticable animals were absent.

It should be kept in mind that in our discussion of hunting, fishing, gathering, animal husbandry, and agriculture, thus far, we have been concerned with only one aspect of these processes, namely, the energy factor. We have not dealt with the tool factor at all so far, and we have ignored environment completely. It is obvious that every culture is determined by instrumental and environmental factors as well as by that of energy, but it is convenient and desirable to treat each one singly while disregarding the other two. In considering the culture process, we may think of any two of these factors as constants while we vary the third. Culture will vary, therefore, as the variable determinant varies. Thus, in the formula $E \times T \times V \rightarrow P$, in which E, T, and P have values as before and V stands for environment, we may hold any two of the three determining factors constant and vary the third. P, the total product, or degree of cultural development, will then vary accordingly. The status, or degree of development, of any actual cultural system will, however, be determined by all three factors working together.

These observations are made at this point to supplement our discussion of cultural development in terms of energy alone. It might be pointed out, for example, that a certain pastoral, or even a hunting or fishing, culture is more advanced, more highly developed as measured in terms of our own standard, the amount of human need-serving goods and services produced per unit of human labor, than a certain culture in which agriculture is practiced. This is quite possible, but it does not affect the validity of our generalizations concerning these modes of life as ways of harnessing energy. An exceptionally favorable environment, or a highly efficient set of tools for the use of energy, or both, might offset an inferior means of harnessing energy. Some hunting or fishing cultures might produce more food per unit of human labor than some primitive horticultural systems. An abundance of game, such as bison in the Plains, especially after the introduction of the horse, or of fish such as salmon in the Northwest Coast area, plus effective means for appropriating such resources, might produce a higher culture than a crude agricultural technique in an unfavorable environment. There are even cases of peoples abandoning horticulture and reverting wholly to hunting. But these facts do not affect the validity of our generalizations concerning the harnessing of energy. They merely illustrate the fact that every cultural system is determined by instrumental and environmental factors as well as by that of energy. We may note, however, that all the lowest cultures have neither agriculture nor herds or flocks; all the highest have agriculture, and in no case has a pastoral system produced a culture as advanced as the highest produced by the cultivation of plants. Our generalizations regarding the relative merits of hunting, fishing, gathering, pastoral, and agricultural systems, as types of control over the forces of nature, are thus supported by culture history in world outline. Subsistence upon wild foods is the most inferior of these methods of control; agriculture, the best.

This does not mean, however, that a people must "pass through these three stages of development" in succession. A *people* may go directly from a wild-food economy to agriculture without ever having flocks or herds at all, as of course many American Indian tribes have done. A people may even give up their gardens and return wholly to a wild-food economy as some North American tribes did, living in or near the Great Plains with its swarming herds of bison, after the introduction of the horse and the beginning of a westward migration of white men. Neither is it necessary for a pastoral stage to precede an agricultural stage in the cultural-evolutionary process. It would be superfluous to mention this, so obvious is it, were it not for the tradition, still extant, that early evolutionists insisted upon a pastoral stage as a prerequisite to an agricultural stage. We know of no reputable anthropologist, however, who ever held such a view.

We are not concerned here with the *history* of the domestication of animals or the cultivation of plants. We might merely mention in passing that it has been animals who live in flocks and herds, like sheep, cattle, and horses, that have played prominent roles in culture building by providing food, hides and fibers, and motive power. Among cultivated plants the cereals are of greatest importance. They have been, as Tylor put it, "the great moving power of civilization";[27] all the great cultures of history have been developed and sustained by the cultivation of cereals.

We may remark also that the domestication of animals was the work of men, principally, as the origin of cultivation of plants was the achievement of women. The male hunter became a pastoralist; the female collector of wild plant foods, a horticulturalist. This division of labor between the sexes has had great import for social organization, in domestic food economies as well as in wild-food cultures.

Environment. We propose to deal at length with the instrumental factor in cultural development later. We may, however, dispose of the environmental factor now, once and for all, so far as evolutionist theory is concerned. Every cultural system exists and functions in a natural habitat, a collocation of flora, fauna, topography, altitude, meteorologic conditions and forces, and so on. And every culture is of course affected by these environmental factors. But the relationship between culture and environment is not a one-to-one correlation by any means. Environment does not "determine" culture in the sense that "given the environment, we can predict the culture."[28] Environments vary, and their influence and effect upon cultures vary likewise. Some habitats are suitable for agriculture, a pastoral economy, or fishing, manufacturing, etc.; others are not; they may even render certain types of cultural adjustment to nature impossible. But the relationship of culture to environment is determined to a very great extent by the degree of cultural development. The region now known as Kansas was not suitable for agriculture for a people with a culture like that of the Dakota Indians in A.D. 1800. The same region is not suited to a hunting economy now. Whether the coal and iron deposits, or the water-power resources, of a region will be exploited or not depends upon the degree of development of the culture of that region. This observation helps to make explicit and apparent an important generalization about the relationship between culture and environment: features of the natural habitat become significant only when and as they are introduced into cultural systems and become incorporated in them as cultural elements. The coal and iron of western Europe, or the water power of England, become significant only at certain levels of cultural development. The flowing streams of England were relatively insignificant culturally in A.D.1200; they became tremendously important as sources of power for industry in the seventeenth and eighteenth centuries; with the development of the steam engine and the exploitation of coal resources, they became relatively insignificant again. Thus we see that although natural habitat exerts an influence upon culture, we can learn more about this influence from a consideration of the culture and its degree of development than by a mere inventory of environmental features.

But a consideration of environmental influence is relevant only to studies of particular cultures; it is not pertinent to a general study of culture as such. If we are concerned with the culture of Egypt in 3000 B.C., of England in A.D. 900, of British Columbia or Kansas in 1850, etc., then one must take the natural habitat into account. But if one is concerned with culture as a distinct class of phenomena, if one wishes to discover how cultural systems are structured and how they function as cultural systems, then one does not need to consider the natural habitat at all. If one wishes to ascertain the relationship between technological instruments and social organization, how and why social systems change, the role of art in social life, the relationship between mode of subsistence and the status of woman, how and why the culture of mankind taken as a whole has grown and developed through the ages, he does not need to consider the environment. The culturologist wants to work out the laws of behavior of cultural systems as such, just as the physicist has worked out laws for falling bodies. To be sure, the natural habitat is always there, and it exerts an influence upon culture at all times and places, just as the nature of the falling body and the density of the atmosphere always affect its fall. An autumn leaf falls in one way, a hailstone in another. A bullet falls one way in the atmosphere, another way in a vacuum. But the law of falling bodies is valuable *precisely because* it ignores the influence of atmosphere and the composition and structure of the falling body. In exactly the same way, the culturologist is trying to formulate laws of behavior of cultural systems in general. Like the physicist, he wants valid universals. If one wishes to deal with particulars, with particular cultures or particular falling bodies, then allowance must of course be made for particular conditions in each instance.

The significance of the origin and development of the agricultural arts, alone or in conjunction with animal husbandry, for the growth of culture was tremendous. For some 990,000 years culture had been developing and accumulating. But at the end of the Paleolithic era it was still on a very low level, comparatively speaking. Man had advanced considerably beyond other animal species, thanks to his use of tools and symbols. But he still subsisted upon wild food as did other animals, lived in small groups, and had neither metals nor writing. In a few thousand years, however, after agriculture got under way, the entire system had undergone a profound transformation. Technologically, the change was from a cultural system based almost wholly upon human energy alone, to one based primarily upon solar energy harnessed in cultivated plants and domesticated animals. There were profound social changes, also. Populations increased greatly in numbers and densities, which in turn found expression in new forms of social organization. Small villages grew into towns, and eventually large cities. Nations and empires took the place of tribe and clan organization. The industrial, aesthetic, and philosophic arts flourished. Metallurgy was developed; writing, mathematics, the calendar, and currency came into use. In short, in a relatively brief time,[29] only a few thousand years, after agriculture had become established as a means of control over forces of nature, the great civilizations of Egypt, Mesopotamia, India, China, and, in the New World, of Mexico, Middle America, and Peru, came into being. The origin and development of agriculture brought about a revolution in culture. The Agricultural Revolution will be the subject of Part Two of this work.

The role of tools. The technological process may be analyzed, as we have noted earlier, into two components or aspects. On the one hand, we have energy, harnessed and expended, and on the other, the mechanical means with which this is accomplished. A woman digs edible roots with a stick; a man shoots a deer with an arrow; corn is ground with a metate or a water mill; an ox draws a plow. Having sketched the course of technological development from the standpoint of energy, we now turn to the aspect of tool, or instrumental, means.

    As Ostwald has pointed out, the structure, use, and development of tools may be illuminated by thinking of them in their relationship to energy. "When a man tools a staff in his hand," he says, "he increased the radius of his muscular energy ... and was therefore able to apply it more usefully. By the use of a club he could accumulate his muscular energy in the form of kinetic energy and bring it into play with sudden force when the club alighted. By this means it was possible to perform work which could not have been accomplished by the unaided activity of his muscular energy in the form of pressure...."[30]

In the bow and arrow, muscular energy is transformed into form energy of the drawn bow, from which it may be released instantaneously and with great intensity. In the crossbow, muscular energy can be stored up indefinitely.

"Another kind of transformation," says Ostwald, "relates to the concentration of energy in small surfaces, as edges and points; both bring it about that muscular work by virtue of the diminution of resistance in the surface, is able to exercise so much greater an intensity of pressure .... Sword and spear unite the increased length of the arm-radius with the concentrated effectiveness of edge and point."[31] Other mechanical devices, such as levers, wheels, ball bearings, etc., have their significance in relation to the most effective or economical expenditure of energy.

The result obtained from an expenditure of energy within a cultural system is of course conditioned by the mechanical means with which the energy is controlled. Means vary; some are more efficient than others. One ax, for example, may be better than another. This is to say, more wood can be chopped per unit of energy expended with one ax than another. We may speak of the quality of the ax, or of instrumental means in general, as its degree of efficiency, or briefly, its efficiency. The efficiency of a tool may vary from none at all—or even less than nothing—to a maximum. We may express this range in terms of percentages: efficiency may range from 0 per cent, or less, to 100 per cent, but not more.

Consider a canoe paddle in a given situation. It might be so long, so slender, or so heavy as to be worthless or even to have a negative value. Its efficiency is then 0 per cent or less. But we can imagine and actually construct a paddle which is of such dimensions and proportions that any change would decrease its efficiency. Its efficiency is now 100 per cent of its capacity, practically as well as theoretically. What is true for a paddle is true for every other mechanical device—for harnessing and expending energy, whether it be a needle, a bow, or type of locomotive, or airplane. Each has a point of maximum efficiency beyond which it cannot be improved. Gains in the efficiency of an instrument may be made by the substitution of one material for another in the composition and manufacture of the instrument, as well as by improvement in design. Thus, an aluminum or plastic paddle might be superior to one of wood; certain alloys might yield greater efficiency in axes or engines than iron or steel. In other words, one type of instrument may be substituted for another type, but each type has a maximum of efficiency. And the number of types made possible through the use of combinations of materials is finite in practice, if not in theory. In final analysis, therefore, improvements in the efficiency of instrumental means must always be confined within certain limits. Practically, as we know from observation, actual limits often fall short of those theoretically possible.

There is an aspect of economy as well as of mechanical efficiency to be considered in evaluating the role of instrumental means of controlling energy. One type of tool may be more economical though no more efficient, or even less efficient, than another. *Economy* is here measured in units of energy required for the production of the tool. Early copper axes or knives were little, if any more, efficient than the stone implements they replaced, according to Childe.[32] But if a stone ax were broken, it would be difficult, if not impossible, to repair it so that another would have to be manufactured to replace it. The copper ax, on the other hand, could be repaired with relative ease. The cost in labor of the stone implement was much greater than that of metal, and so the latter would be preferred at equal degrees of efficiency. The same principle will apply to higher levels of technological development. It is no doubt often possible to make a machine more efficient than one of its type in use, but at a cost, either in energy or money, that would make it less economical to use. Thus considerations of economy may limit the efficiency of tools and machines in many instances. But whether we consider the use of tools from the standpoint of mechanical efficiency or of cost of production, the end result is the same: the tool or instrument that makes possible the greater product per unit of energy expended will tend to replace one yielding the lesser product in processes where the efficient and economical production of goods is the primary consideration.

We need not concern ourselves here with the varying skills with which a tool is used by craftsmen, since they may be reduced to an average, and thus considered a constant.

The social organization of the use of tools and machines is an important aspect of the technological process. Such things as division of labor, specialization, cooperation, systematization, and rationalization may affect the operation of the technological process very considerably, and with it the magnitude of result produced. But we need merely to recognize these facts here; we do not need to take them into account in our consideration of the nature and function of the instruments themselves.

Returning to our formula $E \times T > P$, we may formulate another law of cultural growth: *culture develops as the efficiency or economy of the means of controlling energy increases, other factors remaining constant.* This means, also, that the status, "height," or degree of development of a cultural system is proportional to the efficiency and economy of the mechanical means with which energy is harnessed and expended.[33]

A review of culture history brings out the following: Progress in cultural development, during the long era when cultural systems derived the overwhelming proportion of their motive power from the human organism, was accomplished almost exclusively in the realm of tools. Progress of this sort consisted in adding new tools to the cultural tradition and in the improvement of ones in use.

Mechanical progress was continued during the Agricultural Age also. But here we are confronted by a special situation. In cultivated plants and domestic animals we have both *energy* in definite magnitudes and *means* of harnessing and expending energy, and the two are inseparable. A plant of *Zea mays*, or Indian corn, is not only a certain amount of energy; it is also a means of controlling energy. A cow may be regarded as a means of producing milk, a milk-producing machine, that may be considered from the standpoint of efficiency and economy. Some cows, as machines, are more efficient than others; i.e., they produce more milk and butterfat per unit of diet than others. The same kind of observations could be made about hogs, sheep, and hens as meat-, wool-, and egg-producing machines, respectively. In some cases, such as milk cows, egg producers, etc., it is relatively easy to distinguish the means aspect from the energy aspect. But efficiency as a means, and energy in definite amounts, are virtually one and the same thing in cases such as the cultivation of cereals. A more efficient means of harnessing energy is also a greater magnitude of energy—larger ears of corn, for example.

We may distinguish, therefore, two classes of means of harnessing and expending energy: biological and mechanical. In the latter, instrumental means and energy are easily distinguished. The quality of the ax does not affect the amount of energy offered by the woodsman; the engine neither adds to nor subtracts from the amount of coal burned by it. But as plants or animals become more efficient means of controlling energy, the amount of energy varies also. We may distinguish the two aspects in logical analysis of course, but in actuality they are inseparable.

We may summarize our discussion of energy and tools in the following law of cultural development: *culture advances as the amount of energy harnessed per capita per year increases, or as the efficiency or economy of the means of controlling energy is increased, or both.*[34] Progress was due almost wholly to increase of efficiency or economy of mechanical means in the first stage of cultural development. In subsequent eras development has come from both sources.

It must not be assumed, however, that these two factors, energy and mechanical means, are equally significant merely because both play a part in cultural evolution and progress. The energy factor is much more fundamental and important. The fact that energy is of no significance as a culture builder without mechanical means of expression in no way invalidates this evaluation. If energy is useless without mechanical contrivances, the latter are dead without energy. Furthermore, no amount of addition to, or improvement of, mechanical means can advance culture beyond a certain point so long as the energy factor remains unchanged. Culture would retrogress, even if its tools and machines were perfect—and precisely because they were perfect—if the amount of energy harnessed per capita per year were diminished. On the other hand, an increase in amount of energy harnessed will not only carry culture forward because of this increase but will foster mechanical improvement as well. Mechanical instruments are indeed essential. But they are merely the vehicle, the means, the scaffolding, the skeleton; energy is the dynamic, living force that animates cultural systems and develops them to higher levels and forms.

Notes

1 Frederick Soddy, *Matter and Energy*, Home University Series, Oxford University Press London, 1912, p. 245.

2 The principles of thermodynamics were first formulated in their modern form by the German physicist R.J.E. Clausius (1822-1888), in 1850. The first law is the so-called law of conservation of energy, which says, in effect, that the total amount of energy in the cosmos is a constant. Clausius' formulations of the first and second laws are as follows: "Die Energie der Welt ist constant. Die Entropie der Welt strebt einem Maximum zu" [The energy of the world, or cosmos, is constant. The entropy (a mathematical factor which is a measure of the *un*available energy in a thermodynamic system) of the world, or cosmos, tends, or strives, toward a maximum]. Quoted from Clausius' *Mechanische Wärmetheorie*, Abhand. ix, S. 44, by J. Willard Gibbs in his famous monograph, "On the Equilibrium of Heterogeneous Substances," *Transactions of the Connecticut Academy of Arts and Sciences*, Vol. 3, p. 108, 1874-1878.

3 Ludwig Boltzmann, "Der zweite Haupsatz der mechanischen Wärmetheorie," in *Populäre Schriften*, 1905, pp. 39-40, And today: "The whole web of life is ... a struggle for free energy, whether it be between shrub and tree for a place in the sun, between a locust and a rabbit for the energy-yielding compounds of leaves, or between lion and tiger for the flesh of an antelope. Free energy all living things must have...." Ralph W. Gerard, *Unresting Cells*, Harper & Brothers, New York, 1940, p.209.

4 "Anthropogeny likewise borrows from chemistry, physics and physiology the very basic principles that man, like other organisms, is a sort of solar engine that runs by means of the energy stored up in plant and animal food. It follows that this potential energy forms a hidden prize of great worth, to obtain which all animal life struggles unceasingly. Hence the drama of terrestrial evolution is motivated by the complexly ramifying competition and strife for food and for reproductive

mates; this principle operates as strongly in the latest stages of life as it did in the earliest." William K. Gregory, "The New Anthropogeny: Twenty-five Stages of Vertebrate Evolution, from Silurian Chordate to Man," *Science*, vol. 77, p. 30, 1933.

5   We are following here the argument of Erwin Schrödinger as set forth in *What is Life?* Cambridge University Press, New York, 1944, pp.71-72.

6   Ibid., pp. 72, 75.

7   "... Energies flow through their bodies...this can take place only in such away that the living organism takes up energy of a higher potential and gives it off at a lower potential." Wilhelm Ostwald, "The Relations of Biology and the Neighboring Sciences," *University of California Publications in Physiology*, vol. I, no. 4, p.24, 1903.

8   Alfred J. Lotka, *Elements of Physical Biology*, The Williams & Wilkins Company, Baltimore, 1925, p. 354.

9   Bertrand Russell, *Philosophy*, W. W. Norton & Company, Inc., 1927, p. 27.

10 G.G. Simpson, *The Meaning of Evolution*, Yale University Press, New Haven, Conn., 1949, pp. 256-257.

11 Alfred J. Lotka, "The Law of Evolution as a Maximal Principle," *Human Biology*, vol. 17, p. 185, 1945.

12 "... Natural selection will so operate as to increase the total mass of the organic system, to increase the rate of circulation of matter through the system, and to increase the total energy flux through the system, so long as there is presented an unutilized residue of matter and available energy." Alfred J. Lotka, "Contribution to the Energetics of Evolution," *Proceedings of the National Academy of Sciences*, vol.8, p. 148, 1922.

13 We define *sociocultural system* as the culture possessed by any distinguishable group of people.

14 David Burns, Grieve Lecturer on Physiological Chemistry at the University of Glasgow, reports on experiments in which the amounts of energy required to give lectures were measured, the measurements being expressed in mathematical terms. See *An Introduction to Biophysics*, 1921, p. 329.

15 Soddy, *op. cit.*, pp. 10-11.

16 Erwin Schrödinger, *Science and the Human Temperament*, George Allen & Unwin, Ltd., London, 1935, p. 39.

17 See Leslie A. White, "The Energy Theory of Cultural Development," in *Professor Ghurye Felicitation Volume*, K.M. Kapadia (ed.), 1954, pp. 1-8, for a brief history of this theory.

18 Alfred J. Lotka uses the term "exosomatic"—he speaks of "exosomatic evolution." "The Law of Evolution as a Maximal Principle," *Human Biology*, vol. 17, p. 188, 1945.

19 If, however, the process of cultural development moves in a direction opposite to that specified for the cosmos as a whole by the second law of thermodynamics, the operation of culture within the system of nature is in perfect accord with the cosmic process. In the process of utilizing the energy that it harnesses, culture reduces

it from higher to lower levels of concentration, contributing to a more diffuse distribution of energy in the cosmos. Thus food is transformed and diffused as heat and work and reduced to lower levels of organization, i.e., to inorganic matter. In the burning of coal and oil, energy is transformed from compact, concentrated forms to loose and more diffuse forms. And in harnessing the energy of atomic nuclei, energy in even more concentrated form is released and diffused. Thus, *within* the system that is culture, we find a movement and a direction opposite to that specified for the cosmos by the second law. But in relation to the rest of the cosmos, culture is but a means of furthering the trend described by this law. The cultural process is therefore but an infinitesimally tiny eddy in the vast cosmic flow of things.

20 Soddy, *op. cit.*, p. 25.

21 When we deal with cultures in terms of magnitudes of energy harnessed and put to work we must specify the period of time during which this takes place, since magnitude varies with length of time. We select a year as our unit of time because, in addition to being convenient and easy to work with, it embraces a complete cycle of the seasons, and hence the whole gamut of the routine activities of any cultural system. If, however, we deal with cultures in terms of horsepower, no time period need be specified since horsepower is the rate of doing work.

22 The amount of energy that the human organism is capable of producing will depend largely upon the food-energy intake. Naturally we do not have figures for the diet of primordial man, nor even adequate data for present-day preliterate peoples. We do, however, have statistics for modern nations. The range within which the amount of food energy consumed per capita per diem varies is interesting and significant, especially with respect to animal proteins:

Daily Food Supply per Capita

	All Foods (calories)	Percentage of United States	Animal Proteins (ounces)	Percentage of United States
United States	3,098	100	1.8	100
Sweden	3,171	100.2	2.2	122
Japan	2,230	72	0.4	22
China	2,234	72	0.2	11
India	1,976	64	0.3	17
Mexico	1,855	60	0.7	40

Source: *Point Four*, a mimeographed publication of the U.S. Department of State, 1949, p.109.

23 The reader may be referred to George P. Murdock's excellent book, *Our Primitive Contemporaries*, 1934, for descriptions of cultural systems activated by human energy alone, as well as systems of a higher order.

24 V. Gordon Childe sets the date at about 8000 B.C., in *What Happened in History*,

1946, p. 17; *History*, 1947, p. 7; Robert J. Braidwood at 7000 B.C., plus or minus 1,000 years, in *Prehistoric Men*, 1948, p. 89. The tendency has been, during the last two decades, to shorten the era of food production by bringing the date of its origin closer to our own times.

25 Wool of the domesticated llama and vicuna was used in the Andean highlands in pre-Spanish times, and some Indian tribes of the Northwest Coast of North America used the hair or wool of the domestic dog for textile purposes.

26 "The dense, curly wool of sheep is wholly a product of genetic change and selection under domestication." A.L. Kroeber, *Anthropology*, rev. ed., Harcourt, Brace and Company, Inc., New York, 1948, p. 692; see also E. Cecil Curwen, *Plough and Pasture*, 1946, p. 31, and R.H. Lowie, *An Introduction to Cultural Anthropology*, rev. ed., 1940, p. 52.

27 E.B. Tylor, *Anthropology*, 1881, p.215.

28 "While it is true that cultures are rooted in nature, and can therefore never be completely understood except with reference to that piece of nature in which they occur, they are no more produced by that nature than a plant is produced or caused by the soil in which it is rooted. The immediate causes of cultural phenomena are other cultural phenomena...." A.L. Kroeber, "Cultural and Natural Areas of North America," *University of California Publications in American Archaeology and Ethnology*, 1939, p.1.

29 "... Finds in the Near East seem to indicate that the domestication of plants and animals in that region was followed by an extraordinary flowering of culture." Ralph Linton, "The Present Status of Anthropology," *Science*, vol. 87, p. 245, 1938.

"For a very long time no significant progress was made [in the New World], but eventually there came the discovery of agriculture; and with it increase of population and rapid development of higher culture." A.V. Kidder, "Looking Backward," *Proceedings of the American Philosophical Society*, vol. 83, p. 532, 1940.

30 Wilhelm Ostwald, "The Modern Theory of Energetics," *The Monist*, vol. 17, p. 511, 1907.

31 *Ibid.*, p. 512.

32 V. Gordon Childe, *What Happened in History*, 1946, p. 69.

33 "The degree of efficiency is a very good measure of culture ... for we call every machine and every process better which yields a larger amount of useful energy for an equal amount of raw energy, that is, which works with less waste." Wilhelm Ostwald, "Efficiency," *The Independent*, vol. 71, p. 870, 1911.

34 "... Progress of technical science is characterized by the fact: first, that more and more energy is utilized for human purposes, and secondly, that the transformation of the raw energies into useful forms of energy is attended by ever-increasing efficiency." *Ibid.* Ostwald is here speaking of technical science. But if cultural development as a whole rests upon and is determined by technological advance, what he says here would apply to the evolution of culture in its entirety.

Study Questions

1. How does White characterize the relationship between living systems and theory of thermodynamics?

2. Why is culture a thermodynamic system?

3. What is the role of tools in harnessing energy?

Further Readings

Sahlins, Marshall D., and Service, Elman R. (eds.). 1960. *Evolution and Culture*. Ann Arbor: University of Michigan Press.

Service, Elman R. 1985. *A Century of Controversy*. Orlando, FL: Academic Press.

Steward, Julian. 1972 [1955]. *Theory of Culture Change: The Methodology of Multilinear Evolution*. Champaign: University of Illinois Press.

White, Leslie A. 1949. *The Science of Culture*. New York: Grove Press.

—. 1959. *The Evolution of Culture: The Development of Civilization to the Fall of Rome*. New York: McGraw-Hill.

24

The Epistemology of Cultural Materialism

MARVIN HARRIS

Empirical science, then, is the foundation of the cultural materialist way of knowing. But merely to propose that our strategy should aim at meeting the criteria for scientific knowledge is to say very little about how scientific knowledge of the sociocultural field of inquiry can be acquired. When human beings are the objects of study, the would-be scientist is soon bedeviled by a unique quandary. Alone among the things and organisms studied by science, the human "object" is also a subject; the "objects" have well-developed thoughts about their own and other people's thoughts and behavior. Moreover, because of the mutual translatability of all human languages, what people think about their thoughts and behavior can be learned through questions and answers. What does a Bathonga call his mother? "Mamani." When does a Maring slaughter his pigs? "When the sacred tree has grown." Why are these Yanomamo men setting out to war? "To take vengeance on those who have stolen our women." Why is this Kwakiutl chief distributing blankets? "To shame his rivals."

No aspect of a research strategy more decisively characterizes it than the way in which it treats the relationship between what people say and think as subjects and what they say and think and do as objects of scientific inquiry.

Epistemological Quandaries of Marx and Engels

In *The German Ideology*, Marx and Engels proposed to upend the study of sociocultural phenomena by focusing on the material conditions that determine human existence. A basic aim of their strategy was to demystify social life through the destruction of the socially created illusions that warp human consciousness—for example, the illusion that it is buying and selling rather than labor that creates wealth. Picturing social life as continually evolving out of the daily life of ordinary people, they wrote of the need to identify individuals "not as they may appear in their own or other people's imagination, but as they really are..."

> In direct contrast to German philosophy which descends from heaven to earth, here it is a matter of ascending from earth to heaven. That is to say, not of setting out from what men say, imagine, conceive, nor from men a narrated, thought of, imagined conceived in order to arrive at men in the flesh; but setting out from real, active men.... For the first method of approach, the starting point is consciousness taken as the real living individual; for the second ... it is the real, living individuals themselves .... (Marx and Engels, 1976 [1846]: 36-37)

But what does one mean by "individuals as they *really* are," "*real* active men," and "*real* living individuals"? How does one tell the difference between a real and unreal person? Are all thoughts unreal, or just some? And if the latter, how does one tell them apart?

The epistemological points that Marx and Engels were trying to establish cannot be made by means of the concept of "reality." For scientific materialists, the issue of what is real or unreal is subsumed entirely by the epistemological generalities of the scientific method. If someone claims that shamans can fly, we insist on testable evidence. But our strategy rejects the implication that the thought itself is "unreal." Matter is neither more nor less real than thoughts. The issue of whether ideas or material entities are the basis of reality is not, properly speaking, an epistemological issue. It is an ontological issue—and a sterile one, to boot. Materialists need only insist that material entities exist apart from ideas, that thoughts about things and events are separable from things and events. The central epistemological problem that must be solved then is how one can achieve separate and valid scientific knowledge of the two realms. If materialists wish to solve this problem, I think that they must deal not with "real" and "unreal" but with two different sets of distinctions—first, the distinction between mental and behavioral events, and second, the distinction between **emic** and **etic** events. I shall take these up in turn.

Mental and Behavioral Fields

The scientific study of human social life must concern itself equally with two radically different kinds of phenomena. On the one hand, there are the activities that constitute the human behavior stream—all the body motions and environmental effects produced by such motions, large and small, of all the human beings who have ever lived. On the other hand, there are all the thoughts and feelings that we human beings experience within our minds. The fact that distinctive operations must be used to make scientifically credible statements about each realm guarantees the distinctiveness of each realm. To describe the universe of human mental experiences, one must employ operations capable of discovering what people are thinking about. But to describe body motions and the external effects produced by body motions, one does not have to find out what is going on inside people's heads—at least this is not necessary if one adopts the epistemological stance of **cultural materialism**.

The distinction between mental and behavioral events moves us only halfway toward the solution of Marx and Engels' quandary. There remains the fact that the thoughts and behavior of the participants can be viewed from two different perspectives: from the perspective of the participants themselves, and from the perspective of the observers. In both instances scientific—that is, objective—accounts of the mental and behavioral fields are possible. But in the first instance, the observers employ concepts and distinctions meaningful and appropriate to the participants; while in the second instance, they employ concepts and distinctions meaningful and appropriate to the observers. If the criteria of empirical replicability and testability are met, either perspective may lead to a knowledge of "real," nonimaginary mental and behavioral events, although the accounts rendered may be divergent.

Emics and Etics

Since both the observer's point of view and the participants' point of view can be presented objectively or subjectively, depending on the adequacy of the empirical operations employed by the observer, we cannot use the words "objective" and "subjective" to denote the option in question without creating a great deal of confusion. To avoid this confusion, many anthropologists have begun to use the terms "emic" and "etic," which were first introduced by the anthropological linguist Kenneth Pike in his book *Language in Relation to a Unified Theory of the Structure of Human Behavior*. Emic operations have as their hallmark the elevation of the native informant to the status of ultimate judge of the adequacy of the observer's descriptions and analyses. The test of the adequacy of emic analyses is their ability to generate statements the native accepts as real, meaningful, or appropriate. In carrying out research in the emic mode, the observer attempts to acquire a knowledge of the categories and rules one must know in order to think and act as a native. One attempts to learn, for example, what rule lies behind the use of the same kin term for mother and mother's sister among the Bathonga; or one attempts to learn when it is appropriate to shame one's guests among the Kwakiutl.

Etic operations have as their hallmark the elevation of observers to the status of ultimate judges of the categories and concepts used in descriptions and analyses. The test of the adequacy of etic accounts is simply their ability to generate scientifically productive theories about the causes of sociocultural differences and similarities. Rather than employ concepts that are necessarily real, meaningful, and appropriate from the native point of view, the observer is free to use alien categories and rules derived from the data language of science. Frequently, etic operations involve the measurement and juxtaposition of activities and events that native informants may find inappropriate or meaningless.

I think the following example demonstrates the consummate importance of the difference between emic and etic knowledge. In the Trivandwan district of the state of Kerala, in southern India, I interviewed farmers about the cause of death of their domestic cattle. Every farmer insisted that he would never deliberately shorten the life of one of his animals, that he would never kill it or starve it to death. Every farmer ardently affirmed the legitimacy of the standard Hindu prohibition against the slaughter of domestic bovines. Yet it soon became obvious from the animal reproductive histories I was collecting that the mortality rate of male calves tended to be almost twice as high as the mortality rate of female calves. In fact, male cattle from zero to one years old are outnumbered by female cattle of the same age group in a ratio of 67 to 100. The farmers themselves are aware that male calves are more likely to die than female calves, but they attribute the difference to the relative "weakness" of the males. "The males get sick more often," they say. When I asked farmers to explain why male calves got sick more often, several suggested that the males ate less than the females. One or two suggested that the male calves ate less because they were not permitted to stay at the mother's teats for more than a few seconds. But no one would say that since there is little demand for traction animals in Kerala, males are culled and females reared.

The emics of the situation are that no one knowingly or willingly would shorten the life of a calf. Again and again I was told that every calf has the right to life regardless of its sex. But the etics of the situation are that cattle sex ratios are systematically adjusted to the needs of the local ecology and economy through preferential male "bovicide." Although the unwanted calves are not slaughtered, they are more or less rapidly starved to death. Emically, the systemic relationship between Kerala's cattle sex ratios and local ecological and economic conditions simply does not exist. Yet the consummate importance of this systemic relationship can be seen from the fact that in other parts of India, where different ecological and economic conditions prevail, preferential etic bovicide is practiced against female rather than male cattle, resulting in an adult cattle sex ratio of over 200 oxen for every 100 cows in the state of Uttar Pradesh.

A while back I mentioned the burden of unoperationalized terms, which prevents social scientists from solving puzzles or even communicating effectively about their research. The first simple step toward operationalizing such concepts as status, role, class, caste, tribe, state, aggression, exploitation, family, kinship, and the rest is to specify whether the knowledge one professes to have about these entities has been gained by means of emic or etic operations. All notions of replicability and testability fly up the chimney when the world as seen by the observed is capriciously muddled with the world as seen by the observer. As I hope to show later on, research strategies that fail to distinguish between mental and behavior stream events and between emic and etic operations cannot develop coherent networks of theories embracing the causes of sociocultural differences and similarities. And a priori, one can say that those research strategies that confine themselves exclusively to emics or exclusively to etics do not meet the general criteria for an aim-oriented social science as effectively as those which embrace both points of view.

Etics, Emics, and Objectivity

Kenneth Pike formed the words "etic" and "emic" from the suffixes of the words phon*etic* and phon*emic*. Phonetic accounts of the sounds of a language are based upon a taxonomy of the body parts active in the production of speech utterances and their characteristic environmental effects in the form of acoustic waves. Linguists discriminate etically between voiced and unvoiced sounds, depending on the activity of the vocal cords; between aspirated and nonaspirated sounds, depending on the activity of the glottis; between labials and dentals, depending on the activity of the tongue and teeth. The native speaker does not make these discriminations. On the other hand, emic accounts of the sounds of a language are based on the implicit or unconscious system of sound contrasts that native speakers have inside their heads and that they employ to identify meaningful utterances in their language.

In structural linguistics, phonemes—the minimal units of contrastive sounds found in a particular language—are distinguished from nonsignificant or nondiscriminatory sounds and from each other by means of a simple operational test. If one sound substituted for another in the same sound context results in a change of meaning from that v of one word to another, the two sounds exemplify (belong to the class of) two different phonemes. Thus the spoken *p* and *b* of *pit* and *bit* exemplify two different English phonemes because native speakers recognize *pit* and *bit* (and *pat* and *bat*, *pull* and *bull*, and so forth) as words that have different meanings. The spoken *p* and *b* enjoy the status of phonemes not because they are etically different, but because native speakers perceive them to be in "contrast" when one is substituted for the other in the same context of sounds.

The importance of Pike's distinction is that it leads to a clarification of the meaning of subjectivity and objectivity in the human sciences. To be objective is not to adopt an etic view; nor is it subjective to adopt an emic view. To be objective is to adopt the epistemological criteria discussed in the previous chapter by which science is demarcated from other ways of knowing. It is clearly possible to be objective—i.e., scientific—about either emic or etic phenomena.[1] Similarly, it is equally possible to be subjective about either emic or etic phenomena. Objectivity is the epistemological status that distinguishes the community of observers from communities that are observed. While it is possible for those who are observed to be objective, this can only mean that they have temporarily or permanently joined the community of observers by relying on an operationalized scientific epistemology. Objectivity is not merely intersubjectivity. It is a special form of intersubjectivity established by the distinctive logical and empirical discipline to which members of the scientific community agree to submit.

Pike's Emic Bias

Much controversy has arisen concerning the appropriation by cultural materialists of Pike's emic/etic distinction. In large measure this controversy stems from the fact that Pike is a cultural **idealist** who believes that the aim of social science is to describe and analyze emic systems.

What Pike tried to do was to apply the principles by which linguists discover phonemes and other emic units of language (such as *morphemes*) to the discovery of emic units—which he called "behavioremes"—in the behavior stream. By identifying behavioremes, Pike hoped to extend the research strategy that had proved effective in the analysis of languages to the study of the behavior stream. Pike never considered the possibility of studying the behavior stream etically. He rejected virtually without discussion the possibility that an etic approach to the behavior stream might yield more interesting "structures" than an emic approach. To the extent that one could even talk about the existence of etic units, they were for Pike necessary evils, mere steppingstones to higher emic realms. Observers necessarily begin their analysis of social life with etic categories, but the whole thrust of their analytical task ought to be the replacement of such categories with the emic units that constitute structured systems within the minds of the social actors. In Pike's words (1967:38-39): "etic data provide access into the system—the starting point of analysis." "The initial etic description gradually is refined, and is ultimately—in principle, but probably never in practice—replaced by one which is totally emic."

This position clashes head on with the epistemological assumption of cultural materialism. In the cultural materialist research strategy, etic analysis is not a steppingstone to the discovery of emic structure, but to the discovery of etic structures. The intent is neither to convert etics to emics nor emics to etics, but rather to describe both and if possible to explain one in terms of the other.

Etics, Emics, and Informants

A common source of misunderstanding about the emic/etic distinction is the assumption that etic operations preclude collaboration with native informants.

But as a matter of practical necessity, observers must frequently rely on native informants to obtain their basic information about who has done what. Recourse to informants for such purposes does not automatically settle the epistemological status of the resultant descriptions.

Depending on whose categories establish the framework of discourse, informants may provide either etic or emic descriptions of the event they have observed or participated in. When the description is responsive to the observer's categories of time, place, weights and measure, actor types, numbers of people present, body motion, and a environmental effects, it is etic. Census taking provides the most familiar example. If one merely asks an informant, "Who are the people who live in this house?" the answer will have emic status, since the informant will use the native concept of "lives here" to include and exclude persons present in or absent from the household. Thus in Brazil I had to furnish specific instructions concerning godchildren and servants, who by emic rules could not be considered members of the household in which they were permanent residents. But once my assistant was properly trained in the discriminations that were etically appropriate, the epistemological status of his data was no less etic than my own.

Emics and Consciousness

Pike and others who have used linguistics as the paradigm for emic analysis stress the fact that the immediate products of elicitation do not necessarily furnish the structured models that are the desired end product of emic analysis. For example, in determining whether the two *p*'s in *paper* (the first is aspirated) are phonemically the same or different, one cannot rely on the native's conscious powers of auto-analysis. Native speakers cannot be induced to state their language's phonemic system. Nor can they state the rules of grammar that permit them to generate grammatical statements. It is true, therefore, that many emic descriptions are models of "structures" of which the informant is not conscious. Nonetheless, the validity of such emic models rests on their ability to generate messages that are consciously judged as appropriate and meaningful by the native actor.

Moreover, Pike did provide for what he called *hypostasis*—namely, the elicitation of conscious structural rules, such as "don't use double negatives." When one turns to elicitations concerned with the structure of thought and behavior as distinct from the structure of language, hypostasis is far more common. Questions such as "Why do you do this?" "What is this for?" "Is this the same as that?" and "When or where do you do this?" are no less emic than the question, Does *p'ap' er* (pronounced with two aspirated *p*'s) have the same meaning as *p'aper* (pronounced with one)?

The ethnolinguist Mary Black (1973:524) protests that the "emicist" does not go around "collecting 'verbal statements *about* human action' while an eticist is out there observing human action first hand." Black insists that it is the *structure* of the system of beliefs, including beliefs about action, that is studied in emic research, not the statements about the beliefs themselves: "The idea that ethnoscience is interested in language and linguistics for the purpose of having informants *make statements about their patterns of behavior* is rather simplistic and can be held only by those who have not done ethnosemantic work" (526).

I do not regard it as simplistic to insist that emics are concerned *both* with the conscious content of elicited responses and with the unconscious structures that may be found to underlie surface content. Black cannot maintain that complex emic structures are necessarily unconscious structures which can only be inferred from more superficial elicitations. Many important complex systems of rules are held quite consciously—for example, rules of etiquette, sports, religious rituals, bureaucracies, and governments. Black's notion of what constitutes authentic "ethnosemantic work" would also seem to exclude sociological surveys and opinion polls, whose findings have merely to be tabulated in order to achieve structural significance. Perhaps the fact the most cognitivists have not concerned themselves with manifest hypostatic ideological structures reflects their predilection for dealing with esoteric and politically trivial emic phenomena such as ethnobotanical and kin terminological distinctions.

Mental Etics and Behavioral Emics

If the terms "emic" and "etic" are not redundant with respect to the terms "mental" and "behavioral," there should be four objective operationally definable domains in the sociocultural field of inquiry.[2]

	Emic	*Etic*
Behavioral	I	II
Mental	III	IV

To illustrate with the example of the sacred cow:

    I *Emic/Behavioral*: "No calves are starved to death."
   II *Etic/Behavioral*: "Male calves are starved to death."
  III *Emic/Mental*: "All calves have the right to life."
  IV *Etic/Mental*: "Let the male calves starve to death when feed is scarce."

The epistemological status of domains I and IV creates the thorniest problems. What is the locus of the reality of the emic behavioral statement, "No calves are starved to death"? Does this statement refer to something that is actually in the behavior stream, or is it merely a belief about the behavior stream that exists only inside of the heads of the Indian farmers? Similarly, what is the locus of the reality of the etic mental rule: "Let the male calves starve to death when feed is scarce"? Does this rule exist inside the heads of the farmers, or is it merely something that exists inside of the head of the observer?

Let me turn first to the problem of the status of emic behavioral descriptions. Descriptions of the behavior stream from the actor's point of view can seldom be dismissed as mere figments of the imagination and relegated to a purely mental domain. First of all, there are many instances where there is a very close correspondence between the actor's and observer's views of what is going on in the world. When Indian farmers discuss the steps they take to transplant rice or to get a reluctant cow to let down its milk, their emic descriptions of behavior stream events are as accurate as any ethnographer's etic description would be. Moreover, even when there are sharp divergences between them, the emic and etic viewpoints are not likely to cancel each other out entirely. Even in the present rather extreme example, note that the farmers do not see the culling of unwanted animals as "bovicide" and that the mode of achieving the death of unwanted animals is sufficiently ambiguous to warrant that interpretation. Clearly the amount of discrepancy between the emic and etic versions of events in the behavior stream is an important measure of the degree to which people are mystified about events taking place around them. Only if people were totally mystified could one claim that their behavioral descriptions referred exclusively to mental phenomena.

The other thorny category, the etics of mental life (IV), has similar implications. People can be mystified about their own thoughts as well as about their behavior. Such mystifications may come about as the result of repressing certain thoughts to an unconscious or at least a nonsalient level of attention. In the example under consideration, the existence of the rule "when feed is scarce, let the male calves starve to death" can be inferred from the recurrently lopsided sex ratios. As I mentioned earlier, something very close to this rule can be elicited from some Kerala farmers when they are confronted with the question of why male calves eat less than female calves. Etic descriptions of mental life, in other words, can serve the function of helping to probe the minds of informants concerning less salient or unconscious beliefs and rules.

The road to etic knowledge of mental life is full of pitfalls and impasses. Extreme caution is called for in making inferences about what is going on inside people's heads even when the thoughts are those of our closest friends and relatives. The hazards increase when the thoughts belong to people in other cultures. For example, I became intrigued by the fact that the children in a small Brazilian town frequently came to school wearing only one shoe. When

I asked for an explanation, the children would look embarrassed and say that they had a sore on the unshod foot. However, I never could see anything wrong, with the foot in question. This blatant discrepancy between what I could observe and what the children said about the behavioral situation led me to make a false inference about what was actually motivating them. I supposed that, being children, they preferred to go to school barefoot; since that was not permitted, they did the next best thing. But what was really going on in their heads, as I learned by questioning the children and their parents, was something else. Informants said that it was better to wear two shoes. The reason for wearing only one was to enable siblings to share the same pair of shoes, in order to economize.

Psychoanalysts and their patients are familiar with the dangers of making inferences that contradict what the patient says and that rely solely on the analyst's inferences from behavior. Some psychoanalysts find a hidden motive for everything that happens. Thus if the patients arrive for their session early, they are "anxious." If they arrive on time, they are "compulsive." And if they arrive late, they are "hostile." Clearly anthropologists should use the etic approach to mental life sparingly and should not attempt to override every emic explanation with an etic alternative.

Cross-Cultural Emics

I shall now attempt to clarify the epistemological status of mental phenomena that recur in different cultures. Many anthropologists insist that when mental traits recur cross-culturally, the traits necessarily have an etic status. The focal case concerns the eight key concepts that recurrently figure as components of the world inventory of kin terminological systems.[3] Following Ward Goodenough (1970) and William Sturtevant (1964), Raoul Naroll (1973:3) identifies these as etic concepts: "These are the eight key etic concepts.... The inventory ... is validated by the fact that every known emic kin-term system can be most parsimoniously defined by using the eight etic concepts." Since, as Naroll says, the eight key concepts are derived from emic kin-term systems—systems in which the distinctions are real end appropriate from the participant's point of view—it is difficult to see why they should be called etic concepts. The reason cannot be simply that they recur cross-culturally. When a linguist reports that in a certain language voiced and unvoiced bilabial stops form a phonemic contrast, the epistemological status of [b] and [p] does not shift from phonemic to phonetic. Nor does such a shift take place as a consequence of someone reporting that many other languages including English make the same distinction. Or to take another example: suppose that in describing a particular culture, the ethnographer notes that people believe they have a "soul" that leaves the body at death. What difference does it make if a similar belief is found in a thousand additional cultures? As long as the concept is real, meaningful, and appropriate to the members of those cultures, it remains an emic concept with respect to those cultures.

The explanation for the difference of opinion about the status of the key kinship concepts lies in the use of these concepts to make inferences about mental distinctions in cultures that have yet to be studied emically. The fact is that not all eight distinctions are used in all kin-terminological systems (American kin terminology, for example, ignores relative age and decedence—i.e., whether the kinsperson is alive or dead). In analyzing an unknown system, one would naturally infer that it contains at least some of these distinctions, and in that case the operational status of the inferred distinction would be that of the etics of mental life. I can therefore agree with Ward Goodenough (1970:112) when he says that "emic description requires etics, and by trying to do emic descriptions we add to our etic conceptual resources for subsequent description," provided it is understood that mere recurrence is not the hallmark of etics and that "etic . . . resources for subsequent description" refers exclusively to the etics of mental life. I cannot agree, however, that our etic conceptual resources for the study of the behavior stream are dependent upon emic studies. The etic concepts appropriate for the study of the behavior stream are dependent on their status as productive elements in a corpus of scientific theories.

The Epistemological Status of Speech Acts
Much of the human behavior stream consists of verbal messages sent back and forth between relatives, friends and strangers. Does the emic/etic distinction apply to such events? Since language is the primary mode of human communication, and since it is the function of language to convey meanings, one might conclude that the emic mode is the only feasible approach to language as the conveyor of meaning. This is not necessarily true, however; etic as well as emic approaches to speech acts are possible. One does not have to communicate with communicators in order to understand the meaning of communication acts. For example, psychologists, **ethologists**, and **primatologists** routinely attempt to identify the meaning of communicative acts among infrahuman species by observing the contexts and consequences of such acts. Among chimpanzees one can say that" "bark" means "danger," a loud whooping means "food," an upturned hand is a "begging" gesture, an upturned rump a sign of "submission." If this approach is possible with respect to primate communication, why should it not also be possible in the case of human communication?

When I first thought about this problem in 1964, 1 concluded that the meaning of speech acts was accessible only through emic operations. In 1968 (p.579) I took the same position, stating that "from an etic point of view, the universe of meaning, purposes, goals, motivations, etc., is ... unapproachable."

This was an error. What should be said is that descriptions of mental life based on etic operations do not necessarily uncover the purposes, goals, motivations, and so forth that an emic approach can uncover. For the etic study of speech acts is merely another example of the possibility of an etics of mental life.

The difference between etic meanings and emic meanings of speech acts is the difference between the conventional or "code" meaning of a human utterance and its deeper psychological significance for speaker and hearer respectively. Let me illustrate this distinction with data from a study of speech acts carried out by means of videotape recordings (Dehavenon and Harris, n.d.). The observers intended to measure patterns of superordination and subordination in family life by counting each family member's requests and responses to requests during a week of observation. "Request" is an etic category of speech acts that includes requests for attention ("Mom!"), requests for action ("Take the garbage out"), and requests for information ("What time is it?").

The study was premised on the assumption that the etic meanings which lie on the surface of speech acts correspond in some degree to what is going on inside of the participants' heads. People do not *usually* say "go out" when they mean "come in," or "sit down" when they mean "stand up." But as in other instances of the etics of mental life previously discussed, the inference from what people say etically in the behavior stream to what they mean emically inside their heads can be extremely hazardous. For example, consider the following speech acts involving a mother and her eight-year-old son. At 10:50 A.M. the mother began to request that her son stop playing with the family dog:

Time Request
10:50 Leave him [the dog] alone.
11:01 Leave him alone.
11:09 Leave him alone.
11:10 Hey, don't do that.
11:10 Please leave him alone.
11:15 Leave him alone.
11:15 Leave him alone.
11:15 Why don't you stop teasing him?
11:16 Leave Rex alone, huh?
11:17 Leave him alone.
11:17 Leave him alone.
11:24 Keep away from him.

During the same scene the mother also repeatedly requested the same child to turn down the volume on the radio in the living room, as follows:

Time Request
10:40 Keep your hands off that [radio].
10:41 I don't want to hear that.
11:19 Lower that thing [the radio].
11:20 Come on, knock it off.
11:20 Lower that.
11:20 Get your own [radio in another room].
11:20 Keep your hands off this thing [the radio].
11:26 All right, come on. I've got to have that lowered.
11:27 Leave it alone.
11:27 Leave it alone.
11:29 Turn it off right now.
11:29 You're not to touch that radio.
11:29 Keep your hands off that radio.

One cannot assume that the principal emic component in the meanings of the above requests is the intention of the speaker to be taken seriously about turning the radio off or leaving the dog alone. If the mother intends to be taken seriously, why does she repeat the same requests twelve or thirteen times in less than an hour? One cannot argue that repetition is a token of her seriousness (like a prisoner who repeatedly tries to escape from jail) because she has numerous alternatives—she herself can turn the radio off, for example, or she can segregate the child and the dog in different rooms. Her failure to take decisive action may very well indicate that there are other semantic components involved. Perhaps she really intends merely to show disapproval. Or perhaps her main intention is to punish herself by making requests she knows will not be complied with.

The ambiguities are even more marked when we examine the hearer's role. One possibility is that the child rejects the surface meaning of the request, knowing that his mother isn't really serious. Another possibility is that the child thinks that the mother is serious but rejects her authority. Perhaps the child interprets the repetitions to mean that his mother would rather punish herself than punish him. To disambiguate these meanings, one might employ eliciting operations, the hallmarks of emic status. But the etic meanings of the speech acts viewed as a behavior stream event would remain the same.

To be a human observer capable of carrying out scientific operations presumes that one is competent in at least one natural language. Thus in identifying the etic meaning of speech acts in their own native language, observers are not dependent on eliciting operations and can readily agree that a particular utterance has a specific surface meaning whose locus is in the behavior stream.

This line of reasoning can easily be extended to include foreign speech acts, if we grant the proposition that all human languages are mutually translatable. This means that for every utterance in a foreign language, there is an analogue in one's own. While it is true that successful translation of a foreign speech act is facilitated by the collaboration of a native informant, what the observers intend to find out is which linguistic structures inside their own heads have more or less the same meaning as the utterances in the behavior stream of the foreign actors. Thus the translation amounts to the imposition of the observers' semantic categories on the foreign speech acts. The observers have in effect enlarged their competence to include both languages, and hence they can proceed to identify the surface meanings of foreign speech acts as freely as native speakers of English are able to identify the surface meanings of the English speech acts listed above.

The Emics of the Observer

Partisans of idealist strategies seek to subvert the materialist effort by claiming that "all knowledge is ultimately 'emic'" (Fisher and Werner, 1978:198). The allegation is that in the name of demystifying the nature of social life, the observers merely substitute one brand of illusion for another. After all, who are the "observers"? Why should their categories and beliefs be more credible than those of the actors? The answer to these questions is entirely dependent on whether one accepts the scientific way of knowing as having some special advantages over other ways of knowing. To deny the validity of etic descriptions is in effect to deny the possibility of a social science capable of explaining sociocultural similarities and differences. To urge that the etics of scientific observers is merely one among an infinity of other emics—the emics of Americans and Chinese, of women and men, of blacks and Puerto Ricans, of Jews and Hindus, of rich and poor, and of young and old—is to urge the surrender of our intellects to the supreme mystification of total relativism.

True, the practitioners of science do not constitute a community apart from the rest of humanity, and we are filled with prejudices, preconceptions, and hidden agendas. But the way to correct errors resulting from the value-laden nature of our activity is to demand that we struggle against our strategic competitors and critics of all sorts to improve our accounts of social life, to produce better theories, and to achieve higher, not lower, levels of objectivity with respect to both the emics and etics of mental and behavioral phenomena. Once again we must ask: "What is the alternative?"

Notes

1   Despite my reiteration of this point, Fisher and Werner (1978) have me equating science and ethics.

2   I am indebted to Brian Ferguson for this clarification.
3   These are: (1) consanguinity/affinity; (2) generation; (3) sex; (4) collaterality; (5) bifurcation; (6) relative age; (7) decedence; and (8) genealogical distance.

References

1973. Black, Mary, "Belief Systems," In J. Honnigman, ed., *Handbook of Social and Cultural Anthropology*. Chicago: Rand McNally, pp.509-577.

n.d. Dehavenon, Anna Lou and Marvin Harris, "Hierarchical Behavior in Domestic Groups: A Videotape Analysis."

1978. Fisher, Lawrence and O. Werner, "Explaining Explanation: Tension in American Anthropology." *Journal of Anthropological Research* 34: 194-218.

1970. Goodenough, Ward, *Description and Comparison in Cultural Anthropology*. Chicago: Aldine.

1968. Harris, Marvin, *The Rise of Anthropological Theory*. New York: T.Y. Crowell.

1976 [1846]. Marx, Karl and Frederick Engels, *The German Ideology*. In *Collected Works of Marx and Engels*, Vol. 5. New York: International Publishers, pp. 19-92.

1973. Naroll, Raoul, "Introduction," in R. Naroll and F. Naroll, eds. *Main Currents in Anthropology*. New York: Appleton-Century-Crofts, pp. 1-23.

1967. Pike, K.L., *Language in Relation to a Unified Theory of the Structure of Human Behavior*, 2nd Ed. The Hague: Mouton.

1964. Sturtevant, William, "Studies in Ethnoscience." *American Anthropologist* 66(pt.2): 99-131.

Study Questions
1. How does Harris characterize the difference between "emic" and "etic" forms of analysis?

2. How do emics and etics relate to "behavioural" and "mental" aspects of culture?

3. What advantages does Harris see in the "scientific way of knowing" over other epistemologies?

Further Readings
Harris, Marvin. 1966. The Cultural Ecology of India's Sacred Cattle. *Current Anthropology* 7,1: 51-64.

—. 1968. *The Rise of Anthropological Theory*. New York: Thomas Y. Crowell Company.

—. 1979. *Cultural Materialism: The Struggle for a Science of Culture*. New York: Random House.

—. 1981. *America Now: The Anthropology of a Changing Culture*. New York: Simon and Schuster.

—. 1990 [1974]. *Cows, Pigs, Wars and Witches: The Riddles of Culture*. New York: Random House.

PART IV

TOWARD 2000 AND BEYOND

INTRODUCTION

By and large, and in spite of their many differences, the anthropologists whose writings are the focus of Part Three shared a concern for the reformulation of theories of social and cultural structure. Broadly, British ethnographers adapted the structural-functional concept to explore political processes, conflict, and social integration; the French developed a wholly new understanding of structure as a universalized, internalized logic of the human mind; and American anthropologists concentrated on interpreting cultures as networks of symbolic meaning. Only the materialists and neoevolutionists eschewed this concern for cultural and social structures, to the extent that these were perceived to exclude a concern for scientific analysis. Still, the efforts of White, Harris, and others did not so much break new ground as revive the debates of the late nineteenth and early twentieth centuries, in which the advocates of evolutionism, championed by Tylor, met their match in Durkheimian sociology and, ultimately, its ethnographic application in the work of Malinowski and Radcliffe-Brown. In all cases, these generations of anthropologists "at midlife" contested with one another for authoritative voice within social and cultural anthropology; just as their prewar and "armchair" antecedents had done, anthropologists of the 1940s, 1950s, 1960s, and 1970s vied for the right to say which branch of anthropological theory best represented *the* Truth about human social and cultural life.

These disciplinary approaches did not exist in an academic vacuum, however, and certainly by the late 1960s and early 1970s, more sophisticated social analyses were being developed by theorists working outside of the discipline of anthropology, whose writings would nevertheless bear significantly on future directions of (especially) ethnographic research. In this part, we present a number of selections by theorists who have broadly sought (with varying degrees of success) to develop approaches that transcend objectivity and Cartesian bias, in so far as they have both questioned the possibility of empirically-discernable social structures or objectified cultures, and sought to situate social cultural worlds *within*, rather than apart from, the unfolding of historical time.

The loosely defined, heterogeneous movements within anthropology and other disciplines, which we refer to as "culture and political economy," and "postmodernism," have been deeply influential for their critique of all static and apolitical approaches to the study of social relations. Champions of these "camps" (the term "school" seems far too homogeneous a descriptor for such a diverse assemblage of concepts, disciplines, and personalities) have incorporated several key concerns into their broad project. First, most have moved far afield of Gluckman and his Manchester students in their emphasis on and attention to *power* and its everyday exercise and unformalized influence through time. Crucially, this focus has had ramifications for anthropological understanding of academic knowledge itself, in that anthropologists and others have come to view themselves as bias-laden subjects (the products of particular places and moments in history) and not passive observers of an "objective" world. For this reason, advocates of these perspectives have been unflinching in their demand that researchers pay strict attention both to the conditions under which academic knowledge and texts are produced, and to the biases that inhere in their ethnographic interpretation.

Deconstructing the Ancestors

The anthropological perspective that we are calling "culture and political economy" has roots in eighteenth-century analyses of capitalism and in the historically-grounded Marxist critique of capitalism and the "economies" of class-based power within and between nation-states. Insofar as the contemporary perspective owes its existence to an unabashedly *moral* discourse on the nature of class relations, anthropologists who embrace culture and political economy have incorporated and transformed this critique in such as way as to address the central theoretical concerns of anthropology *vis-à-vis* non-Western societies and cultures. Thus, adoption of this perspective has involved analysis of the effects of Western expansion into, and domination of, the non-Western world. The broadest question for which they have sought an answer might be phrased in this way: "how have indigenous societies of the colonial world been obliged to change in response to the history of military, economic, and ideological dominion imposed upon them since at least the sixteenth century?"

An important aspect of this questioning among anthropologists involved a deepening disciplinary introspection and critique. While there had always been challenges over matters of theory, debates of the 1970s and 1980s attained new levels of critical challenge not only to the logic, coherence, or analytical power of this or that perspective, but to the very methods used to obtain new knowledge and, with increasing vitriol, to the potential for personal flaws and incompetence to enter into the making of anthropological theory.

In Selection 25, "Introduction" and "Critique of the Vulgar Sociobiology," Marshall Sahlins (b. 1930)—who turned from neoevolutionism to French structuralism—challenges the anti-cultural tendencies of anthropologists who employ biologized, evolutionary arguments in their explications of culture. He argues (in the best tradition of Boasian anthropology) that individualized evolutionary motivations cannot account for broad social forms in as much as the latter fail to maximize the reproductive fitness of the former. Selection 26, "Mead's Misconstruing of Samoa," is a chapter from Derek Freeman's (b. 1916) pointed and relentless critique, *Margaret Mead and Samoa* (1983). This essay is an interesting counterpoint to Sahlins, because Freeman marshals historical evidence against what he elsewhere refers to as Mead's "extreme environmentalist conclusion."[1] That is, where Mead shared with Boas and Boasian anthropologists a firm conviction that social environment was foundational to understanding behaviour, Freeman argues that her "faith" led her to compose a work not of scientific anthropology but of ethnographic fiction based on flimsy evidence. He takes the "ancestor" to task not only for her failure to theorize a truly scientific understanding of adolescent Samoan sexuality, but for perpetrating a hoax on the academic establishment, a hoax that, for all its demonstrable flaws, continues to be influential today in how anthropologists think about the influence of culture on the individual and in the "confessional" writing style of much ethnography. Among others, Mead is decried for the inadequacy of her fieldwork methods and for her apparent willingness to accept the fabricated responses of a small number of intimidated (or mocking) field informants at face value—that is, as cultural reality—evidently in order to "see" what she (and her mentor, Boas) "wanted to see": proof positive of the cultural relativity of sexual mores.

While Freeman's writing in the 1980s on Mead and her legacy drew much attention from professional anthropologists (much of it unduly reactionary), he has continued to reflect and write on the matter. Most recently, he published *The Fateful Hoaxing of Margaret Mead: A Historical Analysis of Her Samoan Research* (1999). In this work, he incorporates the surprising testimony of one of young Mead's key field informants—still alive and (in anthropologist Michael Walter's salubrious phrase) "compos mentis" after 60 years.

Beyond the notoriety of its critique, Freeman's account reflects a growing interest among anthropologists in investigating the way in which anthropological knowledge is obtained and constructed. In this case, the critique is employed as a cautionary tale against the pitfalls of nonscientific anthropology and as a clarion call to the "decisive importance" of "indefatigable rational criticism." Although many of the theorists whose work we will cite in subsequent pages, and whose writings are included as selections in this reader, reject such overt scientism, the attention to historical detail in the production of knowledge has continued to be of deep importance to anthropological theory-making.

Culture, Political Economy, and the Colonial Encounter

That such questions about and challenges to the grounding and purpose of anthropological theory became widespread among many anthropologists working in the mid to late 1970s, reflects the degree to which many were disaffected with structural theory that neither accounted for social change nor addressed the many pressing ethical issues related to Euro-America's political, economic, and military influence in the developing world.

Closer to home, many anthropologists found especially troubling their discipline's undeniable historical participation in these relations of inequality. They were haunted by the possibility that they themselves, together with their disciplinary forbears, had played a role—however implicitly—in violating those same non-Western peoples whose right to exist they had championed and for whom they had frequently become self-appointed advocates. Specifically, the colonial "encounter" between Europe and the rest of the world, underway since at least the sixteenth-century voyages of discovery, was not a process from which scholars might easily extract themselves. A new generation of historically-conscious anthropologists attempted to formulate a more dynamic anthropological discipline that took such problematic relations into account. Among the most well-known of the researchers to work within a culture and political economic orientation have been Eric Wolf (1923-99) and Sidney Mintz (b. 1922).

Selections 27 through 29 stand alone as a bloc, in that they represent an interesting exchange between anthropologists seeking to move this debate forward. In Selection 27, Wolf calls for anthropological recognition of the pervasiveness of the capitalist world system and its implications both for the local cultural worlds it has penetrated and, by extension, for ethnographic analysis: how are local social worlds affected and changed by a global, political-economic system? These assertions are repudiated in Selection 28 by Michael Taussig, an historical "Marxist" anthropologist, who castigates both Wolf and Mintz for ethnocentrism in their work, and for being broadly naïve about the authoritative character of their own descriptions. Selection 29 is a final counter-thrust, co-authored by Wolf and Mintz, in which Taussig is himself berated for an apparent inability to appreciate different modes of anthropological analysis. In sum, the three selections are an outstanding, if typical, example of the kinds of debates that have circulated within the discipline as a new generation of anthropologists has sought to discard, once and for all, a static concept of social structure.

These selections also betray what has, as noted above, been a troubling aspect of anthropological research and theory in the closing decades of the twentieth century. However inconvenient to their purposes, many anthropologists have been deeply dismayed at the way in which even the most lauded ethnographic work has depended, and in many cases continues to depend, on the political and economic domination of non-Western peoples. Was the entire legacy of Enlightenment-grounded, Cartesian rationalism and empiricism, and with it all objectivist and empirical approaches to the discipline of anthropology, now to be understood as having been a mere facet of Western military impe-rialism and progressive capitalist expansion? Did this legacy constitute, as Carl Von Clausewitz wrote in an 1812 essay to Crown Prince Friedrich Wilhelm, a "war" that is nothing but "politics by other means"?

Ethical considerations set aside, the postwar disintegration of European colonialism had long since raised questions of importance to anthropological theory about the relationship between the developed and developing worlds. As early as the 1950s, some anthropologists found it increasingly difficult to imag-ine, let alone take for granted, the pristine, timeless, and overwhelmingly rural communities that had been the discipline's *raison d'être* since the time of Tylor and before.

Among the best known of postwar anthropologists to theorize the relations between the Western and non-Western worlds was the American ethnographer Robert Redfield (1897-1958). In distinguishing between "great" and "little" cultural traditions in Mexico, Redfield sought a means to connect in cultural theory what were surely connected in the world as he observed it; that is, the great traditions, which tended to endure in time and space, were locally modi-fied by people living in specific cultural contexts. Perhaps inevitably, such dif-ferences corresponded to social differences within any given society. Thus, the literate, urban social classes of his field studies tended to be guardians of the great traditions, while their illiterate, rural countrymen and women "lagged behind," elaborating perceptions of great traditions in locally meaningful ways—or little traditions. In specifying this integration, Redfield's perspective intentionally contrasted with prevailing British and American theory that still tended to assume a fundamental separation between the cultures of the illiter-ate, magical, rural, and primitive on the one hand and those of the literate, reli-gious, urban, and civilized on the other.

While this approach did indeed imply an integrated social order, the idea that some cultures were but faint echoes of others was tenuous at best. At worst, it resurrected the most ethnocentric aspects of Tylor's nineteenth-century con-cept of "survivals" from the dusty archives of anthropology's earliest days. Moreover, and for all the significance of these first steps to understand a world of interpenetrating, rather than discrete, societies, Redfield's perspective was insufficient for its failure to incorporate political relations. Thus, it was not equipped to address the more problematic ethical concerns of an anthropolog-ical audience that, in addition to expanding its numbers, was growing in sophis-tication and capacity for critical reflection on its own practices. For many, a binary theory of culture that artificially separated the world into the great and the little was hardly a refinement of the older civilized/primitive dichotomy. For this reason, this aspect of Redfield's work was at root dissatisfying and, even when treated generously, raised more questions than it answered. The specter of Tylor could not be easily banished from consideration. If these social inequities existed, how were they socially made to exist? Surely not by the outmoded concept of cultural survival?

Through the 1960s and into the 1970s, the dual conundrums of political relations and intercultural connections continued to gestate within anthropology, without clear resolution or direction. Meanwhile, outside the academy, insurrection and armed insurgency abroad (notably in Africa and Southeast Asia), combined with the feminist, sexual, and antiwar movements in the United States and elsewhere, contributed to an atmosphere in which leftist politics and Marxism became intellectually respectable in various fields of scholarship. While a number of academics incorporated the critique of capitalism into their work, particularly influential for anthropology were the insights of the economist André Gunder Frank and sociologist Immanuel Wallerstein, both strident critics of what they believed to be the destructive processes of global modernization. In analyzing the expansion of Western interests around the world, Gunder Frank proposed a theory of international relations in which "developed" nation-states controlled and exploited "underdeveloped" ones. Through this system of unequal exchange, underdeveloped nations became increasingly dependent on those same powerful, developed states that extracted surplus goods and labour from them—an insidious, vicious circle which accomplished nothing so much as the perpetuation of a two-tiered global order. Writing in the same period as Gunder Frank, Wallerstein likewise observed the growing prosperity of "core" nations in Europe and America, which systematically appropriated wealth generated at the "periphery" of the economic order. Thus, the globe increasingly resembled a "world system" of control, penetration, and subjugation of weaker states by more powerful ones.

These frequently acrimonious debates have concentrated on understanding, or "deconstructing," the foundations of anthropological knowledge so that new, process-oriented approaches could be developed. Culture and political economy as a perspective, and the concern with history that has accompanied it, have certainly been credited with shifting anthropological practice in this direction. Nevertheless, and to the extent that it is legitimate to distinguish analytically between the often seamless character of these arguments, the closing years of the twentieth century have seen the so-called "postmodern turn" in anthropological theory prevail as the preeminent analytical perspective.

After Modernity

While postmodernity has had its most far-reaching effect in the final two decades of the twentieth century, it is best understood when viewed in the context of a constellation of events, both within and outside of the academy, during the 1960s and 1970s. As noted, by the end of the 1960s, the various cultural and academic upheavals in Europe and the United States—the cumulative legacies of feminism, sexual revolution, Cold War, and disintegration of colonialism—precipitated a new questioning of orthodoxy among scholars across a range of academic fields.

As we have seen, among anthropologists these circumstances manifested themselves in an unprecedented level of interest in critiquing, or deconstructing, both the empirical foundations of traditional anthropological research and the disciplinary ancestors who championed them. The culture and political economy school thereby emphasized the ideological, and hence insidious, character of global capitalism and other aspects of Euro-American hegemony around the world. Anthropological political economists perceived, with some justification in our view, that "pre-politicized" anthropology was complicit, if unwittingly so, in a modernization agenda whose public benevolence obscured the worst excesses of industrial capitalism and its prevailing logic—a logic that not only sanctions but insists upon the commodification of human labour and social relations, regardless of those profound social inequities implied by, and which have developed as a result of, such processes.

And yet, there was no immediately obvious "heir apparent" within anthropology to approaches that, in various guises, promoted the "modernist" agenda. Culture and political economy was not as well positioned as it might have been to supplant structural theories, in part due to the intractable character of modernist epistemology within all the natural and social sciences. Wishful thinking aside, anthropology and related disciplines might critique the canonical and methodological opinions on which they had been founded as academic fields, but the empirical and Cartesian biases of the eighteenth century have never been far removed from ways in which research was carried out, and, indeed, they have always been at the roots of how anthropologists go about knowing what they know. Thus, anthropologists of all stripes share at least this basic assumption about the nature of their research and methods: that they are, in principal, capable both of eschewing bias and of apprehending an objective, external world. For this reason, and notwithstanding their explicit commitment to the study of social process and political relations, even proponents of culture and political economy participated in the modernist agenda. In assuming the basic objectivity and authenticity of their own knowledge claims, anthropologists working within this tradition have been open to the accusation of proposing yet another empirical scenario, fully in keeping with the Enlightenment project. The challenge that emerged for anthropologists working in the late 1970s and into the 1980s was how to extract themselves, however imperfectly, from the epistemological orientations that had dominated Western academe since at least the eighteenth century.

Although these insights are now among the most commonplace that exist in anthropology, they emerged only gradually and in response to the challenge posed by scholars working in various disciplines. The contributions of two social theorists will be discussed in light of their enduring influence on a recent generation of anthropologists trying to carve out a new body of truly post "modern," post "structural" social and cultural theory: Michel Foucault and Pierre Bourdieu. Because their work has been so important for social and cultural anthropology in recent years, we include as readings an interview conducted with Foucault and an essay on social theory by Bourdieu.

Among the most influential of social theorists of the past 30 years is the French historian and philosopher Michel Foucault (1926-84), and his work deserves a brief sketch for the impact it has had on anthropological theory. Selection 30, "Truth and Power," which takes the form of an interview between Foucault, Alessandro Fontana, and Pasquale Pasquino, is representative of his theoretical concerns and general perspective. In brief, Foucault was concerned to reveal how sundry non-political institutions, roles, and relationships were in fact eminently political, if tacitly so. Specifically, he believed that social life was characterized generally by a pervasive economy of powerful, circulating "discourses," such that formal political institutions comprised only one set of social mechanisms through which power was exercised. Power was, in other words, inscribed in everyday life, to the extent that many (if not all) taken-for-granted social roles and institutions bore the stamp of power— power to regulate social hierarchies and structures through control of the conditions in which "knowledge" and "truth," and hence socially-accepted "reality," were produced.

In this scenario, therefore, the dominant classes of a given society have had a more effective means of reproducing their own authority than formal politics or legitimate military force alone could provide. Domination has also meant having the capacity to control what people take for granted about the world, as mediated by a host of institutions that reach into the most intimate realms of daily life. Thus, hospitals, schools, universities, laboratories, prisons, asylums, museums, and churches, together with all those who obliviously participate in their function, have been crucibles in which ideology masquerading as objective knowledge has been produced for mass consumption and disciplined acceptance.

Although less clear about what the impetus for any social change could be in this apparently totalizing system, Foucault's detailed historical studies on prisons and state discipline, sexuality, and what he called the "archaeology of knowledge" (that is, discovery of hidden ways-of-knowing that have been marginalized by dominant, powerful social systems; for instance, the spread of Christianity displacing indigeneous religons throughout the Americas and elsewhere) mark the contours of the exercise of social domination and authority in the post-Enlightenment period. This has happened by way of the many mechanisms of control embedded in such pervasive ideological systems as humanism, medicine, and science itself. In contrast, Foucault argued, other configurations of knowledge/power—those not acceptable to orthodoxy—have been rendered illegitimate by their exclusion from everyday discourses.

A second Frenchman whose work has been of great importance to sociocultural theory in the closing decades of the twentieth century is Pierre Bourdieu (b. 1930). Selection 31, taken from one of his most influential theoretical treatises, *Outline of a Theory of Practice* (1977), discusses several of his key ideas, among them, the analytical concept of "habitus." An anthropologist by training, Bourdieu has been concerned with theorizing relations of social power. Indeed, Foucault and Bourdieu advocate similar theories in so far as both view the exercise of power as something that happens in and through routine aspects of life. Bourdieu holds that the individual social actor is central to this process, because it is by way of the individual's cultural practice or "praxis" that symbols are manipulated to assemble social structures and hierarchies. In particular, Bourdieu's agents create, reproduce, and change a variety of taxonomic categories that are the basis for all social relations. These taxonomies do not merely represent the world, but actually make the world what it is for those who inhabit it. Consequently, those who are able to control the character and distribution of some taxonomies to the exclusion of others control the basis for knowledge, authority, and power in any society.

Bourdieu's theory of practice holds that individuals are more than the sum of those powerful social forces (i.e., Foucault's discourses) that discipline them: they are the complex and unique products of personal histories and social positioning (what Bourdieu refers to as the habitus) within various fields of relationships (for instance, artistic, religious, economic, and intellectual). For Bourdieu, the idea of the field replaces that of "culture" in the sense that fields are not conceived of as things or objects, as has been a traditional point of view in anthropology. Far from being organisms, much less superorganic phenomena, fields are porous networks of relations. Although these overlap in time and space, they are nevertheless discrete and integrated according to particular logics that are subject to transformation through the intentioned, creative agency of individuals.

Both Foucault's and Bourdieu's ideas have been influential in stimulating new ways of making anthropological theory and, although these have been deeply insightful, they have likewise proved mystifying for those still seeking certainty and empiricism in social research.

Anthropology in a New Millennium

Much ink has been used by a recent generation of anthropologists both to lauding and bemoaning the dramatic shifts in theory and practice heralded in the work of Foucault, Bourdieu, and others. For anthropology, one unfortunate (if inevitable) consequence of approaches that question or even deny the possibility of authoritative knowledge has been an uncomfortable atmosphere of uncertainty and confusion that greets new students to the field. While the abundance of theoretical perspectives within contemporary anthropology is doubtless exhilarating for many, it remains a discouraging aspect of the discipline for others, who are easily confounded by the sheer volume and complexity of texts and orientations. Many ask whether the anthropological library has in fact grown so large that one no longer sees the forest for the trees?

In grappling with these difficult questions, we have chosen five essays—by Marilyn Strathern (Selection 32), Benedict Anderson (Selection 33), James Clifford (Selection 34), George E. Marcus and Michael M.J. Fischer (Selection 35), and Sherry B. Ortner (Selection 36)—to represent our current period of critical reflection and disciplinary introspection. Significantly, since being penned in the 1980s, several among these have themselves become influential texts in helping to guide a new generation of anthropologists through what often feels like an academic minefield of concepts and methods.

Generally, the current generation of social and cultural anthropologists continues to pay attention to those issues brought to light in the work of Foucault, Bourdieu, and the political economists, but likewise they retain interest in concepts that have been longstanding foci for anthropological research: among them, the importance of history and the manipulation of symbols. Specifically related to current disciplinary interests, Selections 32 and 33 have been chosen for their attention to two important areas of theoretical concern that have preoccupied anthropologists in recent years: gender and nationalism

Strathern's "Self-Interest and the Social Good: Some Implications of Hagen Gender Imaging" and Anderson's "Cultural Roots" reflect concerns that are at once perennial and current. Strathern's essay on gender among the Hagen of Papua New Guinea looks at how notions of maleness and femaleness are culturally constructed and manipulated in local, social, political, and economic context. The concept of personhood ceases to be attributable to discrete individuals who are, in the Western frame of reference, men and women. Rather, among the Hagen, maleness and femaleness are sets of "ethical" attributes that straddle Western perceptions of gender and which may be applied to both sexes. Moreover, Strathern shows how the symbols and meaning linked to maleness and femaleness in this society are both transposable to and affected by other social domains (for instance, the acquisition or loss of social prestige).

Selection 33 by Benedict Anderson is taken from his widely read book, *Imagined Communities* (1991). Anderson's work explains how another taken-for-granted category, that of the modern nation-state, has come to exist through broad historical processes that have taken place in Europe from the early modern period (sixteenth century), in particular response to the demise of a homogeneous religious community and the development and spread of print capitalism. Like Strathern, Anderson shows how meaning is constructed locally and how acts of vernacular creativity—the writing of novels and the proliferation of newspapers—stimulated the widespread imagining of new perceptions of time and, significantly, enduring (indeed, timeless) linguistic and place-centered communities.

While these essays are representative of current approaches to "doing" anthropology, Selections 34 to 36 engage the thorny business of reflecting critically on the past, evaluating the present, and charting a path to a future for the discipline. The "crisis in representation" discussed by Marcus and Fischer in 1986 and the inevitably "partial" truth-value of ethnography described by Clifford in that same year continue to be significant because concern for understanding the interaction of subjectivity and objectivity remains omnipresent among anthropologists. At the beginning of the twenty-first century, these arguments are no longer tinged with the same degree of urgency as they once were; and the anthropologists themselves no longer preoccupied (for the most part) with the potential demise of their discipline. Neither have Ortner's reflections on the destructive polarization of anthropology between a series of artificial oppositions (as we have seen the emic opposed to the etic, the mental to the physical, the idealist to the materialist, the subject to the object, the diachronic to the synchronic, and the local to the global) foreshadowed the end of academic anthropology, notwithstanding a slackening in popularity of Bourdieu-inspired practice theory.

For what reasons, then, are these selections included in this volume? These selections are significant for at least two reasons. First, because they capture the unsettled mood and disquiet of anthropology in the closing years of the twentieth century (each was penned in the mid-1980s), they are themselves already historical texts of considerable import in the discipline. We believe that they will remain barometers that measure, however subjectively, where the twentieth century's ebb and flow of theoretical perspective had brought the field, as practitioners approached the twenty-first century. They continue to evoke, some years after publication, an image of anthropology and anthropologists at a crossroads—a professional community "thinking out loud."

A second point, related to the first, is that, at the time of their original publication, the most troubling implications of postmodernity threatened the very possibility of authoritative knowledge and with it the integrity and *raison d'être* of anthropology. Generally considered six of the most respected voices in contemporary anthropology (then, as now), Clifford, Marcus, Anderson, Fischer, Ortner, and Strathern have been well-positioned to chart the way from which we came as anthropologists, to evaluate the postmodern moment of "crisis" in terms of its consequences for the future of anthropology, and to propose fruitful ways forward. By and large, their anticipation of a discipline in which practitioners pay ever stricter attention to the factors contributing to the production of knowledge has been correct, even as the fears of theory that is endlessly navel-gazing have not. In writing about this moment in the discipline's history, each of these anthropologists has produced elegant and eloquent narratives of our anthropological "culture" that continue to be powerfully insightful in these early days of a new millennium.

Beyond a certain historical value, therefore, these essays are still widely read by students because they highlight a fundamental shift in the perspective of anthropologists. Caught in a perhaps unresolvable tension between the diverse binaries that have characterized (or plagued) the development of anthropological theory, a postmodern generation of anthropologists has increasingly treated subjectivity and objectivity as cultural products in their own right: goals of analysis rather than points of departure. Where is agency located, and how does it operate in the creation of cultural forces such as history, gender, and nationalism? How do social agents—regardless of who or where they are—construct themselves and their surroundings, and how do these same constructions both constrain and enable the transformation of society and culture?

Note

1   In a recent letter published in the American Anthropological Association's newspaper, *Anthropology News* (May, 2000), Freeman cites what he views as fresh evidence (her own words, no less) that Mead was overly credulous when it came to the information supplied by a pair of young Samoan girls. We reprint his letter in its entirety:

I write to inform members of the AAA of the discovery of direct evidence that brings to closure the controversy over Margaret Mead's Samoan fieldwork of 1925-26.

This evidence is contained in a little known book, *All True! The Record of Actual Adventures That Have Happened to Ten Women Today* (1931). The adventure by "Dr. Margaret Mead," entitled "Life as a Samoan Girl," begins with reference to the "group of revered scientists" who in 1925 sent her to study "the problem of which phenomena of adolescence are culturally and which physiologically determined" among the adolescent girls of Samoa, with "no very clear idea" of how she was "to do this." It ends with an account of her journey to the islands of Ofu and Olosega in March 1926 with the "two Samoan girls," as she calls Fa'apua'a and Fofoa. Mead continues, "In all things I had behaved as a Samoan, for only so, only by losing my identity, as far as possible, had I been able to become acquainted with the Samoan girls, received their whispered confidences and learn at the same time the answer to the scientists' questions."

This account *by Mead herself,* is fully confirmed by sworn testimony of Fa'a-pua'a. It is definitive historical evidence that establishes that Martin Orans [see reference to Oran's work in the "Further Readings" following the selection] is in outright error in asserting that it is "demonstrably false that Mead was taken in by Fa'apua'a and Fofoa." It is also evidence that establishes that *Coming of Age in Samoa,* far from being a "scientific classic" is a work of anthropological fiction.

In Chapter 13 of *Coming of Age in Samoa,* Mead concluded unreservedly that the phenomena of adolescence are due not to physiology but to the "social environment." This extreme environmentalist conclusion was very much to the liking of Franz Boas. In 1934, in the *Encyclopedia of Social Sciences,* Boas asserted that "the genetic elements which may determine personality," are *"altogether irrelevant* as compared with the powerful influence of the cultural environment" (emphasis added). This is a succinct statement of the Boasian culturalism that from the late 1920s became, in the words of George Stocking [an eminent historian of anthropology], "fundamental to all American social science."

In Samoa, Mead had acted as Boas' agent and, having been given Boas' enthusiastic commendation, *Coming of Age in Samoa* became one of the most influential texts of the 20th century. We now know that the conclusion to which Mead came is based on evidence that is quite unacceptable scientifically. Furthermore, this also applies to Boasian culturalism, which at the beginning of the 21st century has become a scientifically unacceptable belief system.

This liberating change in the *Zeitgeist* is evident in the fact that the Intercollegiate Studies Institute, in listing the 50 worst and best books of the century, has adjudged Mead's *Coming of Age in Samoa* to be the "very worst" book of the 20th century.

[Readers interested in the ongoing debate over Margaret Mead and her work are referred to the "Further Reading" lists following selections 11 and 26.]

25

Introduction and Critique of the Vulgar Sociobiology [*The Use and Abuse of Biology*]

MARSHALL SAHLINS

Introduction

The publication of Edward O. Wilson's *Sociobiology: The New Synthesis* in the fall of 1975 was greeted, both within and beyond the academy, with a response of historic proportions. At least the reaction was all out of the proportions usually accorded a scholarly work issued by a scholarly press. Actually the storm had been building for years: Mr. Wilson, as he would readily acknowledge, is not the first sociobiologist, although he is clearly the most effective and comprehensive. The book in any case became a "media event," subject of feature stories and even front-page headlines in the *New York Times*, the *Chicago Tribune*, and other leading American dailies. It set off a running debate, as yet without resolution, in the pages of the *New York Review of Books* and in *Science*, the journal of the American Association for the Advancement of Science. By the spring of 1976, lectures and entire courses, pro and con, were being offered on the new discipline of sociobiology at Harvard, the University of Chicago, the University of Michigan, and other distinguished places of higher learning. A critical attack, issued by the Boston-based collective "Science for the People," was being vended at advanced intellectual kiosks across the country. The American Anthropological Association reserved two days of symposia on the subject at its annual Meetings in November, 1976, at which Wilson as well as other biologists and sympathetic anthropologists would argue the case for a major redirection in social-science thinking. In brief, **Sociobiology** has occasioned a crisis of *connaissance* and *conscience*, of knowledge and public consciousness, with overtones as much political or ideological as they have been academic. Willy-nilly, the present essay becomes part of the controversy. It addresses the general intellectual and ideological issues raised by *Sociobiology* and related writings from the particular vantage of a practicing anthropologist, which is to say, from a traditional vantage of what *culture* is. The tenor will be critical but I hope not hysterical.

For the central intellectual problem does come down to the autonomy of culture and of the study of culture. *Sociobiology* challenges the integrity of culture as a thing-in-itself, as a distinctive and symbolic human creation. In place of a social constitution of meanings, it offers a biological determination of human interactions with a source primarily in the general evolutionary propensity of individual genotypes to maximize their reproductive success. It is a new variety of sociological utilitarianism, but transposed now to a biological calculus of the utilities realized in social relations. As a corollary, sociobiologists propose to change the face and structure of the human disciplines. The "New Synthesis" is to include the humanities and social sciences. As the subject matter of these disciplines is not truly unique, they should be incorporated within an evolutionary biology that is prepared to supply their fundamental determinations. "Sociology and the other social sciences," E.O. Wilson writes, "as well as the humanities, are the last branches of biology waiting be included in the **Modern Synthesis**. One of the functions of sociobiology, then, is to reformulate the foundations of the social sciences in a way that draws these subjects into the Modern Synthesis. Whether the social sciences can be truly biologized in this fashion remains to be seen" (1975, p.4)

The answer I suggest here, is that they cannot, because biology, while it is an absolutely necessary condition for culture, is equally and absolutely insufficient: it is completely unable to specify the cultural properties of human behavior or their variations from one human group to another.

The political problems posed by the publication of *Sociobiology* have developed both inside the academy and in the society at large. As for the first, I will say nothing at length. It is only worth noting that the project of encompassment of other disciplines has become practice as well as theory. Anthropologists, sociologists, and others who have been convinced of the correctness of the sociobiological thesis find in it also a means of organized interdisciplinary competition. Sometimes the aggressiveness of the "attack" on the traditional wisdom—for so it has been characterized to me by an anthropologist *cum* sociobiologist—seems designed to describe and prove their theory of human nature at one and the same time.

On the other hand, in the larger society sociobiologists have had to bear vigorous attacks from people of the Left. Most of the discussion in the newspapers and intellectual journals is of this type. Although the practitioners of sociobiology are as bound to their ivory towers as any of us, which is to say that the only politics they know very well are rather of the feudal variety, they suddenly find themselves victimized (as they see it) as archdefenders of a conservative capitalism. Sociobiology is denounced as another incarnation of social Darwinism. The sociobiologists are accused of perpetrating an ideological justification for an oppressive status quo in which they happen to be rather privileged participants. (For a recent version of the debate, see *Bio Science*, March, 1976.) I do not think that Wilson and his coworkers were prepared for this kind of ideological reaction. Some might say that they were unaware of the political dimensions of their argument, but this poses complex issues of criticism which again are presented on two levels.

The first is, what to say about the intentions of the sociobiologists, or more precisely, are their motivations at all relevant? I would say they are not at all relevant, and I should like to refrain from the slightest suggestion of *ad hominem* criticism. This for a principled reason which happens to be one of my main criticisms of the theory itself; namely, that there is no necessary relation between the cultural character of a given act, institution, or belief and the motivations people may have for participating in it. While I do believe that the theory of sociobiology has an intrinsic ideological dimension, in fact a profound historical relation to Western competitive capitalism, this itself is a fact that has to be culturally and meaningfully analyzed—precisely because the lack of agreement between the character of the ideological act and the quality of the intent precludes any easy individualistic explanation.

Furthermore, and this is the second difficulty which criticism must acknowledge, it can he argued that there is no logical isomorphism either between sociobiology and social oppression. In a recent interview in the *Harvard Crimson*, E.O. Wilson is reported to have pointed out that, after all, Noam Chomsky is an "innatist" too—and surely Chomsky is a politically honorable man. But if, the argument runs, we insist scientifically on the infinite plasticity and malleability of human behavior, ignoring the biological constraints on human thought and action, that too is an open invitation to any tinhorn totalitarian to do with us what he will. And we will get no better than what we should. Now while this argument is surely discussable, I should like to concede the point, because again the lack of any strictly rational connection between the innatist outlook and social iniquity could sharpen the cultural dimensions of the issue. How, then, are we to explain the sensitivity of the Left to the thesis of sociobiology? For that sensitivity is surely a social fact. And how are we to account for the fascination of the public and the media? That is another social fact. The ideological controversy provoked by sociobiology is an important cultural phenomenon in itself. It suggests some kind of deep relation between the theory of human action advanced by sociobiology and the self-consciousness Westerners have of their own social existence. There is some relation here between the biological model of the animal kingdom and the natives' model of themselves. Now, if the natives concerned were of some other tribe, the anthropologist would without hesitation think it his task to try to discover that relation. Yet if there is culture

anywhere in humanity, there is culture even in America, and no less obligation on the anthropologist's part to consider it as such, though he find it even
more difficult to work as an observing participant than as a participant
observer. I should like to treat the ideological issues in this kind of ethnographic spirit.

Part 1, Biology and Culture, attempts to determine the inadequacies of
sociobiology as a theory of culture. It consists of a critique in two stages. The
first will be a brief criticism of what I call "the vulgar sociobiology," which is
not so much the work of Wilson as a premise taken up by the New Synthesis
from certain recent predecessors. The premise is that human social phenomena are the direct expression of human behavioral dispositions or emotions
such as aggressiveness, sexuality, or altruism, the dispositions themselves having been laid down in the course of mammalian, primate, or hominid phylogeny. The next and longer section is concerned with "kin selection," which
is a particularly salient form of the idea that human social behavior is determined by a calculus of individual reproductive success; that is, that all kinds
of sociability and asociability can be explained by the evolutionary tendency
of the genetic material to maximize itself over time. The objection to this view
constitutes a critique of "the scientific sociobiology" represented by Wilson
and colleagues.

Part 2, Biology and Ideology, examines the transformations of evolutionary
theory itself that have been occasioned by its ventures into social organization,
especially human social organization. I argue that the traditional understanding
of "natural selection" has been progressively assimilated to the theory of social
action characteristic of the competitive marketplace, theory characteristic of
late and historically specific development of Euro-American culture. From the
idea of differential reproduction dependent on chance genetic and environmental shifts, selection successively became synonymous with optimization or
maximization of individual genotypes and ultimately with the exploitation of
one organism by another in the interest of an egotistical genetic fitness. In the
course of this series of transformations, selection surrenders its theoretical
position as the orienting force of evolution in favor of the genetic maximization project of the individual subject. In the structure of evolutionary argumen-
tation, selection takes the role of a means of the organism's ends. A second section traces the parallel development in the sociological and popular
self-consciousness of Western civilization itself. Ever since Hobbes placed the
bourgeois society he knew in the state of nature, the ideology of capitalism has
been marked by a reciprocal dialectic between the folk conceptions of culture
and nature. Conceived in the image of the market system, the nature thus culturally figured has been in turn used to explain the human social order, and vice
versa, in an endless reciprocal interchange between social Darwinism and natural capitalism. Sociobiology, it is argued, is only the latest phase in this cycle:

the grounding of human social behavior in an advanced or scientific notion of organic evolution, which is in its own terms the representation of a cultural form of economic action. Hence, we have the popular and political reaction that greeted the announcement of this "New Synthesis."

It remains to note that I have written this essay with some sense of urgency, given the current significance of sociobiology, and the good possibility that it will soon disappear as science, only to he preserved in a renewed popular conviction of the naturalness of our cultural dispositions. For this reason the usual scholarly apparatus of extensive footnotes has been dispensed with. Key references are given in the text and the few footnotes explicate technical terms— which I have generally tried to keep to a minimum.

Critique of the Vulgar Sociobiology

"They're trying to kill me," Yossarian told him calmly.
"No one's trying to kill you," Clevinger cried.
"Then why are they shooting at me?" Yossarian asked.
"They're shooting at everyone,*" Clevinger answered. "They're trying to kill everyone."*
"And what difference does that make?"...
"Who's they?" he wanted to know. "Who, specifically, do you think is trying to murder you?"
"Every one of them," Yossarian told him.
"Every one of whom?"
"Every one of whom do you think?"
"I haven't any idea."
"Then how do you know they aren't?"

Joseph Heller, Catch 22

Taken generally, the vulgar sociobiology consists in the explication of human social behavior as the expression of the needs and drives of the human organism, such propensities having been constructed in human nature by biological evolution.

Anthropologists will recognize the close parallel to the "functionalism" of Malinowski, who likewise tried to account for cultural phenomena by the biological needs they satisfied. It has been said that for Malinowski culture was a gigantic metaphorical extension of the physiological processes of digestion.

It would take more effort, however, to recognize the thesis of vulgar sociobiology in the works of scientific biologists such as E.O. Wilson, R.L. Trivers, W.D. Hamilton, R. Alexander, or M. West-Eberhard. These scholars have not been concerned as such to make the case that human social organization represents natural human dispositions. That thesis has been the preoccupation of authors of the recent past, proponents of a less rigorous biological determinism, such as Ardrey, Lorenz, Morris, Tiger, and Fox. Scientific sociobiology is distinguished by a more rigorous and comprehensive attempt to place social behavior on sound evolutionary principles, notably the principle of the self-maximization of the individual genotype, taken as the fundamental logic of natural selection. Yet by the nature of that attempt, the main proposition of the vulgar sociobiology becomes also the necessary premise of a scientific sociobiology. The latter merely anchors the former in genetic-evolutionary processes. The chain of biological causation is accordingly lengthened: from genes through phenotypical dispositions to characteristic social interactions. But the idea of a necessary correspondence between the last two, between human emotions or needs and human social relations, remains indispensable to the scientific analysis.

The position of the vulgar sociobiology is that innate human drives and dispositions, such as aggressiveness or altruism, male "bonding," sexuality of a certain kind or a parental interest in one's offspring, are realized in social institutions of a corresponding character. The interaction of organisms will inscribe these organic tendencies in their social relations. Accordingly, there is a one-to-one parallel between the character of human biological propensities and the properties of human social systems. Corresponding to human aggressiveness we find among all men a taste for violence and warfare, as well as territoriality and systems of social ranking or dominance. Marriage, adultery, harlotry, and (male) promiscuity may be understood as expressions of a bisexual and highly sexual species. A long period of infant dependency finds its cultural analogue in universal norms of motherhood and fatherhood. Note that this kind of reasoning is also implicitly, explicitly, and extensively adopted by Wilson and his coworkers. *Sociobiology* opens with a discussion of the critical relevance of the hypothalmic and limbic centers of the human brain, as evolved by natural selection, to the formulation of any ethical or moral philosophy. These centers are said to "flood our consciousness with emotions" and to "orchestrate our behavioral responses" in such a way as to maximally proliferate the responsible genes. But most generally the thesis of the vulgar sociobiology is built into the scientific sociobiologist's idea of social organization. For him, any Durkheimian notion of the independent existence and persistence of the social fact is a lapse into mysticism. Social organization is rather, and nothing more than, the behavioral outcome of the interaction of organisms having biologically fixed inclinations. There is nothing in society that was not first in the organisms. The ensuing system of statuses and structures is a function of demography and disposition, of the distribution in the group of animals of different age, sex, or other classes, each with its characteristic behavioral propensities. Therefore, we can always resolve the empirical social forms into the behavioral inclinations of the organisms in question, and that resolution will be exhaustive and comprehensive. The idea I want to convey is one of isomorphism between the biological properties and the social properties.

Related to this premise of isomorphism is a mode of discourse characteristic of vulgar sociobiology, which amounts to a nomenclature or classification of social behavior. I refer to the famous temptations of anthropomorphism. Observing animal social relations and statuses, we recognize in them certain similarities to human institutions: as between territorial competition and human warfare, animal dominance and human rank or class, mating and marriage, and so forth. The analogy, the argument runs, is often indeed a functional homology; that is, it is based on common genetic capacities and phylogenetic continuities, an evolutionary identity of the dispositional underpinning. It follows that the social behaviors in question, human and non-human alike, deserve the same designation, which is to say that they belong in the same class of social relations. Usually the English name for the animal activity is taken as the general (or unmarked) label of the class, such that war is subsumed in "territoriality" or chieftainship in "dominance." Sometimes, however, the marked or anthropological term is adopted as the general name for the class and applied also to the animal counterparts. This, of course, smuggles in certain important propositions about the "culture" of animals. Again the anthropomorphic inclination is not confined to the vulgar sociobiology. To take a random and limited sample from Wilson's *Sociobiology: The New Synthesis*, we read of animal societies that have "polygyny," "castes," "slaves," "despots," "matrilineal social organization", "aunts," "queens," "family chauvinism," "culture," "cultural innovation," "agriculture," "taxes," and "investments," as well as "costs, and "benefits."

I shall not be concerned with this anthropomorphic taxonomy, which has been justly and effectively criticized by many others, so much as with the essential anthropological problem in the thesis of vulgar sociobiology. It is a problem that has often recurred in the history of anthropological thought, not only with Malinowski but principally in the "personality and culture" school of the 1940s and 1950s.

The inability to resolve the problem in favor of psychological explanations of culture accounts for the more modest aims of that school at present, as well as for the change of name to "psychological anthropology." The problem is that there is no necessary relation between the phenomenal form of a human social institution and the individual motivations that may be realized or satisfied therein. The idea of a fixed correspondence between innate human dispositions and human social forms constitutes a weak link, a rupture in fact, in the chain of sociobiological reasoning.

Let me explain first by a very simple example, a matter of commonplace observation. Consider the relation between warfare and human aggression—

what Wilson at one point calls "the true, biological joy of warfare." It is evident that the people engaged in fighting wars—or for that matter, any kind of fight-ing—are by no means necessarily aggressive, either in the course of action or beforehand. Many are plainly terrified. People engaged in wars may have any number of motivations to do so, and typically these stand in some contrast to a simple behaviorist characterization of the event as "violence." Men may be moved to fight out of love (as of country) or humaneness (in light of the bru-tality attributed to the enemy), for honor or some sort of self-esteem, from feel-ings of guilt, or to save the world for democracy. It is a priori difficult to con-ceive—and a fortiori even more difficult for an anthropologist to conceive—of any human disposition that cannot be satisfied by war, or more correctly, that cannot be socially mobilized for its prosecution. Compassion, hate, generosity, shame, prestige, emulation, fear, contempt, envy, greed—ethnographically the energies that move men to fight are practically coterminous with the range of human motivations. And that by virtue of another commonplace of anthropo-logical and ordinary experience: that the reasons people fight are not the rea-sons wars take place.

If the reasons why millions of Americans fought in World War II were laid end to end, they would not account for the occurrence or the nature of that war. No more than from the mere fact of their fighting could one understand their reasons. For war is not a relation between individuals but between states (or other socially constituted polities), and people participate in them not in their capacities as individuals or as human beings but as social beings—and indeed not exactly that, but only in a specifically contextualized social capacity. "They're trying to kill me," Yossarian told him calmly. "No one's trying to kill you." 'Then why are they shooting at me?' Yossarian might have had some relief from the answer of a Rousseau rather than a Clevinger. In a stunning pas-sage of the *Social Contract*, Rousseau justifies the title some would give him as the true ancestor of anthropology by arguing the status of war as a phenom-enon of *cultural* nature—precisely against the Hobbesian view of a war of every man against every man grounded in human nature. "War," Rousseau wrote, "is not a relation between man and man, but between State and State, and *individuals are enemies accidentally, not as men, nor even as citizens, but as soldiers*; not as members of their country but as its defenders. Finally, each State can have for enemies only other States, and not men; for between things disparate in nature there can be no real relation" (italics added).

The general point is that human needs and dispositions are not just realized, fulfilled, or expressed in war; they are mobilized. It is certain that a capacity for aggression can be, and often is, symbolically trained and unleashed. But aggression need not be present at all in a man bombing an unseen target in the jungle front a height of 25,000 feet, even as it is always so contingent on the cultural context that, as in the case of the ancient Hawaiians, an army of thousands, upon seeing one of their members successfully dragged off as a sacrifice to the enemy's gods, will suddenly drop its weapons and fly to the mountains. Aggression does not regulate social conflict, but social conflict does regulate aggression. Moreover, any number of different needs may be thus engaged, exactly because satisfaction does not depend on the formal character of the institution but on the meaning attributed to it. For men, emotions are symbolically orchestrated and fulfilled in social actions. As for the actions themselves, as social facts their appropriateness does not lie in their correspondence to human dispositions but in their relations to the cultural context: as an act of war is related to an international power structure, godless Communism, insolent nationalism, diminishing capital funds, and the national distribution of oil.

Is violence an act of aggression, generosity a sign of "altruism"? Ethnographers of Melanesia as well as psychoanalysts of America will readily testify that aggression is often satisfied by making large and unrequited gifts. For as the Eskimo also say, "Gifts make slaves, as whips make dogs." On the other hand, a person may well hit another out of a true concern for the latter's welfare. One man's altruism becomes some child's sore behind; and, "Believe me, I'm doing this for your own good. It hurts me more than it hurts you." There is, in human affairs, a motivational arbitrariness of the social sign that runs parallel to, in fact is due to, Saussure's famous referential arbitrariness of the linguistic sign. Any given psychological disposition is able to take on an indefinite set of institutional realizations. We war on the playing fields of Ann Arbor, express sexuality by painting a picture, even indulge our aggressions and commit mayhem by writing books and giving lectures. Conversely, it is impossible to say in advance what needs may be realized by any given social activity. That is why Ruth Benedict, upon examining diverse patterns of culture, came to the conclusion that one cannot define a given social domain by a characteristic human motive, such as economics by the drive to accumulate wealth or politics by the quest for power. The act of exchange? It may well find inspiration in a hedonistic greed, but just as well in pity, aggression, dominance, love, honor, or duty.

> "Pleasure" (or "satisfaction, or "utility") is not a natural phenomenon like the "five senses" of the physical organism. For every man it is determined by the social medium in which he lives; and consequently when it is adopted as a tool of analysis or a term of explanation of that social order, its adoption means the assumption in advance of all that social fabric of which an explanation is being sought. We hold this truth to be self-evident, that men who live by democracy, or by capital, will find in it their happiness, and that is all that is self-evident (Ayres 1944, p.75).

In sum, the sociobiological reasoning from evolutionary phylogeny to social morphology is interrupted by culture. One could be persuaded to accept the more dubious or unproved assertions at the base of this logical chain; for example, that human emotional dispositions are genetically controlled and that the genetic controls were sedimented by adaptive processes at a time beyond memory. It still would not follow that the constraints of the biological base "orchestrate our behavioral responses" and account thereby for the present social arrangements of men. For between the basic drives that may be attributed to human nature and the social structures of human culture there enters a critical indeterminancy. The same human motives appear in different cultural forms, and different motives appear in the same forms. A fixed correspondence being lacking between the character of society and the human character, there can be no biological determinism.

Culture is the essential condition of this freedom of the human order from emotional or motivational necessity. Men interact in the terms of a system of meanings, attributed to persons and the objects of their existence, but precisely as these attributes are symbolic they cannot be discovered in the intrinsic properties of the things to which they refer. The process rather is one of valuation of certain "objective" properties. An animal stands as an ancestor, and even so the son of a man's brother may be one of the clan of the ancestor's descendants while the son of his sister is an outsider, and perhaps, an enemy. If the matrilineal descent were deemed salient, all this would be reversed and the sister's son not a stranger but one's own proper heir. For the inhabitants of a Polynesian island, the sea is a "higher" social element than the land and the trade winds blowing from east to west likewise are conceived to proceed from "above" to "below." Accordingly, a house is oriented with its sacred sides toward the east and toward the sea, and only men who are of the appropriate chiefly descent should build these sides, which once finished will be the domestic domain of a man and his senior sons, who relative to the women of the family are "chiefly." By the same token, only the men will fish on the deep sea or cultivate in the higher land; whereas, their women work exclusively in the village and inside the reef, that is, the land side of the sea. The social arrangements are constructed on a meaningful logic, which in fact constitutes a human world out of an "objective" one, which call offer to the former a variety of possible distinctions but no necessary significations. Thus, while the human world depends on the senses, and the whole panoply of organic characteristics supplied by biological evolution, its freedom from biology consists in just the capacity to give these their own sense.

In the symbolic event, a radical discontinuity is introduced between culture and nature. The isomorphism between the two required by the sociobiological thesis does not exist. The symbolic system of culture is not just an expression of human nature, but has a form and dynamic consistent with its properties as meaningful, which make it rather an intervention in nature. Culture is not ordered by the primitive emotions of the hypothalmus; it is the emotions which are organized by culture. We have not to deal, therefore, with a biological sequence of events proceeding from the genotype to the social type by way of a phenotype already programmed for social behavior by natural selection. The structure of determinations is a hierarchical one set the other way round: a meaningful system of the world and human experience that was already in existence before any of the current human participants were born, and that from birth engages their natural dispositions as the instruments of a symbolic project. If thus necessary to the symbolic function, these dispositions are in the same measure insufficient to an anthropological explanation since they cannot specify the cultural content of any human social order.

(The proposition that human emotions are culturally constituted, although here stated synchronically, as a recurrent fact of social life could also he extended phylogenetically. As Clifford Geertz [1973] has so effectively argued, to say that a given human disposition is "innate" is not to deny that it was also culturally produced. The biology of mankind has been shaped by culture, which is itself considerably older than the human species as we know it. Culture was developed in the hominid line about three million years ago. The modern species of man, *Homo sapiens*, originated and gained ascendancy about one hundred thousand years ago. It is reasonable to suppose that the dispositions we observe in modern man, and notably the capacity—indeed, the necessity— to organize and define these dispositions symbolically, are effects of a prolonged cultural selection. "Not only ideas," Geertz writes, "but emotions too, are cultural artifacts in man" [ibid., p.81]. When the full implications of this simple but powerful argument are finally drawn, a great deal of what passes today for the biological "basis" of human behavior will be better understood as the cultural mediation of the organism.)

We can see now that the theoretical demand of sociobiology for an isomorphism of behavioral traits and social relations requires an empirical procedure that is equally erroneous. Sociobiology is compelled to take a naive behaviorist view of human social acts. Observing warfare, the sociobiologist concludes he is in the presence of all underlying aggression. Seeing an act of food sharing, he knows it as a disposition toward altruism. For him, the appearance of a social fact is the same thing as its motivation; he immediately places the first within a category of the second. Yet the understanding must remain as superficial as the method, since for people, these are not simply acts but meaningful acts. As for the acts, their cultural reasons for being lie elsewhere, even as the participants' reasons for doing may betray all the appearances.

By a roundabout way we thus return to the true issue in anthropomorphic terminology, for the error in metaphorically assimilating cultural forms to animal behaviors is the same as is involved in translating the contents of social relations in terms of their motivations. Both are procedures of what Sartre (1963) calls "the terror." Sartre applies the phrase to "vulgar Marxist" reductions of superstructural facts to infrastructural determinations, art for example to economics, such that Valéry's poetry becomes "a species of bourgeois idealism"; but it will do as well for the analogous reductions to the human species favored by the vulgar sociobiology. To speak of World War II, the sporadic combats between Australian bands or New Guinea head-hunting as acts of aggression or territoriality is likewise an "inflexible refusal to differentiate," a program of elimination whose aim is "total assimilation at the least possible cost." In a similar way, it dissolves the autonomous and variable cultural contents beyond all hope of recovering them. The method consists of taking the concrete properties of an act such as war, the actual character of World War II or Vietnam, as merely an ostensible appearance. The real truth of such events lies elsewhere; essentially, they are "aggression." But note that in so doing, one provides causes—"aggressions," "sexuality," "egotism," etc.—which themselves have the appearance of being basic and fundamental but are in reality abstract and indeterminate. Meanwhile, in this resolution of the concrete instance to all abstract reason, everything distinctively cultural about the act has been allowed to escape. We can never get back to its empirical specifications—who actually fights whom, where, when, how, and why—because all these properties have been dissolved in the biological characterization. It is, as Sartre says, "a bath of sulphuric acid." To attribute any or all human wars, dominance hierarchies, or the like to human aggressiveness is a kind of bargain made with reality in which an understanding of the phenomenon is gained at the cost of everything we know about it. We have to suspend our comprehension of what it is. But a theory ought to be judged as much by the ignorance it demands as by the knowledge it purports to afford. Between "aggression" and Vietnam, "sexuality" and cross-cousin marriage, "reciprocal altruism" and the exchange rate of red shell necklaces, biology offers us merely an enormous intellectual void. Its place can be filled only by a theory of the nature and dynamics of culture as a meaningful system. Within the void left by biology lies the whole of anthropology.

References
1944. Ayres, Clarence. *The Theory of Economic Progress.* Chapel Hill: University of North Carolina Press.

1973. Geertz, Clifford. *The Interpretation of Cultures.* New York: Basic Books.

1963. Sartre, Jean-Paul. *Search For A Method.* New York: Vintage Books.

1975. Wilson, Edward O. *Sociobiology: The New Synthesis.* Cambridge: Belknap Press of Harvard University Press.

Study Questions

1. How does the vulgar sociobiology threaten the integrity and autonomy of culture, according to Sahlins?

2. How does Sahlins explain the "sensitivity of the Left" to sociobiology?

3. What does Sahlins mean when he says that sociobiological reasoning is "interrupted by culture?"

Further Readings

Thorpe, W.H. 1979. *The Origins and Rise of Ethology.* Westport, CT: Greenwood.

Wilson, Edward O. 1975. *Sociobiology: The New Synthesis.* Cambridge, MA.: Belknap Press of Harvard University.

—. 1994. *Naturalist.* Washington, DC: Island Press.

—. 1994. *On Human Nature.* Cambridge, MA: Harvard University Press.

26

Mead's Misconstruing of Samoa

DEREK FREEMAN

When they were working together in 1927 on the characterization of Samoan culture, Mead and Benedict carried to its logical extreme their deeply felt belief that in human societies the traditional patterns of behavior set the mold into which the raw material of human nature flows. Thus, in *Social Organization of Manu'a*, in her discussion of dominant cultural attitudes, every detail of which had been "thrashed out" with Benedict, Mead wrote of the absolute determination of social pressure in shaping the individuals within its bounds. This notion that cultural determinism was absolute was "so obvious" to Mead that, as we have seen, she also avowed it in *Coming of Age in Samoa*, in respect of adolescent behavior.[1]

That this doctrine of the absoluteness of cultural determinism should have seemed "so obvious" to Mead is understandable. Anthropology, when she began its study in 1922, was dominated by Boas' "compelling idea," as Leslie Spier has called it, of "the complete moulding of every human expression—inner thought and external behavior—by social conditioning," and by the time she left for Samoa in 1925 she had become a fervent devotee of the notion that human behavior could be explained in purely cultural terms. Further, although by the time of Mead's recruitment to its ranks cultural anthropology had achieved its independence, it had done so at the cost of becoming an ideology that, in an actively unscientific way, sought totally to exclude biology from the explanation of human behavior. Thus as Kroeber declared, "the important thing about anthropology is not the science but an attitude of mind"—an attitude of mind, that is, committed to the doctrine of culture as a superorganic entity which incessantly shapes human behavior, "conditioning all responses." It was of this attitude of mind that Mead became a leading proponent, with (as Marvin Harris has observed) her anthropological mission, set for her by Boas, being to defeat the notion of a "panhuman hereditary human nature." She pursued this objective by tirelessly stressing, in publication after publication, "the absence of maturational regularities."[2]

In her own account of this mission, Mead describes it as a battle which she and other Boasians had had to fight with the whole battery at their command, using the most fantastic and startling examples they could muster. It is thus evident that her writings during this period, about Samoa as about other South Seas cultures, had the explicit aim of confuting biological explanations of human behavior and vindicating the doctrines of the Boasian school. By 1939 this battle, according to Mead, had been won. In retrospect, however, it is evident that her eristic approach to anthropological inquiry, which had sprung from the febrile nature-nurture controversy of the 1920s, is fundamentally at variance with the methods and values of science, and there can be no doubt that Mead's fervent desire to demonstrate the validity of the doctrines she held in common with Benedict and Boas led her, in Samoa, to overlook evidence running counter to her beliefs, and to place far too ready a credence in the notion that Manu'a could be put to anthropological use as a "negative instance."[3]

For Mead's readers in North America and elsewhere in the Western world, there could be no more plausible location for the idyllic society of which she wrote than in the South Seas, a region that since the days of Bougainville has figured in the fantasies of Europeans and Americans as a place of preternatural contentment and sensual delight. So, as Mead reports, her announcement in 1925 that she was going to Samoa caused the same breathless stir as if she had been "setting off for heaven." Indeed, there were many in the 1920s, according to Mead, who longed to go to the South Sea islands "to escape to a kind of divine nothingness in which life would be reduced to the simplest physical terms, to sunshine and the moving shadows of palm trees, to bronze-bodied girls and bronze-bodied boys, food for the asking, no work to do, no obligations to meet." Westerners with such yearnings readily succumb to the unfamiliar lushness of a tropical island, and there have been those who have described Samoa in tones of unconcealed rapture. Rupert Brooke, for example, who visited both American and Western Samoa in November 1913, wrote of experiencing there a "sheer beauty, so pure that it's difficult to breathe in it— like living in a Keats world, only ... less syrupy." While the Samoans in this heaven on earth were "the loveliest people in the world, moving and running and dancing like gods and goddesses, very quietly and mysteriously, and utterly content," with "perfect manners and immense kindliness."[4]

It was in comparably euphoric terms that Tahiti had been described to European readers after Bougainville's visit of 1768, as though the Isles of the Blest, of which Horace and Plutarch had written so alluringly, had materialized in the far away South Seas. The New Cythera, they were told, was an earthly paradise, with no other god but love, and with inhabitants who lived in peace among themselves, knowing neither hatred, quarrels, dissension, nor civil war, constituting "perhaps the happiest society which the world knows." This account is so strikingly similar to Mead's depiction of Samoa as to make it evident that in constructing her negative instance, she was, in fundamental ways, influenced by the romantic vision that had possessed the imaginations of Westerners from the eighteenth century onward. The Samoans, she told her readers, among whom free love-making was the pastime *par excellence*, never hate enough to want to kill anyone and are "one of the most amiable, least contentious, and most peaceful peoples in the world."[5]

A romantically beguiling vision, like those of Bougainville and Brooke! Yet, as I have shown in Chapters 9 to 18, these and numerous other components of Mead's depiction of Samoa as a negative instance, on which she based her claims about Samoan adolescence and about the absolute sovereignty of nurture over nature, are fundamentally in error, so that her negative instance is no negative instance at all, and her conclusions are demonstrably invalid. How did the young Margaret Mead come so to misconstrue the ethos and ethnography of Samoa? The fervency of her belief in cultural determinism and her tendency to view the South Seas as an earthly paradise go some way in accounting for what happened, but manifestly more was involved.

The Ph.D. topic that Boas assigned to Mead was the comparative study of canoe-building, house-building, and tattooing in the Polynesian culture area. During 1924 she gathered information on these activities from the available literature on the Hawaiians, the Marquesans, the Maori, the Tahitians, and the Samoans. These doctoral studies did not have any direct relevance to the quite separate problem of adolescence in Samoa that Boas set her in 1925, and, indeed, the fact that her reading was mainly on Eastern rather than Western Polynesia concealed from her the marked extent to which the traditional culture and values of Samoa differ from those of Tahiti. Again, during the spring of 1925 she had little time for systematic preparation for her Samoan researches. Indeed, the counsel she received from Boas about these researches prior to her departure for Pago Pago lasted, she tells us, for only half an hour. During this brief meeting Boas' principal instruction was that she should concentrate on the problem he had set her and not waste time doing ethnography. Accordingly, when in the second week of November 1925 Mead reached Manu'a, she at once launched into the study of adolescence without first acquiring, either by observation or from inquiry with adult informants, a thorough understanding of the traditional values and customs of the Manu'ans. This, without doubt, was an ill-advised way to proceed, for it meant that Mead was in no position to check the statements of the girls she was studying against a well-informed knowledge of the fa'aSamoa.[6]

It is also evident that Mead greatly underestimated the complexity of the culture, society, history, and psychology of the people among whom she was to study adolescence. Samoan society, so Mead would have it, is "very simple," and Samoan culture "uncomplex." In the introduction to *Coming of Age in Samoa* she tells us that while years of study are necessary before a student can begin to understand the forces at work within "complicated civilizations like those of Europe, or the higher civilizations of the East," a "primitive people" presents a much less elaborate problem, with a trained student being able to "master the fundamental structure of a primitive society in a few months."[7]

As any one who cares to consult Augustin Kramer's *Die Samoa-Inseln*, Robert Louis Stevenson's *A Footnote to History*, or J.W. Davidson's *Samoa mo Samoa* will quickly discover, Samoan society and culture are by no means simple and uncomplex; they are marked by particularities, intricacies, and subtleties quite as daunting as those which face students of Europe and Asia. Indeed, the fa'aSamoa is so sinuously complex that, as Stevenson's step-daughter, Isobel Strong, once remarked, "one may live long in Samoa without understanding the whys and wherefores." Mead, however, spent not even a few months on the systematic study of Manu'a before launching upon the study of adolescence immediately upon her arrival in Ta'u in accordance with Boas' instructions. Thus, she has noted that while on her later field trips she had "the more satisfactory task of learning the culture first and only afterwards working on a special problem," in Samoa this was "not necessary."[8]

For some ten weeks prior to her arrival in Manu'a, she had, it is true, been resident in the port of Pago Pago learning the vernacular, and had spent about ten days living with a Samoan family in the village of Vaitogi. But this experience, while it did give her a useful initial orientation, did not amount to the systematic study of the fa'aSamoa that would have enabled her to assess adequately the statements of her adolescent informants on the sexual and other behavior of the Manu'ans. Another problem was that of being able to communicate adequately with the people she was to study. Mead had arrived in Pago Pago without any knowledge of the Samoan language, and although she at once began its study, the ten or so weeks she gave to this task before beginning her researches was far too brief a period for obtaining a fluent command of the formidable Samoan tongue, with its multiple vocabularies stemming from the distinctions of the traditional rank system. In this situation Mead was plainly at some hazard in pursuing her inquiries in Manu'a, for Samoans, when diverted by the stumbling efforts of outsiders to speak their demanding language, are inclined not to take them seriously.

Mead, then, began her inquiries with her girl informants with a far from perfect command of the vernacular, and without systematic prior investigation of

Manu'an society and values. Added to this, she elected to live not in a Samoan household but with the handful of expatriate Americans who were the local representatives of the naval government of American Samoa, from which in 1925 many Manu'ans were radically disaffected. In his introduction of September 1931 to Reo Fortune's *Sorcerers of Dobu*, Bronislaw Malinowski expressed great satisfaction at Fortune's "ruthless avoidance" of both missionary compound and government station in his "determination to live right among the natives."[9] Of the immense advantage that an ethnographer gains by living among the people whose values and behavior he is intent on understanding there can be not the slightest doubt. Mead, however, within six weeks of her arrival in Pago Pago, and before she had spent any time actually staying in a traditional household, had come to feel that the food she would have to eat would be too starchy, and the conditions of living she would have to endure too nerve-racking to make residence with a Samoan family bearable. In Ta'u, she told Boas, she would be able to live "in a white household" and yet be in the midst of one of the villages from which she would be drawing her adolescent subjects. This arrangement to live not in a Samoan household but with the Holt family in their European-style house, which was also the location of the government radio station and medical dispensary, decisively determined the form her researches were to take.

According to Mead her residence in these government quarters furnished her with an absolutely essential neutral base from which she could study all of the individuals in the surrounding village while at the same time remaining "aloof from native feuds and lines of demarcation." Against this exiguous advantage she was, however, depriving herself of the close contacts that speedily develop in Samoa between an ethnographer and the members of the extended family in which he or she lives. Such contacts are essential for the gaining of a thorough understanding of the Samoan language and, most important of all, for the independent verification, by the continuous observation of actual behavior, of the statements being derived from informants. Thus, by living with the Holts, Mead was trapping herself in a situation in which she was forced to rely not on observations of the behavior of Samoans as they lived their lives beyond the precincts of the government station on Ta'u, but on such hearsay information as she was able to extract from her adolescent subjects.[10]

That this was her situation is made clear in Mead's own account of her researches. Her living quarters, she records, were on the back verandah of the dispensary, from where she could look out across a small yard into part of the village of Luma. This part of the government medical dispensary became her research headquarters, and soon the adolescent girls, and later the small girls whom she found she had also to study, came and filled her screen-room "day after day and night after night." When she began her researches in this artificial setting Mead was still only 23 years of age, and was smaller in stature than some of the girls she was studying. They treated her, she says, "as one of themselves."[11]

It is evident then that although, as Mead records, she could "wander freely about the village or go on fishing trips or stop at a house where a woman was weaving" when she was away from the dispensary, her account of adolescence in Samoa was, in the main, derived from the young informants who came to talk with her away from their homes in the villages of Luma, Si'ufaga, and Faleasao. So, as Mead states, for these three villages, from which all her adolescent informants were drawn, she saw the life that went on "through the eyes" of the group of girls on the details of whose lives she was concentrating. This situation is of crucial significance for the assessment of Mead's researches in Manu'a, for we are clearly faced with the question of the extent to which the lens she fashioned from what she was being told by her adolescent informants and through which she saw Samoan life was a true and accurate lens.[12]

As I have documented in Chapters 9 to 18, many of the assertions appearing in Mead's depiction of Samoa are fundamentally in error, and some of them preposterously false. How are we to account for the presence of errors of this magnitude? Some Samoans who have read *Coming of Age in Samoa* react, as Shore reports, with anger and the insistence "that Mead lied." This, however, is an interpretation that I have no hesitation in dismissing. The succession of prefaces to *Coming of Age in Samoa* published by Mead in 1949, 1953, 1961, and 1973 indicate clearly, in my judgment, that she did give genuine credence to the view of Samoan life with which she returned to New York in 1926. Moreover, in the 1969 edition of *Social Organization of Manu'a* she freely conceded that there was a serious problem in reconciling the "contradictions" between her own depiction of Samoa and that contained in "other records of historical and contemporary behavior."[13]

In Mead's view there were but two possibilities: either there was in Manu'a at the time of her sojourn "a temporary felicitous relaxation" of the severe ethos reported by other ethnographers, or the vantage point of the young girl from which she "saw" Samoan society must, in some way, have been responsible. As I have documented in Chapter 8, the mid 1920s were in no way a period of felicitous relaxation in Manu'a, being rather a time of unusual tension during which the majority of Manu'ans, as adherents of the Mau, were in a state of disaffection from the naval government of American Samoa. We are thus left with Mead's second possibility, and with the problem of the way in which her depiction of Samoa might have been affected by the vantage point of the young girls on whose testimony she relied.[14]

Mead's depiction of Samoan culture, as I have shown, is marked by major errors, and her account of the sexual behavior of Samoans by a mind-boggling contradiction, for she asserts that the Samoans have a culture in which female virginity is very highly valued, with a virginity-testing ceremony being "theoretically observed at weddings of all ranks," while at the same time adolescence among females is regarded as a period "appropriate for love-making," with promiscuity before marriage being both permitted and "expected." And, indeed, she actually describes the Samoans as making the "demand" that a female should be "both receptive to the advances of many lovers and yet capable of showing the tokens of virginity at marriage." Something, it becomes plain at this juncture, is emphatically amiss, for surely no human population could be so cognitively disoriented as to conduct their lives in such a schizophrenic way. Nor are the Samoans remotely like this, for, as has been documented in Chapter 16, they are, in fact, a people who traditionally value virginity highly and so disapprove of premarital promiscuity as to exercise a strict surveillance over the comings and goings of adolescent girls. That these values and this regime were in force in Manu'a in the mid 1920s is, furthermore, clearly established by the testimony of the Manu'ans themselves who, when I discussed this period with those who well remembered it, confirmed that the fa'aSamoa in these matters was operative then as it was both before and after Mead's brief sojourn in Ta'u. What then can have been the source of Mead's erroneous statement that in Samoa there is great premarital freedom, with promiscuity before marriage among adolescent girls, being both permitted and expected?[15]

The explanation most consistently advanced by the Samoans themselves for the magnitude of the errors in her depiction of their culture and in particular of their sexual morality is, as Gerber has reported, "that Mead's informants must have been telling lies in order to tease her." Those Samoans who offer this explanation, which I have heard in Manu'a as well as in other parts of Samoa, are referring to the behavior called *tau fa'ase'e*, to which Samoans are much prone. *Fa'ase'e* (literally "to cause to slip") means "to dupe," as in the example given by Milner, *"e fa'ase'e gofie le teine*, the girl is easily duped"; and the phrase *tau fa'ase'e* refers to the action of deliberately duping someone, a pastime that greatly appeals to the Samoans as a respite from the severities of their authoritarian society.[16]

Because of their strict morality, Samoans show a decided reluctance to discuss sexual matters with outsiders or those in authority, a reticence that is especially marked among female adolescents. Thus, Holmes reports that when he and his wife lived in Manu'a and Tutuila in 1954 "it was never possible to obtain details of sexual experience from unmarried informants, though several of these people were constant companions and part of the household." Further, as Lauifi Ili, Holmes's principal assistant, observes, when it comes to imparting information about sexual activities, Samoan girls are "very close-mouthed and ashamed." Yet it was precisely information of this kind that Mead, a liberated young American newly arrived from New York and resident in the government station at Ta'u, sought to extract from the adolescent girls she had been sent to study. And when she persisted in this unprecedented probing of a highly embarrassing topic, it is likely that these girls resorted, as Gerber's Samoan informants have averred, *to tau fa'ase'e*, regaling their inquisitor with counterfeit tales of casual love under the palm trees.[17]

This, then, is the explanation that Samoans give for the highly inaccurate portrayal of their sexual morality in Mead's writings. It is an explanation that accounts for how it was that this erroneous portrayal came to be made, as well as for Mead's sincere credence in the account she has given in *Coming of Age in Samoa*, for she was indeed reporting what she had been told by her adolescent informants. The Manu'ans emphasize, however, that the girls who, they claim, plied Mead with these counterfeit tales were only amusing themselves, and had no inkling that their tales would ever find their way into a book.

While we cannot, in the absence of detailed corroborative evidence, be sure about the truth of this Samoan claim that Mead was mischievously duped by her adolescent informants, we can be certain that she did return to New York in 1926 with tales running directly counter to all other ethnographic accounts of Samoa, from which she constructed her picture of Manu'a as a paradise of free love, and of Samoa as a negative instance, which, so she claimed, validated Boasian doctrine. It was this negative instance that she duly presented to Boas as the ideologically gratifying result of her inquiries in Manu'a.

For Mead, Franz Boas was a peerless intellectual leader who "saw the scientific task as one of probing into a problem now of language, now of physical type, now of art style—-each a deep, sudden, intensive stab at some strategic point into an enormous, untapped and unknown mass of information." Boas continually warned his students, so Mead claims, against premature generalization, which was something he "feared like the plague." Again, in J.R. Swanton's judgment, Boas was "meticulously careful in weighing results and rigidly conservative in announcing conclusions"; while in Robert Lowie's estimation he was a scholar "concerned solely with ascertaining the truth," who controlled the ethnographic literature of the world "as well as anyone." It is pertinent then to take cognizance of Boas' response to the absolute generalization at which Mead had arrived after probing for a few months into adolescent behavior in Samoa. What can be said with certainty is that if Boas, as the instigator and supervisor of Mead's Samoan researches, had taken the elementary precaution of consulting the readily available ethnographic literature on Samoa, as, for example, the writings of Williams, Turner, Pritchard, Stuebel, and Krämer, he would have very quickly found accounts of the sexual and other behavior of the Samoans that are markedly at variance with Mead's picture of life in Manu'a; and further, that if he had done this in a thoroughgoing way, the need to check Mead's findings by an independent replication of her investigations in Samoa would have become unequivocally clear. However, when he read *Coming of Age in Samoa* in manuscript Boas voiced no doubts at all about the absoluteness of its general conclusion, and later in an enthusiastic foreword he wrote of the "painstaking investigation" on which this extreme conclusion was based. He had from the outset, as Mead reports, believed that her work in Samoa would show that culture was "very important." The response of Benedict, Mead's other mentor at Columbia University, was equally uncritical, and a few years later in *Patterns of Culture* she used Mead's conclusions, as had Boas in 1928, as apparently clinching evidence for the doctrine of cultural determinism in which she, like Boas and Mead, so fervently believed.[18]

We are thus confronted in the case of Margaret Mead's Samoan researches with an instructive example of how, as evidence is sought to substantiate a cherished doctrine, the deeply held beliefs of those involved may lead them unwittingly into error. The danger of such an outcome is inherent, it would seem, in the very process of belief formation. Thus, P.D. MacLean has suggested that the limbic system of the human brain "has the capacity to generate strong affective feelings of conviction that we attach to our beliefs regardless of whether they are true or false." In science, as Albert Einstein once remarked, "conviction is a good mainspring, but a poor regulator." In the case of Mead's Samoan researches, certainly, there is the clearest evidence that it was her deeply convinced belief in the doctrine of extreme cultural determinism, for which she was prepared to fight with the whole battery at her command, that led her to construct an account of Samoa that appeared to substantiate this very doctrine. There is, however, conclusive empirical evidence to demonstrate that Samoa, in numerous respects, is not at all as Mead depicted it to be.[19]

A crucial issue that arises from this historic case for the discipline of anthropology, which has tended to accept the reports of ethnographers as entirely empirical statements, is the extent to which other ethnographic accounts may have been distorted by doctrinal convictions, as well as the methodological question of how such distortion can best be avoided. These are no small problems. I would merely comment that as we look back on Mead's Samoan researches we are able to appreciate anew the wisdom of Karl Popper's admonition that in both science and scholarship it is, above all else, indefatigable rational criticism of our suppositions that is of decisive importance, for such criticism by "bringing out our mistakes... makes us understand the difficulties of the problem we are trying to solve," and so saves us from the allure of the "obvious truth" of received doctrine.[20]

Notes

1 R. Benedict, "The Science of Custom," (1929), in V.F. Calverton, ed. *The Making of Man* (New York, 1931), 815; M. Mead, *Social Organization of Manu'a* (Honolulu, 1930), 83; idem, *An Anthropologist at Work* (New York, 1959), 212; idem, Coming of Age in Samoa (New York, 1973), 197.

2 L. Spier, "Some Central Elements in the Legacy," in W. Goldschmidt, ed., *The Anthropology of Franz Boas, Memoirs, American Anthropological Association* 89 (1959): 146; G.W. Stocking, *Race, Culture, and Evolution* (New York, 1968), 303; A.L. Kroeber, "The Anthropological Attitude," *American Mercury* 13 (1928): 490; M. Harris, *The Rise of Anthropological Theory* (London, 1969), 427.

3 M. Mead. *From the South Seas* (New York, 1939), x.

4 M. Mead. "Then Arts of Bali," *Yale Review* 30 (1940): 336; G. Keynes, ed., *The Letters of Rupert Brooke* (London, 1968), 525, 542.

5 J. Ferguson, *Utopias of the Classical World* (London, 1975), 14, 16; G. Daws, *A Dream of Islands* (Milton, Queensland, 1980), 4; L.D. Hammond, ed., *News from New Cythera: A Report of Bourgainville's Voyage, 1766-1769* (Minneapolis, 1970), 27, 44; M. Mead, "Americanization in Samoa," *American Mercury* 16 (1929): 269-; idem, Life as a Samoan Girl," in *All True! The Record of Actual Adventures that have Happened to Ten Women of Today* (New York, 1931), 99; idem, review of *Samoa under the Sailing Gods* by N. Rowe, *The Nation* 133 (1931): 138.

6 M. Mead, *An Inquiry to the Question of Cultural Stability in Polynesia* (New York, 1928), 7; idem, *Blackberry Winter* (New York, 1972), 132, 138.

7 Mead, *Social Organization of Manu'a*, 55; idem, *Coming of Age*, 8, 11.

8 A. Kramer, *Die Samoa-Inseln* (Stuttgart, 1902-1903); R.L. Stevenson, *A Footnote to History*, in *Vailima Papers* (London 1924); J.W. Davidson, *Samoa mo Samoa* (Melbourne, 1967); I. Strong and L. Osbourne, *Memories of Vailima* (New York, 1902), 169; M. Mead, *Blackberry Winter* (New York, 1972), 154.

9 B. Malinowski, in R.F. Fortune, *Sorcerers of Dobu* (London, 1932), xix.

10 Mead, *Social Organization of Manu'a* 4; idem, Coming of Age,vi; cf. P.J. Pelto and G.H. Pelto, *Anthropological Research: The Structure of Inquiry*, 2nd ed. (Cambridge, 1978), 75: "Participant observation is essential for checking and evaluating key-informant data."

11 Mead, *Blackberry Winter*, 150ff.; idem, *Letters from the Field, 1925-1975* (New York, 1977), 55.

12 Mead, *Blackberry Winter*, 151ff; idem, *Social Organization of Manu'a* (Honolulu, 1969), xvii, 224.

13 B.Shore, "Gender and Sexuality in Samoa: Conceptions and Missed Conceptions," in S. Ortner and H. Whitelock, eds. *Sexual Meanings* (Cambridge, 1982), 213, n.2; Mead, *Social Organization of Manu'a* (1969), 227.

14 Mead, *Social Organization of Manu'a* (1969), 228.

15 Mead, *Coming of Age*, 98; 160; idem, "Cultural Contexts of Puberty and Adolescence," *Bulletin of the Philadelphia Association for Psychoanalysis* 9 (1959): 62; idem, "The Sex Life of the Unmarried Adult in Primitive Society," in L.S. Wile,

ed., The *Sex Life of the Unmarried Adult* (London, 1935), 61; idem, *Male and Female* (Harmondsworth, 1962), 119; idem, "Anthropology," in V. Robinson, ed. *Encyclopedia Sexualis* (New York, 1936), 23.

16 E.R. Gerber, "The Cultural Patterning of Emotions in Samoa" (Ph.D. diss, University of California, San Diego, 1975), 126; G.B. Milner, *Samoan Dictionary* (London, 1966, 205.

17 L.D. Holmes, "A Re-Study of Manu'an Culture," Ph.D. diss., Northwestern University, 1957), vii. The view advanced by Gerber's informants is commonplace among Samoans, as Nicholas von Hoffman recounts in his rumbustious account of American Samoa, *Tales from the Margaret Mead Taproom* (Kansas City, 1976), 97ff. Having cited a paragraph from Mead's *Coming of Age in Samoa* ending with a reference to a "the whisper of lovers, until the village rests till dawn," von Hoffman comments: "It's passages like that which have given the South Seas their dishy reputation, although you can find a lot of Samoans who'll tell you that Maggy is a crock. There are supposed to be a bunch of old ladies on the island who claim to be the little girls in Mead's book and who say that they just made up every kind of sexy story for the funny *palagi* lady because she dug dirt."

18 M. Mead, "Apprenticeship Under Boas," in W. Goldschmidt, ed., *The Anthropology of Franz Boas, Memoirs, American Anthropological Association* 89 (1959): 29; J.R. Swanton, "The President Elect," *Science* 73 (1931): 148; R.H. Lowie, review of *Race, Language, and Culture* by Franz Boas, Science 91 (1940):599; idem. *The History of Ethnological Theory* (New York, 1937), 151; R. Benedict, *Patterns of Culture* (London, 1945; orig. 1934), 21.

19 P.D. MacLean, "The Evolution of Three Mentalities," in S.L. Washburn and E.R. McCown, eds., *Human Evolution: Biosocial Perspectives* (Menlo Park, Calif., 1978), 47; A. Einstein, quoted in A.P. French, ed., *Einstein: A Centenary Volume* (London, 1979), 209.

20 K.R. Popper, *Conjectures and Refutations: The Growth of Scientific Knowledge* (London, 1969), vii, 16; cf. E. Gellner, *Legitimation of Belief* (Cambridge, 1974), 171: "Popper's theory is not a descriptive account of humanity's actual cognitive practice but rather a prescription, an ethic, which at the same time also singles out *science* from the rest of putative cognition and explains the secret of its success."

Study Questions

1. What was Franz Boas's influence on Margaret Mead's Samoan research, according to Freeman?

2. In which ways does Freeman perceive Mead's field methods to have been inadequate?

3. Why does Freeman belief that Mead was "duped" by her fieldwork informants?

Further Readings

Côté, James E. 1994. *Adolescent Storm and Stress: An Evaluation of the Mead/Freeman Controversy.* Research Monographs in Adolescence. Hillsdale, NJ: Lawrence Erlbaum Associates.

—. 2000. Was *Coming of Age in Samoa* Based on a "Fateful Hoaxing"? *Current Anthropology* 41,4: 617-20.

Freeman, Derek. 1991. There's Tricks i' th' World: A Historical Analysis of the Researches of Margaret Mead. *Visual Anthropology Review* 7,1.

—. 1999. *The Fateful Hoaxing of Margaret Mead: A Historical Analysis of Her Samoan Research.* Boulder: Westview Press.

—. 2000. Was Margaret Mead Misled or Did She Mislead on Samoa? *Current Anthropology* 41,4: 609-14.

—. 2000. Reply. *Current Anthropology* 41,4: 620-22.

Orans, Martin. 1983. *Not Even Wrong.* Cambridge, MA: Harvard University Press.

—. 2000. Hoaxing, Polemics, and Science. *Current Anthropology* 41,4: 615-16.

27

Introduction
[*Europe and the People Without History*]

ERIC R. WOLF

Introduction

The central assertion of this book is that the world of humankind constitutes a manifold, a totality of interconnected processes, and inquiries that disassemble this totality into bits and then fail to reassemble it falsify reality. Concepts like "nation," "society," and "culture" name bits and threaten to turn names into things. Only by understanding these names as bundles of relationships, and by placing them back into the field from which they were abstracted, can we hope to avoid misleading inferences and increase our share of understanding.

On one level it has become a commonplace to say that we all inhabit "one world." There are ecological connections: New York suffers from the Hong Kong flu; the grapevines of Europe are destroyed by American plant lice. There are demographic connections: Jamaicans migrate to London; Chinese migrate to Singapore. There are economic connections: a shutdown of oil wells on the Persian Gulf halts generating plants in Ohio; a balance of payments unfavorable to the United States drains American dollars into bank accounts in Frankfurt or Yokohama; Italians produce Fiat automobiles in the Soviet Union; Japanese build a hydroelectric system in Ceylon. There are political connections: wars begun in Europe unleash reverberations around the globe; American troops intervene on the rim of Asia; Finns guard the border between Israel and Egypt.

This holds true not only of the present but also of the past. Diseases from Eurasia devastated the native population of America and Oceania. Syphilis moved from the New World to the Old. Europeans and their plants and animals invaded the Americas; the American potato, maize plant, and manioc spread throughout the Old World. Large numbers of Africans were transported forcibly to the New World; Chinese and Indian indentured laborers were shipped to Southeast Asia and the West Indies. Portugal created a Portuguese settlement in Macao off the coast of China. Dutchmen, using labor obtained in

Bengal, constructed Batavia. Irish children were sold into servitude in the West Indies. Fugitive African slaves found sanctuary in the hills of Surinam. Europe learned to copy Indian textiles and Chinese porcelain, to drink native American chocolate, to smoke native American tobacco, to use Arabic numerals.

These are familiar facts. They indicate contact and connections, linkages and interrelationships. Yet the scholars to whom we turn in order to understand what we see largely persist in ignoring them. Historians, economists, and political scientists take separate nations as their basic framework of inquiry. Sociology continues to divide the world into separate societies. Even anthropology, once greatly concerned with how culture traits diffused around the world, divides its subject matter into distinctive cases: each society with its characteristic culture, conceived as an integrated and bounded system, set off against other equally bounded systems.

If social and cultural distinctiveness and mutual separation were a hallmark of humankind, one would expect to find it most easily among the so-called primitives, people "without history," supposedly isolated from the external world and from one another. On this presupposition, what would we make of the archaeological findings that European trade goods appear in sites on the Niagara frontier as early as 1570, and that by 1670 sites of the Onondaga subgroup of the Iroquois reveal almost no items of native manufacture except pipes? On the other side of the Atlantic, the organization and orientations of large African populations were transformed in major ways by the trade in slaves. Since the European slavers only moved the slaves from the African coast to their destination in the Americas, the supply side of the trade was entirely in African hands. This was the "African foundation" upon which was built, in the words of the British mercantilist Malachy Postlethwayt, "the magnificent superstructure of American commerce and naval power." From Senegambia in West Africa to Angola, population after population was drawn into this trade, which ramified far inland and affected people who had never even seen a European trader on the coast. Any account of Kru, Fanti, Asante, Ijaw, Igbo, Kongo, Luba, Lunda, or Ngola that treats each group as a "tribe" sufficient unto itself thus misreads the African past and the African present. Furthermore, trade with Iroquois and West Africa affected Europe in turn. Between 1670 and 1760 the Iroquois demanded dyed scarlet and blue cloth made in the Stroudwater Valley of Gloucestershire. This was also one of the first areas in which English weavers lost their autonomy and became hired factory hands. Perhaps there was an interconnection between the American trade and the onset of the industrial revolution in the valley of the Stroud. Conversely, the more than 5,500 muskets supplied to the Gold Coast in only three years (1658-1661) enriched the gunsmiths of Birmingham, where they were made (Jennings 1977: 99-100; Daaku 1970: 150-151).

If there are connections everywhere, why do we persist in turning dynamic, interconnected phenomena into static, disconnected things? Some of this is owing, perhaps, to the way we have learned our own history. We have been taught, inside the classroom and outside of it, that there exists an entity called the West, and that one can think of this West as a society and civilization independent of and in opposition to other societies and civilizations. Many of us even grew up believing that this West has a genealogy, according to which ancient Greece begat Rome, Rome begat Christian Europe, Christian Europe begat the Renaissance, the Renaissance the Enlightenment, the Enlightenment political democracy and the industrial revolution. Industry, crossed with democracy, in turn yielded the United States, embodying the rights to life, liberty, and the pursuit of happiness.

Such a developmental scheme is misleading. It is misleading, first, because it turns history into a moral success story, a race in time in which each runner of the race passes on the torch of liberty to the next relay. History is thus converted into a tale about the furtherance of virtue, about how the virtuous win out over the bad guys. Frequently, this turns into a story of how the winners prove that they are virtuous and good by winning. If history is the working out of a moral purpose in time, then those who lay claim to that purpose are by that fact the predilect agents of history.

The scheme misleads in a second sense as well. If history is but a tale of unfolding moral purpose, then each link in the genealogy, each runner in the race, is only a precursor of the final apotheosis and not a manifold of social and cultural processes at work in their own time and place. Yet what would we learn of ancient Greece, for example, if we interpreted it only as a prehistoric Miss Liberty, holding aloft the torch of moral purpose in the barbarian night? We would gain little sense of the class conflicts racking the Greek cities, or of the relation between freemen and their slaves. We would have no reason to ask why there were more Greeks fighting in the ranks of the Persian kings than in the ranks of the Hellenic Alliance against the Persians. It would be of no interest to us to know that more Greeks lived in southern Italy and Sicily, then called Magna Graecia, than in Greece proper. Nor would we have any reason to ask why there were soon more Greek mercenaries in foreign armies than in the military bodies of their home cities. Greek settlers outside of Greece, Greek mercenaries in foreign armies, and slaves from Thrace, Phrygia, or Paphalagonia in Greek households all imply Hellenic relations with Greeks and non-Greeks outside of Greece. Yet our guiding scheme would not invite us to ask questions about these relationships.

Nowhere is this myth-making scheme more apparent than in schoolbook versions of the history of the United States. There, a complex orchestration of antagonistic forces is celebrated instead as the unfolding of a timeless essence.

In this perspective, the ever-changing boundaries of the United States and the repeated involvements of the polity in internal and external wars, declared and undeclared, are telescoped together by the teleological understanding that thirteen colonies clinging to the eastern rim of the continent would, in less than a century, plant the American flag on the shores of the Pacific. Yet this final result was itself only the contested outcome of many contradictory relationships. The colonies declared their independence, even though a majority of their population—European settlers, native Americans, and African slaves—favored the Tories. The new republic nearly foundered on the issue of slavery, dealing with it, in a series of problematic compromises, by creating two federated countries, each with its own zone of expansion. There was surely land for the taking on the new continent, but it had to be taken first from the native Americans who inhabited it, and then converted into flamboyant real estate. Jefferson bought the Louisiana territory cheaply, but only after the revolt of the Haitian slaves against their French slave masters robbed the area of its importance in the French scheme of things as a source of food supply for the Caribbean plantations. The occupation of Florida closed off one of the main escape hatches from southern slavery. The war with Mexico made the Southwest safe for slavery and cotton. The Hispanic landowners who stood in the way of the American drive to the Pacific became "bandits" when they defended their own against the Anglophone newcomers. Then North and South—one country importing its working force from Europe, the other from Africa—fought one of the bloodiest wars in history. For a time the defeated South became a colony of the victorious North. Later, the alignment between regions changed, the "sunbelt" rising to predominance as the influence of the industrial Northeast declined. Clearly the republic was neither indivisible nor endowed with God-given boundaries.

It is conceivable that things might have been different. There could have arisen a polyglot Floridian Republic, a Francophone Mississippian America, a Hispanic New Biscay, a Republic of the Great Lakes, a Columbia—comprising the present Oregon, Washington, and British Columbia. Only if we assume a God-given drive toward geopolitical unity on the North American continent would this retrojection be meaningless. Instead, it invites us to account in material terms for what happened at each juncture, to account for how some relationships gained ascendancy over others. Thus neither ancient Greece, Rome, Christian Europe, the Renaissance, the Enlightenment, the industrial revolution, democracy, nor even the United States was ever a thing propelled toward its unfolding goal by some immanent driving spring, but rather a temporally and spatially changing and changeable set of relationships, or relationships among sets of relationships.

The point is more than academic. By turning names into things we create false models of reality. By endowing nations, societies, or cultures with the qualities of internally homogeneous and externally distinctive and bounded objects, we create a model of the world as a global pool hall in which the entities spin off each other like so many hard and round billiard balls. Thus it becomes easy to sort the world into differently colored balls, to declare that "East is East, and West is West, and never the twain shall meet." In this way a quintessential West is counterposed to an equally quintessential East, where life was cheap and slavish multitudes groveled under a variety of despotisms. Later, as peoples in other climes began to assert their political and economic independence from both West and East, we assigned these new applicants for historical status to a Third World of underdevelopment—a residual category of conceptual billiard balls—as contrasted with the developed West and the developing East. Inevitably, perhaps, these reified categories became intellectual instruments in the prosecution of the Cold War. There was the "modern" world of the West. There was the world of the East, which had fallen prey to communism, a "disease of modernization" (Rostow 1960). There was, finally, the Third World, still bound up in "tradition" and strangled in its efforts toward modernization. If the West could only find ways of breaking that grip, it could perhaps save the victim from the infection incubated and spread by the East, and set that Third World upon the road to modernization—the road to life, liberty, and the pursuit of happiness of the West. The ghastly offspring of this way of thinking about the world was the theory of "forced draft urbanization" (Huntington 1968: 655), which held that the Vietnamese could be propelled toward modernization by driving them into the cities through aerial bombardment and defoliation of the countryside. Names thus become things, and things marked with an X can become targets of war.

The Rise of the Social Sciences

The habit of treating named entities such as Iroquois, Greece, Persia, or the United States as fixed entities opposed to one another by stable internal architecture and external boundaries interferes with our ability to understand their mutual encounter and confrontation. In fact, this tendency has made it difficult to understand all such encounters and confrontations. Arranging imaginary building blocks into pyramids called East and West, or First, Second, and Third Worlds, merely compounds that difficulty. It is thus likely that we are dealing with some conceptual shortcomings in our ways of looking at social and political phenomena, and not just a temporary aberration. We seem to have taken a wrong turn in understanding at some critical point in the past, a false choice that bedevils our thinking in the present.

That critical turning point is identifiable. It occurred in the middle of the past century, when inquiry into the nature and varieties of humankind split into separate (and unequal) specialties and disciplines. This split was fateful. It led not only forward into the intensive and specialized study of particular aspects of human existence, but turned the ideological reasons for that split into an intellectual justification for the specialties themselves. Nowhere is this more obvious than in the case of sociology. Before sociology we had political economy, a field of inquiry concerned with "the wealth of nations," the production and distribution of wealth within and between political entities and the classes composing them. With the acceleration of capitalist enterprise in the eighteenth century, that structure of state and classes came under increasing pressure from new and "rising" social groups and categories that clamored for the enactment of their rights against those groups defended and represented by the state. Intellectually, this challenge took the form of asserting the validity of new social, economic, political, and ideological ties, now conceptualized as "society," against the state. The rising tide of discontent pitting "society" against the political and ideological order erupted in disorder, rebellion, and revolution. The specter of disorder and revolution raised the question of how social order could be restored and maintained, indeed, how social order was possible at all. Sociology hoped to answer the "social question." It had, as Rudolph Heberle noted, "an eminently political origin .... Saint Simon, Auguste Comte, and Lorenz Stein conceived the new science of society as an antidote against the poison of social disintegration" (quoted in Bramson 1961: 12, n. 2).

These early sociologists did this by severing the field of social relations from political economy. They pointed to observable and as yet poorly studied ties which bind people to people as individuals, as groups and associations, or as members of institutions. They then took this field of social relations to be the subject matter of their intensive concern. They and their successors expanded this concern into a number of theoretical postulates, using these to mark off sociology from political science and economics. I would summarize these common postulates as follows:

1. In the course of social life, individuals enter into relations with one another. Such relations can be abstracted from the economic, political, or ideological context in which they are found, and treated sui generis. They are autonomous, constituting a realm of their own, the realm of the social.
2. Social order depends on the growth and extension of social relations among individuals. The greater the density of such ties and the wider their scope, the greater the orderliness of society. Maximization of ties of kinship and neighborhood, of group and association, is therefore conducive to social order. Conversely, if these ties are not maximized, social order is called into question. Development of many and varied ties also diminishes the danger of polarization into classes.

3. The formation and maintenance of such ties is strongly related to the existence and propagation of common beliefs and customs among the individuals participating in them. Moral consensus, especially when based on unexamined belief and on nonrational acceptance of custom, furthers the maximization of social ties; expectations of mere utility and the exercise of merely technical reason tend to weaken them.
4. The development of social relations and the spread of associated custom and belief create a society conceived as a totality of social relations between individuals. Social relations constitute society; society, in turn, is the seat of cohesion, the unit to which predictability and orderliness can be ascribed. If social relations are orderly and recurrent, society has a stable internal structure. The extent of that structure is coterminous with the intensity and range of social relations. Where these grow markedly less intense and less frequent, society encounters its boundary.

What is the flaw in these postulates? They predispose one to think of social relations not merely as autonomous but as causal in their own right, apart from their economic, political, or ideological context. Since social relations are conceived as relations between individuals, interaction between individuals becomes the prime cause of social life. Since social disorder has been related to the quantity and quality of social relations, attention is diverted from consideration of economics, politics, or ideology as possible sources of social disorder, into a search for the causes of disorder in family and community, and hence toward the engineering of a proper family and community life. Since, moreover, disorder has been located in the divergence of custom and belief from common norms, convergence in custom and consensus in belief are converted into the touchstone of society in proper working order. And, finally, the postulates make it easy to identify Society in general with a society in particular. Society in need of order becomes a particular society to be ordered. In the context of the tangible present, that society to be ordered is then easily identified with a given nation-state, be that nation-state Ghana, Mexico, or the United States. Since social relations have been severed from their economic, political, or ideological context, it is easy to conceive of the nation-state as a structure of social ties informed by moral consensus rather than as a nexus of economic, political, and ideological relationships connected to other nexuses. Contentless social relations, rather than economic, political, or ideological forces, thus become the prime movers of sociological theory. Since these social relations take place within the charmed circle of the single nation-state, the significant actors in history are seen as nation-states, each driven by its internal social relations. Each society is then a thing, moving in response to an inner clockwork.

Economics and Political Science

This severance of social relations from the economic, political, and ideological contexts in which they are embedded and which they activate was accompanied by the assignment of the economic and political aspects of human life to separate disciplines. Economics abandoned its concern with how socially organized populations produce to supply their polities and became instead a study of how demand creates markets. The guiding theory of this new economics was

> a theory of markets and market interdependence. It is a theory of general equilibrium *in exchange*, extended almost as an afterthought, to cover production and distribution. It is not a theory of a social system, still less of economic power and social class. Households and firms are considered only as market agents, never as parts of a social structure. Their 'initial endowments,' wealth, skills, and property, are taken as given. Moreover, the object of the theory is to demonstrate the tendency towards equilibrium; class and sectoral conflict is therefore ruled out almost by assumption. [Nell 1973: 77-78]

Stated in another form, this new economics is not about the real world at all (Lekachman 1976). It is an abstract model of the workings out of subjective individual choices in relation to one another.

A similar fate befell the study of politics. A new political science severed the sphere of the political from economics and turned to consideration of power in relation to government. By relegating economic, social, and ideological aspects of human life to the status of the "environment," the study of politics divorced itself from a study of how the organization of this environment constrains or directs politics, and moved instead to an inquiry into decision making. The political process is one in which demands are aggregated and translated into decisions, much as in the market model of economics the interplay of demands issues in the production of supplies. As in the market model, such an approach easily slips into the assumption

> that the organized private power forces of the society balance one another so as to preclude concentrated irresponsible rule .... wise public policy is assumed to prevail, explained by a mystique not unlike Adam Smith's invisible hand. [Engler 1968: 199]

Ultimately, in such a model, the willingness to abide by the rules of the political market is necessarily determined not by the market itself but by the orientation and values of the participants, aspects of what political scientists have come to call their "political culture." Much of political science thus focused on the study of decisions, on the one hand, and the study of orientations, understood as constituting together the autonomous political system of a given society, on the other.

Underlying all these specialties is the concept of an aggregate of individuals, engaged in a contract to maximize social order, to truck and barter in the marketplace, and to provide inputs for the formulation of political decisions. Ostensibly engaged in the study of human *behavior*, the various disciplines parcel out the subject among themselves. Each then proceeds to set up a model, seemingly a means to explain "hard," observable facts, yet actually an ideologically loaded scheme geared to a narrow definition of subject matter. Such schemes provide self-fulfilling answers, since phenomena other than those covered by the model are ruled out of the court of specialized discourse. If the models leak like sieves, it is then argued that this is either because they are merely abstract constructs and not expected to hold empirical water, or because troublemakers have poked holes into them. The specialized social sciences, having abandoned a holistic perspective, thus come to resemble the Danae sisters of classical Greek legend, ever condemned to pour water into their separate bottomless containers.

The Development of Sociological Theory
We have seen how sociology stemmed from an attempt to counteract social disorder by creating a theory of social order, by locating order and disorder in the quantity and quality of social relations. An important implication of this approach is that it issues in a polarity between two types of society: one in which social order is maximized because social relations are densely knit and suffused with value consensus; and another in which social disorder predominates over order because social relations are atomized and deranged by dissensus over values. It is only a short step from drawing such a polarity to envisioning social process as a change from one type of society to the other. This seemed consistent with the common view that modern life entails a progressive disintegration of the lifeways that marked the "good old days" of our forebears. In nineteenth-century Europe, where older social ties in fact disintegrated under the twin impact of capitalism and industrialization, such a temporal interpretation of the sociological polarity carried the conviction of experience. Ferdinand Tonnies saw this movement as one from "community," or Gemeinschaft, to "society," or Gesellschaft. Sir Henry Maine phrased it as a shift from social relations based on status to social relations based on contract. Emile Durkheim conceived it as a movement from a kind of social solidarity based on the similarity of all members to a social solidarity based on an "organic" complementarity of differences. The Chicago school of urban sociology saw it as the contrast between a cohesive society and the atomized, heterogeneous, disorganized city. Finally, Robert Redfield drew the various for-

mulations together into a polar model of progression from Folk to Urban Society. In this model the quantity and quality of social relations again were the primary, independent variables. Isolation or paucity of social interaction, coupled with homogeneity or similarity of social ties, generated the dependent variables: orientation toward the group, or "collectivization"; commitment to belief, or "sanctity"; and "organization," the knitting together of understandings in the minds of men. In contrast, contact, or high frequency of contact, coupled with heterogeneity or dissimilarity of social ties, was seen as producing the dependent variables of "individualization," "secularization," and "disorganization." In sum, increases in the quantity and diversity of social interaction caused "the moral order" of the folk to give way to "the technical order" of civilization.

Sociology thus took its departure from a sense that social order was threatened by the atrophy of community. As the twentieth century wore on, however, it gradually came to be taken for granted that society was headed toward increased size and differentiation, and hence also toward the growth of utilitarian and technical relations at the expense of sacred and moral ties. Society was evidently moving toward what Max Weber, using Tonnies's terms, had called *Vergesellschaftung*. By this he meant the expansion of relations resting on

> rationally motivated adjustment of interests or a similarly motivated agreement, whether the basis of rational judgement be absolute values or reasons of expediency. It is especially common, though by no means inevitable, for the associative type of relationship to rest on a rational agreement by mutual consent. [1968:10))

Although Weber himself used the term with ambivalence and misgivings, his latter-day followers embraced the prognosis with enthusiasm. Whereas "traditional society" had fitted people narrowly into inherited positions, and then bound them together tightly in particularistic positions, "modern society" would sever people from inherited ties and allocate the newly mobile population to specialized and differentiated roles responding to the changing needs of an overarching universal society. Such an emerging society would also require a mechanism for setting social goals and a machinery for implementing them. The way the modernizers saw it, goal setting would come out of enlarged popular participation. Implementation of the goals, such as economic development, in turn would require the creation of bureaucracy, defined as organizations capable of marshalling resources rationally and efficiently toward stated goals. Finally, public participation in setting and meeting goals would require a psychic reorientation that could sustain the enactment of such technical and rational norms. Those capable of generating such new arrangements would find themselves launched into modernity. Those incapable of doing so would find their society arrested at the point of transition or mired in traditionalism. In the succession from Max Weber to Talcott Parsons, therefore, *Vergesellschaftung* was transfigured into "modernization" through a simple change of signs. If Gesellschaft had once seemed problematical, after the mid-twentieth century it came to be seen as desirable and forward-looking. The negative pole of the polarity was now allocated to "traditional society," slow to change, inflexible, and lacking in psychic drive toward rational and secular achievement.

Thus, in a reversal of sociology's original critical stance toward the workings of nineteenth-century society, "modernization theory" became an instrument for bestowing praise on societies deemed to be modern and casting a critical eye on those that had yet to attain that achievement. The political leaders of the United States had pronounced themselves in favor of aiding the development of the Third World, and modernization theorists seconded that pronouncement. Yet modernization theory effectively foreclosed any but the most ideologically charged understanding of that world. It used the term *modern*, but meant by that term the United States, or rather an ideal of a democratic, pluralistic, rational, and secular United States. It said *traditional*, but meant all those others that would have to adopt that ideal to qualify for assistance. As theory it was misleading. It imparted a false view of American history, substituting self-satisfaction for analysis. By casting such different entities as China, Albania, Paraguay, Cuba, and Tanzania into the hopper of traditional society, it simultaneously precluded any study of their significant differences. By equating tradition with stasis and lack of development, it denied societies marked off as traditional any significant history of their own. Above all, by dividing the world into modern, transitional, and traditional societies, it blocked effective understanding of relationships among them. Once again each society was defined as an autonomous and bounded structure of social relations, thus discouraging analysis of intersocietal or intergroup interchanges, including internal social strife, colonialism, imperialism, and societal dependency. The theory thus effectively precluded the serious study of issues demonstrably agitating the real world.

Anthropology
If these social sciences have not led to an adequate understanding of the interconnected world, what of anthropology? Anthropology, ambitiously entitled The Science of Man, did lay special claims to the study of non-Western and "primitive" peoples. Indeed, cultural anthropology began as world anthropology. In its evolutionist phase it was concerned with the evolution of culture on a global scale. In its diffusionist phase it was interested in the spread and clustering of cultural forms over the entire face of the globe. The diffusionists also

saw relations between populations exhibiting the same cultural forms—matriliny, blackening of teeth, or tailored clothing—as the outcome of inter-group communication by migration or by copying and learning. They were not much concerned with people, but they did have a sense of global interconnections. They did not believe in the concept of "primitive isolates."

Such interests and understandings were set aside, however, as anthropologists turned from a primary concern with cultural forms to the study of "living cultures," of specified populations and their lifeways in locally delimited habitats. Fieldwork—direct communication with people and participant observation of their ongoing activities *in situ*—became a hallmark of anthropological method. Fieldwork has proved enormously fruitful in laying bare and correcting false assumptions and erroneous descriptions. It has also revealed hitherto unsuspected connections among sets of social activities and cultural forms. Yet the very success of the method lulled its users into a false confidence. It became easy for them to convert merely heuristic considerations of method into theoretical postulates about society and culture.

Limitations of time and energy in the field dictate limitations in the number and locations of possible observations and interviews, demanding concentration of effort on an observable place and on a corps of specifiable "informants." The resulting observations and communications are then made to stand for a larger universe of unrealized observations and communications, and used to construct a model of the social and cultural entity under study. Such a model is no more than an account of "descriptive integration," a theoretical halfway house, and not yet explanation. Functionalist anthropology, however, attempted to derive explanations from the study of the microcosm alone, treating it as a hypothetical isolate. Its features were explained in terms of the contribution each made to the maintenance of this putatively isolated whole. Thus, a methodological unit of inquiry was turned into a theoretical construct by assertion, a priori. The outcome was series of analyses of wholly separate cases.

There were three major attempts to transcend the boundaries of the microcosm. One of these, that of Robert Redfield, had recourse to sociological theory. It applied the polarity of Gemeinschaft and Gesellschaft to anthropological cases by using "communities" as representations or exemplifications of such "imagined types of societies." Thus the communities of X-Cacal and Chan Kom in Yucatan were made to exemplify the folk end of a universal folk-urban continuum of social relations and cultural understandings. The two locations illuminated the theory, but the theory could not explicate the political and economic processes that shaped the communities: X-Cacal as a settlement set up by Maya-speaking rebels during the Caste Wars of the nineteenth century; Chan Kom as a village of cultivators released from the hacienda system by the

Mexican Revolution, settling as newcomers in a frontier area with the support of the Yucatecan Socialist Party. Thus, like Gemeinschaft-Gesellschaft theory in general, Redfield's concepts led only in one direction, up to the theory but not back down from it.

A second attempt to generate a theoretical construct for understanding the microcosm studied in a larger context was Julian Steward's concept of levels of sociocultural integration. The concept, derived from the philosophy of "emergent evolution," was meant to suggest that units of the same kind, when subjected to integrative processes, could yield novel units that not only subsumed those of the lower level but also exhibited qualitatively different characteristics at the higher, emergent level. Steward initially used the concept to counter arguments that treated "the community" as a small replica of "the nation," as if these were qualitatively identical structural phenomena. He then proceeded, however, to construct a conceptual edifice in which units at the family level became parts of a community level, units at the community level became parts of a regional level, and units at the regional level became parts of the level of the nation.

Although the term *integration* suggests a process, the concept is not processual but structural. It suggests an architecture of a whole and its parts, which remain to be specified substantively only after the fact. The model is thus a "hollow" representation of societal complexity, theoretically applicable to all complex sociocultural wholes. Yet it makes no statement about any processes generating the structure, or about the specific features that integrate it, or about the content of any of its parts. Knowledge about processes does not flow from the model but must be added to it. Thus, when Steward turned to the study of "contemporary change in traditional societies," the model remained silent about the penetration of capitalism, the growth of a worldwide specialization and division of labor, and the development of domination by some populations over others. Steward was forced back, unhappily, to the comparative study of separate cases and the unsatisfactory concepts of tradition and modernization.

The third attempt to go beyond the microscopic study of populations in specified locations took the form of a revival of evolutionism. Evolutionary thinking in anthropology, so prominent in the nineteenth century, had been halted by the assertion that "the extensive occurrence of diffusion ... lays the axe to the root of any theory of historical laws" (Lowie 1920: 434). Evolutionists and diffusionists were not so much opposed as interested in quite different phenomena. The evolutionists had recognized the facts of diffusion, but had felt justified in abstracting from these facts to their model of successive stages of social and cultural development. The diffusionists, in turn, sidestepped the problem posed by major inequalities in the technology and organization of different populations to focus instead on the transmission of cultural forms from group to group. Whereas the evolutionists disclaimed an interest in the history of particular societies and cultures, the diffusionists disclaimed any interest in the ecological, economic, social, political, and ideological matrix within which the cultural forms were being transmitted in time and space. The two schools of thought thus effectively talked past each other. The functionalists, in turn, rejected altogether the "conjectural history" of the diffusionists in favor of the analysis of internal functioning in putatively isolated wholes.

When Leslie White reintroduced the evolutionary perspective into American anthropology in the forties and fifties, he did so by reasserting the validity of the earlier model proposed by Tylor, Morgan, and Spencer. To this model of universal or unilineal evolution, Julian Steward opposed a multilineal model that depicted evolution as a process of successive branching. Subsequently Sahlins and Service sought to unify the two approaches by counterposing general and specific evolution as dual aspects of the same evolutionary process. General evolution was defined by them as "passage from less to greater energy exploitation, lower to higher levels of integration, and less to greater all-round adaptability" (Sahlins and Service 1960: 22-23). Specific evolution they defined as "the phylogenetic, ramifying, historic passage of culture along its many lines, the adaptive modification of particular cultures" (1960: 38). Though cognizant of convergence as an aspect of cultural as opposed to biological phylogeny, they defined it in old fashioned diffusionist terms as the diffusion of culture traits, and not as the outcome of multifaceted relationships between interacting culture bearing populations. When they turned to the detailed analysis of specific evolution, they thus emphasized adaptation as "specialization for the exploitation of particular facets of the environment" (1960: 50). They understood that environment included both the physical and the sociocultural matrices of human life, but they laid primary stress on adaptation to different physical environments. In the sixties and seventies, the study of particular ecological "systems" became increasingly sophisticated, without, however, ever transcending the functional analysis of the single case, now hypothesized as an integral, self-regulating ecological whole. Thus, despite its theoretical effort, evolutionary anthropology turned all too easily into the study of ecological adaptation, conducting anthropology back to the comparative study of single cases.

The ecological concentration on the single case is paralleled by the recent fascination with the study and unraveling of what is "in the heads" of single culture-bearing populations. Such studies turn their back on functionalism, including what was most viable in it, the concern with how people cope with the material and organizational problems of their lives. They also disregard material relationships linking the people with others outside. Instead, their interest lies in the investigation of local microcosms of meaning, conceived as autonomous systems.

This turn toward the study of meaning has been influenced strongly by the development of linguistics, notably by de Saussure's structural theory of language as a superindividual social system of linguistic forms that remain normatively identical in all utterances. Such a view relates linguistic sign to linguistic sign without reference to who is speaking to whom, when, and about what. It was originally put forward to oppose the position that a language consisted of an ever-changing historical stream of individually generated utterances, a perspective associated with the names of Humboldt and Vossler. De Saussure, instead, wholly divorced language (*langue*) from utterance (*parole*), defining signs by their mutual relation to one another, without reference to any context external to them. In the same way, meanings were defined in terms of other meanings, without reference to the practical contexts in which they appear.

Clearly, the opposition between the two views requires for its resolution a relational, dialectical perspective, as Volosinov noted fifty years ago. He called into question de Saussure's view of the static linguistic system carried by a faceless and passive collectivity, noting instead that in reality such a collectivity consisted of a population of speakers with diverse "accents" or interests, participating in a historical stream of verbal utterances about diverse, concrete contexts. Contexts should not be thought of as internally homogeneous and externally segregated. For Volosinov, they constituted instead intersections between "differently oriented accents ... in a state of constant tension, of incessant interaction and conflict" (1973: 80). Neither sign nor meaning could be understood without reference to what they are about, their theme in a given situation. The trend within anthropology to treat systems of meaning as wholly autonomous systems threatens to reverse this insight by substituting for it the study of solipsistic discourses generated *in vacuo* by the human mind.

While some anthropologists thus narrow their focus to the ever more intensive study of the single case, others hope to turn anthropology into a science by embarking on the statistical cross-cultural comparisons of coded features drawn from large samples of ethnographically known cases. A good deal of attention has been paid to the methodological problems of how to isolate discrete cases for comparison and how to define the variables to be coded and compared. Are the hundreds of Eskimo local groups separate cases? Are they instances of larger, self-identified clusters such as Copper, Netsilik, and Iglulik? Or do they constitute a single Eskimo case? Other questions deal with the nature of the sample. Can one be sure that the cases are sufficiently separated historically and geographically to constitute distinct cases? Or is the sample contaminated by spatial or temporal propinquity and communication? All the answers to these questions nevertheless assume the autonomy and boundedness of the cases that are selected in the end. Whatever sample is finally chosen, it is interpreted as an aggregate of separate units. These, it is held, either generate cultural traits independently through invention, or borrow them from one another through diffusion. We are back in a world of sociocultural billiard balls, coursing on a global billiard table.

What, however, if we take cognizance of *processes* that transcend separable cases, moving through and beyond them and transforming them as they proceed? Such processes were, for example, the North American fur trade and the trade in native American and African slaves. What of the localized Algonkin-speaking patrilineages, for example, which in the course of the fur trade moved into large nonkin villages and became known as the ethnographic Ojibwa? What of the Chipeweyans, some of whose bands gave up hunting to become fur trappers, or "carriers," while others continued to hunt for game as "caribou eaters," with people continuously changing from caribou eating to carrying and back? What of the multilingual, multiethnic, intermarrying groups of Cree and Assiniboin that grew up in the far northern Plains of North America in response to the stimulus of the fur trade, until the units "graded into one another" (Sharrock 1974: 96)? What of the Mundurucú in Amazonia who changed from patrilocality and patriliny to adopt the unusual combination of matrilocality and patrilineal reckoning in response to their new role as hunters of slaves and suppliers of manioc flour to slave-hunting expeditions? What, moreover, of Africa, where the slave trade created an unlimited demand for slaves, and where quite unrelated populations met that demand by severing people from their kin groups through warfare, kidnapping, pawning, or judicial procedures, in order to have slaves to sell to the Europeans? In all such cases, to attempt to specify separate cultural wholes and distinct boundaries would create a false sample. These cases exemplify spatially and temporally shifting relationships, prompted in all instances by the effects of European expansion. If we consider, furthermore, that this expansion has for nearly 500 years affected case after case, then the search for a world sample of distinct cases is illusory.

One need have no quarrel with a denotative use of the term society to designate an empirically verifiable cluster of interconnections among people, as long as no evaluative prejudgments are added about its state of internal cohesion or boundedness in relation to the external world. Indeed, I shall continue to use the term in this way throughout this book, in preference to other clumsier formulations. Similarly, it would be an error to discard the anthropological insight that human existence entails the creation of cultural forms, themselves predicated on the human capacity to symbol.

Yet the concept of the autonomous, self-regulating and self-justifying society and culture has trapped anthropology inside the bounds of its own definitions. Within the halls of science, the compass of observation and thought has narrowed, while outside the inhabitants of the world are increasingly caught up in continent-wide and global change. Indeed, has there ever been a time when human populations have existed in independence of larger encompassing relationships, unaffected by larger fields of force? Just as the sociologists pursue the will-o'-the-wisp of social order and integration in a world of upheaval and change, so anthropologists look for pristine replicas of the precapitalist, preindustrial past in the sinks and margins of the capitalist, industrial world. But Europeans and Americans would never have encountered these supposed bearers of a pristine past if they had not encountered one another, in bloody fact, as Europe reached out to seize the resources and populations of the other continents. Thus, it has been rightly said that anthropology is an offspring of imperialism. Without imperialism there would be no anthropologists, but there would also be no Dene, Baluba, or Malay fishermen to be studied. The tacit anthropological supposition that people like these are people without history amounts to the erasure of 500 years of confrontation, killing, resurrection, and accommodation. If sociology operates with its mythology of Gemeinschaft and Gesellschaft, anthropology all too frequently operates with its mythology of the pristine primitive. Both perpetuate fictions that deny the facts of ongoing relationships and involvements.

These facts clearly emerge in the work of anthropologists and historians who have specialized in what has come to be known as ethnohistory. Perhaps "ethnohistory" has been so called to separate it from "real" history, the study of the supposedly civilized. Yet what is clear from the study of ethnohistory is that the subjects of the two kinds of history are the same. The more ethnohistory we know, the more clearly "their" history and "our" history emerge as part of the same history. Thus, there can be no "Black history" apart from "White history," only a component of a common history suppressed or omitted from conventional studies for economic, political, or ideological reasons.

These remarks echo those made by the anthropologist Alexander Lesser who, in a different context, asked years ago that "we adopt as a working hypothesis the universality of human contact and influence"; that we think "of human societies—prehistoric, primitive, or modern—not as closed systems, but as open systems"; that we see them "as inextricably involved with other aggregates, near and far, in weblike, netlike connections" (1961: 42). The labors of the ethnohistorians have demonstrated the validity of this advice in case after case. Yet it remains merely programmatic until we can move from a consideration of connections at work in separate cases to a wider perspective, one that will allow us to connect the connections in theory as well as in empirical study.

In such a perspective, it becomes difficult to view any given culture as a bounded system or as a self-perpetuating "design for living." We thus stand in need of a new theory of cultural forms. The anthropologists have shown us that cultural forms—as "determinate orderings" of things, behavior, and ideas—do play a demonstrable role in the management of human interaction. What will be required of us in the future is not to deny that role, but to understand more precisely how cultural forms work to mediate social relationships among particular populations.

The Uses of Marx

If we grant the existence of such connections, how are we to conceive of them? Can we grasp a common process that generates and organizes them? Is it possible to envision such a common dynamic and yet maintain a sense of its distinctive unfolding in time and space as it involves and engulfs now this population, now that other?

Such an approach is possible, but only if we can face theoretical possibilities that transcend our specialized disciplines. It is not enough to become multidisciplinary in the hope that an addition of all the disciplines will lead to a new vision. A major obstacle to the development of a new perspective lies in the very fact of specialization itself. That fact has a history and that history is significant, because the several academic disciplines owe their existence to a common rebellion against political economy, their parent discipline. That discipline strove to lay bare the laws or regularities surrounding the production of wealth. It entailed a concern with how wealth was generated in production, with the role of classes in the genesis of wealth, and with the role of the state in relation to the different classes. These concerns were common to conservatives and socialists alike. (Marx addressed himself to them when he criticized political economists for taking as universals what he saw as the characteristics of historically particular systems of production.) Yet these concerns have been expunged so completely from the repertory of the social sciences that the latest *International Encyclopedia of the Social Sciences* does not even include entries under "political economy" and "class." Today, concern with such matters is usually ascribed only to Marxists, even though Marx himself wrote in a letter to a friend (Joseph Weydemeyer, March 5, 1852):

> no credit is due me for discovering the existence of classes in society nor yet the struggle between them. Long before me bourgeois historians had described the historical development of this class struggle and bourgeois economists the economic anatomy of the classes. [quoted in Venable 1945: 6, n.3]

It is likely that it was precisely the conception of political economy as a structure of *classes* that led the nascent social sciences to turn against the concept of class. If social, economic, and political relations were seen to involve a division into antagonistic classes, endowed by the structure of the political economy itself with opposing interests and capabilities, then the pursuit of order would indeed be haunted forever by the specter of discord. This was what led James Madison, in his tough-minded *Federalist Papers*, to define the function of government as the regulation of relations among antagonistic classes. The several social science disciplines, in contrast, turned their back on political economy, shifting instead to the intensive study of interaction among individuals—in primary and secondary groups, in the market, in the processes of government. They thus turned away also from concern with crucial questions about the nature of production, class, and power: If production is the condition of being human, how is production to be understood and analyzed? Under what conditions does production entail the rise of classes? What are the implications of class division for the allocation of resources and the exercise of power? What is the nature of the state?

Although these questions were abandoned by the social sciences, they persist as their hidden agenda. Because Marx raised these questions most persistently and systematically, he remains a hidden interlocutor in much social science discourse. It has been said, with reason, that the social sciences constitute one long dialogue with the ghost of Marx. If we are to transcend the present limits and limitations of the specialized disciplines, we must return to these unanswered questions and reconsider them.

Marx is important for this reconsideration in several ways. He was one of the last major figures to aim at a holistic human science, capable of integrating the varied specializations. Contrary to what is all too often said about him, he was by no means an economic determinist. He was a materialist, believing in the primacy of material relationships as against the primacy of "spirit." Indeed, his concept of production (*Produktion*) was conceived in opposition to Hegel's concept of *Geist*, manifesting itself in successive incarnations of spirit. For him, production embraced at once the changing relations of humankind, to nature, the social relations into which humans enter in the course of transforming nature, and the consequent transformations of human symbolic capability. The concept is thus not merely economic in the strict sense but also ecological, social, political, and social-psychological. It is relational in character.

Marx further argued—against those who wanted to universalize Society, or the Market, or the Political Process—the existence of different modes of production in human history. Each mode represented a different combination of elements. What was true of one mode was not true of another: there was therefore no universal history. But Marx was profoundly historical. Both the elements constituting a mode of production and their characteristic combination had for him a definable history of origin, unfolding, and disintegration. He was neither a universal historian nor a historian of events, but a historian of configurations or syndromes of material relationships. Most of his energy was, of course, spent on efforts to understand the history and workings of one particular mode, capitalism, and this not to defend it but to effect its revolutionary transformation. Since our specialized disciplinary discourse developed as an antidote to revolution and disorder, it is understandable that this ghostly interrogator should have been made unwelcome in the halls of academe.

Yet the specter has vital lessons for us. First, we shall not understand the present world unless we trace the growth of the world market and the course of capitalist development. Second, we must have a theory of that growth and development. Third, we must be able to relate both the history and theory of that unfolding development to processes that affect and change the lives of local populations. That theory must be able to delineate the significant elements at work in these processes and their systemic combinations in historical time. At the same time, it ought to cut finely enough to explain the significant differences marking off each such combination from all the others—say, capitalism from other historically known combinations. Finally, theoretically informed. history and historically informed theory must be joined together to account for populations specifiable in time and space, both as outcomes of significant processes and as their carriers.

Among those who have contributed to a theoretically informed history of the world to which capitalism has given rise, two names standout, both for the trenchancy of their formulations and the scope of their research effort. One of these is Andre Gunder Frank, an economist, who began to question the modernization approach to economic development in the early 1960s. Frank clearly articulated the heretical proposition that development and underdevelopment were not separate phenomena, but were closely bound up with each other (1966, 1967). Over the past centuries, capitalism had spread outward from its original center to all parts of the globe. Everywhere it penetrated, it turned other areas into dependent satellites of the metropolitan center. Extracting the surpluses produced in the satellites to meet the requirements of the metropolis, capitalism distorted and thwarted the development of the satellites to its own benefit. This phenomenon Frank called "the development of underdevelopment." The exploitative relation between metropolis and satellite was, moreover, repeated within each satellite itself, with the classes and regions in closer contact with the external metropolis drawing surplus from the hinterland and distorting and thwarting its development. Underdevelopment in the satellites was therefore not a phenomenon sui generis, but the outcome of relations between satellite and metropolis, ever renewed in the process of surplus transfer and ever reinforced by the continued dependency of the satellite on the metropolis.

Similar to Frank's approach is Immanuel Wallerstein's explicitly historical account of capitalist origins and the development of the "European world-economy." This world-economy, originating in the late fifteenth and early sixteenth centuries, constitutes a global market, characterized by a global division of labor. Firms (be they individuals, enterprises, or regions) meet in this market to exchange the goods they have produced in the hope of realizing a profit. The search for profit guides both production in general and specialization in production. Profits are generated by primary producers, whom Wallerstein calls proletarians, no matter how their labor is mobilized. Those profits are appropriated through legal sanctions by capitalists, whom Wallerstein classifies as bourgeois, no matter what the source of their capital. The growth of the market and the resulting worldwide division of labor generate a basic distinction between the core countries (Frank's metropolis) and the periphery (Frank's satellites). The two are linked by "unequal exchange," whereby "high-wage (but low-supervision), high-profit, high-capital intensive" goods produced in the core are exchanged for "low-wage (but high-supervision), low-profit, low-capital intensive goods" produced in the periphery (see Wallerstein 1974: 351). In the core, goods are produced mainly by "free" wage remunerated labor; in the periphery goods are produced mainly by one kind or another of coerced labor. Although he adduces various factors to explain this difference, Wallerstein has recourse to what is basically a demographic explanation. He argues that the growth of free wage labor in the core area arose in response to the high densities of population that made workers competitive with one another and hence willing to submit to market discipline, while in the periphery low population densities favored the growth of labor coercion. We shall have occasion to look critically at some of these propositions. Yet what is important about both Frank's and Wallerstein's work is that they have replaced the fruitless debates about modernization with a sophisticated and theoretically oriented acount of how capitalism evolved and spread, an evolution and spread of intertwined and yet differentiated relationships.

Both Frank and Wallerstein focused their attention on the capitalist world system and the arrangements of its parts. Although they utilized the findings of anthropologists and regional historians, for both the principal aim was to understand how the core subjugated the periphery, and not to study the reactions of the micro-populations habitually investigated by anthropologists. Their choice of focus thus leads them to omit consideration of the range and variety of such populations, of their modes of existence before European expansion and the advent of capitalism, and of the manner in which these modes were penetrated, subordinated, destroyed, or absorbed, first by the growing market and subsequently by industrial capitalism. Without such an examination, however, the concept of the "periphery" remains as much of a cover term as "traditional society." Its advantage over the older term lies chiefly in its implications: it points to wider linkages that must be investigated if the processes at work in the periphery are to be understood. Yet this examination still lies before us if we wish to understand how Mundurucú or Meo were drawn into the larger system to suffer its impact and to become its agents.

This book undertakes such an examination. It hopes to delineate the general processes at work in mercantile and capitalist development, while at the same time following their effects on the micro-populations studied by the ethnohistorians and anthropologists. My view of these processes and their effects is historical; but in the sense of history as an analytic account of the development of material relations, moving simultaneously on the level of the encompassing system and on the micro-level. I therefore look first at the world in 1400, before Europe achieved worldwide dominance. I then discuss some theoretical constructs that might allow us to grasp the determining features of capitalism and the modes that preceded it. Next I turn to the development of European mercantile expansion and to the parts played by various European nations in extending its global sway. Following the global effects of European expansion leads to a consideration of the search for American silver, the fur trade, the slave trade, and the quest for new sources of wealth in Asia. I then trace the transition to capitalism in the course of the industrial revolution, examine its impact on areas of the world supplying resources to the industrial centers, and sketch out the formation of working classes and their migrations within and between continents. In this account, both the people who claim history as their own and the people to whom history has been denied emerge as participants in the same historical trajectory.

References

Bramson, Leon. 1961. *The Political Context of Sociology.* Princeton, NJ: Princeton University Press.

Daaku, Kwame Yeboa. 1970. *Trade and Politics on the Gold Coast 1600-1720: A Study of the African Reaction to European Trade.* Oxford: Clarendon Press.

Engler, Robert. 1968. Social Science and Social Consciousness: The Shame of the Universities. In *The Dissenting Academy.* Theodore Roszak, ed. Pp. 182-207. New York: Vintage Books.

Frank, Andre Gunder. 1966. The Development of Underdevelopment. *Monthly Review* 18: 17-31.

—. 1967. Sociology of Development and Underdevelopment of Sociology. *Catalyst* (Buffalo), No. 3: 20-73.

Huntington, Samuel P. 1968. The Bases of Accommodation. *Foreign Affairs* 46: 642-656.

Jennings, Francis. 1976. *The Invasion of America: Indians, Colonialism, and the Cant of Conquest*. New York: W.W. Norton.

Lekachman, Robert. 1976. *Economists at Bay*. New York: McGraw-Hill.

Lesser, Alexander. 1961. Social Fields and the Evolution of Society. *Southwestern Journal of Anthropology* 17: 40-48.

Lowie, Robert H. 1920. *Primitive Society*. New York: Boni and Liveright.

Nell, Edward. 1973. Economics: The Revival of Political Economy. In *Ideology in Social Science: Readings in Critical Social Theory*. Robin Blackburn, ed. Pp. 76-95. New York: Vintage Books/Random House.

Rostow, Walt Whitman. 1960. *The Stages of Economic Growth: A Non-Communist Manifesto*. Cambridge: Cambridge University Press.

Sahlins, Marshall D., and Elman R. Service, eds. 1960. *Evolution and Culture*. Ann Arbor: University of Michigan Press.

Sharrock, Susan R. 1974. Crees, Cree-Assinboines and Assiniboines: Inter-ethnic Social Organization on the Far Northern Plains. *Ethnohistory* 21:95-122.

Venable, Vernon. 1945. *Human Nature: The Marxian View*. New York: Knopf.

Volosinov, Valentin N. 1973. *Marxism and the Philosophy of Language*. New York and London: Seminar Press. (First pub. in Russian 1930.)

Wallerstein, Immanuel. 1974. *The Modern World-System: Capitalist Agriculture and the Origins of the European World-Economy in the Sixteenth Century*. New York: Academic Press.

Weber, Max. 1968. *On Charisma and Institution Building: Selected Papers*. Shmuel N. Eisenstadt, ed. Chicago: University of Chicago Press.

Study Questions
1. How does Wolf characterize the relationship between the Western world and non-Western peoples?

2. In what ways have different social scientific disciplines severed social relations from political, economic, and ideological context?

3. Specify some ways in which anthropologists have attempted to transcend the "boundaries of the microcosm."

Further Readings

Gunder Frank, André. 1967. *Capitalism and Underdevelopment in Latin America*. New York and London: Monthly Review Press.

Redfield, Robert. 1971 [1956]. *Peasant Society and Culture: An Anthropological Approach to Civilization*. Chicago: University of Chicago Press.

Wallerstein, Emmanuel. 1976. *The Modern World System*. New York: Academic Press.

Wolf, Eric R. 1966. *Peasants*. Englewood Cliffs, NJ: Prentice-Hall.

—. 1982. *Europe and the People Without History*. Berkeley: University of California Press.

28

History as Commodity in Some Recent American (Anthropological) Literature[1]

MICHAEL TAUSSIG

*There are no facts **as such**. We must always begin by introducing a mean-*
ing in order for there to be a fact.
    —Nietzsche, quoted in R. Barthes, "The Discourse of History"

Sundering truth from falsehood is the goal of the materialist method, not
its point of departure. In other words, its point of departure is the object
riddled with error, with conjecture. The distinctions with which the mate-
rialist method, discriminative from the outset, starts are distinctions
within this highly mixed object, and it cannot present this object as mixed
or uncritical enough.
    —Walter Benjamin, "Addendum to 'The Paris of the Second
                                            Empire in Baudelaire'"

Guide Books

Two highly polished books about commodities have recently been launched
onto the U.S. market. The results of lifetimes of thought, both seize on the commodity in the belief or the hope that the firmer they grasp it, the more likely
they are to shake us free of the illusions we have about explaining society. Pre-
eminently they are guide books for American Anthropology, which they wish
to save from various fates—a descent into triviality, losing sense of purpose.
It's as if Anthropology, once an item in a dull university catalog, had like the
commodity itself risen from mere thinghood to acquire life and soul, albeit
sickly and deformed and in need of saving.

> Studies of the everyday in modern life, of the changing character of mundane
> matters like food, viewed from the joined perspective of production and con-
> sumption, use and function, and concerned with the differential emergence
> and variation of meaning, may be one way to inspirit a discipline now dan-

gerously close to losing its sense of purpose (Sidney Mintz, *Sweetness and Power*, p. 213).

In 1968 1 wrote that anthropology needed to discover history, a history that could account for the ways in which the social system of the modern world came into being, and that would strive to make analytic sense of all societies, including our own [because] our methods were becoming more sophisticated but their yield seemed increasingly commmonplace. To stem a descent into triviality, I thought we needed to search out the causes of the present in the past. Only in this way could we come to comprehend the forces that impel societies and cultures here and now. This book grew out of these convictions (Eric Wolf, *Europe and the People without History*, p. ix).

Lifesavers

I have been thrown two life jackets, one to inspire, the other to stem descent, yet I fear the sea is too cold and choppy to use them, much as I might want to. Like Kafka I'm sure there's hope, but I'm not sure if it's for us. This is the sea of commodities, vast and treacherous. Most of the time the best one can do is tread water. Kafka said he suffered from seasickness on dry land, but the builders of these life jackets don't have much time for that sort of talk, and I suppose that befits the grim purpose of saving lives. Not for them the resort to play or trickery, the slow digesting of experience(s), the place of dream in the commodity as utopian wishing, emotions, interpretation, and all that goes along with observing oneself observing. Yet sometimes I think the designers of these jackets do not realize quite how serious our situation is, how the sea surrounds us on all sides, commodities determining the very way we try to size up things, **objectify** and **subjectify** the world and in doing so create colliding realities, how the horizon wavers, advances and recedes, making us giddy as the currents from the deep pull and tear us in all directions. More mysterious than table-turning, Marx said in his famous chapter on the fetishism of commodities and its secret— therewith bringing to a close that massive first step of an introduction to *Capital* concerned not merely with the vexing question of value but with *problematizing the **commodity**-form itself.* Marx was not happy with the solid, open-faced appearance that commodities acquired as things, complete unto themselves. And with what fiendish delight did he point to the dazzling epistemological somersaults undertaken by commodities and upon ourselves, first as things, then as spirits. Fetishism was the term he used and we, in a post-Frankfurt/Adorno/Benjamin age, are now somewhat accustomed not only to attempts to work through the effects of the coupling and decoupling of reification with **fetishization** but also to the shocking conclusions that Adorno, for one, drew; namely, that this somersaulting, this coupling and decoupling, constituted the basis of capitalist culture as well as the insuperable block to the Kantian antimonies. There could be no solution inside philosophy to the epistemological problems posed by our type of economy. Ours was the age of contradiction par excellence, an age of fragmentation and incoherence in which (according to the *Communist Manifesto* and Marshall Berman) "all that is sold melts into air." Georg Lukács, in a classic paper on reification, opined in the mid-1920s that at this stage of capitalism there was no problem that did not lead back to the question of the commodity-form, the central structural problem of capitalist society in *all* its aspects. The basis of this commodity-form, he wrote, "is that a relation between people takes on the character of a thing and thus acquires a 'phantom objectivity,' an autonomy that seems so strictly rational and all-embracing as to conceal every trace of its fundamental nature; the relation between people." Exceedingly strange, therefore, that our two commodity authors should be attempting to save us without so much as a nod to Marx for his warnings about the commodity's two-facedness and double-dealing—especially when we consider the dependence on him they manifest throughout their work. On looking over their books one is tempted to conclude that works which cannot trade blow for blow with the commodity as thing and the commodity as fetish are destined to reproduce the very phantom objectivity Lukacs pointed to. And they do this not only in the name of critique, but to save us.

Titles

There is Sidney Mintz's book *Sweetness and Power: The Place of Sugar in Modern History*, and Eric Wolf's *Europe and the People without History*. Both titles have something to tell us. Professor Mintz's is congenial in assuring me that there is an entity, Modern History, with *places* in it for commodities like shelving in the supermarket. Our task is to find where the sugar is kept, and in search of it, we learn much about the whole. As a guide, Mintz is charming and modest. His text depends much on the subjunctive mood, a lot of perhaps and maybe, a nudge here and there, every now and then a grand slam where bits are smooshed together to the benefit of capital and power. In short it is a text, a poetics, of sweetness *and* power. As such it is to be sharply distinguished from the poetics of Wolf's commodity-book, which proceeds in a straight line through History seen as progressive stages in the unfolding of a Totality. Wolf knows the supermarket so well that all he has to do is pull a few items off the shelves to illustrate the interlocking connections that constitute aforesaid Totality, and his tone is authoritative. The poetics of sweetness and power takes on added significance when Mintz speaks eloquently of a sense of mystery he found in sugar from the beginning of his Caribbean awakening, a mystery that is largely but not completely put to rest by finding out about and being able to envision as so many internal relations of sugar the trading relations between Europe, Africa, and the sugar islands and land south of Florida; the stupendous importance of sugar in the development of capitalism; the complex puzzle of Demand (as in Supply and Demand); aristocratic luxury taste and lower-class imitating; the possible role of sugar in sweetening and fueling the bitter life of the English laborer; and so forth. But the mystery lingers. No matter how many connections of (what one might chose [sic] to call) the historical sort Mintz brings to light, it is we, with our specific conventions, convictions, and curiosity, who provide that light (of intelligibility) —and thereby continue to puzzle about the connections between meaning (sweetness) and power.

Wolf's entitling is, to put it mildly, a study in irony, for the implication is that many or all Third World people have been *falsely* portrayed (particularly by anthropologists, he will say) as not having History (First Irony). Then there is the Marxist or Marxist-Populist convention by which it is a sign of revolutionary solidarity to affirm the existence of those passive objects of others' History-making, "people (truly) without history" (Second Irony). Both formulations effortlessly reify History as some-thing to be possessed, and both are subject in his book to a Third or meta-irony by the surprising absence of the Histories of the people without history. It is Wolf's way of looking at History as the History of the Commodity that causes this dehistoricization of History. He takes the materialist or bourgeois meaning of the commodity, not the one that bedevils Marx in the long first section of *Capital*, with the result that History itself becomes a fetish, a live being with a spirit of its own. This fetish-power Wolf renders as Capital Accumulation. People then become things, truly without History.

Men Make Stories

"Men make history," states Wolf in his Afterword, following Marx, "but not under conditions of their own choosing." Men (and women) make stories too, and since the Enlightenment they have often called them Histories. The wonder is how such stories, removed from the authority of the lived experience of the story-teller, are constructed so as to seem (in the words of Roland Barthes) *to tell themselves*. Like the commodity, (hi)story has two modes; in its thing-form it is something that the (hi)storian can rise above and manipulate; in its fetish-form it is self-empowered and irresistibly real. As commodity, therefore, History is the story that men make and makes men. In this way the Historian humbly finds that privileged position, that Archimedean point, outside of History whereby History in its telling can be evaded. This point outside and above history is the phantom to which the historian striving for objectivity, the phantom objectivity of Lukács, aspires. Both of these books about the commodity and history are phantomized in this way.

Irresistibly Real

In this type of History "everything happens," writes Barthes, "as if the discourse or the linguistic existence was merely a pure and simple 'copy' of another existence, situated in an extra-structural field, the 'real.'"

Not so much "arguments" and "points" but first the creation and sustenance of a feeling of the real, out there—this is the major ideological task of the discourse of history, and it involves a mode of **representation** which denies the act of representing. Raymond Williams writes that language is not merely an instrument but also a source of experience. Yet to the sustenance of the "reality-effect" of historical discourse it is essential that writing be understood as only instrumental—our instrument with which we copy reality out there, reality serene in its independence from its representation. (The reality with which we are not so much concerned as involved, of course, is the one that asks us not about the existence of this table or that tree but about social relationships, social knowledge in both its implicit and its explicit dimensions, labor and labor-power.)

The Reality of Modernity

Might not commodity fetishism create modes of representation which undo as well as sustain this "effect of the real"?

Barthes writes that historical discourse is the only one in which the referent is addressed as external to the discourse, though without its ever being possible to reach it outside this discourse.

This superb and supreme insolubility of the referent, smug in its own thinghood, is of course a phantom, a contrivance that masquerades as self-made in its occupying Lukács's space of phantom objectivity. Its very phantasmic character, however, beckons us toward modes of representation in which representation itself is represented. These modes are Modernism. And it is their task to link arms with phantoms so as to problematize reference. They do not openly contest the fetishism of commodities so much as trip them up in their own epistemological murk.

Professor Mintz calls not only for an "anthropology of modern life" and "of the changing character of mundane matters like food," but for an anthropology that retains "a full appreciation of humanity's historical nature as a species" (p. 213). He invokes the modern against the primitive. He sees Primitivism as an essential part of anthropologists' undoing and castigates Romanticism, that whipping boy of Realists.

Yet is not his very insistence here testimony to the dependence of the modern on Primitivism? What could be more archaic, if not primitive, than the impassioning appeal to humanity's historical nature as species? And might not the commodity itself, which is what his book is about, be testimony to this precise dependence and conflation of Primitivism and Modernism? Think here of Walter Benjamin's *Passagenwerk*, the Paris Arcades Project of the 1930s, with his pointed concern to show us the ways by which the commodity, in its very modernity and mundaneness, conjured up the archaic and the exotic, the primitive and the mythic. It was as if, in our secular and scientific age, fancy found its home no longer in the stories and gods of times gone by but in commodities, as fetishes and as things.[2] A dreamworld lay before us in the mythic meanings of commodities, the promise they held. The primitive was made anew by the new, and it was the child's fresh eye that brought the always-the-same in the commodity to the adult's sense of change and "progress" in this age of the modern—this age for which Mintz wants an anthropology. But little of this implosion of the made-up past in the present meets Mintz's adult eye, despite his poignant call for an anthropology of the modern in the mundane. Like the way both he and Professor Wolf eye the commodity, so modernity is here deproblematized; it is the latest slice in the homogenous flow of time.

Marlboro Man

In leather and denim he sits, high on his galloping horse, way above the freeway, swinging his lariat yet perfectly relaxed as the cars hum and the semis scream past underneath, their drivers half in and half out of consciousness in that funny semi-awake/semi-dream state of near hypnosis that characterizes not only highway driving but much of modernity as well. And what could be more rationalistic than the freeway, the shortest distance between two points in a straight line, cruise control, every exit numbered. Progress too. He's high already. Must be fifty feet up there dwarfing us, going too fast to do more than glimpse him galloping in another century through the grey midwestern summer sky as we approach Detroit or cross the Bay Bridge to Oakland.

Visceral Meaning

Tobacco: a capital substance, and a mystical one too; a killer and a necessity. It enters not only the freeway of our imagination, as it does for shamans in the Orinoco Delta, but the blood that is our biological life-stream. Its meanings overwhelm us. Up there in the sky with his lariat and with the gods, more alive than you or me, the Marlboro Man. But sugar, where rides its champion? This is a question not so much of "advertising" (a term that instantly makes one switch off one's politico-aesthetic scanner) but of the mythification of substances in a non-mythifying age of marketing rationality. Why tobacco one way and sugar another? Why should Mintz's book on the meaning-and-power of sugar in modern history contain next to nothing that can help us? And what happens to "meaning" when it becomes "taste"? Might not we call on Mintz, by the material facts of the matter, to create a new field not of power and meaning but of power and ... visceral meaning? And what might that be? (With some surprise I note that what people mean by meaning, when they regard it as secondary to something "more basic" like "power" or one or another of *les grandes recits*, is so terribly staid, so framed, cognitive, and uptight. No place for emotions or visceral meanings here.)

Ritual

The study of "consumption" is essential to Mintz's mystery of sugar. The commodity passes in its life-circuit from exchange-value to use-value where, anthropologist as he is, Mintz scents the strategic importance of ritual in creating and maintaining sugar's demand. In doing so he subtly reminds us of some of anthropology's claim to distinction, what makes it different from other human sciences. He is using anthropology, showing us its power. Yet his doing so weakens its power, for what we get are textbookish cliches about ritual as a crude functionalizer: rituals into which sugar was "wedged" (*sic*) reproduce social status and social divisions; sugar drifts down the social ladder as it becomes cheaper and more plentiful and drifts down further to be used as a sign of ... one is not sure exactly, but it is used in rituals of separation and departure and, of course, the ritual of tea and the tea break in work. But we seem to be sliding, for what a ritual banquet of the ruling class or the ritual of a funeral means is not quite the same as what we mean when we speak of the ritual of a cup of tea in modern times, one of the many "rituals" of everyday life. In fact, we do not say ritual (that's more a professionalized anthropological smirk). What people say are things like (recalling my childhood) "a cuppa tea, a Bex, and a good lie down"—a sigh of pleasure/a cry of pain and muted protest, associated particularly with or attributed to working-class women in Sydney (Bex is an across-the-counter analgesic). It is a pity that Mintz never takes us into one of these rituals of the modern everyday so often named and hence claimed in the explanation of consumption. But perhaps modernity would stretch anthropology out of shape.

—We can drink it black, Stephen said. There's a lemon in the locker.
—O, damn you and your Paris fads, Buck Mulligan said. I want Sandycove milk.
Haines came in from the doorway and said quietly:
—That woman is coming up with the milk.
—The blessings of God on you, Buck Mulligan cried, jumping up from his chair. Sit down. Pour out the tea there. The sugar is in the bag. Here I can't go fumbling at the damned eggs. He hacked through the fry on the dish and slapped it out on three plates saying:
—*In nomine Patris et Filii et Spiritus Sancti*. Haines sat down to pour out the tea.

—I'm giving you two lumps each, he said. But, I say, Mulligan, you do make strong tea, don't you?

Buck Mulligan hewing thick slices from the loaf said in an old woman's wheedling voice:

—When I makes tea, I makes tea, as old Mother Grogan said. And when I makes water, I makes water.

—By Jove, it's tea, Haines said.

Buck Mulligan went on hewing and wheedling:

—So I do, Mrs Cahill, says she. *Begob, ma'am*, says Mrs Cahill, *God send you don't make them in the one pot.* He lunged towards his messmates in turn a thick slice of bread, impaled on his knife.

—That's folk, he said very earnestly, for your book Haines.

An unusual group in some ways only, students in James Joyce's Dublin, July 16, 1904. Yet this is clearly life surging around the sugary rite, and how its sense differs from the naming and claiming and functionalizing of the rites of that what we might call a premodern Anthropology, enmeshed in the fiction of the real, wishes to recruit for the explanation of demand! How its sudden swerves of pace and direction, its gathering of angles, imprecisions, and layers, suggest conflicting realities at work in any instant of Modernity! But where would that leave an anthropology of the modern everyday[?]

Practices

Mintz talks of practices of consumption (p. 154) as well as of rituals, and in much the same way. Practices of consumption "mark the distribution of power" within the organization of society, for example. Comforting words are "mark" and "organization," reassuringly solid for the necessary task of bestowing a sense of coherence on the world. But of "power," the wished-for bedrock, there are other views. Michel de Certeau, for example, writes on what he calls the logic of everyday practices and, more pointedly, on the complication posed for the study of such practices by the constant disruption of such logic. In his words, "these practices themselves alternately exacerbate and disrupt our logics" (note, exacerbate *and* disrupt). Research into these practices, as much as the practices themselves, contains what he calls "regrets"—the havoc played on the logic of explanation and of analysis by the play of chance in everyday life-practice, the ineffability of certain experiences constituting those practices, the grayness of the epistemic murk habituating our life-forms. The study of practices in everyday modern life leads, he concludes, to a "*polemological* analysis of culture. Like law (one of its models), culture articulates conflicts and alternately legitimizes, displaces, or controls the superior force. It develops in an atmosphere of tensions, and often of violence [and] the tactics of consumption, the ingenious ways in which the weak make use of the strong, thus lend a political dimension to everyday practices."[3]

De Certeau thus sees power as not only entailed in practices of consumption but destabilized as well. This is quite distinct—as writing practice—from what a text like Mintz's achieves. *Sweetness and Power*, in the very earnestness with which it continuously strives to reduce such things as "practices of consumption" to "power" as the bedrock, constantly affirms and sustains that power. Just as the commodity is deproblematized, and the Modern too (seen as the latest slice in the flow of homogenous time), so power itself is reified, and critique cast in conventional terms sustains convention.

Slipperiness and Power
One of the things that amazes me reading a book like this, with its wealth of materials and enormity of scope and drama, is how little it amazes me. There is no estrangement. Not only is this anthropology of the everyday textualized so that the everyday remains everyday, but the sense of slipperiness of power, what de Certeau conveys, is anathema to it. Instead the text itself is slippery, to grease the huge determinisms of capital's narrative. This is a text that creates its effects with the subjunctive, the perhaps, the subtle, the sugary understatement—yet it is implacable as the closing of a coffin-lid in sealing fate. One example:

> The history of sugar in the United Kingdom has been marked by many "accidental" events, such as the introduction of bitter stimulant beverages in the mid-seventeenth century. But sugar consumption's rise there-after was not accidental; it was the direct consequence of underlying forces in British society and of the excercise of power. (p.150).

Symboling
Mintz writes (p. 153-54) that "birth and death are universal in the sense that they happen to all human beings; our capacity to symbolize, to endow anything with meaning and then act in terms of that meaning, is similarly universal and intrinsic to our nature—like learning to walk or to speak (or being born or dying). But which materials we link to events and endow with meaning are unpredictably subject to cultural and historical forces."

Meaning is thus subject (unpredictably) to forces. But what is the meaning of those forces? How did they escape symbolization? Where is the privileged point outside meaning whereby judgement on meaning can be rendered?

In Mintz's book this point is social relations and the distribution of power in society. Unlike birth and death such relations are not subject to our capacity to symbolize. There lies our hope. They escape fate.

History and Difference

"If there is any explanation it is historical." With these words Professor Mintz banishes hermeneutics to intellectual purgatory. Meaning becomes History. "When we pass onto our children the meanings of what we do, our explanation consists largely of instructions to what we learned to do before them" (p. 158). It is left to the historian's historian to ask about the learner's learning, and history is thus what exists—truly "the past in the present," to quote Professor Wolf. But one has questions about a view that chains the present to the past in this way. Do not the children pass something onto their elders?

What most anthropologists think about meaning can he summed up, Mintz says, by paraphrasing Clifford Geertz: human beings are caught in webs of signification they themselves have spun. Mintz strongly objects. Not only is meaning historical, it is also determined by differences between groups in society (in an older earthier discourse, by class struggle). "The assumption of a homogenous web," he writes, "may mask, instead of reveal, how meanings are generated and transmitted. This is perhaps the point where meaning and power touch most clearly" (p. 158).

Touching

"The profound changes in dietary and consumption patterns in eighteenth and nineteenth century Europe were not random or fortuitous, but the direct consequence of the same momentum that created a world economy, shaping the asymmetrical relationship between metropolitan centers and their colonies [and] the tremendous productive apparatuses, both technical and human, of modern capitalism. But this is not to say that these changes were intended" (pp. 158-59).

Touching is the trope which Professor Mintz uses to displace the "web of meaning." Touching is what sweetness-and-power is all about. Touching consists in:

(a) listing dates and prices and volumes of sugar production and consumption; and
(b) giving some (to my mind extraordinarily limited) sense of the symbolism of sugar; and
(c) touching (a) with (b), implying some meaningful connection exists between the two

when in fact what makes the connection meaningful in Mintz' text is a quality brought from outside—from Reality, from History, from the great narrative of Capitalism ("the same momentum that created a world economy").

Sweetness and Power

Touching involves the artful confounding of "cause" with metonymy. Although historical discourse of the type Mintz employs strains to give the appearance of manifesting, if not establishing, "causal" connections, what it really gives us is the continuous parading and constellating of bits and pieces to an imagined whole—bits and pieces of the world and world history in sugar.

When, at the very close of his book, and with his perennial charm and modesty, Professor Mintz suggests that his "connecting so minor a matter as sugar to the state of the world in general may seem like yet another chorus of the bone song—the hip bone's connected to the leg bone, etc." (p. 214)—we see quite clearly how the artful confounding of metonymic with causal analysis works. It succeeds (throughout the text, not just here at the strategic moment of closure) through Mintz's very sweetness, the sense of the author that the text tirelessly creates, with his wonderfully developed poetics of understatement, modesty, and subtlety.

Thus can the very next sentence after the bone song-disclaimer read, in a slashingly different key, "But we have already seen how sucrose, this 'favored child of capitalism'—in Fernando Ortiz' lapidary phrase—epitomized the transition from one kind of society to another."

Thus does the bone song become, through its own sweetness, power—the power of the story that seems to tell itself.

Undoing History

Because of its furtive yet complete dependence on a narrative, that of Capitalism, to make its metonymic connections appear causal ones that can make "meaning" seem like something secondary to "History," Mintz's contribution to an Anthropology of the Modern Everyday does little more than reproduce a premodern anthropology chained ever more firmly to its past. To adopt the jargon: the task is not to do history but to undo it.

One way of doing this is precisely that of the bone song. We consciously dismiss the commodified storytelling of causal analysis and instead make the juxtaposition of metonyms our way of "doing history" through its undoing—not for us the rosary beads and chains of causes and effects. Then would we be confronted not by the power of Historical Discourse but by a quite different collation of meaning and power as generated by a modernist text of the modern and the mundane, striking with the left hand (the hand of accident and fortuity so abhorred by Mintz), irregularly challenging the inviolablity of the referent, constantly problematizing reality instead of sustaining it by resort to the awesome power of Capital.

Stemming Descent

I am sitting in a hot and waterless sugar plantation town in western Colombia, reading Professor Wolf's book about commodities and colonies, *Europe and the People without History*. I have been coming back to this town every year since 1969. Everything Wolf writes in his book about plantation development strikes me as curiously over-general and, when applied to what I know about the history of the people of this town and of the surrounding plantations, wrong. What am I to make of the sort of knowledge this book creates, this book aimed at stemming a descent into triviality?

Wolf's book is built on the impassioned appeal to make broader connections. Part One is titled "Connections," in bold type above a double-page reproduction of one of the de Brys's engravings made in the year 1599, depicting a moving caravan of armed traders together with their laden camels and mules. Why with this demand to broaden the context is there a terrible narrowing of interest? Why with the demand to look for connection is there blindness to the unexpected?

There are no surprises in this history of history-less peoples, and no escaping it either. It is more remorseless than fate. Making connections here means referring the part to the whole. The whole is already known. It is the world of trade and production. It is the whole world as a metaphysical entity. Its driving force is Capital Accumulation. Its destination is History.

Incidentally, the de Brys' engravings, several of them dramatically featured in this book, are now emblematic of the European conquest of the New World, a graphic cliché like the use of Mayan glyphs to serve as signs of Latin America. But the de Brys, commissioned by Protestant Dutch and English merchants, rivals of the Spanish, never traveled far from Paris and certainly never saw the New World. Their task was to create images with which others—such as us, today—would see that world's newness. And they peopled it with humans taken from Classical ideals, from (the idea of) ancient Greece.

What sort of connections does the use of such imagery suggest we make? Perpetuated conventions raise the question of how we can ever see the newness of the New World. Could that be the true aim of history?

How strange that this book, so enthusiastically rooted in the deep soil of historical determinism, should itself be able to escape the ways by which history transmutes connections into conventions.

The plentiful use of maps of the world and its parts is interesting in this regard, because maps function to authorize, even more than photographs, the idea of the real. If the de Brys images authorize the "once upon a time" of History, then the maps complement that realization with the notion that reality is not so much represented as copied.

This book is like a map, a copy, of the world. It looks down onto the world. But where does it look from, and how did it get there?

Curious, how one reads and says, So what? Is this not all terribly obvious, or an academicization of the obvious? It produces a strange effect. I, the reader, must be missing something—and the book is no longer obvious but mysterious. It's all very well to talk so much about Historical Political Economy and of The Three Modes of Production that constitute World History. But aren't there other modes of production to consider? What about the mode of textual production, alongside if not prior to the kinship, the tributary, and the capitalist modes of production? What about modes of production of the real? And anyway, didn't Marx subtitle his *Capital* a *critique* of political economy?

Overarching, thrusting, penetrating, choking, consolidating, expanding, shifting of gears, more thrusting—these are the terms this book pours forth. We seem to be caught between a machine and certain sorts of sexual acts, the colony a woman's thighs, capitalism a penis, capitalism as juggernaut. The text evinces a strange pleasure in recounting this activity. It seems to be more than the pleasure of always being right. (In Kafka's penal colony the official in charge of the torture machine puts himself into it and then sets it going, inscribing the death sentence in words on his very body. He enjoys it.)

> —"External warfare, trade, and internal consolidation created new states in Europe [and] agriculture ceased to grow, perhaps because the available technology reached the limits of its productivity. The climate worsened" (p. 108).
> —"Trade and warfare necessarily fed upon each other."
> —"The State needed the merchants."

Thus does this writing animate things and abstractions of things; war becomes a person, a spirit, or a god. It creates States. So does trade. They feed on each other. Internal consolidation also creates (States). Agriculture stops growing. Technology reaches. And all this spiritualization of things is on a par with natural process; "the climate worsened." This mode of production of reality parallels Marx's ironic, teasing observations about commodity fetishism whereby people become like things and things become like people. Only Wolf's fetishism is not ironic. He is serious. He animates things in the same way as Capital. But as we know, the life thereby endowed is spectral.

A text that so closely reproduces the life-force of capital as its own innermost mode of production is a bullying text. In its attempt at critique through relentless repetition of the terrific power of capital, such a text joins forces with that power. Grim determinism and grim determination to "face reality" combine. How could we undo this combination in a way that would never let itself be assimilated to capital's fetish power?

Authoritarian realism: in siding with the power of capital through this mode of reality production, everything loose is nailed down, as the expression goes. Nailed down to what? To an integrated (imaginary) whole.

This totality is made in part through the continuous use of violent verbs in the passive voice. The usage not only makes the violence of the text strategically ambivalent—both violent and controlled (by whom? by what?)—but also creates the sense of past-perfect action completed, action finalized. It makes it difficult to see history as a living force in the present. Instead history comes across as judgment, and the Final one at that.

I keep coming back to the question What is history? What is historical explanation? What is historical understanding? The answer seems to be taken for granted in the text. I must be the only one who doesn't follow. Surely, "history," like religion, is here endowed with the moral authority of the past?

One gets only a negative idea of what historical understanding is: it is not what anthropologists did or still do in studying so-called primitives as pristine survivals from a timeless past. But one cannot define history and historical understanding from their (supposed) absence, like filling an empty bucket. Everything is securely established in this text, and the first thing securely established is the inviolability of the text's own procedures and modes of explaining. History is never given the chance to marshal a counterattack and devour the means by which it is invoked.

"There were several reasons for Huron success in this role" is typical of the text's attempts to recreate a world in which everything has its reasonable reason. In this instance of the Hurons' relationship with the French, the Hurons "occupied a strategic location for [trade] exchanges." In fact it boils down not to several but to one Reason capable of infinite multiplication.

Explanation is thus a matter of "unravelling the chains of causes and effects at work in the lives of particular populations" as "the totality [which is the world] developed over time" (p.385). What more could one say? As against "the totality" not people, but "populations."

What about people, the "people without history"? Wolf distinguishes his way of creating historical understanding from that of the (now largely defunct) Modernization School (with its concept of "traditional society"), and from that of André Gunder Frank and of Immanuel Wallerstein, by the fact that they all omit considerations of the precapitalist modes of existence of the "micropopulations habitually studied by anthropologists," and "of the manner in which these modes were penetrated, subordinated, destroyed, or absorbed, first by the growing market and subsequently by industrial capitalism" (p. 23). Wolf distinguishes his own position by its undertaking an examination of just such penetration, subordination, destruction, and absorption—of how (for example) "Mundurucú or Meo were drawn into the larger system to suffer its impact and to become its agents" (p. 23). The totality rests its immense weight on this examination.

I read statistics and see maps bordered with anthropological jargon of authenticity and titles of classes (the planter class, peasants, wage labor, serfdom). Categories unfold like the Stations of the Cross: the scenes are static, but with faith the believer is moved toward the great ascent. In the section "The Movement of Commodities" the first example of how Wolf's Historical Political Economy will shatter anthropological understanding of the dreadful ahistorical variety concerns rice and the concept of the "loosely structured social system" advanced by John Embree in 1950 to characterize, so Wolf writes, Thai society. There is a growling and huffing in the text at this crucial point, but one gathers that anthropological discourse concerning Thai society is both single-voiced and intent on claiming nonhistorical "reasons" for such looseness of structure. "Yet," continues and concludes Wolf, "the features of [the Thai village] Bang Chan that led to its characterization as 'loosely structured'—like the features of other Thai villages caught up in the rice economy in other ways—must [*sic*] be understood not merely as social structure of a certain kind but as the outcome of the expansion of commodity production" (p. 321).

That's Rice. That's the examination and illustration of how the people without history in Thailand got theirs—enormously inconclusive; a mouse's squeak. And remember, this is the book that begins with the plea to make connections. Next comes Meat. The Aborigines of Australia are fitted into Meat, where we find one paragraph of eleven lines about the people without history, a paragraph that tells us (a) pastoralists and natives clashed over land and water, and the natives were largely overrun, some like "the Walbiri" (people without history are rarely differentiated) becoming wage hands, and (b) the anthropologist Mervyn Megitt "noted that in the mid-1950s the Walbiri made use of their increased leisure, freed from the stringent demands of food collecting by the transition to wage work, to intensify their social and ceremonial activities" (p. 321). Next, Bananas.

Not a word inviting us to wonder what those "ceremonial activities" might be saying to us about commodification as seen from the central desert—about the meat that enters into labor-power and the labor-power that enters into meat —let alone what it means to have time bourgeoisified into "work" and "leisure time." Instead, this supposed critique of commodities sustains their very cultural categories.

Bananas. Here the "examination" of the effect on "populations" of the movement of commodities, the examination designed to manifest the unraveling of chains of causes and effects as they intertwine in the totality, concludes in the same spirit as Meat, with a similarly curiously out-of-place "set-piece" apparently aimed at showing the causative role of the commodity economy on "culture" as "effect"—that mechanization was probably the main cause of a "native millenarian movement" (note the jargon) among banana plantation workers in western Panama.

There cannot be even a whisper in a totalizing project such as Professor Wolf's that this native millenarian movement may have something to teach us about the equally millenarian movement of commodities. Its function in history is to be his example. But might there not be in this "reaction" in western Panama a theory of history and the commodity from which we could all "react" in *our* turn, so as to gain not that sublime point outside history to which Professor Wolf strives, but the see-sawing inside-and-outside mobility of positions required to match and mismatch the fetishized view of commodified reality to which Wolf's text grants such eloquent, indeed overwhelming, testimony.

Additional Author's Note
This essay was written as long ago as November 1986 in Puerto Tejada in the canefields of western Colombia, and in Bogota, capital of that beleagured Republic. It was written in response to a request from Professor S. Kaplan, one of the editors of the journal *Food and Foodways*, asking me to write an article-length review of Professor S. Mintz's book, *Sweetness and Power*, as a contribution to the issue of the journal devoted in its entirety to an examination of that book. Sensing that the rhetorical energy in the Mintz book, focussing on History and on the Commodity, overlapped with Professor E. Wolf's intentions in his work, *Europe and the People Without History*, a book I had not seriously studied, and that the contemporary revivalist enthusiasm for History in American Anthropology was—to say the least—naive, untheorized, and unself-critical, I undertook to write a review that included my working through the Wolf book as well as *Sweetness and Power*, a review which set forth in its form as well as in its content—as if these could ever be separated—the challenge and implications that the commodity-principle, understood historically, delivers to writing and rewriting the real. The late Bob Scholte, on the editorial board of *Critique of Anthropology*, (note *Critique*), wanted very much to also publish this review-article on its completion in December 1986 in that journal. Its belated publication now serves to acknowledge his singular encouragement.

Notes
1   The version if Michael Taussig's review printed here appeared in *Food and Foodways*, Vol. 2, pp. 151-169, (© 1987 Harwood Academic Publishers Gmb). We are grateful to the editor and publishers of that journal for granting us permission to reprint the article. This text embodies some slight modifications to the original draft submitted to *Critique of Anthropology*, the version to which Professors Mintz and Wolf addressed their reply. Although we did offer to publish the original ver-

sion, the author asked us to reprint the modified text, with an addition of the author's note on the writing of the piece at the end of the article.

2   See Susan Buck-Morss's article on the *Passagenwerk* in *New German Critique* no. 29 (1983), which is especially helpful on this argument.

3   Michel de Certeau, *The Practice of Everyday Life* (Berkeley: University of California Press, 1984), pp. xvi-xvii.

Study Questions

1.   In Taussig's understanding, what is the major ideological task of historical discourse?

2.   According to Taussig, how does "Meaning become History" in the work of Sidney Mintz?

3.   What does Taussig mean when he says of Wolf's book that it is "able to escape the ways by which history transmutes connections into conventions"?

Further Readings

Taussig, Michael T. 1980. *The Devil and Commodity Fetishism in South America.* Chapel Hill: The University of North Carolina Press.

—. 1984. History as Sorcery. *Representations* 7: 87-109.

29

Reply to Michael Taussig

SIDNEY W. MINTZ AND ERIC R. WOLF

We have had ample opportunity to study Michael Taussig's objections to our work, which he originally intended to publish in two versions in two places, although, in the event, only one has appeared. At the risk of making Taussig's commentary more intelligible than he may have intended it to be, we will begin by outlining what we understand to be our critic's difficulties with *Sweetness and Power* (which he was once asked to review; hereafter *S&P*), and *Europe and the People Without History* (which he was not asked to review, but reviewed anyway; hereafter *EPWH*).

Taussig does not like either book. *He* does not like what we say, and *he* does not like the way we say it. Taussig seems unwilling to imagine that others might have projects different from his own. This makes him readier than he ought to be to rely upon a rhetoric of denunciation. Venting his own "visceral" reactions, he has turned an ancient argument among many different figures in the sociocultural disciplines into a discursus that struck us as more than slightly self-referential. According to him, we are historical when we should be **hermeneutical**; we study the history of commodities, rather than studying commodity fetishism; we treat commodities as things, rather than as fetish objects *and* things; we talk of causes instead of talking of "visceral meanings," and by our naturalizing we appear to make inevitable in capitalism what is really only contingent. This listing gives Taussig's critique more coherence than it possesses, but we see no need to replicate either his longwindedness or his vagueness.

We are not the positivist, naturalizing devils Taussig makes us out to be. We have even had our share of encounters with the problems of subjectivity and reflexivity. Mintz once authored a book entitled *Worker in the Cane: A Puerto Rican Life History* (1960); and Wolf (with Edward Hansen) wrote a multiperspectival, "Brechtian" presentation of *The Human Condition in Latin America* (1972). But it is indeed the case that, in *S&P* and *EPWH*, we take the position that human arrangements are best understood by a grasp of the bases and workings of material life, through what Marx, in *A Contribution to the Critique of Political Economy,* called "production and productive consumption" and "consumption and consumptive production." We have tried to apply this approach in historically specific ways, and not only abstractly. Our insistence on a historical orientation is not new for either of us. It is exemplified, for instance, in the first paper we published together (Mintz and Wolf 1950), and in much of our subsequent work. We employ historical perspectives because both of us feel that material conditions and their consequences for social life are best weighed and best understood when seen in their development over time.

Contrary to what Taussig says of our work, we have no interest in **teleological** history. We do not see history as a series of stepping-stones toward the achievement of some transcendental goal. We are also unconcerned with history as a discourse that installs the effects of the real. Our concern with history is primarily methodological. Studying phenomena in their temporal dimension is not an end in itself, but a way of getting at causal forces and their incremental or diminishing consequences. Taussig concluded that we are antiquated fuddy-duddies because we look for chains of cause and effect. But our aim is to explain human arrangements as well as to interpret them. We believe that explanation requires conceptions of causality; we want to clarify causation because we aspire to understand why human beings make their own history, but under determinant and constraining conditions. We do not believe that history is just what people feel it is; we think we have a commitment to try to understand the "facts" that undergird their lives. From where we stand, both action *and* choice obey a causal structure of possibilities. We want to know what determines the shape of these structures of possibilities, in both time and space. In our books, we devoted our efforts to the history of the processes by which particular goods became commodities within world capitalism. *S&P* deals with one such commodity, *EPWH* with a number of different commodities. But Taussig says we don't study commodity fetishism, which is what he would have studied had he been us. Worse, we cavalierly fail to acknowledge our debt to the man who gave the world the concept of commodity fetishism, Karl Marx. Taussig thinks that by our not dealing with the fetishistic nature of commodities, we fall into the trap of falsely hypostatizing things; we treat things as if they were things. Dopes (he says) ... can't you see that they're *not* things? Don't you recognize that they can *only* be understood if their fetishistic nature is given as much importance as their thing-nature? That's what Marx was talking about ... he tells us. By treating things as things, by favoring history over visceral reactions (thus banishing "hermeneutics to intellectual purgatory"), we make everything inevitable, and we take the magic away from the relationship between persons and things. Not for us, he chides us, "the resort to play or trickery, the slow digesting of experience(s), the place of dream in the commodity as utopian wishing, emotions, interpretation, and all that goes along with observing oneself observing."

We would answer that, no, we don't resort intentionally to play or trickery. We *have* done some digesting of experience, and both *S&P* and *EPWH* embody portions of our experience (though they might not be recognizable as such by everybody). As for the place of dream in the commodity as ... etc, etc, it is after all simply that we were trying to do something else. Most readers and reviewers seemed to notice as much without prodding. Now, "All that goes along with observing oneself observing" sounds like ... well, you know, I mean like *great*, man. But do we all have to do it?

We suggest that there is a difference between tracing the history of particular commodities in the western world, and employing Marx's concept of commodity fetishism to interpret the relationships among persons as mediated through commodities. The world of commodities, as Marx sought to describe it, was an emerging capitalist world of producers and consumers, a world remade by their changing relations to the means of production, and by the changing significance of exchange in that world. Through these changes producers and consumers of commodities came to stand in qualitatively different relationships to each other. But this new world of commodities as defined by Marx did not arise with a thunderclap; it did not appear overnight; it did not happen everywhere at the same time, or at the same rate, or in exactly the same way. We remain in doubt about the total variety of ways in which such transitions may occur; we are not yet confident that we can abstract from a large number of well-understood cases in order to frame universal rules about how the world became capitalistic. We believe that studies of single cases can help us understand what happened, but without always clarifying the general processes they exemplify. Hence we recognize that to speak of "capitalist" and "precapitalist," while highly convenient to swift and tidy exposition, is also risky ... a shortcut and an abstraction. The uneven process by which things became commodities was gradual and many-sided and took centuries; it has not ended and there persist serious arguments about when it began. All this admitted, it is nonetheless possible to study, as part of the rise of capitalism, how particular commodities came to be produced for sale in distant markets, within organizations created by capitalist entrepreneurs, uniting labor, land, capital goods and variable amounts of capital in new settings. Such commodities reached consumers whose relationships to the new world market differed widely, and in many different ways, from those of their specific producers. If one studies how palm oil or sugar or cocoa or oil or diamonds become commodities within an expanding world market, one notes that the relationships between their specific producers and consumers were similarly specific. The fetishism characteristic of the perception of those commodities is not a property of the commodities themselves but of their phenomenological status in systems of production, exchange and consumption of a capitalist kind. But all parts of those systems are not necessarily evolved to the same degree or in the same fashion. The parts of the world taken up into the system started out much differentiated among themselves, culturally, economically and otherwise. Those outsiders who came to engineer them into the system shared with each other their eventual intentions, perhaps, but not much else. Oil here, woven cloth there; sharecropping here, contract labor there; alienated land here, rented land there. Different systems of kinship, of religious belief, were invoked within newly organized ways of doing familiar things differently, or of doing different things in familiar ways.

To address the challenge of adequate analysis of this variety, it should not be enough to say that the victims have been put on the capitalist road; nor to explore, however imaginatively, their subjective reactions to their plight. That they are victims is likely; that the outcomes vary is certain; that there is much more to the story is even more certain. Both of us in different ways tried in the books reviewed to grapple with the worrisome questions which a study of the cultural history of commodities brings in its wake. If the commodities whose history we study as a means of explaining the progress of capitalism outside Europe are to be interpreted in terms of their fetishistic character, then this is a *different* task from analyzing the growth of a world in which the relationships between producers and consumers come to be analyzable through commodities. Neither such kind of study can be labelled "wrong" because it exists. They are different kinds of study.

The study of the fetishism of commodities has become interesting to many scholars now, inside and outside of anthropology. That interest rests heavily upon analyses of the ways that contemporary consumers in the West integrate their consumption into the regnant framework of "buyers' culture." But this, too, is different from the study of the history of commodities; from the study of how these *particular* things became commodities; and from the study of the variety of processes involved in the emergence of uneven and widely distributed capitalist forms, inside the West as well as outside it. To learn about the concept of commodity fetishism (and to teach about it), to make its study part of anthropology, is a useful activity. We pointed to the importance of the concept ourselves, in a joint paper first published slightly more than thirty years ago (Wolf and Mintz 1957). But neither of the books causing Taussig's distress were aimed at analyzing this concept. We wonder what useful purpose it serves ... though we have no doubt that it serves some ... to attack us for not having written books different from the ones we wrote.

Taussig favors over our methods a methodology of "collation of meanings and power as generated by a modernist text of the modern and the mundane." This is not what we do, and we are not convinced that it is a procedure superior to our own.

Extrapolating and juxtaposing tell-tale meanings ripped—doubtless with lots of gut feeling—from tattered books of life provides one way of apprehending something called reality; but there's the rub. Such *bricolage*, even when inspired, leads not to explanation but to revelation. No wonder Taussig festoons his discussion with quotations from Fredrich Nietzsche and Walter Benjamin, the latter a seeker after deliverance for whom the goal of knowledge was Messianic redemption, the former a prophet of nihilism for whom the value of an idea lay in its power to enhance "life."

Life, yes; but for whom and against whom? Taussig prefers such inspirational soundings to what he calls "the rosary beads and chains of causes and effects." No materialist rosary in his musings, we concede in our role as fuddy-duddies; but not much responsibility to reality, either. Instead, Prometheus-Taussig invites us to transcend "the inviolability of the referent," presumably through "collation." But "collation" sounds dangerously like a methodology that emphasizes style of presentation more than it does "the referent." The referent sometimes gets lost in the text altogether, because of what turns out to be irresistible temptations to show off, to sound off, and to take it off ... on the determinate causes of which we do not comment.

Taussing says we want to install a "fetishized view of commodified reality." He is exercised by what he understands as our invocation of a "fetish-power" (his words) called Capitalist Accumulation. In our tracings of commodities and their implications for people's lives, he finds us "trivializing" anthropology. What appeals to *him* in Marx is the Old Man's "unhappiness" about commodity fetishism. It is clear that Taussig has read Part I of *Das Kapital*. But his reading is heavily social-psychological, cosmological, and culturalist, with rather less attention to Marx's demonstration of how this form of fetishism informs the division of labor under capitalism. Perhaps he failed to read Part VII of that same work by Marx, called *The Accumulation of Capital*. Wolf, in his book, tried to show how people's lives became intertwined in the production and movement of particular commodities (including, yes, meat), and how their lives were changed as a consequence of these intertwined connections. Mintz wrote his book about how sucrose ... sugar ... penetrated and altered the lives of its users: the ways its meanings changed, and the way they changed its meanings. Neither of us sought to write a history or sociology or social psychology of commodities as such; we used the trajectories of commodities as "tracers" through the veins and arteries of a developing political and economic system. If people do not live the way they did in 1400, how does one account for how they live now? Looking for causes we found them in the ways by which people were drawn into the circuits of capital and became increasingly subject to the processes that Marx labelled "the accumulation of capital." Taussig dislikes this "fetishized view of a commodified reality". Does he think this is something we imposed upon that reality?

We assure Taussig that we don't much care for capitalism, either. Nonetheless, we were greatly intrigued, as we read his interpretation, by his apparent success in staying entirely outside the system of commodity production and consumption in the course of his own social reproduction. How, indeed, does Dr. Taussig do it? Does he shave with obsidian chips of his own manufacture? Does he live in a tent of buffalo hide? Are his feet sheathed in the skins of alligators that he has himself harpooned? Can we learn to do it, too? And if not, why not? And if this impression, which we gather from his criticisms of our work, is incorrect; if he has not managed, Houdini-like, to stay entirely independent of this system we all apparently dislike, perhaps he can explain to us why the same question we put to him should not be put to Iroquois fur hunters, to Mundurucu, to Meo, or to Caribbean plantation laborers. What are the ways in which they were drawn into the capitalist world? May we not ask them what we ask Dr. Taussig?

That people can react differentially and in contradictory fashion to these involvements is hardly news. Even Taussig's own project of opposing our "fetishized view of a commodified reality" with one that is presumably non-fetishized and non-commodified is clearly predicated upon some sort of involvement with a commodified world. In the end, then, perhaps we can comprehend Taussig's motivations for such an attempt. But we would question both the reasoning that underlies it, and the fashion in which it has been put forward.

Study Questions

1. How do Mintz and Wolf characterize the difference between "commodity fetishism" and the "history of commodities"?

2. Why do Mintz and Wolf feel it is important to study the history of commodities, and how do they relate this to Marxist theory?

Further Readings

Mintz, Sidney W. 1960. *Worker in the Cane: A Puerto Rican Life History.* New Haven: Yale University Press.

—. 1986. *Sweetness and Power: The Place of Sugar in Modern History.* New York: Penguin Books.

Roseberry, William. 1989. *Anthropologies and Histories: Essays in Culture, History, and Political Economy.* New Brunswick, NJ: Rutgers University Press.

Wolf, Eric R. 1969. *Peasant Wars of the Twentieth Century.* New York: Harper and Row.

30

Truth and Power[1]

MICHEL FOUCAULT

Q. Could you briefly outline the route which led you from your work on madness in the classical age to the study of criminality and delinquency?

M.F. When I was studying during the early 1950s, one of the great problems that arose was that of the political status of science and the ideological functions which it could serve. It wasn't exactly the Lysenko business which dominated everything, but I believe that around that sordid affair—which had long remained buried and carefully hidden—a whole number of interesting questions were provoked. These can all be summed up in two words: power and knowledge. I believe I wrote *Madness and Civilization* to some extent within the horizon of these questions. For me, it was a matter of saying this: if, concerning a science like theoretical physics or organic chemistry, one poses the problem of its relations with the political and economic structures of society, isn't one posing an excessively complicated question? Doesn't this set the threshold of possible explanations impossibly high? But on the other hand, if one takes a form of knowledge (*savoir*) like psychiatry, won't the question be much easier to resolve, since the epistemological profile of psychiatry is a low one and psychiatric practice is linked with a whole range of institutions, economic requirements, and political issues of social regulation? Couldn't the interweaving of effects of power and knowledge be grasped with greater certainty in the case of a science as "dubious" as psychiatry? It was this same question which I wanted to pose concerning medicine in *The Birth of the Clinic*: medicine certainly has a much more solid scientific armature than psychiatry, but it, too, is profoundly enmeshed in social structures. What rather threw me at the time was the fact that the question I was posing totally failed to inter-

---

1   This interview with Michel Foucault was conducted by Alessandro Fontana and
    Pasquale Pasquino. Foucault's response to the last question was given in writing.

est those to whom I addressed it. They regarded it as a problem which was politically unimportant and epistemologically vulgar.

I think there were three reasons for this. The first is that for Marxist intellectuals in France (and there they were playing the role prescribed for them by the PCF [*Parti communiste francais*]), the problem consisted in gaining for themselves the recognition of the university institutions and establishment. Consequently they found it necessary to pose the same theoretical questions as the academic establishment, to deal with the same problems and topics: "We may be Marxists, but for all that we are not strangers to your preoccupations; rather, we are the only ones able to provide new solutions for your old concerns." Marxism sought to win acceptance as a renewal of the liberal university tradition—just as, more broadly, during the same period the Communists presented themselves as the only people capable of taking over and reinvigorating the nationalist tradition. Hence, in the field we are concerned with here, it followed that they wanted to take up the "noblest," most academic problems in the history of the sciences: mathematics and physics, in short the themes valorized by Duhem, Husserl, and Koyré. Medicine and psychiatry didn't seem to them to be very noble or serious matters, nor to stand on the same level as the great forms of classical rationalism.

The second reason is that post-Stalinist Stalinism, by excluding from Marxist **discourse** everything that wasn't a frightened repetition of the already said, would not permit the broaching of uncharted domains. There were no ready-made concepts, no approved terms of vocabulary available for questions like the power effects of psychiatry or the political function of medicine, whereas, on the contrary, innumerable exchanges between Marxists and academics, from Marx via Engels and Lenin down to the present, had nourished a whole tradition of discourse on "science," in the nineteenth-century sense of that term. The price Marxists paid for their fidelity to the old positivism was a radical deafness to a whole series of questions posed by science.

Finally, there is perhaps a third reason, but I can't be absolutely sure that it played a part. I wonder, nevertheless, whether among intellectuals in or close to the PCF there wasn't a refusal to pose the problem of internment, of the political use of psychiatry, and, in a more general sense, of the disciplinary grid of society. No doubt little was then known in 1955-60 of the real extent of the Gulag, but I believe that many sensed it; in any case, many had a feeling that it was better not to talk about those things: it was a danger zone, marked by warning signs. Of course it's difficult in retrospect to judge people's degree of awareness. But in any case, you well know how easily the Party leadership—which knew everything of course—could circulate instructions preventing people from speaking about this or that, or precluding this or that line of research. At any rate, if the question of Pavlovian psychiatry did get discussed among a few doctors close to the PCF, psychiatric politics and psychiatry as politics were hardly considered to be respectable topics.

What I myself tried to do in this domain was met with a great silence among the French intellectual left. And it was only around 1968, and in spite of the Marxist tradition and the PCF, that all these questions came to assume their political significance, with a sharpness that I had never envisaged, showing how timid and hesitant those early books of mine had still been. Without the political opening created during those years, I would surely never have had the courage to take up these problems again and pursue my research in the direction of penal theory, prisons, and disciplines.

Q. So there is a certain "discontinuity" in your theoretical trajectory. Incidentally, what do you think today about this concept of discontinuity, on the basis of which you have been all too rapidly and readily labeled a "structuralist" historian?

M.F. This business about discontinuity has always rather bewildered me. In the new edition of the Petit Larousse it says: "Foucault: a philosopher who founds his theory of history on discontinuity." That leaves me flabbergasted. No doubt I didn't make myself sufficiently clear in *The Order of Things*, though I said a good deal there about this question. It seemed to me that in certain empirical forms of knowledge, like biology, political economy, psychiatry, medicine, etc., the rhythm of transformation doesn't follow the smooth, continuist schemas of development which are normally accepted. The great biological image of a progressive maturation of science still underpins a good many historical analyses; it does not seem to me to be pertinent to history. In a science like medicine, for example, up to the end of the eighteenth century one has a certain type of discourse whose gradual transformation, within a period of twenty-five or thirty years, broke not only with the "true" propositions which it had hitherto been possible to formulate, but also, more profoundly, with the ways of speaking and seeing, the whole ensemble of practices which served as supports for medical knowledge. These are not simply new discoveries; there is a whole new "regime" in discourse and forms of knowledge. And all this happens in the space of a few years. This is something which is undeniable, once one has looked at the texts with sufficient attention. My problem was not at all to say, *"Voila,* long live discontinuity, we are in the discontinuous and a good thing too," but to pose the question, "How is it that at certain moments and in certain orders of knowledge, there are these sudden take-offs, these hastenings of evolution, these transformations which fail to correspond to the calm, continuist image that is normally accredited?" But the important thing here is not that such changes can be rapid and extensive, or rather it is that this extent and rapidity are only the sign of something else: a modification in the rules of formation of statements which are accepted as scientifically true. Thus it is not a change of content (refutation of old errors, recovery of old truths), nor is it a change of theoretical form (renewal of paradigm, modification of systematic ensembles). It is a question of what *governs* statements, and the way in which they *govern* each other so as to constitute a set of propositions which are scientifically acceptable, and hence capable of being verified or falsified by scientific procedures. In short, there is a problem of the regime, the politics of the scientific statement. At this level it's not so much a matter of knowing what external power imposes itself on science, as of what effects of power circulate among scientific statements, what constitutes, as it were, their internal regime of power, and how and why at certain moments that regime undergoes a global modification.

It was these different regimes that I tried to identify and describe *in The Order of Things*, all the while making it clear that I wasn't trying for the moment to explain them, and that it would be necessary to try and do this in a subsequent work. But what was lacking here was this problem of the "discursive regime," of the effects of power peculiar to the play of statements. I confused this too much with systematicity, theoretical form, or something like a paradigm. This same central problem of power, which at that time I had not yet properly isolated, emerges in two very different aspects at the point of junction of *Madness and Civilization* and *The Order of Things*.

Q. We need, then, to locate the notion of discontinuity in its proper context. And perhaps there is another concept which is both more difficult and more central to your thought—the concept of an event. For, in relation to the event, a whole generation was long trapped in an impasse, in that following the works of ethnologists, some of them great ethnologists, a dichotomy was established between structures (the *thinkable*) and the event considered as the site of the irrational, the unthinkable, that which doesn't and cannot enter into the mechanism and play of analysis, at least in the form which this took in structuralism. In a recent discussion published in the journal *L'Homme*, three eminent anthropologists posed this question once again about the concept of event, and said: the event is what always escapes our rational grasp, the domain of "absolute contingency"; we are thinkers who analyze structures, history is no concern of ours, what could we be expected to have to say about it, and so forth. This opposition, then, between event and structure is the site and the product of a certain anthropology. I would say this has had devastating effects among historians who have finally reached the point of trying to dismiss the event and the *évèmentiel* as an inferior order of history dealing with trivial facts, chance occurrences, and so on. Whereas it is a fact that there are nodal problems in history which are neither a matter of trivial circumstances nor of those beautiful structures that are so orderly, intelligible, and transparent to analysis. For instance, the "great internment" which you described in *Madness and Civilization* perhaps represents one of these nodes which elude the dichotomy of structure and event. Could you elaborate from our present standpoint on this renewal and reformulation of the concept of event?

M.F. One can agree that structuralism formed the most systematic effort to evacuate the concept of the event, not only from ethnology but from a whole series of other sciences and in the extreme case from history. In that sense, I don't see who could be more of an anti-structuralist than myself. But the important thing is to avoid trying to do for the event what was previously done with the concept of structure. It's not a matter of locating everything on one level, that of the event, but of realizing that there is actually a whole order of levels of different types of events, differing in amplitude, chronological breadth, and capacity to produce effects.

The problem is at once to distinguish among events, to differentiate the networks and levels to which they belong, and to reconstitute the lines along which they are connected and engender one another. From this follows a refusal of analyses couched in terms of the symbolic field or the domain of signifying structures, and a recourse to analyses in terms of the genealogy of relations of force, strategic developments, and tactics. Here I believe one's point of reference should not be to the great model of language (*langue*) and signs, but to that of war and battle. The history which bears and determines us has the form of a war rather than that of a language: relations of power, not relations of meaning. History has no "meaning," though this is not to say that it is absurd or incoherent. On the contrary, it is intelligible and should be susceptible to analysis down to the smallest detail—but this in accordance with the intelligibility of struggles, of strategies and tactics. Neither the dialectic, as logic of contradictions, nor semiotics, as the structure of communication, can account for the intrinsic intelligibility of conflicts. "Dialectic" is a way of evading the always open and hazardous reality of conflict by reducing it to a Hegelian skeleton, and "semiology" is a way of avoiding its violent, bloody, and lethal character by reducing it to the calm Platonic form of language and dialogue.

Q. In the context of this problem of discursivity, I think one can be confident in saying that you were the first person to pose the question of power regarding discourse, and that at a time when analyses in terms of the concept or object of the "text," along with the accompanying methodology of semiology, structuralism, etc., were the prevailing fashion. Posing for discourse the question of power means basically to ask whom does discourse serve? It isn't so much a matter of analyzing discourse into its unsaid, its implicit meaning, because (as you have often repeated) discourses are transparent, they need no interpretation, no one to assign them a meaning. If one reads "texts" in a certain way, one perceives that they speak clearly to us and require no further supplementary sense or interpretation. This question of power that you have addressed to discourse naturally has particular effects and implications in relation to methodology and contemporary historical researches. Could you briefly situate within your work this question you have posed—if indeed it's true that you have posed it?

M.F. I don't think I was the first to pose the question. On the contrary, I'm struck by the difficulty I had in formulating it. When I think back now, I ask myself what else it was that I was talking about, in *Madness and Civilization* or *The Birth of the Clinic*, but power? Yet I'm perfectly aware that I scarcely ever used the word and never had such a field of analyses at my disposal. I can say that this was an incapacity linked undoubtedly with the political situation we found ourselves in. It is hard to see where, either on the right or the left, this problem of power could then have been posed. On the right, it was posed only in terms of constitution, sovereignty, etc., that is, in juridical terms; on the Marxist side, it was posed only in terms of the state apparatus. The way power was exercised—concretely and in detail—with its specificity, its techniques and tactics, was something that no one attempted to ascertain; they contented themselves with denouncing it in a polemical and global fashion as it existed among the "others," in the adversary camp. Where Soviet socialist power was in question, its opponents called it totalitarianism; power in Western capitalism was denounced by the Marxists as class domination; but the mechanics of power in themselves were never analyzed. This task could only begin after 1968, that is to say, on the basis of daily struggles at the grass-roots level, among those whose fight was located in the fine meshes of the web of power. This was where the concrete nature of power became visible, along with the prospect that these analyses of power would prove fruitful in accounting for all that had hitherto remained outside the field of political analysis. To put it very simply, psychiatric internment, the mental normalization of individuals, and penal institutions have no doubt a fairly limited importance if one is only looking for their economic significance. On the other hand, they are undoubtedly essential to the general functioning of the wheels of power. So long as the posing of the question of power was kept subordinate to the economic instance and the system of interests which this served, there was a tendency to regard these problems as of small importance.

Q. So a certain kind of Marxism and a certain kind of phenomenology constituted an objective obstacle to the formulation of this problematic?

M.F. Yes, if you like, to the extent that it's true that, in our student days, people of my generation were brought up on these two forms of analysis—one in terms of the constituent subject, the other in terms of the economic, in the last instance, ideology and the play of superstructures and infrastructures.

Q. Still, within this methodological context, how would you situate the genealogical approach? As a questioning of the conditions of possibility, modalities, and constitution of the "objects" and domains you have successively analyzed, what makes it necessary?

M.F. I wanted to see how these problems of constitution could be resolved within a historical framework, instead of referring them back to a constituent object (madness, criminality, or whatever). But this historical contextualization needed to be something more than the simple relativization of the **phenomenological** subject. I don't believe the problem can be solved by historicizing the subject as posited by the phenomenologists, fabricating a subject that evolves through the course of history. One has to dispense with the constituent subject, to get rid of the subject itself, that's to say, to arrive at an analysis which can account for the constitution of the subject within a historical framework. And this is what I would call genealogy, that is, a form of history which can account for the constitution of knowledges, discourses, domains of objects, etc., without having to make reference to a subject which is either transcendental in relation to the field of events or runs in its empty sameness throughout the course of history.

Q. Marxist phenomenology and a certain kind of Marxism have clearly acted as a screen and an obstacle; there are two further concepts which continue today to act as a screen and an obstacle: ideology, on the one hand, and repression, on the other.

All history comes to be thought of within these categories which serve to assign a meaning to such diverse phenomena as normalization, sexuality, and power. And regardless of whether these two concepts are explicitly utilized, in the end one always comes back, on the one hand to ideology—where it is easy to make the reference back to Marx—and on the other to repression, which is a concept often and readily employed by Freud throughout the course of his career. Hence I would like to put forward the following suggestion. Behind these concepts and among those who (properly or improperly) employ them, there is a kind of nostalgia; behind the concept of ideology, the nostalgia for a quasi-transparent form of knowledge, free from all error and illusion, and behind the concept of repression, the longing for a form of power innocent of all coercion, discipline, and normalization. On the one hand, a power without a bludgeon and, on the other hand, knowledge without deception. You have called these two concepts, ideology and repression, negative, "psychological," insufficiently analytical. This is particularly the case in *Discipline and Punish*, where, even if there isn't an extended discussion of these concepts, there is nevertheless a kind of analysis that allows one to go beyond the traditional forms of explanation and intelligibility which, in the last (and not only the last) instance, rest on the concepts of ideology and repression. Could you perhaps use this occasion to specify more explicitly your thoughts on these matters? With *Discipline and Punish*, a kind of positive history seems to be emerging, which is free of all the negativity and psychologism implicit in those two universal skeleton-keys.

M.F. The notion of ideology appears to me to be difficult to make use of, for three reasons. The first is that, like it or not, it always stands in virtual opposition to something else which is supposed to count as truth. Now I believe that the problem does not consist in drawing the line between that in a discourse which falls under the category of scientificity or truth, and that which comes under some other category, but in seeing historically how effects of truth are produced within discourses which in themselves are neither true nor false. The second drawback is that the concept of ideology refers, I think necessarily, to something of the order of a subject. Third, ideology stands in a secondary position relative to something which functions as its infrastructure, as its material, economic determinant, etc. For these three reasons, I think that this is a notion that cannot be used without circumspection.

The notion of repression is a more insidious one, or at all events I myself have had much more trouble in freeing myself of it, insofar as it does indeed appear to correspond so well with a whole range of phenomena which belong among the effects of power. When I wrote *Madness and Civilization*, I made at least an implicit use of this notion of repression. I think, indeed, that I was positing the existence of a sort of living, voluble, and anxious madness which the mechanisms of power and psychiatry were supposed to have come to repress and reduce to silence. But it seems to me now that the notion of repression is quite inadequate for capturing what is precisely the productive aspect of power. In defining the effects of power as repression, one adopts a purely juridical conception of such power; one identifies power with a law which says no; power is taken above all as carrying the force of a prohibition. Now I believe that this is a wholly negative, narrow, skeletal conception of power, one which has been curiously widespread. If power were never anything but repressive, if it never did anything but to say no, do you really think one would be brought to obey it? What makes power hold good, what makes it accepted, is simply the fact that it doesn't only weigh on us as a force that says no, but that it traverses and produces things, it induces pleasure, forms knowledge, produces discourse. It needs to be considered as a productive network which runs through the whole social body, much more than as a negative instance whose function is repression. In *Discipline and Punish*, what I wanted to show was how, from the seventeenth and eighteenth centuries onward, there was a veritable technological take-off in the productivity of power. Not only did the monarchies of the classical period develop great state apparatuses (the army, the police and fiscal administration), but above all there was established in this period what one might call a new "economy" of power, that is to say, procedures which allowed the effects of power to circulate in a manner at once continuous, uninterrupted, adapted, and "individualized" throughout the entire social body. These new techniques are both much more efficient and much less wasteful (less costly economically, less risky in their results, less open to loopholes and resistances) than the techniques previously employed, which were based on a mixture of more or less forced tolerances (from recognized privileges to endemic criminality) and costly ostentation (spectacular and discontinuous interventions of power, the most violent form of which was the "exemplary," because exceptional, punishment).

Q. Repression is a concept used above all in relation to sexuality. It was held that bourgeois society represses sexuality, stifles sexual desire, and so forth. And when one considers, for example, the campaign launched against masturbation in the eighteenth century, or the medical discourse on homosexuality in the second half of the nineteenth century, or discourse on sexuality in general, one does seem to be faced with a discourse of repression. In reality, however, this discourse serves to make possible a whole series of interventions, tactical and positive interventions of surveillance, circulation, control, and so forth, which seem to have been intimately linked with techniques that give the appearance of repression, or are at least liable to be interpreted as such. I believe the crusade against masturbation is a typical example of this.

M.F. Certainly. It is customary to say that bourgeois society repressed infantile sexuality to the point where it refused even to speak of it or acknowledge its existence. It was necessary to wait until Freud for the discovery at last to be made that children have a sexuality. Now if you read all the books on pedagogy and child medicine—all the manuals for parents that were published in the eighteenth century—you find that children's sex is spoken of constantly and in every possible context. One might argue that the purpose of these discourses was precisely to prevent children from having a sexuality. But their *effect* was to din it into parents' heads that their children's sex constituted a fundamental problem in terms of their parental educational responsibilities, and to din it into children's heads that their relationship with their own bodies and their own sex was to be a fundamental problem as far as *they* were concerned; and this had the consequence of sexually exciting the bodies of children while at the same time fixing the parental gaze and vigilance on the peril of infantile sexuality. The result was a sexualizing of the infantile body, a sexualizing of the bodily relationship between parent and child, a sexualizing of the familial domain. "Sexuality" is far more of a positive product of power than power was ever repression of sexuality. I believe that it is precisely these positive mechanisms that need to be investigated, and here one must free oneself of the juridical schematism of all previous characterizations of the nature of power. Hence a historical problem arises, namely, that of discovering why the West has insisted for so long on

seeing the power it exercises as juridical and negative rather than as technical and positive.

Q. Perhaps this is because it has always been thought that power is mediated
through the forms prescribed in the great juridical and philosophical theories,
and that there is a fundamental, immutable gulf between those who exercise
power and those who undergo it.

M.F. I wonder if this isn't bound up with the institution of monarchy. This
developed during the Middle Ages against the backdrop of the previously
endemic struggles between feudal power agencies. The monarchy presented
itself as a referee, a power capable of putting an end to war, violence, and pillage and saying no to these struggles and private feuds. It made itself acceptable by allocating itself a juridical and negative function, albeit one whose limits it naturally began at once to overstep. Sovereign, law, and prohibition
formed a system of representation of power which was extended during the
subsequent era by the theories of right: political theory has never ceased to be
obsessed with the person of the sovereign. Such theories still continue today to
busy themselves with the problem of sovereignty. What we need, however, is a
political philosophy that isn't erected around the problem of sovereignty, nor
therefore around the problems of law and prohibition. We need to cut off the
king's head: in political theory that has still to be done.

Q. The king's head still hasn't been cut off, yet already people are trying to
replace it by discipline, that vast system instituted in the seventeenth century,
comprising the functions of surveillance, normalization and control, and, a little later, those of punishment, correction, education, and so on. One wonders
where this system comes from, why it emerges, and what its use is. And today
there is rather a tendency to attribute a subject to it, a great, molar, totalitarian
subject, namely, the modern state, constituted in the sixteenth and seventeenth
centuries and bringing with it (according to the classical theories) the professional army, the police, and the administrative bureaucracy.

M.F. To pose the problem in terms of the state means to continue posing it in
terms of sovereign and sovereignty, that is to say, in terms of law. If one
describes all these phenomena of power as dependent on the state apparatus,
this means grasping them as essentially repressive: the army as a power of
death, police and justice as punitive instances, etc. I don't want to say that the
state isn't important; what I want to say is that relations of power, and hence
the analysis that must be made of them, necessarily extend beyond the limits of
the state. In two senses: first of all because the state, for all the omnipotence of
its apparatuses, is far from being able to occupy the whole field of actual power
relations, and further because the state can only operate on the basis of other,
already existing power relations. The state is superstructural in relation to a
whole series of power networks that invest the body, sexuality, the family, kin-

ship, knowledge, technology, and so forth. True, these networks stand in a conditioning-conditioned relationship to a kind of "metapower" which is structured essentially around a certain number of great prohibition functions; but this metapower with its prohibitions can only take hold and secure its footing where it is rooted in a whole series of multiple and indefinite power relations that supply the necessary basis for the great negative forms of power. That is just what I was trying to make apparent in my book.

Q. Doesn't this open up the possibility of overcoming the dualism of political struggles that eternally feed on the opposition between the state, on the one hand, and revolution, on the other? Doesn't it indicate a wider field of conflicts than that of those where the adversary is the state?

M.F. I would say that the state consists in the codification of a whole number of power relations which render its functioning possible, and that revolution is a different type of codification of the same relations. This implies that there are many different kinds of revolution, roughly speaking, as many kinds as there are possible subversive recodifications of power relations, and further that one can perfectly well conceive of revolutions which leave essentially untouched the power relations which form the basis for the functioning of the state.

Q. You have said about power as an object of research that one has to invert Clausewitz's formula so as to arrive at the idea that politics is the continuation of war by other means. Does the military model seem to you, on the basis of your most recent researches, to be the best one for describing power; is war here simply a metaphorical model, or is it the literal, regular, everyday mode of operation of power?

M.F. This is the problem I now find myself confronting. As soon as one endeavors to detach power with its techniques and procedures from the form of law within which it has been theoretically confined up until now, one is driven to ask this basic question: Isn't power simply a form of warlike domination? Shouldn't one therefore conceive all problems of power in terms of relations of war? Isn't power a sort of generalized war which assumes at particular moments the forms of peace and the state? Peace would then be a form of war, and the state a means of waging it.

A whole range of problems emerges here. Who wages war against whom? Is it between two classes, or more? Is it a war of all against all? What is the role of the army and military institutions in this civil society where permanent war is waged? What is the relevance of concepts of tactics and strategy for analyzing structures and political processes? What is the essence and mode of transformation of power relations? All these questions need to be explored. In any case it's astonishing to see how easily and self-evidently people talk of warlike relations of power or of class struggle without ever making it clear whether some form of war is meant, and if so what form.

Q. We have already talked about this disciplinary power whose effects, rules, and mode of constitution you describe in *Discipline and Punish*. One might ask here: Why surveillance? What is the use of surveillance? Now there is a phenomenon that emerges during the eighteenth century, namely, the discovery of population as an object of scientific investigation; people begin to inquire into birth rates, death rates, and changes in population and to say for the first time that it is impossible to govern a state without knowing its population. Moheau, for example, who was one of the first to organize this kind of research on an administrative basis, seems to see its goal as lying in the problems of political control of a population. Does this disciplinary power then act alone and of itself, or doesn't it, rather, draw support from something more general, namely, this fixed conception of a population that reproduces itself in the proper way, composed of people who marry in the proper way and behave in the proper way, according to precisely determined norms? One would then have, on the one hand, a sort of global, molar body, the body of the population, together with a whole series of discourses concerning it, and then, on the other hand and down below, the small bodies, the docile, individual bodies, the microbodies of discipline. Even if you are only perhaps at the beginning of your researches here, could you say how you see the nature of the relationships (if any) which are engendered between these different bodies: the molar body of the population and the microbodies of individuals?

M.F. Your question is exactly on target. I find it difficult to reply because I am working on this problem right now. I believe one must keep in view the fact that along with all the fundamental technical inventions and discoveries of the seventeenth and eighteenth centuries, a new technology of the exercise of power also emerged, which was probably even more important than the constitutional reforms and new forms of government established at the end of the eighteenth century. In the camp of the left, one often hears people saying that power is that which abstracts, which negates the body, represses, suppresses, and so forth. I would say instead that what I find most striking about these new technologies of power introduced since the seventeenth and eighteenth centuries is their concrete and precise character, their grasp of a multiple and differentiated reality. In feudal societies, power functioned essentially through signs and levies. Signs of loyalty to the feudal lords, rituals, ceremonies, and so forth, and levies in the form of taxes, pillage, hunting, war, etc. In the seventeenth and eighteenth centuries, a form of power comes into being that begins to exercise itself through social production and social service. It becomes a matter of obtaining productive service from individuals in their concrete lives. And, in consequence, a real and effective "incorporation" of power was necessary, in the sense that power had to be able to gain access to the bodies of individuals, to their acts, attitudes, and modes of everyday behavior. Hence the significance of methods like school discipline, which succeeded in making children's bodies the object of highly complex systems of manipulation and conditioning. But, at the same time, these new techniques of power needed to grapple with the phenomena of population, in short, to undertake the administration, control, and direction of the accumulation of men (the economic system that promotes the accumulation of capital and the system of power that ordains the accumulation of men are, from the seventeenth century on, correlated and inseparable phenomena): hence there arise the problems of demography, public health, hygiene, housing conditions, longevity, and fertility. And I believe that the political significance of the problem of sex is due to the fact that sex is located at the point of intersection of the discipline of the body and the control of the population.

Q. Finally, a question you have been asked before: The work you do, these preoccupations of yours, the results you arrive at, what use can one finally make of all this in everyday political struggles? You have spoken previously of local struggles as the specific site of confrontation with power, outside and beyond all such global, general instances as parties or classes. What does this imply about the role of intellectuals? If one isn't an "organic" intellectual acting as the spokesman for a global organization, if one doesn't purport to function as the bringer, the master of truth, what position is the intellectual to assume?

M.F. For a long period, the "left" intellectual spoke and was acknowledged the right of speaking in the capacity of master of truth and justice. He was heard, or purported to make himself heard, as the spokesman of the universal. To be an intellectual meant something like being the consciousness/conscience of us all. I think we have here an idea transposed from Marxism, from a faded Marxism indeed. Just as the proletariat, by the necessity of its historical situation, is the bearer of the universal (but its immediate, unreflected bearer, barely conscious of itself as such), so the intellectual, through his moral, theoretical, and political choice, aspires to be the bearer of this universality in its conscious, elaborated form. The intellectual is thus taken as the clear, individual figure of a universality whose obscure, collective form is embodied in the proletariat.

Some years have now passed since the intellectual was called upon to play this role. A new mode of the "connection between theory and practice" has been established. Intellectuals have become used to working, not in the modality of the "universal," the "exemplary," the "just-and-true-for-all," but within specific sectors, at the precise points where their own conditions of life or work situate them (housing, the hospital, the asylum, the laboratory, the university, family, and sexual relations). This has undoubtedly given them a much more immediate and concrete awareness of struggles. And they have met here with problems which are specific, "nonuniversal," and often different from those of the proletariat or the masses. And yet I believe intellectuals have actually been drawn closer to the proletariat and the masses, for two reasons. Firstly, because it has been a question of real, material, everyday struggles, and secondly because they have often been confronted, albeit in a different form, by the same adversary as the proletariat, namely, the multinational corporations, the judicial and police apparatuses, the property speculators, etc. This is what I would call the "specific" intellectual as opposed to the "universal" intellectual.

This new configuration has a further political significance. It makes it possible, if not to integrate, at least to rearticulate categories which were previously kept separate. The intellectual *par excellence* used to be the writer: as a universal consciousness, a free subject, he was counterposed to those intellectuals who were merely *competent instances* in the service of the state or capital-technicians, magistrates, teachers. Since the time when each individual's specific activity began to serve as the basis for politicization, the threshold of *writing*, as the sacralizing mark of the intellectual, has disappeared. And it has become possible to develop lateral connections across different forms of knowledge and from one focus of politicization to another. Magistrates and psychiatrists, doctors and social workers, laboratory technicians and sociologists have become able to participate, both within their own fields and through mutual exchange and support, in a global process of politicization of intellectuals. This process explains how, even as the writer tends to disappear as a figurehead, the university and the academic emerge, if not as principal elements, at least as "exchangers," privileged points of intersection. If the universities and education have become politically ultrasensitive areas, this is no doubt the reason why. And what is called the crisis of the universities should not be interpreted as a loss of power, but on the contrary as a multiplication and reinforcement of their power effects as centers in a polymorphous ensemble of intellectuals who virtually all pass through and relate themselves to the academic system. The whole relentless theorization of writing which we saw in the 1960s was doubtless only a swansong. Through it, the writer was fighting for the preservation of his political privilege; but the fact that it was precisely a matter of theory, that he needed scientific credentials, founded in linguistics, semiology, psychoanalysis, that this theory took its references from the direction of Saussure or Chomsky, etc., and that it gave rise to such mediocre literary products, all this proves that the activity of the writer was no longer at the focus of things.

It seems to me that this figure of the "specific" intellectual has emerged since the Second World War. Perhaps it was the atomic scientist (in a word, or rather a name: Oppenheimer) who acted as the point of transition between the universal and the specific intellectual. It's because he had a direct and localized relation to scientific knowledge and institutions that the atomic scientist could make his intervention; but, since the nuclear threat affected the whole human race and the fate of the world, his discourse could at the same time be the discourse of the universal. Under the rubric of this protest, which concerned the entire world, the atomic expert brought into play his specific position in the order of knowledge. And for the first time, I think, the intellectual was hounded by political powers, no longer on account of a general discourse which he conducted, but because of the knowledge at his disposal: it was at this level that he constituted a political threat. I am speaking here only of Western intellectuals. What happened in the Soviet Union is analogous with this on a number of points, but different on many others. There is certainly a whole study that needs to be made of scientific dissidence in the West and the socialist countries since 1945.

It is possible to suppose that the "universal" intellectual, as he functioned in the nineteenth and early twentieth centuries, was in fact derived from a quite specific historical figure: the man of justice, the man of law, who counterposes to power, despotism, and the abuses and arrogance of wealth the universality of justice and the equity of an ideal law. The great political struggles of the eighteenth century were fought over law, right, the constitution, the just in reason and law, that which can and must apply universally. What we call today "the intellectual" (I mean the intellectual in the political, not the sociological sense of the word; in other words, the person who utilizes his knowledge, his competence, and his relation to truth in the field of political struggles) was, I think, an offspring of the jurist, or at any rate of the man who invoked the universality of a just law, if necessary against the legal professions themselves (Voltaire, in France, is the prototype of such intellectuals). The "universal" intellectual derives from the jurist or notable, and finds his fullest manifestation in the writer, the bearer of values and significations in which all can recognize themselves. The "specific" intellectual derives from quite another figure, not the jurist or notable, but the savant or expert. I said just now that it's with the atomic scientists that this latter figure comes to the forefront. In fact, it was preparing in the wings for some time before, and was even present on at least a corner of the stage from about the end of the nineteenth century. No doubt it's with Darwin or, rather, with the post-Darwinian evolutionists that this figure begins to appear clearly. The stormy relationship between evolutionism and the socialists, as well as the highly ambiguous effects of evolutionism (on sociology, criminology, psychiatry, and eugenics, for example), marks the important moment when the savant begins to intervene in contemporary political struggles in the name of a "local" scientific truth—however important the latter may be. Historically, Darwin represents this point of inflection in the history of the Western intellectual. (Zola is very significant from this point of view: he is the type of the "universal" intellectual, bearer of law and militant of equity, but he ballasts his discourse with a whole invocation of nosology and evolutionism, which he believes to be scientific, grasps very poorly in any case, and whose political effects on his own discourse are very equivocal.) If one were to study this closely, one would have to follow how the physicists, at the turn of the century, reentered the field of political debate. The debates between the theorists of socialism and the theorists of relativity are of capital importance in this history.

At all events, biology and physics were to a privileged degree the zones of formation of this new personage, the specific intellectual. The extension of technico-scientific structures in the economic and strategic domain was what gave him his real importance. The figure in which the functions and prestige of this new intellectual are concentrated is no longer that of the "writer of genius," but that of the "absolute savant"; no longer he who bears the values of all, opposes the unjust sovereign or his ministers, and makes his cry resound even beyond the grave. It is, rather, he who, along with a handful of others, has at his disposal, whether in the service of the state or against it, powers which can either benefit or irrevocably destroy life. He is no longer the rhapsodist of the eternal, but the strategist of life and death. Meanwhile we are at present experiencing the disappearance of the figure of the "great writer."

Now let's come back to more precise details. We accept, alongside the development of technico-scientific structures in contemporary society, the importance gained by the specific intellectual in recent decades, as well as the acceleration of this process since around 1960. Now the specific intellectual encounters certain obstacles and faces certain dangers. The danger of remaining at the level of conjunctural struggles, pressing demands restricted to particular sectors. The risk of letting himself be manipulated by the political parties or trade union apparatuses which control these local struggles. Above all, the risk of being unable to develop these struggles for lack of a global strategy or outside support; the risk, too, of not being followed, or only by very limited groups. In France we can see at the moment an example of this. The struggle around the prisons, the penal system, and the police-judicial system, because it has developed "in solitary," among social workers and ex-prisoners, has tended increasingly to separate itself from the forces which would have enabled it to grow. It has allowed itself to be penetrated by a whole naive, archaic ideology which makes the criminal at once into the innocent victim and the pure rebel—society's scapegoat—and the young wolf of future revolutions. This return to anarchist themes of the late nineteenth century was possible only because of a failure of integration of current strategies. And the result has been a deep split between this campaign with its monotonous, lyrical little chant, heard only among a few small groups, and the masses who have good reason not to accept it as valid political currency, but who also—thanks to the studiously cultivated fear of criminals—

tolerate the maintenance, or rather the reinforcement, of the judicial and police apparatuses.

It seems to me that we are now at a point where the function of the specific intellectual needs to be reconsidered. Reconsidered but not abandoned, despite the nostalgia of some for the great "universal" intellectuals and the desire for a new philosophy, a new world-view. Suffice it to consider the important results which have been achieved in psychiatry: they prove that these local, specific struggles haven't been a mistake and haven't led to a dead end. One may even say that the role of the specific intellectual must become more and more important in proportion to the political responsibilities which he is obliged willynilly to accept, as a nuclear scientist, computer expert, pharmacologist, etc. It would be a dangerous error to discount him politically in his specific relation to a local form of power, either on the grounds that this is a specialist matter which doesn't concern the masses (which is doubly wrong: they are already aware of it, and in any case implicated in it), or that the specific intellectual serves the interests of state or capital (which is true, but at the same time shows the strategic position he occupies), or, again, on the grounds that he propagates a scientific ideology (which isn't always true, and is anyway certainly a secondary matter compared with the fundamental point: the effects proper to true discourses).

The important thing here, I believe, is that truth isn't outside power, or lacking in power: contrary to a myth whose history and functions would repay further study, truth isn't the reward of free spirits, the child of protracted solitude, nor the privilege of those who have succeeded in liberating themselves. Truth is a thing of this world: it is produced only by virtue of multiple forms of constraint. And it induces regular effects of power. Each society has its regime of truth, its "general politics" of truth: that is, the types of discourse which it accepts and makes function as true; the mechanisms and instances which enable one to distinguish true and false statements, the means by which each is sanctioned; the techniques and procedures accorded value in the acquisition of truth; the status of those who are charged with saying what counts as true.

In societies like ours, the "political economy" of truth is characterized by five important traits. "Truth" is centered on the form of scientific discourse and the institutions which produce it; it is subject to constant economic and political incitement (the demand for truth, as much for economic production as for political power); it is the object, under diverse forms, of immense diffusion and consumption (circulating through apparatuses of education and information whose extent is relatively broad in the social body, notwithstanding certain strict limitations); it is produced and transmitted under the control, dominant if not exclusive, of a few great political and economic apparatuses (university, army, writing, media); lastly, it is the issue of a whole political debate and social confrontation ("ideological" struggles).

It seems to me that what must now be taken into account in the intellectual is not the "bearer of universal values." Rather, it's the person occupying a specific position—but whose specificity is linked, in a society like ours, to the general functioning of an apparatus of truth. In other words, the intellectual has a threefold specificity: that of his class position (whether as petty-bourgeois in the service of capitalism or "organic" intellectual of the proletariat); that of his conditions of life and work, linked to his condition as an intellectual (his field of research, his place in a laboratory, the political and economic demands to which he submits or against which he rebels, in the university, the hospital, etc.); lastly, the specificity of the politics of truth in our societies. And it's with this last factor that his position can take on a general significance and that his local, specific struggle can have effects and implications which are not simply professional or sectoral. The intellectual can operate and struggle at the general level of that regime of truth which is so essential to the structure and functioning of our society. There is a battle "for truth," or at least "around truth"—it being understood once again that by truth I do not mean "the ensemble of truths which are to be discovered and accepted," but rather "the ensemble of rules according to which the true and the false are separated and specific effects of power attached to the true," it being understood also that it's a matter not of a battle "on behalf" of the truth, but of a battle about the status of truth and the economic and political role it plays. It is necessary to think of the political problems of intellectuals not in terms of "science" and "ideology," but in terms of "truth" and "power." And thus the question of the professionalization of intellectuals and the division between intellectual and manual labor can be envisaged in a new way.

All this must seem very confused and uncertain. Uncertain indeed, and what I am saying here is above all to be taken as a hypothesis. In order for it to be a little less confused, however, I would like to put forward a few "propositions"—not firm assertions, but simply suggestions to be further tested and evaluated.

"Truth" is to be understood as a system of ordered procedures for the production, regulation, distribution, circulation, and operation of statements.

"Truth" is linked in a circular relation with systems of power which produce and sustain it, and to effects of power which it induces and which extends it. A "regime" of truth.

This regime is not merely ideological or superstructural; it was a condition of the formation and development of capitalism. And it's this same regime which, subject to certain modifications, operates in the socialist countries (I leave open here the question of China, about which I know little).

The essential political problem for the intellectual is not to criticize the ideological contents supposedly linked to science, or to ensure that his own scientific practice is accompanied by a correct ideology, but that of ascertaining the possibility of constituting a new politics of truth. The problem is not changing people's consciousnesses—or what's in their heads—but the political, economic, institutional regime of the production of truth.

It's not a matter of emancipating truth from every system of power (which would be a chimera, for truth is already power), but of detaching the power of truth from the forms of hegemony, social, economic, and cultural, within which it operates at the present time.

The political question, to sum up, is not error, illusion, alienated consciousness, or ideology; it is truth itself. Hence the importance of Nietzsche.

Study Questions

1. How does history relate to ideology in Foucault's perspective?

2. Under what conditions is power accepted and embraced?

3. What is the concept of surveillance in Foucault's work?

Further Readings

Dreyfus, Hubert, and Rabinow, Paul. 1982. *Michel Foucault Beyond Structuralism and Hermeneutics.* Chicago: University of Chicago Press.

Foucault, Michel. 1973. *The Order of Things.* New York: Vintage Press.

—. 1978. *The History of Sexuality: Volume I.* Trans. Robert Hurley. New York: Pantheon Books.

—. 1979. *Discipline and Punish: The Birth of the Prison.* Trans. Alan Sheridan. New York: Pantheon Books.

—. 1982. *The Archaeology of Knowledge.* New York: Pantheon Books.

Rabinow, Paul (ed.). 1984. *The Foucault Reader.* New York: Pantheon.

31

Structures, Habitus, and Practices

PIERRE BOURDIEU

Trans. Richard Nice

The **habitus**, the durably installed generative principle of regulated improvisa-tions, produces **practices** which tend to reproduce the regularities immanent in the objective conditions of the production of their generative principle, while adjusting to the demands inscribed as objective potentialities in the situation, as defined by the cognitive and motivating structures making up the habitus. It follows that these practices cannot be directly deduced either from the objec-tive conditions, defined as the instantaneous sum of the stimuli which may appear to have directly triggered them, or from the conditions which produced the durable principle of their production. These practices can be accounted for only by relating the objective *structure* defining the social conditions of the production of the habitus which engendered them to the conditions in which this habitus is operating, that is, to the *conjuncture* which, short of a radical transformation, represents a particular state of this structure. In practice, it is the habitus, history turned into nature, i.e. denied as such, which accomplishes practically the relating of these two systems of relations, in and through the production of practice. The "unconscious" is never anything other than the for-getting of history which history itself produces by incorporating the objective structures it produces in the second natures of habitus: "... in each of us, in varying proportions, there is part of yesterday's man; it is yesterday's man who inevitably predominates in us, since the present amounts to little compared with the long past in the course of which we were formed and from which we result. Yet we do not sense this man of the past, because he is inveterate in us; he makes up the unconscious part of ourselves. Consequently we are led to take no account of him, any more than we take account of his legitimate demands. Conversely, we are very much aware of the most recent attainments of civi-lization, because, being recent, they have not yet had time to settle into our unconscious."

Genesis amnesia is also encouraged (if not entailed) by the objectivist apprehension which, grasping the product of history as an *opus operatum*, a *fait accompli*, can only invoke the mysteries of pre-established harmony or the prodigies of conscious orchestration to account for what, apprehended in pure synchrony, appears as objective meaning, whether it be the internal coherence of works or institutions such as myths, rites, or bodies of law, or the objective co-ordination which the concordant or conflicting practices of the members of the same group or class at once manifest and presuppose (inasmuch as they imply a community of dispositions).

Each agent, wittingly or unwittingly, willy nilly, is a producer and reproducer of objective meaning. Because his actions and works are the product of a *modus operandi* of which he is not the producer and has no conscious mastery, they contain an "objective intention," as the Scholastics put it, which always outruns his conscious intentions. The schemes of thought and expression he has acquired are the basis for the *intentionless invention* of regulated improvisation. Endlessly overtaken by his own words, with which he maintains a relation of "carry and be carried," as Nicolai Hartmann put it, the virtuoso finds in the *opus operatum* new triggers and new supports for the *modus operandi* from which they arise, so that his discourse continuously feeds off itself like a train bringing along its own rails. If witticisms surprise their author no less than their audience, and impress as much by their retrospective necessity as by their novelty, the reason is that the *trouvaille* appears as the simple unearthing, at once accidental and irresistible, of a buried possibility. It is because subjects do not, strictly speaking, know what they are doing that what they do has more meaning than they know. The habitus is the universalizing mediation which causes an individual agent's practices, without either explicit reason or signifying intent, to be none the less "sensible" and "reasonable." That part of practices which remains obscure in the eyes of their own producers is the aspect by which they are objectively adjusted to other practices and to the structures of which the principle of their production is itself the product.

One of the fundamental effects of the orchestration of habitus is the production of a commonsense world endowed with the *objectivity* secured by consensus on the meaning (*sens*) of practices and the world, in other words the harmonization of agents' experiences and the continuous reinforcement that each of them receives from the expression, individual or collective (in festivals, for example), improvised or programmed (commonplaces, sayings), of similar or identical experiences. The homogeneity of habitus is what—within the limits of the group of agents possessing the schemes (of production and interpretation) implied in their production—causes practices and works to be immediately intelligible and foreseeable, and hence taken for granted. This practical comprehension obviates the "intention" and "intentional transfer into the Other" dear to the phenomenologists, by dispensing, for the ordinary occasions of life, with close analysis of the nuances of another's practice and tacit or explicit inquiry ("What do you *mean*? ") into his intentions. Automatic and impersonal, significant without intending to signify, ordinary practices lend themselves to an understanding no less automatic and impersonal: the picking up of the objective intention they express in no way implies "reactivation" of the "lived" intention of the agent who performs them." "Communication of consciousnesses" presupposes community of "unconsciouses" (i.e. of linguistic and cultural competences). The deciphering of the objective intention of practices and works has nothing to do with the "reproduction" (*Nachbildung*, as the early Dilthey puts it) of lived experiences and the reconstitution, unnecessary and uncertain, of the personal singularities of an "intention" which is not their true origin.

The objective homogenizing of group or class habitus which results from the homogeneity of the conditions of existence is what enables practices to be objectively harmonized without any intentional calculation or conscious reference to a norm and mutually adjusted *in the absence of any direct interaction* or, *a fortiori*, explicit co-ordination. "Imagine," Leibniz suggests, "two clocks or watches in perfect agreement as to the time. This may occur in one of three ways. The first consists in mutual influence; the second is to appoint a skilful workman to correct them and synchronize them at all times; the third is to construct these clocks with such art and precision that one can be assured of their subsequent agreement." So long as, retaining only the first or at a pinch the second hypothesis, one ignores the true principle of the conductorless orchestration which gives regularity, unity, and systematicity to the practices of a group or class, and this even in the absence of any spontaneous or externally imposed organization of individual projects, one is condemned to the naive artificialism which recognizes no other principle unifying a group's or class's ordinary or extraordinary action than the conscious co-ordination of a conspiracy. If the practices of the members of the same group or class are more and better harmonized than the agents know or wish, it is because, as Leibniz puts it, "following only (his) own laws", each "nonetheless agrees with the other." The habitus is precisely this immanent law, *lex insita*, laid down in each agent by his earliest upbringing, which is the precondition not only for the co-ordination of practices but also for practices of co-ordination, since the corrections and adjustments the agents themselves consciously carry out presuppose their mastery of a common code and since undertakings of collective mobilization cannot succeed without a minimum of concordance between the habitus of the mobilizing agents (e.g. prophet, party leader, etc.) and the dispositions of those whose aspirations and world-view they express.

So it is because they are the product of dispositions which, being the internalization of the same objective structures, are objectively concerted that the practices of the members of the same group or, in a differentiated society, the same class are endowed with an objective meaning that is at once unitary and systematic, transcending subjective intentions and conscious projects whether individual or collective." To describe the process of objectification and orchestration in the language of *interaction* and mutual adjustment is to forget that the interaction itself owes its form to the objective structures which have produced the dispositions of the interacting agents and which allot them their relative positions in the interaction and elsewhere. Every confrontation between agents in fact brings together, in an *interaction* defined by the *objective structure* of the relation between the groups they belong to (e.g. a boss giving orders to a subordinate, colleagues discussing their pupils, academics taking part in a symposium), systems of dispositions (carried by "natural persons") such as a linguistic competence and a cultural competence and, through these habitus, all the objective structures of which they are the product, structures which are active only when *embodied* in a competence acquired in the course of a particular history (with the different types of bilingualism or pronunciation, for example, stemming from different modes of acquisition).

Thus, when we speak of class habitus, we are insisting, against all forms of the occasionalist illusion which consists in directly relating practices to properties inscribed in the situation, that "interpersonal" relations are never, except in appearance, *individual-to-individual* relationships and that the truth of the interaction is never entirely contained in the interaction. This is what social psychology and **interactionism** or **ethnomethodology** forget when, reducing the objective structure of the relationship between the assembled individuals to the conjunctural structure of their interaction in a particular situation and group, they seek to explain everything that occurs in an experimental or observed interaction in terms of the experimentally controlled characteristics of the situation, such as the relative spatial positions of the participants or the nature of the channels used. In fact it is their present and past positions in the social structure that biological individuals carry with them, at all times and in all places, in the form of dispositions which are so many marks of *social position* and hence of the social distance between objective positions, that is, between social persons conjuncturally brought together (in physical space, which is not the same thing as social space) and correlatively, so many reminders of this distance and of the conduct required in order to "keep one's distance" or to manipulate it strategically, whether symbolically or actually, to reduce it (easier for the dominant than for the dominated), increase it, or simply maintain if (by not "letting oneself go," not "becoming familiar," in short, "standing on one's dignity," or on the other hand, refusing to "take liberties" and "put oneself forward," in short "knowing one's place" and staying there).

Even those forms of interaction seemingly most amenable to description in terms of "intentional transfer into the Other," such as sympathy, friendship, or love, are dominated (as class homogamy attests), through the harmony of habitus, that is to say, more precisely, the harmony of ethos and tastes—doubtless sensed in the imperceptible cues of body *hexis*—by the objective structure of the relations between social conditions. The illusion of mutual election or predestination arises from ignorance of the social conditions for the harmony of aesthetic tastes or ethical leanings, which is thereby perceived as evidence of the ineffable affinities which spring from it.

In short, the habitus, the product of history, produces individual and collective practices, and hence history, in accordance with the schemes engendered by history. The system of dispositions—a past which survives in the present and tends to perpetuate itself into the future by making itself present in practices structured according to its principles, an internal law relaying the continuous exercise of the law of external necessities (irreducible to immediate conjunctural constraints)—is the principle of the continuity and regularity which objectivism discerns in the social world without being able to give them a rational basis. And it is at the same time the principle of the transformations and regulated revolutions which neither the extrinsic and instantaneous determinisms of a mechanistic sociologism nor the purely internal but equally punctual determination of voluntarist or spontaneist subjectivism are capable of accounting for.

It is just as true and just as untrue to say that collective actions produce the event or that they are its product. The conjuncture capable of transforming practices objectively co-ordinated because subordinated to partially or wholly identical objective necessities, into *collective action* (e.g. revolutionary action) is constituted in the dialectical relationship between, on the one hand, a habitus, understood as a system of lasting, transposable dispositions which, integrating past experiences, functions at every moment as a *matrix of perceptions, appreciations*, and *actions* and makes possible the achievement of infinitely diversified tasks, thanks to analogical transfers of schemes permitting the solution of similarly shaped problems, and thanks to the unceasing corrections of the results obtained, dialectically produced by those results, and on the other hand, an *objective event* which exerts its action of conditional stimulation calling for or demanding a determinate response, only on those who are disposed to constitute it as such because they are endowed with a determinate type of dispositions (which are amenable to reduplication and reinforcement by the "awakening of class consciousness," that is, by the direct or indirect possession of a discourse capable of securing symbolic mastery of the practically mastered principles of the class habitus). Without ever being totally co-ordinated, since they are the product of "causal series" characterized by different structural durations, the dispositions and the situations which combine synchronically to constitute a determinate conjuncture are never wholly independent, since they are engendered by the objective structures, that is, in the last analysis, by the economic bases of the social formation in question. The hysteresis of habitus, which is inherent in the social conditions of the reproduction of the structures in habitus, is doubtless one of the foundations of the structural lag between opportunities and the dispositions to grasp them which is the cause of missed opportunities and, in particular, of the frequently observed incapacity to think historical crises in categories of perception and thought other than those of the past, albeit a revolutionary past.

If one ignores the dialectical relationship between the objective structures and the cognitive and motivating structures which they produce and which tend to reproduce them, if one forgets that these objective structures are themselves products of historical practices and are constantly reproduced and transformed by historical practices whose productive principle is itself the product of the structures which it consequently tends to reproduce, then one is condemned to reduce the relationship between the different social agencies (*instances*), treated as "different translations of the same sentence"—in a Spinozist metaphor which contains the truth of the objectivist language of "articulation"—to the logical formula enabling any one of them to be derived from any other. The unifying principle of practices in different domains which objectivist analysis would assign to separate "sub-systems," such as matrimonial strategies, fertility strategies, or economic choices, is nothing other than the habitus, the locus of practical realization of the "articulation" of fields which objectivism (from Parsons to the structuralist readers of Marx) lays out side by side without securing the means of discovering the real principle of the structural homologies or relations of transformation objectively established between them (which is not to deny that the structures are objectivities irreducible to their manifestation in the habitus which they produce and which tend to reproduce them). So long as one accepts the canonic opposition which, endlessly reappearing in new forms throughout the history of social thought, nowadays pits "humanist" against "structuralist" readings of Marx, to declare diametrical opposition to subjectivism is not genuinely to *break* with it, but to fall into the fetishism of social laws to which objectivism consigns itself when in establishing between structure and practice the relation of the virtual to the actual, of the score to the performance, of essence to existence, it merely substitutes for the creative man of subjectivism a man subjugated to the dead laws of a natural history. And how could one underestimate the strength of the ideological couple subjectivism/objectivism when one sees that the critique of the *individual* considered as *ens realissimum* only leads to his being made an epiphenomenon of hypostatized structure, and that the well-founded assertion of the primacy of objective relations results in products of human action, the structures, being credited with the power to develop in accordance with their own laws and to determine and overdetermine other structures?

Just as the opposition of language to speech as mere execution or even as a preconstructed object masks the opposition between the objective relations of the language and the dispositions making up linguistic competence, so the opposition between the structure and the individual against whom the structure has to be won and endlessly rewon stands in the way of construction of the dialectical relationship between the structure and the dispositions making up the habitus.

If the debate on the relationship between "culture" and "personality" which dominated a whole era of American anthropology now seems so artificial and sterile it is because, amidst a host of logical and epistemological fallacies, it was organized around the relation between two complementary products of the same realist, substantialist representation of the scientific object. In its most exaggerated forms, the theory of "basic personality" tends to define personality as a miniature replica (obtained by "moulding") of the "culture" to be found in all members of the same society, except deviants. Cora Du Bois's celebrated analyses on the Alor Island natives provide a very typical example of the confusions and contradictions resulting from the theory that "culture" and personality can each be deduced from the other: determined to reconcile the anthropologist's conclusions, based on the postulate that the same influences produce the same basic personality, with her own clinical observations of four subjects who seem to her to be "highly individual characters," each "moulded by the specific factors in his individual fate," the psychoanalyst who struggles to find individual incarnations of the basic personality is condemned to recantations and contradictions. Thus, she can see Mangma as "the most typical" of the four ("his personality corresponds to the basic personality structure") after having written: "It is difficult to decide how typical Mangma is. I would venture to say that if he were typical, the society could not continue to exist." Ripalda, who is passive and has a strong super-ego, is "atypical," So is Fantan, who has "the strongest character formation, devoid of inhibitions toward women" (extreme heterosexual inhibition being the rule), and "differs from the other men as much as a city-slicker differs from a farmer." The fourth, Malekala, whose biography is typical at every point, is a well-known prophet who tried to start a revivalist movement, and his personality seems to resemble that of Ripalda, another sorcerer who, as we have seen, is described as atypical. All this is capped by the analyst's observation that "characters such as Mangma, Ripalda and Fantan can be found in any society." Anthony F. Wallace, from whom this critique is taken, is no doubt right in pointing out that the notion of modal personality has the advantage of avoiding the illogicalities resulting from indifference to differences (and thus to statistics) usually implicit in recourse to the notion of basic personality. But what might pass for a mere refinement of the measuring and checking techniques used to test the validity of a theoretical construct amounts in fact to the substitution of one object for another: a system of hypotheses as to the *structure* of personality, conceived as a homeostatic system which changes by reinterpreting external pressures in accordance with its own logic, is replaced by a simple description of the central tendency in the distribution of the values of a variable, or rather a combination of variables. Wallace thus comes to the tautological conclusion that in a population of Tuscarora Indians the modal personality type defined by reference to twenty-seven variables is to be found in only 37 per cent of the subjects studied. The construction of a class *ethos* may, for example, make use of a reading of statistical regularities treated as *indices*, without the principle which unifies and explains these regularities being reducible to the regularities in which it manifests itself. In short failing to see in the notion of "basic personality" anything other than a way of pointing to a directly observable "datum," i.e. the "personality type" shared by the greatest number of members of a given society, the advocates of this notion cannot, in all logic, take issue with those who submit this theory to the test of statistical critique, in the name of the same realist representation of the scientific object.

The habitus is the product of the work of inculcation and appropriation necessary in order for those products of collective history, the objective structures (e.g. of language, economy, etc.) to succeed in reproducing themselves more or less completely, in the form of durable dispositions, in the organisms (which one can, if one wishes, call individuals) lastingly subjected to the same conditionings, and hence placed in the same material conditions of existence. Therefore sociology treats as identical all the biological individuals who, being the product of the same objective conditions, are the supports of the same habitus: social class, understood as a system of objective determinations, must be brought into relation not with the individual or with the "class" as a *population*, i.e. as an aggregate of enumerable, measurable biological individuals, but with the class habitus, the system of dispositions (partially) common to all products of the same structures. Though it is impossible for *all* members of the same class (or even two of them) to have had the same experiences, in the same order, it is certain that each member of the same class is more likely than any member of another class to have been confronted with the situations most frequent for the members of that class. The objective structures which science apprehends in the form of statistical regularities (e.g. employment rates, income curves, probabilities of access to secondary education, frequency of holidays, etc.) inculcate, through the direct or indirect but always convergent experiences which give a social environment its *physiognomy*, with its "closed doors," "dead ends," and limited "prospects," that "art of assessing likelihoods," as Leibniz put it, of anticipating the objective future, in short, the sense of reality or realities which is perhaps the best-concealed principle of their efficacy.

In order to define the relations between class, habitus and the organic individuality which can never entirely be removed from sociological discourse, inasmuch as, being given immediately to immediate perception (*intuitus personae*), it is also socially designated and recognized (name, legal identity, etc.) and is defined by a *social trajectory* strictly speaking irreducible to any other, the habitus could be considered as a subjective but not individual system of internalized structures, schemes of perception, conception, and action common to all members of the same group or class and constituting the precondition for all objectification and apperception: and the objective coordination of practices and the sharing of a world-view could be founded on the perfect impersonality and interchangeability of singular practices and views. But this would amount to regarding all the practices or representations produced in accordance with identical schemes as impersonal and substitutable, like singular intuitions of space which, according to Kant, reflect none of the peculiarities of the individual ego. In fact, it is in a relation of homology, of diversity within homogeneity reflecting the diversity within homogeneity characteristic of their social conditions of production, that the singular habitus of the different members of the same class are united; the homology of world-views implies the systematic differences which separate singular world-views, adopted from singular but concerted standpoints. Since the history of the individual is never anything other than a certain specification of the collective history of his group or class, *each individual system of dispositions* may be seen as a *structural variant* of all the other group or class habitus, expressing the difference between trajectories and positions inside or outside the class. "Personal" style, the particular stamp marking all the products of the same habitus, whether practices or works, is never more than a *deviation* in relation to the *style* of a period or class so that it relates back to the common style not only by its conformity—like Phidias, who, according to Hegel, had no "manner"—but also by the difference which makes the whole "manner."

The principle of these individual differences lies in the fact that, being the product of a chronologically ordered series of structuring determinations, the habitus, which at every moment structures in terms of the structuring experiences which produced it the structuring experiences which affect its structure, brings about a unique integration, dominated by the earliest experiences, of the experiences statistically common to the members of the same class. Thus, for example, the habitus acquired in the family underlies the structuring of school experiences (in particular the reception and assimilation of the specifically pedagogic message), and the habitus transformed by schooling, itself diversified, in turn underlies the structuring of all subsequent experiences (e.g. the reception and assimilation of the messages of the culture industry or work experiences), and so on, from restructuring to restructuring.

Springing from the encounter in an integrative organism of relatively independent causal series, such as biological and social determinisms, the habitus makes coherence and necessity out of accident and contingency: for example, the equivalences it establishes between positions in the division of labour and positions in the division between the sexes are doubtless not peculiar to societies in which the division of labour and the division between the sexes coincide almost perfectly. In a class society, all the products of a given agent, by an essential *overdetermination*, speak inseparably and simultaneously of his class—or, more, precisely, his position in the social structure and his rising or falling trajectory—and of his (or her) body—or, more precisely, all the properties, always socially qualified, of which he or she is the bearer—sexual properties of course, but also physical properties, praised, like strength or beauty, or stigmatized.

Study Questions
1. How does Bourdieu define the "habitus"?
2. What is the relationship between individual "dispositions" and "class habitus"?
3. In Bourdieu's theory, how is the "commonsense world" endowed with objectivity?

Further Readings
Bourdieu, Pierre. 1977. *Outline of a Theory of Practice.* Trans. Richard Nice. New York: Cambridge University Press.

—. 1979. *Algeria 1960.* New York: Cambridge University Press.

—. 1984. *Distinction.* Cambridge, MA.: Harvard University Press.

—. 1984. *Homo Academicus.* Paris: Editions de Minuit.

Bourdieu, Pierre, and Wacquant, Loïc J.D. 1992. *An Invitation to Reflexive Sociology.* Chicago: University of Chicago Press.

Calhoun, Craig, LiPuma, Edward, and Postone, Moishe (eds.). 1993. *Bourdieu: Critical Perspectives.* Chicago: University of Chicago Press.

32

Self-Interest and the Social Good: Some Implications of Hagen Gender Imagery

MARILYN STRATHERN

Introduction

In 1976 in the Papua New Guinea Highlands, I was roundly criticized for taking two Hagen women friends for a drive. My critics were men, who said that women should not sit in the front of the vehicle—it was not their place. I shall use implications of this incident to comment upon some issues in gender analysis.[1]

Consider for a moment some of the remarks made by men and women in the discussion surrounding the incident. One of the vehicle owners was the man whose scathing views about women in general I had recorded twelve years before: "They are little rubbish things who stay at home simply, don't you see!" (M. Strathern 1972: 161). On this occasion, talking about the car purchase, he added a rather different observation: "Some women are rubbish, they do not think of earning money. [But] some women are strong and help their husbands by taking food to market; they earn money and contribute to buying a car or to bridewealth and they help their husbands." Wives of the vehicle owners gave an account of themselves in similar terms. "I may give the money to X [her husband] or Y [her son] or buy things for the children—some I put aside for myself and this I don't eat. I don't buy things for myself, I just put it by. Later if the men need money, if they are in trouble [and have to pay compensation], I help them." One woman spoke of how she and her husband always pooled their resources. "The coffee we pick together and sell together. When we get money some R [the husband] gets and some he gives to me.... R picked a first lot of coffee and earned K 100 which he put towards the car.[2] This was R's coffee, we just picked it together and I helped him. It is our car. R didn't take the money and drink beer, it was our car [which he spent our money on] and I felt it was all right."

I choose this incident for the way in which it highlights certain issues in the understanding of gender concepts. There has always been an implicit contrast in Hagen men's statements between categorical denigration of females and contextual evaluation of particular women. The women's remarks quoted here hint as well at a perspective on their involvement in men's affairs that is not unlike the perspective of the men. Much has been written on how men have captured the anthropological imagination and imposed their worldview on the resulting ethnographies. Is it simply the case that Hagen men have managed to impose their view on Hagen women?[3]

On the anthropological analysis of male-female relations two points are generally separated: (a) gender stereotypes, the symbolic representation of the sexes, and the way these often underpin formal relations of authority or power; (b) how women adapt to their position, the maneuvers and stratagems to which they resort, their informal power and interpersonal influence. These may be set against one another. Rosaldo and Lamphere comment that "although the formal authority structure of a society may declare that women are impotent and irrelevant, close attention to women's strategies and motives ... indicates that even in situations of overt sex role asymmetry women have a good deal more power than conventional theorists have assumed" (1974: 9). Faithorn's conclusions about the ethnography of the Papua New Guinea Highlands is that Highlands women have been "neglected" and characterizations of male-female relations "over-simplified" (1976: 86). Her essay, taking to task the emphasis of reporting relations between the sexes as antagonistic and women as restricted to the domestic domain, is entitled "Women as Persons."

Hageners' own definitions of male and female, and of persons, suggest that we should, however, be particularly careful of our levels of analysis. They lead me to make three points.

First, dissatisfaction with an androcentric bias in anthropology, with constructs such as "political power" or (male) "group," cannot be met by concentrating on women as actors in the system, as persons "in their own right," individuals outside the formal male/anthropological model. No doubt Weiner is right in saying that "any study that does not include the role of women—as seen by women—as part of the way the society is structured remains only a partial study of that society" (1976: 228). But I would question her ensuing comments: "Whether women are publicly valued or privately secluded, whether they control politics, a range of economic commodities, or merely magic spells, they function within that society, not as objects but as individuals with some measure of control. We cannot begin to understand ... why and how women in so many cases have been relegated to secondary status until we *first* reckon with the power women do have, even if this power *appears* limited and seems outside the political field" (1976: 228-9, her italics). An analysis of individual action can surely not *compensate* for a cultural bias in gender constructs. It can only show us the extent to which this impinges upon action.

I do not wish to ignore the many questions associated with the nature of ideological construction (cf. Asad 1979); nevertheless, there is a sense in which any understanding of the meaning with which action is endowed must consider the symbolic structure as it is. Bias in the reporting of events is one thing; but a remedy of bias in this area cannot compensate for bias in the symbolic order. A closer look at interaction between men and women is likely to reveal only the organizational impact of people's models. The models themselves are already constructed at a distance from behavior. Certainly we should not simply reproduce people's own symbols in our analysis of events and behavior. But neither can a symbolic antithesis between male and female somehow be readjusted by taking up one of its terms—characteristics associated with femaleness—and showing that actual women do not fit the image.

A concentration on "the individual" as a unit of analysis brings into focus the nature of interpersonal power. For example, Faithorn seeks to show that Kafe women exert considerable power in broad areas of their daily lives, while Weiner talks of the kinds of decision-making control that Trobriand women have. (She also makes the point that women's power is not to be valued simply in relation to men's, but is a domain in its own right.) All this is very proper in terms of our overall understanding of society. Because a male-female antithesis is of symbolic importance we should not therefore imagine that it governs all that men and women do, or that there is a simple identity between the ideal and the actual. Yet we cannot turn to "the individual" as a self-evident analytical category to rescue us from the conceptual bias of the symbolic order.

My second point concerns conceptualizations of personhood. In the previous citations, Weiner talks of individuals, Faithorn of persons. There is tremendous rhetorical force behind the exhortation to consider women as "individuals" or "persons." To my mind the rhetoric is suspect. It draws on cultural obsessions of our own, which view the person as a political entity ("in his/her own right") with interests opposed to those of society. When "society" is identified as a male construct, women's strategies can thus be taken up on the basis of their being "individuals": people set apart from the social system, actors manipulating structure. The "real" state of affairs is thus revealed. To endow the "individual" with such superior reality (Evens 1977) is mistaken concretism. At the least attention should be given to the ideological status of such an entity in the society being studied, and to the cultural presuppositions about behavior based on this. In Hagen the individual as a "person" stands in a specific relationship to ideas about gender that cannot be preempted by the kind of antithesis suggested by Faithorn and Weiner.

The terms "person" and "individual" are used in a number of ways, sometimes as synonyms, sometimes diacritically, sometimes in antithesis. In this essay I shall argue that we can usefully talk of Hagen ideas of the person, in an analytic sense, provided we do not conflate the construct with the ideological "individual" of Western culture. This latter is best seen as a particular cultural type (of person) rather than as a self-evident analytical category itself. The point can be made from Dumont's (1977) formulations. He takes "individual" as his key word, and distinguishes two meanings. First is the "subject of speech, thought, and will, the indivisible sample of mankind," and I retain "individual" for this. His second definition refers to a culturally constituted moral entity, one defined by its potential autonomy and independence from others like it. For this, I shall use the term "person." Dumont's own formula in fact fuses a general description (the autonomous moral being) with a particular case (the "nonsocial" being "as found primarily in our modern ideology of man and society" (Dumont 1977: 8)). In Western notions of personhood, bounded units of the species are seen as *ipso facto* morally self-contained, and further are set in opposition to nature and society. Social science notions of personhood that emically oppose "the individual" to "society" are best understood as flowing from this specifically Western conception. But in other cultures, the ethical entity, the person, may be conceived along rather different axes. Certainly Hagen notions of the person are embedded in neither a mind/matter nor an individual/society contrast insofar as these presuppose some kind of relationship between nature and culture (cf. M. Strathern 1980).

In concentrating on the concept of "person" as an ethical entity, I refer back to Read (1955) who also wished to make "person" stand for just such an ethical category, although he argued that it was not to be found in the Gahuka Gama moral system.[4] My usage also fits Poole's description of personhood in Bimin-Kuskusmin, as the "attributes, capacities, and signs of 'proper' social persons that mark a moral career" (1979: 3). He specifically sets this conception of the person apart from the western "individual." Expectations about how people behave as persons enter into Hagen calculations and evaluations of others. It remains to be seen how far Hagen ideas of the person share elements of our folk concept "the individual."

The final point is that we need to distinguish interests and viewpoints that identify particular sections of society from models that set up such categories in symbolic opposition. The issue here is raised by Reay's observation that besides the perspective of women, New Guinea Highlands ethnographers have neglected the perspective of rubbish men (1976: 13). Yet not all potential positions offering a particular perspective on events are likely to receive the same symbolic emphasis. Thus Hagen old people certainly share characteristics that mark them as a category, but as the basis of a contrast with youth or middle age these are of little metaphorical value.

We are led here to what I believe has been an underappreciated dimension of Papua New Guinea "sex antagonism"—that the male-female opposition *is* of metaphoric value (see Buchbinder and Rappaport 1976; Kelly 1976). And where metaphor exists, we must be clear about its function. We should not *assume* for cultures that make heavy symbolic use of the antithesis between male and female that it literally divides men and women into social classes—so that we then have to account for each class having its own model. This may well be true for certain ideological structures. But insistence on looking for alternative models entails the premise that ideologies are exclusively about dominance and power relations, and that the symbols they employ are to be understood in their own terms. Thus (so the argument goes) images of maleness and femaleness refer only to men and women, and a model with a male "bias" must be about men's control of women. Hence, there must be a woman's version of equal validity.

As a medium through which the activities of men and women are perceived, models that focus on male and female may indeed misrepresent or mystify modes of interaction. They may obscure the bases of production and trivialize women's contribution. They may support men's (actual) domination over women in some contexts. Yet even in doing all of these things, male-female models often do something else as well. If I tend to concentrate on gender as a mode of creating symbolization, at the expense of its other dimensions, it is to underline a single significant point. Our understanding of gender constructs in Hagen cannot stop at what they tell us about men and women. Through the imagery of sexually based differences is ordered a wide range of values.[5] In what they sometimes set up as a "problem of women," Hageners—of both sexes—are also spelling out certain implications of personhood, of the alignment between self-interest and group action, in short, what is to them a "problem of people."

The Case of the Appropriated Landcruiser

The car over which I caused so much trouble belonged to a subclan of the Kawelka tribe who have settled away from their former territory in a lucrative cash cropping area. Spouses usually see themselves as working together in growing coffee (the chief cash crop), although as in the case of food production much routine care falls on women. Men are energetic at the height of the harvest season and in the subsequent processing of the bean. They also plant most of the coffee, which is therefore in their "name," but the division of proceeds goes generally by quantity. When more than about K5 is being sold, men take the bulk. The significant fact is the division into large and small sums. Householders vary in their arrangements. If the wife is selling she may hand the total sum to her husband, or hand over most and keep a small amount for herself; if he sells, he may keep it all, or give some to her. This figure also represents the ceiling of what women expect to earn at market (K2-4 per trip). The marketing of vegetable produce, planted by themselves, is almost entirely in their hands. Normally the wife keeps all this money herself.[6]

Money figures in transactions where traditional valuables are employed (A. Strathern 1976). The ideal is to produce money off the land or raise it through finance; wage labor tends to be denigrated (M. Strathern 1975), for the laborer must consume a high proportion of what he earns. Investment is valued over consumption. Money of any significant amount should be channeled into ceremonial exchange or some productive enterprise such as vehicle purchase, productive both of prestige and further financial enterprises. "The people with cars are able to travel around, and they taunt others—'You haven't bought anything [big] with your money: you have eaten the money yourselves at home. You don't do anything good with what you earn!'" (male driver of the Kawelka car).

The Dispute
The vehicle (a Landcruiser) cost K6000, purchased in the name of ten men. It was seen as enabling them to travel to exchange partners, transport pigs, take women to market, and earn money from fare-paying passengers. The designated driver was a man; typically some men would accompany him in the cab, while their wives sat with others in the back.

The ten owners were proud that they had bought it before the 1976 coffee season was underway, for this indicated the strength of their resources. Through contributions raised on their personal networks, each man had donated the substantial sum that marked his "ownership." By no means their first car, it was also further proof of their prosperity as pioneers in this area; and a politically precious object, for the money had been raised in rivalry against men of the pair subclan.

As a minor contributor and a driver I had a lien on the vehicle.[7] I had gone to visit a friend in another tribe, taking with me Ann and Lucy (pseudonyms) who were married to two of the owners. We all sat in the cab. We returned to a crowd at the roadside, and to a quite virulent attack. Two men rushed up, one of them demanding heatedly of my companions who they thought they were to ride in the front, and insisting that the proper place for women was in the back with the netbags and produce—they would endanger the vehicle. He protested over and again that the car had only been recently purchased, and what were the women doing in the men's place. Other men pressed around, and the affair escalated into an altercation.

The attack was not just about the women. The chief accuser belonged to a faction within the subclan that was highly critical of the general way the car was deployed. The basic criticism in such situations is always that the car is being used for consumption rather than investment. The point of course is that one person's investment is another's consumption. A driver who attends exclusively to the fund-raising affairs of one set of people will be looked upon by those left out as gadding around for pleasure. What began as an object of group prestige will seem to have degenerated into one of personal benefit for some.

The two factions comprised Lucy's husband, Michael, the subclan's regular driver, along with his close associate who had originally planned the purchase, and Edward, an aging minor big-man whose chief followers were dependent sister's sons living with him. It was one of the sister's sons who led the attack. As the driver whose personal agreement was inevitably involved in the daily journeying, Michael felt himself much put upon. Now he became the main object of Edward's recriminations. Their open argument quickly reached the point of Michael saying that they would return Edward's money. Then Edward and his cronies could go and buy their own car—Michael would even give them some extra money to start them off! If, after the money was returned, Edward forgot himself and begged a lift, why he would be no better than a dog! Edward demanded the withdrawal.

Some interesting issues came to light when money was indeed returned the following day. Lucy and Ann were no longer participants in the dispute, their actions neither defended by their menfolk nor the basis for further public recrimination. But others of their sex were very much involved. Edward's contribution had included money given him by women. His adult son, an owner in his own name, was treated as a separate person, it being up to him whether he withdrew his share (he did not). It was assumed that the sister's two sons—whose names were subsumed under Edward's—would go along with Edward. But also involved were Rachel, the mother of these men, and Katherine his wife. Between them, sister and wife had privately provided at least the equal of Edward's personal share. Two very different interpretations were made of this by men of the other faction.

Edward was said to have been shamed by the revelation of how little was his "own" money. He had claimed to have put in K400 in his own name, but only K70 was discovered to have been raised independently of his household. To show self-sufficiency is to be "strong"; if dependency on others is made a public matter, one is displaying "weakness."[8] Thus females who are categorically dependent upon males are "weak." Here the rubbishing of Edward was bound with bringing into the open his dependency on women. Edward suffered a diminution of personal status both from the publication of the fact and because his actions were ultimately against his own enduring self-interest. Others could imagine a time when there would be conflict within himself—between his wanting to use the car and this emphatic withdrawal. If he ever lost awareness of the social consequences of his actions and gave in to petulance, he would be something less than human—a dog, Michael said.

Rachel and Katherine themselves had turned upon Edward and said they did not want to take back their money. This was acknowledged as a feasible course of action; they were treated, like Edward's son, as autonomous persons with a self-interest in the matter. Their claims to the car were never made in terms of ownership but of usufruct. Rachel stressed that she relied on it to take produce to market, for she was an old woman now and the netbags heavy. Both of them also underlined their right to independent action in terms of specific social relationships. Rachel noted that it had been her own decision to reside on her brother's land where she could plant cash crops (earn money to help him among others), and she was not going to forfeit her position. Katherine said she had had her children (not just her own offspring but the junior generation in general) in mind when she contributed to the car and refused to make them argue by withdrawing her money. The women's autonomy was respected; only Edward and his sister's sons were given back their shares, and Edward received much less than he had originally given in his name.

Edward's association with females was thus used to show up his own weakness, a device that rested on categorical attributes of "femaleness." His wife and sister, by gender "weak," were symbols for Edward's lack of personal strength. Yet when it came to considering the consequences of Rachel's and Katherine's contributions in the matter of returning the money, the men organizing this dropped these symbolic equations and put in their place certain assumptions about women as persons. This switch in attitude reveals something of the connections Hageners themselves make between the categorical use of gender attributes ("male" and "female" behavior) and reference to the actor as a person, whose sex may or may not be relevant.

Women as persons

The male owners of the Landcruiser had, like Edward, almost all received money from women—wives, mothers, sisters, a mother-in-law.[9] One or two such contributions exceeded or equaled those of some men. Money the owners initially put forward as their "own" would have included earnings based upon women's labor, but this prior appropriation is done in the name of the household as a joint unit. The cash women in addition gave specifically for the car came from further tiny amounts earned and kept by themselves.

Contributing money did not make a woman an owner: She had no independent claims on financial returns from the vehicle, her relationship to the enterprise being mediated through the son or husband who had counted her money in with his. From the man's point of view her support was in the nature not of transaction but domestic production, money raised as food and pigs were raised from home resources (M. Strathern 1972: 133-42). Nor did the women make any claims to be considered among the owners, although they regarded themselves as entitled to particular attention when they wanted to use the car.[10]

Women save money, then, and contribute it toward group enterprises. The expectation of this is an element in men's calculations of the support they can give other men. Women whom I spoke to were proud of their contributions; several stressed their self-sufficiency—it was specifically money they themselves had earned (*na nanemnga-ko*, "myself my own"). Another of Michael's wives told me she had secretly saved cash that her husband assumed she was spending on herself and the children. She and her co-wife,[11] she said, wanted to provide substantial sums because it mattered to them what others, especially the older wives in the subclan who were also contributing, would think of them.

Her colleague corroborated this. "Our husband did not help in the gardens and it was hard work earning the money. Now the money is gone on the car we feel bad. But if we didn't give to the car then other women would gossip about it. They would say: 'All the time you take food to the market [i.e. earn money] yet you don't help your husband.' The other women would wonder what we did with our cash, and if we did not contribute to a big thing, would talk against us." There are three assumptions here: (*a*) women should assist in group enterprises; (*b*) they do so through individually helping their husbands; (*c*) money is ideally invested in "big" things. Wives do not simply aid the husband in the attainment of his goals, but make these goals theirs.

Men encourage this and accord prestige to women whose interests are demonstrated to coincide with their own. Michael praised these two wives (privately to me) for working hard and promoting his welfare. Lucy, the third wife, had yet to prove herself: Would she eat all the money she earned, throw it about, spend it on food and clothes, or would she also save and contribute toward important things? He will wait, he told me, and see how she behaves, what she does with her money.

Both sexes are evaluating women's behavior in terms of personal volition. A wife cannot be coerced: She must be motivated from within to identify her interests with her husband's. Hageners express this by saying that the *noman* is set on a particular road. *Noman* is mind, consciousness, conscience, desire, the capacity to translate wishes or intentions into action. It spans the individuality of decision making and the social nature of a person's orientations (see the discussion in A. Strathern, in press). Behavior is under its control. Observable actions are explained by the state of an individual's *noman*, and there need be no reference to anything else other than that he/she is behaving "as him/herself" (*elemnga noman-nt*). If people are persuaded to do something, then, it is seen as the product of internalization. Women, like men, are amenable to persuasion, comprehend general social values, and have the opportunity to incorporate such values within a personal framework of action. Indeed, Rachel and Katherine both gave voice to a self-image as "social persons," bearers of a configuration of statuses. They reminded Edward that they were not only *his* wife and sister, but were attached to others of the subclan whose concerns they were also thinking of. They thus implied the contrast between acting for the sake of wider social ends and for the narrow personal ends that men so often attribute to women. Although their recognized efforts were not of the same order as the men's, and did not bring them owner status, the women contributors to the car were perceived as having behaved in a socially responsible manner, evidence of good *noman*.

Here we have something of a Hagen theory of "the person." Individuals act under volition in the acquisition of prestige; corporate effort is seen to arise from the combining of people's several self-interests.

But if women have wills subject to influence they also have wills of their own. A person is autonomous precisely because the *noman* is within. Ultimately, aims, values, and interests are accessible only to him or herself. The *noman*'s orientation has to be judged from external behavior, as Michael said of Lucy. The positive side of this is self-sufficiency, that people strive on their own. In treating women as persons Hagen men demand of them commitment, loyalty, the capacity to perceive "social" interests, in short an active engagement of their volition and purposefulness. But on what may sometimes be regarded as a negative side, self-interest also provides a reference point independent of other people's goals. Men and women alike may follow aims of their own.

Edward's autonomy in getting his money back was seen by his opponents as an exercise in futile self-interest. Had the sum been larger it would have threatened group solidarity; as it was his motives were obscure, judged in the light of his history of unreliable participation in subclan matters now joining in, now swearing never to join again. His self-interest had ends only of its own, leading to behavior not only irresponsible but ultimately self-destructive. His wife and sister, on the other hand, exercised autonomy very much at his expense and through an appeal to wider issues. They had a choice of roles before them: their self-interest, in maintaining use rights to the car, was explained by reference to attachment to the land or their position within the whole subclan as against a particular relationship to Edward. It is in such situations of choice that "the person" is made visible—it has been shown that there is nothing automatic about the role the actor is playing.

One aspect of Hagen ideas should be made clear. What I gloss as "autonomy" comprises self-sufficiency, privacy, the person as a self-governing agent, to the extent that behavior can on occasion be assessed independently of those statuses and roles that also define the actor. There is an ethical dimension here insofar as such elements are taken into account in the way behavior is evaluated. Yet these ideas do not incorporate a contrast between the naturally constituted biological "individual" and the conventional, culturally contrived constraints of society. Rather, personhood is shown in the engagement of the mind in enterprises, in purposefulness (A. Strathern, in press). The dual connotations of the Hagen *noman* is aptly paralleled in Rosaldo's description of the way Ilongots speak of "hearts": "to indicate those aspects of the self that *can be alienated—or engaged—*in social interaction" (1980:43, my italics). When Hageners consider the nature of purposeful action, men and women emerge as persons.

The person is made visible, then, when an actor draws attention to the volitional, self-governing aspects of his or her socially acceptable role behavior. When he/she does not consider alternative social interests, and discards one set of such interests without reference to any others, then self-interest alone emerges, and the person is seen to go against social concerns. Here the person is no longer a manifestation of social values (as were Rachel and Katherine) but acts in contradistinction to them. Edward was judged by Michael in these terms.

Although men and women may equally subscribe to social goals or be judged as antisocial, from the stereotyped behavior of males and females Hageners draw certain symbols for these same possibilities. Unaligned self-interest is portrayed as typically female. Hageners also posit that constitutionally females are not the same kind of "persons" as males. This moves us into another realm of symbolism.

Women as Females

I use "female" rather than "woman" when I wish to draw attention to gender constructs.

The *noman* may be classified by gender. Thus through the different ways it works, females are held to be less capable than males of pursuing rational goals. This contrast is one of many tied to that of male-female. The most salient and embracing is between the prestigeful (*nyim*) and the rubbish (*korpa*). Prestige is particularly to be gained through ceremonial exchange but in general is associated with public matters in which men play the major part. A man is able to both enhance his own status and contribute to that of his clan or subclan, so that his acquisition of prestige has a moral dimension. The big-man is the successful transactor, skillful in deploying wealth and influencing others. Males as a category have an aptitude for big-manship. Females, on the other hand, carry out worthy and necessary tasks, attaining prestige only when their activities are seen as contributing to male enterprises. In themselves they may be called "rubbish."

There is a concomitant distinction between investment—males put their resources to social use—and consumption—females want to eat the fruits of their labors. Consumption is waste, spending on oneself for items that do not carry the prestige that gives a social dimension to individual behavior.

If males can usually claim some "social" benefit from their use of resources, females who demand clothes, tradestore food, school fees for their children, are "eating" money all the time. They are archetypical consumers because they spend money on domestic concerns.

Both men and women may situationally apply gender images (for example, the symbolized male or female) to persons of the other sex without implying that such a classification is totally encompassing. To consume or to be weak may be female characteristics, but do not thereby completely define women. The car-owning husbands who subscribed to the belief that females cannot do anything for themselves but are dependent upon males also solicited money from the women, relying as much upon women's sense of commitment as upon their independent earnings.

Yet when men think of themselves and not their wives as the owners of a vehicle, it is because males are investors. They (it is stressed) have planned and negotiated the purchase and now drive the car. Drivers in Hagen are invariably men, and although in the case of the Landcruiser there was only one regular driver, the cab is a marked male area. Wives, on journeys to market or to see relatives, sit in the back, benefiting from the men's enterprise, and are also encouraged to use the car for small enterprises of their own. Only prostitutes are said to sit in the front of vehicles. Whereas wives consume what their husbands give them (the husband initially cleared the land they grow their food on), prostitutes are seen as extractive, making a man squander his resources and turning him into a consumer like themselves. It so happened that the reputations of my two companions were already somewhat at risk on this last count.

Buchbinder and Rappaport consider the male-female distinction as summating a host of other oppositions; they write, "in taking gender to be a metaphor for the conventional oppositions they impose upon the world, people establish forever these oppositions in their own bodies" (1976: 33). The attack on the women in the car was a clear example of this. Whatever incidental justification we had for being there, I chose an unfortunate moment, when men were arguing among themselves in terms of consumption and investment, to present to them actual living women sitting in the front of the car, returned from a private visit. This sight provided the most perfect symbol Michael's critics could have wished for, a switch between back and front, female and male, between rubbishness and prestige itself.[12] The ensuing dispute did not, of course, turn only on our actions.[13] Rather, where my companions sat was used to reveal the car's general misuse.

In their evaluation of types of behavior as sex-linked, Hageners construct a set of symbols they can apply to other areas of behavior. Thus the domains male-female and *nyim-korpa* (prestige and rubbishness) are brought together into a metaphorical relationship (cf. Kelly 1976: 51). Each "symbolizes" the other; but neither signifies the totality of the other. It is certain *contrastive* elements in *nyim-korpa* that are imaged through the male-female distinction, and vice versa. Here the relationship is mutual: A dismissal of a rubbish man as "like a woman" entails also the equation of being female and rubbish. In the case of self-interest, an element itself ambiguous is differentially evaluated by reference to male-female. Autonomy expressed in some ways is typically male, in others female.

The contrast between "wider" and "narrower" goals, even between what is of "social" and what of "personal" concern, is largely contextual, contingent on an actor's standpoint. The differing interests of some may be brought together under the rubric of common goals, whereas the divergence of others may be branded as "antisocial." However, Hagen political units, tribes, clans and their subdivisions are seen to operate *ipso facto* on the basis of solidarity and the meeting of interests; and these units are to some extent defined through their male membership. When they act as bodies it is in activities where men are predominant. Hence men appear to have a vested interest in a type of corporate action that women cannot fully share. The demands of clan morality give a further shape to the use of gender symbols and, in the equation of "collective" concerns with male, attribute to the female goals of an emphatically "personal" nature.

It is in this context that I return to the original issue of how in analyses of other societies we tend to oppose the individual as actor to the kinds of cultural definitions involved in gender designations.

The logic of Hagen gender symbolism has been treated in other recent articles (M. Strathern 1978, in press). In the present account I am concerned with the accommodation Hageners make between these constructs and their notions of personhood, and in particular how this affects women—whose femaleness is denigrated, and who are less than men able to align "personal" with ostensible "social" goals. That Rachel and Katherine's socially oriented decisions contrasted nicely in this case with Edward's selfishness should not blind us to the way in which Hagen stereotypes are frequently used by both sexes to presuppose that males generally have a somewhat larger and females a narrower social horizon. But my argument is that in a situation that denigrates femaleness, women nevertheless have a position of some substance and maneuverability, and this is inherent in the cultural categorizations Hageners themselves make.

The Problem of People
As a preface to further discussion, let me summarize features of Hagen constructs that turn upon differences between male and female.

Gender imagery faces two ways. On the one hand it affects the identity individuals claim, and influences the evaluation of men's and women's activities;
on the other, notions of maleness and femaleness receive input from specific
cultural concerns (such as the acquisition of prestige) and in turn can be used
to evaluate other ideas and activities. Insofar as the latter is true, gender is not
just "about" men and women but "about" other things as well. I have already
noted that in Hagen the contrast between success (being *nyim*) and failure
(being *korpa*), and a contrast between public and private orientations, are both
linked to an antithesis between maleness and femaleness.

The attachment of these other ideas to gender employs gender as a ranking
mechanism. It is essential to such a mechanism that one sex should carry connotations of inferior status. Men's and women's affairs are frequently classified
in terms of a distinction between the public and private (e.g., Rosaldo 1974) or
the large scale and small scale (Langness 1976: 101). The way in which
women's power is thus *valued* in respect of men's draws on a model of cross-
sex ties in which a significant component is the relative position of male and
female to one another. Ortner (1974: 71) has asked how we are to explain the
universal devaluation of women. She suggests that women everywhere have
come to symbolize a realm, "nature," which is in opposition to the higher order
"culture." My point is that the object of denigration may be less crucially
women themselves than what they *stand for*. That a contrast between male and
female is used to symbolize a disjunction of values does not *ipso facto* imply
an antagonism between men and women.

Hagen females are represented as wayward, individualistic and antisocial.
Those who value integrative, universal concerns are going to devalue socially
fragmenting, particularistic ones and thus devalue the "female" (cf. Ortner
1974: 79). But who are the "those"? Although the relationship between social
and personal concerns, as well as the antithesis between the prestigious and
the rubbish, are symbolized in stereotypes based on gender, the values themselves are held across the sex divide, by men and women alike. Women can
dissociate themselves from the handicap of being female, as men have to
prove they can utilize the potential of being male, because these gender mark-
ers do not totally encompass the person. An individual Hagen woman is not
entirely identified with the stereotypes of her sex. In using gender to structure
other values, then, Hageners detach posited qualities of maleness and femaleness from actual men and women. A person of either sex can behave in a male
or female way.

The substance of the symbols—that it is "male" to have higher-order interests at heart—perhaps makes us think we are dealing only with men's models.
This would be an illusory concretism, for the same prestige values also separate the rich from the poor, the energetic from the lethargic, the intelligent from

the stupid, adults from children, and so on. Indeed in terms of capacity for prestige such categories are more realistically distinguished than are actual men and women.

Yet insofar as maleness is on the superior side of the equation and insofar as these values are realized most fully in activities in which men take the most active social roles, this model of the relationship between gender and prestige appears to have a marked male bias. I believe most Hagen men and women take these associations for granted. It is true that in certain contexts men use these equations to bolster their power in relation to women, and that women perceive the equations as favoring men. At the same time, the ranking of the sexes in terms, for example, of *nyim-korpa* primarily concerns the allocation of public prestige, and although men attempt to generalize this model and use it to represent power relations between the sexes (cf. M. Strathern 1978), such relations are not their central focus, and men are not very successful in their endeavor. Men use the notion in a rhetorical manner to support situational power, but the concept itself is predicated on the idea of achievement, rather than simply on the idea of male control over females.

Nevertheless, we are left with the question of why women allow "female" to have connotations of inferiority. The acceptability of the model rests on three notions: that women agree with the basic social values at issue, which involve matters other than the relations between the sexes themselves; that all that is put on the female side is not in fact negative, even though it may appear antisocial; and that as persons women can free themselves from the gender stereotype.

Gender and the Person

As a formal entity in Hagen structure, the person is both symbolically linked to and differentiated from gender. Far from revealing an alternative cosmology, the way in which Hagen women act and are perceived of as persons turns out to uncover one basis for their apparent acceptance of the kinds of public models men also hold.

"Women" can be distinguished from stereotypes and symbols of "females" not simply as the theoretical "social actors" of the anthropologist's framework, but as "persons" within the Hagen worldview. The "self interest" of persons in Hagen is seen not merely as a maximization of individuality, but as a mechanism through which individuals, male and female, may be committed to socially oriented roles (cf. Wagner 1972b). Indeed women do make such commitments, and their behavior can be calculated accordingly. At the same time, such commitments tie women into the very structure of cultural expression that uses the male-female antithesis to conceptualize commitment to as against divergence from social goals, ability as against inability to attain success. This is only apparently paradoxical. To become *nyim* ("successful") has to be seen as within the reach of all men and women, for it is the medium through which common aims are presented; it underlies group (clan) morality and (as I shall argue) relations between big-men and others. At the same time, *nyim* must be marked off from its opposite, *korpa* ("rubbish"); and the sex contrast, established at a general level by the contrast between men's and women's spheres of activity, provides an image of boundary.

One result of this is that certain orientations of self-interest come to be labeled "male" and others "female." The autonomous big-man projects male success though merging group interests with personal ones (and gets away with it), but the willful wife and the recalcitrant clansman show equally a "female" irresponsibility ultimately destructive of the self. Obviously, when private interests can be aligned with social goals, they are cloaked under the rubrics of collective action. Women, whose actions are classified under fewer "social" idioms than those of men accordingly more often appear autonomous in the negative sense. And men, failing to align a personal with a collective interest, appear as women. Thus gender comes to classify types of autonomy in relation to social goals.

But the point is that the sex stereotyping of modes of orientation is in many ways the precondition for the visibility of the "person" as a genderless locus of orientation. Individuals of either sex can be seen to act in a manner typical of the other. The weak, dependent man is "like a woman," a divergence from the male ideal; the strong, committed woman is "like a man," congruent with it. The deviation of individuals from their gender type makes the "person" visible. Women commit themselves to the attainment of prestige as persons setting their self-interest in an approved direction (positive autonomy); men flying in the face of corporate concerns are following their self-interest to destruction (negative autonomy). The Landcruiser dispute shows people switching from one frame of reference to another in their evaluations: The men and women involved are seen by other men and women to act out gender stereotypes, to exemplify self-interests of particular kinds, and to behave as autonomous persons. It is the point at which the frame of reference is shifted, the issue that selects one evaluation over another, that reveals the moral imperatives behind the symbols.

Hagen men's and women's ideas about the person are not just a set of residual notions dealing with aspects of individuality and personality that social categories leave out. They amount to an ideology of personhood, and give a special place to the factor of self-interest in social interaction. This is both a source of morality—the process by which individuals acknowledge the values held by others implies a specific orientation on their part—and a problem—for the self also has its own goals. When men switch from deriding women as weak and dependent females to urging them as persons to consider rational, long-term aims, they are not simply playing tricks to extract the best out of those they keep down. In the imagery of cross-sex relationships are symbols for the bases upon which people as such interact—coercion, persuasion, and the threat of indifference.

The "Problem of People" in Relations of Production

There is a more general issue at the back of gender symbols in this society. Among Hageners the problem of aligning individual interest to social goals takes the particular form of reconciling striving for achievement, differential prestige, and inequality between individuals with a positive emphasis upon egalitarianism and autonomy. Achievement in social terms is seen by Hageners to rest on the bringing together of multiple personal interests: This is the essential skill and technique at the heart of big-man systems. It entails a high evaluation of individual autonomy, and Douglas has pointed to the paradox. "A society so strongly centred on a structure of ego-focussed grid is liable to recurrent breakdown from its inherent moral weakness. It cannot continually sustain the commitment of all its members to an egalitarian principle that favours a minority. It has no way of symbolising or activating the collective conscience" (1970: 139).[14] In Hagen this is precisely what the symbols of gender provide. Douglas's point is that in such societies questions about the identity and value of the self are only soluble in manifestations of success and only the few can be successful. By linking the capacity for success to gender, Hageners sustain an image of the person in which the *orientation* and not just the results are a reward. People's intentions and endeavors are seen to be set on certain ends, and these are symbolized as "male" or "female."

Egalitarianism and solidarity are represented in same-sex images (the bond between clansman is that of fraternity); differential achievement, in cross-sex images (not everyone has the same potential for success) (see Forge 1972: 536). Another kind of differential is also encompassed in these metaphors, I have suggested, for collective action is held to spring not from solidarity alone but also from the alignment of disparate interests. The male-female contrast is used to point up potential disparity in the differing orientations that individuals are bound to have, and provides something of a model for crossing the gap.

I want to bring out two points: (a) insofar as male-female is used to symbolize achievement differential, men have an interest in keeping domestic and political relations on a qualitatively contrasting basis, to separate labor and wealth; (b) at the same time cross-sex relations within the domestic unit, between husband and wife, are to some extent modeled on and provide models for intraclan and interclan relationships between men. That male-female can provide such symbols I take to stem from particular relations of production between the sexes. Gender ideology is anchored primarily in the husband-wife dyad; in the relationship of spouses are mirrored issues to do precisely with the meeting of autonomy and collective action.

Gender is the chief axis of the economic division of labor in Hagen—not between males and females working as teams but within the household between spouses. The domestic dyad is the primary unit of stock raising and gardening; yet not the sole source of wealth. Through their exchange partners men traditionally had access to shell valuables (which Western money has to some extent replaced). This source of wealth is of singular importance to their self-definition as males (A. Strathern 1979). The circulation of shells is interlocked with that of pigs, which are, from a man's point of view to be gained partly from transactions with others and partly from the pig-raising efforts of his wives at home. Vegetables, produced mainly by women, and the foodstuff of pigs as well as people, are not valuables and are not objects of public exchange.

Women regard their labor as entitling them to some control over the disposal of pigs, for they own no counterpart to men's shells.[15] Whereas a wife converts garden produce into pork, but has to relinquish some control over animals entering the exchange system, the husband, through his shell exchanges, brings other pigs into the household. Nevertheless, men are dependent on women, both for personal daily sustenance and for the tending of pigs, for they replace those kept by their wives with those kept by other women.

The problem of production is not so much that of resources as of labor, and the problem of labor is its effective mobilization-the degree of work women are willing to put into producing a surplus of foodstuff necessary to maintain the stock. The ultimate problem, then, is people's motivation. A husband sees himself as having to encourage his wife to work for their mutual benefit. In precisely the same way, big-men can carry their personal aspirations only so far as individuals. Men's deployment of pigs in transaction converts produce into wealth, but it takes group-based collective displays to convert wealth into prestige. Although individual exchange transactions enhance a man's reputation, ultimately personal success lies in the success of the clan or subclan of which he is a part. Thus clan members have to be *encouraged* to join in group enterprises. Hagen men see a parallel between the management of persons within the clan and within the household.

I am here extrapolating from various remarks made by men and women rather than reporting a systematic symbolism. Nevertheless, it is significant that the wife who "listens" to what her husband says is described in the same terms as the clan brother who takes his mates' interests to heart. One Kawelka man told me how men became *nyim* (important) in two ways. "Those who have talk [are public orators, planners] and those who have things [wealth] they are both *nyim* ... A man who has few things but good talk, we don't blame him. And a man who has no talk but owns something, *he helps us too* [my emphasis]. But a man who owns nothing, has no talk either, doesn't help his brothers, he is *korpa* ('rubbish'). He doesn't contribute to anything. He hides his things. A man who doesn't help others [to him they say], 'You have no feelings for your brothers or your fathers, you are rubbish' ... A woman who looks after pigs and gardens, who doesn't round and decorate [like a potential prostitute], she is *nyim* ... She thinks of her work and her gardens and her children, she is *nyim* even if she has no talk. The woman who gives no heed to things, her children, she has no name. But a strong woman who works in the gardens, *she helps her husband* [my emphasis] so they will both have a reputation, this kind of woman is *nyim*." Earlier he had said, "Women who humbug, who don't hear the talk of men, they are *korpa*, they don't listen to what their husband says, don't give food or valuables to people ... they don't have good thoughts ... Some men, too, they eat things, they lie, they don't return their debts, we say they are rubbish ... The men who are *korpa* ('rubbish'), they don't make *moka* ('ceremonial exchange')."

The implicit presumption here is that husbands and wives cooperate as clansmen do: They have interests in common, and the husband directs these interests as big-men influence lesser men. It is a presumption of mutuality and hierarchy, providing a context for women's labor and effort; when women assist their husbands they are engaged in a "social" enterprise. Wives are thus made out to be dependent upon men to give this value to their work. But a crucial second factor is the degree of influence actual men have over their spouses, and women's willingness to perceive things their way. It is the *husband-wife* relationship, and not other male-female pairing, that provides a particular combination of mutuality and separateness, in terms of the division of labor, for it is only over the labor of their own wives that men have a controlling voice.

A big-man haranguing his followers treats them as persons, acknowledging their autonomy but hoping to set their minds on a particular course of action. In putting pressure upon the lazy or uninterested, the would-be leader is likely to use a symbolic antithesis between male and female. However he uses only one side of the contrast. He is not likely to use the image of wives helping their husbands, for such help can be appealed to on the more immediate basis of fraternal solidarity. He may well however use the second image: Those who do not contribute to joint enterprises are like socially irresponsible females, interested only in "eating" and in their own petty concerns. Here again we find the antithesis between investment and consumption.

Hagen political structure is acephalous, leadership being a matter not of office or administration but interpersonal influence. Big-men see themselves as manipulating others. They are supremely autonomous in Read's (1959) sense, in that they strive to create a situation in which clan enterprises and their own ambitions are reciprocally enhancing. But their autonomy to act in the light of their own interests can be preserved only at the cost of attributing this autonomy to others also. The price in fact raises their own value. It is *because* individuals have their own selves to consider that influence over others is an achievement. The renown of a big-man rests on his being seen to have engineered solidarity. We might say it is in his interest that such action should not be perceived as mechanical but as the combining of multitudinous self-governing individuals: It is he who has drawn them together. (One term for big-man is *wua peng mumuk*, "the head man who gathers [everything] together"—A. Strathern 1971: 188, 190.) The problem is that only an individual can commit himself. In intraclan relations (as opposed to those mediated by exchange or hostility) collective action must be based on a perceived *mutuality* of interest. If men are making an effort to involve women by setting themselves (men) up as agents of social transformation, they also use a disjunction between the sexes to symbolize problems of joint action among themselves.

Let me give an example: Hagen men and women agree that one cannot force a girl to marry against her will. For the marriage to succeed, her own commitment is important—to some extent the arrangement must be presented as in her self-interest also. Yet at the prospect of an impending breakup they will point to the wife's wanting to run away as an example of a heedless and typically female pursuit of self-interest in the face of responsibility. They may agree post facto that her mind had been averse to the match from the start, but once the marriage relationships had been set up the woman was in a situation that demanded that she take notice of the interests of others. Someone who goes his or her own way is not behaving illegitimately (a person has a "right" to follow his/her self-interest). Rather, spouses, like clan members, should also take other people's interests into account. Females are regarded as specially prone to acts of irresponsibility.

Men who do not join in clan enterprises are criticized for staying at home, being interested only in sex and other forms of consumption, giving in to short-term desires rather than pursuing long-term plans. By succumbing to such gratification (*kum*) they are seen as dependent upon comfort and domesticity; they are "like woman." Female dependency on males, in men's view, both expresses their subordinate position and integrates them into "society" (through the mediating husband); male dependency upon the female, on the other hand, deflects men away from wider social concerns. Economic dependency is one thing (both sexes privately acknowledge that it is wives who make their husbands *nyim*); whereas an exaggerated social dependency is seen to detract from other commitments, and is actually set up in symbolic antithesis to them. Men who spend all their time with women are rubbish. Autonomous insofar as they go against the wishes of their clansmen, by ignoring group interests they ultimately destroy themselves. Kum, the greed that leads to loss of reason (*noman*), forces one to eat and in the end, Hageners say, itself eats one up.

It is possible for an ambitious man to bring his group prestige through a selfish manipulation of relationships; a woman cannot bring prestige to anyone by pushing her own interests exclusively, because she cannot thereby bring prestige to herself. Females much more frequently than males are seen to pursue idiosyncratic and personal goals. This representation is not a simple devaluation of *women*, but an ideological comment upon self-interest. In its association with the unprestigious, uncommited female, strong controls are put on the direction in which men are made to see their personal interests as lying. Converting personal interests into social ones is a matter of trying to influence other people's self-orientations. The power of the male-female symbolism is to suggest that the contrast between social and antisocial orientations is axiomatic and self-evident, not the matter of context an outsider might see it as. In fact wives may be cast into the role of ally or enemy as well as helpmate. Sometimes they are kept sweet with gifts, sometimes coerced, sometimes urged to help. In their individual lives particular couples may make any of these terms dominant. In men's imagery of the female, and specifically the female as wife, all three are run together. The wife-as-enemy is classified as untrustworthy, liable to succumb to hostile impulses, as treacherous as male enemies are, to be beaten into submission; wife-as-ally can be counted upon most of the times, but must be flattered, complimented, given the generous attention that will make her feel good; wife-as-clan-member is appealed to as a rational person who can see where long-term interests lie, who acknowledges the significance of group affairs and is bent upon common goals. All three involve notions of females as persons with orientations of their own; they differ in the degree of disjunction between husband and wife and the method of coping with this. Do cross-sex relationships mirror some of the alternatives that men are faced with in their dealings with others'? If there is a mutual symbolization here, the husband-wife dyad is the crucial locus, for it is the chief relationship in which the sexes come together on the basis of their differences.[16]

Men's and Women's Models

Shirley Ardener (1975) has found useful the distinction between dominant and muted models. A society may be dominated or overdetermined by models generated from a particular group within it. For that group there will be a fit between their perception of surface events and the underlying structure, where-as the muted group is faced with problems of accommodation. In the case of Hagen I argue that we should not take the focus of the model—men defining themselves as prestigious "social" beings in contradistinction to unfortunate females—in terms of its own apparent value hierarchy. That "female" is not given positive value in this instance does not imply that women are to be defined as subscribing to values forever in antithesis. On the contrary, I think I have shown the extent to which Hagen men and woman do share common goals. My concern has been to demonstrate that one of the enabling condi-tions—by which men and woman may share goals and yet notions of male and female be used to differentiate expected orientations—lies in the idea of per-son. People, of either sex, can act independently of the stereotypes that define their gender.

Nonetheless, one can detect some difference in emphasis in the way men and women make use of gender symbolism. My companions were told to get down because of the gender associations of the driver's cab. They complied rather resentfully. Such equations are louder in the mouths of men than women, although women also give them voice. But what do women think of some of the assumptions, that, for example, to be female is to be spendthrift? There was an element of glee in the way Michael's wives explained how they would sur-prise him by revealing what they had actually managed to save. This would show: (a) that they were acting responsibly; (b) as far as their own behavior was concerned, they were not going to conform to this particular female stereo-type, but present rather the more role-grounded image of the "good wife." From the men's point of view, such attitudes are already accommodated in their mod-els: Women can be treated as persons, or if they show exemplary devotion to male affairs are regarded as behaving "like men."

When women talk of other women as "like men" it is with less approval and more insinuation of presumptuousness. They use the terms *nyim* and *korpa*, readily enough to brand their personal enemies in the derogatory idioms men use of females in general. I suspect that women think of themselves as "per-sons" in subjective assessment of their own worth, applying symbols of female to others as appropriate. However, they do not operate a symbolic system that apportions connotations of male-female in any radically different way.[17] If they use the ideology of autonomy more than men do, this is to assert particular counter interests, and is a maneuver that concepts of the person take into account.

Wives grumble that their husbands do not help enough, do not buy them clothes, make exchanges with their kin. Yet they concur in the view that large sums of money should not be frittered away but allocated to collective enter-prises. They accept it as the order of things that when coffee is sold any sum of magnitude will be appropriated by the man. Their minor share is "for eating," separated conceptually from the resources men will feed into ceremonial exchange, compensation, bridewealth, and so on. In fact, they may save their share, only to contribute it at a later stage. The contrast is between money for personal and for wider purposes. Women become bitter when husbands use money in the pursuit of what they interpret as narrow interests, as when it is consumed in gambling and drink. If men interpret the "social good" as evinced in transactions that will bring them renown, perhaps women find it in the benefits that flow back from the men's involvement in collective action— exchanges with their kinsfolk, a car on whose journeying they have claim, a successful bridewealth for their children, pigs they will eat.[18]

It is men who seem to be put on the side of morality, to represent the "social" dimension of commitment, to be rewarded when their self-interest coincides with the public good. But that is precisely the appearance that the images of gender assume. Qualitative differences in the spheres of action between men and women are used to symbolize values shared by both sexes and to differentiate the prestigious of either sex from the nonprestigious. These formulations also support activities such as clan affairs and the major institutions of ceremonial exchange and warfare in which men play leading roles; they justify an exclusion of women from cult performances and other spiritual matters. It follows that women may well have a perspective on the matter, but not necessarily countermodels or a definitive domain of power. Indeed, I have suggested that the autonomy that defines persons as beings with wills of their own opens up the way for women to be subjectively involved in some of men's affairs.

At the same time, insofar as an extremely high cultural value is put upon autonomy, people are not, as it were, only social creatures. The point is that which is socially oriented is not the only good, and a high valuation of autonomy may override contextual evaluations of the "inferior" female. Whereas prestige must rest upon the opinions of others, self-interest has its own ends, and the exercise of autonomy, whatever others may think, is a payoff in itself. This social versus personal antithesis, to the extent that it is developed, is much more fraught with ambivalence than the *nyim-korpa* ("prestige-rubbish") one. But it is certainly not completely obvious that male is, in this case, always on the preferred side.

To be true to Hageners' representation of themselves, one cannot reduce group interests to a matter of transactions between individuals (Evens 1977: 588-9; Cohen 1977). Gender imagery is, among other things, a symbolic mechanism whereby "collective" and "personal" interests are made to seem to be of different orders. Yet I have suggested that this distinction is not to be equated in an unexamined manner with the Western opposition between "society" and the "individual." Hagen notions of autonomy, for example, do not conceive it as a "natural" condition upon which the artifice that is society has to work. A study of situations in which people display autonomy could not thus yield an analysis in some privileged sense more true or more real than those presented in the rhetoric of collective action. When Hagen women are seen to act autonomously they are, quite as much as the socially oriented men, providing exemplars of ideologically constituted behavior.

I have followed the Hagen definition of the person to show how notions of autonomy mesh with sexual symbols. These are not themselves simply statements of power. Prestige is also at issue, and it is through the possibility of women as well as men acquiring a measure of prestige that they can both demonstrate their personhood as purposeful beings with interests of their own, and at the same time accept the equation male equals social equals group enterprise. We certainly need to ask also why men accept that women often go "their own way, and why they feel it necessary to engage their commitment as well as their labor. Are they seeking evidence of volition behind the action, the person behind the role"? The effort of "social" achievement paradoxically rests in this society upon a high evaluation of the person as an autonomous entity. But to be visible it must also be set apart. The autonomous female is as crucial to men's values as hardworking wives are to their success.

We may surmise that women themselves have an interest in promoting men's sense of the "social." In their everyday lives they are much concerned with focusing men's attention upon their status as wives, mothers, sisters, and so on. A polygynist's wives demand that he manage their separate relations with scrupulous fairness—men say ruefully that a polygynist never rests, for whichever house he sleeps in he always has to remember the others. Another stereotyped dilemma points to the hapless distributor of pork who in satisfying all the demands upon him can keep none for himself. Keeping numerous ends in view is a burden the manager places upon himself, and one that women encourage insofar as they demand that they be taken into men's calculations. Perhaps indeed it is the very image of female as consumer as well as producer that anchors men's affairs to women, making women the end as much as the beginning of their endeavors.

Indeed, Van Baal wonders if women's self-selected role of care giving has not led them to invent politics, putting men into debt with one another over their marriage contracts, creating a mythical need for protection "to lure men into marriage, into willingness to submit themselves to their loving cares" (1975: 113). He suggests that among the Nalum of the Star Mountains (West Irian) men feel themselves encapsulated by women's cares, and the netbags in which children are carried become a threatening symbol of embrace.[19] If Hagen women encapsulate men it is within a domesticity that lies conceptually opposed to the domain of public affairs. Yet at the same time women may also be considered as socially responsible persons whose own orientations include the goals men pursue. Not only food and children but also wealth is carried in their netbags, and wealth is inevitably destined for some man. Women's productive capacities do not belong in some alternative social cosmos with its own scale of values, but are regarded by both sexes to have a value contingent upon other aspects of social life. Where women themselves perhaps differ from men is less in having a model that obliterates the distinction between private and public worth, than in rating their domestic chores and personal enterprises more highly. This is largely seen as a matter of the different interests that are bound to affect people. In itself it does not point to some structural inconsistency, nor even a classlike cleavage between men and women. On the contrary, for all that Hageners use gender stereotypes to represent a contrast between social and personal goals, every woman, as well as every man, is visibly a person in the way she or he works out his or her own accommodation between self-interest and the social good.

Notes

1 I have received fieldwork assistance from several institutions in the past, including Cambridge University and the Australian National University. In 1976 I was making some inquiries on my own account. I am very grateful to Andrew Strathern and Jerry Leach for their detailed comments, to Peter Gow, and to Marie Reay for remarks on another paper, which stimulated me to write this one. I thank the Women in Society study group in Cambridge, and members of anthropology departments in Cambridge, London, and Oxford for their helpful criticisms; the editors of this volume have made several constructive points. Finally I should acknowledge my debt to Gillian Gillison for general discussions on gender that have influenced my presentation here.

2 K=Kina (Papua New Guinea currency); KI is worth roughly $1.20 Australian

3 Woman's accommodation of the "male world" is the theme of Strathern (1972). My perspective has since shifted. The present essay does however illuminate this original formulation—that in spite of Hagen women's own viewpoints and interests, there is no "female world." It reiterates some of the material found in Strathern (1978), to which the reader is directed for fuller information on gender stereotypes, although again I have moved on from the standpoint taken there.

4 Among the early writings on the Papua New Guinea Highlands was an article by Read, which specifically explored the difference between "Western" and Gahuka Gama notions of self. These Highlanders, he argued, have an idiosyncratic sense of self without the higher consciousness of person—by which he meant an ethically discrete entity of intrinsic worth. Behavior is judged according to an individual's social status rather than his worth as a "person." Hageners have specific ideas about people's behavior that are to be understood independently, of their

roles or statuses, and that are taken into account in the assessment of actions and may constrain or modify any reaction. In this sense I talk of "person." Two further points should be made. First, I have not elsewhere been consistent in my usage of the terms "person" and "individual." Second, although it will be clear that the Hagen "person" is constituted with a social orientation, I am not referring to person in the sociological sense of an ensemble of statuses (cf. Fortes 1969), nor on the other hand the "oneness" of the person that Cohen (1977) describes as self hood. The self is only one referent of the Hagen person.

5 Ortner made this general point when she insisted that we should sort out "levels of the problem" (the relationship between women's subordination and specific ideologies): "it [would be] a misguided endeavour to focus only upon women's actual though culturally unrecognized and unvalued powers in any given society, without first understanding the overarching ideology and deeper assumptions ... that render such powers trivial" (1974: 69). La Fontaine applies a similar idea to the study of initiation (1977: 422-3; see also 1978: I-2). It should be clear that my concern is with "gender" as a set of ideas constructed in reference to male and female, and not with the process of self-definition by which individuals make sense of their genital characteristics.

6 It was pointed out (by both Hagen men and women) that men get the major proceeds from coffee even if women's labor has gone into weeding and tending as well as the picking. Women claim the proceeds from vegetable produce, even if men's labor has gone into clearing the gardens.

7 Hagen women do not drive. I fall myself into the stereotype of the "strong" woman (resolutely set on my work) with something of the ambiguity of "waywardness," a reputation stemming from 1964 when I first set up house apart from my husband.

8 "Dependency" on clansmen or allies in a positive light is glossed as common solidarity, friendship, contract, etc. The small amount Edward was shown to have actually contributed himself was picked on by seniors of Michael's faction as evidence that he could not be considered a true "owner." Many other men had in fact been "helpers," like the women. What differentiated them from the owners was that (a) they had not taken part in the basic planning but were approached for assistance afterwards; (b) the amounts they gave were relatively small; and (c) they gave to specific members of the owning core in personal transactions. Men who helped in this way claimed rights to the use of the car. The denigration of Edward was largely internal to Michael's faction; I was not present when the money was returned, but was told that the men saved his face by giving him K 100 (and K 130 to his supporters) because they did not want to make his shameful situation too intolerable.

9 In a subsequent quarrel within his faction, Michael was himself accused in the same idiom of having no money of his own and having to depend on his womenfolk. The total amount from women was 20-25 percent.

10 In other purchases women occasionally claim to have contributed substantial sums in their own name; A. Strathern (1979) gives an example of a money moles (exchange) in which a woman is given token donor status. This account of gender

ideology in money transactions was written about the same time but quite independently of the first draft of the present essay, and I regard it as corroborating my analysis.

11 Michael had three wives, Lucy being the most recently married and much less established than these two. The pair had both received gifts from their brothers, which they also put toward the car.

12 Possibly an example of symbolic innovation (Wagner 1972a: 8). I had not previously heard categorical statements that women should never ride in the front, although it is a well-established custom. The only exception—apart from the case of prostitutes, which is the idea stated in reverse—is made for dignitaries such as the mother of a Council President. Once voiced the other men did not dispute it (there was no argument as to whether the women did have the right).

13 Many other social issues not mentioned here also involved the men at the time. For example, Edward's sister's sons had been involved in recent disputes with outsiders in which the Kawelka had refused to support them. They also originated from a clan that happened to be an enemy of Lucy and Ann's clan of origin (they were classificatory sisters).

14 She illustrates this class of society by Papua New Guinea examples. "In New Guinea a leader's dependence on his followers creates a sensitive feedback system. Everyone who transacts with others subscribes to the respect for reciprocity, and feels as sensitive to shame as to glory. These moral restraints are generated in the competition itself. Though they inform the concept of the upright man, the honest broker, they do nothing further to relate the individual to any final purposes of the community as such" (1970: 135).

15 Pigs are an ambiguous category, both food and valuable. Husbands and wives clashing over their disposal can each use the idioms of consumption and transaction. A husband whose wife wants to send a particular animal to her own kin may regard this either as a legitimate transactional claim or as her wanting to "eat" it herself— i.e., not dispose of it in some more "productive" way (in light of his own interests). Women support their claims by pointing to the hard work they had done, in return for which they want to "eat," i.e., consume it themselves, or else to the pressures they are under from their kin as partners of the husband. Note that pigs are only part of men's strategic resource, not the whole.

16 Barth (1975: 206) suggests that the Baktaman contrast between male and female metaphorizes transactions between men and ancestor, and in-group versus outgroup. In Hagen it is not simply that females are outsiders, but that male-female interaction may carry analogies for either internal or external actions among men.

17 Any role or status position will afford a particular "perspective" upon events. would restrict the term "model" to concepts and structures that are to some extent objectified, that is, given voice by a self-conscious segment of society.

18 Pork is consumed primarily in the context of exchanges, being distributed widely through personal ties after public events involving an initial group prestation (as at bridewealth, *moka*, or funeral). Opportunity thus depends upon the scope of one's network, for this potentially brings in meat all year round. When meat is finally

divided up for consumption, women receive the bulk and receive first. (Men hope to eat later from pieces their wives will have saved for them.)

19 Van Baal's account is based on Hylkema's analysis (S. Hylkema 1974: *Mannen in het Draagnet.* Verhandelingen van het Koninklijk Instituut voor Taal-, Land- en Volkenkunde vol. 67, The Hague, Nijhoff).

References

Asad, T. 1979. "Anthropology and the analysis of ideology." *Man* (N.S.) 14: 607-27.

Ardener, S. 1975. Introduction to *Perceiving women*, ed. S. Ardener, pp. vii-xxiii London: Dent.

Barth, F. 1975. *Ritual and knowledge among the Baktaman of New Guinea.* New Haven: Yale University Press.

Buchbinder, G. and R.A. Rappaport. 1976. "Fertility and death among the Marin." In *Man and woman in the New Guinea Highlands*, ed. P. Brown and G. Buchbinder. pp. 13-35. Washington, D.C.: Special publication America Anthropological Association, No. 8.

Cohen, A. 1977. "Symbolic action and the structure of the self." In *Symbols and sentiments*, ed. I. Lewis. New York: Academic.

Douglas, M. 1970. *Natural symbols.* London: The Cresset Press.

Dumont, L. 1977. *From Mandeville to Marx.* Chicago: University of Chicago Press.

Evens, T.M.S. 1977. "The predication of the individual in anthropological interactionism." *American Anthropologist* 79: 579-97.

Faithorn, E. 1976. "Women as persons: aspects of female life and male-female relationships among the Kafe." In *Man and woman in the New Guinea Highlands*, ed. P. Brown and G. Buchbinder, pp. 86-106. Washington, D.C: Special publication American Anthropological Association, No. 8.

Forge, A. 1972. "The Golden Fleece." *Man* (N.S.) 7: 527-40.

Fortes, M. 1969. *Kinship and the social order.* Chicago: Aldine.

Kelly, R.C. 1976. "Witchcraft and sexual relations: an exploration in the social and semantic implications of the structure of belief." In *Man and woman in the New Guinea Highlands*, ed. P. Brown and G. Buchbinder, pp. 36-53. Washington. D.C.: Special publication, American Anthropological Association, No. 8.

Langness, L.L. 1976. "Discussion." In *Man and woman in the New Guinea Highlands*, ed. P. Brown and G. Buchbinder, pp. 96-105. Washington, D.C. Special publication, American Anthropological Association, No. 8.

LaFontaine, J.S. 1977. "The power of rights." *Man* (N.S.) 12: 421-37.

—1978. Introduction to *Sex and age as principles of social differentiation*, ed. J.S. LaFontaine, pp. 1-20. ASA Monograph 7. New York: Academic.

Ortner, S.B. 1974. "Is female to male as nature is to culture?" In *Woman, culture and society*, ed. M.Z. Rosaldo and L. Lamphere, pp. 67-87. Stanford: Stanford University Press.

Poole, F.J.P. 1979. "The ritual forging of identity: aspects of person and self in Bimin-Kuskusmin initiation." Paper presented to Association for Social Anthropologists of Oceania meetings.

Reade, K.E. 1955. "Morality and the concept of the person among the GahakuGama." *Oceania* 25: 233-82.

—1959. "Leadership and consensus in a New Guinea society." *American Anthropologist* 61: 425-36.

Reay, M. 1976. "The politics of a witch-killing." *Oceania* 47: I-20.

Rosaldo, M.Z. 1974. "Woman, culture and society: a theoretical overview." In *Woman, culture and society*, ed. M.Z. Rosaldo and L. Lamphere, pp. 17-42. Stanford: Stanford University Press.

—1980. *Knowledge and passion: Ilongot notions of self and social life*. Cambridge Cambridge University Press.

Rosaldo, M.Z. and L. Lamphere. 1974. Introduction to *Woman, culture and society*, ed. M.Z. Rosaldo and L. Lamphere, pp. 1-15. Stanford: Stanford University Press.

Strathern, A. 1971. *The rope of moka*. Cambridge: Cambridge University Press.

—1976. "Transactional continuity in Mount Hagen." In *Transaction and meaning*, ed. B. Kapferer, pp. 277-87. Philadelphia: Institute for the Study of Human Issues.

—1979. "Gender, ideology and money in Mount Hagen." *Man* (N.S..) 14: 530-48.

—in press. *"Noman*: representations of identity in Mount Hagen." In *The structure of folk models*, ed. L. Holy and M. Stuchlik. ASA Monograph. New York: Academic.

Strathern, M. 1972. *Women in between*. London: Seminar (Academic) Press.

—1975. *No money on our skins: Hagen migrants in Port Moresby*, New Guinea Research Bulletin 61, Canberra: Australian National University.

—1978. "The achievement of sex: paradoxes in Hagen gender thinking." In *The yearbook of symbolic anthropology* 1, ed. E. Schwimmer, pp. 171-202. London: Hurst.

—1980. "No nature, no culture: the Hagen case." In *Nature, culture and gender*, ed C. MacCormack and M. Strathern, pp. 174-222. Cambridge: Cambridge University Press.

—in press. "Domesticity and the denigration of women." In *Women in Oceania*, ed. D. O'Brien and S. Tiffany. ASAO Monograph.

Van Baal, J. 1975. *Reciprocity and the position of women*. Amsterdam: Van Gorcum.

Wagner. R. 1972a. *Habu*. Chicago: University of Chicago Press.

—1972b "Incest and identity: a critique and theory on the subject of exogamy and incest prohibition." *Man* (N.S..) 7: 601-13.

Weiner, A.B. 1976. *Women of value, men of renown*. Austin: University of Texas Press.

Study Questions

1. How does Hagen gender construction differ from Western models?

2. How are perceptions of "gender" differentiated from those of the "person" in Hagen culture?

3. How is a cultural emphasis on differential prestige in Hagen society reconciled with a local ethic of egalitarianism?

Further Readings

MacCormack, Carol, and Strathern, Marilyn (eds.). 1981. *Nature, Culture, and Gender*. Cambridge: Cambridge University Press.

Strathern, Marilyn. 1984. Dislodging a World View: Challenge and Counter-Challenge in the Relationship Between Feminism and Anthropology. *Changing Paradigms: The Impact of Feminist Theory Upon the World of Scholarship*. Ed. Susan Magarey. Sydney: Hale and Iremonger.

—. 1992. *Reproducing the Future*. London and New York: Routledge.

—. 1995. *Shifting Contexts: Transformations in Anthropological Knowledge (The Uses of Knowledge)*. London and New York: Routledge.

—. 1999. *Property, Substance and Effect: Anthropological Essays on Persons and Things*. London: Athlone Press.

33

Cultural Roots

BENEDICT ANDERSON

No more arresting emblems of the modern culture of nationalism exist than cenotaphs and tombs of Unknown Soldiers. The public ceremonial reverence accorded these monuments precisely because they are either deliberately empty or no one knows who lies inside them, has no true precedents in earlier times.[1] To feel the force of this modernity one has only to imagine the general reaction to the busybody who "discovered" the Unknown Soldier's name or insisted on filling the cenotaph with some real bones. Sacrilege of a strange, contemporary kind! Yet void as these tombs are of identifiable mortal remains or immortal souls, they are nonetheless saturated with ghostly *national* imaginings.[2] (This is why so many different nations have such tombs without feeling any need to specify the nationality of their absent occupants. What else could they be *but* Germans, Americans, Argentinians ...?)

The cultural significance of such monuments becomes even clearer if one tries to imagine, say, a Tomb of the Unknown Marxist or a cenotaph for fallen Liberals. Is a sense of absurdity avoidable? The reason is that neither Marxism nor Liberalism are much concerned with death and immortality. If the nationalist imagining is so concerned, this suggests a strong affinity with religious imaginings. As this affinity is by no means fortuitous, it may be useful to begin a consideration of the cultural roots of nationalism with death, as the last of a whole gamut of fatalities.

If the manner of a man's dying usually seems arbitrary, his mortality is inescapable. Human lives are full of such combinations of necessity and chance. We are all aware of the contingency and ineluctability of our particular genetic heritage, our gender, our life-era, our physical capabilities, our mother-tongue, and so forth. The great merit of traditional religious world-views (which naturally must be distinguished from their role in the legitimation of specific systems of domination and exploitation) has been their concern with man-in-the-cosmos, man as species being, and the contingency of life. The

573

extraordinary survival over thousands of years of Buddhism, Christianity or Islam in dozens of different social formations attests to their imaginative response to the overwhelming burden of human suffering—disease, mutilation, grief, age, and death. Why was I born blind? Why is my best friend paralyzed? Why is my daughter retarded? The religions attempt to explain. The great weakness of all evolutionary/progressive styles of thought, not excluding Marxism, is that such questions are answered with impatient silence.[3] At the same time, in different ways, religious thought also responds to obscure intimations of immortality, generally by transforming fatality into continuity (karma, original sin, etc.) In this way, it concerns itself with the links between the dead and the yet unborn, the mystery of re-generation. Who experiences *their* child's conception and birth without dimly apprehending a combined connectedness, fortuity, and fatality in a language of "continuity"? (Again, the disadvantage of evolutionary/progressive thought is an almost Heraclitean hostility to any idea of continuity.)

I bring up these perhaps simpleminded observations primarily because in Western Europe the eighteenth century marks not only the dawn of the age of nationalism but the dusk of religious modes of thought. The century of the Enlightenment, of rationalist secularism, brought with it its own modern darkness. With the ebbing of religious belief, the suffering which belief in part composed did not disappear. Disintegration of paradise: nothing makes fatality more arbitrary. Absurdity of salvation: nothing makes another style of continuity more necessary. What then was required was a secular transformation of fatality into continuity, contingency into meaning. As we shall see, few things were (are) better suited to this end than an idea of nation. If nation-states are widely conceded to be "new" and "historical," the nations to which they give political expression always loom out of an immemorial past,[4] and, still more important, glide into a limitless future. It is the magic of nationalism to turn chance into destiny. With Debray we might say, "Yes, it is quite accidental that I am born French; but after all, France is eternal."

Needless to say, I am not claiming that the appearance of nationalism towards the end of the eighteenth century was "produced" by the erosion of religious certainties, or that this erosion does not itself require a complex explanation. Nor am I suggesting that somehow nationalism historically "supersedes" religion. What I am proposing is that nationalism has to be understood by aligning it, not with self-consciously held political ideologies, but with the large cultural systems that preceded it, out of which-as well as against which—it came into being.

For present purposes, the two relevant cultural systems are the *religious community* and the *dynastic realm*. For both of these, in their heydays, were taken-for-granted frames of reference, very much as nationality is today. It is therefore essential to consider what gave these cultural systems their self-evident plausibility, and at the same time to underline certain key elements in their decomposition.

The Religious Community

Few things are more impressive than the vast territorial stretch of the Ummah Islam from Morocco to the Sulu Archipelago, of Christendom from Paraguay to Japan, and of the Buddhist world from Sri Lanka to the Korean peninsula. The great sacral cultures (and for our purposes here it may be permissible to include "Confucianism") incorporated conceptions of immense communities. But Christendom, the Islamic Ummah, and even the Middle Kingdom—which, though we think of it today as Chinese, imagined itself not as Chinese, but as central—were imaginable largely through the medium of a sacred language and written script. Take only the example of Islam: if Maguindanao met Berbers in Mecca, knowing nothing of each other's languages, incapable of communicating orally, they nonetheless understood each other's ideographs, *because* the sacred texts they shared existed only in classical Arabic. In this sense, written Arabic functioned like Chinese characters to create a community out of signs, not sounds. (So today mathematical language continues an old tradition. Of what the Thai call + Rumanians have no idea, and vice versa, but both comprehend the symbol.) All the great classical communities conceived of themselves as cosmically central, through the medium of a sacred language linked to a superterrestrial order of power. Accordingly, the stretch of written Latin, Pali, Arabic, or Chinese was, in theory, unlimited. (In fact, the deader the written language—the farther it was from speech—the better: in principle everyone has access to a pure world of signs.)

Yet such classical communities linked by sacred languages had a character distinct from the imagined communities of modern nations. One crucial difference was the older communities' confidence in the unique sacredness of their languages, and thus their ideas about admission to membership. Chinese mandarins looked with approval on barbarians who painfully learned to paint Middle Kingdom ideograms. These barbarians were already halfway to full absorption.[5] Half-civilized was vastly better than barbarian. Such an attitude was certainly not peculiar to the Chinese, nor confined to antiquity. Consider, for example, the following "policy on barbarians" formulated by the early-nineteenth-century Colombian liberal Pedro Fermin de Vargas:

> To expand our agriculture it would be necessary to hispanicize our Indians. Their idleness, stupidity, and indifference towards normal endeavours causes one to think that they come from a degenerate race which deteriorates in proportion to the distance from its origin ... it would be very desirable that the Indians be extin-

guished, by miscegenation with the whites, declaring them free of tribute and other charges, and giving them private property in land.[6]

How striking it is that this liberal still proposes to "extinguish" his Indians in part by "declaring them free of tribute" and "giving them private property in land," rather than exterminating them by gun and microbe as his heirs in Brazil, Argentina, and the United States began to do soon afterwards. Note also, alongside the condescending cruelty, a cosmic optimism: the Indian is ultimately redeemable—by impregnation with white, "civilized" semen, and the acquisition of private property, *like everyone else.* (How different Fermin's attitude is from the later European imperialist's preference for "genuine" Malays, Gurkhas, and Hausas over "half-breeds," "semi-educated natives," "wogs," and the like.)

Yet if the sacred silent languages were the media through which the great global communities of the past were imagined, the reality of such apparitions depended on an idea largely foreign to the contemporary Western mind: the non-arbitrariness of the sign. The ideograms of Chinese, Latin, or Arabic were emanations of reality, not randomly fabricated representations of it. We are familiar with the long dispute over the appropriate language (Latin or vernacular) for the mass. In the Islamic tradition, until quite recently, the Qur'an was literally untranslatable (and therefore untranslated), because Allah's truth was accessible only through the unsubstitutable true signs of written Arabic. There is no idea here of a world so separated from language that all languages are equidistant (and thus interchangeable) signs for it. In effect, ontological reality is apprehensible only through a single, privileged system of re-presentation: the truth-language of Church Latin, Qur'anic Arabic, or Examination Chinese.[7] And, as truth-languages, imbued with an impulse largely foreign to nationalism, the impulse towards conversion. By conversion, I mean not so much the acceptance of particular religious tenets, but alchemic absorption. The barbarian becomes "Middle Kingdom," the Rif Muslim, the Ilongo Christian. The whole nature of man's being is sacrally malleable. (Contrast thus the prestige of these old world-languages, towering high over all vernaculars, with Esperanto or Volapük, which lie ignored between them.) It was, after all, this possibility of conversion through the sacred language that made it possible for an "Englishman" to become Pope[8] and a "Manchu" Son of Heaven.

But even though the sacred languages made such communities as Christendom imaginable, the actual scope and plausibility of these communities can not be explained by sacred script alone: their readers were, after all, tiny literate reefs on top of vast illiterate oceans.[9] A fuller explanation requires a glance at the relationship between the literati and their societies. It would be a mistake to view the former as a kind of theological technocracy. The languages they sustained, if abstruse, had none of the self-arranged abstruseness of lawyers' or economists' jargons, on the margin of society's idea of reality. Rather, the literati were adepts, strategic strata in a cosmological hierarchy of which the apex was divine.[10] The fundamental conceptions about "social groups" were centripetal and hierarchical, rather than boundary-oriented and horizontal. The astonishing power of the papacy in its noonday is only comprehensible in terms of a trans-European Latin-writing clerisy, *and* a conception of the world, shared by virtually everyone, that the bilingual intelligentsia, by mediating between vernacular and Latin, mediated between earth and heaven. (The awesomeness of excommunication reflects this cosmology.)

Yet for all the grandeur and power of the great religiously imagined communities, their *unselfconscious coherence* waned steadily after the late Middle Ages. Among the reasons for this decline, I wish here to emphasize only the two which are directly related to these communities' unique sacredness.

First was the effect of the explorations of the non-European world, which mainly but by no means exclusively in Europe "abruptly widened the cultural and geographic horizon and hence also men's conception of possible forms of human life."[11] The process is already apparent in the greatest of all European travel-books. Consider the following awed description of Kublai Khan by the good Venetian Christian Marco Polo at the end of the thirteenth century:[12]

The grand khan, having obtained this signal victory, returned with great pomp and triumph to the capital city of Kanbalu. This took place in the month of November, and he continued to reside there during the months of February and March, in which latter was *our* festival of Easter. Being aware that this was one of our principal solemnities, he commanded all the Christians to attend him, and to bring with them *their* Book, which contains the four Gospels of the Evangelists. After causing it to be repeatedly perfumed with incense, in a ceremonious manner, he devoutly kissed it, and directed that the same should be done by all his nobles who were present. This was his usual practice upon each of the principal Christian festivals, such as Easter and Christmas; and he observed the same at the festivals of the Saracens, Jews, and idolaters. Upon being asked his motive for this conduct, he said: "There are four great Prophets who are reverenced and worshipped by the different classes of mankind. The Christians regard Jesus Christ as their divinity; the Saracens, Mahomet; the Jews, Moses; and the idolaters, Sogomombar-kan, the most eminent among their idols. I do honour and show respect to all the four, and invoke to my aid *whichever amongst them is in truth supreme in heaven*." But from the manner in which his majesty acted towards them, it is evident that he regarded the faith of the Christians as the truest and the best

...

What is so remarkable about this passage is not so much the great Mongol dynast's calm religious relativism (it is still a *religious* relativism), as Marco Polo's attitude and language. It never occurs to him, even though he is writing for fellow-European Christians, to term Kublai a hypocrite or an idolater. (No doubt in part because "in respect to number of subjects, extent of territory, and amount of revenue, he surpasses every sovereign that has heretofore been or that now is in the world.")[13] And in the unselfconscious use of "our" (which becomes "their"), and the description of the faith of the Christians as "truest," rather than "true," we can detect the seeds of a territorialization of faiths which foreshadows the language of many nationalists ("our" nation is "the best"—in a competitive, *comparative field*).

What a revealing contrast is provided by the opening of the letter written by the Persian traveller "Rica" to his friend "Ibben" from Paris in "1712":[14]

> The Pope is the chief of the Christians; he is an ancient idol, worshipped now from habit. Once he was formidable even to princes, for he would depose them as easily as our magnificent sultans depose the kings of Iremetia or Georgia. But nobody fears him any longer. He claims to be the successor of one of the earliest Christians, called Saint Peter, and it is certainly a rich succession, for his treasure is immense and he has a great country under his control.

The deliberate, sophisticated fabrications of the eighteenth-century Catholic mirror the naive realism of his thirteenth-century predecessor, but by now the "relativization" and "territorialization" are utterly selfconscious, and political in intent. Is it unreasonable to see a paradoxical elaboration of this evolving tradition in the Ayatollah Ruhollah Khomeini's identification of The Great Satan, not as a heresy, nor even as a demonic personage (dim little Carter scarcely fitted the bill), but as a *nation*?

Second was a gradual demotion of the sacred language itself. Writing of mediaeval Western Europe, Bloch noted that "Latin was not only the language in which teaching was done, it was the *only language taught.*"[15] (This second "only" shows quite clearly the sacredness of Latin—no other language was thought worth the teaching.) But by the sixteenth century all this was changing fast. The reasons for the change need not detain us here: the central importance of print capitalism will be discussed below. It is sufficient to remind ourselves of its scale and pace. Febvre and Martin estimate that 77% of the books printed before 1500 were still in Latin (meaning nonetheless that 23% were already in vernaculars).[16] If of the 88 editions printed in Paris in 1501 all but 8 were in Latin, after 1575 a majority were always in French.[17] Despite a temporary come-back during the Counter-Reformation, Latin's hegemony was doomed. Nor are we speaking simply of a general popularity. Somewhat later, but at no less dizzying speed, Latin ceased to be the language of a pan-European high intelligentsia. In the seventeenth century Hobbes (1588-1678) was a figure of continental renown because he wrote in he truth-language. Shakespeare (1564-1616), on the other hand, composing in the vernacular, was virtually unknown across the Channel.[18] And had English not become, two hundred years later, the pre-eminent world-imperial language, might he not largely have retained his original insular obscurity? Meanwhile, these men's cross-Channel near-contemporaries, Descartes (1596-1650) and Pascal (1623-1662) conducted most of their correspondence in Latin; but virtually all of Voltaire's (1694-1778) was in the vernacular.[19] "After 1640, with fewer and fewer books coming out in Latin, and more and more in the vernacular languages, publishing was ceasing to be an international [sic] enterprise."[20] In a word, the fall of Latin exemplified a larger process in which the sacred communities integrated by old sacred languages were gradually fragmented, pluralized, and territorialized.

The Dynastic Realm

These days it is perhaps difficult to put oneself empathetically into a world in which the dynastic realm appeared for most men as the only imaginable "political" system. For in fundamental ways "serious" monarchy lies transverse to all modern conceptions of political life. Kingship organizes everything around a high centre. Its legitimacy derives from divinity, not from populations, who, after all, are subjects, not citizens. In the modern conception, state sovereignty is fully, flatly, and evenly operative over each square centimetre of a legally demarcated territory. But in the older imagining, where states were defined by centres, borders were porous and indistinct, and sovereignties faded imperceptibly into one another.[21] Hence, paradoxically enough, the ease with which pre-modern empires and kingdoms were able to sustain their rule over immensely heterogeneous, and often not even contiguous, populations for long periods of time.[22]

One must also remember that these antique monarchical states expanded not only by warfare but by sexual politics—of a kind very different than that practised today. Through the general principal of verticality, dynastic populations brought together diverse populations under new auspices. Paradigmatic in the respect was the House of Habsburg. As the tag went, *Bella gerant alii tu felix Austria nube!* Here, in somewhat abbreviated form, is the later dynasts' titulature.[23]

> Emperor of Austria; King of Hungary, of Bohemia, of Dalmatia, Croatia, Slavonia, Galicia, Lodomeria, and Illyria; King of Jerusalem, etc; Archduke of Austria [sic]; Grand Duke of Tuscany and Cracow; Duke of Loth[a]ringia, of Salzburg, Styria, Carinthia, Carniola, and Bukovina; Grand Duke of Transylvania, Margrave of Moravia; Duke of Upper and Lower Silesia, of Modena, Parma,

Piacenza, and Guastella, of Ausschwitz and Sator, of Teschen, Friaul, Ragusa, and Zara; Princely Count of Habsburg and Tyrol, of Kyburg, Görz, and Gradiska; Duke of Trient and Brizen; Margrave of Upper and Lower Lausitz and in Istria; Count of Hohenembs, Feldkirch, Bregenz, Sonnenberg, etc; Lord of Trieste, of Cattaro, and above the Windisch Mark; Great Voyvod of the Voyvodina, Servia, etc.

This, Jászi justly observes, was, "not without a certain comic aspect ... the record of the innumerable marriages, hucksterings and captures of the Habsburgs."

In realms where polygyny was religiously sanctioned, complex systems of tiered concubinage were essential to the integration of the realm. In fact, royal lineages often derived their prestige, aside from any aura of divinity, from, shall we say, miscegenation?[24] For such mixtures were signs of a superordinate status. It is characteristic that there has not been an "English" dynasty ruling in London since the eleventh century (if then); and what "nationality" are we to assign to the Bourbons?[25]

During the seventeenth century, however—for reasons that need not detain us here—the automatic legitimacy of sacral monarchy began its slow decline in Western Europe. In 1649, Charles Stuart was beheaded in the first of the modern world's revolutions, and during the 1650s one of the more important European states was ruled by a plebeian Protector than a king. Yet even in the age of Pope and Addison, Anne Stuart was still healing the sick by the laying on of royal hands, cures committed also by the Bourbons, Louis XV and XVI, in Enlightened France till the end of the *ancien régime*.[26] But after 1789 the principle of Legitimacy had to be loudly and self-consciously defended, and, in the process, "monarchy" became a semi-standardized model. Tennô and Son of Heaven became "Emperors." In far-off Siam Rama V (Chulalongkorn) sent his sons and nephews to the courts of St. Petersburg, London and Berlin to learn the intricacies of the world-model. In 1887, he instituted the requisite principle of succession-by-legal-primogeniture, thus bringing Siam "into line with the 'civilized' monarchies of Europe."[27] The new system brought to the throne in 1910 an erratic homosexual who would certainly have been passed over in an earlier age. However, inter-monarchic approval of his ascension as Rama VI was sealed by the attendance of his coronation of princelings from Britain, Russia, Greece, Sweden, Denmark—and Japan![28]

As late as 1914, dynastic states made up the majority of the membership of the world political system, but, as we shall be noting in detail below, many dynasts had for some time been reaching for a "national" cachet as the old principle of Legitimacy withered silently away. While the armies of Frederick the Great (r. 1740-1786) were heavily staffed by "foreigners," those of his great-nephew Friedrich Wilhelm III (r. 1797-1840) were, as a result of Scharnhorst's, Gneisenau's and Clausewitz's spectacular reforms, exclusively "national-Prussian."[29]

Apprehensions of Time

It would be short-sighted, however, to think of the imagined communities of nations as simply growing out of and replacing religious communities and dynastic realms. Beneath the decline of sacred communities, languages and lineages, a fundamental change was taking place in modes of apprehending the world, which, more than anything else, made it possible to "think" the nation.

To get a feeling for this change, one can profitably turn to the visual representations of the sacred communities, such as the reliefs and stained-glass windows of mediaeval churches, or the paintings of early Italian and Flemish masters. A characteristic feature of such presentations is something misleadingly analogous to "modern dress." The shepherds who have followed the star to the manger where Christ is born bear the features of Burgundian peasants. The Virgin Mary is figured as a Tuscan merchant's daughter. In many paintings the commissioning patron, in full burgher or noble costume, appears kneeling in adoration alongside the shepherds. What seems incongruous today obviously appeared wholly natural to the eyes of mediaeval worshippers. We are faced with a world in which the figuring of imagined reality was overwhelmingly visual and aural. Christendom assumed its universal form through a myriad of specificities and particularities: this relief, that window, this sermon, that tale, this morality play, that relic. While the transEuropean Latin-reading clerisy was one essential element in the structuring of the Christian imagination, the mediation of its conceptions to the illiterate masses, by visual and aural creations, always personal and particular, was no less vital. The humble parish priest, whose forebears and frailties everyone who heard his celebrations knew, was still the direct intermediary between his parishioners and the divine. This juxtaposition of the cosmic-universal and the mundane-particular meant that however vast Christendom might be, and was sensed to be, it manifested itself *variously* to particular Swabian or Andalusian communities as replications of themselves. Figuring the Virgin Mary with "Semitic" features or "first-century" costumes in the restoring spirit of the modern museum was unimaginable because the mediaeval Christian mind had no conception of history as an endless chain of cause and effect or of radical separations between past and present.[30] Bloch observes that people thought they must be near the end of time, in the sense that Christ's second coming could occur at any moment: St.Paul had said that "the day of the Lord cometh like a thief in the night." It was thus natural for the great twelfth-century chronicler Bishop Otto of Freising to refer repeatedly to "we who have been placed at the end of time." Bloch concludes that as soon as mediaeval men "gave themselves up to meditation, nothing was farther from their thoughts than the prospect of along future for a young and vigorous human race."[31]

Auerbach gives an unforgettable sketch of this form of consciousness:[32]

> If an occurrence like the sacrifice of Isaac is interpreted as prefiguring the sacrifice of Christ, so that in the former the latter is as it were announced and promised and the latter "fulfills" ... the former, then a connection is established between two events which are linked neither temporally nor causally—a connection which it is impossible to establish by reason in the horizontal dimension.... It can be established only if both occurrences are vertically linked to Divine Providence, which alone is able to devise such a plan of history and supply the key to its understanding ... the here and now is no longer a mere link in an earthly chain of events, it is *simultaneously* something which has always been, and will be fulfilled in the future; and strictly, in the eyes of God, it is something eternal, something omnitemporal, something already consummated in the realm of fragmentary earthly event.

He rightly stresses that such an idea of *simultaneity* is wholly alien to our own. It views time as something close to what Benjamin calls Messianic time, a simultaneity of past and future in an instantaneous present.[33] In such a view of things, the word "meanwhile" cannot be of real significance.

Our own conception of simultaneity has been a long time in the making, and its emergence is certainly connected, in ways that have yet to be well studied, with the development of the secular sciences. But it is a conception of such fundamental importance that, without taking it fully into account, we will find it difficult to probe the obscure genesis of nationalism. What has come to take the place of the mediaeval conception of simultaneity-along-time is, to borrow again from Benjamin, an idea of "homogeneous, empty time," in which simultaneity is, as it were, transverse, cross-time, marked not by prefiguring and fulfillment, but by temporal coincidence, and measured by clock and calendar.[34]

Why this transformation should be so important for the birth of the imagined community of the nation can best be seen if we consider the basic structure of two forms of imagining which first flowered in Europe in the eighteenth century: the novel and the newspaper.[35] For these forms provided the technical means for "re-presenting" the *kind* of imagined community that is the nation.

Consider first the structure of the old-fashioned novel, a structure typical not only of the masterpieces of Balzac but also of any contemporary dollar-dreadful. It is clearly a device for the presentation of simultaneity in "homogeneous, empty time," or a complex gloss upon the word "meanwhile." Take, for illustrative purposes, a segment of a simple novel-plot, in which a man (A) has a wife (B) and a mistress (C), who in turn has a lover (D). We might imagine a sort of time-chart for this segment as follows:

Time:	I	II	III
Events:	A quarrels with B	A telephones C	D gets drunk in a bar
	C and D make love	B shops	A dines at home with B
		D plays pool	C has an ominous dream

Notice that during this sequence A and D never meet, indeed may not even be aware of each other's existence if C has played her cards right.[36] What then actually links A to D? Two complementary conceptions: First, that they are embedded in "societies" (Wessex, Lubeck, Los Angeles). These societies are sociological entities of such firm and stable reality that their members (A and D) can even be described as passing each other on the street, without ever becoming acquainted, and still be connected.[37] Second, that A and D are embedded in the minds of the omniscient readers. Only they, like God, watch A telephoning C, B shopping, and D playing pool all *at once*. That all these acts are performed at the same clocked calendrical time, but by actors who may be largely unaware of one another, shows the novelty of this imagined world conjured up by the author in his readers' minds.[38]

The idea of a sociological organism moving calendrically through homogeneous, empty time is a precise analogue of the idea of the nation, which also is conceived as a solid community moving steadily down (or up) history.[39] An American will never meet, or even know the names of more than a handful of his 240,000-odd fellow-Americans. He has no idea of what they are up to at any one time. But he has complete confidence in their steady, anonymous, simultaneous activity.

The perspective I am suggesting will perhaps seem less abstract if we turn to inspect briefly four fictions from different cultures and different epochs, all but one of which, nonetheless, are inextricably bound to nationalist movements. In 1887, the Father of Filipino "Nationalism," Jose Rizal, wrote the novel *Noli Me Tangere*, which today is regarded as the greatest achievement of modern Filipino literature. It was also almost the first novel written by an "Indio."[40] Here is how it marvellously begins:[41]

> Towards the end of October, Don Santiago de los Santos, popularly known as Capitan Tiago, was giving a dinner party. Although, contrary to his usual practice, he had announced it only that afternoon, it was already the subject of every conversation in Binondo, in other quarters of the city, and even in [the walled inner city of] Intramuros. In those days Capitan Tiago had the reputa-

tion of a lavish host. It was known that his house, like his country, closed its doors to nothing, except to commerce and to any new or daring idea.

So the news coursed like an electric shock through the community of parasites, spongers, and gatecrashers whom God, in His infinite goodness, created, and so tenderly multiplies in Manila. Some hunted polish for their boots, others looked for collar-buttons and cravats. But one and all were preoccupied with the problem of how to greet their host with the familiarity required to create the appearance of longstanding friendship, or, if need be, to excuse themselves for not having arrived earlier.

The dinner was being given at a house on Anloague Street. Since we do not recall the street number, we shall describe it in such a way that it may still be recognized—that is, if earthquakes have not yet destroyed it. We do not believe that its owner will have had it torn down, since such work is usually left to God or to Nature, which, besides, holds many contracts with our Government.

Extensive comment is surely unnecessary. It should suffice to note that right from the start the image (wholly new to Filipino writing) of a dinner-party being discussed by hundreds of unnamed people, who do not know each other, in quite different parts of Manila, in a particular month of a particular decade, immediately conjures up the imagined community. And in the phrase "a house on Anloague Street" which "we shall describe in such a way that it may still be recognized," the would-be recognizers are we-Filipino-readers. The casual progression of this house from the "interior" time of the novel to the "exterior" time of the [Manila] reader's everyday life gives a hypnotic confirmation of the solidity of a single community, embracing characters, author and readers, moving onward through calendrical time.[42] Notice too the tone. While Rizal has not the faintest idea of his readers' individual identities, he writes to them with an ironical intimacy, as though their relationships with each other are not in the smallest degree problematic.[43]

Nothing gives one a more Foucauldian sense of abrupt discontinuities of consciousness than to compare *Noli* with the most celebrated previous literary work by an "Indio," Francisco Balagtas (Baltazar)'s *Pinagdaanang Buhay ni Florante at ni Laura sa Cahariang Albania* [The Story of Florante and Laura in the Kingdom of Albania], the first printed edition of which dates from 1861, though it may have "been composed as early as 1838."[44] For although Balagtas was still alive when Rizal was born, the world of his masterpiece is in every basic respect foreign to that of *Noli*. Its setting—a fabulous mediaeval Albania—is utterly removed in time and space from the Binondo of the 1880s. Its heroes—Florante, a Christian Albanian nobleman, and his bosom-friend Aladin, a Muslim ("Moro") Persian aristocrat—remind us of the Philippines only by the Christian-Moro linkage. Where Rizal deliberately sprinkles his Spanish prose with Tagalog words for "realistic", satirical, or nationalist effect, Balagtas unselfconsciously mixes Spanish phrases into his Tagalog quatrains simply to heighten the grandeur and sonority of his diction. *Noli* was meant to be read, while *Florante at Laura* was to be sung aloud. Most striking of all is Balagtas's handling of time. As Lumbera notes, "the unravelling of the plot does not follow a chronological order. The story begins *in medias res*, so that the complete story comes to us through a series of speeches that serve as flashbacks."[45] Almost half of the 399 quatrains are accounts of Florante's childhood, student years in Athens, and subsequent military exploits, given by the hero in conversation with Aladin.[46] The "spoken flashback" was for Balagtas the only alternative to a straightforward single-file narrative. If we learn of Florante's and Aladin's "simultaneous" pasts, they are connected by their conversing voices, not by the structure of the epic. How distant this technique is from that of the novel: "In that same spring, while Florante was still studying in Athens, Aladin was expelled from his sovereign's court..." In effect, it never occurs to Balagtas to "situate" his protagonists in "society," or to discuss them with his audience. Nor, aside from the mellifluous flow of Tagalog polysyllables, is there much "Filipino" about his text.[47]

In 1816, seventy years before the writing of *Noli*, José Joaquín Fernandez de Lizardi wrote a novel called *El Periquillo Sarniento* [The Itching Parrot], evidently the first Latin American work in this genre. In the words of one critic, this text is "a ferocious indictment of Spanish administration in Mexico: ignorance, superstition and corruption are seen to be its most notable characteristics."[48] The essential form of this "nationalist" novel is indicated by the following description of its content:[49]

> From the first, [the hero, the Itching Parrot] is exposed to bad influences—ignorant maids inculcate superstitions, his mother indulges his whims, his teachers either have no vocation or no ability to discipline him. And though his father is an intelligent man who wants his son to practise a useful trade rather than swell the ranks of lawyers and parasites, it is Periquillo's over-fond mother who wins the day, sends her son to university and thus ensures that he will learn only superstitious nonsense ... Periquillo remains incorrigibly ignorant despite many encounters with good and wise people. He is unwilling to work or take anything seriously and becomes successively a priest, a gambler, a thief, apprentice to an apothecary, a doctor, clerk in a provincial town ... These episodes *permit the author to describe hospitals, prisons, remote villages, monasteries*, while at the same time driving home one major point—that Spanish government and the education system encourage parasitism and laziness... Periquillo's adventures several times take him among Indians and Negroes ...

Here again we see the "national imagination" at work in the movement of a solitary hero through a sociological landscape of a fixity that fuses the world inside the novel with the world outside. This picaresque *tour d'horison*—hospitals, prisons, remote villages, monasteries, Indians, Negroes—is nonetheless not a *tour du monde*. The horizon is clearly bounded: it is that of colonial Mexico. Nothing assures us of this sociological solidity more than the succession of plurals. For they conjure up a social space full of *comparable* prisons, none in itself of any unique importance, but all representative (in their simultaneous, separate existence) of the oppressiveness of *this* colony.[50] (Contrast prisons in the Bible. They are never imagined as *typical* of this or that society. Each, like the one where Salome was bewitched by John the Baptist, is magically alone.)

Finally, to remove the possibility that, since Rizal and Lizardi both wrote in Spanish, the frameworks we have been studying are somehow "European", here is the opening of *Semarang Hitam* [Black Semarang], a tale by the ill-fated young Indonesian communist-nationalist Mas Marco Kartodikromo,[51] published serially in 1924:[52]

> *It was 7 o'clock, Saturday evening;* young people in Semarang never stayed at home on Saturday night. On this night however nobody was about. Because the heavy day-long rain had made the roads wet and very slippery, all had stayed at home.
>
> For the workers in shops and offices Saturday morning was a time of anticipation—anticipating their leisure and the fun of walking around the city in the evening, but on this night they were to be disappointed—because of lethargy caused by the bad weather and the sticky roads in the kampungs. The main roads usually crammed with all sorts of traffic, the footpaths usually teeming with people, all were deserted. Now and then the crack of a horse-cab's whip could be heard spurring a horse on its way—or the clip-clop of horses' hooves pulling carriages along.
>
> Semarang was deserted. The light from the rows of gas lamps shone straight down on the shining asphalt road. Occasionally the clear light from the gas lamps was dimmed as the wind blew from the east....
>
> A young man was seated on a long rattan lounge reading a newspaper. He was totally engrossed. His occasional anger and at other times smiles were a sure sign of his deep interest in the story. He turned the pages of the newspaper, thinking that perhaps he could find something that would stop him feeling so miserable. All of a sudden he came upon an article entitled:
>
> PROSPERITY
> A destitute vagrant became ill and died on the side of the road from exposure.

The young man was moved by this brief report. He could just imagine the suffering of the poor soul as he lay dying on the side of the road ... One moment he felt an explosive anger well up inside. Another moment he felt pity. Yet another moment his anger was directed at the social system which gave rise to such poverty, while making a small group of people wealthy.

Here, as in *El Periquillo Sarniento*, we are in a world of plurals: shops, offices, carriages, kampungs, and gas lamps. As in the case of *Noli*, we-the-Indonesian-readers are plunged immediately into calendrical time and a familiar landscape; some of us may well have walked those "sticky" Semarang roads. Once again, a solitary hero is juxtaposed to a socioscape described in careful, *general* detail. But there is also something new: a hero who is never named, but who is frequently referred to as "*our* young man." Precisely the clumsiness and literary naivety of the text confirm the unselfconscious "sincerity" of this pronominal adjective. Neither Marco nor his readers have any doubts about the reference. If in the jocular-sophisticated fiction of eighteenth- and nineteenth-century Europe the trope "our hero" merely underlines an authorial play with a(ny) reader, Marco's "our young man," not least in its novelty, *means* a young man who belongs to the collective body of readers of *Indonesian*, and thus, implicitly, an embryonic Indonesian "imagined community." Notice that Marco feels no need to specify this community by name: it is already there. (Even if polylingual Dutch colonial censors could join his readership, they are excluded from this "ourness," as can be seen from the fact that the young man's anger is directed at "the," not "our," social system.)

Finally, the imagined community is confirmed by the doubleness of our reading about our young man reading. He does not find the corpse of the destitute vagrant by the side of a sticky Semarang road, but imagines it from the print in a newspaper.[53] Nor does he care the slightest who the dead vagrant individually was: he thinks of the representative body, not the personal life.

It is fitting that in *Semarang Hitam* a newspaper appears embedded in fiction, for, if we now turn to the newspaper as cultural product, we will be struck by its profound fictiveness. What is the essential literary convention of the newspaper? If we were to look at a sample front page of, say, *The New York Times*, we might find there stories about Soviet dissidents, famine in Mali, a gruesome murder, a coup in Iraq, the discovery of a rare fossil in Zimbabwe, and a speech by Mitterrand. Why are these events so juxtaposed? What connects them to each other? Not sheer caprice. Yet obviously most of them happen independently, without the actors being aware of each other or of what the others are up to. The arbitrariness of their inclusion and juxtaposition (a later edition will substitute a baseball triumph for Mitterrand) shows that the linkage between them is imagined.

This imagined linkage derives from two obliquely related sources. The first is simply calendrical coincidence. The date at the top of the newspaper, the single most important emblem on it, provides the essential connection—the steady onward clocking of homogeneous, empty time.[54] Within that time, "the world" ambles sturdily ahead. The sign for this: if Mali disappears from the pages of *The New York Times* after two days of famine reportage, for months on end, readers do not for a moment imagine that Mali has disappeared or that famine has wiped out all its citizens. The novelistic format of the newspaper assures them that somewhere out there the "character" Mali moves along quietly, awaiting its next reappearance in the plot.

The second source of imagined linkage lies in the relationship between the newspaper, as a form of book, and the market. It has been estimated that in the 40-odd years between the publication of the Gutenberg Bible and the close of the fifteenth century, more than 20,000,000 printed volumes were produced in Europe.[55] Between 1500 and 1600, the number manufactured had reached between 150,000,000 and 200,000,000.[56] "From early on ... the printing shops looked more like modern workshops than the monastic workrooms of the Middle Ages. In 1455, Fust and Schoeffer were already running a business geared to standardised production, and twenty years later large printing concerns were operating everywhere in all [sic] Europe."[57] In a rather special sense, the book was the first modern-style mass-produced industrial commodity.[58] The sense I have in mind can be shown if we compare the book to other early industrial products, such as textiles, bricks, or sugar. For these commodities are *measured* in mathematical amounts (pounds or loads or pieces). A pound of sugar is simply a quantity, a convenient load, not an object in itself. The book, however—and here it prefigures the durables of our time—is a distinct, self-contained object, exactly reproduced on a large scale.[59] One pound of sugar flows into the next; each book has its own eremitic self-sufficiency. (Small wonder that libraries, personal collections of mass-produced commodities, were already a familiar sight, in urban centres like Paris, by the sixteenth century.)[60]

In this perspective, the newspaper is merely an "extreme form" of the book, a book sold on a colossal scale, but of ephemeral popularity. Might we say: one-day best-sellers?[61] The obsolescence of the newspaper on the morrow of its printing—curious that one of the earlier mass-produced commodities should so prefigure the inbuilt obsolescence of modern durables—nonetheless, for just this reason, creates this extraordinary mass ceremony: the almost precisely simultaneous consumption ("imagining") of the newspaper-as-fiction. We know that particular morning and evening editions will overwhelmingly be consumed between this hour and that, only on this day, not that. (Contrast sugar, the use of which proceeds in an unclocked, continuous flow; it may go bad, but it does not go out of date.) The significance of this mass ceremony—Hegel observed that newspapers serve modern man as a substitute for morning prayers—is paradoxical. It is performed in silent privacy, in the lair of the skull.[62] Yet each communicant is well aware that the ceremony he performs is being replicated simultaneously by thousands (or millions) of others of whose existence he is confident, yet of whose identity he has not the slightest notion. Furthermore, this ceremony is incessantly repeated at daily or half-daily intervals throughout the calendar. What more vivid figure for the secular, historically clocked, imagined community can be envisioned?[63] At the same time, the newspaper-reader, observing exact replicas of his own paper being consumed by his subway, barbershop, or residential neighbours, is continually reassured that the imagined world is visibly rooted in everyday life. As with *Noli Me Tangere*, fiction seeps quietly and continuously into reality, creating that remarkable confidence of community in anonymity which is the hallmark of modern nations.

Before proceeding to a discussion of the specific origins of nationalism, it may be useful to recapitulate the main propositions put forward thus far. Essentially, I have been arguing that the very possibility of imagining the nation only arose historically when, and where, three fundamental cultural conceptions, all of great antiquity, lost their axiomatic grip on men's minds. The first of these was the idea that a particular script-language offered privileged access to ontological truth, precisely because it was an inseparable part of that truth. It was this idea that called into being the great transcontinental sodalities of Christendom, the Islamic Ummah, and the rest. Second was the belief that society was naturally organized around and under high centres monarchs who were persons apart from other human beings and who ruled by some form of cosmological (divine) dispensation. Human loyalties were necessarily hierarchical and centripetal because the ruler, like the sacred script, was a node of access to being and inherent in it. Third was a conception of temporality in which cosmology and history were indistinguishable, the origins of the world and of men essentially identical. Combined, these ideas rooted human lives firmly in the very nature of things, giving certain meaning to the everyday fatalities of existence (above all death, loss, and servitude) and offering, in various ways, redemption from them.

The slow, uneven decline of these interlinked certainties, first in Western Europe, later elsewhere, under the impact of economic change, "discoveries" (social and scientific), and the development of increasingly rapid communications, drove a harsh wedge between cosmology and history. No surprise then that the search was on, so to speak, for a new way of linking fraternity, power and time meaningfully together. Nothing perhaps more precipitated this search, nor made it more fruitful, than print-capitalism, which made it possible for rapidly growing numbers of people to think about themselves, and to relate themselves to others, in profoundly new ways.

Notes

1 The ancient Greeks had cenotaphs, but for specific, known individuals whose bodies, for one reason or another, could not be retrieved for regular burial. I owe this information to my Byzantinist colleague Judith Herrin.

2 Consider, for example, these remarkable tropes: 1. "The long grey line has never failed us. Were you to do so, a million ghosts in olive drab, in brown khaki, in blue and grey, would rise from their white crosses, thundering those magic words: Duty, honour, country." 2. "My estimate of [the American man-at-arms] was formed on the battlefield many, many years ago, and has never changed. I regarded him then, as I regard him now, as one of the world's noblest figures; not only as one of the finest military characters, but also as one of the most stainless [sic].... He belongs to history as furnishing one of the greatest examples of successful patriotism [sic]. He belongs to posterity as the instructor of future generations in the principles of liberty and freedom. He belongs to the present, to us, by his virtues and his achievements." Douglas MacArthur, "Duty, Honour, Country," Address to the U.S. Military Academy, West Point, May 12, 1962, in his *A Soldier Speaks*, pp. 354 and 357.

3 Cf. Régis Debray. "Marxism and the National Question," *New Left Review* 105 (September-October 1977), p. 29. In the course of doing fieldwork in Indonesia in the 1960s I was struck by the calm refusal of many Muslims to accept the ideas of Darwin. At first I interpreted this refusal as obscurantism. Subsequently I came to see it as an honourable attempt to be consistent: the doctrine of evolution was simply) not compatible with the teachings of Islam. What are we to make of a scientific materialism which formally accepts the findings of physics about matter, yet makes so little effort to link these findings with the class struggle, revolution, or whatever. Does not the abyss between protons and the proletariat conceal an unacknowledged metaphysical conception of man? But see the refreshing texts of Sebastiano Timpanaro, *On Materialism* and *The Freudian Slip*, and Raymond Williams' thoughtful response to them in "Timpanaro's Materialist Challenge," *New Left Review*, 109 (May-June 1978), pp. 3-17.

4 The late President Sukarno always spoke with complete sincerity of the 350 years of colonialism that his "Indonesia" had endured, although the very concept "Indonesia" is a twentieth-century invention, and most of today's Indonesia was only conquered by the Dutch between 1850 and 1910. Preeminent among contemporary Indonesia's national heroes is the early nineteenth-century Javanese Prince Diponegoro, although the Prince's own memoirs show that he intended to "conquer [not liberate!] *Java*," rather than expel "the Dutch." Indeed, he clearly had no concept of "the Dutch" as a collectivity. See Harry J. Benda and John A. Larkin, eds., *The World of Southeast Asia*, p. 158; and Ann Kumar, "Diponegoro (1778?-1855)," *Indonesia*,13 (April 1972), p. 103. Emphasis added. Similarly

Kemal Atatürk named one of his state banks the Eti Banka (Hittite Bank) and another the Sumerian Bank. (Seton-Watson, *Nations and States*, p. 259). These banks flourish today, and there is no reason to doubt that many Turks, possibly not excluding Kemal himself, seriously saw, and see, in the Hittites and Sumerians their Turkish forebears. Before laughing too hard, we should remind ourselves of Arthur and Boadicea, and ponder the commercial success of Tolkien's mythographies.

5 Hence the equanimity with which Sinicized Mongols and Manchus were accepted as Sons of Heaven.

6 John Lynch, *The Spanish-American Revolutions, 1808-1826*, p. 260. Emphasis added.

7 Church Greek seems not to have achieved the status of a truth-language. The reasons for this "failure" are various, but one key factor was certainly the fact that Greek remained a *living* demotic speech (unlike Latin) in much of the Eastern Empire. This insight I owe to Judith Herrin.

8 Nicholas Brakespear held the office of pontiff between 1154 and 1159 under the name Adrian IV.

9 Marc Bloch reminds us that "the majority of lords and many great barons [in mediaeval times] were administrators incapable of studying personally a report or an account." *Feudal Society*, I, p. 81.

10 This is not to say that the illiterate did not read. What they read, however, was not words but the visible world. "In the eyes of all who were capable of reflection the material world was scarcely more than a sort of mask, behind which took place all the really important things; it seemed to them also a language, intended to express by signs a more profound reality." Ibid. p. 83.

11 Erich Auerbach, *Mimesis*, p. 282.

12 Marco Polo, *The Travels of Marco Polo*, pp. 158-59. Emphases added. Notice that, though kissed, the Evangel is not read.

13 *The Travels of Marco Polo*, p. 152.

14 Henri de Montesquieu, *Persian Letters*, p. 81. The *Lettres Persanes* first appeared in 1721.

15 Bloch, *Feudal Society*, I, p. 77. Emphasis added.

16 Lucien Febvre and Henri-Jean Martin, *The Coming of the Book*, pp. 248-49.

17 Ibid., p. 321.

18 Ibid., p. 330.

19 Ibid., pp. 331-32.

20 Ibid., pp. 232-33. The original French is more modest and historically exact: "Tandis que l'on édite de moins en moins d'ouvrages en latin, et une proportion toujours plus grande de textes en langue nationale, le commerce du livre se morcelle en Europe." *L'Apparition du Livre*, p. 356.

21 Notice the displacement in rulers' nomenclature that corresponds to this transformation. Schoolchildren remember monarchs by their first names (what *was* William the Conqueror's surname?), presidents by their last (what was *Ebert's* Christian name?). In a world of citizens, all of whom are theoretically eligible for

the presidency, the limited pool of "Christian" names makes them inadequate as specifying designators. In monarchies, however, where rule is reserved for a single surname, it is necessarily "Christian" names, with numbers, or sobriquets, that supply the requisite distinctions.

22 We may here note in passing that Nairn is certainly correct in describing the 1707 Act of Union between England and Scotland as a "patrician bargain," in the sense that the union's architects were aristocratic politicians. (See his lucid discussion in *The Break-up of Britain*, pp. 136f.). Still, it is difficult to imagine such a bargain being struck between the aristocracies of two republics. The conception of a United *Kingdom* was surely the crucial mediating element that made the deal possible.

23 Oscar Jászi, *The Dissolution of the Habsburg Monarchy*, p. 34.

24 Most notably in pre-modern Asia. But the same principle was at work in monogamous Christian Europe. In 1910, one Otto Forst put out his *Ahnentafel Seiner Kaiserlichen und Koniglichen Hoheit des durchlauchtigsten Hern Erzherzogs Franz Ferdinand*, listing 2,047 of the soon-to-be-assassinated Archduke's ancestors. They included 1,486 Germans, 124 French, 196 Italians, 89 Spaniards, 52 Poles, 47 Danes, 20 Englishmen/women, as well as four other nationalities. This "curious document" is cited in ibid., p.136, no.1. I can not resist quoting here Franz Joseph's wonderful reaction to the news of his erratic heir-apparent's murder: "In this manner a superior power has restored that order which I unfortunately was unable to maintain" (ibid., p. 125).

25 Gellner stresses the typical foreignness of dynasties, but interprets the phenomenon too narrowly: local aristocrats prefer an alien monarch because he will not take sides in their internal rivalries. *Thought and Change*, p. 136.

26 March Bloch, *Les Rois Thaumaturges*, pp. 390 and 398-99.

27 Noel A. Battye, "The Military, Government and Society in Siam, 1868-1910," PhD thesis, Cornell 1974, p. 270.

28 Stephen Greene, "Thai Government and Administration in the Reign of Rama VI (1910-1925)," PhD thesis, University of London 1971, p. 92.

29 More than 1,000 of the 7,000-8,000 men on the Prussian Army's officer list in 1806 were foreigners. "Middle-class Prussians were outnumbered by foreigners in their own army; this lent colour to the saying that Prussia was not a country that had a army, but an army that had a country. In 1798, Prussian reformers had demanded reduction by one half of the number of foreigners, who still amounted to about 50% of the privates...." Alfred Vagts, *A History of Militarism*, pp. 64 and 85.

30 For us the idea of "modern dress," a metaphorical equivalencing of past with present, is a backhanded recognition of their fatal separation.

31 Bloch, *Feudal Society*, I, pp. 84-86.

32 Auerbach, *Mimesis*, p. 64. Emphasis added. Compare St. Augustine's description of the Old Testament as "the shadow of [i.e. cast backwards by] the future." Cited in Bloch, *Feudal Society*, I, p. 90.

33 Walter Benjamin, *Illuminations*, p. 265.

34 Ibid., p. 263. So deep-lying is this new idea that one could argue that every essential modern conception is based on a conception of "meanwhile."

35 While the *Princesse de Clèves* had already appeared in 1678, the era of Richardson, Defoe and Fielding is the early eighteenth century. The origins of the modern newspaper lie in the Dutch gazettes of the late seventeenth century but the newspaper only became a general category of printed matter after 1700. Febvre and Martin, *The Coming of the Book*, p. 197.

36 Indeed, the plot's grip may *depend* at Times I, II, and III on A, B, C and D not knowing what the others are up to.

37 This polyphony decisively marks off the modern novel even from so brilliant a forerunner as Petronius's *Satyricon*. Its narrative proceeds single file. If Encolpius bewails his young lover's faithlessness, we are not simultaneously shown Gito in bed with Ascyltus.

38 In this context it is rewarding to compare any historical novel with documents or narratives from the period fictionalized.

39 Nothing better shows the immersion of the novel in homogeneous, empty time than the absence of those prefatory genealogies, often ascending to the origin of man, which are so characteristic a feature of ancient chronicles, legends, and holy books.

40 Rizal wrote this novel in the colonial language (Spanish), which was then the lingua franca of the ethnically diverse Eurasian and native elites. Alongside the novel appeared also for the first time a "nationalist" press, not only in Spanish but in such "ethnic" languages as Tagalog and Ilocano. See Leopoldo Y. Yabes, "The Modern Literature of the Philippines," pp. 287-302, in Pierre-Bernard Lafont and Denys Lombard (eds), *Littératures Contemporaines de l'Asie du Sud-Est*.

41 José Rizal, *Noli Me Tangere* (Manila: Instituto Nacional de Historia, 1978), p.1. My translation. At the time of the original publication of *Imagined Communities*, I had no command of Spanish, and was thus unwittingly led to rely on the instructively corrupt translation of Leon Maria Guerrero.

42 Notice, for example, Rizal's subtle shift, in the same sentence, from the past tense of "created" (*crió*) to the all-of-us-together present tense of "multiplies" (*multiplica*).

43 The obverse side of the readers' anonymous obscurity was/is the author's immediate celebrity. As we shall see, this obscurity/celebrity has everything to do with the spread of print-capitalism. As early as 1593 energetic Dominicans had published in Manila the *Doctrina Christiana*. But for centuries thereafter print remained under tight ecclesiastical control. Liberalization only began in the 1860s. See Bienvenido L. Lumbera, *Tagalog Poetry 1570-1898: Tradition and Influences in its Development*, pp. 35, 93.

44 Ibid., p. 115.

45 Ibid., p. 120.

46 The technique is similar to that of Homer, so ably discussed by Auerbach, *Mimesis*, ch. 1 ("Odysseus' Scar").

47 "Paalam Albaniang pinamamayanan
ng casama, t, lupit, bangis caliluhan,
acong tangulan mo, i, cusa mang pinatay
sa iyo, i, malaqui ang panghihinayang."

"Farewell, Albania, kingdom now
of evil, cruelty, brutishness and deceit!
I, your defender, whom you now murder
Nevertheless lament the fate that has befallen you."

This famous stanza has sometimes been interpreted as a veiled statement of Fil-ipino patriotism, but Lumbera convincingly shows such an interpretation to be an anachronistic gloss. *Tagalog Poetry*, p. 125. The translation is Lumbera's. I have slightly altered his Tagalog text to conform to a 1973 edition of the poem based on the 1861 imprint.

48 Jean Franco, *An Introduction to Spanish-American Literature*, p. 34.

49 Ibid., pp. 35-36. Emphasis added.

50 This movement of a solitary hero through an adamantine social landscape is typ-ical of many early (anti-)colonial novels.

51 After a brief, meteoric career as a radical journalist, Marco was interned by the Dutch colonial authorities in Boven Digul, one of the world's earliest concentra-tion camps, deep in the interior swamps of western New Guinea. There he died in 1932, after six years confinement. Henri Chambert-Loir, "Mas Marco Kartodikro-mo (c. 1890-1932) ou L'Education Politique," p. 208, in *Littératures contempo-raines de l'Asie du Sud-Est*. A brilliant recent full-length account of Marco's career can be found in Takashi Shiraishi, *An Age in Motion: Popular Radicalism in Java, 1912-1926*, chapters 2-5 and 8.

52 As translated by Paul Tickell in his *Three Early Indonesian Short Stories by Mas Marco Kartodikromo (c. 1890-1932)*, p. 7. Emphasis added.

53 In 1924, a close friend and political ally of Marco published a novel titled *Rasa Merdika* [Feeling Free/The Feel of Freedom]. Of the hero of this novel (which he wrongly attributes to Marco) Chambert-Loir writes that "he has no idea of the meaning of the word 'socialism': nonetheless he feels a profound malaise in the face of the social organization that surrounds him and he feels the need to enlarge his horizons by two methods: *travel and reading*." ("Mas Marco", p. 208. Emphasis added.) The Itching Parrot has moved to Java and the twentieth century.

54 Reading a newspaper is like reading a novel whose author has abandoned any thought of a coherent plot.

55 Febvre and Martin, *The Coming of the Book*, p. 186. This amounted to no less than 35,000 editions produced in no fewer than 236 towns. As early as 1480, presses existed in more than 110 towns, of which 50 were in today's Italy, 30 in Germany, 9 in France, 8 each in Holland and Spain, 5 each in Belgium and Switzerland, 4 in England, 2 in Bohemia, and 1 in Poland. "From that date it may be said of Europe that the printed book was in universal use." (p. 182).

56 Ibid., p. 262. The authors comment that by the sixteenth century books were read-ily available to anyone who could read.

57 The great Antwerp publishing house of Plantin controlled, early in the sixteenth century, 24 presses with more than 100 workers in each shop. Ibid., p. 125.

58 This is one point solidly made amidst the vagaries of Marshall McLuhan's *Gutenberg Galaxy* (p. 125). One might add that if the book market was dwarfed by the markets in other commodities, its strategic role in the dissemination of ideas nonetheless made it of central importance to the development of modern Europe.

59 The principle here is more important than the scale. Until the nineteenth century, editions were still relatively small. Even Luther's Bible, an extraordinary best-seller, had only a 4,000-copy first edition. The unusually large first edition of Diderot's *Encyclopedie* numbered no more than 4,250. The average eighteenth century run was less than 2,000. Febvre and Martin, *The Coming of the Book*, pp, 218-20. At the same time, the book was always distinguishable from other durables by its inherently limited market. Anyone with money can buy Czech cars; only Czech-readers will buy Czech-language books. The importance of this distinction will be considered below.

60 Furthermore, as early as the late fifteenth century the Venetian publisher Aldus had pioneered the portable "pocket edition."

61 As the case of *Semarang Hitam* shows, the two kinds of best-sellers used to be more closely linked than they are today. Dickens too serialized his popular novels in popular newspapers.

62 "Printed materials encouraged silent adherence to causes whose advocates could not be located in any one parish and who addressed an invisible public from afar." Elizabeth L. Eisenstein, "Some Conjectures about the Impact of Printing on Western Society and Thought," *Journal of Modern History*, 40:1 (March 1968), p. 42.

63 Writing of the relationship between the material anarchy of middle-class society and an abstract political state-order, Nairn observes that "the representative mechanism converted real class inequality into the abstract egalitarianism of citizens, individual egotisms into an impersonal collective will, what would otherwise be chaos into a new state legitimacy." *The Break-up of Britain*, p. 24. No doubt. But the representative mechanism (elections?) is a rare and moveable feast. The generation of the impersonal will is, I think, better sought in the diurnal regularities of the imagining life.

Bibliography

Auerbach, Erich. 1957. *Mimesis: The Representation of Reality in Western Literature.* Willard Trask, trans. Garden City, NY: Doubleday Anchor.

Battye, Noel A. 1974. "The Military, Government and Society in Siam, 1868-1910," PhD thesis, Cornell University.

Benda, Harry J., and John A. Larkin, eds. 1967. *The World of Southeast Asia.* New York: Harper and Row.

Benjamin, Walter. 1973. *Illuminations.* London: Fontana.

Bloch, Marc. 1961. *Feudal Society* (Vol. I). I.A. Manyon, trans. Chicago: University of Chicago Press.

— 1924. *Les Rois Thaumaturges*. Strasbourg: Librairie Istra

Chambert-Loir, Henri. 1974. "Mas Marco Kartodikromo (c. 1890-1932) ou L'Education Politique," In *Littératures contemporaines de l'Asie du Sud-Est*. Pierre Bernard Lafont and Denys Lombard, eds. Pp. 203-214. Paris: L'Asiathèque.

Debray, Régis. 1977. "Marxism and the National Question." *New Left Review* 105: 25-41.

Eisenstein, Elizabeth L. 1968. "Some Conjectures about the Impact of Printing on Western Society and Thought: A Preliminary Report." *Journal of Modern History* 40,1: 1-56.

Febvre, Lucien and Henri-Jean Martin. 1976. *The Coming of the Book: The Impact of Printing, 1450-1800*. London: New Left Books.

Franco, Jean. 1969. *An Introduction to Spanish-American Literature*. Cambridge: Cambridge University Press.

Gellner, Ernest. 1964. *Thought and Change*. London: Weidenfeld and Nicholson.

Greene, Stephen. 1971. "Thai Government and Administration in the Reign of Rama VI (1910-1925)," PhD thesis, University of London.

Jászi, Oscar. 1929. *The Dissolution of the Habsburg Monarchy*. Chicago: University of Chicago Press.

Kumar, Ann. 1972. "Diponegoro (1778?-1855)," *Indonesia* 13: 69-118.

Lumbera, Bienvenido L. 1986. *Tagalog Poetry 1570-1898, Tradition and Influences in its Development*. Quezon City: Ateneo de Manila Press.

Lynch, John. 1973. *The Spanish-American Revolutions, 1808-1826*. New York: Norton.

MacArthur, Douglas. 1965. *A Soldier Speaks*. New York: Praeger

McLuhan, Marshall. 1962. *The Gutenberg Galaxy: The Making of Typographic Man*. Toronto: University of Toronto Press.

Montesquieu, Henri de. 1973. *Persian Letters*. C.J. Betts, trans. Harmondsworth: Penguin.

Nairn, Tom. 1977. *The Break-Up of Britain*. London: New Left Books

Polo, Marco. 1946. *The Travels of Marco Polo*. William Marsden, trans. and ed. London and New York: Everyman's Library.

Rizal, José. 1978. *Noli Me Tangere*. Manila: Instituto Nacional de Historia.

Seton-Watson, Hugh. 1977. *Nations and States: An Enquiry into the Origins of Nations and the Politics of Nationalism.* Boulder, Colorado: Westview Press.

Shiraishi, Takashi. 1990. *An Age in Motion: Popular Radicalism in Java, 1912-1926.* Ithaca: Cornell University Press.

Tickell, Paul. 1981. *Three Early Indonesian Short Stories by Mas Marco Kartodikromo (c. 1890-1932).* Melbourne: Monash University, Center of Southeast Asian Studies.

Timpanaro, Sebastiano. 1975. *On Materialism.* London: New Left Books.

—1976. *The Freudian Slip.* London: New Left Books.

Vagts, Alfred. 1959. *A History of Militarism, Civilian and Military.* Rev. ed. New York: The Free Press.

Williams, Raymond. 1978. "Timpanaro's Materialist Challenge," *New Left Review* 109: 3-17.

Yabes, Leopoldo Y. 1974. "The Modern Literature of the Philippines." In *Littératures Contemporaines de l'Asie du Sud-Est.* Pierre-Bernard Lafont and Denys Lombard, eds. pp. 287-302. Paris: L'Asiathèque.

Study Questions

1. What was the relation of "sacred silent languages" to the rise of nationalism in early modern Europe?

2. How does Anderson characterize the role of print capitalism in the rise of the imagined community?

3. How did the novel and newspapers affect vernacular perceptions of time in early modern Europe?

Further Readings

Anderson, Benedict. 1996. Introduction. *Mapping the Nation.* Ed. Gopal Balakrishan. London and New York: Verso Books.

—. 1998. *The Spectre of Comparisons: Nationalism, Southeast Asia, and the World.* London and New York: Verso Press.

34

Introduction: Partial Truths
[*Writing Culture*]

JAMES CLIFFORD

Interdisciplinary work, so much discussed these days, is not about con-
fronting already constituted disciplines (none of which, in fact, is willing
to let itself go). To do something interdisciplinary it's not enough to choose
a "subject" (a theme) and gather around it two or three sciences. Inter-
disciplinarity consists in creating a new object that belongs to no one.
Roland Barthes, "Jeunes Chercheurs"

You'll need more tables than you think.
  Elenore Smith Bowen, advice for fieldworkers, in Return to Laughter

Our frontispiece shows Stephen Tyler, one of this volume's contributors, at
work in India in 1963. The ethnographer is absorbed in writing—taking dictation? fleshing out an interpretation? recording an important observation? dash-
ing off a poem? Hunched over in the heat, he has draped a wet cloth over his
glasses. His expression is obscured. An interlocutor looks over his shoulder—
with boredom? patience? amusement? In this image the ethnographer hovers at
the edge of the frame—faceless, almost extraterrestrial, a hand that writes. It is
not the usual portrait of anthropological fieldwork. We are more accustomed to
pictures of Margaret Mead exuberantly playing with children in Manus or
questioning villagers in Bali. Participant-observation, the classic formula for
ethnographic work, leaves little room for texts. But still, somewhere lost in his
account of fieldwork among the Mbuti pygmies—running along jungle paths,
sitting up at night singing, sleeping in a crowded leaf hut—Colin Turnbull
mentions that he lugged around a typewriter.

  In Bronislaw Malinowski's *Argonauts of the Western Pacific*, where a photograph of the ethnographer's tent among Kiriwinan dwellings is prominently
displayed, there is no revelation of the tent's interior. But in another photo,
carefully posed, Malinowski recorded himself writing at a table. (The tent flaps

are pulled back; he sits in profile, and some Trobrianders stand outside, observing the curious rite.) This remarkable picture was only published two years ago—a sign of our times, not his.[1] We begin, not with participant-observation or with cultural texts (suitable for interpretation), but with writing, the making of texts. No longer a marginal, or occulted, dimension, writing has emerged as central to what anthropologists do both in the field and thereafter. The fact that it has not until recently been portrayed or seriously discussed reflects the persistence of an ideology claiming transparency of representation and immediacy of experience. Writing reduced to method: keeping good field notes, making accurate snaps, "writing up" results.

The essays collected here assert that this ideology has crumbled. They see culture as composed of seriously contested codes and representations; they assume that the poetic and the political are inseparable, that science is in, not above, historical and linguistic processes. They assume that academic and literary genres interpenetrate and that the writing of cultural descriptions is properly experimental and ethical. Their focus on text making and rhetoric serves to highlight the constructed, artificial nature of cultural accounts. It undermines overly transparent modes of authority, and it draws attention to the historical predicament of ethnography, the fact that it is always caught up in the invention, not the representation, of cultures (Wagner 1975). As will soon be apparent, the range of issues raised is not literary in any traditional sense. Most of the essays, while focusing on textual practices, reach beyond texts to contexts of power, resistance, institutional constraint, and innovation.

Ethnography's tradition is that of Herodotus and of Montesquieu's Persian. It looks obliquely at all collective arrangements, distant or nearby. It makes the familiar strange, the exotic quotidian. Ethnography cultivates an engaged clarity like that urged by Virginia Woolf: "Let us never cease from thinking—what is this 'civilization' in which we find ourselves? What are these ceremonies and why should we take part in them? What are these professions and why should we make money out of them? Where in short is it leading us, the procession of the sons of educated men?" (1936: 62-63). Ethnography is actively situated *between* powerful systems of meaning. It poses its questions at the boundaries of civilizations, cultures, classes, races, and genders. Ethnography decodes and recodes, telling the grounds of collective order and diversity, inclusion and exclusion. It describes processes of innovation and structuration, and is itself part of these processes.

Ethnography is an emergent interdisciplinary phenomenon. Its authority and rhetoric have spread to many fields where "culture" is a newly problematic object of description and critique. The present book, though beginning with fieldwork and its texts, opens onto the wider practice of writing about, against, and among cultures. This blurred purview includes, to name only a few developing perspectives, historical ethnography (Emmanuel Le Roy Ladurie, Natalie Davis, Carlo Ginzburg), cultural poetics (Stephen Greenblatt), cultural criticism (Hayden White, Edward Said, Fredric Jameson), the analysis of implicit knowledge and everyday practices (Pierre Bourdieu, Michel de Certeau), the critique of hegemonic structures of feeling (Raymond Williams), the study of scientific communities (following Thomas Kuhn), the semiotics of exotic worlds and fantastic spaces (Tzvetan Todorov, Louis Marin), and all those studies that focus on meaning systems, disputed traditions, or cultural artifacts.

This complex interdisciplinary area, approached here from the starting point of a crisis in anthropology, is changing and diverse. Thus I do not want to impose a false unity on the exploratory essays that follow. Though sharing a general sympathy for approaches combining poetics, politics, and history, they frequently disagree. Many of the contributions fuse literary theory and ethnography. Some probe the limits of such approaches, stressing the dangers of estheticism and the constraints of institutional power. Others enthusiastically advocate experimental forms of writing. But in their different ways they all analyze past and present practices out of a commitment to future possibilities. They see ethnographic writing as changing, inventive: "History," in William Carlos Williams's words, "that should be a left hand to us, as of a violinist."

"Literary" approaches have recently enjoyed some popularity in the human sciences. In anthropology influential writers such as Clifford Geertz, Victor Turner, Mary Douglas, Claude Lévi-Strauss, Jean Duvignaud, and Edmund Leach, to mention only a few, have shown an interest in literary theory and practice. In their quite different ways they have blurred the boundary separating art from science. Nor is theirs a new attraction. Malinowski's authorial identifications (Conrad, Frazer) are well known. Margaret Mead, Edward Sapir, and Ruth Benedict saw themselves as both anthropologists and literary artists. In Paris surrealism and professional ethnography regularly exchanged both ideas and personnel. But until recently literary influences have been held at a distance from the "rigorous" core of the discipline. Sapir and Benedict had, after all, to hide their poetry from the scientific gaze of Franz Boas. And though ethnographers have often been called novelists manqué (especially those who write a little too well), the notion that literary procedures pervade any work of cultural representation is a recent idea in the discipline. To a growing number, however, the "literariness" of anthropology—and especially of ethnography—appears as much more than a matter of good writing or distinctive style.[2] Literary processes—metaphor, figuration, narrative—affect the ways cultural phenomena are registered, from the first jotted "observations," to the completed book, to the ways these configurations "make sense" in determined acts of reading.[3]

It has long been asserted that scientific anthropology is also an "art," that ethnographies have literary qualities. We often hear that an author writes with style, that certain descriptions are vivid or convincing (should not every accurate description be convincing?). A work is deemed evocative or artfully composed in addition to being factual; expressive, rhetorical functions are conceived its decorative or merely as ways to present an objective analysis or description more effectively. Thus the facts of the matter may be kept separate, at least in principle, from their means of communication. But the literary or rhetorical dimensions of ethnography can no longer be so easily compartmentalized. They are active at every level of cultural science. Indeed, the very notion of a "literary" approach to a discipline, "anthropology," is seriously misleading.

The present essays do not represent a tendency or perspective within a coherent "anthropology" (*pace* Wolf 1980). The "four-field" definition of the discipline, of which Boas was perhaps the last virtuoso, included physical (or biological) anthropology, archaeology, cultural (or social) anthropology, and linguistics. Few today can seriously claim that these fields share a unified approach or object, though the dream persists, thanks largely to institutional arrangements. The essays in this volume occupy a new space opened up by the disintegration of "Man" as *telos* for a whole discipline, and they draw on recent developments in the fields of textual criticism, cultural history, semiotics, hermeneutic philosophy, and psychoanalysis. Some years ago, in a trenchant essay, Rodney Needham surveyed the theoretical incoherence, tangled roots, impossible bedfellows, and divergent specializations that seemed to be leading to academic anthropology's intellectual disintegration. He suggested with ironic equanimity that the field might soon be redistributed among a variety of neighboring disciplines. Anthropology in its present form would undergo "an iridescent metamorphosis" (1970: 46). The present essays are part of the metamorphosis.

But if they are post-anthropological, they are also post-literary. Michel Foucault (1973), Michel de Certeau (1983), and Terry Eagleton (1983) have recently argued that "literature" itself is a transient category. Since the seventeenth century, they suggest, Western science has excluded certain expressive modes from its legitimate repertoire: rhetoric (in the name of "plain," transparent signification), fiction (in the name of fact), and subjectivity (in the name of objectivity). The qualities eliminated from science were localized in the category of "literature." Literary texts were deemed to be metaphoric and allegorical, composed of inventions rather than observed facts; they allowed a wide latitude to the emotions, speculations, and subjective "genius" of their authors. De Certeau notes that the fictions of literary language were scientifically condemned (and esthetically appreciated) for lacking "univocity," the purportedly unambiguous accounting of natural science and professional history. In this schema, the discourse of literature and fiction is inherently unstable; it "plays on the stratification of meaning; it narrates one thing in order to tell something else; it delineates itself in a language from which it continuously draws effects of meaning that cannot be circumscribed or checked" (1983: 128). This discourse, repeatedly banished from science, but with uneven success, is incurably figurative and polysemous. (Whenever its effects begin to be felt too openly, a scientific text will appear "literary"; it will seem to be using too many metaphors, to be relying on style, evocation, and so on.)[4]

By the nineteenth century, literature had emerged as a bourgeois institution closely allied with "culture" and "art." Raymond Williams (1966) shows how this special, refined sensibility functioned as a kind of court of appeals in response to the perceived dislocations and vulgarity of industrial, class society. Literature and art were, in effect, circumscribed zones in which nonutilitarian, "higher" values were maintained. At the same time they were domains for the playing out of experimental, avant-garde transgressions. Seen in this light, the ideological formations of art and culture have no essential or eternal status. They are changing and contestable, like the special rhetoric of "literature." The essays that follow do not, in fact, appeal to a literary practice marked off in an esthetic, creative, or humanizing domain. They struggle, in their different ways, against the received definitions of art, literature, science, and history. And if they sometimes suggest that ethnography is an "art," they return the word to an older usage—before it had become associated with a higher or rebellious sensibility—to the eighteenth-century meaning Williams recalls: art as the skillful fashioning of useful artifacts. The making of ethnography is artisanal, tied to the worldly work of writing.

Ethnographic writing is determined in at least six ways: (1) contextuality (it draws from and creates meaningful social milieux); (2) rhetorically (it uses and is used by expressive conventions); (3) institutionally (one writes within, and against, specific traditions, disciplines, audiences); (4) generically (an ethnography is usually distinguishable from a novel or a travel account); (5) politically (the authority to represent cultural realities is unequally shared and at times contested); (6) historically (all the above conventions and constraints are changing). These determinations govern the inscription of coherent ethnographic fictions.

To call ethnographies fictions may raise empiricist hackles. But the word as commonly used in recent textual theory has lost its connotation of falsehood, of something merely opposed to truth. It suggests the partiality of cultural and historical truths, the ways they are systematic and exclusive. Ethnographic writings can properly be called fictions in the sense of "something made or fashioned," the principal burden of the word's Latin root, *fingere*. But it is important to preserve the meaning not merely of making, but also of making up, of inventing things not actually real. (*Fingere*, in some of its uses, implied a degree of falsehood.) Interpretive social scientists have recently come to view good ethnographies as "true fictions," but usually at the cost of weakening the oxymoron, reducing it to the banal claim that all truths are constructed. The essays collected here keep the oxymoron sharp. For example, Vincent Crapanzano portrays ethnographers as tricksters, promising, like Hermes, not to lie, but never undertaking to tell the whole truth either. Their rhetoric empowers *and subverts* their message. Other essays reinforce the point by stressing that cultural fictions are based on systematic, and contestable, exclusions. These may involve silencing incongruent voices ("Two Crows denies it!") or deploying a consistent manner of quoting, "speaking for," translating the reality of others. Purportedly irrelevant personal or historical circumstances will also be excluded (one cannot tell all). Moreover, the maker (but why only one?) of ethnographic texts cannot avoid expressive tropes, figures, and allegories that select and impose meaning as they translate it. In this view, more Nietzschean than realist or hermeneutic, all constructed truths are made possible by powerful "lies" of exclusion and rhetoric. Even the best ethnographic texts—serious, true fictions—are systems, or economies, of truth. Power and history work through them, in ways their authors cannot fully control.

Ethnographic truths are thus inherently *partial*—committed and incomplete. This point is now widely asserted—and resisted at strategic points by those who fear the collapse of clear standards of verification. But once accepted and built into ethnographic art, a rigorous sense of partiality can be a source of representational tact. A recent work by Richard Price, *First-Time: The Historical Vision of an Afro-American People* (1983), offers a good example of self-conscious, serious partiality. Price recounts the specific conditions of his fieldwork among the Saramakas, a Maroon society of Suriname. We learn about external and self-imposed limits to the research, about individual informants, and about the construction of the final written artifact. (The book avoids a smoothed-over, monological form, presenting itself as literally pieced-together, full of holes.) *First-Time* is evidence of the fact that acute political and epistemological self-consciousness need not lead to ethnographic self-absorption, or to the conclusion that it is impossible to know anything certain about other people. Rather, it leads to a concrete sense of why a Saramaka folktale, featured by Price, teaches that "knowledge is power, and that one must never reveal all of what one knows" (1983: 14).

A complex technique of revelation and secrecy governs the communication (reinvention) of "First-Time" knowledge, lore about the society's crucial struggles for survival in the eighteenth century. Using techniques of deliberate frustration, digression, and incompleteness, old men impart their historical knowledge to younger kinsmen, preferably at cock's crow, the hour before dawn. These strategies of ellipsis, concealment, and partial disclosure determine ethnographic relations as much as they do the transmission of stories between generations. Price has to accept the paradoxical fact that "any Saramaka narrative (including those told at cock's crow with the ostensible intent of communicating knowledge) will leave out most of what the teller knows about the incident in question. A person's knowledge is supposed to grow only in small increments, and in any aspect of life people are deliberately told only a little bit more than the speaker thinks they already know" (10).

It soon becomes apparent that there is no "complete" corpus of First-Time knowledge, that no one—least of all the visiting ethnographer—can know this lore except through an open-ended series of contingent, power-laden encounters. "It is accepted that different Saramaka historians will have different versions, and it is up to the listener to piece together for himself the version of an event that he, for the time being, accepts" (28). Though Price, the scrupulous fieldworker and historian, armed with writing, has gathered a text that surpasses in extent what individuals know or tell, it still "represents only the tip of the iceberg that Saramakas *collectively* preserve about First-Time" (25),

The ethical questions raised by forming a written archive of secret, oral lore are considerable, and Price wrestles with them openly. Part of his solution has been to undermine the completeness of his own account (but not its seriousness) by publishing a book that is a series of fragments. The aim is not to indicate unfortunate gaps remaining in our knowledge of eighteenth-century Saramaka life, but rather to present an inherently imperfect mode of knowledge, which produces gaps as it fills them. Though Price himself is not free of the desire to write a complete ethnography or history, to portray a "whole way of life" (24), the message of partiality resonates throughout *First-Time*.

Ethnographers are more and more like the Cree hunter who (the story goes) came to Montreal to testify in court concerning the fate of his hunting lands in the new James Bay hydroelectric scheme. He would describe his way of life. But when administered the oath he hesitated: "I'm not sure I can tell the truth .... I can only tell what I know."

It is useful to recall that the witness was speaking artfully, in a determining context of power. Since Michel Leiris's early essay of 1950, "L'Ethnographe devant le colonialisme" (but why so late?), anthropology has had to reckon with historical determination and political conflict in its midst. A rapid decade, from 1950 to 1960, saw the end of empire become a widely accepted project, if not an accomplished fact. Georges Balandier's *"situation coloniale"* was suddenly visible (1955), Imperial relations, formal and informal, were no longer the accepted rule of the game—to be reformed piecemeal, or ironically distanced in various ways. Enduring power inequalities had clearly constrained ethnographic practice. This "situation" was felt earliest in France, largely because of the Vietnamese and Algerian conflicts and through the writings of an ethnographically aware group of black intellectuals and poets, the *négritude* movement of Aimé Césaire, Léopold Senghor, René Ménil, and Léon Damas. The pages of *Présence Africaine* in the early fifties offered an unusual forum for collaboration between these writers and social scientists like Balandier, Leiris, Marcel Griaule, Edmond Ortigues, and Paul Rivet. In other countries the *crise de conscience* came somewhat later. One thinks of Jacques Maquet's influential essay "Objectivity in Anthropology" (1964), Dell Hymes's *Reinventing Anthropology* (1973), the work of Stanley Diamond (1974), Bob Scholte (1971, 1972, 1978), Gerard Leclerc (1972), and particularly of Talal Asad's collection *Anthropology and the Colonial Encounter* (1973), which has stimulated much clarifying debate (Firth et al. 1977).

In popular imagery the ethnographer has shifted from a sympathetic, authoritative observer (best incarnated, perhaps, by Margaret Mead) to the unflattering figure portrayed by Vine Deloria in *Custer Died for Your Sins* (1969). Indeed, the negative portrait has sometimes hardened into caricature— the ambitious social scientist making off with tribal lore and giving nothing in return, imposing crude portraits on subtle peoples, or (most recently) serving as dupe for sophisticated informants. Such portraits are about as realistic as the earlier heroic versions of participant-observation. Ethnographic work has indeed been enmeshed in a world of enduring and changing power inequalities, and it continues to be implicated. It enacts power relations. But its function within these relations is complex, often ambivalent, potentially counter-hegemonic.

Different rules of the game for ethnography are now emerging in many parts of the world. An outsider studying Native American cultures may expect, perhaps as a requirement for continuing research, to testify in support of land claim litigation. And a variety of formal restrictions are now placed on field-work by indigenous governments at national and local levels. These condition in new ways what can, and especially cannot, be said about particular peoples. A new figure has entered the scene, the "indigenous ethnographer" (Fahim, ed. 1982; Ohnuki-Tierney 1984). Insiders studying their own cultures offer new angles of vision and depths of understanding. Their accounts are empowered and restricted in unique ways. The diverse post- and neocolonial rules for ethnographic practice do not necessarily encourage "better" cultural accounts. The criteria for judging a good account have never been settled and are changing. But what has emerged from all these ideological shifts, rule changes, and new compromises is the fact that a series of historical pressures have begun to reposition anthropology with respect to its "objects" of study. Anthropology no longer speaks with automatic authority for others defined as unable to speak for themselves ("primitive," "pre-literate," "without history"). Other groups can less easily be distanced in special, almost always past or passing, times—represented as if they were not involved in the present world systems that implicate ethnographers along with the peoples they study. "Cultures" do not hold still for their portraits. Attempts to make them do so always involve simplification and exclusion, selection of a temporal focus, the construction of a particular self-other relationship, and the imposition or negotiation of a power relationship.

The critique of colonialism in the postwar period—an undermining of "The West's" ability to represent other societies—has been reinforced by an important process of theorizing about the limits of representation itself. There is no way adequately to survey this multifarious critique of what Vico called the "serious poem" of cultural history. Positions proliferate: "hermeneutics," "structuralism," "history of mentalities," "neo-Marxism," "genealogy," "post-structuralism," "post-modernism," "pragmatism"; also a spate of "alternate epistemologies"—feminist, ethnic, and non-Western. What is at stake, but not always recognized, is an ongoing critique of the West's most confident, characteristic discourses. Diverse philosophies may implicitly have this critical stance in common. For example, Jacques Derrida's unraveling of logocentrism, from the Greeks to Freud, and Walter J. Ong's quite different diagnosis of the consequences of literacy share an overarching rejection of the institutionalized ways one large group of humanity has for millennia construed its world. New historical studies of hegemonic patterns of thought (Marxist, Annaliste, Foucaultian) have in common with recent styles of textual criticism (semiotic, reader-response, post-structural) the conviction that what appears as "real" in history, the social sciences, the arts, even in common sense, is always analyzable as a restrictive and expressive set of social codes and conventions. Hermeneutic philosophy in its varying styles, from Wilhelm Dilthey and Paul Ricoeur to Heidegger, reminds us that the simplest cultural accounts are intentional creations, that interpreters constantly construct themselves through the others they study. The twentieth-century sciences of "language," from Ferdinand de Saussure and Roman Jacobson to Benjamin Lee Whorf, Sapir, and Wittgenstein, have made inescapable the systematic and situational verbal structures that determine all representations of reality. Finally, the return of rhetoric to an important place in many fields of study (it had for millennia been at the core of Western education) has made possible a detailed anatomy of conventional expressive modes. Allied with semiotics and discourse analysis, the new rhetoric is concerned with what Kenneth Burke called "strategies for the encompassing of situations" (1969: 3). It is less about how to speak well than about how to speak at all, and to act meaningfully, in the world of public cultural symbols.

The impact of these critiques is beginning to be felt in ethnography's sense of its own development. Noncelebratory histories are becoming common. The new histories try to avoid charting the discovery of some current wisdom (origins of the culture concept, and so forth); and they are suspicious of promoting and demoting intellectual precursors in order to confirm a particular paradigm. (For the latter approach, see Harris 1968 and Evans-Pritchard 1981). Rather, the new histories treat anthropological ideas as enmeshed in local practices and institutional constraints, as contingent and often "political" solutions to cultural problems. They construe science as a social process. They stress the historical discontinuities, as well as continuities, of past and present practices, as often as not making present knowledge seem temporary, in motion. The authority of a scientific discipline, in this kind of historical account, will always be mediated by the claims of rhetoric and power.[5]

Another major impact of the accumulating political/theoretical critique of anthropology may be briefly summarized as a rejection of "visualism." Ong (1967, 1977), among others, has studied ways in which the senses are hierarchically ordered in different cultures and epochs. He argues that the truth of vision in Western, literate cultures has predominated over the evidences of sound and interlocution, of touch, smell, and taste. (Mary Pratt has observed that references to odor, very prominent in travel writing, are virtually absent from ethnographies.)[6] The predominant metaphors in anthropological research have been participant-observation, data collection, and cultural description, all of which presuppose a standpoint outside-looking at, objectifying, or, somewhat closer, "reading," a given reality. Ong's work has been mobilized as a critique of ethnography by Johannes Fabian (1983), who explores the consequences of positing cultural facts as things observed, rather than, for example, heard, invented in dialogue, or transcribed. Following Frances Yates (1966), he argues that the taxonomic imagination in the West is strongly visualist in nature, constituting cultures as if they were theaters of memory, or spatialized arrays.

In a related polemic against "Orientalism" Edward Said (1978) identifies persistent tropes by which Europeans and Americans have visualized Eastern and Arab cultures. The Orient functions as a theater, a stage on which a performance is repeated, to be seen from a privileged standpoint. (Barthes [1977] locates a similar "perspective" in the emerging bourgeois esthetics of Diderot.) For Said, the Orient is "textualized"; its multiple, divergent stories and existential predicaments are coherently woven as a body of signs susceptible of virtuoso reading. This Orient, occulted and fragile, is brought lovingly to light, salvaged in the work of the outside scholar. The effect of domination in such spatial /temporal deployments (not limited, of course, to Orientalism proper) is that they confer on the other a discrete identity, while also providing the knowing observer with a standpoint from which to see without being seen, to read without interruption.

Once cultures are no longer prefigured visually—as objects, theaters, texts—it becomes possible to think of a cultural poetics that is an interplay of voices, of positioned utterances. In a discursive rather than a visual paradigm, the dominant metaphors for ethnography shift away from the observing eye and toward expressive speech (and gesture). The writer's "voice" pervades and situates the analysis, and objective, distancing rhetoric is renounced. Renato Rosaldo has recently argued, and exemplified, these points (1984, 1985). Other changes of textual enactment are urged by Stephen Tyler in this volume. (See also Tedlock 1983.) The evocative, performative elements of ethnography are legitimated. And the crucial poetic problem for a discursive ethnography becomes how "to achieve by written means what speech creates, and to do it without simply imitating speech" (Tyler 1984c:25). From another angle we notice how much has been said, in criticism and praise, of the ethnographic gaze. But what of the ethnographic ear? This is what Nathaniel Tarn is getting at in an interview, speaking of his experience as a tricultural French/Englishman endlessly becoming an American.

> It may be the ethnographer or the anthropologist again having his ears wider open to what he considers the exotic as opposed to the familiar, but I still feel I'm discovering something new in the use of language here almost every day. I'm getting new expressions almost every day, as if the language were growing from every conceivable shoot. (1975:9)

An interest in the discursive aspects of cultural representation draws attention not to the interpretation of cultural "texts" but to their relations of production. Divergent styles of writing are, with varying degrees of success, grappling with these new orders of complexity—different rules and possibilities within the horizon of a historical moment. The main experimental trends have been reviewed in detail elsewhere (Marcus and Cushman 1982; Clifford 1983a). It is enough to mention here the general trend toward a *specification of discourses* in ethnography: who speaks? who writes? when and where? with or to whom? under what institutional and historical constraints?

Since Malinowski's time, the "method" of participant-observation has enacted a delicate balance of subjectivity and objectivity. The ethnographer's personal experiences, especially those of participation and empathy, are recognized as central to the research process, but they are firmly restrained by the impersonal standards of observation and "objective" distance. In classical ethnographies the voice of the author was always manifest, but the conventions of textual presentation and reading forbade too close a connection between authorial style and the reality represented. Though we discern immediately the distinctive accent of Margaret Mead, Raymond Firth, or Paul Radin, we still cannot refer to Samoans as "Meadian" or call Tikopia a "Firthian" culture as freely as we speak of Dickensian or Flaubertian worlds. The subjectivity of the author is separated from the objective referent of the text. At best, the author's personal voice is seen as a style in the weak sense: a tone, or embellishment of the facts. Moreover, the actual field experience of the ethnographer is presented only in very stylized ways (the "arrival stories" discussed below by Mary Pratt, for example). States of serious confusion, violent feelings or acts, censorships, important failures, changes of course, and excessive pleasures are excluded from the published account.

In the sixties this set of expository conventions cracked. Ethnographers began to write about their field experience in ways that disturbed the prevailing subjective/ objective balance. There had been earlier disturbances, but they were kept marginal: Leiris's aberrant *L'Afrique fantôme* (1934); *Tristes Tropiques* (whose strongest impact outside France came only after 1960); and Elenore Smith Bowen's important *Return to Laughter* (1954). That Laura Bohannan in the early sixties had to disguise herself as Bowen, and her fieldwork narrative as a "novel," is symptomatic. But things were changing rapidly, and others—Georges Balandier (*L' Afrique ambigüe* 1957), David Maybury-Lewis (*The Savage and the Innocent* 1965), Jean Briggs (*Never in Anger* 1970), Jean-Paul Dumont (*The Headman and I* 1978), and Paul Rabinow (*Reflections on Fieldwork in Morocco* 1977)—were soon writing "factually" under their own names. The publication of Malinowski's Mailu and Trobriand diaries (1967) publicly upset the applecart. Henceforth an implicit mark of interrogation was placed beside any overly confident and consistent ethnographic voice. What desires and confusions was it smoothing over? How was its "objectivity" textually constructed?[7]

A subgenre of ethnographic writing emerged, the self-reflexive "fieldwork account." Variously sophisticated and naive, confessional and analytic, these accounts provide an important forum for the discussion of a wide range of issues, epistemological, existential, and political. The discourse of the cultural analyst can no longer be simply that of the "experienced" observer, describing and interpreting custom. Ethnographic experience and the participant—observation ideal are shown to be problematic. Different textual strategies are attempted. For example, the first person singular (never banned from ethnographies, which were always personal in stylized ways) is deployed according to new conventions. With the "fieldwork account" the rhetoric of experienced objectivity yields to that of the autobiography and the ironic self-portrait. (See Beaujour 1980, Lejeune 1975.) The ethnographer, a character in a fiction, is at center stage. He or she can speak of previously "irrelevant" topics: violence and desire, confusions, struggles and economic transactions with informants. These matters (long discussed informally within the discipline) have moved away from the margins of ethnography, to be seen as constitutive, inescapable (Honigman 1976).

Some reflexive accounts have worked to specify the discourse of informants, as well as that of the ethnographer, by staging dialogues or narrating interpersonal confrontations (Lacoste-Dujardin 1977, Crapanzano 1980, Dwyer 1982, Shostak 1981, Mernissi 1984). These fictions of dialogue have the effect of transforming the "cultural" text (a ritual, an institution, a life history, or any unit of typical behavior to be described or interpreted) into a speaking subject, who sees as well as is seen, who evades, argues, probes back. In this view of ethnography the proper referent of any account is not a represented "world"; now it is specific instances of discourse. But the principle of dialogical textual production goes well beyond the more or less artful presentation of "actual" encounters. It locates cultural interpretations in many sorts of reciprocal contexts, and it obliges writers to find diverse ways of rendering negotiated realities as multisubjective, power-laden, and incongruent. In this view, "culture" is always relational, an inscription of communicative processes that exist, historically, *between* subjects in relations of power (Dwyer 1977, Tedlock 1979).

Dialogical modes are not, in principle, autobiographical; they need not lead to hyper self-consciousness or self-absorption. As Bakhtin (1981) has shown, dialogical processes proliferate in any complexly represented discursive space (that of an ethnography, or, in his case, a realist novel). Many voices clamor for expression. Polyvocality was restrained and orchestrated in traditional ethnographies by giving to one voice a pervasive authorial function and to others the role of sources, "informants," to be quoted or paraphrased. Once dialogism and polyphony are recognized as modes of textual production, monophonic authority is questioned, revealed to be characteristic of a science that has claimed to *represent* cultures. The tendency to specify discourses—historically and intersubjectively—recasts this authority, and in the process alters the questions we put to cultural descriptions. Two recent examples must suffice. The first involves the voices and readings of Native Americans, the second those of women.

James Walker is widely known for his classic monograph *The Sun Dance and Other Ceremonies of the Oglala Division of the Teton Sioux* (1917). It is a carefully observed and documented work of interpretation. But our reading of it must now be complemented—and altered—by an extraordinary glimpse of its "makings." Three titles have now appeared in a four-volume edition of documents he collected while a physician and ethnographer on the Pine Ridge Sioux Reservation between 1896 and 1914. The first (Walker, *Lakota Belief and Ritual* 1982a, edited by Raymond DeMallie and Elaine Jahner) is a collage of notes, interviews, texts, and essay fragments written or spoken by Walker and numerous Oglala collaborators. This volume lists more than thirty "authorities," and wherever possible each contribution is marked with the name of its enunciator, writer, or transcriber. These individuals are not ethnographic "informants." *Lakota Belief* is a collaborative work of documentation, edited in a manner that gives equal rhetorical weight to diverse renditions of tradition. Walker's own descriptions and glosses are fragments among fragments.

The ethnographer worked closely with interpreters Charles and Richard Nines, and with Thomas Tyon and George Sword, both of whom composed extended essays in Old Lakota. These have now been translated and published for the first time. In a long section of *Lakota Belief* Tyon presents explanations he obtained from a number of Pine Ridge shamans; and it is revealing to see questions of belief (for example the crucial and elusive quality of "wakan") interpreted in differing, idiosyncratic styles. The result is a version of culture in process that resists any final summation. In *Lakota Belief* the editors provide biographical details on Walker, with hints about the individual sources of the writings in his collection, brought together from the Colorado Historical Society, the American Museum of Natural History, and the American Philosophical Society.

The second volume to have appeared is *Lakota Society* (1982b), which assembles documents roughly relating to aspects of social organization, as well as concepts of time and history. The inclusion of extensive Winter Counts (Lakota annals) and personal recollections of historical events confirms recent tendencies to question overly clear distinctions between peoples "with" and "without" history (Rosaldo 1980; Price 1983). Volume three is *Lakota Myth* (1983). And the last will contain the translated writings of George Sword. Sword was an Oglala warrior, later a judge of the Court of Indian Offenses at Pine Ridge. With Walker's encouragement, he wrote a detailed vernacular record of customary life, covering myth, ritual, warfare and games, complemented by an autobiography.

Taken together, these works offer an unusual, multiply articulated record of Lakota life at it crucial moment in its history—a three-volume anthology of ad hoc interpretations and transcriptions by more than a score of individuals occupying a spectrum of positions with respect to "tradition," plus an elaborated view of the ensemble by a well-placed Oglala writer. It becomes possible to assess critically the synthesis Walker made of these diverse materials. When complete, the five volumes (including *The Sun Dance*) will constitute an expanded (dispersed, not total) text representing a particular *moment* of ethnographic production (not "Lakota culture"). It is this expanded text, rather than Walker's monograph, that we must now learn to read.

Such an ensemble opens up new meanings and desires in an ongoing cultural *poesis*. The decision to publish these texts was provoked by requests to the Colorado Historical Society from community members at Pine Ridge, where copies were needed in Oglala history classes. For other readers the "Walker Collection" offers different lessons, providing, among other things, a mock-up for an ethnopoetics with history (and individuals) in it. One has difficulty giving these materials (many of which are very beautiful) the timeless, impersonal identity of, say, "Sioux myth." Moreover, the question of *who writes* (performs? transcribes? translates? edits?) cultural statements is inescapable in an expanded text of this sort. Here the ethnographer no longer holds unquestioned rights of salvage: the authority long associated with bringing elusive, "disappearing" oral lore into legible textual form. It is unclear whether James Walker (or anyone) can appear as author of these writings. Such lack of clarity is a sign of the times.

Western texts conventionally come with authors attached. Thus it is perhaps inevitable that *Lakota Belief, Lakota Society*, and *Lakota Myth* should be published under Walker's name. But as ethnography's complex, plural *poesis* becomes more apparent—and politically charged—conventions begin, in small ways, to slip. Walker's work may be an unusual case of textual collaboration. But it helps us see behind the scenes. Once "informants" begin to be considered as co-authors, and the ethnographer as scribe and archivist as well as interpreting observer, we can ask new, critical questions of all ethnographies. However monological, dialogical, or polyphonic their form, they are hierarchical arrangements of discourses.

A second example of the specification of discourses concerns gender. I shall first touch on ways in which it can impinge on the reading of ethnographic texts and then explore how the exclusion of feminist perspectives from the present volume limits and focuses its discursive standpoint. My first example, of the many possible, is Godfrey Lienhardt's *Divinity and Experience: The Religion of the Dinka* (1961), surely among the most finely argued ethnographies in recent anthropological literature. Its phenomenological rendition of Dinka senses of the self, of time, space, and "the Powers" is unparalleled. Thus it comes as a shock to recognize that Lienhardt's portrayal concerns, almost exclusively, the experience of Dinka men. When speaking of "the Dinka" he may or may not be extending the point to women. We often cannot know from the published text. The examples he chooses are, in any case, overwhelmingly centered on males. A rapid perusal of the book's introductory chapter on Dinka and their cattle confirms the point. Only once is a woman's view mentioned, and it is in affirmation of men's relation to cows, saying nothing of how women experience cattle. This observation introduces an equivocation in passages such as "Dinka often interpret accidents or coincidences as acts of Divinity distinguishing truth from falsehood by signs which appear to men" (p. 47). The intended sense of the word "men" is certainly generic, yet surrounded exclusively by examples from male experience it slides toward a gendered meaning. (Do signs appear to women? in significantly different ways?) Terms such as "the Dinka," or "Dinka," used throughout the book, become similarly equivocal.

The point is not to convict Lienhardt of duplicity; his book specifies gender to an unusual extent. What emerges, instead, are the history and politics that intervene in our reading. British academics of a certain caste and era say "men" when they mean "people" more often than do other groups, a cultural and historical context that is now less invisible than it once was. The partiality of gender in question here was not at issue when the book was published in 1961. If it were, Lienhardt would have directly addressed the problem, as more recent ethnographers now feel obliged to (for example, Meigs 1984:xix). One did not read "The Religion of the Dinka" then as one now must, as the religion of Dinka men and only perhaps Dinka women. Our task is to think historically about Lienhardt's text and its possible readings, including our own, as we read.

Systematic doubts about gender in cultural representation have become widespread only in the past decade or so, in certain milieux, under pressure of feminism. A great many portrayals of "cultural" truths now appear to reflect male domains of experience. (And there are, of course, inverse, though much less common cases: for example, Mead's work, which often focused on female domains and generalized on this basis about the culture as a whole.) In recognizing such biases, however, it is well to recall that our own "full" versions will themselves inevitably appear partial; and if many cultural portrayals now seem more limited than they once did, this is an index of the contingency and historical movement of all readings. No one reads from a neutral or final position. This rather obvious caution is often violated in new accounts that purport to set the record straight or to fill a gap in "our" knowledge.

When is a gap in knowledge perceived, and by whom? Where do "problems" come from?[8] It is obviously more than a simple matter of noticing an error, bias, or omission. I have chosen examples (Walker and Lienhardt) that underline the role of political and historical factors in the discovery of discursive partiality. The epistemology this implies cannot be reconciled with a notion of cumulative scientific progress, and the partiality at stake is stronger than the normal scientific dictates that we study problems piecemeal, that we must not over-generalize, that the best picture is built up by an accretion of rigorous evidence. Cultures are not scientific "objects" (assuming such things exist, even in the natural sciences). Culture, and our views of "it," are produced historically, and are actively contested. There is no whole picture that can be "filled in," since the perception and filling of a gap lead to the awareness of other gaps. If women's experience has been significantly excluded from ethnographic accounts, the recognition of this absence, and its correction in many recent studies, now highlights the fact that men's experience (as gendered subjects, not cultural types—"Dinka" or "Trobrianders") is itself largely unstudied. As canonical topics like "kinship" come under critical scrutiny (Needham 1974; Schneider 1972, 1984), new problems concerning "sexuality" are made visible. And so forth without end. It is evident that we know more about the Trobriand Islanders than was known in 1900. But the "we" requires historical identification. (Talal Asad argues in this volume that the fact that this knowledge is routinely inscribed in certain "strong" languages is not scientifically neutral.) If "culture" is not an object to be described, neither is it a unified corpus of symbols and meanings that can be definitively interpreted. Culture is contested, temporal, and emergent. Representation and explanation—both by insiders and outsiders—is implicated in this emergence. The specification of discourses I have been tracing is thus more than a matter of making carefully limited claims. It is thoroughly historicist and self-reflexive.

In this spirit, let me turn to the present volume. Everyone will be able to think of individuals or perspectives that should have been included. The volume's focus limits it in ways its authors and editors can only begin to make apparent. Readers may note that its anthropological bias neglects photography, film, performance theory, documentary art, the nonfiction novel, "the new journalism," oral history, and various forms of sociology. The book gives relatively little attention to new ethnographic possibilities emerging from non-Western experience and from feminist theory and politics. Let me dwell on this last exclusion, for it concerns an especially strong intellectual and moral influence in the university milieux from which these essays have sprung. Thus its absence cries out for comment. (But by addressing this one exclusion I do not mean to imply that it offers any privileged standpoint from which to perceive the partiality of the book.) Feminist theorizing is obviously of great potential significance for rethinking ethnographic writing. It debates the historical, political construction of identities and self/other relations, and it probes the gendered positions that make all accounts of, or by, other people inescapably partial.[9] Why, then, are there no essays in this book written from primarily feminist standpoints?

The volume was planned as the publication of a seminar limited by its sponsoring body to ten participants. It was institutionally defined as an "advanced seminar," and its organizers, George Marcus and myself, accepted this format without serious question. We decided to invite people doing "advanced" work on our topic, by which we understood people who had already contributed significantly to the analysis of ethnographic textual form. For the sake of coherence, we located the seminar within, and at the boundaries of, the discipline of anthropology. We invited participants well known for their recent contributions to the opening up of ethnographic writing possibilities, or whom we knew to be well along on research relevant to our focus. The seminar was small and its formation ad hoc, reflecting our specific personal and intellectual networks, our limited knowledge of appropriate work in progress. (I shall not go into individual personalities, friendships, and so forth, though they are clearly relevant.)

Planning the seminar, we were confronted by what seemed to us an obvious—important and regrettable—fact. Feminism had not contributed much to the theoretical analysis of ethnographies as texts. Where women had made textual innovations (Bowen 1954, Briggs 1970, Favret-Saada 1980, 1981) they had not done so on feminist grounds. A few quite recent works (Shostak 1981, Cesara 1982, Mernissi 1984) had reflected in their form feminist claims about subjectivity, relationality, and female experience, but these same textual forms were shared by other, nonfeminist, experimental works. Moreover, their authors did not seem conversant with the rhetorical and textual theory that we wanted to bring to bear on ethnography. Our focus was thus on textual theory as well as on textual form: a defensible, productive focus.

Within this focus we could not draw on any developed debates generated by feminism on ethnographic textual practices. A few very initial indications (for example, Atkinson 1982; Roberts, ed. 1981) were all that had been published. And the situation has not changed dramatically since. Feminism clearly has contributed to anthropological theory. And various female ethnographers, like Annette Weiner (1976), are actively rewriting the masculinist canon. But feminist ethnography has focused either on setting the record straight about women or on revising anthropological categories (for example, the nature/culture opposition). It has not produced either unconventional forms of writing or a developed reflection on ethnographic textuality as such.

The reasons for this general situation need careful exploration, and this is not the place for it.[10] In the case of our seminar and volume, by stressing textual form and by privileging textual theory, we focused the topic in ways that excluded certain forms of ethnographic innovation. This fact emerged in the seminar discussions, during which it became clear that concrete institutional forces—tenure patterns, canons, the influence of disciplinary authorities, global inequalities of power—could not be evaded. From this perspective, issues of content in ethnography (the exclusion and inclusion of different experiences in the anthropological archive, the rewriting of established traditions) became directly relevant. And this is where feminist and non-Western writings have made their greatest impact.[11] Clearly our sharp separation of form from content—and our fetishizing of form—was, and is, contestable. It is a bias that may well be implicit in modernist "textualism." (Most of us at the seminar, excluding Stephen Tyler, were not yet thoroughly "post-modern"!)

We see these things better, of course, now that the deed is done, the book finished. But even early on, in Santa Fe, intense discussions turned on the exclusion of several important perspectives and what to do about them. As editors, we decided not to try and "fill out" the volume by seeking additional essays. This seemed to be tokenism and to reflect an aspiration to false completeness. Our response to the problem of excluded standpoints has been to leave them blatant. The present volume remains a limited intervention, with no aspiration to be comprehensive or to cover the territory. It sheds a strong, partial light.

A major consequence of the historical and theoretical movements traced in this Introduction has been to dislodge the ground from which persons and groups securely represent others. A conceptual shift, "tectonic" in its implications, has taken place. We ground things, now, on a moving earth. There is no longer any place of overview (mountaintop) from which to map human ways of life, no Archimedian point from which to represent the world. Mountains are in constant motion. So are islands: for one cannot occupy, unambiguously, a bounded cultural world from which to journey out and analyze other cultures. Human ways of life increasingly influence, dominate, parody, translate, and subvert one another. Cultural analysis is always enmeshed in global movements of difference and power. However one defines it, and the phrase is here used loosely, a "world system" now links the planet's societies in a common historical process.[12]

A number of the essays that follow grapple with this predicament. Their emphases differ. How, George Marcus asks, can ethnography—at home or abroad—define its object of study in ways that permit detailed, local, contextual analysis and simultaneously the portrayal of global implicating forces? Accepted textual strategies for defining cultural domains, separating micro and macro levels, are no longer adequate to the challenge. He explores new writing possibilities that blur the distinction between anthropology and sociology, subverting an unproductive division of labor. Talal Asad also confronts the systematic interconnection of the planet's societies. But he finds persistent, glacial inequalities imposing all-too-coherent forms on the world's diversity and firmly positioning any ethnographic practice. "Translations" of culture, however subtle or inventive in textual form, take place within relations of "weak" and "strong" languages that govern the international flow of knowledge. Ethnography is still very much a one way street. Michael Fischer's essay suggests that notions of global hegemony may miss the reflexive, inventive dimensions of ethnicity and cultural contact. (And in a similar vein, my own contribution treats all narratives of lost authenticity and vanishing diversity as self-confirming allegories, until proven otherwise.) Fischer locates ethnographic writing in a syncretic world of ethnicity rather than a world of discrete cultures and traditions. Post-modernism, in his analysis, is more than a literary, philosophical, or artistic trend. It is a general condition of multicultural life demanding new forms of inventiveness and subtlety from a fully reflexive ethnography.

Ethnography in the service of anthropology once looked out at clearly defined others, defined as primitive, or tribal, or non-Western, or pre-literate, or nonhistorical—the list, if extended, soon becomes incoherent. Now ethnography encounters others in relation to itself, while seeing itself as other. Thus an "ethnographic" perspective is being deployed in diverse and novel circumstances. Renato Rosaldo probes the way its rhetoric has been appropriated by social history and how this makes visible certain disturbing assumptions that have empowered fieldwork. The ethnographer's distinctively intimate, inquisitive perspective turns up in history, literature, advertising, and many other unlikely places. The science of the exotic is being "repatriated" (Fischer and Marcus 1986).

Ethnography's traditional vocation of cultural criticism (Montaigne's "On Cannibals," Montesquieu's *Persian Letters*) has reemerged with new explicitness and vigor. Anthropological fieldworkers can now realign their work with pioneers like Henry Mayhew in the nineteenth century and, more recently, with the Chicago school of urban sociology (Lloyd Warner, William F. Whyte, Robert Park). Sociological description of everyday practices has recently been complicated by ethnomethodology (Leiter 1980): the work of Harold Garfinkel, Harvey Sacks, and Aaron Cicourel (also neglected in the present volume) reflects a crisis in sociology similar to that in anthropology. Meanwhile a different rapprochement between anthropological and sociological ethnography has been taking place under the influence of Marxist cultural theory at the Birmingham Centre for Contemporary Cultural Studies (Stuart Hall, Paul Willis). In America fieldworkers are turning their attention to laboratory biologists and physicists (Latour and Woolgar 1979, Traweek 1982), to American "kinship" (Schneider 1980), to the dynastic rich (Marcus 1983), to truckers (Agar 1985), to psychiatric clients (Estroff 1985), to new urban communities (Krieger 1983), to problematic traditional identities (Blu 1980). This is only the beginning of a growing list.

What is at stake is more than anthropological methods being deployed at home, or studying new groups (Nader 1969). Ethnography is moving into areas long occupied by sociology, the novel, or avant-garde cultural critique (Clifford 1981), rediscovering otherness and difference within the cultures of the West. It has become clear that every version of an "other," wherever found, is also the construction of a "self," and the making of ethnographic texts, as Michael Fischer, Vincent Crapanzano, and others in this volume show, has always involved a process of "self-fashioning" (Greenblatt 1980). Cultural *poesis*—and politics—is the constant reconstitution of selves and others through specific exclusions, conventions, and discursive practices. The essays that follow provide tools for the analysis of these processes, at home and abroad.

These essays do not prophesy. Taken as a whole, they portray historical constraints on the making of ethnographies, as well as areas of textual experiment and emergence. Talal Asad's tone is sober, preoccupied (like Paul Rabinow) with institutional limits on interpretive freedom. George Marcus and Michael Fischer explore concrete examples of alternative writing. Stephen Tyler evokes what does not (cannot?) yet exist, but must be imagined—or, better, sounded. Many of the essays (especially those of Renato Rosaldo, Vincent Crapanzano, Mary Pratt, and Talal Asad) are occupied with critical ground clearing-dislodging canons to make space for alternatives. Rabinow identifies a new canon, post-modernism. Other essays (Tyler on oral and performative modes, my own treatment of allegory) recapture old rhetorics and projects for use now. "For use now!" Charles Olson's poetic rule should guide the reading of these essays: they are responses to a current, changing situation, interventions rather than positions. To place this volume in a historical conjuncture, as I have tried to do here, is to reveal the moving ground on which it stands, and to do so without benefit of a master narrative of historical development that can offer a coherent direction, or future, for ethnography.[13]

One launches a controversial collection like this with some trepidation, hoping it will be seriously engaged—not simply rejected, for example, as another attack on science or an incitement to relativism. Rejections of this kind should at least make clear why close analysis of one of the principal things ethnographers do—that is, write—should not be central to evaluation of the results of scientific research. The authors in this volume do not suggest that one cultural account is as good as any other. If they espoused so trivial and self-refuting a relativism, they would not have gone to the trouble of writing detailed, committed, critical studies.

Other, more subtle, objections have recently been raised to the literary, theoretical reflexivity represented here. Textual, epistemological questions are sometimes thought to be paralyzing, abstract, dangerously solipsistic—in short, a barrier to the task of writing "grounded" or "unified" cultural and historical studies.[14] In practice, however, such questions do not necessarily inhibit those who entertain them from producing truthful, realistic accounts. All of the essays collected here point toward new, better modes of writing. One need not agree with their particular standards to take seriously the fact that in ethnography, as in literary and historical studies, what counts as "realist" is now a matter of both theoretical debate and practical experimentation.

The writing and reading of ethnography are overdetermined by forces ultimately beyond the control of either an author or an interpretive community. These contingencies—of language, rhetoric, power, and history—must now be openly confronted in the process of writing. They can no longer be evaded. But the confrontation raises thorny problems of verification: how are the truths of cultural accounts evaluated? Who has the authority to separate science from art? realism from fantasy? knowledge from ideology? Of course such separations will continue to be maintained, and redrawn; but their changing poetic and political grounds will be less easily ignored. In cultural studies at least, we can no longer know the whole truth, or even claim to approach it. The rigorous partiality I have been stressing here may be a source of pessimism for some readers. But is there not a liberation, too, in recognizing that no one can write about others any longer as if they were discrete objects or texts? And may not the vision of a complex, problematic, partial ethnography lead, not to its abandonment, but to more subtle, concrete ways of writing and reading, to new conceptions of culture as interactive and historical? Most of the essays in this volume, for all their trenchant critiques, are optimistic about ethnographic writing. The problems they raise are incitements, not barriers.

These essays will be accused of having gone too far: poetry will again be banned from the city, power from the halls of science. And extreme self-consciousness certainly has its dangers—of irony, of elitism, of solipsism, of putting the whole world in quotation marks. But I trust that readers who signal these dangers will do so (like some of the essays below) *after* they have confronted the changing history, rhetoric, and politics of established representational forms. In the wake of semiotics, post-structuralism, hermeneutics, and deconstruction there has been considerable talk about a return to plain speaking and to realism. But to return to realism one must first have left it! Moreover, to recognize the poetic dimensions of ethnography does not require that one give up facts and accurate accounting for the supposed free play of poetry. "Poetry" is not limited to romantic or modernist subjectivism: it can be historical, precise, objective. And of course it is just as conventional and institutionally determined as "prose." Ethnography is hybrid textual activity: it traverses genres and disciplines. The essays in this volume do not claim ethnography is "only literature." They do insist it is always writing.

I would like to thank the members of the Santa Fe seminar for their many suggestions incorporated in, or left out of, this Introduction. (I have certainly not tried to represent the "native point of view" of that small group.) In graduate seminars co-taught with Paul Rabinow at the University of California at Berkeley and Santa Cruz, many of my ideas on these topics have been agreeably assaulted. My special thanks to him and to the students in those classes. At

Santa Cruz, Deborah Gordon, Donna Haraway, and Ruth Frankenberg have helped me with this essay, and I have had important encouragement and stimulus from Hayden White and the members of the Research Group on Colonial Discourse. Various press readers made important suggestions, particularly Barbara Babcock. George Marcus, who got the whole project rolling, has been an inestimable ally and friend.

Notes

1 Malinowski 1961: 17. The photograph inside the tent was published in 1983 by George Stocking in *History of Anthropology* 1: 101. This volume contains other telling scenes of ethnographic writing.

2 A partial list of works exploring this expanded field of the "literary" in anthropology includes (not mentioning contributors to the present volume): Boon 1972, 1977, 1982; Geertz 1973, 1983; Turner 1974, 1975; Fernandez 1974; Diamond 1974; Duvignaud 1970, 1978; Favret-Saada 1980; Favret-Saada and Contreras 1981; Dumont 1978; Tedlock 1983; Jarnin 1979, 1980, 1985; Webster 1982; Thornton 1983, 1984.

3 See the work of Hayden White (1973, 1978) for a tropological theory of "prefigured" realities; also Latour and Woolgar (1979) for a view of scientific activity as "inscription."

4 "It might be objected that *figurative style* is not the only style, or even the only poetic style, and that rhetoric also takes cognizance of what is called *simple* style. But in fact this is merely a less decorated style, or rather, a style decorated more simply, and it, too, like the lyric and the epic, has its own special figures. A style in which figure is strictly absent does not exist," writes Gerard Genette (1982:47).

5 I exclude from this category the various histories of "anthropological" ideas, which must always have a Whiggish cast. I include the strong historicism of George Stocking, which often has the effect of questioning disciplinary genealogies (for example, 1968:69-90). The work of Terry Clark on the institutionalization of social science (1973) and of Foucault on the sociopolitical constitution of "discursive formations" (1973) points in the direction I am indicating. See also: Hartog (1980), Duchet (1971), many works by De Certeau (e.g., 1980), Boon (1982), Rupp-Eisenreich (1984), and the yearly volume *History of Anthropology*, edited by Stocking whose approach goes well beyond the history of ideas or theory. An allied approach can be found in recent social studies of science research: e.g., Knorr-Cetina (1981), Latour (1984), Knorr-Cetina and Mulkay (1983).

6 An observation by Pratt at the Santa Fe seminar. The relative inattention to sound is beginning to be corrected in recent ethnographic writing (e.g., Feld 1982). For examples of work unusually attentive to the sensorium, see Stoller (1984a, b).

7 I have explored the relation of personal subjectivity and authoritative cultural accounts, seen as mutually reinforcing fictions, in an essay on Malinowski and Conrad (Clifford 1985a).

8 "The stork didn't bring them!" (David Schneider, in conversation). Foucault described his approach as a "history of problematics" (1984).

9 Many of the themes I have been stressing above are supported by recent feminist work. Some theorists have problematized all totalizing, Archimedian perspectives (Jehlen 1981). Many have seriously rethought the social construction of relationship and difference (Chodorow 1978, Rich 1976, Keller 1985). Much feminist practice questions the strict separation of subjective and objective, emphasizing processual modes of knowledge, closely connecting personal, political, and representational processes. Other strands deepen the critique of visually based modes of surveillance and portrayal, linking them to domination and masculine desire (Mulvey 1975, Kuhn 1982). Narrative forms of representation are analyzed with regard to the gendered positions they reenact (de Lauretis 1984). Some feminist writing has worked to politicize and subvert all natural essences and identities, including "femininity" and "woman" (Wittig 1975, Irigaray 1977, Russ 1975, Haraway 1985). "Anthropological" categories such as nature and culture public and private, sex and gender have been brought into question (Ortner 1974, MacCormack and Strathern 1980, Rosaldo and Lamphere 1974, Rosaldo 1980, Rubin 1975).

10 Marilyn Strathern's unpublished essay "Dislodging a World View" (1984), also discussed by Paul Rabinow in this volume, begins the investigation. A fuller analysis is being worked out by Deborah Gordon in a dissertation for the History of Consciousness program, University of California, Santa Cruz. I am indebted to conversations with her.

11 It may generally be true that groups long excluded from positions of institutional power, like women or people of color, have less concrete freedom to indulge in textual experimentations. To write in an unorthodox way, Paul Rabinow suggests in this volume, one must first have tenure. In specific contexts a preoccupation with self-reflexivity and style may be an index of privileged estheticism. For if one does not have to worry about the exclusion or true representation of one's experience, one is freer to undermine ways of telling, to focus on form over content. But I am uneasy with a general notion that privileged discourse indulges in esthetic or epistemological subtleties, whereas marginal discourse "tells it like it is." The reverse is too often the case. (See Michael Fischer's essay in this volume.)

12 The term is, of course Wallerstein's (1976). I find, however, his strong sense of a unitary direction to the global historical process problematic, and agree with Ortner's reservations (1984: 142-43).

13 My notion of historicism owes a great deal to the recent work of Fredric Jameson (1980, 1981, 1984a, b). I am not, however, persuaded by the master narrative (a global sequence of modes of production) he invokes from time to time as an alternative to post-modern fragmentation (the sense that history is composed of various local narratives). The partiality I have been urging in this introduction always presupposes a local historical predicament. This historicist partiality is not the unsituated "partiality and flux" with which Rabinow (see p.252) taxes a somewhat rigidly defined "post-modernism."

14 The response is frequently expressed informally. It appears in different forms in Randall (1984), Rosen (1984), Ortner (1984: 143), Pullum (1984), and Darnton (1985).

References

Agar, Michael. 1985. *Independents Declared: The Dilemma of Independent Trucking*. Washington, DC: Smithsonian Institution.

Atkinson, Jane. 1982. "Anthropology." *Signs* 8: 236-58.

Asad, Talal. 1973. *Anthropology and the Colonial Encounter*. London: Ithaca Press.

Bakhtin, Mikhail. 1981. "Discourse in the Novel." In *The Dialogical Imagination*. Michael Holquist, ed. Pp. 259-442. Austin, Tex.: University of Texas Press.

Balandier, Georges. 1955. *Sociologie actuelle de L'Afrique noire*. Paris: Presses universitaires de la France.

—. *L'Afrique ambigüe*. Paris: Plon.

Barthes, Roland. 1977. *Image Music Text*. New York: Hill and Wang.

Beaujour, Michel. 1980. *Miroirs d'Encre*. Paris: Le Seuil.

Boon, James. 1972. *From Symbolism to Structuralism: Levi-Strauss in a Literary Tradition*. New York: Harper and Row.

—. 1977. *The Anthropological Romance of Bali, 1597-1972*. Cambridge: Cambridge University Press.

—. 1982. *Other Tribes Other Scribes*. Ithaca, NY: Cornell University Press.

Bowen, Elenore Smith [Pseud. of Laura Bohannan]. 1954. *Return to Laughter*. New York: Harper and Row.

Briggs, Jean. 1970. *Never in Anger*. Cambridge, Mass.: Harvard University Press.

Burke, Kenneth. 1969. *A Rhetoric of Motives*. Berkeley and Los Angeles: University of California Press.

Cesara, Manda. 1982. *Reflections of a Woman Anthropologist: No Hiding Place*. New York: Academic Press.

Chowdorow, Nancy. 1978. *The Reproduction of Mothering*. Berkeley and Los Angeles: The University of California Press.

Clark, Terry. 1973. *Prophets and Patrons: The French University and the Emergence of the Social Sciences*. Cambridge, Mass.: Harvard University Press.

Clifford, James. 1981. "On Ethnographic Surrealism." *Comparative Studies in Society and History* 23,4: 539-64.

—. 1983. "On Ethnographic Authority." *Representations* 1,2: 118-46.

—. 1985. "On Ethnographic Self-Fashioning: Conrad and Malinowski." In *Reconstructing Individualism*. Stanford, Calif.: Stanford University Press.

Crapanzano, Vincent. 1980. *Tuhami: Portrait of a Moroccan*. Chicago: University of Chicago Press.

Darnton, Robert. 1985. "Revolution sans Revolutionaires." *New York Review of Books*, January 31st, 1985, 21-28.

De Certeau, Michel. 1980. "Writing vs. Time: History and Anthropology in the Works of Lafitau." *Yale French Studies* 59: 37-64.

—. 1983. "History: Ethics, Science, and Fiction." In *Social Sciences as Moral Inquiry*. Hahn *et. al.*, eds. Pp. 173-209. New York: Columbia University Press.

De Lauretis, Teresa. 1984. *Alice Doesn't: Feminism, Semiotics, Cinema*. Bloomington, Ind.: University of Indiana Press.

Deloria, Vine. 1969. *Custer Died For Your Sins*. New York: Macmillan Co.

Diamond, Stanley. 1974. *In Search of the Primitive: A Critique of Civilization*. New Brunswick, NJ: E.P. Dutton.

Duchet, Michele. 1971. *Anthropologie et histoire au siècle des lumières*. Paris: Masparo.

Dumont, Jean-Paul. 1978. *The Headman and I*. Austin, Tex.: University of Texas Press.

Duvignaud, Jean. 1970. *Change at Shebika: Report from a North African Village*. New York: Vintage Books.

—. 1973. *Le Langage Perdu: Essai sur la différence anthropologique*. Paris: Presses universitaires de France.

Dwyer, Kevin. 1977. "The Dialogic of Anthropology." *Dialectical Anthropology* 2: 143-51.

—. 1982. *Moroccan Dialogues*. Baltimore: Johns Hopkins University Press.

Eagleton, Terry. 1983. *Literary Theory*. Oxford: Oxford University Press.

Estroff, Sue E. 1985. *Making it Crazy: An Ethnography of Psychiatric Clients in an American Community*. Berkeley and Los Angeles: University of California Press.

Evans-Pritchard, Edward E. 1981. *A History of Anthropological Thought*. London: Faber and Faber.

Fabian, Johannes. 1983. *Time and the Other: How Anthropology Makes Its Object*. New York: Columbia University Press.

Fahim, Hussein, ed. 1982. *Indigenous Anthropology in Non-Western Countries*. Durham, NC: Carolina Academic Press.

Favret-Saada, Jeanne. 1980. *Deadly Words: Witchcraft in the Bocage*. London: Cambridge University Press.

Favret-Saada, Jeanne, and Josee Contreras. 1981. *Corps pour corps: Enquête sur la sorcellerie dans le bocage*. Paris: Gallimard.

Feld, Steven. 1982. *Sounds and Sentiment: Birds, Weeping, Poetics, and Song in Kaluli Expression*. Philadelphia: University of Pennsylvania Press.

Fernandez, James. 1974. "The Mission of Metaphor in Expressive Culture." *Current Anthropology* 15: 119-45.

Firth, Raymond, *et.al.* 1977. "Anthropological Research in British Colonies: Some Personal Accounts." *Anthropological Forum* 4,2.

Foucault, Michel. 1973. *The Order of Things*. New York: Vintage Press.

—. 1984. "Polemics, Politics, and Problemizations." In *The Foucault Reader*. Paul Rabinow, ed. Pp. 381-90. New York: Pantheon.

Geertz, Clifford. 1973. *The Interpretation of Cultures*. New York: Basic Books.

—. 1983. "Slide-Show: Evans-Pritchard's African Transparencies." *Raritan Review*, Fall. Pp. 62-80

Genette, Gerard. 1982. *Figures of Literary Discourse*. New York: Columbia University Press.

Greenblatt, Stephen. 1980. *Renaissance Self-Fashioning: From More to Shakespeare*. Chicago: University of Chicago Press.

Haraway, Donna. 1985. "A Manifesto for Cyborgs: Science, Technology, and Socialist Feminism in the 1980s." *Socialist Review* 15, 2: 65-108.

Harris, Marvin. 1968. *The Rise of Anthropological Theory*. New York: Thomas Crowell.

Hartog, François. 1980. *Le Miroire d'Hérodote*. Paris: Gallimard.

Honigman, John J. 1976. "The Personal Approach in Cultural Anthropological Research." *Current Anthropology* 16: 243-61.

Hymes, Dell, ed. 1974. *Reinventing Anthropology*. New York: Vintage.

Irigaray, Luce. 1977. *Ce sexe qui n'en est pas un*. Paris: Editions de Minuit.

Jamin, Jean. 1979. "Une Initiation au réel: À propos de Segalen." *Cahiers internatiounaux de la sociologie* 66:125-39.

—. 1980. "Un Sacré collège, ou les apprenties sorciers de la sociologie." *Cahiers internationaux de la sociologie* 68:5-32.

Jamin, Jean, ed. 1985. "Le Texte ethnographique." Special issue of *Etudes rurales*, nos. 97-98.

Jameson, Fredric. 1980. "Marxism and Historicism." *New Literary History*, Spring 1980. Pp. 41-73.

—. 1981. *The Political Unconscious: Narrative as a Socially Symbolic Act.* Ithaca, NY: Cornell University Press.

—. 1984a. "Postmodernism, or the Cultural Logic of Late Capitalism." *New Left Review* 146: 53-92.

—. 1984b. "Periodizing the 60s." In *The Sixties Without Apology.* S. Sayers, *et. al.*, eds. Pp 178-215. Minneapolis, Minn.: University of Minnesota Press.

Jehlen, Myra. 1981. "Archimedes and the Paradox of Feminist Criticism." *Signs* 6,4: 575-601.

Keller, Evelyn Fox. 1985. *Reflections on Gender and Science.* New Haven, Conn.: Yale University Press.

Knorr-Cetina, Karin. 1981. *The Manufacture of Knowledge.* Oxford: Pergamon Press.

Knorr-Cetina, Karin and Michael Mulkay. 1983. *Science Observed: Perspectives on the Social Study of Science.* Beverley Hills, Calif.: Sage Publications.

Krieger, Susan. 1983. *The Mirror Dance: Identity in a Woman's Community.* Philadelphia: Temple University Press.

Kuhn, Annette. 1982. *Women's Pictures: Feminism and Cinema.* London: Routledge & Kegan Paul.

Lacoste-Dujardin, Camille. 1977. *Dialogue des femmes en ethnologie.* Paris: Maspero.

Latour, Bruno. 1984. *Les Microbes: Guerre et paix, suivi des irréductions.* Paris: Metailie

Latour, Bruno and Steve Woolgar. 1979. *Laboratory Life: The Social Construction of Scientific Facts.* Beverley Hills, Calif.: Sage Publiations.

Leclerc, Gerard. 1972. *Anthropologie et colonialisme: essai sur l'histoire de l'africanisme.* Paris: Fayard.

Leiter, Kenneth. 1980. *A Primer on Ethnomethodology.* Oxford: Oxford University Press.

Leiris, Michel. 1984. *L'Afrique fantôme.* Paris: Gallimard.

Lejeune, Phillipe. 1975. *Le Pacte autobiographique.* Paris: Seuil.

Lévi-Strauss, Claude. 1975. *Tristes Tropiques.* New York: Atheneum.

Lienhardt, Godfrey. 1961. *Divinity and Experience: The Religion of the Dinka.* Oxford: Oxford University Press.

MacCormack, Carol and Marilyn Strathern. 1980. *Nature, Culture and Gender.* Cambridge: Cambridge University Press.

Malinowski, Bronislaw. 1961. *Argonauts of the Western Pacific*. New York: E.P. Dutton.

—. 1967. *A Diary in the Strict Sense of the Term*. New York: Harcourt, Brace, & World.

Maquet, Jacques. 1964. "Objectivity in Anthropology." *Current Anthropology* 5: 47-55.

Marcus, George, ed. 1983. *Elites: Ethnographic Issues*. Albuquerque, N.Mex.: University of New Mexico Press.

Marcus, George and Dick Cushman. 1982. "Ethnographies as Text." *Annual Review of Anthropology* 11: 25-69.

Maybury-Lewis, David. 1965. *The Savage and the Innocent*. Cleveland: World Publishing Co.

Meigs, Anna. 1984. *Food, Sex, and Pollution: A New Guinea Religion*. New Brunswick, N.J.: Rutgers University Press.

Mernissi, Fatima. 1984. *Le Maroc raconté par ses femmes*. Rabat: Société marocaine des éditeurs réunis.

Mulvey, Laura. 1975. "Visual Pleasure and Narrative Cinema." *Screen* 16, 3: 6-18.

Nader, Laura. 1969. "Up the Anthropologist—Perspectives Gained from Studying Up." In *Reinventing Anthropology*. Dell Hymes, ed. Pp. 284-311. New York: Pantheon.

Needham, Rodney. 1970. "The Future of Anthropology: Disintegration or Metamorphosis?" In *Anniversary Contributions to Anthropology*. Pp. 34-47. Leiden: Brill.

—. 1974. *Remarks and Inventions: Skeptical Essays on Kinship*. London: Tavistock Publications.

Ohnuki-Tierney, Emiko. 1984. " 'Native' Anthropologists." *American Ethnologist* 11, 3: 584-86.

Ong, Walter J. 1967. *The Presence of the Word*. New Haven, Conn.: Yale University Press.

—. 1977. *Interfaces of the Word*. Ithaca, NY: Cornell University Press.

Ortner, Sherry B. 1974. "Is Female to Male as Nature is to Culture?" In *Women, Culture, and Society*. Michele Rosaldo and Louise Lamphere, eds. Pp. 67-87. Stanford, Calif.: Stanford University Press.

—. 1984. "Theory in Anthropology Since the Sixties." *Comparative Studies in Society and History 26,1*: 126-66.

Price, Richard. 1983. *First-Time: The Historical Vision of an Afro-American People*. Baltimore: Johns Hopkins University Press.

Pullum, Geoffrey K. 1984. "The Revenge of the Methodological Moaners." *Natural Language and Linguistic Theory* 1,4: 583-88.

Rabinow, Paul. 1977. *Reflections on Fieldwork in Morocco*. Berkeley and Los Angeles: University of California Press.

Randall, Frederika. 1984. "Why Scholars Become Storytellers." *New York Times Book Review*, January 29: 1-2.

Rich, Adrienne. 1976. *Of Woman Born*. New York: Norton.

Roberts, Helen, ed. 1981. *Doing Feminist Research*. London: Routledge & Kegan Paul.

Rosaldo, Renato. 1980. *Ilongot Headhunting 1883-1974: A Study in Society and History*. Stanford, Calif.: Stanford University Press.

Rosaldo, Michele. 1980. "The Use and Abuse of Anthropology: Reflections on Feminism and Cross-Cultural Understanding." *Signs* 5,3: 389-417.

—. 1984. "Grief and a Headhunter's Rage: On the Cultural Force of Emotions." In *Text, Play, and Story*. E. Bruner, ed. Pp. 178-95. Seattle: American Ethnological Society.

—. 1985. "Where Objectivity Lies: The Rhetoric of Anthropology." MS.

Rosaldo, Michele and Louise Lamphere, eds. 1974. *Woman, Culture and Society*. Stanford, Calif.: Stanford University Press.

Rosen, Lawrence. 1984. Review of *Moroccan Dialogues*, by Kevin Dwyer. American Ethnologist 11,3: 597-98.

Rubin, Gayle. 1975. "The Traffic in Women: Notes on the 'Political Economy' of Sex." In *Towards an Anthropology of Women*. Rayna Reiter, ed. Pp. 157-210. New York: Monthly Review Press.

Rupp-Eisenreich, Britta, ed. 1984. *Histoires de l'anthropologie: XIV-XIX siècles*. Paris: Klincksieck.

Russ, Joanna. 1975. *The Female Man*. New York: Bantam.

Said, Edward. 1978. *Orientalism*. New York: Pantheon

Schneider, David. 1972. "What is Kinship All About?" *In Kinship Studies in the Morgan Centennial Year*. P. Reining, ed. Pp. 32-63. Washington, DC: Anthropological Society of Washington.

—. 1980. *American Kinship*, 2nd edition.: Chicago: University of Chicago Press.

—. 1984. *A Critique of the Study of Kinship*. Ann Arbor, Mich.: University of Michigan Press.

Scholte, Bob. 1971. "Discontents in Anthropology." *Social Research* 38, 4: 777-807.

—. 1972. "Toward a Reflexive and Critical Anthropology." In *Reinventing Anthropology*. Dell Hymes, ed. Pp. 430-57. New York: Pantheon.

—. 1978. "Critical Anthropology Since Its Reinvention." *Anthropology and Humanism Quarterly* 3,1-2: 4-17.

Shostak, Marjorie. 1981. *Nisa: The Life and Words of a !Kung Woman*. Cambridge, Mass.: Harvard University Press.

Stocking, George. 1968. "Arnold, Tylor and the Uses of Invention." In *Race, Culture, and Evolution*. Pp.69-90. New York: Free Press.

Stoller, Paul. 1984a. "Sound in Songhay Cultural Experience." *American Ethnologist* 12,3: 91-112.

—. 1984b. "Eye, Mind and Word in Anthropology." *L'Homme* 24, 3-4: 91-114.

Strathern, Marilyn. 1984. "Dislodging a World View: Challenge and Counter-Challenge in the Relationship Between Feminism and Anthropology." Lecture at the Research Center for Women's Studies, University of Adelaide, July 4, 1984. Forthcoming in *Changing Paradigms: The Impact of Feminist Theory Upon the World of Scholarship*. Susan Mageray, ed. (Sydney: Hale and Iremonger); a version will also appear in *Signs*.

Tarn, Nathaniel. 1975. "Interview with Nathaniel Tarn." *Boundary* 24, 1: 1-34.

Tedlock, Dennis. 1979. "The Analogical Tradition and the Emergence of a Dialogical Anthropology." *Journal of Anthropological Research* 35: 387-400.

—. 1983. *The Spoken Word and the Work of Interpretation*. Philadelphia: University of Pennsylvania Press.

Thornton, Robert J. 1983. "Narrative Ethnography in Africa, 1850-1920." *Man* 18: 502-20.

—. 1984. "Chapters and Verses: Classification as Rhetorical Trope in Ethnographic Writing." Paper presented at the School of American Research Seminar, "The Making of Ethnographic Texts," April 1984.

Traweek, Sharon. 1982. "Uptime, Downtime, Spacetime and Power: An Ethnography of U.S. and Japanese Particle Physics." PhD thesis. University of California, Santa Cruz, History of Consciousness Program.

Turner, Victor. 1974. *Dramas, Fields, and Metaphors: Symbolic Action in Human Society*. Ithaca, NY: Cornell University Press.

—. 1975. *Revelation and Divination in Ndembu Ritual*. Ithaca, NY: Cornell University Press.

Tyler, Stephen A. 1984. "The Vision Quest in the West, or What the Mind's Eye Sees." *Journal of Anthropological Research* 40,1: 23-40.

Wagner, Roy. 1980. *The Invention of Culture*. Chicago: University of Chicago Press.

Walker, James. 1917. *The Sun Dance and Other Ceremonies of the Oglala Division of the Teton Sioux*. New York, AMS Press, 1979.

—. 1982a. *Lakota Belief and Ritual*. Raymond J. DeMallie and Elaine A. Jahner, eds. Lincoln, Nebr.: University of Nebraska Press.

—. 1982b. *Lakota Society*. Raymond J. DeMallie, ed. Lincoln, Nebr.: University of Nebraska Press.

—. 1983. *Lakota Myth*. Elaine A. Jahner, ed. Lincoln, Nebr.: University of Nebraska Press.

Wallerstein, Immanuel. 1976. *The Modern World System: Capitalist Agriculture and the Origins of the European World-Economy in the Sixteenth Century*. New York: Academic Press.

Webster, Steven. 1982. "Dialogue and Fiction in Ethnography." *Dialectical Anthropology* 7,2: 91-114.

Weiner, Annette. 1976. *Women of Value, Men of Renown*. Austin, Tex.: University of Texas Press.

White, Hayden. 1973. *Metahistory*. Baltimore: Johns Hopkins University Press.

—. 1978. *Tropics of Discourse*. Baltimore: Johns Hopkins University Press.

Williams, Raymond. 1966. *Culture and Society: 1780-1950*. New York: Harper and Row.

Wittig, Monique. 1975. *The Lesbian Body*. David LeVay, trans. New York: Avon.

Wolf, Eric. 1980. "They Divide and Subdivide and Call it Anthropology." *New York Times*, November 30th.

Woolf, Virginia. 1936. *Three Guineas*. New York: Harcourt, Brace & World.

Yates, Francis. 1966. *The Art of Memory*. Chicago: University of Chicago Press.

Study Questions

1. What does Clifford mean by the phrase "partial truth?"

2. How is the rejection of "visualism" important in the critique of anthropology?

3. How is the concept of the "reflexive account" significant for contemporary anthropology?

Further Readings

Clifford, James. 1981. On Ethnographic Surrealism. *Comparative Studies in Society and History* 23: 539-64.

—. 1983. Power and Dialogue in Ethnography: Marcel Griaule's Initiation. *Observers Observed: Essays on Ethnographic Fieldwork.* Ed. George W. Stocking, Jr. Madison: University of Wisconsin Press.

—. 1983. On Ethnographic Authority. *Representations* 2: 132-143.

—. 1988. *The Predicament of Culture: Twentieth-Century Ethnography, Literature, and Art.* Cambridge, MA.: Harvard University Press.

Clifford, James, and Marcus, George E. (eds.). 1986. *Writing Culture: The Poetics and Politics of Ethnography.* Berkeley: University of California Press.

35

A Crisis of Representation in
the Human Sciences

GEORGE E. MARCUS AND MICHAEL M.J. FISCHER

The present is a time of reassessment of dominant ideas across the human sciences (a designation broader than and inclusive of the conventional social sciences), extending to law, art, architecture, philosophy, literature, and even the natural sciences. This reassessment is more salient in some disciplines than in others, but its presence is pervasive. It is not just the ideas themselves that are coming under attack but the paradigmatic style in which they have been presented. Particularly in the social sciences, the goal of organizing disciplines by abstract, generalizing frameworks that encompass and guide all efforts at empirical research is being fundamentally challenged.

Clifford Geertz's paper, "Blurred Genres" (1980), attempted to characterize the current trend by noting the fluid borrowing of ideas and methods from one discipline to another. Geertz did not, however, attempt to analyze the dilemmas of the various disciplines. While the problem of the loss of encompassing theories remains the same from discipline to discipline, the formulation of and responses to this predicament are varied. For example, in **literary criticism**, there has been the waning of the "new criticism," a paradigm which asserted that the meaning of texts was fully explorable in terms of their internal construction. Now, literary critics have incorporated, among other moves, social theories of literary production and reception (see Lentricchia 1980 and the excellent discussion in the late Elizabeth Bruss's *Beautiful Theories*, 1982). In law, there have arisen demystifying critiques by the Critical Legal Studies movement of the long authoritative model of legal reasoning (see, for example, Livingston 1982). In art, architecture, as well as literature, techniques that once had shock value or reoriented perception, such as surrealism, today have lost their original force, thus stimulating a debate about the nature of postmodernist aesthetics (see Jameson 1984). In social theory, the trend is reflected in challenges to establishment positivism (see Giddens 1976, 1979). In neoclassical economics, it is expressed in a crisis of forecasting and economic policy (see

Thurow 1983) as well as in a critique of the ideal of growth in economic theory (see Hirsch 1976, and Piore and Sabel 1984). In philosophy, it takes the form of a recognition of the devastating implications of issues of contextuality and indeterminacies in human life for the construction of abstract systems, based on clearly derived and universal principles of justice, morality, and discourse (see Ungar 1976, 1984; Rorty 1979). In the current lively debate about the possibility of artificial intelligence, a key issue is precisely that of an adequate language of description (see Dennett 1984: 1454). Finally, in the natural sciences (physics, especially) and mathematics, the trend is indicated by a preference among some theorists for concentrating less on elegant theoretical visions of order, and more on the micropatterns of disorder—for example, the attention that "chaos" theory has recently gotten in physics, chemistry, biology, and mathematics (for a popular account of this development, see Gleick 1984).

Present conditions of knowledge are defined not so much by what they are as by what they come after. In general discussion within the humanities and social sciences, the present indeed is often characterized as "postparadigm"—postmodernism, poststructuralism, postMarxism, for example. It is striking that in Jean-François Lyotard's acute exploration of *The Postmodern Condition: A Report on Knowledge* (1984 [1979]), he too should cite the contemporary "incredulity towards metanarratives" which previously legitimated the rules of science. He speaks of a "crisis of narratives" with a turn to multiple "language games" that give rise to "institutions in patches." "Postmodern knowledge," he says, "is not simply a tool of the authorities; it refines our sensitivity to differences and reinforces our ability to tolerate the incommensurable" (p. xxv). The key feature of this moment, then, is the loosening of the hold over fragmented scholarly communities of either specific totalizing visions or a general paradigmatic style of organizing research. The authority of "grand theory" styles seems suspended for the moment in favor of a close consideration of such issues as contextuality, the meaning of social life to those who enact it, and the explanation of exceptions and indeterminants rather than regularities in phenomena observed—all issues that make problematic what were taken for granted as facts or certainties on which the validity of paradigms had rested.

The part of these conditions in which we are most interested is what we call a crisis of representation. This is the intellectual stimulus for the contemporary vitality of experimental writing in anthropology. The crisis arises from uncertainty about adequate means of describing social reality. In the United States, it is an expression of the failure of post-World War II paradigms, or the unifying ideas of a remarkable number of fields, to account for conditions within American society, if not within Western societies globally, which seem to be in a state of profound transition.

This trend may have much to do with the unfavorable shift in the relative position of American power and influence in the world, and with the widespread perception of the dissolution of the ruling postwar model of the liberal welfare state at home. Both the taste for totalizing frameworks and the predominance in many academic disciplines of general models of stability in the social and natural order seemed to have coincided with the previously more confident and secure national mood. The current exhaustion of this style of theorizing merely points up the politicized context in which post-World War II intellectual trends have been shaped all along.

The questioning of *specific* postwar paradigms, such as the social theory of Talcott Parsons, gained its force during the 1960s when there was a widespread politicization of academic thought in the United States. Yet, those times were sufficiently dominated by hopes for (or reactions to) images of massive, revolutionary transformations of society that grand, abstract theoretical visions themselves remained in vogue. While retaining its politicized dimension as a legacy of the 1960s, social thought in the years since has grown more suspicious of the ability of encompassing paradigms to ask the right questions, let alone provide answers, about the variety of local responses to the operation of global systems, which are not understood as certainly as they were once thought to be under the regime of "grand theory" styles. Consequently, the most interesting theoretical debates in a number of fields have shifted to the level of method, to problems of epistemology, interpretation, and discursive forms of representation themselves, employed by social thinkers. Elevated to a central concern of theoretical reflection, problems of description become problems of representation. These are issues that have been most trenchantly explored by philosophical and literary theories of interpretation—thus their prominence now as a source of inspiration for theoretical and self-critical reflection in so many disciplines.

The intellectual historian must have a sense of déja vù in contemplating these recent developments, for they recapitulate issues debated in other periods, most proximately during the 1920s and 1930s. There is often a circular motion to intellectual history, a return with fresh perspectives to questions explored earlier, forgotten or temporarily resolved, and then reposed in attempts to manage intractable contemporary dilemmas. Yet, this history is better conceived as spiral rather than circular. Rather than mere repetition, there is cumulative growth in knowledge, through the creative rediscovery of older and persistent questions in response to keenly experienced moments of dissatisfaction with the state of a discipline's practice tied to perceptions of unprecedented changes in the world.

Ours is once again a period rich in experimentation and conceptual risk-taking. Older dominant frameworks are not so much denied—there being nothing so grand to replace them—as suspended. The ideas they embody remain intellectual resources to be used in novel and eclectic ways. The closest such previous period was the 1920s and 1930s when evolutionary paradigms, laissez-faire liberalism, and revolutionary socialism and marxism all came under energetic critiques. Instead of grand theories and encyclopedic works, writers devoted themselves to the essay, to documenting diverse social experiences at close quarters, and to fragmentary illuminations. The atmosphere was one of uncertainty about the nature of major trends of change and the ability of existing social theories to grasp it holistically. The essay, experience, documentation, intensive focus on fragments and detail—these were the terms and vocabulary of the generation of Walter Benjamin, Robert Musil, Ludwig Wittgenstein, the surrealists, and the American documentary realists of the 1920s and 1930s.

Fascism and World War II brought to fruition the worst fears of the prewar speculations about the effects of the social transformations in industrial capitalism, communications /propaganda, and commodity production. In the aftermath, America emerged as the dominant economic force, and it created a new creed of can-do modernization. In the social sciences, Parsonian sociology became a hegemonic framework, not merely for sociology, but for anthropology, psychology, political science, and models of economic development as well. Based on his synthesis of the major systems of nineteenth-century social theory (including Weber and Durkheim, but excluding Marx), Parsons provided a comprehensive, abstract vision of the social system, and its relationship to the separate systems of culture and personality. His theoretical project promised to coordinate and unify conceptually the empirical work of all the social sciences. It was an intellectual effort of such vast scope and ambition that it occupied minds and disciplines for some time.

During the 1960s, Parsonian sociology rapidly lost its hold, to disappear quite as dramatically from open terms of reference by the time Parsons died as had, for example, Spencerian sociology before it. The apolitical and ahistoric character of Parsonian theory could not be sustained through the upheavals of the 1960s. In purely analytic terms, reducing the richness of social life, especially conflict, to the notions of function and system equilibrium on which the Parsonian vision depended, proved unsatisfactory. Parsonian social theory has not vanished; too many generations of students, now prominent scholars, were trained in terms of it for that to happen. But the theoretical edifice of Parsons has been thoroughly delegitimated, though many ideas within it remain intellectual resources at present, along with a multitude of other influences.

Furthermore, it is not that contemporary attempts to revive Parsonian sociology do not sometimes occur (as in the work of Niklas Luhmann 1984 and Jeffrey Alexander 1982-83) or that different, but equally ambitious efforts at grand theory do not arise (for example, sociobiology, "the new synthesis"—see Wilson 1975). It is simply that they each become just one more voice to be heard at the moment, with little likelihood of achieving hegemonic status. Indeed, if Talcott Parsons were writing today, his synthetic scheme would merely take its place among several other grand, and not so grand, programs and suggestions for research, each capturing its own fragment among scholars within and across disciplines.

So, too, in the contemporary period a similar diffusion of legitimacy and authority attends Marxism. Marxism is a nineteenth-century paradigm which presented itself as a natural science of society that not only had an intellectual identity but also a political one. It was a grand theory to be enacted and measured against history. In the period of Parsonian hegemony in the United States, Marxism maintained itself as an alternative, suppressed and awaiting its release. Today, there are still those who desire to preserve the framework, dogma, and canonic terminology of Marxism—formalists like Maurice Godelier and Louis Althusser. But there are also more interpretive Marxists, accepting the framework loosely as a realm of shared discourse, but probing within it to find out in cultural and experiential terms what concepts such as mode of production, commodity fetishism, or relations and forces of production might mean under diverse and changing world conditions. The label Marxist itself has become increasingly ambiguous; the use of Marxist ideas in social thought has become diffuse and pervasive; and there no longer seem to be any clear paradigmatic boundaries to Marxism. There is indeed a new empirical, and essentially ethnographic/documentary mood in Marxist writing (see Anderson 1984). It is just this sort of diffusion of ideas across boundaries that is to be expected in a period such as this when paradigmatic styles of social thought are suspended. Old labels are thus a poor guide to the current fluidity and cross-currents in intellectual trends. While Marxism as a system of thought remains strong as an image, in practice, it is difficult to identify Marxists anymore, or to locate a contemporary central tradition for it.

Parsonian social theory and Marxism (as well as French structuralism, more recently) have all served prominently during the postwar period as paradigms or disciplined frameworks for research in the human sciences. All remain today as sources of concepts, methodological questions, and procedures, but none authoritatively guides research programs on a large scale. They have become merely alternatives among many others that are used or discarded at will by researchers operating much more independently. The current period, like the 1920s and 1930s before it, is thus one of acute awareness of the limits of our conceptual systems as systems.

So far we have viewed the present crisis of representation as one distinctive, alternate swing of a pendulum between periods in which paradigms, or totalizing theories, are relatively secure, and periods in which paradigms lose their legitimacy and authority—when theoretical concerns shift to problems of the interpretation of the details of a reality that eludes the ability of dominant paradigms to describe it, let alone explain it. It is worth playing back this broadly conceived vision of intellectual history, which sets the context of the present experimentation with anthropological writing in terms that specifically capture the literary and rhetorical qualities of such shifts. To do so, we consult the pioneering study by Hayden White, *Metahistory* (1973), which traces the major changes in nineteenth-century European history and social theory, registered at the level of techniques for writing about society. In briefly considering White's framework, we see twentieth-century anthropology, as well as any other discipline which has depended on discursive, essentially literary accounts of its subjects, as comparable to the efforts of nineteenth-century historiography to establish a science of society through presenting realistic and accurate portraits of conditions and events.

Any historical (or anthropological) work exhibits emplotment, argument, and ideological implication, according to White. These three elements may be at odds with one another as well as being in an unstable relation to the facts they attempt to encompass and order. From these instabilities come shifting modes of writing which also show connections with broader social currents. The struggle to reconcile conflicts among these elements in the writing of texts, especially of important, influential works, poses problems of method for other practicing historians that define a theoretical discourse about the interpretation of reality. White's scheme is of interest to us here precisely because it translates the problem of historical (and anthropological) explanation, most often conceived as a clash of theoretical paradigms, into the writer's problem of representation.

Nineteenth-century historical writing, according to White, began and ended in an ironic mode. Irony is unsettling: it is a self-conscious mode that senses the failure of all sophisticated conceptualizations; stylistically, it employs rhetorical devices that signal real or feigned disbelief on the part of the author toward the truth of his own statements; it often centers on the recognition of the problematic nature of language, the potential foolishness of all linguistic characterizations of reality; and so it revels—or wallows—in satirical techniques. Yet, the irony at the end of the Enlightenment was quite different from that at the end of the nineteenth century. In between, historians and social theorists attempted at least three major alternatives to break out of the conditions of irony and thus to find a proper (read paradigmatic) representation of historical process.

In White's literary terms, these alternatives are best conceived as strategies of emplotment in constructing works of history and social theory—Romance,

Tragedy, and Comedy. Romance is the empathetic self-identification by the writer with quests that transcend specific periods of world history: in ethnology, an example would be Sir James Frazer who envisioned *The Golden Bough* as a quest of reason battling through centuries of superstition. Tragedy is a heightening of the sense of conflicting social forces, in which the individual or the event is merely an unhappy locus, one, however, in which there can be a gain in consciousness and understanding through experiencing the power of social conflicts. It is more world-wise than Romance; an example would be Marx's vision of class conflict, derived from his earlier explorations of the alienation of human labor. Comedy is the reverse side of Tragedy: it cultivates the sense that there can be temporary triumphs and reconciliations, often figured in the euphoria of festivals and rituals that bring competitors together and temporarily still conflict. An example would be the vision of social solidarity in Durkheim's *Elementary Forms of Religious Life*.

For nineteenth-century historiography, White describes a movement from Romance to Tragedy to Comedy, ending finally in a deep ironic mode. The irony at the end of the nineteenth century was different from that at the end of the Enlightenment. Nineteenth-century historiography was uniformly less abstract, and more empirical than that of the Enlightenment. During the nineteenth century there had been a sustained series of efforts to find a "realist" mode of description. All ended in irony, however, because there were a number of equally comprehensive and plausible, yet apparently mutually exclusive conceptions of the same events. At the end of the nineteenth century, writers such as Nietzsche and Croce took the ironic consciousness of the age as their problem and attempted to find ways of overcoming its unsettling, self-conscious inability to have faith in itself. Croce attempted the romantic move again, trying to purge history of irony by assimilating it to art, but he succeeded only in driving deeper the awareness of the ironic conditions of knowledge.

Twentieth-century human sciences have not so much repeated the cycle White describes for the nineteenth century; rather they have exhibited a persistent oscillation between more realist modes of description and irony. For example, the later work of the anthropologist Clifford Geertz, who was among those prominent in developing the idea of the cultural system out of the Parsonian framework discussed earlier, turns away from Parsons and represents a romantic move. Like Croce, he utilizes an image or symbol to uncover, define, and impose a recognizable pattern in cultural thought, be it the cockfight to explore the patterning of Balinese thought, or the theater state to discuss an aspect of politics undervalued in Western thought. At the same time, however, his mode of selecting such symbols and images draws attention to questions of perspective and questions assumptions of "scientific" objectivity. Similarly, the persistent contemporary interest in Marxist perspectives continues the tragic move in the writing of Marx himself, while also exhibiting increasing concern about issues of epistemology. Thus, throughout the twentieth century, irony has remained consistently strong and has become particularly salient during the two periods—the 1920s and 1930s and the 1970s and 1980s—that have exhibited a pervasive suspension of faith in the idea of grand covering theories and reigning paradigms of research in a number of fields.

The task, particularly now, is not to escape the deeply suspicious and critical nature of the ironic mode of writing, but to embrace and utilize it in combination with other strategies for producing realist descriptions of society. The desirability of reconciling the persistence of irony with other modes of representation derives in turn from a recognition that because all perspectives and interpretations are subject to critical review, they must finally be left as multiple and open-ended alternatives. The only way to an accurate view and confident knowledge of the world is through a sophisticated epistemology that takes full account of intractable contradiction, paradox, irony, and uncertainty in the explanation of human activities. This seems to be the spirit of the developing responses across disciplines to what we described as a contemporary crisis of representation.

Periods of heightened irony in the means of representing social reality seem to go with heightened perceptions throughout society of living through historic moments of profound change. The content of social theory becomes politicized and historicized; the limiting conditions of theory become clearer. Those fields most closely tied in their concerns to describing and explaining social phenomena undergoing complex changes exhibit strong internal challenges to reigning paradigms, and to the idea of paradigms itself. Thus, during the 1970s and early 1980s, we find such generalist works on social theory as Anthony Giddens's *New Rules of Sociological Method* (1976) and *Central Problems of Social Theory: Action Structure, and Contradiction in Social Analysis* (1979), Alvin Gouldner's *The Coming Crisis in Western Sociology* (1970), R.J. Bernstein's *The Restructuring of Social and Political Theory* (1976), and Pierre Bourdieu's *Outline of a Theory of Practice* (1977). Simultaneously, the problems posed in such works of theoretical discourse are more directly and cogently being addressed in the research process itself, which for fields such as cultural anthropology and history, is significantly a matter of representing in a narrative form social and cultural realities. Empirical research monographs, through self-conscious attention to their writing strategies, equally become works of heightened theoretical significance and ambition. Intellectually, then, the problem of the moment is less one of explaining changes within broad encompassing frameworks of theory from a concern to preserve the purpose and legitimacy of such theorizing, than of exploring innovative ways of describing at a microscopic level the process of change itself.

A jeweler's-eye view of the world is thus urgently needed, and this is precisely where the strength and attractiveness of cultural anthropology reside at the moment. As we will see in the next chapter, anthropology's distinctive method of research, ethnography, has long been focused precisely on problems of the recording, interpretation, and description of closely observed social and cultural processes. While long associated by its public with the study of so-called primitive, isolated societies, anthropology in fact has been applying its "jeweler's-eye" method for some time to complex nation-state societies, including, increasingly, our own. Moreover, the contemporary innovations in anthropological writing, occasioned by the same crisis of representation affecting other disciplines, are moving it toward an unprecedentedly acute political and historical sensibility that is transforming the way cultural diversity is portrayed. With its concerns firmly established across the traditional divide of the social sciences and humanities, anthropology (among other disciplines such as literary criticism) is thus serving as a conduit for the diffusion of ideas and methods from one to the other. The current changes in past conventions for writing about other cultures are the locus of operation for this strategic contemporary function of anthropology.

Within anthropology itself, the current absence of paradigmatic authority is registered by the fact that there are presently many anthropologies: efforts to revitalize old research programs such as **ethnosemantics**, British functionalism, French structuralism, cultural ecology, and psychological anthropology; efforts to synthesize Marxist approaches with structuralism, semiotics, and other forms of symbolic analysis; efforts to establish more encompassing frameworks of explanation such as sociobiology to achieve the aim of a more fully "scientific" anthropology; efforts to merge the influential study of language in anthropology with the concerns of social theory. All of these have merits and problems in different measure; yet, all are inspired by and inspire the practice of ethnography as a common denominator in a very fragmented period.

The explicit discourse that reflects on the doing and writing of ethnography itself is what we call interpretive anthropology. It grew out of the cultural anthropology of the 1960s, gradually shifting in emphasis from the attempt to construct a general theory of culture to a reflection on ethnographic fieldwork and writing. It has a major spokesman in Clifford Geertz, whose work has made it the most influential style of anthropology among the wider intellectual public. It is, as well, the trend in the anthropology of the 1960s from which the contemporary experimental ethnographies, our central concern in this essay, took off.

We now turn from the broader intellectual trend affecting anthropology to this inside story. We first discuss the central role that the ethnographic method, and especially the production of ethnographic texts, has occupied in modern cultural anthropology. Then we trace the emergence of interpretive anthropology as a discourse on this central research practice, to its revision in response to the crisis of representation we have discussed in this chapter.

References

Alexander, Jeffrey. 1982-83. *Theoretical logic in sociology*. 4 vols. Berkeley: University of California Press.

Anderson, Perry. 1984. *In the tracks of historical materialism*. Chicago: University of Chicago Press.

Bernstein, Richard J. 1976. *The restructuring of social and political theory*. Philadelphia: University of Pennsylvania Press.

Bourdieu, Pierre. 1977. *Outline of a theory of practice*. Cambridge: Cambridge University Press.

Bruss, Elizabeth. 1982. *Beautiful theories: The spectacle of discourse in contemporary criticism*. Baltimore: The Johns Hopkins University Press.

Dennet, Dennis. 1984. Computer models and the mind—a view from the East Pole. *Times Literary Supplement*, p. 1454.

Geertz, Clifford. 1980. Blurred genres. *American Scholar* 49: 165-79.

Giddens, Anthony. 1976. *New rules of the sociological method*. New York: Basic Books.

—. 1979. *Central Problems in social theory: Action, structure and contradiction in social analysis*. Berkeley: University of California Press.

Gleick, James. 1984. Solving the mathematical riddle of chaos. *New York Times Magazine*, June 10, pp.30-32.

Gouldner, Alvin W. 1970. *The coming crisis of Western sociology*. New York: Basic Books.

Hirsch, Fred. 1976. *The social limits to growth*. Cambridge, Mass.: Harvard University Press.

Jameson, Fredric. 1984. Postmodernism, or the cultural logic of late capitalism. *New Left Review* 146: 53-93.

Livingston, Debra. 1982. 'Round and 'round the bramble bush: from legal realism to critical legal scholarship. *Harvard Law Review* 95: 1670-76.

Luhmann, Niklas. 1984. *Soziale Systeme: Grundrisse einer allegemeinen Theorie*. Frankfurt am Main: Suhrkamp.

Lyotard, Jean-François. 1984 [1979]. *The postmodern condition: A report on knowledge*. Minneapolis: University of Minnesota Press.

Piore, Michael J. and Charles F. Sabel. 1984. *The second industrial divide*. New York: Basic Books.

Rorty, Richard. 1979. *Philosophy and the mirror of nature*. Princeton: Princeton University Press.

Thurow, Lester. 1983. *Dangerous currents: The state of economics*. New York: Random House.

Ungar, Roberto M. 1976. *Law and modern social theory*. New York: Free Press.

—. 1984. *Passion: An essay on personality*. New York: Free Press.

White, Hayden V. 1973. *Metahistory: The historical imagination in nineteenth century Europe*. Baltimore: The Johns Hopkins University Press.

Wilson, E.O. 1975. *Sociobiology: The new synthesis*. Cambridge, Mass.: Harvard University Press.

Study Questions
1. What is the "crisis in representation" which Marcus and Fischer refer to?

2. What is meant by an "ironic mode of writing?"

3. How do the authors characterize the "motion" of intellectual history?

Further Readings
Fischer, Michael M.J. 1984. Toward a Third World Poetics: Seeing through Fiction and Film in the Iranian Culture Area. *Knowledge and Society* 5: 171-241.

—. 1986. Ethnicity and post-modern arts of memory. *Writing Culture: The Poetics and Politics of Ethnography*. Eds. James Clifford and George E. Marcus. Berkeley: University of California Press.

Marcus, George E., and Cushman, Dick. 1982. Ethnographies as Texts. *Annual Review of Anthropology* 11: 25-69.

36

Theory in Anthropology Since the Sixties

SHERRY B. ORTNER

Every year, around the time of the meetings of the American Anthropological Association, the *New York Times* asks a Big Name anthropologist to contribute an op-ed piece on the state of the field. These pieces tend to take a rather gloomy view. A few years ago, for example, Marvin Harris suggested that anthropology was being taken over by mystics, religious fanatics, and California cultists; that the meetings were dominated by panels on shamanism, witchcraft, and "abnormal phenomena"; and that "scientific papers based on empirical studies" had been willfully excluded from the program (Harris 1978). More recently, in a more sober tone, Eric Wolf suggested that the field of anthropology is coming apart. The sub-fields (and sub-sub-fields) are increasingly pursuing their specialized interests, losing contact with each other and with the whole. There is no longer a shared discourse, a shared set of terms to which all practitioners address themselves, a shared language we all, however idiosyncratically, speak (Wolf 1980).

The state of affairs does seem much as Wolf describes it. The field appears to be a thing of shreds and patches, of individuals and small coteries pursuing disjunctive investigations and talking mainly to themselves. We do not even hear stirring arguments any more. Although anthropology was never actually unified in the sense of adopting a single shared paradigm, there was at least a period when there were a few large categories of theoretical affiliation, a set of identifiable camps or schools, and a few simple epithets one could hurl at one's opponents. Now there appears to be an apathy of spirit even at this level. We no longer call each other names. We are no longer sure of how the sides are to be drawn up, and of where we would place ourselves if we could identify the sides.

Yet as anthropologists we can recognize in all of this the classic symptoms of liminality—confusion of categories, expressions of chaos and antistructure. And we know that such disorder may be the breeding ground for a new and perhaps better order. Indeed, if one scrutinizes the present more closely, one may even discern within it the shape of the new order to come. That is what I propose to do in this article. I will argue that a new key symbol of theoretical orientation is emerging, which may be labeled "practice" (or "action" or "praxis"). This is neither a theory nor a method in itself, but rather, as I said, a symbol in the name of which a variety of methods are being developed. In order to understand the significance of this trend, however we must go back at least twenty years and see where we started from, and how we got to where we are now.

Before launching this enterprise it is important to specify its nature. This essay will be primarily concerned with the *relations* between various theoretical schools or approaches, both within periods of time, and across time. No single approach will be exhaustively outlined or discussed in itself; rather, various themes or dimensions of each will be highlighted insofar as they relate to the larger trends of thought with which I am concerned. Every anthropologist will probably find his or her favorite school oversimplified, if not outright distorted, insofar as I have chosen to emphasize features that do not correspond to what are normally taken, among the practitioners, to be its most important theoretical features. Thus readers seeking more exhaustive discussions of particular approaches, and/or discussions pursued from a point of view more interior to the approaches, will have to seek elsewhere. The concern here, again, is with elucidating relations.

The Sixties: Symbol, Nature, Structure

Although there is always some arbitrariness in choosing a starting point for any historical discussion, I have decided to begin in the early 1960s. For one thing, that is when *I* started in the field, and since I generally assume the importance of seeing any system, at least in part, from the actor's point of view, I might as well unite theory and practice from the outset. It is thus fully acknowledged that this discussion proceeds not from some hypothetical external point, but from the perspective of this particular actor moving through anthropology between 1960 and the present.

But actors always wish to claim universality for their particular experiences and interpretations. I would further suggest then that, in some relatively objective sense, there was in fact a major set of revolutions in anthropological theory, beginning in the early sixties. Indeed it appears that such revisionist upheaval was characteristic of many other fields in that era. In literary criticism, for example,

by the 1960's a volatile mixture of linguistics, psychoanalysis and semiotics, structuralism, Marxist theory and reception aesthetics had begun to replace the older moral humanism. The literary text tended to move towards the status of phenomenon: a socio-psycho-culturo-linguistic and ideological event, arising from the offered competencies of language, the available taxonomies of narrative order, the permutations of genre, the sociological options of structural formation, the ideological constraints of the infra-structure .... [There was a] broad and contentious revisionist perception. (Bradbury 1981:137)

In anthropology at the close of the fifties, the theoretical *bricoleur's* kit consisted of three major, and somewhat exhausted, paradigms—British structural-functionalism (descended from A.R. Radcliffe-Brown and Bronislaw Malinowski), American cultural and psychocultural anthropology (descended from Margaret Mead, Ruth Benedict, et al.), and American evolutionist anthropology (centered around Leslie White and Julian Steward, and having strong affiliations with archaeology). Yet it was also during the fifties that certain actors and cohorts central to our story were trained in each of these areas. They emerged at the beginning of the sixties with aggressive ideas about how to strengthen the paradigms of their mentors and ancestors, as well as with, apparently, much more combative stances vis-à-vis the other schools. It was this combination of new ideas and intellectual aggressiveness that launched the three movements with which this account begins: symbolic anthropology, cultural ecology, and structuralism.

Symbolic Anthropology

"Symbolic anthropology" as a label was never used by any of its main proponents in the formative period—say, 1963-66. Rather it was a shorthand tag (probably invented by the opposition), an umbrella for a number of rather diverse trends. Two of its major variants appear to have been independently invented, one by Clifford Geertz and his colleagues at the University of Chicago, and the other by Victor Turner at Cornell.[1] The important differences between the Geertzians and the Turnerians are probably not fully appreciated by those outside the symbolic anthropology scene. Whereas Geertz was primarily influenced by Max Weber (via Talcott Parsons), Turner was primarily influenced by Emile Durkheim. Further, Geertz clearly represents a transformation upon the earlier American anthropology concerned mainly with the operations of "culture," while Turner represents a transformation upon the earlier British anthropology concerned mainly with the operations of "society."

Geertz's most radical theoretical move (1973b) was to argue that culture is not something locked inside people's heads, but rather is embodied in public symbols, symbols through which the members of a society communicate their worldview, value-orientations, ethos, and all the rest to one another, to future generations—and to anthropologists. With this formulation, Geertz gave the hitherto elusive concept of culture a relatively fixed locus, and a degree of objectivity, that it did not have before. The focus on symbols was for Geertz and many others heuristically liberating: it told them where to find what they wanted to study. Yet the point about symbols was that they were ultimately vehicles for meanings; the study of symbols as such was never an end in itself. Thus, on the one hand, Geertzians[2] have never been particularly interested in distinguishing and cataloguing the varieties of symbolic types (signals, signs, icons, indexes, et cetera—see, in contrast, Singer 1980); nor, on the other hand (and in contrast with Turner to whom we will get in a moment), have they been particularly interested in the ways in which symbols perform certain practical operations in the social process—heal people through curing rites, turn boys and girls into men and women through initiation, kill people through sorcery— and so forth. Geertzians do not ignore these practical social effects, but such operations have not been their primary focus of interest. Rather, the focus of Geertzian anthropology has consistently been the question of how symbols shape the way social actors see, feel, and think about the world, or, in other words, how symbols operate as vehicles of "culture."

It is further worth noting, in anticipation of the discussion of structuralism, that Geertz's heart has always been more with the "ethos" side of culture than with the "worldview," more with the affective and stylistic dimensions than with the cognitive. While of course it is very difficult (not to say unproductive and ultimately wrong-headed) to separate the two too sharply, it is nonetheless possible to distinguish an emphasis on one or the other side. For Geertz, then (as for Benedict, especially, before him), even the most cognitive or intellectual of cultural systems—say, the Balinese calendars—are analyzed not (only) to lay bare a set of cognitive ordering principles, but (especially) to understand how the Balinese way of chopping up time stamps their sense of self, of social relations, and of conduct with a particular culturally distinctive flavor, an ethos (1973e).[3]

The other major contribution of the Geertzian framework was the insistence on studying culture "from the actor's point of view" (e.g., 1975). Again, this does not imply that we must get "into people's heads." What it means, very simply, is that culture is a product of acting social beings trying to make sense of the world in which they find themselves, and, if *we* are to make sense of a culture, we must situate ourselves in the position from which it was constructed. Culture is not some abstractly ordered system, deriving its logic from hidden structural principles, or from special symbols that provide the "keys" to its coherence. Its logic—the principles of relations that obtain among its elements—derives rather from the logic or organization of action, from people operating within certain institutional orders, interpreting their situations in order to act coherently within them (1973d). It may be noted here, however, that while the actor-centered perspective is fundamental to Geertz's framework, it is not systematically elaborated: Geertz did not develop a theory of action or practice as such. He did, however, firmly plant the actor at the center of his model, and much of the later practice-centered work builds on a Geertzian (or Geertzo-Weberian) base, as we shall see.

The other major figure in the Chicago school of symbolic anthropology has been David Schneider. Schneider, like Geertz, was a product of Parsons, and he, too, concentrated primarily on refining the culture concept. But his efforts went toward understanding the *internal logic* of systems of symbols and meanings, by way of a notion of "core symbols," and also by way of ideas akin to Claude Lévi-Strauss's concept of structure (e.g., 1968, 1977). Indeed, although Geertz prominently used the phrase "cultural *system*" (emphasis added), he never paid much attention to the systemic aspects of culture, and it was Schneider who developed this side of the problem much more fully. Schneider in his own work cut culture off from social action much more radically than Geertz did. Yet, perhaps precisely because social action ("practice," "praxis") was so radically separated from "culture" in Schneider's work, he and some of his students were among the earliest of the symbolic anthropologists to see practice itself as a problem (Barnett 1977; Dolgin, Kemnitzer, and Schneider 1977).

Victor Turner, finally, comes out of quite a different intellectual background. He was trained in the Max Gluckman variant of British structural-functionalism, which was influenced by Marxism, and which stressed that the normal state of society is not one of solidarity and harmonious integration of parts, but rather one of conflict and contradiction. Thus, the analytic question was not, as for the straight line descendants of Durkheim, how solidarity is fine-tuned, reinforced, and intensified, but rather how it is constructed and maintained in the first place over and above the conflicts and contradictions that constitute the normal state of affairs. To the American reader, this may appear to be only a minor variant on the basic functionalist project, since for both schools the emphasis is on the maintenance of integration, and specifically on the maintenance of the integration of "society" —actors, groups, the social whole—as opposed to "culture." But Gluckman and his students (including Turner) believed their differences from the mainstream to be quite deep. Moreover, they always constituted a minority within the British establishment. This background may account in part for Turner's originality vis-à-vis his compatriots, leading ultimately to his independently inventing his own brand of an explicitly symbolic anthropology.

Despite the relative novelty of Turner's move to symbols, however, there is in his work a deep continuity with British social anthropological concerns, and, as a result, profound differences between Turnerian and Geertzian symbolic anthropology. For Turner, symbols are of interest not as vehicles of, and analytic windows onto, "culture,"—the integrated ethos and worldview of a society—but as what might be called operators in the social process things that, when put together in certain arrangements in certain contexts (especially rituals), produce essentially social transformations. Thus, symbols in Ndembu curing or initiation or hunting rituals are investigated for the ways in which they move actors from one status to another, resolve social contradictions, and wed actors to the categories and norms of their society (1967). Along the way toward these rather traditional structural-functional goals, however, Turner identified or elaborated upon certain ritual mechanisms, and some of the concepts he developed have become indispensable parts of the vocabulary of ritual analysis—liminality, marginality, antistructure, communitas, and so forth (1967, 1969).[4]

Turner and the Chicago symbolic anthropologists did not so much conflict with one another as simply, for the most part, talk past one another. Yet the Turnerians[5] added an important, and characteristically British, dimension to the field of symbolic anthropology as a whole, a sense of the *pragmatics* of symbols. They investigated in much more detail than Geertz, Schneider, et al., the "effectiveness of symbols," the question of how symbols actually do what all symbolic anthropologists claim they do: operate as active forces in the social process (see also Lévi-Strauss 1963; Tambiah 1968; Lewis 1977; Fernandez 1974).

In retrospect, one may say that symbolic anthropology had a number of significant limitations. I refer not to the charges that it was unscientific, mystical, literary, soft-headed, and the like leveled at it by practitioners of cultural ecology (see below). Rather, one may point to symbolic anthropology's lack, especially in its American form, of a systematic sociology; its underdeveloped sense of the politics of culture; and its lack of curiosity concerning the production and maintenance of symbolic systems. These points will be discussed more fully in the course of this article.

Cultural Ecology[6]

Cultural ecology represented a new synthesis of, and a further development upon, the materialist evolutionism of Leslie White (1943, 1949), Julian Steward (1953, 1955), and V. Gordon Childe (1942). Its roots go back to Lewis Henry Morgan and E.B. Tylor in the nineteenth century, and ultimately back to Marx and Engels, although many of the 1950s evolutionists, for understandable political reasons, were not encouraged to emphasize the Marxist connection.[7]

White had been investigating what came to be labeled "general evolution," or the evolution of culture-in-general, in terms of stages of social complexity and technological advancement. These stages were subsequently refined by Elman Service (1958), and by Marshall Sahlins and Elman Service (1960), into the famous bands-tribes-chiefdoms-states scheme. The evolutionary mechanisms in White's framework derived from more or less fortuitous events: technological inventions that allowed for the greater "capture of energy," and population growth (and perhaps warfare and conquest) that stimulated the development of more complex forms of social/political organization and coordination. Steward (1953) attacked both the focus on the evolution of culture-in-general (as opposed to specific cultures), and the lack of a more systematically operative evolutionary mechanism. Instead, he emphasized that specific cultures evolve their specific forms in the process of adapting to specific environmental conditions, and that the apparent uniformity of evolutionary stages is actually a matter of similar adaptations to similar natural conditions in different parts of the world.

If the idea that culture was embodied in public, observable symbols was the key to the liberation of symbolic anthropology from earlier American cultural anthropology, the concept that played a similar role in cultural ecology was "adaptation." (See Alland 1975 for a summary.) Just as Geertz had trumpeted that the study of culture as embodied in symbols removed the problem of getting inside people's heads, so Sahlins proclaimed the focus on adaptation to environmental factors as the way around such amorphous factors as cultural *gestalten* and historical dialectics (1964). There was a large-scale rejection of the study of the inner workings of both culture in the American sense and society in the British sense. Internal dynamics were seen as hard to measure, and even harder to choose among for purposes of assigning causal primacy, whereas external factors of natural and social environment were amenable to treatment as fixed, measurable, "independent variables:"

> For decades, centuries now, intellectual battle has been given over which sector of culture is the decisive one for change. Many have entered the lists under banners diverse. Curiously, few seem to fall. Leslie White champions technological growth as the sector most responsible for cultural evolution; Julian Huxley, with many others, sees "man's view of destiny" as the deciding force; the mode of production and the class struggle are still very much in contention. Different as they are, these positions agree in one respect, that the impulse to development is generated from within .... The case for internal causes of development may be bolstered by pointing to a mechanism, such as the Hegelian dialectic, or it may rest more insecurely on an argument from logic .... In any event, an unreal and vulnerable assumption is always there, that cultures are closed systems.... It is precisely on this point that cultural ecology offers a new perspective.... [I]t shifts attention to the relation between

inside and outside; it envisions as the mainspring of the evolutionary movement the interchange between culture and environment. Now which view shall
prevail is not to be decided on a sheet of paper .... But if adaptation wins over
inner dynamism, it will be for certain intrinsic and obvious strengths. Adaptation is real, naturalistic, anchored to those historic contexts of cultures that
inner dynamism ignores. (Sahlins 1964:135136)[8]

The Sahlins and Service version of cultural ecology, which was also adhered to
by the mainstream of the archaeology wing of anthropology, was still fundamentally evolutionist. The primary use of the adaptation concept was in
explaining, the development, maintenance, and transformation of social forms.
But there was another variant of cultural ecology, which developed slightly
later, and which came to dominate the materialist wing in the sixties. Its position, expressed most forcefully by Marvin Harris (e.g., 1966) and perhaps most
elegantly by Roy Rappaport (1967), drew heavily on systems theory. It shifted
the analytic focus away from evolution, and toward explaining the existence of
particular bits of particular cultures in terms of the adaptive or system-main-
taining functions of those bits. Thus, the Maring *kaiko* ritual prevented the
degradation of the natural environment (Rappaport 1967), the Kwakiutl potlatch maintained a balance of food distribution over tribal segments (Piddocke
1969), and the sacredness of the cow in India protected a vital link in the agricultural food chain (Harris 1966). In these studies, the interest has shifted from
how the environment stimulates (or prevents) the development of social and
cultural forms, to the question of the ways in which to social and cultural forms
function to maintain an existing relationship with the environment. It was these
latter sorts of studies that came to represent cultural ecology as a whole in the
sixties.

One would have had to be particularly out of touch with anthropological theory at the time not to have been aware of the acrimonious debate between the
cultural ecologists and the symbolic anthropologists. Whereas the cultural ecologists considered the symbolic anthropologists to be fuzzy-headed mentalists,
involved in unscientific and unverifiable flights of subjective interpretation, the
symbolic anthropologists considered cultural ecology to be involved with
mindless and sterile scientism, counting calories and measuring rainfall, and
willfully ignoring the one truth that anthropology had presumably established
by that time: that culture mediates all human behavior. The Manichaean struggle between "materialism" and "idealism," "hard" and "soft" approaches, interpretive "emics" and explanatory "etics," dominated the field for a good part of
the decade of the sixties, and in some quarters well into the seventies.

That most of us thought and wrote in terms of such oppositions may be partly rooted in more pervasive schemes of Western thought: subjective/objective,

nature/culture, mind/body, and so on. The practice of fieldwork itself may further contribute to such thinking, based as it is on the paradoxical injunction to participate and observe at one and the same time. It may be then that this sort of polarized construction of the intellectual landscape in anthropology is too deeply motivated, by both cultural categories and the forms of practice of the trade, to be completely eliminated. But the emic/etic struggle of the sixties had a number of unfortunate effects, not the least of which was the prevention of adequate self-criticism on both sides of the fence. Both schools could luxuriate in the faults of the other, and not inspect their own houses for serious weaknesses. In fact, both sides were weak not only in being unable to handle what the other side did (the symbolic anthropologists in renouncing all claims to "explanation," the cultural ecologists in losing sight of the frames of meaning within which human action takes place); both were also weak in what neither of them did, which was much of any systematic sociology.[9]

Indeed, from the point of view of British social anthropology, the whole American struggle was quite meaningless, since it seemed to leave out the necessary central term of all proper anthropological discussion: society. Where were the social groups, social relationships, social structures, social institutions, that mediate *both* the ways in which people think ("culture") *and* the which people experience and act upon their environment? But this set of questions could not be answered (had anybody bothered to ask them) in terms of British social anthropological categories, because the British were having their own intellectual upheavals, to which we will return in due course.

Structuralism

Structuralism, the more-or-less single-handed invention of Claude Lévi-Strauss, was the only genuinely new paradigm to be developed in the sixties. One might even say that it is the only genuinely original social science paradigm (and humanities [paradigm] too, for that matter) to be developed in the twentieth century. Drawing on linguistics and communication theory, and considering himself influenced by both Marx and Freud, Lévi-Strauss argued that the seemingly bewildering variety of social and cultural phenomena could be rendered intelligible by demonstrating the shared relationships of those phenomena to a few simple, underlying principles. He sought to establish the universal grammar of culture, the ways in which units of cultural discourse are created (by the principle of binary opposition), and the rules according to which the units (pairs of opposed terms) are arranged and combined to produce the actual cultural productions (myths, marriage rules, totemic clan arrangements, and the like) that anthropologists record. Cultures are primarily systems of classification, as well as the sets of institutional and intellectual productions built upon those systems of classification and performing further operations upon them. One of the most important secondary operations of culture in relation to its own taxonomies is precisely to mediate or reconcile the oppositions which are the bases of those taxonomies in the first place.

In practice, structural analysis consists of sifting out the basic sets of oppositions that underlie some complex cultural phenomena—a myth, a ritual, a marriage system—and of showing the ways in which the phenomenon in question is both an expression of those contrasts and a reworking of them, thereby producing a culturally meaningful statement of, or reflection upon, order. Even without the full analysis of a myth or ritual, however, the sheer enumeration of the important sets of oppositions in a culture is taken to be a useful enterprise because it reveals the axes of thought, and the limits of the thinkable, within that and related cultures (e.g., Needham 1973b). But the fullest demonstration of the power of structural analysis is seen in Lévi-Strauss's four-volume study, *Mythologiques* (1964-71). Here the method allows the ordering of data both on a vast scale (including most of indigenous South America, and parts of native North America as well), and also in terms of explicating myriad tiny details— why the jaguar covers his mouth when he laughs, or why honey metaphors are used to describe the escape of game animals. The combination of wide scope and minute detail is what lends the work its great power.

Much has been made of the point that Lévi-Strauss ultimately grounds the structures he discerns beneath society and culture in the structure of the mind. Both the point itself, and the criticism of it, are perhaps somewhat irrelevant for anthropologists. It seems incontrovertible that all humans, and all cultures, classify. This suggests in turn an innate mental propensity of some sort, but it does not mean that any particular scheme of classification is inevitable, [any] more than the fact that all humans eat motivates some universal system of food categories.

The enduring contribution of Lévi-Straussian structuralism lies in the perception that luxuriant variety, even apparent randomness, may have a deeper unity and systematicity, derived from the operation of a small number of underlying principles. It is in this sense that Lévi-Strauss claims affinity with Marx and Freud, who similarly argue that beneath the surface proliferation of forms, a few relatively simple and relatively uniform mechanisms are operating (DeGeorge and DeGeorge 1972). Such a perception, in turn, allows us to distinguish much more clearly between simple transformations, which operate within a given structure, and real change, revolution if you will, in which the structure itself is transformed. Thus, despite the naturalistic or biologistic base of structuralism, and despite Lévi-Strauss's personal predilection for considering that *plus ça change, plus c'est la même chose*, the theory has always had important implications for a much more historical and/or evolutionary anthro-

pology than that practiced by the master. The work of Louis Dumont in particular has developed some of these evolutionary implications in analyzing the
structure of the Indian caste system, and in articulating some of the profound
structural changes involved in the transition from caste to class (1965, 1970;
see also Goldman 1970, Barnett 1977, Sahlins 1981).[10]

Structuralism was never all that popular among American anthropologists.
Although it was seen at first (mostly by the cultural ecologists) as a variant of
symbolic anthropology, its central assumptions were in fact rather distant
from those of the symbolic anthropologists (with the partial exception of the
Schneiderians). There were a number of reasons for this, which can be only
very briefly sketched: (1) the very pure cognitive emphasis of Lévi-Strauss's
notion of meaning, as against the Americans' interest in ethos and values; (2)
Lévi-Strauss's rather austere emphasis on arbitrariness of meaning (all meaning is established by contrasts, nothing carries any meaning in itself), as
against the Americans' interest in relations between the *forms* of symbolic
constructs, and the *contents* for which they are vehicles;[11] and (3) the explicitly abstract locus of structures, divorced in every way from the actions and
intentions of actors, as against the symbolic anthropologists' fairly consistent,
if variably defined, actor-centrism (again, Schneider is a partial exception to
this point). For all these reasons, and probably more, structuralism was not as
much embraced by American symbolic anthropologists as might have
appeared likely at first glance.[12] It was granted what might be called fictive
kinship status, largely because of its tendency to focus on some of the same
domains that symbolic anthropologists took as their own—myth, ritual, etiquette, and so forth.

The main impact of structuralism outside of France was in England, among
some of the more adventurous British social anthropologists (see especially
Leach 1966). Lévi-Strauss and the British were in fact more truly kin to one
another, born of two lines of descent from Durkheim. In any event, structuralism in the British context underwent a number of important transformations.
Avoiding the question of mind, and of universal structures, British anthropologists primarily applied structural analysis to particular societies and particular cosmologies (e.g., Leach 1966, 1969; Needham 1973a; Yalman 1969; the
point also applies to Dumont [1970] in France). They also focused in more
detail on the process of mediation of oppositions, and produced a number
of quite original ruminations upon anomaly and antistructure, especially
Mary Douglas's *Purity and Danger* (see also Turner 1967, 1969; Leach 1964;
Tambiah 1969).

However, there was also an important way in which many of the British
purged structuralism of one of its more radical features—the eradication of the
Durkheimian distinction between the social "base" and the cultural "reflection"

of it. Lévi-Strauss had claimed that if mythic structures paralleled social structures, it was not because myth reflected society, but because both myth and social organization shared a common underlying structure. Many of the British structuralists (Rodney Needham is the major exception), on the other hand, went back to a position more in the tradition of Durkheim and Marcel Mauss, and considered myth and ritual as reflecting and resolving "at the symbolic level" oppositions taken to be fundamentally social.[13] As long as British structuralism was confined to the study of myth and ritual, then, it was possible for it to fit nicely into British anthropology without having a very profound effect upon it. It became their version of cultural or symbolic anthropology, their theory of superstructure. It was only later, when a structural (i.e., structural-Marxist) eye was turned on the British concept of social structure itself, that the sparks began to fly.

In a number of fields—linguistics, philosophy, history—there was a strong reaction against structuralism by the early seventies. Two interrelated features—the denial of the relevance of an intentional subject in the social and cultural process, and the denial of any significant impact of history or "event" upon structure—were felt to be particularly problematic, not to say unacceptable. Scholars began to elaborate alternative models, in which both agents and events played a more active role. These models did not, however, get much play in anthropology until the late seventies, and they will be discussed in the final section of the essay. In anthropology during most of that decade, structuralism itself, with all its flaws (and virtues), became the basis of one of the dominant schools of theory, structural Marxism. We move now to that decade.

The Seventies: Marx

The anthropology of the 1970s was much more obviously and transparently tied to real-world events than that of the preceding period. Starting in the late 1960s, in both the United States and France (less so in England), radical social movements emerged on a vast scale. First came the counterculture, then the antiwar movement, and then, just a bit later, the women's movement: these movements not only affected the academic world, they originated in good part within it. *Everything* that was part of the existing order was questioned and criticized. In anthropology, the earliest critiques took the form of denouncing the historical links between anthropology on the one hand, and colonialism and imperialism on the other (e.g., Asad 1973, Hymes 1974). But this merely scratched the surface. The issue quickly moved to the deeper question of the nature of our theoretical frameworks, and especially the degree to which they embody and carry forward the assumptions of bourgeois Western culture.

The rallying symbol of the new criticism, and of the theoretical alternatives offered to replace the old models, was Marx. Of all the great nineteenth-century antecedents of modern social science, Marx had been conspicuously absent from the mainstream theoretical repertoire. Parson's *structure of social action,* one of the sacred texts of the Harvard-trained symbolic anthropologists, surveyed the thought of Durkheim and Weber, and of two economic theorists, Alfred Marshall and Vilfredo Pareto, whose main significance in that context seemed to be that they were Not Marx. The British, including both the symbolic anthropologists and the structuralists, were still firmly embedded in Durkheim. Lévi-Strauss claimed to have been influenced by Marx, but it took a while for anyone to figure out what he meant by that. Even the cultural ecolog[ists], the only self-proclaimed materialists of the sixties, hardly invoked Marx at all; indeed Marvin Harris specifically repudiated him (1968). One does not need to be an especially subtle analyst of the ideological aspects of intellectual history to realize that the absence of a significant Marxist influence before the seventies was just as much a reflex of real-world politics as was the emergence of a strong Marxist influence in the seventies.

There were at least two distinct Marxist schools of anthropological theory: structural Marxism, developed mainly in France and England, and political economy, which emerged first in the United States, and later in England as well. There was also a movement that might be called cultural Marxism, worked out largely in historical and literary studies, but this was not picked up by anthropologists until recently, and will be addressed in the final section of the essay.

Structural Marxism

Structural Marxism was the only one of the schools developed entirely within the field of anthropology, and probably for that reason was also the earliest in its impact. Within it, Marx was used to attack and/or rethink, or at the very least to expand, virtually every theoretical scheme on the landscape—symbolic anthropology, cultural ecology, British social anthropology, and structuralism itself. Structural Marxism constituted a would-be total intellectual revolution, and if it did not succeed in establishing itself as the only alternative to everything else we had, it certainly succeeded in shaking up most of the received wisdom. This is not to say that it was necessarily the actual writings of the structural Marxists themselves (e.g., Althusser 1971; Godelier 3 1977; Terray 1972; Sahlins 1972; Friedman 1975) that had this effect; it was simply that structural Marxism was the original force within anthropology for promulgating and legitimating "Marx," "Marxism," and "critical inquiry" in the discourse of the field as a whole (see also Diamond 1979).

The specific advance of structural Marxism over its antecedent forms of materialist anthropology lay in its locating the determinative forces not in the natural environment and/or in technology, but specifically within certain structures of social relations. Ecological considerations were not excluded, but they were encompassed by and subordinated to the analysis of the social, and especially political, organization of production. Cultural ecology was thus attacked as "vulgar materialism," reinforcing rather than undoing the classical capitalist fetishization of "things," the domination of subjects by objects rather than by the social relations embodied in, and symbolized by, those objects (see especially Friedman 1974). The critical social relations in question, referred to as the mode(s) of production, are not to be confused with the surface organization of social relations traditionally studied by British social anthropologists—lineages, clans, moieties, and all the rest. These surface forms of what the British called "social structure" are seen as native *models* of social organization that have been bought by anthropologists as the real thing, but that actually mask or at least only partially correspond to, the hidden asymmetrical relations of production that are driving the system. Here, then, was situated the critique of traditional British social anthropology (see especially Bloch 1971, 1974, 1977; Terray 1975).

In addition to critiquing and revising both cultural ecology and British social anthropology, structural Marxists turned their attention to cultural phenomena. Unlike the cultural ecologists, the structural Marxists did not dismiss cultural beliefs and native categories as irrelevant to the real or objective operations of society, nor, alternatively, did they set about to show that apparently irrational cultural beliefs, such as the sacred cow, actually had practical adaptive functions. Just as the New Left in the real world took cultural issues (life style, consciousness) more seriously than the Old Left had done, so the structural Marxists allocated to cultural phenomena (beliefs, values, classifications) at least one central function in their model of the social process. Specifically, culture was converted to "ideology" and considered from the point of view of its role in social reproduction: legitimating the existing order, mediating contradictions in the base, and mystifying the sources of exploitation and inequality in the system (O'Laughlin 1974; Bloch 1977; Godelier 1977).

One of the virtues of structural Marxism, then, was that there was a place for everything in its scheme. Refusing to see inquiries into material relations and into "ideology" as opposed enterprises, its practitioners established a model in which the "two levels" were related to one another via a core of social/political/economic processes. In this sense, they offered an explicit mediation between the "materialist" and "idealist" camps of sixties anthropology. The mediation was rather mechanical, as we will discuss in a moment, but it was there.

More important, to my mind, the structural Marxists put a relatively powerful sociology back into the picture period. They cross-fertilized British social anthropological categories with Marxist ones, and produced an expanded model of social organization ("mode of production") which they then proceeded to apply systematically to particular cases. Whereas other Marxisms emphasized relations of political/economic organization ("production") almost exclusively, the structural Marxists were, after all, anthropologists, trained to pay attention to kinship, descent, marriage, exchange, domestic organization, and the like. They thus included these elements within their considerations of political and economic relations (often giving them a more Marxist ring by calling them "relations of reproduction") and the total effect was to produce rich and complex pictures of the social process in specific cases. Given the relative paucity, mentioned earlier, of detailed sociological analysis in the various sixties schools, this was an important contribution.

All this having been said, one may nonetheless recognize that structural Marxism had a number of problems. For one thing, the narrowing of the culture concept to "ideology," which had the powerful effect of allowing analysts to connect cultural conceptions to specific structures of social relations, was too extreme, and posed the problem of relating ideology back to more general conceptions of culture. For another, the tendency to see culture/ideology largely in terms of mystification gave most of the cultural or ideological studies in this school a decided functionalist flavor, since the upshot of these analyses was to show how myth, ritual, taboo, or whatever maintained the status-quo. Finally, and most seriously, although structural Marxists offered a way of mediating the material and ideological "levels," they did not actually challenge the notion that such levels are analytically distinguishable in the first place. Thus despite criticizing the Durkheimian (and Parsonian) notion of "the social" as the "base" of the system, they merely offered a deeper and allegedly more real and objective "base." And despite attempting to discover more important functions for the "superstructure" (or despite claiming that what is base and what is superstructure varies culturally and/or historically, or even occasionally and rather vaguely that the superstructure is part of the base) they continued to reproduce the idea that it is useful to maintain such a set of analytic boxes.

In this sense, it may be seen that structural Marxism was still very much rooted in the sixties. While it injected a healthy dose of sociology into the earlier scheme of categories, and while this sociology was itself relatively originally conceived, the basic pigeonholes of sixties thought were not radically revised. Further, unlike the political economy school and other more recent approaches to be discussed shortly, structural Marxism was largely nonhistorical, a factor which, again, tied it to earlier forms of anthropology. Indeed one may guess that it was in part this comfortable mix of old categories and assumptions wrapped up in a new critical rhetoric that made structural Marxism so appealing in its day. It was in many ways the perfect vehicle for academics who had been trained in an earlier era, but who, in the seventies, were feeling the pull of critical thought and action that was exploding all around them.

Political Economy

The political economy school has taken its inspiration primarily from world-systems and underdevelopment theories in political sociology (Wallerstein 1976; Gunder Frank 1967). In contrast to structural Marxism, which focused largely, in the manner of conventional anthropological studies, on relatively discrete societies or cultures, the political economists have shifted the focus to large-scale regional political/economic systems (e.g., Hart 1982). Insofar as they have attempted to combine this focus with traditional fieldwork in specific communities or microregions, their research has generally taken the form of studying the effects of capitalist penetration upon those communities (e.g., American Ethnologist 1978; Schneider and Schneider 1976). The emphasis on the impact of external forces, and on the ways in which societies change or evolve largely in adaptation to such impact, ties the political economy school in certain ways to the cultural ecology of the sixties, and indeed many of its current practitioners were trained in that school (e.g., Ross 1980). But whereas for sixties cultural ecolog[ists], often studying relatively "primitive" societies, the important external forces were those of the natural environment, for the seventies political economists, generally studying "peasants," the important external forces are those of the state and the capitalist world system.

At the level of theory, the political economists differ from their cultural ecology forebears partly in showing a greater willingness to incorporate cultural or symbolic issues into their inquiries (e.g., Schneider 1978; Riegelhaupt 1978). Specifically, their work tends to focus on symbols involved in the development of class or group identity, in the context of political/economic struggles of one sort or another.The political economy school thus overlaps with the burgeoning "ethnicity" industry, although the literature in the latter field is too vast and too amorphous for me to do more than nod to here. In any event, the willingness of the political economists to pay attention, in however circumscribed fashion to symbolic processes, is part of the general relaxation of the old materialism/idealism wars of the sixties.

The emphasis of this school upon larger regional processes is also salutary, at least up to a point. Anthropologists do have a tendency to treat societies, even villages, as if they were islands unto themselves, with little sense of the larger systems of relations in which these units are embedded. The occasional work (e.g., Edmund Leach's *Political Systems of Highland Burma*) that has viewed societies in larger regional context has been something of an unclassifiable (if admired) freak. To ignore the fact that peasants are part of states, and that even "primitive" societies and communities are invariably involved in wider systems of exchanges of all sorts, is to seriously distort the data, and it is the virtue of the political economists that they remind us of this.

Finally, the political economists must be given leading credit for stressing very strongly the importance of history for anthropological study. They are not the first to have done so, nor are they the only ones doing so now, and I will say more about anthropology's rapprochement with history in the conclusions of this essay. Nonetheless, it is certainly the members of this school who appear the most committed to a fully historical anthropology, and who are producing sustained and systematic work grounded in this commitment.

On the negative side of the ledger, we may complain first that the political economy model is too economic, too strictly material. One hears a lot about wages, the market, the cash nexus, economic exploitation, underdevelopment, and so forth, but not enough about the relations of power, domination, manipulation, control, and the like which those economic relations play into, and which for actors constitute much of the experienced pain of economic injustice. Political economy, in other words, is not political enough.

My main objection, however, is located deeper in the theoretical model of political economy. Specifically, I find the capitalism-centered view of the world questionable, to say the least, especially for anthropology. At the core of the model is the assumption that virtually everything we study has already been touched ("penetrated") by the capitalist world system, and that therefore much of what we see in our fieldwork and describe in our monographs must be understood as having been shaped in response to that system. Perhaps this is true for European peasants, but even here one would want at least to leave the question open. When we get even further from the "center," however, the assumption becomes very problematic indeed. A society, even a village, has its own structure and history, and this must be as much part of the analysis as its relations with the larger context within which it operates. (See Joel Kahn [1980] for a more balanced view.)

The problems derived from the capitalism-centered worldview also affect the political economists' view of history. History is often treated as something that arrives, like a ship, from outside the society in question. Thus we do not get the history *of* that society, but the impact of (our) history *on* that society. The accounts produced from such a perspective are often quite unsatisfactory in terms of traditional anthropological concerns: the actual organization and culture of the society in question. Traditional studies of course had their own problems with respect to history. They often presented us with a thin chapter on "historical background" at the beginning and an inadequate chapter on "social change" at the end. The political economy study inverts this relationship, but only to create the inverse problem.

The political economists, moreover, tend to situate themselves more on the ship of (capitalist) history than on the shore. They say in effect that we can never know what the other system, in its unique, "traditional," aspects, really looked like anyway. By realizing that much of what we see as tradition is in fact a response to Western impact, so the argument goes, we not only get a more accurate picture of what is going on, but we acknowledge at the same time the pernicious effects of our own system upon others. Such a view is also present, but in modes of anger and/or despair rather than pragmatism, in a number of recent works that question philosophically whether we can ever truly know the "other"—Edward Said's *Orientalism* is the prime example (see also Rabinow 1977; Crapanzano 1980; Riesman 1977).

To such a position we can only respond: Try. The effort is as important as the results, in terms of both our theories and our practices. The attempt to view other systems from ground level is the basis, perhaps the only basis, of anthropology's distinctive contribution to the human sciences. It is our capacity, largely developed in fieldwork, to take the perspective of the folks on the shore, that allows us to learn anything at all—even in our own culture—beyond what we already know. (Indeed, as more and more anthropologists are doing fieldwork in Western cultures, including the United States, the importance of maintaining a capacity to see otherness, even next door, becomes more and more acute.) Further, it is our location "on the ground" that puts us in a position to see people not simply as passive reactors to and enactors of some "system," but as active agents and subjects of their own history.

In concluding this section, I must confess that my placement of the political economy school in the seventies is something of an ideological move. In fact political economy is very much alive and well in the eighties, and it will probably thrive for some time. My periodization is thus, like that of all histories, only partly related to real time. I have included political economy and structural Marxism within this period/category because both schools continue to share a set of assumptions distinct from what I wish to emphasize for the anthropology of the eighties. Specifically, both assume, together with earlier anthropologies, that human action and historical process are almost entirely structurally or systemically determined. Whether it be the hidden hand of structure or the juggernaut of capitalism that is seen as the agent of society/history, it is certainly not in any central way real people doing real things. These are precisely the views from which at least some anthropologists, as well as practitioners in many other fields, appear to be struggling to break free as we move into the present decade.

Into the Eighties: Practice

I began this article by noting the apparent accuracy of Wolf's remarks to the effect that the field of anthropology is disintegrating, even granting the low degree of integration it had in the past. I also suggested that one could find scattered over the landscape the elements of a new trend that seems to be gathering force and coherence. In this final section I call attention to this new trend, sketch it, and subject it to a preliminary critique.

For the past several years, there has been growing interest in analysis focused through one or another of a bundle of interrelated terms: practice, praxis, action, interaction, activity, experience, performance. A second, and closely related, bundle of terms focuses on the doer of all that doing: agent, actor, person, self, individual, subject.

In some fields, movement in this direction began relatively early in the seventies, some of it in direct reaction to structuralism. In linguistics, for example, there was an early rejection of structural linguistics and a strong move to view language as communication and performance (e.g., Bauman and Sherzer 1974; Cole and Morgan 1975). In anthropology, too, there were scattered calls for a more action based approach. In France, Pierre Bourdieu published his *Outline of a Theory of Practice* in 1972. In the United States, Geertz attacked both hypercoherent studies of symbolic systems (many of them inspired by his own programmatic papers) and what he saw as the sterile formalism of structuralism, calling instead for anthropologists to see "human behavior ... as ... symbolic action" (1973a:10; see also Dolgin, Kemnitzer, and Schneider 1977; Wagner 1975; T. Turner 1969). In England, there was a minority wing that criticized traditional views of "social structure" not from the point of view of structural Marxism, but from the perspective of individual choice and decision making (e.g., Kapferer 1976).[14]

For much of the seventies, however, the structural Marxists and, later, the political economists, remained dominant, at least within anthropology. For them, social and cultural phenomena were to be explained largely by being referred to systemic/structural mechanisms of one sort or another. It was only in the late seventies that the hegemony of structural Marxism, if not that of political economy, began to wane. An English translation of Bourdieu's book was published in 1978, and it was at about that time that the calls for a more practice-oriented approach became increasingly audible. Here is a sampler:

> The instruments of reasoning are changing and society is less and less represented as an elaborate machine or a quasi-organism than as a serious game, a sidewalk drama, or a behavioral text. (Geertz 1980a:168)

> We need to watch these systems [of kinship] in action, to study tactics and strategy, not merely the rules of the game. (Barnes 1980:301)

> [G]ender conceptions in any society are to be understood as functioning aspects of a cultural system through which actors manipulate, interpret, legit-

imize, and reproduce the patterns ... that order their social world. (Collier and Rosaldo 1981:311)[15]

What do actors want and how can they get it? (Ortner 1981:366)

If structural/semiotic analysis is to be extended to general anthropology on the model of its pertinence to "language," then what is lost is not merely history and change, but practice-human action in the world. Some might think that what is lost is what anthropology is all about. (Sahlins 1981:6)

As was the case with the strong revisionist trend in the sixties, the present movement appears much broader than the field of anthropology alone. In linguistics, Alton Becker, in a much-cited article, has emphasized issues of text building over and against reification of The Text (1979). In sociology, symbolic interactionism and other forms of so-called microsociology appear to be attracting new attention,[16] and Anthony Giddens has dubbed the relationship between structure and "agency" one of the "central problems" of modern social theory (1979). In history, E.P. Thompson has railed against theorists (every[one] from Parsonians to Stalinists) who treat "history as a 'process without a subject' [and] concur in the eviction from history of human agency" (1978:79). In literary studies, Raymond Williams insists that literature must be treated as the product of particular practices, and accuses those who abstract literature from practice of performing "an extraordinary ideological feat" (1977:46). If we push further—and here we skirt dangerous ground—we might even see the whole sociobiology movement as part of this general trend, insofar as it shifts the evolutionary mechanism from random mutation to intentional choice on the part of actors seeking to maximize reproductive success. (I should probably say, right here and not in a footnote, that I have a range of very strong objections to sociobiology. Nonetheless, I do not think it is too farfetched to see its emergence as part of the broad movement to which I am drawing attention here.)

The practice approach is diverse, and I will not attempt to compare and contrast its many strands. Rather I will select for discussion a number of works that seem to share a common orientation within the larger set, an orientation that seems to me particularly promising. I do not wish to canonize any single one of these works, nor do I wish to provide a label for the subset and endow it with more reality than it has. What I do here is more like beginning to develop a photograph, to coax a latent form into something recognizable.

We may begin by contrasting, in a general way, this (subset of) newer practice-oriented work with certain more established approaches, especially with symbolic interactionism in sociology (Blumer 1962; Goffman 1959; see also

Berreman 1962, and more recently Gregor 1977 in anthropology) and with what was called transactionalism in anthropology (Kapferer 1976, Marriott 1976, Goody 1978, Barth 1966, Bailey 1969). The first point to note is that these approaches were elaborated in opposition to the dominant, essentially Parsonian/Durkheimian, view of the world as ordered by rules and norms.[17] Recognizing that institutional organization and cultural patterning exist, the symbolic interactionists and transactionalists nonetheless sought to minimalize or bracket the relevance of these phenomena for understanding social life:

> From the standpoint of symbolic interaction, social organization is a frame-
> work inside of which acting units develop their actions. Structural features,
> such as "culture," "social systems," "social stratification," or "social roles," set
> conditions for their action but do not determine their action. (Blumer
> 1962:152).

The newer practice theorists, on the other hand, share a view that "the system" (in a variety of senses to be discussed below) does in fact have very powerful, even "determining," effect upon human action and the shape of events. Their interest in the study of action and interaction is thus not a matter of denying or minimizing this point, but expresses rather an urgent need to understand where "the system" comes from—how it is produced and reproduced, and how it may have changed in the past or be changed in the future. As Giddens argues in his important recent book (1979), the study of practice is not an antagonistic alternative to the study of systems or structures, but a necessary complement to it.

The other major aspect of the newer practice orientation, differentiating it significantly from earlier interactionist and transactionalist approaches, resides in a palpable Marxist influence carrying through from the seventies. Partly this is visible in the way in which things like culture and/or structure are viewed. That is, although the newer practice theorists share with sixties anthropology a strong sense of the shaping power of culture/structure, this shaping power is viewed rather darkly, as a matter of "constraint," "hegemony," and "symbolic domination." We will come back to this position in greater detail later. More generally, the Marxist influence is to be seen in the assumption that the most important forms of action or interaction for analytic purposes are those which take place in asymmetrical or dominated relations, that it is these forms of action or interaction that best explain the shape of any given system at any given time. Whether it is a matter of focusing directly on interaction (even "struggle") between asymmetrically related actors, or whether it is more broadly a matter of defining actors (whatever they are doing) in terms of roles or statuses derived from asymmetrical relations in which they participate, the approach tends to highlight social asymmetry as the most important dimension of both action and structure.

Not all current practice work manifests the Marxist influence. Some of it—like symbolic interactionism and transactionalism themselves—is more in the spirit of Adam Smith. The members of the subset with which I am concerned, however, implicitly or explicitly share at least the critical flavor of seventies anthropology, if not a systematic allegiance to Marxist theory per se.

Yet to speak of a Marxist influence in all of this is actually to obscure an important aspect of what is going on: an interpenetration, almost a merger, between Marxist and Weberian frameworks. In the sixties, the opposition between Marx and Weber, as "materialist" and "idealist," had been emphasized. The practice theorists, in contrast, draw on a set of writers who interpret the Marxist corpus in such a way as to render it quite compatible with Weber's views. As Weber put the actor at the center of his model, so these writers emphasize issues of human praxis in Marx. As Weber subsumed the economic within the political, so these writers encompass economic exploitation within political domination. And as Weber was centrally concerned with ethos and consciousness, so these writers stress similar issues within Marx's work. Choosing Marx over Weber as one's theorist of reference is a tactical move of a certain sort. In reality, the theoretical framework involved is about equally indebted to both. (On theory, see Giddens 1971; Williams 1976; Avineri 1971; Ollman 1971; Bauman 1973; Habermas 1973; Goldmann 1977. For substantive case analyses in this Weberian-Marxist vein, see Thompson 1966; Williams 1973; Genovese 1976.)

I will proceed to explicate and evaluate the "new practice" position by way of posing a series of questions: What is it that a practice approach seeks to explain? What is practice? How is it motivated? And what sorts of analytic relationships are postulated in the model? Let me emphasize very strongly that I do not offer here a coherent theory of practice. I merely sort out and discuss, in a very preliminary fashion, some of the central axes of such a theory.

What Is Being Explained?

As previously indicated, modern practice theory seeks to explain the relationship(s) that obtain between human action on the one hand, and some global entity which we may call "the system" on the other. Questions concerning these relationships may go in either direction—the impact of the system on practice, and the impact of practice on the system. How these processes work will be taken up below. Here we must say a few words about the nature of "the system."

In two recent works in anthropology that explicitly attempt to elaborate a practice-based model (Bourdieu 1978 [1972]; and Sahlins 1981), the authors nominally take a French structuralist view of the system (patterns of relations between categories, and of relations between relations). In fact, however, both Bourdieu's *habitus* and Sahlin's "cosmological dramas" behave in many ways like the American concept of culture, combining elements of ethos, affect, and value with more strictly cognitive schemes of classification. The choice of a French or American perspective on the system does have certain consequences for the shape of the analysis as a whole, but we will not pursue these here. The point is that practice anthropologists assume that society and history are not simply sums of ad hoc responses and adaptations to particular stimuli, but are governed by organizational and evaluative schemes. It is these (embodied, of course, within institutional, symbolic, and material forms) that constitute the system.

The system, further, is not broken up into units like base and superstructure, or society and culture, but is rather a relative seamless whole. An institution—say a marriage system—is at once a system of social relations, economic arrangements, political processes, cultural categories, norms, values, ideals, emotional patterns, and so on and on. No attempt is made to sort these components into levels and to assign primacy to one or the other level. Nor, for example, is marriage as a whole assigned to "society," while religion is assigned to "culture." A practice approach has no need to break the system into artificial chunks like base and superstructure (and to argue over which determines which), since the analytic effort is not to explain one chunk of the system by referring it to another chunk, but rather to explain the system as an integral whole (which is not to say a harmoniously integrated one) by referring it to practice.

But if the system is an integral whole, at the same time all of its parts or dimensions do not have equal analytic significance. At the core of the system, both forming it and deforming it, are the specific realities of asymmetry, inequality, and domination in a given time and place. Raymond Williams, a Marxist literary/cultural historian, sums up both the insistence upon holism and the privileged position of domination characteristic of this view. Picking up Antonio Gramsci's term "hegemony" as his label for the system, he argues that

> "hegemony is a concept which at once includes and goes beyond two powerful earlier concepts: that of "culture" as a "whole social process," in which men define and shape their whole lives; and that of "ideology" in any of its Marxist senses, in which a system of meanings and values is the expression or projection of a particular class interest.
>
> "Hegemony" goes beyond "culture" in its insistence on relating the "whole social process" to specific distributions of power and influence. To say that men define and shape their whole lives is true only in abstraction. In any actual society there are specific inequalities in means and therefore in capacity to realize this process .... Gramsci therefore introduces the necessary recognition of dominance and subordination in what has still, however, to be recognized as a whole process.

It is in just this recognition of the wholeness of the process that the concept of "hegemony" goes beyond "ideology." What is decisive is not only the
conscious system of ideas and beliefs, but the whole lived social process as
practically organized by specific and dominant meanings and values ....

[Hegemony] is in the strongest sense a "culture," but a culture which has
also to be seen as the lived dominance and subordination of particular classes. (Williams 1977:108-109, 110)

What a practice theory seeks to explain, then, is the genesis, reproduction, and
change of form and meaning of a given social/cultural whole, defined in—
more or less—this sense.

What Is Practice?

In principle, the answer to this question is almost unlimited: anything people
do. Given the centrality of domination in the model, however, the most significant forms of practice are those with intentional or unintentional political
implications. Then again, almost anything people do has such implications. So
the study of practice is after all the study of all forms of human action, but from
a particular—political—angle.

Beyond this general point, further distinctions may be introduced. There is
first of all the question of what are taken to be the acting units. Most practice
anthropology to date takes these units to be individual actors, whether actual
historical individuals, or social types ("women," "commoners," "workers,"
"junior siblings," et cetera). The analyst takes these people and their doings as
the reference point for understanding a particular unfolding of events, and/or
for understanding the processes involved in the reproduction or change of some
set of structural features. In contrast to a large body of work in the field of history, there has been relatively little done in anthropology on concerted collective action (but see Wolf 1969; Friedrich 1970; Blu 1980; see also the literature
on cargo cults, especially Worsley 1968). Even in studies of collective action,
however, the collectivity is handled methodologically as a single subject. We
shall be discussing, throughout this section, some of the problems that arise
from the essential individualism of most current forms of practice theory.

A second set of questions concerns the temporal organization of action.
Some authors (Bourdieu is an example) treat action in terms of relatively ad
hoc decision making, and/or relatively short-term "moves." Others suggest,
even if they do not develop the point, that human beings act within plans or programs that are always more long range than any single move, and indeed that
most moves are intelligible only within the context of these larger plans
(Sahlins [1981] implies this, as do Ortner [1981] and Collier and Rosaldo
[1981]; for an older example, see Hart and Pilling [1960]). Many such plans are

culturally provided (the normative life cycle, for example), but many others must be constructed by actors themselves. Even projects generated ("creatively") by actors, however, tend to take stereotyped forms, insofar as the constraints and the resources of the system are relatively constant for actors in similar positions. In any event, an emphasis on larger "projects" rather than particular "moves" underlines the point that action itself *has* (developmental) structure, as well as operating *in*, and in relation *to*, structure.

Finally, there is the question of the kinds of action taken to be analytically central to the current approach. Everyone seems to agree in opposing a Parsonian or Saussurian view in which action is seen as sheer en-actment or execution of rules and norms (Bourdieu 1978; Sahlins 1981; Giddens 1979). Moreover, everyone seems also to agree that a kind of romantic or heroic "voluntarism," emphasizing the freedom and relatively unrestricted inventiveness of actors, will not do either (e.g., Thompson 1978). What is left, then, is a view of action largely in terms of pragmatic choice and decision making, and/or active calculating and strategizing. I will have more to say about the strategic model in the next section, when I discuss the views of motivation entailed in practice theory. Here, however, I wish to question whether the critique of enactment or execution may not have gone too far. Indeed, despite the attacks on Parsons by Bourdieu and Giddens, both recognize the central role of highly patterned and routinized behavior in systemic reproduction. It is precisely in those areas of life—especially in the so-called domestic domain—where action proceeds with little reflection, that much of the conservatism of a system tends to be located. Either because practice theorists wish to emphasize the activeness and intentionality of action, or because of a growing interest in change as against reproduction, or both, the degree to which actors really do simply enact norms because "that" was the way of our ancestors may be duly undervalued.

What Motivates Action?

A theory of practice requires some sort of theory of motivation. At the moment, the dominant theory of motivation in practice anthropology is derived from interest theory. The model is that of an essentially individualistic, and somewhat aggressive, actor, self-interested, rational, pragmatic, and perhaps with a maximizing orientation as well. What actors do, it is assumed, is rationally go after what they want, and what they want is what is materially and politically useful for them within the context of their cultural and historical situations.

Interest theory has been raked over the coals many times before. Here it is sufficient simply to note a few points that have particular relevance for anthropological studies of practice.

Insofar as interest theory is, even if it pretends not to be, a psychological theory, it is clearly far too narrow. In particular, although pragmatic rationality is certainly one aspect of motivation, it is never the only one, and not always even the dominant one. To accord it the status of exclusive motivating force is to exclude from the analytic discourse a whole range of emotional terms—need, fear, suffering, desire, and others—that must surely be part of motivation.

Unfortunately, anthropologists have generally found that actors with too much psychological plumbing are hard to handle methodologically, and practice theorists are no exception. There is, however, a growing body of literature which explores the variable construction of self, person, emotion, and motive in cross-cultural perspective (e.g., M. Rosaldo 1980, 1981; Friedrich 1977; Geertz 1973a, 1975; Singer 1980; Kirkpatrick 1977; Guemple 1972). The growth of this body of work is itself part of the larger trend toward an interest in elaborating an actor-centered paradigm, as is the fact that the sub-field of psychological anthropology seems to be enjoying something of a renaissance (e.g., Paul 1982; Kracke 1978; Levy 1973). One may hope for some cross-fertilization between the more sociologically oriented practice accounts, with their relatively denatured views of motive, and some of these more richly textured accounts of emotion and motivation.

If interest theory assumes too much rationality on the part of actors, it also assumes too much activeness. The idea that actors are always pressing claims, pursuing goals, advancing purposes, and the like may simply be an overly energetic (and overly political) view of how and why people act. We may recall here the distinction, underscored by Geertz, between interest theory and strain theory (1973c). If actors in interest theory are always actively striving for gains, actors in strain theory are seen as experiencing the complexities of their situations and attempting to solve problems posed by those situations. It follows from these points that the strain perspective places greater emphasis on the analysis of the system itself, the forces in play upon actors, as a way of understanding where actors, as we say, are coming from. In particular, a system is analyzed with the aim of revealing the sorts of binds it creates for actors, the sorts of burdens it places upon them, and so on. This analysis, in turn, provides much of the context for understanding actors motives, and the kinds of projects they construct for dealing with their situations (see also Ortner 1975, 1978).

While strain theory does not rectify the psychological shortcomings of interest theory, it does at least make for a more systematic exploration of the social forces shaping motives than interest theory does. Indeed, one may say that strain theory is a theory of the social, as opposed to psychological, production of "interests," the latter being seen less as direct expressions of utility and advantage for actors, and more as images of solutions to experienced stresses and problems.

Finally, an interest approach tends to go hand in hand with seeing action in terms of short-term tactical "moves," rather than long-term developmental "projects." From a tactical point of view, actors seek particular gains, whereas from a developmental point of view, actors are seen as involved in relatively far-reaching transformations of their states of being—of their relationships with things, persons, and self. We may say, in the spirit of Gramsci, that action in a developmental or "projects" perspective is more a matter of "becoming" than of "getting" (1957). Intrinsic to this latter perspective is a sense of motive and action as shaped not only by problems being solved, and gains being sought, but by images and ideals of what constitutes goodness in people, in relationships, and in conditions of life.

It is a peculiarity of interest theory that it is shared across a broad spectrum of analysts, Marxist and non-Marxist, "old" and "new" practice theorists. The popularity and durability of the perspective, despite numerous attacks and criticisms, suggest that especially deep changes in our own practices will be required if anything is to be dislodged in this area.

The Nature of Interactions between Practice and the System

1. How does the system shape practice? Anthropologists—American ones, anyway—have for the most part long agreed that culture shapes, guides, and even to some extent dictates behavior. In the sixties, Geertz elaborated some of the important mechanisms involved in this process, and it seems to me that most modern practice theorists, including those who write in Marxist and/or structuralist terms, hold an essentially Geertzian view. But there are certain changes of emphasis, derived from the centrality of domination within the practice framework. For one thing, as noted earlier, the emphasis has shifted from what culture allows and enables people to see, feel, and do, to what it restricts and inhibits them from seeing, feeling, and doing. Further, although it is agreed that culture powerfully constitutes the reality that actors live in, this reality is looked upon with critical eyes: why this one and not some other? And what sorts of alternatives are people being dis-abled from seeing?

It is important to note that this view is at least partly distinct from a view of culture as mystification. In a mystification view, culture (= "ideology") tells lies about the realities of people's lives, and the analytic problem is to understand how people come to believe these lies (e.g., Bloch 1977). In the approach under discussion here, however, there is only one reality, and it is culturally constituted from top to bottom. The problem is not that of the system telling lies about some extrasystemic "reality," but of why the system as a whole has a certain configuration, and of why and how it excludes alternative possible configurations.

In any event, in terms of the specific question of how the system constrains practice, the emphasis tends to be laid on essentially cultural and psychological mechanisms: mechanisms of the formation and transformation of "consciousness." Although constraints of material and political sorts, including force, are fully acknowledged, there seems to be general agreement that action is constrained most deeply and systematically by the ways in which culture controls the definitions of the world for actors, limits their conceptual tools, and restricts their emotional repertoires. Culture becomes part of the self. Speaking of the sense of honor among the Kabyle, for example, Bourdieu says:

> [H]onour is a permanent disposition, embedded in the agents' very bodies in the form of mental dispositions, schemes of perception and thought, extremely general in their application, such as those which divide up the world in accordance with the oppositions between the male and the female, east and west, future and past, top and bottom, right and left, etc., and also, at a deeper level, in the form of bodily postures and stances, ways of standing, sitting, looking, speaking, or walking. What is called the sense of honour is nothing other than the cultivated disposition, inscribed in the body schema and the schemes of thought. (1978:15)

In a similar vein, Foucault says of the discourse of "perversions":

> The machinery of power that focuses on this whole alien strain did not aim to suppress it, but rather to give it an analytical, visible, and permanent reality: it was implanted in bodies, slipped in beneath modes of conduct, made into a principle of classification and intelligibility, established as a raison d'être and a natural order of disorder .... The strategy behind this dissemination was to strew reality with them and incorporate them into the individual. (1980:44)

Thus insofar as domination is as much a matter of cultural and psychological processes as of material and political ones, it operates by shaping actors' dispositions such that, in the extreme case, "the agents' aspirations have the same limits as the objective conditions of which they are the product" (Bourdieu 1978:166; see also Rabinow 1975; Barnett and Silverman 1979; Rabinow and Sullivan 1979).

At the same time, however, those authors who emphasize cultural domination also place important limits on the scope and depth of cultural controls. The extreme case is never reached, and often never even approached. Thus while accepting the view of culture as powerfully constraining, they argue that hegemony is always more fragile than it appears, and never as total as it (or as traditional cultural anthropology) would claim. The reasons given for this state of affairs are various, and relate directly to the ways in which the different authors conceptualize systemic change. This brings us to our final set of questions.

2. *How does practice shape the system?* There are really two considerations here—how practice reproduces the system, and how the system may be changed by practice. A unified theory of practice should ideally be able to account for both within a single framework. At the moment, however, it is clear that a focus on reproduction tends to produce a rather different picture from a focus on change, and we will thus take these issues separately.

Beginning with reproduction, there is of course a long tradition in anthropology of asking how it is that norms, values, and conceptual schemes get reproduced by and for actors. Prior to the sixties, at least in American anthropology, emphasis was laid upon socialization practices as the as the primary agents of this process. In England, however, the influence of the Durkheimian paradigm generated an emphasis on ritual. It was through the enactment of rituals of various kinds that actors were seen as coming to be wedded to the norms and values of their culture, and/or to be purged, at least temporarily, of whatever dissident sentiments they might harbor (e.g., Gluckman 1955; V. Turner 1969; Beidelman 1966). The ritual focus, or what might be called the focus on extraordinary practice, became even stronger in the sixties and seventies. American symbolic anthropologists took up the view that ritual was one of the primary matrices for the reproduction of consciousness (Geertz 1973b; Ortner 1978), even if they dissented from certain aspects of the British approach. The structural Marxists, too, placed great weight on the power of ritual to mediate social structural contradictions and mystify the workings of the system. Ritual in fact is a form of practice—people *do* it—and to study the reproduction of consciousness, mystified or otherwise, in the processes of ritual behavior is to study at least one way in which practice reproduces the system.

The newer practice approaches, by contrast, place greater emphasis on the practices of ordinary living. Although these were not by any means ignored in earlier work, they assume greater prominence here. Thus despite his stress on the highly intentionalized moments of practice, Bourdieu also pays close attention to the little routines people enact, again and again, in working, eating, sleeping, and relaxing, as well as the little scenarios of etiquette they play out again and again in social interaction. All of these routines and scenarios are predicated upon, and embody within themselves, the fundamental notions of temporal, spatial, and social ordering that underlie and organize the system as a whole. In enacting these routines, actors not only continue to be shaped by the underlying organizational principles involved, but continually re-endorse those principles in the world of public observation and discourse.

One question lurking behind all of this is whether in fact *all* practice, everything everybody does, embodies and hence reproduces the assumptions of the system. There is actually a profound philosophic issue here: how, if actors are fully cultural beings, they could ever do anything that does not in some way carry forward core cultural assumptions. On the more mundane level, the question comes down to whether divergent or nonnormative practices are simply variations upon basic cultural themes, or whether they actually imply alternative modes of social and cultural being.

These two formulations are grounded in two quite different models of systemic change. One is the classic Marxist model, in which the divisions of labor and the asymmetries of political relations create, in effect, incipient counter-cultures within the dominant system. At least some of the practices and modes of consciousness of dominated groups "escape" the prevailing hegemony. Change comes about as a result of class struggle in which formerly dominated groups succeed to power and institute a new hegemony based on their own distinctive ways of seeing and organizing the world.

There are a variety of problems with this model that I will not review here. I will simply note that it appears to overstate the differences of conceptual, as opposed to tactical, orientations between classes or other asymmetrically related entities. The model seems to work best when class differences are also, historically, cultural differences, as in cases of colonialism and imperialism (e.g., Taussig 1980). It works less well for many other sorts of cases with which anthropologists typically deal—culturally homogeneous systems in which inequities and asymmetries of various kinds (based on gender, age, or kinship, for example) are inseparable from complementarities and reciprocities that are equally real and equally strongly felt.

Recently, Marshall Sahlins has offered a model which derives systemic change from changes in practices in a rather different way. Sahlins argues that radical change need not be equated with the coming to power of groups with alternative visions of the world. He emphasizes instead the importance of changes of meaning of existing relations.

In a nutshell, Sahlins argues that people in different social positions have different "interests" (a term Sahlins worries over, and uses in an extended sense), and they act accordingly. This does not in itself imply either conflict or struggle, nor does it imply that people with different interests hold radically different views of the world. It does imply, however, that they will seek to enhance their respective positions when opportunities arise, although they will do so by means traditionally available to people in their positions. Change comes about when traditional strategies, which assume traditional patterns of relations (e.g., between chiefs and commoners, or between men and women), are deployed in relation to novel phenomena (e.g., the arrival of Captain Cook in Hawaii) which do not respond to those strategies in traditional ways. This change of context, this refractoriness of the real world to traditional expectations, calls into question both the strategies of practice and the nature of the relationships which they presuppose:

[T]he pragmatics had its own dynamics: relations that defeated both intention and convention. The complex of exchanges that developed between Hawaiians and Europeans ...brought the former into uncharacteristic conditions of internal conflict and contradiction. Their differential connections with Europeans thereby endowed their own relationships to each other with novel functional content. This is structural transformation. The values acquired in practice return to structure as new relationships between its categories. (Sahlins 1981:50)

Sahlins' model is appealing in a number of ways. As already noted, he does not equate divergence of interest with an almost countercultural formation, and is thus not forced to see change in terms of actual replacement of groups (although there is some of this, eventually, in the Hawaiian case, too). Further, in arguing that change may come about largely through (abortive) attempts to apply traditional interpretations and practices, his model unites mechanisms of reproduction and transformation. Change, as he says, is failed reproduction. And finally, in stressing changes of *meaning* as an essentially revolutionary process, he renders revolution itself less extraordinary (if no less dramatic, in its own way) than the standard models would have it.

One may nonetheless register a few quibbles. For one thing, Sahlins is still struggling with the interest perspective. He confronts it briefly, and he offers a formula that attempts to soften some its more ethnocentric qualities, but he does not really grapple with the full range of thought and feeling that moves actors to act, and to act in complex ways.

Further, one may suggest that Sahlins makes change appear a bit too easy. Of course the book is short, and the model only sketched. Moreover, the relative "openness" of any given system, and of different types of systems, is probably empirically variable (see, e.g., Yenogoyan 1979). Nonetheless, Sahlins notes only in passing the many mechanisms that tend, in the normal course of events, to hold a system in place despite what appear to be important changes in practices. The moves to maintain the status quo by those who have vested interests are perhaps the least of these, and in any event they may backfire or produce unintended novel results. More important is the sort of "drag" introduced into the system by the fact that, as a result of enculturation, actors embody the system as well as living within it (see Bourdieu 1978). But mature actors are not all that flexible. An adequate model of the capacity of practice to revise structure must thus in all probability encompass a long-term, two- or three-generation developmental framework.

A related point derives from the fact that much of systemic reproduction takes place via the routinized activities and intimate interactions of domestic life. To the degree that domestic life is insulated from the wider social sphere (a degree generally much greater than is the case in Polynesia), important practices—of gender relations and child socialization—remain relatively untouched, and the transmission of novel meanings, values, and categorical relations to succeeding generations may be hindered. At the very least, what gets transmitted may be significantly—and conservatively—modified.

In short, there are probably far more linkages and far more possibilities of slippage, in the route leading back from practice to structure than Sahlins' relatively smooth account allows for. Nonetheless, if the course of structural change is more difficult than he makes it appear, Sahlins presents a convincing account of how it may be easier than some would claim.

I close this final section with two reservations beyond those already expressed. The first concerns the centrality of domination within the contemporary practice framework, or at least within that segment of it upon which we have focused here. I am as persuaded as many of the authors that to penetrate into the workings of asymmetrical social relations is to penetrate to the heart of much of what is going on in any given system. I am equally convinced, however, that such an enterprise, taken by itself, is one-sided. Patterns of cooperation, reciprocity, and solidarity constitute the other side of the coin of social being. In this post-seventies context, views of the social in terms of sharing, exchange, and moral obligation—in David Schneider's famous phrase, "diffuse, enduring solidarity"—are treated largely as ideology. Often of course they *are* ideological. Yet a Hobbesian view of social life is surely as biased as one that harks back to Rousseau. An adequate model must encompass the full set.

My second point is not so much a critical reservation as a kind of fingering of an irony at the core of the practice model. The irony, although some may not feel it as such, is this: that although actors' intentions are accorded central place in the model, yet major social change does not for the most part come about as an *intended* consequence of action. Change is largely a by-product, an *unintended* consequence of action, however rational action may have been. Setting out to conceive children with superior mana by sleeping with British sailors, Hawaiian women became agents of the spirit of capitalism in their society. Setting out to preserve structure and reduce anomaly by killing a "god" who was really Captain Cook, the Hawaiians put in motion a train of events that ultimately brought down their gods, their chiefs, and their world as they knew it. To say that society and history are products of human action is true, but only in a certain ironic sense. They are rarely the products the actors themselves set out to make.[18]

Conclusions and Prospects

It has not been my intention, as I said earlier, to give an exhaustive account of any single school of anthropological thought over the last two decades. Rather

I have been concerned with the relations between various intellectual trends in the field, within and across time. Nor has this been, as is surely obvious, a wholly disinterested inquiry. The strands of thought I have chosen to emphasize are those which I see as being most important in bringing the field to a certain position today, and my representations concerning where we are today are themselves clearly selective.

Much of what has been said in this essay can be subsumed within Peter Berger and Thomas Luckmann's little epigram: "Society is a human product. Society is an objective reality. Man [sic] is a social product" (1967:61). Most prior anthropologies have emphasized the second component of this set: society (or culture) has been regarded as an objective reality in some form or another, with its own dynamics divorced in large part from human agency. The American cultural and psychocultural anthropologists, in addition, have emphasized the third component, the ways in which society and culture shape personality, consciousness, ways of seeing and feeling. But until very recently, little effort has been put toward understanding how society and culture themselves are produced and reproduced through human intention and action. It is around this question, as I see it, that eighties anthropology is beginning to take shape, while at the same time maintaining—ideally—a sense of the truths of the other two perspectives.

I have thus taken practice as the key symbol of eighties anthropology. I am aware, however, that many would have chosen a different key symbol: history. Around this term cluster notions of time, process, duration, reproduction, change, development, evolution, transformation (see Cohn 1981). Rather than seeing the theoretical shift in the field as a move from structures and systems to persons and practices, it might thus be seen as a shift from static, synchronic analyses to diachronic, processual ones. Viewing the shift in this way, the practice approach comprises only one wing of the move to diachrony, emphasizing microdevelopmental processes—transactions, projects, careers, developmental cycles, and the like.

The other wing of the move to diachrony is macroprocessual or macrohistorical, and itself comprises at least two trends. On the one side, there is the political economy school already discussed, which attempts to understand change in the small-scale societies typically studied by anthropologists by relating that change to large-scale historical developments (especially colonialism and capitalist expansion) external to the societies in question. On the other, there is a more ethnographic sort of historical investigation, which pays greater attention to the internal developmental dynamics of particular societies over time. External impingements are taken into account, but there is greater effort to delineate forces of both stability and change at work within a given system, as well as the social and cultural filters operating to select and/or reinterpret whatever may be coming in from outside (e.g., Geertz 1980b; Blu 1980; R. Rosaldo 1980; Wallace 1980; Sahlins 1981; Ortner 1989; Kelly 1985).

Anthropology's rapprochement with history is in my view an extremely important development for the field as a whole. If I have chosen in this essay not to emphasize it, it is only because, at the moment, the trend is too broad. It covers, rather than reveals, important distinctions. Insofar as history is being amalgamated with virtually every kind of anthropological work, it offers a pseudointegration of the field which fails to address some of the deeper problems. As argued in this essay, those deeper problems were generated by the very successes of systems and structuralist approaches, which established the reality of the thinglike nature of society, but which failed to ask, in any systematic way, where the thing comes from and how it might change.

To answer these questions with the word "history" is to avoid them, if by history is meant largely a chain of external events to which people react. History is not simply something that happens to people, but something they make—within, of course, the very powerful constraints of the system within which they are operating. A practice approach attempts to see this making, whether in the past or in the present, whether in the creation of novelty or in the reproduction of the same old thing. Rather than fetishizing history, a practice approach offers, or at least promises, a model that implicitly unifies both historical and anthropological studies.[19]

There have, of course, been attempts to put human agency back in the picture before. These attempts, however, yielded either too much or too little to the systems/ structures perspective. In the case of Parsons's "general theory of action," action was seen almost purely as en-actment of the rules and roles of the system. In the cases of symbolic interactionism and transactionalism, systemic constraints were minimized, the system itself being viewed as a relatively unordered reservoir of "resources" that actors draw upon in constructing their strategies. The modern versions of practice theory, on the other hand, appear unique, in accepting all three sides of the Berger and Luckmann triangle: that society is a system, that the system is powerfully constraining, and yet that the system can be made and unmade through human action and interaction.

All of which is not to say either that the practice perspective represents the end of the intellectual dialectic or that it is perfect. I have touched upon many of its defects in the present essay. Like any theory, it is a product of its times. Once, practice had the romantic aura of voluntarism—"man," as the saying went, "makes himself." Now practice has qualities related to the hard times of today: pragmatism, maximization of advantage, "every man," as the saying goes, "for himself." Such a view seems natural in the context of the failure of many of the social movements of the sixties and seventies, and in the context of a disastrous economy and a heated up nuclear threat. Yet however realistic it may appear at the moment, such a view is as skewed as voluntarism itself. A lot of work remains to be done.

Notes

1 For the discussion of the sixties and the seventies, I will for the most part invoke only the most representative figures and works. In an article of this length, many interesting developments must be bypassed. One important figure of this period who gets left by the wayside is Gregory Bateson (e.g., 1972), who, though himself clearly a powerful and original thinker, never really founded a major school in anthropology.

2 E.g., Ortner 1975; M. Rosaldo 1980; Blu 1980; Meeker 1979; Rosen 1978.

3 If culture itself had been an elusive phenomenon, one may say that Geertz has pursued the most elusive part of it, the ethos. It may also be suggested that this, among other things, accounts for his continuing and broad-based appeal. Perhaps the majority of students who go into anthropology, and almost certainly the majority of nonanthropologists who are fascinated by our field, are drawn to it because they have been struck at some point in their experience by the "otherness" of another culture, which we would call its ethos. Geertz's work provides one of the very few handles for grasping that otherness.

4 Another point of contrast between Turner and Geertz is that Turner's concept of meaning, at least in those early works that launched his approach, is largely referential. Meanings are things that symbols point to or refer to, like "matriliny" or "blood." Geertz, on the other hand, is primarily concerned with what might be called Meaning with a capital M—the purpose, or point, or larger significance of things. Thus he quotes Northrop Frye: "You wouldn't go to *Macbeth* to learn about the history of Scotland—you go to it to learn what a man feels like after he's gained a kingdom and lost his soul" (Geertz 1973f:450).

5 E.g., Munn 1969; Myerhoff 1974; Moore and Myerhoff 1975; Babcock 1978.

6 This section is partly based on readings, partly on semiformal interviews with Conrad P. Kottak and Roy A. Rappaport, and partly on general discussions with Raymond C. Kelly. Absolution is extended to all of the informants.

7 White and Childe were fairly explicit about the Marxist influence on their work.

8 This was the programmatic position. In practice, Sahlins did pay a good deal of attention to internal social dynamics.

9 The early Turner is a partial exception to this point, but most of his successors are not.

10 Dumont is another of those figures who deserve more space than can be afforded here.

11 This is not to imply that American symbolic anthropologists deny the doctrine of arbitrariness of symbols. But they do insist that the choice of a particular sym-

bolic form among several possible, equally arbitrary, symbols for the same conception, is not only not arbitrary, but has important implications that must be investigated.

12 James Boon (e.g., 1972) has devoted a fair amount of effort to reconciling Lévi-Strauss and/or Schneider on the one side, with Geertz on the other. The outcome is generally heavily in favor of structuralism. (See also Boon and Schneider 1974.)

13 Lévi-Strauss himself moved from a Durkheim/Mauss position in "La Geste d'Asdiwal" (1967) to the more radical structuralist position in *Mythologigues*. It is no accident that Leach, or whoever made the decision, chose to present "La Geste d'Asdiwal" as the lead essay in the British collection, *The Structural Study of Myth and Totemism* (1967).

14 The transactionalist tradition in British anthropology may of course be traced back further.

15 I would argue, if I had more space, that feminist anthropology is one of the primary contexts in which a practice approach has been developing. The Collier and Rosaldo (1981) article is a good example. See also Ortner (1981).

16 Mayer Zald, personal communication, at the Social Science History Seminar (University of Michigan), 1982.

17 Parsons and his colleagues gave the term "action" central place in their scheme (1962 [1951]), but what they meant by this was essentially *en*-actment of rules and norms. Bourdieu, Giddens, and others have pointed this out, and have cast their arguments in part against this position.

18 Michel Foucault, whose later work (1979 and 1980) is certainly part of the current practice trend, and who is making an impact in at least some quarters of anthropology, has put this point nicely: "People know what they do; they frequently know why they do what they do; but what they don't know is what they do does" (quoted in Dreyfus and Rabinow 1982:187). I regret having been unable to incorporate Foucault into the discussions of this section. In particular, he has been struggling against some of the ramifications of the individualism at the heart of much of practice theory, although he has wound up tying himself into other knots—such as "intentionality without a subject, [and] a strategy without a strategist" (ibid.)—in the process.

19 It might be objected that the political economists themselves put practice in a central position in their model. As external events impinge, actors in a given society react and attempt to deal with those impingements. The problem here is that action is primarily re-action. The reader might object in turn that re-action is central to Sahlins's model too. But the point in Sahlins is that the nature of the reaction is shaped as much by internal dynamics as by the nature of the external events.

References

Alland, Alex. 1975. "Adaptation," in *Annual Review of Anthropology*, 4. Palo Alto: Annual Reviews, Inc.

Althusser, Louis. 1971. *Lenin and Philosophy*, Ben Brewster, trans. New York and London: Monthly Review Press.

American Ethnologist. 1978. Special issue on Political Economy (5:3).

Asad, Talal, ed. 1973. *Anthropology and the Colonial Encounter*. London: Ithaca Press.

Avineri, Shlomo. 1971. *The Social and Political Thought of Karl Marx*. Cambridge: Cambridge University Press.

Babcock, Barbara, ed. 1978. *The Reversible World: Symbolic Inversion in Art and Society*. Ithaca, New York: Cornell University Press.

Bailey, F.G. 1969. *Strategems and Spoils*. New York: Schocken.

Barnes, J.A. 1980. "Kinship Studies: Some Impressions on the Current State of Play." *Man*, 14:2, 293-303.

Barnett, Steve. 1977. "Identity Choice and Caste Ideology," in *Symbolic Anthropology*, J. Dolgin, D. Kemnitzer, and D. Schneider, eds. New York: Columbia University Press.

Barnett, Steve, and Silverman, Martin G. 1979. *Ideology and Everyday Life*. Ann Arbor: University of Michigan Press.

Barth, Fredrik. 1966. "Models of Social Organization." Royal Anthropological Institute of Great Britain and Ireland, Occasional Papers 23.

Bateson, Gregory. 1972. *Steps to an Ecology of Mind*. New York: Ballantine Books.

Bauman, Richard, and Sherzer, Joel, eds. 1974. *Explorations in the Ethnography of Speaking*. Cambridge: Cambridge University Press.

Bauman, Zygmund. 1973. *Culture as Praxis*. London and Boston: Routledge and Kegan Paul.

Becker, A.L. 1979. "Text-Building, Epistemology, and Aesthetics in Japanese Shadow Theater," in *The Imagination of Reality*, A.L. Becker and A.A. Yengoyan, eds. Norwood, New Jersey: Ablex.

Beidelman, Thomas. 1966. "Swazi Royal Ritual." *Africa*, 36:4, 373-405.

Berger, Peter, and Luckmann, Thomas. 1967. *The Social Construction of Reality*. Garden City, New York: Doubleday.

Berreman, Gerald. 1962. *Behind Many Masks: Ethnography and Impression Management in a Himalayan Village*. Monograph 4. Ithaca, New York: Society for Applied Anthropology.

Bloch, Maurice. 1971. "The Moral and Tactical Meaning of Kinship Terms." *Man*, 6:1, 79-87.

—. 1974. "The Long Term and the Short Term: The Economic and Political Significance of the Morality of Kinship," in *The Character of Kinship*, J. Goody, ed. Cambridge: Cambridge University Press.

—. 1977. "The Disconnection between Power and Rank as a Process." *Archives Européene de Sociologie*, 18:107-18.

Blu, Karen. 1980. *The Lumbee Problem: The Making of an American Indian People*. Cambridge: Cambridge University Press.

Blumer, Herbert. 1962. "Society as Symbolic Interaction," in *Human Behavior and Social Processes*, A.M. Rose, ed. Boston: Houghton Mifflin.

Boon, James A. 1972. "Further Operations of 'Culture' in Anthropology: A Synthesis of and for Debate." *Social Science Quarterly*, 52 (September), 221-52.

Boon, James A., and Schneider, David M. 1974. "Kinship vis-à-vis Myth: Contrasts in Lévi-Strauss' Approach to Cross-cultural Comparison." *American Anthropologist*, 76:4, 794-817.

Bourdieu, Pierre. 1978 [1972]. *Outline of a Theory of Practice*, Richard Nice, trans. Cambridge: Cambridge University Press.

Bradbury, Malcolm. 1981. Comment on "Modern Literary Theory: Its Place in Teaching." *Times Literary Supplement* (6 February), 137.

Childe, V. Gordon. 1942. *What Happened in History*. New York: Penguin.

Cohn, Bernard S. 1981. "Anthropology and History in the 1980's." *Journal of Interdisciplinary History*, 12: 2, 227-52.

Cole, P., and Morgan, J., eds. 1975. *Syntax and Semantics 3: Speech Acts*. New York: Academic Press.

Collier, Jane, and Rosaldo, Michelle Z. 1981. "Politics and Gender in Simple Societies," in *Sexual Meanings: The Cultural Construction of Gender and Sexuality*, Sherry B. Ortner and Harriet Whitehead, eds. Cambridge and New York: Cambridge University Press.

Crapanzano, Vincent. 1980. *Tuhami: Portrait of a Moroccan*. Chicago: University of Chicago Press.

DeGeorge, Richard, and DeGeorge, Femande, eds. 1972. *The Structuralists from Marx to Lévi-Strauss*. Garden City, New York: Doubleday.

Diamond, Stanley, ed. 1979. *Toward a Marxist Anthropology*. The Hague: Mouton.

Dolgin, J., Kemnitzer, D., and Schneider, D.M. 1977. "As People Express Their Lives, So They Are ..." in their *Symbolic Anthropology*. New York: Columbia University Press.

Douglas, Mary. 1966. *Purity and Danger*. New York: Frederick A. Praeger.

Dreyfus, Hubert L., and Rabinow, Paul. 1982. *Michel Foucault: Beyond Structuralism and Hermeneutics*. Chicago: University of Chicago Press.

Dumont, Louis. 1965. "The Modern Conception of the Individual: Notes on Its Genesis." *Contributions to Indian Sociology*, 8:1, 13-61.

—. 1970. *Homo Hierarchicus: Art Essay on the Caste System*, M. Sainsbury, trans. Chicago: University of Chicago Press.

Fernandez, James. 1974. "The Mission of Metaphor in Expressive Culture." *Current Anthropology*, 15:2, 119-45.

Firth, Raymond. 1963 [1951]. *Elements of Social Organization*. Boston: Beacon Press.

Foucault, Michel. 1979. *Discipline and Punish: The Birth of the Prison*, Alan Sheridan, trans. New York: Random House.

—. 1980. *The History of Sexuality*. Volume I, Robert Hurley, trans. New York: Vintage.

Friedman, Jonathan. 1974. "Marxism, Structuralism, and Vulgar Materialism." *Man*, n.s. 9:3, 444-69.

—. 1975. "Tribes, States and Transformations," in *Marxist Analyses and Social Anthropology*, M. Bloch, ed. New York: John Wiley and Sons.

Friedrich, Paul. 1970. *Agrarian Revolt in a Mexican Village*. Englewood Cliffs, New Jersey: Prentice-Hall.

—. 1977. "Sanity and the Myth of Honor: The Problem of Achilles." *Ethos*, 5.3, 281-305.

Geertz, Clifford. 1973. *The Interpretation of Cultures*. New York: Basic Books.

—. 1973a. "Thick Description: Toward an Interpretive Theory of Culture," in Geertz, *Interpretation of Cultures*.

—. 1973b. "Religion as a Cultural System," in Geertz, *Interpretation of Cultures*.

—. 1973c. "Ideology as a Cultural System," in Geertz, *Interpretation of Cultures*.

—. 1973d. "The Cerebral Savage: On the Work of Claude Lévi-Strauss," in Geertz, *Interpretation of Cultures*.

—. 1973e. "Person, Time and Conduct in Bali," in Geertz, *Interpretation of Cultures*.

—. 1973f. "Deep Play: Notes on the Balinese Cockfight," in Geertz, *Interpretation of Cultures*.

—. 1975. "On the Nature of Anthropological Understanding." *American Scientist*, 63:1, 47-53.

—. 1980a. "Blurred Genres: The Refiguration of Social Thought." *The American Scholar*, 49: 2, 165-79.

—. 1980b. *Negara: The Theater-State in Nineteenth Century Bali.* Princeton: Princeton University Press.

Genovese, Eugene D. 1976. *Roll, Jordan, Roll: The World the Slaves Made.* New York: Random House.

Giddens, Anthony. 1971. *Capitalism and Modern Social Theory.* Cambridge: Cambridge University Press.

—. 1979. *Central Problems in Social Theory: Action, Structure and Contradiction in Social Analysis.* Cambridge: Cambridge University Press.

Gluckman, Max. 1955. *Custom and Conflict in Africa.* Glencoe, Illinois: The Free Press.

Godelier, Maurice. 1977. *Perspectives in Marxist Anthropology*, Robert Brain, trans. Cambridge: Cambridge University Press.

Goffman, Erving. 1959. *The Presentation of Self in Everyday Life.* Garden City, New York: Doubleday.

Goldman, Irving. 1970. *Ancient Polynesian Society.* Chicago: University of Chicago Press.

Goldmann, Lucien. 1977. *Cultural Creation in Modern Society*, Bart Grahl, trans. Oxford: Basil Blackwell.

Goody, Esther N., ed. 1978. *Questions and Politeness: Strategies in Social Interaction*, New York: Cambridge University Press.

Gramsci, Antonio. 1957. *The Modern Prince and Other Writings*, Louis Marks, trans. New York: International Publishers.

Gregor, Thomas. 1977. *Mehinaku: The Drama of Daily Life in a Brazilian Indian Village.* Chicago: University of Chicago Press.

Guemple, Lee. 1972. Panel on "Cultural Basis of Social Relations: Kinship, Person, and Actor." Annual Meetings of the American Anthropological Association, Toronto.

Gunder Frank, André. 1967. *Capitalism and Underdevelopment in Latin America.* New York and London: Monthly Review Press.

Habermas, Jurgen. 1973. *Theory and Practice*, John Viertel, trans. Boston: Beacon Press.

Harris, Marvin. 1966. "The Cultural Ecology of India's Sacred Cattle." *Current Anthropology*, 7:1, 51-64.

—. 1968. *The Rise of Anthropological Theory*. New York: Crowell.

—. 1978. "No End of Messiahs." *New York Times* (26 November), sec. 4, p. 21.

Hart, Keith. 1982. *The Development of Commercial Agriculture in West Africa*. Cambridge: Cambridge University Press.

Hart, C.W.M., and Pilling, Arnold R. 1960. *The Tiwi of North Australia*. New York: Holt, Rinehart, Winston.

Hymes, Dell, ed. 1974. *Reinventing Anthropology*. New York: Vintage.

Kahn, Joel S. 1980. *Minangkabau Social Formations: Indonesian Peasants and the World Economy*. Cambridge: Cambridge University Press.

Kapferer, Bruce, ed. 1976. *Transaction and Meaning: Directions in the Anthropology of Exchange and Human Behavior*. Philadelphia: ISHI Publications.

Kelly, Raymond. 1985. *The Nuer Conquest: The Structure and Development of an Expansionist System*. Ann Arbor: University of Michigan Press.

Kirkpatrick, John T. 1977. "Person, Hierarchy, and Autonomy in Traditional Yapese Theory," in *Symbolic Anthropology*, Dolgin, Kemnitzer, and Schneider, eds.

Kracke, Waud H. 1978. *Force and Persuasion: Leadership in an Amazonian Society*. Chicago: University of Chicago Press.

Leach, Edmund. 1954. *Political Systems of Highland Burma*. Boston: Beacon Press.

—. 1960. "The Sinhalese of the Dry Zone of Northern Ceylon," in *Social Structure in Southeast Asia*, G. P. Murdock, ed. London: Tavistock.

—. 1964. "Anthropological Aspects of Language: Animal Categories and Verbal Abuse," in *New Directions in the Study of Language*, E. H. Lenneberg, ed. Cambridge: MIT Press.

—. 1966. *Rethinking Anthropology*. London School of Economics Monographs on Social Anthropology, no. 22. New York: Humanities Press.

—. 1969. *Genesis as Myth and Other Essays*. London: Jonathan Cape.

Leach, Edmund, ed. 1967. *The Structural Study of Myth and Totemism*. London: Tavistock.

Lévi-Strauss, Claude. 1963. "The Effectiveness of Symbols," in his *Structural Anthropology*, C. Jacobson and B. G. Schoepf, trans. New York: Basic Books.

—. 1964-71. *Mythologiques (Introduction to a Science of Mythology)*. 4 vols. Paris: Plon.

—. 1967. "La Geste d'Asdiwal," in *Structural Study of Myth and Totemism*, Leach, ed.

Levy, Robert. 1973. *Tahitians: Mind and Experience in the Society Islands*. Chicago: University of Chicago Press.

Lewis, Gilbert. 1977. "A Mother's Brother to a Sister's Son," in *Symbols and Sentiments*, I. Lewis, ed. London: Academic Press.

Marriott, McKim. 1976. "Hindu Transactions: Diversity without Dualism," in *Transaction and Meaning*, Kapferer, ed.

Meeker, Michael E. 1979. *Literature and Violence in North Arabia*. Cambridge: Cambridge University Press.

Moore, Sally Falk, and Myerhoff, Barbara G., eds. 1975. *Symbols and Politics in Communal Ideology*, Ithaca, New York: Cornell University Press.

Munn, Nancy. 1969. "The Effectiveness of Symbols in Murngin Rite and Myth," in *Forms of Symbolic Action*, R. Spencer, ed. Seattle: University of Washington Press.

Myerhoff, Barbara G. 1974. *Peyote Hunt: The Sacred Journey of the Huichol Indians*. Ithaca, New York: Cornell University Press.

Needham, Rodney. 1973a. "The Left Hand of the Mugwe: An Analytical Note on the Structure of Meru Symbolism," in *Right and Left*, Needham, ed.

Needham, Rodney, ed. 1973b. *Right and Left: Essays on Dual Symbolic Classification*. Chicago: University of Chicago Press.

O'Laughlin, Bridget. 1974. "Mediation of a Contradiction: Why Mbum Women Do Not Eat Chicken," in *Woman, Culture and Society*, M. Rosaldo and L. Lamphere, eds. Stanford: Stanford University Press.

Ollman, Bertell. 1971. *Alienation: Marx's Conception of Man in Capitalist Society*. Cambridge: Cambridge University Press.

Ortner, Sherry B. 1975. "Gods' Bodies, Gods' Food: A Symbolic Analysis of a Sherpa Ritual," in *The Interpretation of Symbolism*, R. Willis, ed. London: Malaby Press.

—. 1978. *Sherpas through their Rituals*. Cambridge: Cambridge University Press.

—. 1981. "Gender and Sexuality in Hierarchical Societies: The Case of Polynesia and Some Comparative Implications," in *Sexual Meanings*, S. Ortner and H. Whitehead, eds. Cambridge: Cambridge University Press.

—. 1989. *High Religion: A Cultural and Political History of Sherpa Buddhism*. Princeton: Princeton University Press.

Parsons, Talcott. 1949 [1937]. *The Structure of Social Action*. New York: The Free Press of Glencoe.

Parsons, Talcott, and Shils, Edward A., eds. 1962 [1951]. *Toward a General Theory of Action*. New York: Harper and Row.

Paul, Robert A. 1982. *The Tibetan Symbolic World: Psychoanalytic Explorations*. Chicago: University of Chicago Press.

Piddocke, Stuart. 1969. "The Potlatch System of the Southern Kwakiutl: A New Perspective," in *Environment and Cultural Behavior*, A.P. Vayda, ed. Austin: University of Texas Press.

Rabinow, Paul. 1975. *Symbolic Domination: Cultural Form and Historical Change in Morocco*. Chicago: University of Chicago Press.

—. 1977. *Reflections on Fieldwork in Morocco*. Berkeley: University of California Press.

Rabinow, Paul, and Sullivan, William M. 1979. "The Interpretive Turn: Emergence of an Approach," in their *Interpretive Social Science: A Reader*. Berkeley: University of California Press.

Rappaport, Roy A. 1967. *Pigs for the Ancestors*. New Haven: Yale University Press.

Riegelhaupt, Joyce. 1978. "The Revolt of Maria da Fonte: Peasants, 'Women,' and the State." Manuscript.

Riesman, Paul. 1977. *Freedom in Fulani Social Life: An Introspective Ethnography*. Chicago: University of Chicago Press.

Rosaldo, Michelle Z. 1980. *Knowledge and Passion: Ilongot Notions of Self and Social Life*. Cambridge: Cambridge University Press.

—. 1981. "Towards an Anthropology of Self and Feeling." Manuscript.

Rosaldo, Renato. 1980. *Ilongot Headhunting, 1883-1974*. Stanford: Stanford University Press.

Rosen, Lawrence. 1978. "The Negotiation of Reality: Male-Female Relations in Sefrou, Morocco," in *Women in the Muslim World*, L. Beck and N. Keddie, eds. Cambridge: Harvard University Press.

Ross, Eric B., ed. 1980. *Beyond the Myth of Culture: Essays in Cultural Materialism*, New York and London: Academic Press.

Sahlins, Marshall. 1964. "Culture and Environment," in *Horizons of Anthropology*, S. Tax, ed. Chicago: Aldine.

—. 1972. *Stone Age Economics*. Chicago: Aldine.

—. 1981. *Historical Metaphors and Mythical Realities: Structure in the Early History of the Sandwich Islands Kingdom*. Ann Arbor: University of Michigan Press.

Sahlins, Marshall, and Service, Elman R., eds. 1960. *Evolution and Culture*. Ann Arbor: University of Michigan Press.

Said, Edward W. 1979. *Orientalism*. New York: Vintage.

Schneider, David M. 1968. *American Kinship: A Cultural Account*, Englewood Cliffs, New Jersey: Prentice-Hall.

—. 1977. "Kinship, Nationality, and Religion in American Culture: Toward a Definition of Kinship," in *Symbolic Anthropology*, Dolgin, Kemnitzer, and Schneider, eds.

Schneider, Jane. 1978. "Peacocks and Penguins: The Political Economy of European Cloth and Colors," *American Ethnologist*, 5:3, 413-47.

Schneider, Jane, and Schneider, Peter. 1976. *Culture and Political Economy in Western Sicily*. New York: Academic Press.

Service, Elman, R. 1958. *Profiles in Ethnology*, New York: Harper and Row.

Singer, Milton. 1980. "Signs of the Self: An Exploration in Semiotic Anthropology," *American Anthropologist*, 82:3, 485-507.

Steward, Julian H. 1953. "Evolution and Process," in *Anthropology Today*, A.L. Kroeber, ed. Chicago: University of Chicago Press.

—. 1955. *Theory of Culture Change*. Urbana: University of Illinois Press.

Tambiah, Stanley J. 1968. "The Magical Power of Words." *Man*, n.s. 3:2, 175-208.

—. 1969. "Animals Are Good to Think and Good to Prohibit." *Ethnology*, 8:4, 423-59.

Taussig, Michael T. 1980. *The Devil and Commodity Fetishism in South America*. Chapel Hill: University of North Carolina Press.

Terray, Emmanuel. 1972. *Marxism and "Primitive" Societies*, Mary Klopper, trans. New York: Monthly Review Press.

—. 1975. "Classes and Class Consciousness in the Abron Kingdom of Gyaman," in *Marxist Analyses and Social Anthropology*, M. Bloch, ed. New York: John Wiley and Sons.

Thompson, E.P. 1966. *The Making of the English Working Class*. New York: Vintage.

—. 1978. *The Poverty of Theory and Other Essays*. New York: Monthly Review Press.

Turner, Terence S. 1969. "Oedipus: Time and Structure in Narrative Form," in *Forms of Symbolic Action*, R. Spencer, ed. Seattle: University of Washington Press.

Turner, Victor. 1967. *The Forest of Symbols*. Ithaca, New York: Cornell University Press.

—. 1969. *The Ritual Process*. Chicago: Aldine.

Wagner, Roy. 1975. *The Invention of Culture*. Chicago: University of Chicago Press.

Wallace, Anthony F.C. 1980. *Rockdale: The Growth of an American Village in the Early Industrial Revolution*. New York: W.W. Norton.

Wallerstein, Emmanuel. 1976. *The Modern World System*. New York: Academic Press.

White, Leslie A. 1943. "Energy and the Evolution of Culture." *American Anthropologist*, 45:3, 335-56.

—. 1949. *The Science of Culture*. New York: Farrar Straus.

Williams, Raymond. 1973. *The Country and the City*. New York: Oxford University Press.

—. 1976. *Keywords: A Vocabulary of Culture and Society*. New York: Oxford University Press.

—. 1977. *Marxism and Literature*. Oxford: Oxford University Press.

Wolf, Eric R. 1969. *Peasant Wars of the Twentieth Century*. New York: Harper and Row.

—. 1980. "They Divide and Subdivide and Call it Anthropology." *New York Times* (30 November), Ideas and Trends Section, p. E9.

Worsley, Peter. 1968. *The Trumpet Shall Sound: A Study of "Cargo" Cults in Melanesia*. New York: Schocken.

Yalman, Nur. 1969. "The Structure of Sinhalese Healing Rituals," in *Forms of Symbolic Action*, R. Spencer, ed. Seattle: University of Washington Press.

Yengoyan, A.A. 1979. "Cultural Forms and a Theory of Constraints," in *The Imagination of Reality*, A.L. Becker and A.A. Yengoyan, eds. Norwood, New Jersey: Ablex.

Study Questions

1. According to Ortner, what is the position of "practice theory" in the history of anthropology?

2. What is the relationship between practice and "the system"?

―――――――――

Further Readings
Ortner, Sherry B. 1978. *Sherpas through their Rituals*. Cambridge: Cambridge University Press.

―. 1981. Gender and Sexuality in Hierarchical Societies: The Case of Indonesia and Some Comparative Implications. *Sexual Meanings*. Eds. S. Ortner & H. Whitehead. Cambridge: Cambridge University Press.

―. 1989. *High Religion: A Cultural and Political History of Sherpa Buddhism*. Princeton, NJ: Princeton University Press.

CONCLUSION
MAKING ANTHROPOLOGICAL HISTORIES

In this volume, we have employed a select canon of well-known texts to present a history of anthropological theory. As we have seen in these readings, anthropologists and their disciplinary ancestors have had very diverse perspectives concerning the origins and character of human life and social behaviour. So diverse, in fact, that it is often difficult for students entering the field to perceive the connections between the sundry schools of thought that anthropologists—generally writing for and against each other, as opposed to a public readership—implicitly champion as "Truth." To some extent, this is to be expected. Anthropology is, after all, no different than any other scholarly field in that practitioners have developed their own professional lexicon, nomenclature, and conventions of writing and research; they possess, in short, their own jargon or dialect, which frequently baffles outsiders. Indeed, this much should be evident from the length of the various "References" and "Citations" sections one finds among our selections for Part Four. The anthropological library has certainly grown large in recent decades, and with it the need for those entering anthropology to master (or at least acquaint themselves with) a broader variety of texts and theoretical orientations than had heretofore been necessary.

Conscious of the difficulties which these disciplinary idiosyncrasies pose for the uninitiated, we have attempted in our introductions to provide readers with a context in which to understand the various connections between the central perspectives and personalities of anthropological theory. Likewise, we have tried to put "flesh on the bones," as it were, by showing how events outside academia have influenced the directions taken by anthropologists in developing new foci for research and theory-building. Still, by linking this corpus of heterogeneous writing together in a single text, our task has not been limited to identifying *differences* in perspective. Though it is important to characterize anthropology with respect to what it is not, we have also sought to show how the discipline of anthropology has emerged, over the centuries of its existence, as a *unified* group of researchers, theorists, and writers.

In so doing, we agree with Marcus and Fischer when they reflect that there "exists a circular motion to intellectual history," in which the same themes rise to the surface time and again. In the 1980s, they wrote of anthropology that there is and has been a "persistent oscillation between more realist modes of description and irony," wherein the "Holy Grail" of objectivity (or realism) is offset by an abiding uncertainty about the very possibility of such knowledge at all. Early in the twenty-first century, the concerns raised by these and other researchers of the past generation remain; within the mainstream of social and cultural anthropology, the pendulum has yet to swing back to an overtly Cartesian agenda. It is perhaps more useful to agree with Ortner, for whom the axis of subjectivity and objectivity are a false dichotomy, representing different modes of understanding within the same, largely unified Western intellectual project.

Whatever position one takes on these abstract issues, a key challenge and responsibility for us—as editors of a book that purports to be a "history"—has been to select readings that reflect this steady ebb and flow of practitioners, approaches, methods, subject matter, and theories that have been the substance of anthropology. As academic historians of a self-conscious, "reflexive" discipline, we acknowledge the cultural embeddedness of our way of knowing, without relinquishing its analytical power. If anthropology is distinctive, we must ask how and why is it so? Why have we selected from among the texts written by this group of scholars, in particular? What makes their work and theory distinctive from that practiced by members of other disciplines in the social sciences and humanities? How are we, finally, to characterize the disciplinary centre (if, in fact, there is one) around which anthropologists and their ideas pivot?

In this conclusion, we suggest that the search for such a centre or core, per se, can be misleading, precisely because of the variety of approaches to doing anthropology that have existed—again, we run the risk of overlooking the forest for the trees—and which are so eloquently discussed in the work of Marcus and Fischer, Ortner, and others throughout this volume. Rather than recapitulate the substance of their arguments, we wish to point out that from the formal beginning of their profession, anthropologists have found more unity in the scope of questions they ask and the ways they go about asking them, than in the particular explanations of culture and society they propose. In particular, a focus for understanding is revealed by looking at the way anthropologists tell tales of their own "kind." In short, what can we learn about the anthropological present from interpretations of an anthropological past?

Past Theory and Theories of the Past

Though a full discussion of anthropological perspectives on anthropological history is well beyond the scope of this conclusion, we can still make some preliminary observations about how anthropology has been transformed, as a discipline, through a progressive tendency to look inward, to be "subjective."

A maxim of contemporary American popular culture is that "history is written by the victors." This phrase expresses the idea that whatever objective reality historical discourse might ultimately describe, it always does so from a particular—and political—point of view: that of the subject. The past few years of anthropological theory have invited students to revisit the whole range of human social and cultural phenomena with this in mind. Part of the great excitement generated by the postmodern revolution is that beliefs, behaviours, and institutions whose existence we took for granted have become, over the course of a few years, akin to Shakespeare's "undiscovered country." The politics and contingency of *all* knowledge, and not solely that of the non-Western world, now form a focus for disciplinary research.

In this way, institutions like "religion," "language," and "nation" are no longer taken for granted, but are investigated for how they are socially produced, by whom, under what conditions, and for what reasons. Of course, as the selections in this reader attest, these have been of interest to anthropologists since the foundations of the discipline. But anthropologists working today take far more seriously the idea that *all* social phenomena (regardless of where and among whom they are found) are constructed to seem natural and objective in the contexts of their use. The institutions cited above, for instance, frequently serve to confer official status and legitimacy and are among the most telling diacritics of social power. Inversely, implicit in the notions of the "cult," "dialect," and "ethnicity" are ideas about political weakness and social marginality.

In other words, to construct and employ such meanings, practices, and institutions is to engage in fundamentally political activity that has *real* impact on the experienced world. More than this, it is to create genuine structures that, notwithstanding the fact that they are made by people and thus "invented," have social force and meaning. For all that, these are not static (as a past generation of structural-functionalists or structuralists would have it) but can be and are transformed by individuals in and through what they say, what they do, and what they are *allowed* by those same, *constraining* structures to say and do.

Similarly, this maxim is appropriate for describing the views of anthropologists themselves, insofar as these, too, are selective and partial interpretations that connect particular personalities, theories, and circumstances together in such a way as to objectively explain or justify the present. Like the subjects of Anderson's "imagined communities," anthropologists link themselves to a legacy of professional interests and perform their membership through the various "rituals" of academic anthropology: the attendance of conferences, the writing and publication of articles and books, and the teaching of students. Our understanding of ourselves, no less than that of the communities we study ethnographically is, as Geertz has said, "foreign, faded, full of ellipses, incoherencies, suspicious emendations, and tendentious commentaries." As we have seen, this perspective (common today) differs markedly from older anthropologies, in which the certainty of progress, order, rationality, and above all objectivity were assured—within anthropology, science, and in the world beyond.

Anthropologists are today far more conscious and critical of the subjective aspects of their discipline: a fact made abundantly apparent by Part Four's collection of critical and introspective selections. In addition to casting doubt over the objectivity of ethnographic analyses, a gradual trend toward increasing reflexivity has involved a revisiting of and sustained dialogue with our own anthropological past, in which few aspects of anthropological tradition escape scrutiny. For instance, anthropological historian Adam Kuper, in his book *Anthropology and Anthropologists* (1983), has cited Edmund Leach commenting on the prophet-like quality of Malinowski, "who had no doubts about his own greatness." Whereas Kluckhohn dismissed him as a "pretentious Messiah of the credulous," it is hardly a stretch to imagine Malinowski as, in the sense employed by Max Weber, a charismatic, larger-than-life figure who brought methodological rigor and concern for detail to a profession too well mired in its armchairs. Like Prometheus bringing fire to humanity, the hero Malinowski thus emancipated a torpid anthropology from nineteenth-century anachronism. According to a conventional reading, fieldwork among the Trobriand islanders allowed Malinowski to sweep aside the vestiges of an imperfect discipline and pave the way for a new, more empirically sound era in ethnographic research. He has become the founder-ancestor, whose prolific corpus of writing and systematic methodology are still looked to by undergraduates seeking to understand the near mythical origins of anthropology. It is likewise hardly a coincidence that graduate students at Yale University make an annual pilgrimage (albeit with tongues firmly in cheek) to Malinowski's grave in New Haven, in order to "pay homage" to the progenitor of Our Kind.

As this example testifies, a certain cultural bias has clearly underscored anthropologists' understandings of their own ancestors, no matter how objective these understandings might appear. Our "tales" of Western science and discovery are, as it turns out, not so different from the tales of the non-Western peoples who remain a focus for much of anthropological research. Accordingly we, as editors, do not insist on the objectivity of the tale told in these pages, and admit to the deliberate omission of some writings for the sake of including others. Indeed, it is for this reason that we have entitled our book *Readings For A History of Anthropological Theory*, rather than "Readings For *The* History of Anthropological Theory." Generally speaking, however, the history we present in this book is one that is conventional within the discipline and may be briefly sketched as follows.

The early selections presented in this book show how, at least from its beginnings in the Victorian era, anthropological theory has been split into two competing epistemological branches. On the one hand, empiricism and Cartesian bias were the base for structural and evolutionary approaches that considered the study of human life as the proper object of scientific scrutiny, much in the same way as the rest of the natural world. On the other hand, culture-historical study maintained that particular, meaningful, historically-situated human cultures, and not "Culture," were the appropriate objects of anthropological study and (where possible) preservation. While, epistemologically, one broadly stressed an "etic" and the other an "emic" focus, both perspectives assumed, in keeping with the Enlightenment, that human societies and cultures were indeed objects that could be dispassionately viewed and understood by way of anthropological theory. Though periodically updated in the guise of "materialist" and "symbolist" and "objectivist" and "subjectivist" dichotomies, this original division has continued to be a central tension within the discipline and is still reflected in the kinds of theories devised to account for human societies and cultures.

Important changes in anthropological theory occurred from the middle decades of the twentieth century, which witnessed dramatic transformations in political relations between Euro-America and the non-Western world. The often violent demise of colonial empires following World War II and emerging consciousness of a gulf between the "developed" and "developing" worlds precipitated an infusion of political consciousness into anthropology. Subsequently, at least two generations of political and politicized anthropologists have defied the heritage of a discipline preoccupied with empiricism and structure by asserting the contingency and historicity of all knowledge and the ways in which various forms of power shape and control its character—a process that has reached its apogee in the "postmodern turn" of the late twentieth century.

An important question, posed above, asked what can be learned about the unity of anthropology from the kind of narrative we outline throughout this book and summarize here. Again we suggest that one significant insight lies in the shifting nature of the questions posed by anthropologists: a shift that we characterize as transforming the focus of theory from the "why" to the "how" of society and culture.

Conclusions: The Why and the How of Anthropological Theory

Despite the cacophony of debate at conferences and the heated rhetoric that is spilled across the pages of professional journals, anthropologists are seldom driven from the discipline because they perceive it to lack coherence. Rather the reverse is true, as many who choose to become professionals find a degree of disciplinary harmony precisely through focus on those questions that divide them, questions that we believe to be of universal and perennial interest. Perhaps the most important, if general, is: how to understand a species that remains a single humanity, in spite of all its diversity?

It is no mistake that the key word in this observation is *"how"* rather than "for what purpose," and this is perhaps a watershed in anthropological thought from the time of Tylor to the present day. Armchairs long since abandoned, most modern anthropologists have likewise ceased their ancestors' quest to determine the truth of philosophy and metaphysics, such as the theories of Spencer or Durkheim, which sustained the functional, structural, and psychosocial assumptions of at least two generations of anthropologists in the early twentieth century. And though many (perhaps most) no longer see themselves as narrowly empiricist, the prevailing professional stance is one in which philosophy and metaphysics are best left to others. In their place, anthropologists now ask questions that begin with *how*. How do human-beings have Culture? Society? Language? Gender? Hierarchy? Ethnicity? Nationality? History? How are "we" similar to and different from "them?" How do we perceive gods, spirits, or a transcendent order of existence, and how are such phenomena invested with meaning? How do we have economies, kinship, and rituals? How do we understand what it means "to do" anything, and how does "meaning" itself shape the lives of those who "have" it?

In asking how these human phenomena are variously evolved, thought about, constructed, or performed in explicitly *historical* and *political* contexts, anthropologists of the past 40 or more years have increasingly grounded their work in an important (though unstated) and nearly universal ethic in the discipline that prevails today: that social and cultural categories, forms, and meanings be understood within a holistic, local context. Even the most seemingly objective aspects of the world and universe around us are thereby subject to an anthropological gaze that probes searchingly for new levels of understanding about how these and other very "real" phenomena are nevertheless made through cultural and social behaviour.

Some will no doubt find cause for concern in the failure of contemporary anthropological theory to draw bold new conclusions about society and culture—grand meta-theories in keeping with the faith in empiricism and "progress"—that still rages in the broader public imagination. In fact, most anthropologists do indeed accept that very few universal conclusions can be drawn about the "nature" of humanity from anthropological research and that multiple theoretical perspectives are needed to develop full-blooded knowledge of human societies always rooted in place and time. Paradoxically, this insight is possibly itself the very grand Truth, or meta-theory which earlier generations hoped to discover.

Perhaps this observation is a cornerstone that continues to support the edifice of a discipline still freighted with the interrelated baggage of imperialism, sexism, and ethnocentrism. Anthropologists of many stripes share in this singularly important insight of their discipline: that they were among the first to reject the idea that these questions were the "natural" province of an elite few, those graced by birth with superior culture, morals, biology, or all of these. At a time when it was hardly popular to do so, anthropologists and their immediate forerunners were among the first to articulate and champion a principle which so many now take for granted: that these and other questions endure in all times and places and for all people.

Ironically then, what appears at first blush to be a fatal weakness may just prove to be anthropology's greatest strength, or even the heart which pumps blood to the disciplinary extremities (to again indulge what we have seen to be an oft-used organic metaphor): the study of human diversity does not yield, ultimately, to a monochrome, two-dimensional, or oversimplified perspective. To the contrary, the study of humankind has evoked among practitioners a greater appreciation, and even awe, of the rich and colorful pageant of human ingenuity and creative genius. Distinguishing it from many other disciplines, anthropology therefore becomes more, not less, cohesive through the development of new theory.

Finally, an enduring insight of anthropology has been that questions about society and culture are perhaps impossible to resolve definitively, at least by way of the European-derived scientific method. Hence, like human communities everywhere, anthropologists build their knowledge piecemeal, making allowance for circumstance and always adjusting to the world around them. More and more, they view themselves as "writing culture"—as makers of social and cultural history (their own included) that they had intended only to observe. In light of our shared Cartesian heritage, this is as true for biological anthropologists, paleoanthropologists, and archaeologists as it is of linguistic, social, and cultural anthropologists. Nevertheless, anthropologists may be justifiably proud of their collective contribution to defining and expanding these questions, as well as of the role they have played in helping answer them, however tentatively or provisionally.

Reference
Kuper, Adam. 1983. *Anthropology and Anthropologists: The Modern British School*. Rev. ed. London and New York: Routledge.

Glossary

acculturation. The process of acquiring characteristics of another culture.

Achilles. The hero of Homer's *Iliad*, invincible except in the heel.

Adair. James Adair (*c*.1709-*c*.1783), influential American writer about American Indians.

affinity. Kinship relationship through marriage, or "in-laws," according to Lewis Henry Morgan.

ancient transmission. The inheritance of psychological states from the distant past of humanity.

Andamans. Inhabitants of the Andaman Islands near India in the Bay of Bengal.

Animism. The widespread belief in spirits and souls, a concept explored by Edward Burnett Tylor.

Anjou. A province of western France.

Ankole. A central African region, centered in Uganda, inhabited by groups of Bantu-speaking pastoralists.

a priori. Before the fact, or prior to experience.

apriorists. Thinkers who rely on *a priori* logic contrasted with experience.

Ascidians. Members of the zoological class Ascidiacea, comprising saclike marine animals.

autochthonous. Native, or aboriginal.

Bachofen. Johann Bachofen (1815-87), German ethnologist and classical cultural evolutionist.

Balfour. H. Balfour, nineteenth-century writer on decorative art.

Banks Islander. An inhabitant of Banks Island in the western Arctic Archipelago.

Banyankole. An ethnic and linguistic group inhabiting the Ankole region of central Africa.

barbarism. In the cultural evolutionary schema of Lewis Henry Morgan, the middle period of culture from the invention of pottery to the invention of writing.

Bastian. Adolf Bastian (1826-1905), German ethnographer who held that all people share the same "psychic unity."

Bechuana. A member of a Bantu-speaking group in Botswana in southern Africa.

Bemba. A Bantu-speaking group inhabiting south-central Africa.

berdache. Men who in certain cultures perform cultural roles of women.

bilateral. Pertaining to kinship reckoned through both the male and the female lines.

Blackstone. William Blackstone (1723-80), British jurist and author of the *Commentaries*.

Boswell. James Boswell (1740-95), Scottish lawyer and biographer of Dr. Samuel Johnson.

bourgeoisie. In Marxist analysis, the middle class of capitalists, oppressors of the proletariat.

branchiae. Breathing organs, such as gills.

bundle societies. American Indian cultures using bundles, or packages of paraphernalia with supernatural or medicinal properties.

bureaucratic. Pertaining to bureaucracy, or governance through permanent office, contrasted by Max Weber with charismatic governance.

burgesses. Citizens of early English towns.

burghers. In the Middle Ages, members of the mercantile class.

Byzantium. A former Greek city, forerunner of Constantinople, capital of the Byzantine Empire.

Cambridge school. A group of early twentieth-century British social anthropologists who pioneered the "genealogical method" of fieldwork.

Canon Callaway. A nineteenth-century missionary who worked in southern Africa.

capital. In Marxist analysis, the wealth of the bourgeoisie, derived from oppression of the proletariat.

cartesian. Pertaining to the philosophy of René Descartes (1596-1650).

Casalis. Eugene Casalis, nineteenth-century missionary who studied the material culture of the Basotho of southern Africa.

catalepsy. A disassociative mental state associated with epilepsy.

cephalic index. The breadth of a human skull divided by its length and multiplied by 100.

Cervantes. Miguel de Cervantes Saavedra (1547-1616), Spanish author and creator of the fictional character Don Quixote.

charismatic. Pertaining to charisma, or governance through powerfully persuasive personality, contrasted by Max Weber with bureaucratic governance.

Chauncey Wright. American mathematician (1830-75), philosopher, and promoter of the scientific mode of inquiry.

Cholulans. Inhabitants of Cholula, Mexico, site of the ancient pyramid of Quetzalcoatl.

chromatic. Pertaining to musical scales.

cicerone. A sightseeing guide, or in scholarship, a learned authority.

civilization. In the cultural evolutionary schema of Lewis Henry Morgan, the latest period of culture beginning with the invention of writing.

civitas. According to Lewis Henry Morgan, societies based mainly on property, contrasted with *societas*.

collective representations. According to Émile Durkheim, representations of social reality that reinforce social solidarity.

colligation. A binding together.

commodity. An object that is valuable in relation to other such objects, and that can therefore be used in economic exchange. This is distinguished from "gifts," the value of which rests in the relations between the giver and the receiver, rather than in the commodity itself.

componential analysis. A major method of cognitive anthropology, used to generate folk taxonomies of a semantic domain.

congeners. Members of the same kind or group.

consanguinity. Kinship relationship through descent, or "blood," according to Lewis Henry Morgan.

Copernican. Pertaining to Nicolaus Copernicus (1473-1543), Polish astronomer who promoted the idea that the earth revolves around the sun.

corpora. Bodies, as bodies of written work or scholarship.

corpus inscriptionum Kiriwiniensium. A body of writings in the Kiriwinian language.

cosmogony. The study of the evolution of the universe.

cosmology. The study of the nature and structure of the universe.

Court of Versailles. The retinue of French monarch Louis XIV (1638-1714).

Cuchulain Mythical hero who defended Ulster against the rest of Ireland.

cultural materialism A theoretical orientation that distinguishes emic from etic perspectives and mental from behavioral domains, advocating material causation.

Cushing. Frank Hamilton Cushing (1857-1901), ethnographer of Southwestern American Indians.

Dahome. Or Dahomey, a former west African state in Benin.

Dalton. John Dalton (1766-1844), British chemist who formulated the theory of atoms and atomic weights.

Dasent. George Webbe Dasent (1817-96), English Scandinavian scholar.

deme. A township of ancient Greece.

d'Entrecasteaux. The d'Entrecasteaux Islands in the southwest Pacific Ocean.

Dewey. John Dewey (1859-1952), American philosopher and educator.

diachronic. Historical, or oriented to change through time.

dialectic. Exposing contradictions in the argument of an opponent, then resolving them; or, according to philosopher Friedrich Hegel (1770-1831), a logical process whereby something generates its opposite, which then generates their synthesis.

diffusion. The spread of cultural traits by borrowing or migration.

Dinka. A Nilotic group inhabiting southern Sudan.

Dionysian. Pertaining to Dionysius (*c*.430-367 BC), Greek tyrant prone to irrational excess.

discourse. A term derived from both linguistics and cultural studies. In anthropology, the study of discourses is often linked with the project of French theorist Michel Foucault to look at connections between various kinds of communications, the formation and maintenance of knowledge, and the exercise of social power.

Dobu. A region of New Guinea inhabited by Dobuans, whom Ruth Benedict characterized as "paranoid."

Don Quixote. A fictional romantic character and impractical idealist created by Miguel de Cervantes.

Dulcinea. Dulcinea del Toboso, love interest of Don Quixote.

Durkheim. Émile Durkheim (1858-1917), French theoretical sociologist.

Elliot Smith. Grafton Elliot Smith (1871-1937), British diffusionist anthropologist.

Elsie Clews Parsons. American feminist (1874-1941), sociologist, and anthropologist.

embodied. In anthropology, referring to the ways in which social power and ideas are formulated with reference to, and expressed through, the human body.

emic. Derived from phonemic, the epistemological perspective of the investigated, or the "inside point of view," contrasted with etic.

empirical. Scientific, or based on observation.

eponymic. Pertaining to eponymy, the practice of deriving the name of a geographical region or institution from the name of a person.

Escurial. Or Escorial, a former royal residence near Madrid, Spain completed in 1584.

escutcheon. A shield-like emblem with a coat of arms.

ethnocentricity. Or ethnocentrism, the belief in the superiority of one's own ethnic group.

ethnomethodology. A school of micro-sociology that seeks to discover in language the everyday methods that actors bring to bear in discrete social situations.

ethnoscience. A term for the collection of methods used in cognitive anthropology.

ethnosemantics. The study of emic meaning, particularly as it is constructed linguistically.

ethologists. Practitioners of ethology. Human ethologists employ a hereditarian approach to the study of human behavior derived in part from Darwinism and employing the analytical constructs of fixed action pattern, innate releasing mechanism, and key stimulus.

ethos. Predominating value system.

etic. Derived from phonetic, the epistemological perspective of the investigator, or the "outside point of view," contrasted with emic.

etymological. Pertaining to etymology, the study of the historical development of words.

eugenic. Pertaining to eugenics, or human selective breeding.

Ewe. A people of western Africa.

exegesis. A theological term meaning "explanation"; in anthropology, a term describing the "emic" or insider point of view.

fetichism. Or fetishism, worshiping objects believed to have magical powers.

fetishization. The "fetish" is an object believed to possess metaphysical power (such as an object employed in ritual), and fetishization involves orienting to a particular object, person, or idea as if it were a fetish.

Foy. Willy Foy (1873-1929), German diffusionist and collaborator of Fritz Graebner.

Frazer. James Frazer (1854-1941), British classical cultural evolutionist.

Fuegians. Inhabitants of Tierra del Fuego at the southern tip of South America.

fulvous. Tawny, or dull yellowish-gray.

Galton. Francis Galton (1822-1911), English statistician, eugenicist, and cousin of Charles Darwin.

gens. Singular of gentes, or patrilineal clans.

gentes. Plural of gens, or a patrilineal clan.

geocentric. Earth-centered, or pertaining to the view that the earth is the center of the universe.

Gerland. Georg Gerland, nineteenth-century ethnologist.

gerontocracy. Government by elders.

Gordian knot. An extraordinarily complicated problem, sometimes said to be "cut" by a bold measure.

Graebner. Fritz Graebner (1877-1934), German diffusionist ethnographer.

Gros Ventre. A river originating in northwest Wyoming.

guildmaster. In the Middle Ages, a high-ranking member of a society of merchants or artisans.

habitus. A term used by French social theorist Pierre Bourdieu to describe the capacity of individuals to innovate social and cultural form, based on their personal histories and social positioning within a community.

Haddon. Alfred Cort Haddon (1855-1940), British anthropologist and member of the "Cambridge school."

Heinrich Schurtz. German scholar (1863-1903) who studied social organization, secret societies, and religion.

hermeneutical. Hermeneutical anthropology refers to the practice of interpreting cultures as if they were literary text, and has been a prominent orientation within interpretive and symbolic anthropology.

Herodotus. Greek historian of the fifth century BC, sometimes called "the father of history."

Hidatsa. A Siouan-speaking group of American Indians inhabiting northern Plains States.

Hobhouse. Leonard Hobhouse (1864-1929), English sociologist.

Holmes. William Henry Holmes (1846-1933), ethnographer active in the Bureau of American Ethnology.

Holy Inquisition A former Roman Catholic Church tribunal aimed at suppressing heresy.

homologies. Similarities among organisms due to common evolution or descent.

horde. A group of people, usually nomadic.

hypostasis. The essential character of something, as opposed to its surface characteristics.

idealist. Pertaining to idealism, a general perspective in the social sciences that looks to systems of ideas and meanings, as opposed to the material conditions of existence, as the wellspring of human society and culture.

in abstracto. In the abstract.

Indirect Rule. The former British colonial policy of governing without the deployment of direct force.

informant. An individual who gives an anthropologist information about a culture.

interactionism. Or "symbolic interactionism," a sociological perspective that stresses the emergent character of social interaction and self knowledge.

interstitial. Occurring between interstices, or narrow spaces between parts.

Isola Bella. An island in European Lake Maggiore visited by Napoleon.

Johnson. Dr. Samuel Johnson (1709-84), English author and conversationalist.

journeyman. In the Middle Ages, someone who had completed an apprenticeship in a trade or craft and was ready for employment.

Jung. Carl Gustav Jung (1875-1961), Swiss psychologist.

Kamchatka. The Kamchatka Peninsula of northeastern Siberia.

Kant. Immanuel Kant (1724-1824), German philosopher who posited basic categories of a priori thought.

Kede. An ethnic group inhabiting northern Nigeria.

Kiriwinian. The language of aboriginal Trobriand Islanders, named after the main island Kiriwana.

Kroeber. Alfred Louis Kroeber (1876-1960), American anthropologist.

Kubary. John Stanislaw Kubary (1846-96), Polish naturalist and ethnographer.

Kula. A cultural and economic exchange network among inhabitants of the Trobriand Islands and studied by Bronislaw Malinowski.

Kwakiutl. An aboriginal American group inhabiting coastal British Columbia.

laissez faire. "Free-hand," or the doctrine that governments should not interfere with international trade.

lakotoi. As described by Bronislaw Malinowski, heavy canoes used by the Motu of Port Moresby.

Leibnitz. Gottfried Wilhelm von Leibnitz (1646-1716), German philosopher and mathematician.

Leslie Spier. American anthropologist (1893-1961) and student of Franz Boas.

libertinage. Situational freedom from traditional moral constraint.

libidinal. According to Sigmund Freud, pertaining to the libido, or the part of the human psyche expressing instinct.

literary criticism. An academic discipline that takes for its subject matter the analysis of literature, and which has in recent years been very influential for anthropologists concerned with subjectivity in the writing of ethnographic texts.

Logoli. An ethnic group inhabiting western Kenya.

Louisiades. The Louisiade Archipelago, islands of Papua New Guinea.

Lowie. Robert Lowie (1883-1957), American anthropologist and ethnologist.

Lubbock. John Lubbock (1834-1913), English prehistorian.

Lucretius. Titus Lucretius Carus (c.96-55BC), Roman poet and philosopher.

Lumpenproletariat. According to Karl Marx and Friedrich Engels, the lowest stratum of the proletariat, sometimes characterized as "rabble."

Lynd. Robert Lynd (1892-1970) or Helen Lynd (1894-1982), authors of the sociological study *Middletown* (1929).

MacIver. Robert MacIver (1882-1970), author of *Society* (1931).

MacLennan. John MacLennan (1827-81), British classical cultural evolutionist.

Maidu. An aboriginal American group formerly inhabiting central California.

Maine. Henry Maine (1822-88), British classical cultural evolutionist.

Manchesterian. Pertaining to the nineteenth-century Manchester school of economics stressing free trade.

Masai. A member of an African people inhabiting Kenya and Tanzania.

Massim. A region of islands east of the main island of New Guinea and including the d'Entrescasteaux and Trobriand Islands.

matriliny. Also called a matrilineage, a unilineal kinship system reckoned through the female line.

Mauss. Marcel Mauss (1872-1950), French sociologist and nephew of Émile Durkheim.

Max Müller. Friedrich Maximillian Müller (1823-1900), German-born linguist who traced European myths and folklore back to Sanskrit.

means of production. In Marxist analysis, how people make a living in the material world.

menage. Persons living together, as in a household.

Mencius. A fourth-century BC Chinese philosopher, also known as Meng-tse.

Meng-tse. A fourth-century BC Chinese philosopher, also known as Mencius.

metaphysics. The branch of philosophy investigating the nature of reality.

metes and bounds. Property boundaries.

metonymy. The substitution of a part for a whole.

Middletown. A fictionalized American community studied by Robert and Helen Lynd as representing middle-class values.

Milton. John Milton (1608-74), English poet.

modern synthesis. Edward O. Wilson's name for sociobiology, referring to its alleged neo-Darwinian embrace of a wide range of natural and social sciences.

moieties. Halves of society defined by rules of kinship.

Morgan. Lewis Henry Morgan, nineteenth-century American ethnologist and classical cultural evolutionist.

mound-builders. Mythical builders of prehistoric North American Indian mounds.

natural selection. According to Charles Darwin, the biological evolutionary outcome of the struggle for existence among individuals.

Neolithic. A cultural evolutionary stage characterized chiefly by the domestication of plants and animals.

neuroses. According to Sigmund Freud, disturbed psychological states resulting from maladjustment to the demands of civilization.

Newtonian. Pertaining to Isaac Newton (1642-1727), English mathematical philosopher who developed the law of universal gravitation.

Nicene Creed. A formal statement of the tenets of Christianity, including the Trinity, set forth in the fourth century AD.

nominal. In linguistics, pertaining to nouns.

nominalism. The philosophical doctrine, contrasted with realism, that general concepts are not real, but exist only as names.

noumenon. An intuited object, contrasted with a perceived object, or phenomenon.

Nuer. A pastoralist people of eastern Africa studied by Edward Evan Evans-Pritchard.

Nupe. An ethnic group inhabiting western Africa.

objectify. In anthropology, the process of defining a person or culture as an "object." In recent years, objectification of different cultures and societies has been seen as increasingly problematic for its lack of concern with the subjectivity of the analyst, and also because of the term's static implications.

Occidental. Pertaining to the Occident, or the Western nations of Europe and North America, contrasted with the Orient.

orthogenetic. Straight-lined and predetermined.

Parsons. Talcott Parsons (1902-79), American functionalist sociologist.

parvenu. A social upstart.

Patagonians. Inhabitants of Patagonia near the southern tip of South America.

pathos. A quality that arouses sympathy or pity.

patriliny. Also called a patrilineage, a unilineal kinship system reckoned through the male line.

patrimony. A family inheritance, usually from a father.

Paviotso. A Shoshonean-speaking group of American Indians inhabiting what is now Nevada.

penumbra. An area of partial shadowing.

Peschel. Oscar Peschel, nineteenth-century ethnologist.

petty bourgeoisie. In Marxist analysis, insignificant members of the bourgeoisie, or middle class.

phenomenological. Referring to phenomenology, a sociological and anthropological term meaning the study of the ways in which people experience everyday life.

philologist. One who practices philology, the historical study of languages.

phleme. Or fleam, a sharp surgical instrument or lancet used for opening veins.

phonetic. Pertaining to phonetics, the study of the sound systems of language.

phratry. A kin-based exogamous subdivision of a tribe comprising two or more clans.

pidgin. Simplified, or linguistically-mixed.

plastids. Specialized structures in the cells of plants and plant-like organisms.

Plato. Greek philosopher (*c*.427-*c*.347 BC) of idealism.

polyandrous. Pertaining to polyandry, the mating or marriage of one women and more than one man.

polygamy. Mating or marriage involving multiple partners of either sex.

polysynthetic. Pertaining to a language in which many linguistic elements are combined into a single utterance.

Port Moresby. The capital city of Papua New Guinea.

positive. According to the positive philosophy of Auguste Comte (1798-1857).

postilion. A rider who guides horses drawing a coach.

practices. Or praxis, a concept pioneered by French theorist Pierre Bourdieu holding that society and culture are constructed by purposeful creative agents who enact social life through talk and activity, producing these as objective, "natural" facts.

Priestly. Joseph Priestly (1733-1804), British chemist who discovered oxygen.

primatologists. Those who study non-human primates, whether in natural or artificial settings

Prince Kropotkin. Peter Kropotkin (1842-1921), Russian anarchistic prince who renounced his title.

Professor Pearson. Karl Pearson (1857-1936), English scientist who applied statistics to biology.

proletariat. In Marxist analysis, the working class of capitalism, oppressed by the bourgeoisie.

Puritan. Member of a group of sixteenth- and seventeenth-century English Protestants who advocated religious simplification and strict religious discipline.

Putnam. Frederic Ward Putnam (1839-1915), American anthropologist and archaeologist.

Pythagorean. Pertaining to Pythagoras, sixth-century BC Greek philosopher who described reality in terms of arithmetical relationships.

Quadrumana. A group of animals with four feet and opposable digits.

Quetelet. Adolphe Quetelet (1796-1874), French statistician.

ratiocination. Reasoning methodically and logically.

rationalists. Thinkers who rely primarily on reason or logic rather than experience, as do empiricists.

Ratzel. Friedrich Ratzel (1844-1904), German ethnologist and geographer.

realism. The philosophical doctrine, contrasted with nominalism, that general concepts are real and not merely names.

relations of production. In Marxist analysis, the social organization of how people make a living in the material world.

rentiers. Those who derive income from rents or returns on other investments.

representation. In anthropology, the act of writing about other peoples is an act of representation. Since at least the 1980s, ethnographic representation has been increasingly complicated by the postmodern turn and concern for subjectivity.

ritual. Prescribed behaviour that is periodically repeated and that links the actions of the individual or group to a metaphysical order of existence.

Rivers. William H.R. Rivers (1864-1922), British anthropologist and member of the "Cambridge school."

Roi Soleil. The "Sun King," Louis XIV (1638-1715) of France.

Romulian. Pertaining to Romulus, mythical founder of Rome and twin brother of Remus.

Rossel Island. Part of the Louisiade Archipelago of Papua New Guinea.

ruling class. In Marxist analysis, the oppressor class, such as the bourgeoisie.

Ruth Benedict. American psychological anthropologist (1887-1948), student, and colleague of Franz Boas.

Ruth Bunzel. American anthropologist (1898-1990) and student of Franz Boas.

Sacred Book of the Mormons. The textual basis of the religious beliefs of the Church of Jesus Christ of Latter-Day Saints, or Mormons.

sago. A starch obtained from the sago palm.

Saint Francis. Francis of Assisi (*c*.1182-1226), charismatic founder of the Christian order of Franciscans.

Sapir. Edward Sapir (1884-1939), American anthropologist, linguist, and student of Franz Boas.

savagery. In the cultural evolutionary schema of Lewis Henry Morgan, the earliest period of culture up to the invention of pottery.

scholia. Explanatory notes or comments.

segmentary system. The flexible division of society into unilateral kinship groups, as among the Nuer of eastern Africa.

Seligman. Charles Seligman (1873-1940), British anthropologist and member of the "Cambridge school."

semiology. Or semiotics, the science of signs, pertaining to the relationship between symbols and what they represent.

semiotic. About semiotics, or semiology, the science of signs, pertaining to the relationship between symbols and what they represent.

sexual selection. According to Charles Darwin, the biological evolutionary mechanism of competition among members of one sex for reproductive access to the other sex.

Shaka. Shaka Zulu (1785-1828), militaristic leader of the Zulu people.

shamans. Magico-religious specialists who wield supernatural power to cure people or solve social problems.

Shasta. The Shasta Indian "nation" of northern California and Oregon.

Shoshoneans. Members of an aboriginal American people inhabiting parts of the western United States.

sib. A group of kinspeople.

signs. Generally, things which "stand for" or represent other things.

Sir Henry Maine. British jurist (1822-88) and anthropologist.

societas. According to Lewis Henry Morgan, societies based mainly on interpersonal relations, contrasted with *civitas*.

sociobiology. An investigation of the biological basis of social behavior using the evolutionary principles of kin selection and inclusive fitness.

Solomonic. Pertaining to Solomon, "wise" king of Israel in the tenth century BC.

somatology. The anatomical study of human bodies, a former synonym for physical anthropology.

Sorokin. Pitirim Sorokin, Russian-American sociologist and historian.

Spencer. Herbert Spencer (1820-1903), English social evolutionist.

Stanley Hall. Granville Stanley Hall (1846-1924), American psychologist and founder of the child-study movement.

Stolpe. Hjalmar Stolpe (1841-1905), Scandinavian ethnographer and archaeologist.

structuralism. In British social anthropology, the synchronic concern with social structure, the social matrix of behavior, sometimes called social morphology; in French structural anthropology, the concern with the elementary forms of minds and cultures.

struggle for existence. As expounded by Charles Darwin, biological evolutionary competition among individuals that results in natural selection.

subjectify. In anthropological writing, to give "voice" to the peoples being studied, such that they are empowered within ethnographic accounts to assist in the building of explanatory models for their own social worlds.

sublimation. According to Sigmund Freud, the process of rechanneling libidinous instincts in socially productive ways.

sui generis. Of its own kind, or unique.

Sumner. William Graham Sumner (1840-1910), American sociologist and economist.

superorganic. "Above biology," or the autonomous realm of culture, according to Alfred Louis Kroeber.

survivals. According to Edward Burnett Tylor, vestiges of past cultural states.

symbols. As employed by Clifford Geertz, the vehicles for meanings that intersect to form culture; in the usage of Victor Turner, manipulations of ritual to create social solidarity.

synchronic. Present-oriented, without reference to history.

Tallensi. A west African group inhabiting Ghana and studied by British social anthropologist Meyer Fortes.

Tartary. A region of eastern Europe and Asia occupied by Tartars in the thirteenth and fourteenth centuries.

teknonymy. The practice of designating an individual only as the parent of a named child.

teleological. The idea that a current form, meaning, or perspective is the inevitable outcome of past events.

ten-hour bill. The Ten Hours Act passed by the British Parliament in 1847 limiting factory workers to working ten hours per day.

termini technici. Technical terms or terminology.

thick description. In the interpretive anthropology of Clifford Geertz, the process of interpreting culture as meaningful text.

third estate. Commoners, a class of citizens.

Thirty Years' War. A series of European religious wars 1618-48.

Toda. A polyandrous ethnic group inhabiting India.

totemism Objects of collective cultural veneration, a term that Sigmund Freud employed to represent father figures and that Émile Durkheim employed to refer to certain ritual objects that embody the sacred sentiments of a society and stimulate feelings of "effervescence" and of a greater reality existing outside the individual.

transcendental. Philosophically, rising above common thoughts or ideas.

Trobriand Archipelago. A group of islands east of New Guinea where Bronislaw Malinowski conducted ethnographic fieldwork.

Tylor. Edward Burnett Tylor (1832-1917), English classical cultural evolutionist.

unilateral. Pertaining to kinship reckoned through either the male or the female line.

unilinear evolution. Cultural evolution in an obligatory series of stages.

Vedda. An aboriginal people of Sri Lanka.

vesicle A small cell or cavity containing fluid, such as a bladder.

von den Steinen. Karl von den Steinen (1855-1929), German anthropologist who worked in central Brazil.

Wesleyan. Pertaining to John Wesley (1703-91), British founder of Methodism.

Wiener Wald. A hilly wooded area outside Vienna.

Wilhelm von Humboldt. Prussian linguist (1767-1835) and brother of explorer Alexander von Humboldt.

Woodlark Island. An eastern part of Papua New Guinea.

Zulu. A large Bantu-speaking group, or "nation," inhabiting southeastern Africa.

ACKNOWLEDGEMENTS

The Editors of the book and the Publisher have made every attempt to locate the authors of the copyrighted material or their heirs or assigns, and would be grateful for any information that would allow them to correct any errors or omissions in a subsequent edition of the work.

Anderson, Benedict. From *Imagined Communities: Reflections on the Origin and Spread of Nationalism*. Verso, 1991: 9-36. Reprinted by permission of the publisher.

Benedict, Ruth. Reprinted from *Patterns in Culture*, 1959. Reprinted by permission of Routledge and Kegan Paul.

Boas, Franz. From *Race, Language and Culture*. The Free Press, 1940. Reprinted with the permission of Scribner, a Division of Simon & Schuster. Copyright 1940 by Franz Boas; copyright renewed © 1968 by Franziska Boas Nichelson.

Bourdieu, Pierre. "Structures, Habitus, and Practices" from *Outline of a Theory of Practice*. Trans. Richard Nice. Cambridge University Press, 1977: 78-87. © in the English language Cambridge University Press 1977. The original edition, entitled *Esquisse d'une théorie de la pratique, précédée de trois études d'ethnologie kabyle*, was published by Librairie Droz S.A., Switzerland, 1972. Reprinted by permission of Cambridge University Press.

Clifford, James. "Introduction: Partial Truths" from *Writing Culture: The Poetics and Politics of Ethnography*, ed James Clifford and George E. Marcus. University of California Press, 1986: 1-26. Copyright © 1986 The Regents of the University of California. Reprinted by permission of the University of California Press.

Durkheim, Émile. From *The Elementary Forms of the Religious Life*, translated by Joseph Ward Swain. Routledge (Allen & Unwin), 1915. Reprinted by permission of the publisher.

Fortes, M. and E.E. Evans-Pritchard. From *African Political Systems*, Oxford University Press, 1940. Reprinted 1994 by Kegan Paul. Reprinted by permission of Kegan Paul.

Foucault, Michel. From *Power/Knowledge: Selected Interviews and Other Writings by Michel Foucault 1972-1977*, edited by Colin Gordon. Copyright

1972, 1975, 1976, 1977 by Michel Foucault. Reprinted by permission of Georges Borchardt, Inc.

Freeman, Derek. "Mead's Misconstruing of Samoa," from *Margaret Mead and Samoa: The Making and Unmaking of an Anthropological Myth*, Harvard University Press, 1983: 281-93. Reprinted by permission of the author. "21st Century Boasian Culturalism," a letter from Derek Freeman to *Anthropology News* (May 2000). Reprinted by permission of the author and the American Anthropological Association.

Freud, Sigmund. From *Civilization and Its Discontents*, translated by James Strachey. Copyright © 1961 by James Strachey, renewed 1989 by Alix Strachey. Used by permission of W.W. Norton & Company, Inc. Also: Sigmund Freud © Copyrights, The Institute of Psycho-Analysis and The Hogarth Press, permission to quote from *The Standard Edition of the Complete Psychological Works of Sigmund Freud*, translated and edited by James Strachey. Reprinted by permission of The Random House Group, Ltd.

Geertz, Clifford. From *The Interpretation of Cultures*. Copyright © 1973 by Basic Books, Inc. Reprinted by permission of Basic Books, a member of Perseus Books, L.L.C. and by HarperCollins Publishers, UK.

Gluckman, Max. "The Utility of the Equilibrium Model in the Study of Social Change." Reproduced by permission of the American Anthropological Association from *American Anthropologist* 70:2 (1968): 219-37. Not for further reproduction.

Harris, Marvin. From *Cultural Materialism* by Marvin Harris. Copyright © 1979 by Marvin Harris. Reprinted by permission of Random House, Inc.

Kroeber, A.L. "What Anthropology is About" from *Anthropology* by A.L. Kroeber, copyright 1948 by Harcourt, Inc., and renewed 1972 by Theodore Kroeber Quinn. Reprinted by permission of the publisher.

Leach, Edmund. "Structuralism in Social Anthropology" from *Structuralism: An Introduction. Wolfson College Lectures 1972*, edited by David Robey (1973). Copyright © Oxford University Press 1973. Reprinted by permission of Oxford University Press.

Lévi-Strauss, Claude. From *The Scope of Anthropology*, Jonathan Cape, 1967: 16-30, 46-50. Reprinted by permission of the publisher.

Lowie, Robert H. From *Primitive Society*. Copyright © 1920 by Horace Liveright. Copyright 1947 by Liveright Publishing Corporation, renewed © 1975 by L. Winifred Cole Lowie. Used by permission of Liveright Publishing Corporation.

Marcus, George and M.J. Fischer, "A Crisis of Representation in the Human Sciences" from *Anthropology as Cultural Critique*. University of Chicago

Press, 1986: 7-16. © 1986 by the University of Chicago Press, all rights reserved. Reprinted by permission of the University of Chicago Press.

Marx, Karl and Friedrich Engels. From *The Communist Manifesto*, translated by Samuel H. Beer, copyright © 1955 by Appleton-Century-Crofts Inc. Used by permission of Dutton, a division of Penguin Putnam, Inc.

Mead, Margaret. From *Coming of Age in Samoa*. Copyright © 1928, 49, 55, 61, 73 by Margaret Mead. Reprinted by permission of HarperCollins Publishers, Inc.

Mintz, Sidney and Eric Wolf, "Reply to Michael Taussig" from *Critique of Anthropology* 9:1 (1989): 25-31. Reprinted by permission of Sage Publications.

Ortner, Sherry B. "Theory in Anthropology Since the Sixties" from *Culture/Power/History: A Reader in Contemporary Social Theory*, ed. Nicholas B. Dirks *et al.*, Princeton University Press, 1994: 372-411. © 1993 by Princeton University Press. Reprinted by permission of Princeton University Press.

Radcliffe-Brown, Alfred Reginald. From *Method in Social Anthropology*. Copyright © 1958 by the University of Chicago Press. Reprinted by permission of The University of Chicago Press.

Sahlins, Marshall. From *The Use and Abuse of Biology* (Ann Arbor: University of Michigan Press, 1976): 3-26. Copyright © 1976 by the University of Michigan, all rights reserved. Reprinted by permission of the publisher.

Sapir, Edward. From *Selected Writings of Edward Sapir in Language, Culture, and Personality*, translated/edited by David Mandelbaum, University of California Press, 1949: 544-59. Copyright © 1949 The Regents of the University of California. Reprinted by permission of the publisher.

Strathern, Marilyn, "Self-Interest and the Social Good: Some Implications of Hagen Gender Imagery," from *Sexual Meanings: The Cultural Construction of Gender and Sexuality*, edited by Sherry B. Ortner and Harriet Whitehead, Cambridge University Press, 1981: 166-91. Reprinted by permission of Cambridge University Press.

Taussig, Michael. "History as Commodity in some Recent American (Anthropological) Literature. *Critique of Anthropology* 9:1 (1989): 7-23. Reprinted by permission of Sage Publications.

Turner, Victor. "Symbols in Ndembu Ritual" from *The Forest of Symbols: Aspects of Ndembu Ritual*. Cornell University Press, 1967.

Weber, Max. "The Sociology of Charismatic Authority" from *Max Weber: Essays in Sociology* by Max Weber, edited by H.H. Gerth and C. Wright Mills, translated by H.H. Gerth and C. Wright Mills, copyright 1946, 1958 by H.H. Gerth and C. Wright Mills. Used by permission of Oxford University Press.

Wolf, Eric R. "Introduction" from *Europe and the People Without History*. University of California Press, 1983: 3-23. Copyright © 1983 The Regents of the University of California. Reprinted by permission of the publisher.